AF660810

A DICTIONARY OF INDIAN LITERATURE

A Dictionary of Indian Literature

ONE

Beginnings — 1850

SUJIT MUKHERJEE

Orient Longman

ORIENT LONGMAN LIMITED

Registered Office
3-6-272 Himayatnagar, Hyderabad 500 029 (A.P.), India

Other Offices
Bangalore, Bhopal, Bhubaneshwar, Calcutta, Chandigarh, Chennai, Ernakulam, Guwahati,Hyderabad, Jaipur, Lucknow, Mumbai, New Delhi, Patna

© Orient Longman Limited 1998
First Published 1999

ISBN 81 250 1453 5

Typeset by
Scribe Consultants
New Delhi

Printed in India at
Baba Barkha Nath Printers
New Delhi

Published by
Orient Longman Limited
1/24 Asaf Ali Road
New Delhi 110 002

To
J. Rameshwar Rao
Who encouraged me to complete this work
but did not wait to see it in print

Preface

This is a dictionary only in the sense of its being "a work of informative character arranged alphabetically". It began as a by-product of some work I did as a Senior Fellow of the Central Institute of Indian Languages, Mysore, during 1978–79. My area of interest was Indian Literature in general, not confined to any particular language. Quite often I found that when I needed any preliminary information on an Indian author or literary work of an earlier century—and even of more recent times—I would have to work my way through several books before I could get what I was seeking. There was no single reference work I could consult. So I used to prepare an index card noting the information I had gathered and put it aside for future reference.

From the examples of Bangla, Hindi and Marathi (languages which I can read with varying degrees of comprehension), I know there is in print some comprehensive reference work in Bangla for Bengali literature, in Hindi for Hindi literature, in Marathi for Marathi literature, and I presume this would be true of all the major literary languages of India, modern as well as ancient. What we did not have then is a reference work covering the literature of all Indian languages. We do have *vishwa-kosh* kind of works in most Indian languages but these cover much else besides literature, hence their literary information is necessarily limited.

As the above-mentioned index cards grew in number and my fellowship tenure neared its end, I began to nurse the idea of producing a handy reference volume for Indian Literature in the English language. During the twenty-odd years that have passed since I wrote my first few index cards, the Kerala Sahitya Akademi produced their two-volume opus somewhat misleadingly entitled *Comparative Indian Literature* (1984; 1985) published in English by Macmillan Co. of India; the comparisons have to be effected by the reader because the entries relate closely to single languages. The central Sahitya Akademi at New Delhi has enlarged upon this by preparing and publishing a six-volume *Encylopaedia of Indian Literature* (1987–94), also in English. For all its commissions and omissions, it is our only truly national pan-Indian literature reference work. But the whole set costs (or used to in 1995) Rs 3000, whereas my hope and prayer was to produce something that the Indian scholar, teacher and student—or simply reader—could afford without too much strain. That will explain the brevity of the entries to be found here, perhaps also the paucity of their number.

The present volume covers an ambitious span 'from the beginnings' to 1850. The upper limit cannot be specified but a selection of works and authors in Vedic, Sanskrit, Pali and the Prakrits have been included because so much of later literature derives from them. The lower limit was fixed at 1850 mainly in order to reduce the work-load for this volume. A subsequent volume covering 1851 to 2000 is being planned. The cut-off point of 1850 stands for works composed not later than that this year and authors born before it.

For literature in the so-called Modern Indian Languages, information was derived initially from the various histories of literature in particular languages commissioned and published by Sahitya Akademi. These sources were supplemented by other histories of literature of these languages written (in English) by Indian scholars and published in India. Thirdly, two compilations by Sureshchandra Banerji, *A Companion to Sanskrit Literature* (Motilal Banarsidass, 1971) and *A Companion to Middle Indo-Aryan Literature* (Firma K.L. Mukhopadhyay, 1977), have been drawn upon for information on older literary works and authors.

In the context of this project, 'literature' has been taken to mean, generally, works of the imagination. But other works necessary for the study of literature (viz. grammars, dictionaries, commentaries etc.) have also been included. The more obviously literary items chosen relate to literary works, authors, forms, terms and movements.

When this work was in progress, sample checking of entries and notes was done at CIIL, Mysore, by Shri Balaram Prasad (for Maithili), Smt. Rajashri Subbiah (for Marathi), Smt. Shyamala Kumari (for Malayalam) and Shri Ranjit Singh (for Punjabi). The first round of material collected for Assamiya, Bangla, Gujarati, Hindi and Kannada appeared in successive issues of *Vagartha*, a Delhi-based literary quarterly devoted to the study of Indian Literature.

Since this compilation is meant for the general user rather than for the specialist, a popular mode of transcription (in roman) has been followed for names, terms and titles, instead of the orthodox practice using diacritical marks. As guide to further reading, English translations of literary works have been mentioned below relevant entries.

☆ ☆ ☆

But for the generosity and encouragement of Orient Longman Ltd., this work would have remained unpublished. That was the melancholy prospect when it was offered, successively, to National Book Trust, M/s Motilal Banarsidass, and the Central Institute of Indian Languages.

21 August 1998 SUJIT MUKHERJEE
Haidarabad

A

Abdul Rauf Bhatti (1682–1752): poet in Sindhi from Hala village. His two known works, *Maulud* and *Madahe*, were both written to glorify Hazrat Muhammad. These contain early examples of Farsi metres being used in Sindhi poetical works.

Abdur Rahim Khankhana (*c*1556–1613): poet in Hindi and military commander under Akbar. He knew several languages (Turki, Farsi, Arabic, Sanskrit) but composed mainly in Brajbhasha and Avadhi. Among his other works are *Barvaynayika-bhed, Shringar dortha, Madana-shatak, Rasa-Panchadhyayi*. He also prepared a diwan in Farsi and translated *Bakyat bavri* from Turki into Farsi. The standard collection *Rahim satsai* (or *dohavali*) consists of 400 doha couplets about Krishna. While he is best known for his doha verses, he also composed in other metres and forms and is said to have innovated the barvay metre of Hindi.

Abhang (Marathi): verse metre, used especially in composition of devotional songs from about end-13th. The word (literally meaning unbroken or completed) also came to mean a poem or verses in this metre. It derived from the folk-verse form known as ovi and was developed by the Warkari (Vaishnav) sant-poets like Jnaneshwar, Namadev, Eknath, Tukaram and others. The abhang remained popular till end-17th and Tukaram's compositions are generallly regarded as the finest examples of the form.

Abhaya-deva Suri (?C): this name has been assigned as author of works such as *Mahavira-charita* (in Apabhramsh), *Jaya-tihuyana-stotra* (in Prakrit), *Rishabha-jina-stotra* (in Prakrit), and *Dharma-suri-stuti* (in Apabhramsh). He may have been the disciple of Jayasingha Suri, while Hemachandra Suri was his disciple. The Abhayadeva who wrote a number of commentaries is probably another person; there have been other Jaina scholars in 13th to 15th India bearing this name.

Abhidha (Sanskrit): term in poetics representing the function by which a word denotes its primary or conventional sense.

Abhidhana-ppadipika (late 12th; Pali) of Mogallanna: a lexicon modelled on the Sanskrit *Amarakosha*; deals, in three parts, with synonyms, homonyms and undeclinables. The author is to be distinguished from the grammarian with the same name.

Abhijnana-shakuntala (?5C; Sanskrit;) of Kalidasa: the most famous drama in Sanskrit; consisting of seven acts, is available in four recensions. It presents the Dushyanta-Shakuntala story to be found in *Mahabharata* (Adi), also in *Padma-Purana* (Swarga), but Kalidasa has introduced many new elements like the curse of Durvasa and the ring-episode. The latter also appears in a story of *Katthahari-jataka*.

Tr. William Jones, Calcutta, 1790; Emeneau,Berkeley; 1962; Coulson, Harmondsworth, 1981; Chandra Rajan, New Delhi, 1989.

Abhimanyu Samanta Simhara (1757–1807): poet in Oriya whose major work is *Vidagdha-chintamani*; also composed *Sulakshana, Rasavati, Prema-kala, Prema-chintamani*. He belonged to a kshatriya family of Rohilkhand (in Uttar Pradesh) settled for several generations in Orissa. When young, he wrote poems like *Bagha-gita* about a tiger-hunt and *Chadai-gita* about sparrow fights; these are realistic and full of action. Later he came under the influence of scholar and poet Sadananda Kavisurya, and imbibed the best as well as the worst qualities of ornate poetry, also of popular Vaishnav faith.

Abhimaraka (?3C; Sanskrit) of Bhasa: play in six acts depicting the romance between prince Abhimaraka and Kurangi, grand-daughter of Raja Kuntibhoj. The plot is based on a folk-tale; the erotic element predominates in the presentation.

Abhinava-bharati (early 11th; Sanskrit) of Abhinavagupta: commentary on *Natyasastra*.

Abhinava Dashakumara-charit (*c*1100; Kannada) of Chaundarasa: a champu rendering of Dandi's prose epic. Generally faithful to the original, it shows revision and alteration at places.

Abinava-gupta (late10th/early 11th): famous Kashmiri scholar of Sanskrit, literary theorist, and authoriy on Kashmir Shaivism. At least 41 of his works, all in Sanskrit are known. Among his most influential commentaries on literature are *Lochana* (or *Kavyalokalochana*), *Abinavabharati* and *Abhivyakti-vada*.

Abhinaya (Sanskrit): term in dramaturgy for the means by which a performer presents the rasas effectively through physical action on the stage.

Abhinaya-darpana (?C;Sanskrit) attributed to Nandikeshwara: work on histrionics associated with dance and drama, dealing mainly with gestures and postures.
Tr. M. Ghosh, Calcutta, 1957.

Abhinaya-shastra (?C; Sanskrit) of Kohala: treatise on dramatic performance, extant only in an abbreviated version.

Abhisheka (?3rd) of Bhasa: play in six acts based on *Ramayana*. It begins with the killing of Vali and crowning of Sugriva; ends with the ordeal of Sita and consecration of Rama. The special feature is Bhasa's sympathetic characterisation of Vali and Ravana.

Abhivyakti-vada: doctrine of Sanskrit poetics expounded by Abhinavagupta.

Abru [Najmuddin Shah Mubarak (1622–1747)]: poet in Urdu; came from Gwalior to settle in Delhi. A relative and disciple of Khan-e-Arzu, also influenced by Valli, he was one of the earliest poets in North India to compose only in Urdu. Apart from ghazals and some descriptive poems, he wrote a masnavi entitled *Dar Mauaz-e-Araish-e-Mashuq* which advises a young boy on how to enhance his attractiveness by paying attention to items of dress and toilet. His poetry is marked by the eiham goi style and he also began the writing of poems in the wasokht form.

Acca Tenugu (Pure Telugu) also known as 'Desyandramu': a kind of Telugu which abjures Sanskrit words absorbed into the language; much in vogue during 17th in Andhradesha.

Achaldas Khichi Ri Vachanika (*c*1430; Rajasthani) of Shivadas Charan: a relatively short work written in 'vachanika' style; except in prose portions, the verse mainly uses 'doha' metre. It describes the attack on Achaldas Khichi of Gaguran (near mod. Kota) in 1423 by Sultan Hoshang Shah of Mandavgarh (Mandu). Achaldas fights until death, his son Palhanasi is persuaded to leave the fort, the women commit 'jauhar'. The earliest version of the work is likely to have been an eye-witness account since Shivadas was probably the court poet of Achaldas.

Achyuat|abhyudayamu (*c*1630; Telugu) of Raghunatha Nayaka: biography by ruler of Thanjavur of his father; written in dvipadi metre, this work became a model for verse biographies in Telugu.

Achyutananda Dasa (16th): youngest of the Pancha-sakha poets in Oriya; prolific writer and social reformer. Born into a respectable Karana family, he lived for a time among the Keutas (fishermen) and the Gaudas (cowherds) in order to help them improve their lot; is honoured by them even now as their patron saint; mainly for their benefit, composed *Kaivarta Gita* and *Gopalanka-ogala*. He is supposed to have written altogether one lakh treatises in Oriya verse on various religious subjects. This gave rise to the notion that there were several poets using the same name. However, the works mentioned above as well as others like *Gurubhakti Gita, Anakar-samhita, Chahayalisa-patala*, were composed by the same Achyutananda; His major work is *Harivamsha* in Oriya.

Ada Kisna (earlier 18th): charan poet in Hindi (Dingal) who was attached to the court of Rana Bhimsingh of Mewar; author of *Bhim-vilas* (1722), an account of the Rana's life, and *Raghubarjasprakas* (1724), a work on poetics which contains a valuable description of the metres in Dingal. Kisna had helped Colonel Tod to collect material about Rajasthan.

Adbhuta Ramayana (?C; Sanskrit) attributed to Valmiki: a kind of sequel to *Ramayana* in 27 sections, the work narrates the earlier part of the epic story and describes the real nature of Sita, who is said to have killed a hundred-headed Ravana whom Rama could not defeat.

Addahaman [Abdul Rahman (12th); poet in Prakrit: probably lived in Multan; also scholar of Sanskrit and Apabhramsha. He is the author of *Sandes rasak*, the only known literary work in Apabhramsh written by a Muslim.

Addanki Gangadhar Kavi (late 16th); poet in Telugu: lived in Golkonda; wrote the prabandha work *Tapati Samvaranopakhyanamu*. He dedicated it to Golkonda ruler Ibrahim Quli Qutb Shah (r. 1550–80).

Adho Duraso (*c*1538–1651): poet in Rajasthani, leading composer of heroic poems. Among his longer works are *Virud chhihattari, Doha Solanki Viramdevji ra, Jhulana Rav Surtan ra, Jhulana Rav Amarsingh Gajasinghota ra, Kirtan Bhavani*;

he also composed shorter poems in marsiya and kavitta forms in celebration of contemporary minor heroes and events. Born into a poor family of Adha village (hence the name 'Adho') of Marwar, he died in Panchatiya village near Jodhpur. Apart from occupying a place of honour in many Rajput courts, he is said to have been given due recognition by Emperor Akbar.

Adhyatma-pariksha (late 17th; Prakrit) of Yashovijaya: a work of 184 verses, dealing with spiritual matters, especially the controversy between the Digambara and Swetambara sects. The author (1608–88; of *Tapogaccha*) also wrote a Sanskrit commentary on the subject, entitled *Jnana | bindu-prakarana.*

Adhyatma-Ramayana (?C; Sanskrit): considered as part of *Brahmanda-purana*. Consisting of 4000 verses and divided into seven books, the work has the form of a mahakavya, but is actually a manual of devotion and is tantric in character. As in many tantras, the teaching is presented in the form of a dialogue between Shiva and Uma. Here Rama is essentially Vishnu; the Sita abducted by Ravana is an illusion; the real Sita, who is Lakshmi and Prakriti, emerges after the fire-ordeal at the end of the book.
Tr. Lala Baijnath, Allahabad, 1913.

Adhyatma Ramayanam Kilippattu (early 17th; Malayalam) of Ezhuttacchan: a re-telling of the Sanskrit work in kilippattu form. It also draws upon the Valmiki *Ramayana*, Kalidas's Raghuvamsha and the Malayalam work *Kannassa Ramayana*. Possibly influenced by the ongoing bhakti movement, the poet decided to recast the original in a popular language.

Adhyatma Ramayanamu (middle-18th; Telugu) of Munipalli Subrahmanya: a retelling of the Sanskrit work which became popular because it could be set to tunes and sung.

Adi Granth (1601/04; Panjabi): the holy book of the Sikhs, also known as 'Guru Granth' or 'Granth Saheb' or 'Guru Granth Sahib', these being condensed forms of the full title, *Adi Siri Guru Granth Saheb*. Originally known simply as 'pothi', it was compiled in 1601 or 1604 by Arjan Dev, the fifth Guru. The work came to be called 'Guru Granth' since 1708 after Guru Gobind (1666–1708), the tenth Guru added the works of his father and the ninth Guru, Tegh Bahadur, to the compilation and nominated the book as the permanent successor of the gurus. The prefix 'Adi' was added to distinguish it from another anthology, *Dasham Granth*, which contained the works of the tenth Guru. Consisting of 3384 hymns running to 15,575 stanzas of verse in the 'Middle Stage' of various North Indian languages related to Panjabi, the volume presents the works of 35 persons from different parts of India and belonging to various castes and creeds. The authors are (a) six Gurus, all of whom call themselves 'Nanak' in their compositions; (b) sants and bhagats known to India of that age viz., Kabir, Namdev, Ravidas, Sheik Farid, Jaidev, Sadhana, Surdas, etc.; (c) popular composers of the time like Balwand, Jalap, Bhikha, etc; (d) Sundar, probably a descendant of Amar Das, the third Guru.

Adinatha-charita (*c*1103; Prakrit) of Vardhamana: a puranic work in verse dealing with the life of the first tirthankar Adinath.

Adipurana or **Adi-tirthankar-purana** (*c*940; Kannada) of Pampa: an adaptation, in champu style, of the Sanskrit *Purva-purana of* Jinasenacharya. The work tells the story of the first tirthankar, Purudeva or Vrishabhaswami, also known as Adinath. Among the elements added by Pampa is an account of the conflict between the sons of Purudeva, king Bharatesha and his younger brother Bahubali.

Adiyarkku Nallar (12th/13th): scholar of Tamil and author of a commentary on *Silappadikaram* covers the entire work and also refers to other ancient Tamil works on verse, prose and drama. 'Adiyarkku Nallar' is not his real name but a phrase denoting an attribute of the god Shiva.

Adrishta-purana (17th; Asamiya) of Shiva Sharma: long verse tale which narrates how the servant of a prince attempts to foil the romance between the prince and princess.

Advaita-prakasa (*c*1564; Bangla): biography of Shri Chaitanya by one of his companions.

Afsos [Mir Sher Ali (1732–1809)]: Urdu writer: lived in Lakhnau and Patna before he was appointed as a translator in Fort William College of Calcutta. Here he tranalated Shaikh Sadi's *Gulistan* from Farsi into Urdu. He also wrote *Arayise mahfil* which deals with Indian history and geography. He revised the kulliyat of Sauda for new publication.

Agattiyam (?C; Tamil) of Agattiyar: the first grammar in the language. It dealt with 'iyal' (poetry), 'isai' (music) and 'natakam' (dance and drama).

Agattiyar or **Akattiyar** (?C): legendary progenitor and patriarch of Tamil literature. He is said to have been a primary member of the First Sangam in Ten Madurai; wrote the first grammar of Tamil, *Agattiyam*; had twelve disciples all of whom became great authors in due course (like Tolkappiyar, Adankottasan, Panambaranar, etc). According to one tradition, Agattiyar is the same as the Sanskrit puranic character Agastya; this tradition makes him a close associate of Shiva, who initiated him into the mysteries of Tamil language and literature and sent him south to put the Tamil South on footing with the Sanskrit North.

Aggal Lilavati see *Chandraprabha puran* of Aggal.

Aggavamsa (late 12th): also known as Aggapandita: author of noted grammatical work on Pali, *Saddaniti*, which utilises earlier works like *Ashtadhyayi*. He was the tutor of king Narapati-sithu of Pagan (1167–1202). According to *Gandha-vamsa*, he was a native of India; it has also been claimed he was of Burmese origin.

Agni-das (late 17th/early 18th): poet in Marathi: composed the powada on Afzal Khan's meeting with Shivaji, which is regarded as the first famous composition in this form. It is believed that this powada was heard in person by Shivaji and Jijabai.

Agni-purana (?C; Sanskrit): one of the later puranas, important to literature because it includes discussions of literary topics. Thus, it describes Vedic literature (chs. 259–271); deals with metrics, phonetics, grammar, lexicography, poetics and dramaturgy (chs. 336–46). Besides deriving topics from *Natyashastra*, it seems to have drawn also from Bhamaha, Dandin, Vamana and Dhananjaya. The extant purana probably attained its full form in the 17th.
Tr. M.N. Dutta, Calcutta, 1901.

Agra (late 18th): poet in Panjabi: often regarded as the first writer of var works in the language. Nothing is known about his life. From the pure Panjabi used in his *Hakikat Rai di var* (?1796), it seems he was a resident of Lahore.

Agra-das (d.1575): Ram-bhakta poet in Hindi in the Ramanand tradition; guru of Nabhadas, contemporary of Tulsidas; lived in Galta, near Jaipur. Among his works are *Hitopadesh upakhyan bavani*, *Dhyan-manjari*, *Ramadhyan-manjari*.

Ahalya-samkrandanamu (18th; Telugu) of Samukh Venkatkrishnan Naikuru: an erotic kavya in three sections dealing with Indra's illicit affair with Ahalya, wife of Gautam Muni.

Aha-pporul (?C; Tamil) of Iraiyanar: grammatical work of 60 'suttinams' (propositions) which depict the theme of clandestine love. The work was also known as *Kalaviyal*; later, as *Iraiyanar Ahapporul*. Dating the work has ranged from 2nd to 11th.

Aha-pporul-vilakkam (11th; Tamil) of Narkavi Nambi: the work discusses various aspects of love. The author was a Jaina scholar.

Ahashanka Vijayamu (18th; Telugu) of Shesha Venkatpati: a kavya work in five 'aswas' (sections) telling of the romance between the moon-god Chandra and a housewife named Tara. Erotic elements predominate in this work.

Ahmad Shah Gujjar (17th); poet in Panjabi: the first Muslim poet to write a verse-narrative on the Hir-Ranjha story. His work, entitled *Hir Ahonad* (1692), deviates from the story-line presented by his predecessor Damodar, but later Muslim poets have preferred to follow Ahmad Shah's version. Ahmad Shah was also the earliest poet in Panjabi to employ the baiet metre.

Ahmad Yar (1768–1875): qissa writer in Panjabi: first made a name for himself in Lahore by writing a history of the Khalsa. Enjoying the patronage of Sikh sardars, he studied books on Islam for several years and wrote more than 40 qissas—the largest number by any single author. Among these are *Hatim nama, Kam Rup, Chander Badan, Saiful Maluk, Yusuf Zulekha, Raj Bibi*, etc., most of which are in swaiya chhand metre. He used a lot of Farsi words and his stories resemble those composed in West Asian countries.

Aihole inscription (634); of Chalukya king Pulakesin II (r.609–642): who ruled in West Dakhan. This inscription in Sanskrit is important to literary history because it mentions Kalidas (also Bharavi), thus providing a lower terminus for dating him.

Ai-nam (Asamiya): term for songs in praise of Shitala, the goddess who ordains smallpox; sung to propitiate her when there is an affliction in the family.

Ain-kurunuru (?C; Tamil) of Kutalur Kizhar: one of the *Ettuttogai* anthologies, consists of 500 akam poems representing the work of five poets. The poems range from three to six lines and are in akaval metre. The anthology is in five sections of 100 poems each; each 100 is divided into 10 poems each. Each poet dealt with a particular tinai—thus, Orampokiyar with 'muratam', Ammuvanar with 'neytal', Kapilar with 'kurinchi', Otalantiyar with 'palai', Peynar with 'mulai'. Some scholars believe this was the earliest of the Sangam anthologies. Also, see Akamo.

Aiyadigal Kadavar Kon (?6C): sant-poet in Tamil and one of the 63 Nayanmars; he appears to have been a Pallava king, Simmavarman (*c* 550/575); abdicated his throne in favour of his son and went around Tamilnadu visiting all the sacred shrines; composed his hymns during this period, and these were collected as *Kshetra Tiruvenba*.

Ajamil upakhyan: this puranic story has been retold in Asamiya by Shankaradeva, Bhushan Dvija and others.

Ajan Fakirar Jikir (18th; Asamiya): songs attributed to the mendicant Ajan Fakir and the poet-composer Sah Milan. These preach a blend of Hinduism and Islam wherein the world is regarded as maya and Allah the only refuge of the individual.

Ajita-santi-laghu-stavana (early 12th; Prakrit) of Jinavallabha: a hymn in 17 verses; also known as *Ullasi-kama-thaya*.

Ajitnath-purana (?C; Kannada) of Ranna: a champu work dealing with the second tirthankar, Ajitnath; it also tells about Ayodhya ruler Sagara who lost all his 60,000 sons. The poem's depiction of vairagya is of a very high order.

Ajitsimha, Maharaja (1678–1724): Jodhpur ruler and poet in Rajasthani. Among works ascribed to him are *Gunasar*, a compilation consisting of about ten works on various themes; *Bhava virahi*, another miscellaneous compilation which includes poems reflecting on the death of his Sisodiya wife; *Gaja uddhar grantha*, based on a story from Bhagavata; *Durgapatha bhasha*, said to be a recreation of an older work. The last-named has not been recovered.

Ajna-patra (1715; Marathi) of Ramachandra Panta Amatya: a prose work on statecraft relating generally to the Maratha kingdom established by Shivaji. The author served three Maratha rulers over nearly 40 years.

Akam or **Aham** (Tamil): term for a broad category of poems of the Third Sangam period. These are the 'interior' poems concerning all phases of love between man and woman. True love is either 'karpu' (wedded) or 'kalavu' (clandestine or extra-marital) and has five aspects - 'punartal' (union), 'pirital' (separation), 'iruttal' (patience in separation), 'irangal' (bewailing), and 'udal' (sulking). These are, in turn, related to specific 'tinai' (geographic regions); thus, 'marutam' (agricultural), 'neytal' (coastal), 'kurinci' (mountain), 'palai' (desert), and 'mullai' (forest). The idealised poetic treatment of love is known as 'akattinai'. According to Sangam classification, whatever is not akam is 'puram'; see later.

Akha-nanuru or **Aha-nanuru** (?C; Tamil) of Urutirasammanar: one of the *Ettuttogai* collections, consists of 400 akam poems on love, representing the work of 145 poets. The length of these poems varies from 13 to 37 lines. The collection is in three parts - 'Kalitriyani-nirai' (the array of male elephants); 'Manipadai-pavalam' (a string of corals interspersed with gems); 'Nittilakkovai' (a necklace of pearls). It was compiled at the instance of Pandyan king Ukkirapperu Valhudi. The work is also cknown as *Neduntogai*.

Akharavat (late 16th; Hindi) of Jayasi: work in Avadhi, in which the sequence of the Devanagri alphabet is discussed philosophically.

Akhdai (Bangla): a semi-classical style of singing that came into vogue in Calcutta towards end-18th under the patronage of Raja Nabokrishna Deb. The song consisted of three stanzas—the first invoked the giddess; the second spoke of secular love; the third lamented a night spent without the beloved. Due to formal constraints, it failed to become popular; whereupon an attempt was made to popularise it by introducing elements of Kabiwala songs. This modified form came to be called 'haf-akhdai', meaning semi-akhdai.

Akhe-gita (1649; Gujarati) of Akho: a long metaphysical poem dealing mainly with knowledge of the Absolute.

Akho (1600–55): poet in Gujarati; belonged to Jitalpur village near Ahmedabad and was a goldsmith by profession. According to legend he renounced his profession when his honesty was questioned; turned to spiritual quests and visited sacred places like Varanasi; adopted Gokulnath, grandson of Vallabhacharya, as his guru. He appears to have begun writing only around

1641; initially a poet of bhakti in the Vaishnav tradition, later he laid more stress on knowledge and renunciation. Among his works that have been reliably dated are *Panchi-karana* (1645), *Guru-sishya-samvada* (1645), *Akhe-gita* (1649); among others are *Anubhava-bindu, Sakhi-duha, Chappa*. The last became a popular classic. Akho composed a few poems in Braj early in his career; later he wrote some substantial works in Hindi.

Akhyan-kavya (Rajasthani): the term in Rajasthani literature for puranic or historical stories that were sung. Gujarati also uses the same term.

Akhyana: originally a Sanskrit term for a tale, generally having to do with the gods or great kings of the past. Two more Sanskrit terms, 'upakhyana' and 'akhyanaka', have also been used with the same meaning. Narrative hymns and short legends in *Rigveda* are the earliest known specimens of akhyana.

Akhyana (Gujarati): a popular genre in medieval Gujarat, it was a mythological or religious story, in verse and set to tune, recited by professional story tellers known as Mana-bhattas or Gagari-bhattas. The reciter also acted out parts of the story. The recitation was in three parts. The first part ('mukhabandh') introduced the story; the second ('dhal') narrated the story in detail; the third ('valan') summed up the story. These three parts taken together was known as 'kadavun' (stanzas), and only stories recited with 'kadava' were known as akhyana.

Akhyana-git (Asamiya): old ballads based on Assamese history and legend. Among these are 'Badan Baraphukanar git', 'Jayamati Kumvarir git', 'Maniram Devanar git', 'Mayanamati-Gopichandra git', 'Teji Malar git'.

Akrura-gaman (?C; Asamiya) of Namati Gosai; a 'bhavana' play first staged during the reign of Ahom ruler Kamaleshwar Simha.

Akshar-mala (Kannada): a poetic form in which the initial letters of each line are in alphabetic order. Ponna's *Jinakshar-mala* is one such poem; it eulogises Jina in 39 lines.

Akshaykumar Datta (1820–86): prose writer in Bangla; editor of *Tattvabodhini*, a journal for which he wrote many essays on religion, science, archaeology, etc. His essays were later collected in three volumes under the title *Charupath* (1852–53). As seen in these essays, he succeeded in creating a prose medium flexible enough to tackle a variety of subjects.

Alahuniya (Panjabi): song of lamentation sung by a group of women when somebody dies.

Alam (*c*1580–1625): poet in Hindi from near Jaunpur in Uttar Pradesh. According to tradition he was born into a brahman family but, on falling in love with a Muslim 'rangrejin' (dyer woman), he converted to Islam in order to marry her. Prince Muazzam (later the emperor Bahadur Shah), son of Aurangzeb, is said to have been his patron. Four works attributed to him are *Madhavanala-Kamakandala, Sudama-charitra, Shyam-sunehi* and *Alamkeli*. He composed in Avadhi as well as in Brajbhasa.

Alam-keli (*c*1600; Hindi): see above.

Alamkara (Sanskrit): literally meaning 'ornament', the term is used in a general sense for poetic (or literary) beauty; consequently, the study of poetry (or literary criticism) is known as 'alamkar-shastra'. In a more restricted sense, alamkara means any figure of speech used in literary composition. The earliest discussion of figures or tropes is to be found in *Natyashastra*.

Alamkara-chandrodaya (*c*1720; Sanskrit) of Rasik Sumati: prose work based on *Kuvalayananda*.

Alamkara-darpana (Prakrit) of unknown date and authorship: a work on poetics.

Alamkara-kaustubha (early 16th; Sanskrit) of Kavikarnapura: a work on poetics, the most important among several works with the same title. This work consists of ten chapters called 'kirana' and the treatment of subject matter follows *Kavyaprakasha*. Most of the illustrative verses are in praise of Krishna.

Alamkara'sarvaswa (?12th; Sanskrit) of Ruyyaka: a work on poetics, consisting of sutra and vritti. Some scholars hold that while Ruyyaka wrote the sutra portion, the vritti was written by somebody else, probably Mankhaka. The work deals only with poetic figures and introduces two new ones, 'vikalpa' and 'vichitra'. Many later rhetoricians (Vishwanatha, Vidyanatha, Appayya Dikshita) have drawn upon it, while Ruyyaka has quoted *Kavyaprakasha* of Mammata at many places. There are two other works with the same title, one by an unknown author, another probably by Keshava Mishra.

Alaol (*c*1607–80): leading Muslim poet in Bangla; lived mostly in Arakan (now in Myanmar) and received the patronage of a succession of chiefs and nobles of that region. His best and most famous work, *Padmavati* (1645), is a free translation of the long poem in Avadhi by Malik Muhammad Jayasi, *Padumavat*; he also translated *Saiful-mulk Badiuz-zamal* (from Farsi), *Tohfa* (from Arabic), *Sapta-paikar* (from Farsi), *Dara-Sikandarnama* (from Farsi). He completed *Sati Mainamati*, the famous poem left unfinished by Daulat Kazi; wrote a treatise on music, *Raga-nama*. When Shah Shuja, son of Emperot Jahangir, took refuge in Arakan he and Alaol became friends; the murder of Shuja brought Alaol under suspicion. He was imprisoned and all his property confiscated; even after release he lived amid much hardship and poverty for ten years.

Alata (?C): also called Alaka or Allata; son of Rajanaka Jayanaka; appears to have been a Kashmiri. He wrote the small portion of *Kavyaprakasha* left incomplete by Mammata; also wrote a commentary on *Haravijaya* of Ratnakara.

Alha (Hindi): the metre in which *Alha-khand* of Jaganik was composed; also known as 'savagya' or 'vira'.

Alha-khand (*c*1176; Hindi) of Jaganik: a giti-kavya narrating the brave deeds of two brothers Alha and Udal, who were chiefs under Parmal (or Parmardidev), ruler of Kalinjar. At a very young age they fought and killed the chieftain Karingarai (or Kalingarai) who had murdered their father Dassaraj (or Desraj) and uncle Bachharaj. Later they were involved in the great battle of Mahoba between Prithviraj, ruler of Delhi, and Paramardidev. This fraternal strife became famous as 'the Mahabharat of Mahoba'. The work describes as many as 52 separate combats; apart from the feats of Alha and Udal, the bravery of others like Malkhan, Lakhan. Brahamjit and Talhan Syed is also mentioned. On account of oral transmission, the original language of the work has been wholly lost over the centuries; later versions refer even to more modern weapons like pistols and muskets. Though the literary merit of the work is negligible, it has been preserved by popular practice and is sung even today, during the monsoons, in Hindi-speaking areas like Bihar, eastern Uttar Pradesh, northern Madhya Pradesh. No manuscript has ever been found; in 1880, Charles Eliot collected oral versions;

later George Grierson enlarged the text. The work is also called *Parmal raso.*

Ali Haidar (1690–1785): sant poet in Panjabi, also a scholar of Farsi and Arabic. Five siharfi works, one baramaha and an incomplete *Hir-Ranjha* have been attributed to him; these were collectively published in 1907 under the title *Mukammal Majmua Abiat Ali Haidar*. He was born and brought up in Multan, now in Pakistan.

Ali-nama (*c*1570; Urdu) of Nusrati: a masnavi work dealing with the wars of Bijapur sultan Ali Adil Shah with the Mughals and the Marathas.

Aliraja (?18th); Muslim poet in Bangla: lived mostly in Chatgaon (now in Bangladesh). Also known as Kanu Fakir, he is the author of *Jnana-sagar*, which deals with the philosophy of fakirs; *Siraj-kulup*, which tells of the creation of the universe and its destruction; *Dhyana-mala*, a treatise on music. He also wrote many Vaishnav padas and at least two songs on the goddess Kali (called Shyama).

Allahabad Inscription (*c*370): praise of king Samudragupta (*c*335–375) composed in Sanskrit; important to literary history because it proves that kavya composition had already achieved fairly developed form by this date. Composed by the court-poet, Harisena, the panegyric inscribed on a stone-pillar consists of eight verses, a long prose passage, and a concluding verse.

Allama Prabhu (12th): poet in Kannada and religious leader; composed more than a thousand vachanas. He led the Virshaiva movement in Karnataka and was the guru of Basaveshwar.

Allasani Peddanna (*c*1510–75): poet in Telugu; foremost among the 'Ashta-diggaja' poets at the court of Krishnadevaraya of Vijayanagar. Also known as 'Andhra-kavita Pithamahudu' (grandfather of Andhra poetry), he originated the 'prabandha' form in his work *Manucharitramu.*

Allur Nanmullai (1st/2nd): woman poet in Tamil; her work appears in anthologies like *Ahananuru*, etc. Some of her poems present the incipient revolt of a housewife who would like to but cannot defy social strictures that limit women's freedom of action.

Alvar (Azhvar): term for the 12 Vaishnav sant-poets of Tamilnadu whose songs and personal example launched and sustained the Bhakti movement in that region upto 10th century A.D. Their compositions were later collected by Nathamuni in the anthology *Divya Prabandham.* The Alvars recognized by the canon are Poygai, Bhudam, Pey, Tirumalisai, Nammalvar, Madhurakan, Peryalvar, Andal, Tiruppan, Tondaraddipodi, Kulasekara and Tirumangai. The first three belong to 5th/6th; of the rest, the most eminent are Andal (8th) and Nammalvar (9th). Andal was a woman.

Amanat [Agha Hasan Amanat (1815–59)]: poet in Urdu; who settled in Lakhnau. His most famous work is *Inder Sabha*, a musical drama which was much favoured by Avadh's last nawab, Wajid Ali Shah. Among Amanat's other works are the long poem *Wasokht Wat* (1846–59) and the collection *Guldasta-i-Amanat* (1853). His diwan, *Khazain-ul-Fasahat*, was published in 1868.

Amardas, Guru (1479–1547): third guru of the Sikhs and composer of hymns in Panjabi; 5122 stanzas of his composition are to be found in *Guru Granth.* Born in Basarke village, near Amritsar, he became a Sikh quite late in life; his poetry is in the style of folk songs and his diction is predominantly Panjabi.

Amara-kosha: see *Namalinganushasana.*

Amarakosha-bhasanama-Samhita (?C; Marathi) of unknown author: a lexicon.

Amara-simha (?4th): Bouddhist scholar of Sanskrit; author of *Namalinganushasana*, popularly known as *Amara-kosha.* According to tradition, he was one of the nine distinguished men ('nava-ratna') of the court of Vikramaditya.

Amarnath-samvad (?11th; Marathi) work attributed to Gorakhnath: or another of the Nath following in Maharashtra.

Amaru-shataka (7th/8th; Sanskrit) of Amaru or Amaruka: an erotic poem which presumably consisted of one hundred verses. It is extant in four recensions; the number of verses vary from 96 to 115, of which 51 are common to all recensions. The poem presents differrent mental states of the lover and the beloved. Very little is known about the poet's life; since he is quoted by Vamana and Anandavardhana, he lived before 9C. He may have been a king of Kashmir. According to legend, Shankaracharya entered the dead king's body and experienced different aspects of love.

Ambika-vilasa (*c*1780; Oriya) of Brajanath Badajena: kavya work on the marriage of Shiva and Parvati. It has also been ascribed to Keonjhar ruler, Birbhadra Bhanja, under whom Brajanath served for some time.

Ambikapati Kovai (late 12th; Tamil) of Ambikapati: an unusual 'kovai' work inasmuch as it was not composed to praise any patron and is named after the author himself. Also, it exceeds the 400 verses stipulated for a kovai. It is believed that the poet was Kamban's son; may have been a Shaiva.

Amir Hamzah (18th: Bangla) a jangnama begun by Garibullah in early 18th and completed by Saiyad Hamzah in 1792–94.

Amir Khusro or **Khusrau** (1253–1325): scholar of Arabic and Farsi, wrote poetry in Old Hindi. His real name was Abul Hasan; belonged to Patiali (Pata) in Etah district in Uttar Pradesh; was tutor of prince Muhammad and court-poet of Sultan Ghiyasuddin Balban. At a time when Dingal and Apabhramsha were in use, he composed verse in the earliest known form of Kharibolі, to which he gave the name 'Hindvi'; it tends towards Brajbhasha. His most famous work is *Khaliq-bari*; he is famous also for having composed every variety of paheliyan; more than 90 works are attributed to him. A singer who also composed music, he is said to have invented the sitar.

Amir Minai (1829–1900): poet and scholar in Urdu from Lakhnau. He joined the court of Wajid Ali Shah in 1853; during the Revolt moved to Kakori; invited to Rampur State, spent the most productive period of his life here, 1859–87; left Rampur after the death of Nawab Yusuf Ali Khan and visited Patna, Bhopal, Haidarabad (Dakhan) in search of patronage. His religious thought is represented in a work like *Mahamid-e-Khatimunnabeen* (1872); among his ghazal collections is *Sanam-khana-e-Ishq* (1896); a large Urdu dictionary project he took up in 1884, *Amri-ul-Lughat*, remained unfinished at his death. He is said to have written more than 40 books, many of which await publication.

Amitrakshar chhand (Bangla): the name given to the kind of blank verse innovated by Maikel Madhusudan Datta for the purpose of composing epic poetry on the Western model.

Ammuvanar (?1st): poet in Tamil; real name is Muvan. One hundred of his poems appear in the anthology *Ainnukuṛunuru*. From geographic references in his work it would appear that he belonged to the west coast; many ancient cities of the Chera region (modern Kerala) are named in his poems.

Amogha-raghavam (*c*1299; Sanskrit) of Divakara: the first champu work composed by a poet of Kerala.

Amritakara (*c*1400–82): a contemporary of Vidyapati in Mithila; belonged to the family of dewans of the kingdom. Primarily involved in political affairs, he was also a man of letters; perhaps a poet or dramatist in Maithili.

Amrit-anubhava (1320; Marathi) of Jnaneshwar: an original philosophic work, which is at times at variance with *Jnaneshwari* in exposition of the Vedantic doctrine of Advaita. It is also a much shorter work, in 10 chapters, consisting of 800 ovi stanzas.

Amrita-raya (1698–1753): poet in Marathi; author of works like *Durvasa-yatra*, *Draupadi-vastraharan*, *Dhruva-charitra*, etc.; innovated the katav metre. Born and brought up in a village near Buldana in Old Berar, he lived and died in Aurangabad.

Amukta-malyada (early 16th; Telugu) of Krishnadeva Raya, king of Vijayanagar: a 'prabandha' named after the heroine Godadevi who is also called Amuktamalyada (meaning, a girl who offers to the gods a garland worn first by her). The work in six sections is also known as *Vishnuchittiyamu* after Vishnuchitta, the father of Godadevi. She is an incarnation of goddess Lakshmi, given as a foundling to the childless Vishnuchitta, and later married to Shrirangeshwara (another form of Vishnu). As narrated in the introductory section, Krishnadeva Raya was told the story by Vishnu in a dream when the king stopped overnight at a temple in Shrikakulam district (Andhra Pradesh) on his way to Kalinga. The prabandha contains two other stories and long descriptions of the various seasons of the year; there is also ample mention of the customs, religious beliefs and practices of the age.

Anadipatan-kavya (16th; Asamiya) of Shankaradeva: long philosophical poem based on *Bhagavata*, *Vishnu-Purana*, etc; deals mainly with Vaishnav cosmogony. The work later became a source book for composers of dehabicharar git.

Anagata-vamsha (?C; Pali) of Kassapa: a work which discusses the forthcoming decadence and eventual extinction of Buddhism. One version is in 142 verses, written in the form of prophesies supposed to have been made by Gautam Buddha himself. Another version, part-verse and part-prose, is in the form of a dialogue between Buddha and Sariputta. The author may have belonged to Chola country; other works attributed to him are *Buddha-vamsha* and *Moha-vichhedani* or *Vimati-chhedani*.

Ananda-brindavan champu (16th; Sanskrit) of Kavikarnapura: champu kavya based on the life of Shri Krishna with special attention to his role as lover.

Ananda-ghan (1604–74): Jaina sadhu and poet in Gujarati; his original name was Labhanand and he belonged to Tapagaccha; lived in Gujarat as well as in Rajasthan, hence the use of Rajasthani diction. Of his *Anandaghan-chovisi*, 22 and not 24 verses are available; in *Anandghan-bahoteri*, different manuscripts show different numbers of verses. His religious poems resemble those of Kabir, Surdas, Mira, etc., and sometimes their compositions have been shown as his in certain manuscripts.

Ananda-lahari (8th/9th; Sanskrit) attributed to Shankaracharya: a poem of about 104 verses in praise of Tripurasundari and conveying some mystical doctrine.

Ananda-raghunandan (early 18th; Hindi) of Vishwanath Singh: a play on Rama which uses both verse and prose. The author was ruler of Rewa (r. 1721–40).

Anandarai Makhi (late 17th/early 18th): writer in Sanskrit; chief minister of Thanjavur rulers Shahji (r.1684–1710) and Sarfoji (r.1711–20). He is the author of two symbolist plays in Sanskrit: *Vidya-parinayan*, which blends Vedanta with erotic sentiment, and *Jivanandan*, which has various diseases as dramatic characters.

Anandaram Dhekial Phukan (1829–59): prose writer in Asamiya who was also a strong advocate of using Asamiya in educational institutions and law courts. He published a series of articles on the subject in the newly founded periodical, *Orunodoy*; also wrote a pamphlet in English entitled *A Few Remarks on the Assamese Language* (1849) pleading for reinstatement of Asamiya. He propagated Assamese culture and dressed in Assamese costume even while attending office as a subordinate court official. He is the subject of Gunabhiram Barua's famous biography.

Anandaram Dhekial Phukanar Jibon Charitra (1880; Asamiya) of Gunbhiram Barua: first biographical work in modern Asamiya. The author, only eight years younger than his subject, was related to him and shared the life of the time. The work is thus autobiographical at places. The introductory chapter can be read as socio-political history of Assam.

Ananda-sundari (mid-18th; Prakrit) of Ghanashyama: a 'sattaka' play. The author was a poet in the court of Thanjavur-ruler Tulaji.

Ananda-tanaya (?C): poet in Marathi from Thanjavur district. He composed about twenty akhyana poems of which the better works are *Sita-swayamvar, Radha-vilas, Putane-vadha*.

Ananda-vardhana (late 9th): scholar of Sanskrit and literary critic from Kashmir, also wrote some poetry in Sanskrit and Prakrit. A contemporary of king Avantivarman (r. 855–83) of Kashmir and possibly also of the next ruler Shankaravarman (r. 883–902), he is best-known as the author of *Dhvanyaloka*. Other works ascribed to him are the Sanskrit poems *Devi-shataka* (or *Devi stotra*) and *Arjuna-harita*, the Prakrit poem *Vishamabanalila*, the treatise *Tattvaloka*. He has himself claimed authorship of *Dharmottama*, a commentary on *Pramana-vinischaya* of Dharmakirti. He is mentioned in *Rajatarangini* (v:34).

Ananga-bhasa-sahitam (?C; Marathi) of unknown author: work on erotics.

Ananga'harsha Amatraraja

(?8th): playwright in Sanskrit and son of a king named Narendravardhana; author of the play *Tapasa vatsa Raja* and *Udatta'Raghava*.

Ananga-ranga (16th; Sanskrit) of Kalyanamalla: a work on erotics.

Tr. anon. for Kamasutra Society, London & Benares, 1885.

Anant Phandi (1744–1821): poet and performer in Marathi; innovated the phataka metre. Born at Sangamner (Ahmednagar district) into a brahman family of bankers, he joined tamasha performing parties, for whom he used to compose powadas and lavanis; later, took to serious literature under the influence of Ahilya Bai, the saintly queen of Indore.

Ananta Acharya (18th): court-poet of Ahom king Shiva Simha; author of *Ananta-lahari*; see below.

Ananta Dasa (16th): one of the Pancha-sakha poets in Oriya.

Ananta Kandali (16th): poet and disciple of Shankaradeva with whom he collaborated in rendering *Bhagavat*a into Asamiya. He is the author of *Sahasra-nama-vrittanta, Kumari-haran, Mahiravan-vadh*, and other kavyas that have been lost; also composed an abridged version of *Ramayana*.

Ananta-lahari (*c*1730; Asamiya) of Ananta Acharya: a paean to the goddess Durga, based on the Sanskrit *Saundarya-lahari*. The poem ends with an eulogy of the queen-consort of Ahom king Shiva Simha.

Anantanath-puran (mid-13th; Kannada) of Janna: a champu work in fourteen chapters about the 14th tirthankar Anantanath. However, at the core of this work is the story of Chandasasan and his illicit passion for Sunanda, the wife of his friend Vasudev.

Anantapura-varnam (early 14th; Malayalam) of unknown author: a devotional poem in Manipravalam, in praise of Vishnu as enshrined in Anantapura (Thiruvanantapuram or Trivandrum). The work contains a seemingly realistic description of the city.

Anargha'raghava (late 9th/early 10th; Sanskrit) of Murari: play in seven acts based on *Ramayana*. The prologue says Murari was the son of Vardhamanka and Tantumati.

Andal (?6th): one of the 12 Alvars of Tamilnadu and the only woman among them. Her hymns in Tamil have been collected in the anthology *Divya Prabandha*. She was a foundling, discovered in a tulsi bush by Perialvar who was himself a devotee of Vishnu and a composer of hymns. After she grew up and her devotion to Krishna was revealed to her foster-father, she was taken to Shrirangam and she worshipped in that temple thereafter. Two separate poetical works composed by her are *Tiruppavai* and *Nachir Tirumozhi*; in both she assumes the role of the bride of Krishna.

Andayya (13th): poet in Kannada, known mainly as author of the champu work *Kabbigara kava*. In it the poet seems to have made an attempt to identify the hero Kama with the Kadamba king Kamadeva (1130–1217) who was the poet's near contemporary. Also, in paying tribute to earlier poets, the latest one he mentions is Janna (d.1230) Hence it is inferred that Andayya lived and wrote in the first half of 13th. He was a Jain by birth.

Andhra-bhasa-bhusanamu (*c*1250; Telugu) of Mulaghatika Ketana: a grammatical treatise which the author claimed was the first of its kind in Telugu.

Andhra-bhasarnavamu (*c*1760; Telugu) of Mudurapati Venkatanarayudu: a lexicon in verse, prepared under the patronage of Vijayaraghunatha Tondaman (r. 1730–69), ruler at Pudukkotai.

Andhra-mahabharatamu (11th/14th; Telugu): the oldest extant literary work in Telugu, this rendering of *Mahabharata* into Telugu was carried out by three poets. Nannaya began the work in 11th and translated Adi-parva, Sabha-parva and a part of Vana-parva. Subsequently, Tikkana (13th) translated all fifteen books after Vana-parva. It was left to Errapragada (14th) to do the rest of Vana-parva and complete the work.

Andhra-shabda-chintamani (?11th; Sanskrit) ascribed to Nannaya Bhatta: a grammar of Telugu. The work was unknown until Bal Saraswati wrote a commentary on it sometime between 1575 and 1625. Most scholars believe that before starting his literary career Nannaya prepared this grammar of Telugu in order to give the language some fixity. Until he began composing in Telugu, it was not considered a language fit for literary composition.

Anga: a class of veda-like works of the Jaina religion, composed generally in Prakrit using verse as well as prose forms. There are 12 authoritative angas; 14 works outside this cannon are called 'angavahya'.

Angom Gopi (1710–80): poet in Manipuri; introduced Sanskrit and Bangla literature to Manipur through translation. He adopted two parts of Gangadas' *Mahabharata* and the whole of Krittibas' *Ramayana* from Bangla into Manipuri.

Aniruddha-deva (*c*1553–1626): poet in Asamiya Vaishnav scholar; disciple of Gopal Ata and founder of the Mayamara sect. He translated parts of *Bhagavata* into Asamiya verse; composed many religious songs, including 182 baragita lyrics; his *Bhaktimangal-ghosa* contains 805 choral verses.

Aniruddha-charit (?C; Asamiya) of Chidananda Deva: a biography of Aniruddha.

Anis [Anis Mir Baber Ali (1803–74)]: poet in Urdu, particularly famous for marsiya compositions.

Anka (Sanskrit): division of a play. *Natyashastra* lays down the number of ankas for a particular kind of play and what each anka is expected to contain.

Ankar-arya (?C; Asamiya) of unknown authorship: treatise on dances and dance poses, probably based on the Sanskrit *Srihasta-muktavali*.

Ankitam (Telugu): the dedication of a literary work. An early example in Telugu is Nannaya's dedicating his part translation of *Mahabharata* to Rajaraja Narendra.

Ankiya-nat (Asamiya): one-act plays in prose, a form innovated by Shankaradeva for the purpose of spreading Vaishnav faith. The term 'ankiya' derives from Sanskrit 'anka' but the Asamiya form differs considerably. The form was also known in Mithila and the influence of Maithili compositions is seen in the occasional verse portions where a mixture of Asamiya and Maithili of a corrupt Asamized Maithili is used, not unlike the Brajabuli of Bengal. Among the best-known ankiya-nats composed by Shankaradeva are *Rama-vijay, Kaliya-daman, Parijat-haran, Rukmini-haran, Patni-prasad*.

Annada-mangal (1750–53; Bangla) of Bharatchandra Raye: a trilogy comprising three practically independent poems; (i) *Annada-mangal* proper, describing the Shiva-Parvati story with the poet's own innovation of Parvati becoming 'Annada' (the foodgiving goddess) by offering cooked food to a famished Shiva; work was written to support the worship of Annada newly instituted by the poet's patron, Raja Krishnachandra; (ii) *Vidya-Sundar*, an erotic romance about Vidya and Sundar; (iii) *Mansimha*, a historical romance, intended to glorify the founder of Raja Krishnachandra's family. The whole work, also known as *Kalika-mangal*, was the greatest Bangla poem of 18th.

Annamacharya or **Annamayya** (1424–1503): sant poet in Telugu from Tirupati; according to tradition he composed as many as 32,000 songs in his life time. These songs are known as 'sankirtana' and they are meant for community singing. Annamacharya also wrote a treatise in Sanskrit. *Sankirtana lakshmanam*, in which he formulated rules for composing sankirtana.

Anubhava (Sanskrit): term in poetics for that which follows and strengthens a mood; a factor of rasa. In Kannada, the term is used for 'mystical meaning' in philosophical works.

Anubhava-saram (early 13th; Telugu) of Palakuriki Somnatha: series of verses in vritta metre borrowed from Sanskrit prosody.

Anu-Gita: a part of *Mahabharata* (Bk xiv, 16–51); contains the spiritual instruction to Arjuna by Krishna after the Kurukshetra battle is over. It also narrates the legend of Utanka, the preservation of the foetus of Uttara, and the Ashwamedha-yajna performed by Yudhisthira.
Tr. Telang, Oxford, 1932.

Anukramani (Sanskrit): generic term for catalogues, indexes or lists relating to the contents of Vedic samhitas.

Anukriti (Sanskrit): term in drama aesthetics, first used by Bharata. Broadly indicating 'imitation', more specifically it indicates the relation of the poem and the world, or of the actor and the character, or of this poem and other poems.

Anumiti-vada (Sanskrit): doctrine of Sanskrit poetics expounded by Shankuka, according to whom rasa is to be inferred ('anuman' = inference).

Anurag Bansuri (late 18th; Hindi) of Nur Muhammad: an allegorical kavya which seeks to preach Islam.

Anuraga-balli (*c*1697; Bangla) of Manohardas: a biography of Shri Chaitanya.

Anuruddha (late 12th): Bouddha scholar and author of works in Pali, *Abhidhamma-samgraha* and *Paramartha-vinicchaya*. Born somewhere in Tamilnadu, he lived for some time in Thanjavur and settled finally in the Mulsomavihara in Sri Lanka.

Anyokti (Sanskrit): term for an expression which means something different from what it states. Anyokti (or anyapadesha) was a popular device of Sanskrit writers and was widely adopted by writers in other Indian languages.

Apabhramsha: generic name for Indo-Aryan dialects which represent the stage of development following the Prakrits. The Apabhramsas began to be used in folk as well as formal literature after A.D. 500. The Modern Indo-Aryan languages (the Bhashas) emerged from the Apabhramshas.

Apadana (Pali): the thirteenth part of *Khuddaniyaka*; Composed in verse, it comprises the biography of 550 men and 40 women who belonged to the monastic order; deals mainly with their heroic and pious deeds and, like the Jataka tales, contains stories of the past as well as the present; also has close correspondence with Avadana works in Sanskrit.

Appa'kavi (17th): poet in Telugu and authority on prosody; author of *Andhra shabda chintamani* (1656). It is also believed that he wrote a yakshagana named *Ambikavadamu* and a kavya named *Anantavrata-kalpa*, but neither has been found. Of the original eight chapters of his work on prosody, *Appakaviyamu*, only five have been recovered.

Appar (7th): Shaiva sant-poet in Tamil; one of the four great Nayanmars; composed 3000 hymns which make up the 4th, 5th and 6th *Tirumurai* collections. Originally named Marul Nikkiyar, he became a Jain in early youth and took the name Dharmasena; later, under the influence of his sister Tilakavati, changed to Shaiva faith and was named Tirunavukkarasar (Prince of the sacred word). For some time he was persecuted by Pallava king Mahendravarman (*c*600/630), a Jaina, but the ruler himself became a Shaiva later. Tirunavukkarusu visited all the sacred shrines of Tamilnadu and composed his hymns. At Siyali he met the younger Nayanmar, Sambandhar, who addressed him affectionately as 'Appar' (Father); this is the name by which he was referred to thereafter.

Appayya Dikshita (1520–93): Shaiva philosopher and Sanskrit scholar; author of three works in Sanskrit on poetics—*Kuvalaya-nanda, Chitra-mimamsa* and *Vritti-vartika*. The lost work ascribed to him, *Lakshana-ratnavali*, probably dealt with dramaturgy. Also called Appa or Apya, he is to be distinguished from other authors named Appayya Dikshita.

Aranimal' (late 18th): see Arinmal.

Aranyaka (Sanskrit): generic name for texts appended to the Brahmanas. These are mystical works, dealing mainly with the symbolism of sacrifice and with priestly philosophy. They belong to the various Vedic schools; thus, 'Aitareya-aranyaka' to *Rig-veda*, 'Taittiriya-aranyaka to *Yajur-veda*, and so on.

Arappalisur Shatakam (18th; Tamil) of Ampalvanakkavirayar: 100 verses in 'achriya viruttam' metre on various subjects. Each poem makes reference to the poet's patron Matvel, to the god Koluli worshipped by him, and to the hill-top temple of Arappali where the presiding deity was Shiva.

Arayirappadi (12th; Tamil) of Pillan: prose commentary on the songs of Nammalvar, especially of his *Tiruvaymoli*. The prose used is Manipravala.

Ardha-kathanak (*c*1641; Hindi) of Banarsidas Jain: perhaps the first autobiographical work in the language. Though a trader by profession, Banarsidas aspired to be a writer and began writing his memoirs at the age of 55. The work refers to many events and places known at first hand to the author. It is composed in 675 couplets, mostly in 'doha' and 'chaupayi' forms.

Ardha-magadhi: a Prakrit language of Koshal (Avadh). Language areawise it lay between Magadhi (of Magadh) and Sauraseni (of Surasen): later it came to be known as Ardhamagadhi. The Jains adopted this language for many of their sacred books.

Ardhanemi-purana (early 13th; Kannada) of Nemichandra: a champu work dealing with the 22nd tirthankar Neminath. It is an incomplete kavya and the poet probably died before he could complete it; therefore it is called 'ardha-Nemi' (half of Nemi).

Aricchandir-puranam (*c*1520; Tamil) of Virkavirayar: a kavya work in ten 'kanda' telling the story of Raja Harischandra. The main metre is venba, but other metres have also been used. The poet has employed Sanskrit words occasionally.

Arinmal (*c*1750–1800): woman song-writer in Kashmiri; said to have ushered in the Lol era in Kashmiri literature. Her 'lol' (love-song) compositions have a bearing on her own marriage (to Munshi Bhabanidas Kachru), and expressed both her fulfilled love of her husband and her pain of separation when he was attracted by other women. She has influenced the style of composition of geet and ghazal in Kashmiri.

Arjan Dev, Guru (1565–1605): the fifth Guru, compiler of *Adi Granth*; poet in Panjabi; author of *Sukhwani*, a long mystical poem of about 60,000 lines in 24 ashtapadi stanzas with 24 introductory shlokas. He also wrote three expositions of Sikh mysticism, *Bavan akhri, Bara mah,* and *Gatha.*

Arjun-bhanjan (16th; Asamiya) of Madhavadeva: a play based on an episode from the childhood of Krishna. Once his mother Yashoda put him down from her lap in order to attend to milk being boiled;

offended by this, he breaks the butter pots and distributes the butter to monkeys; as punishment Yashoda tries to tie him to a post but when they come close to two arjun trees, these break and topple to the ground.

Arjun Dasa (15th/16th): poet in Oriya and Jagannath-bhakta of a pre-Chaitanya period, probably 1450–1525. Of two poetical works discovered so far, *Rama-bibaha* is earlier; it is in puranic style and has divisions as in a kavya-work. The later work, *Kavya-lata*, portrays fictitious character involved in shringara-featured activities. He was a pioneer in Oriya poetry inasmuch as he adapted the Sanskrit mahakavya form to his language.

Arpudattirubamdadi (6th; Tamil) of Karekkal Ammaiyar: a collection of verse fragments composed by this Shiva-devoted woman-poet.

Artha-prakriti (Sanskrit): term of dramaturgy; element of plot in drama. There are five elements- 'bija' (germ from which the action originates); 'bindu' (drop which spreads out like oil in water); 'pataka' (chain of episodes); 'prakari' (particular incident); 'karya' (denouement). A play passes through these 'avastha' (conditions).

Artha-shastra (?C; Sanskrit) of Kautilya: a treatise on politics and statecraft. The author is identified by tradition as Chanakya Vishnugupta, minister or counsellor of Chandragupta Maurya (4th century B.C) The work is divided into 15 sections (adhikarana) and 180 subsections. It is written in short prose sentences.

Arumuga Navalar (1822–79): Shaiva scholar and Tamil author from Jafna, Sri Lanka. Apart from religious books, he wrote a book on Sri Lanka geography, another on Tamil grammar, and several textbooks for schoolgoers. He developed Tamil prose into a medium for modern expository writing.

Arunachalak Kavirayar (1712–79): Tamil composer and singer; author of *Rama-natakam* (1771), which became very popular because of its simple language and lively tunes. He is said to have narrowed the gap between spoken Tamil and written Tamil. Among his other works are *Sikazhit talapuranam*, *Sikazhikkovai, Anumar pillaittamil, Asomukhi natakam.*

Arunagiri-nathar (early 15th): bhakti poet in Tamil who composed a number of works in honour of Muruga; regarded as chief exponent of the Kaumara sect which worships Muruga. His most famous work is the collection of hymns called *Tiruppugazh*; among his other works are *Kandar antadi*, *Kandar anubhuti*, *Kandar alankaram*.

Arunodai (also **Orunodai**): first ever periodical in Asamiya; published by the American Baptist Mission from Sibsagar; began publication 1848 and continued upto 1882.

Arya (Marathi): a verse-metre popularised by Moropant, especially in his version of *Mahabharata*. He took the metre over from Sanskrit and gave it a new polish and variety.

Arya-bharata (mid-17th; Marathi) of Moropant: an abridged version of *Mahabharata* in Marathi, composed mainly in arya metre.

Arya-saptasati (*c*1200; Sanskrit) of Govardhan: collection of over 700 verses Sanskrit) in arya metre, arranged under appropriate headings. The verses are generally erotic in character. The work was modelled on *Sattasai* of Hala. The author was one of the five 'gems' who adorned the court of king Lakshman Sen of Bengal.

Aryasura (3rd/4th): Bouddha preacher and prose writer in Sanskrit; author of *Jatakamala* (or *Bodhisattvardanamala*), which tells 34 legends about the noble deeds of Buddha in his previous births.

Asaf-ud-daula, Nawab (1775–97) ruler of Avadh, during whose reign the capital shifted from Faizabad to Lakhnau and made the latter a centre of literary patronage.

Asaga (mid-9th): poet in Sanskrit of Karnataka who is known from reference by other poets. He is said to have composed *Shanti-puran* and *Vardhaman-puran* in Sanskrit. The 10th poet in Apabhramsha, Dhaval, has praised Asaga in his *Harivamsha-puran*.

Asamiya (abbrevated as Assamese here for reference): the language of about 22 million people mainly in the state of Assam in N E India; spoken along the Brahmaputra valley, also in other north-eastern states like Meghalaya, Nagaland and Arunachal. Asamiya shares with Bangla and Oriya a common source in Magadhi Apabhramsha; also shares the script with Bangla. It emerged as a separate speech probably by 7th century A.D. For writing, a script known as 'Kutilalipi' was used until early 19th. The British used the word 'Assamese' to refer to the language as well as to the people.

Asayit Thakar (late 14th): poet in Gujarati, also singer and storyteller; is said to have innovated the 'bhavai' form of folk-theatre. His major work *Hamsauli* is in four parts; the first part tells of the marriage between Hamsavali and Naravahan; the remaining three parts describe the feats of their two sons, Hamsaraj and Bachharaj.

Ascharya-chudamani (?9th; Sanskrit) of Shaktibhadra: play in seven acts on the *Ramayana* story; reveals knowledge of Bhavabhuti's drama. The title refers to the magic crest-jewel of Sita used as a token of recognition. This work is regarded by some scholars as the oldest drama of South India, assigned to 9th.
Tr. Kuppusvami Sastri, Madras, 1926, 1927.

Ashta-chhap (or, Eight stamped seals): name of the group of sant-poets in Hindi established by Vitthalnath around 1600. The poets are Surdas, Kundandas, Parmananddas, Krishnadas, Chitswami, Govindaswami, Chaturbhujdas and Nandadas. The first four were disciples of Vitthalnath, the latter of Vallabhacharya.

Ashtadhyayi (?5C; Sanskrit) of Panini: earliest extant and most authoritative grammar. The work is divided into eight 'adhyaya' (chapters), each sub-divided into four sub-sections called 'pada'. Containing nearly 4000 aphorisms by Panini and supplementary rules called 'Vartika-sutra' by Katyayana, it deals not only with classical Sanskrit but also analyses Vedic. Apart from the grammar, the work documents the socio-cultural milieu of the time. There have been many commentaries on *Ashtadhyayi*; among the more important are *Varttika* of Katyayana or Vararuchi (4th/3rd B.C.), *Mahabhashya* of Patanjali (2nd B.C.), *Kashika* of Jayadittya and Vamana (7th), *Nyasa* of Jinendrabuddhi (7th/8th), *Padamanjari* of Haridatta (12th), *Durghatavritti* of Sharanadeva (13th), *Siddhanta-kaumudi* of Bhattoji Dikshit (16th).
Tr. Bohtlingk, Leipzeig, 1887.

Ashta-diggaja (Eight elephants of the quarters bearing the earth): name given to a group of eight great poets in Telugu attached to the court of Krishnadeva Raya (1509–30). They are Allasani Peddana, Nandi Timmanna, Ramabhadra Kavi, Madayagari Mallana, Pingali Suranna, Bhattumurti, Dhurjati and Tenali Ramakrishna. There is some doubt, however, whether Pingali and Bhattumurti belonged to this court.

Ashta-nayika-vivaha (?C; Marathi) of Elhana: kavya work based on 10th skandha of *Bhagavata*; describes the eight weddings of Krishna, the particular god of the sect.

Ashta-prabandham (12th; Tamil) of Perumal Ayyangar: anthology of eight poetical works celebrating Narayan. These are: 1. *Shri Ranga kalambakam* (100 poems); 2. *Shri Ranga-mala* (111); 3. *Shri Ranga antadi* (100); 4. *Shri Ranganayaka dolika* (32); 5. *Shri Venkatesh-mala* (100); 6. *Shri Venkatesh antadi* (100); 7. *Alkar antadi*; 8. *Ashatottarsata tirtha* (108).

Ashwaghosa (?1st): name of the author of *Buddha-charita, Saundarananda* and *Gandistotra-gatha*, all works in verse; also wrote a play, *Sariputra* or *Saradavatiputra-prakarana*. Born a brahman, he became a Bouddha and probably belonged to the Hinayana sect; he is said to be a contemporary of the Kushana king, Kanishka.

Asir [Syed Muzaffar Ali Khan 'Asir'; (1800–81)]: poet in Urdu fom Lakhnau. He was associated for about nine years with Nawab Wajid Ali Shah who conferred on him titles such as 'Tadbir-ud-daulah' and 'Mukaddar-ul-mulk'. His poems have been collected in six volumes; he also wrote a number of poems in Farsi. He was specially known for marsiya and qasida compositions.

Asiriyam (Tamil): name of a verse metre.

Asiriyargal Panniru-tirumurai (?C; Tamil): collective title of the 12 books of Shaiva hymns that are central to the tradition in Tamilnadu. These were composed over five to six centuries by various poets and were later organised into canonical books. The major sant-poets concerned are Sambandar (or Jnana-sambandar), Appar (or Tirunakkarasar), Sundarar, Manikkavachakar, Tirumular.

Asiyo Bankidas (1781–1833): poet in Rajasthani counted among the most eminent 'charana kavis' of his time; belonged to Jodhpur. Well versed in Sanskrit, Farsi, Braj and Rajasthani, he composed numerous works on a variety of subjects.

Aswathi Thirunal (1756–94): poet in Malayalam; member of the Travancore royal family. His poetical talent was discovered by his elder brother, Kartika Thirunal Maharaja, who was already well-known as a writer of Kathakali scripts. Aswathi also wrote scripts for Kathakali works like *Paundrakavadham, Ambarishacharitam, Rukminiswayamvaram*.

Atharvana Dvityacharya (13th): Jain scholar of Andhra; composed a Telugu grammar, *Trilinga-shabdananushasana*, and a work on prosody, *Atharvana-chhandas*.

Athvara (Panjabi): poem describing eight days. For seven days the seeker waits anxiously for god; at the end of the eighth day, when he has nearly given up hope, he finds himself in god's embrace.

Atibadi Jagannatha Dasa (b. 1450): poet in Oriya, one of the 'Pancha Sakha' group; best known for his translation of *Bhagavata* into Oriya. Among his many other works are *Krishnabhakti kalpalata, Nityaguptamala, Upasana shataka, Niladri shataka*, etc.

Atish [Khwaja Haidar Ali (1778–1847)]: poet in Urdu who migrated from Delhi to Lakhnau and became a leading light of the Lakhnau school of Urdu poetry. His special contribution was a new style of ghazal.

Atma-bodha (?C; Sanskrit) attributed to Shankaracharya: a philosophical poem in 67 stanzas.

Atma-charit (Sanskrit; Hindi): autobiography or autobiographical account. Terms such as 'atmajivani' or 'atmakatha' mean the same thing.

Attakatha (Malayalam): the text used for a Kathakali performance. The literary form may have derived from *Gita Govinda*; words of the poet are usually given as shlokas while words of the characters are given as 'gana' (songs). The text is divided into so many sequences and each sequence is introduced with a narrative quatrain in Sanskrit or Manipravala, called 'pada'. The padas are sung in classical modes.

Atta-prakaram (Malayalam): manuals explaining how a koodiyattam is to be performed. These were written in prose. The earliest such manuals were no doubt written by Tholan, who developed the koodiyattam form sometime between 9th and 11th. Also see 'kramadipika'.

Attaru-ppade (Tamil): literally means a poem which shows the way. Five of the ten long poems of *Pattuppattu* belong to this category. In it a poet or artist is returning home after receiving some reward from his patron; on the way he meets another poor poet or artist and tells him how to reach that patron.

Attha-Katha (Pali): a class of

works which offer commentary on *Tripitaka*. These were preserved in Anuradhapura (Sri Lanka) and later translated into Sinhala.

Attha Katha (Prakrit): generic term for commentaries, like 'artha-katha' in Sanskrit.

Atukuri Molla (16th): the first woman poet in Telugu, whose best work is a version of *Ramayana* popularly known as *Molla Ramayanamu*. Born in a family of potters, she was a contemporary of Vijayanagar king Krishnadeva Raya. It is believed she was acquainted with another Telugu poet of the time, Tenali Ramakrishna.

Auchitya (Sanskrit): term in poetics for propriety or appropriateness. According to Kshemendra, whatever is improper detracts from rasa, hence is to be eschewed.

Auchitya-vichara-charcha (11th; Sanskrit) of Kshemendra: work in poetics, which develops the concept of 'auchitya' or propriety as essential to the sentiment depicted in a literary work. Apart from the importance of this concept, the work is rich in illustrations and contains valuable criticism of what Kshemendra regards as literary flaws or defects.

Tr. Suryakanta, Pune, 1954.

Avadana (Sanskrit): generic name for a class of Buddhist works containing stories of the past lives of Boddhisattva. For each there is an introduction stating where and on what occasion the Buddha related the story; the lesson deduced by him from the story is given as conclusion. These are composed in prose, with occasional metrical passages; not of high literary merit, but these illustrate a type of early narrative literature in Sanskrit. The more notable examples are *Avadhana-shataka, Divyavadana, Mahavastu* and *Lalitavistara*.

Avadhanam (Telugu): a form of poetical composition in which the poet is required to compose extempore on a specific topic and in a stipulated metre. The poet has to perform in response to what the audience requires.

Avadhi: the speech of Avadh. It emerged from Ardhamagadhi Prakrit; was spoken in four or five districts of Avadh around Ayodhya. *Padumavat* shows its chaste form, *Ramacharitmanas* its finest literary use.

Avadhuta Narayan Swami (13th/14th): author of the earliest prose work in Oriya, *Rudrasudhanidhi*. Nothing is known about him except that he had lived for some time in Bhubaneswar; from his work it appears that he was a learned person who renounced the world and became a wandering mendicant (hence 'Avadhut') of Shaiva faith.

Avanti-sundari-katha (?C; Sanskrit) of Dandin: a fragmentary prose work. Some scholars suggest that this is the last 'purvapithika' of *Dashakumaracharita*.

Avastha (Sanskrit): term in dramaturgy indicating stage of development of dramatic action. There are five stages —'arambha' (beginning with the desire to attain some end); 'prayatna' (determined effort to secure that end); 'praptyasa' (possibility of success); 'niyatapti' (certainty of success), 'phalagama' (attainment of the end desired and pursued).

Aviveka-purna Guru-kathai

(*c*1730; Tamil) of Constantius Beschi: a satirical tale in prose.

Avvaiyar (?C): woman poet in Tamil of the Sangam period. The word Avvaiyar means 'respectable woman' and it cannot be a natural proper name; but there have been several poets of this name.

Ayyalla Raju Ramabhadra (early 16th): also known as Pillala Ramabhadrayya ('Ramabhadrayya with many children'); scholar and poet in Telugu; author of *Vasucharitra*.

Azad [Muhammad Husain Azad (1830–1910)]: scholar and educationist, also prose writer in Urdu. He is credited with the establishment of Urdu in public life. His *Ab-i-Hayat* is the first history of the language; he also wrote *Darbar-i-Akbari, Nairang-i-Khayal, Sukhandan-i-Fars*, and other books. He belonged to Delhi but eventually settled in Lahore, and retired from a teaching post in the Oriental College there.

B

Baba Farid (1173–1266): also known as Baba Sheikh Farid or Baba Fariduddin Shakarganj; a Sufi poet of Panjab. His verses were composed in the Lahnda speech of West Panjab; four hymns and 112 shlokas of his were later included in *Adi Granth*. The maturity of his poetry suggests there was a growing literature preceding him; but no trace of this or what followed in the next three centuries have been found. Guru Nanak is said to have received Baba Farid's verses most probably from Sheikh Ibrahim, a direct descendant of Baba Farid whose verses were preserved until then by his apostolic successors.

Baba Padmanji (1831–1906): prose-writer in Marathi from Belgaum. He became a Christian in 1854; began writing mainly to propagate Christianity; later wrote on a variety of subjects. His main works are *Yamunaparyatan*, a novel; *Nibandha-mala*, a collection of essays; *Marathi-Angreji Kosh*, a dictionary; *Maharashtra deshacha samkshipta itihas*, history; and *Khristi lokanche kartaryasar*.

Babbar (mid-11th): poet in Old Hindi. He belonged to Tripuri village in Jabalpur district (Madhya Pradesh); was the court-poet of Raja Karna of Kalchuri. Only fragments of his verse have been found.

Ba-chautisa (late 17th; Oriya) of Lokanath: an unusual work in the chautisa form. Entirely secular and socio-political in character, it was probably composed at a time of political instability and social confusion. In it, king Yudhisthir asks brother Sahadeva, his minister, what the Kali-yuga will be like; Sahedeva's reply sounds like an account of the times in which the poem was composed.

Baccha Dasa (14th/15th): poet in Oriya who pre-dates Sarala Dasa. His only known work, *Kalasa chautisa*, is thus the earliest extant literary composition in Oriya.

Badu Chandidas (?C): poet in Bangla; presumed author of *Shri Krishna-kirtan*. 'Badu' indicates his profession, brahman menial of a temple. He was probably a subordinate priest or temple attendant of the goddess Basuli. The site of this temple is not known.

Baeit (Panjabi): a verse metre based on couplets, used most often in qissa poems: earliest use was probably in *Hir Ahmad* (1692).

Bagdavat (Rajasthani): name for a particular genre of heroic verse-tales concerning 24 Devda Chauhans of 10th who fought among each other and died. These tales are sung by the Bhopa folk.

Bagh-o-bahar (1801/02; Urdu) of Mir Amman Dehalvi: a re-telling of *Qissa chahar darvesh*.

Baidehisha Bilas (mid-17th; Oriya) of Upendra Bhanja: one of the four Ram-katha kavyas composed by this poet.

Baily: see Benjamin Baily.

Bakhar (Marathi): term for prose chronicles which began to be written systematically from late-17th and continued till the end of the Maratha rule in early 19th. These provide invaluable source material for history. Some representative specimens are *Vakenavis-bakhar, Sabhasadi-bakhar, Ajna-patra, Shiva- digvijaya.* The term is probably derived from the Farsi word 'khabar' meaning news; those who wrote bakhars were known as 'bakharkars'.

Bakhtiyar Singh (1813–91): poet and prose-writer in Hindi. Born in Basi village in Rajasthan; obtained patronage of the maharanas of Udaipur. Among his works are *Sajjan-yash prakash, Anyokti prakash, Kehar prakash.*

Bal-avatara (?C; Pali): a grammatical work, based on *Kacchayana-vyakarana*. Its authorship is traditionally attributed to Dhammakitti; but according to *Gandhavamsha*, it was composed by Vachissara.

Tr. H.T. De Silva and K.O. Thera, revised Woodward, Pegu, 1915.

Bala-bhakti (end-17th): a Ram-bhakti poet in Hindi; composed *Neha-prakash* and *Dayal'manjari*.

Bala-bharata (late 9th/early 10th; Sanskrit) of Rajasekhara: drama based on the *Mahabharata* story, of which only two acts are available. The first deals with Draupadi's swayamvara, the second with the dyuta-sabha. This work may have been left incomplete by the author.

Bala-charita (?C; Sanskrit) of Bhasa: play in five acts, presenting the feats of the child Krishna.

Bala-ramayana (late 9th/early 10th; Sanskrit) of Rajasekhara: drama in ten acts, depicting the *Ramayan* story up to the coronation of Rama. Among changes in the story are Ravana's being presented as a rival to Rama for the hand of Sita.

Balaram Dasa (b. 1472): the oldest and most talented of the Panchasakha group of poets in Oriya. His major work is an *Oriya Ramayan*; wrote a number of devotional works. *Vedantasara-gita, Gupta-gita, Virata-gita, Saptanga-yogasara-gita*; also many shorter works, *Bhava-samudra, Mriguini-stuti, Lakshmipurana suanga*. A pious man, originally not without capacity for free thought, he came under the influence of Shri Chaitanya in middle age and became like one possessed; came to be called 'Matta' (intoxicated or mad) Balaram by the common man in Puri.

Balaram Ramayana (early 16th; Oriya): the Oriya rendering by Balaram Dasa, also known as *Oriya Ramayan*. Like the *Mahabharata* of Sarala Dasa, this work also makes epic characters look human and natural, and is tinged with local colour. Composed in dandi-vritti metre, the narrative is made effective because of the naturalistic dialogue and character-portrayal.

Balaramdas: at least 19 poets of this name in Bangla can be found in the Vaishnav tradition. Among these, five have composed notable lyrics: (1) Balaramdas of Dagachi village in Bardhaman district of West Bengal; a follower of Nityanandaprabhu; (2) Balaramdas of Telia-Budhri village in Murshidabad district; disciple of Ramchandra Kaviraj; (3) Balaramdas of Srikhanda village in Bardhaman district; disciple of Jahnavi Devi, wife of Nityanandaprabhu; (4) the author of *Krishnalilamrita*; gave himself the bhanita 'Deena Balarama'; (5) gave himself the bhanita 'Basu Balaram'.

Balbhadra Mishra (late 16th): poet in Hindi from Orchha in M.P.; known especially for the work *Nakha-shikha* which offers erotic description of a heroine's body. According to him he also wrote *Balbhadri vyakaran, Hanumannatak* and *Gobardhan satsai*. In his verses, riti poetry is seen in its early form. He was a contemporary of Keshavdas.

Bali-bandha (?C) of unknown authorship and date: a lost play, possibly in Sanskrit, mentioned in Patanjali's *Mahabhashya*.

Balkrishna Bhatta (1844–1914): Hindi journalist and essayist; associated continuously for 33 years with the journal *Hindi pradip* through which he propagated his social, political and literary ideas. His important writings have been collected in *Bhatta nibandhavali.*

Bammera Potana (*c*1400–75): poet in Telugu; rendered *Bhaghavathapuranam* into Telugu; also wrote the long poem *Virabhadra-vijaya* in praise of Shiva.

Bana-bhatta or **Bana Bhatta** (*c*630): author of *Kadambari* and *Harsha-charita*, both prose-works in Sanskrit. A devotional lyric, Chandi-shataka, has also been ascribed to him. Harshavardhana, Maukhari king of Thaneshwar (r. 606–647), was his patron; his parents were Chitrabhanu and Rajyadevi.

Banamali Dasa (late 18th): poet in Oriya and one of the most popular padavali composers of his time. Born into a kayastha family of Puri, his original title was Pattanayak; after initiation as a Vaishnav he was named Ballabhananda Dasa. But because he was already well-known as a poet in his own name, he preferred to be called Banamali Dasa. Despite his popularity, his padas were collected and published for the first time only in 1934. Of three other poets in Oriya known by this name, one wrote *Chata ichabati* probably in 16th; another, of the same period, was also called Siva Banamali; the third belonged to late 18th and is the author of *Bhojaraja champu*.

Banarsi Das (b. 1586): poet and prose writer in Hindi, Jain by faith; known mainly for his autobiographical work entitled *Ardha-kathanak.* He also wrote *Samaysar natak, Banarsi paddhati, Kalyanmandir bhasha*. After his death one Jagjivan collected 75 of his poems and called the collection *Banarsi vilas*.

Banasura-katha (?C; Kashmiri) of Bhatavatar: a long poem on the Usha-Aniruddha story.

Banda Nawaz Gesu Daraz

(d. 1442): Sufi sant and poet in Dakhni (Urdu); migrated from Dehli to Gulbarga, a Bahmani kingdom in Dakhan; author of *Merajul Asiqin* and about 100 other mystical treatises dealing with various aspects of esoteric experience and rituals connected with folklore and tradition. Among works ascribed to him are *Shikar-nama*, a collection of prose riddles in the form of stories; *Chakki-nama*, a poetic rendering of mystic thoughts into tunes popular with rural women folk at the time of corn grinding; *Hidayat-nama; Sehbara*. The first of these works, if truly composed by him, makes him the earliest known writer of Urdu prose.

Bangla: main language of Bengal province of undivided India; now spoken by about 200 million persons in the state of West Bengal in east India and in Bangladesh (formerly East Pakistan). The speakers are known as Bangali; in British usage, the language as well as its speakers were named Bangla. Descended from a late Middle Indo-Aryan language sometime about A.D. 800 its immediate ancestor was Avahatta. The earliest known compositions in the language, the *Charya* songs and poems, have been dated between A.D. 1000 and 1200. No samples are available for the next 300 years but from *C* 1500 onwards there has been continuous composition in Bangla. Although full of Sanskrit words, during 1500–1800 it abscribed a large number of Turki, Farsi and Arabic words. The script originated from an eastern variety of the northern Brahmi alphabet; the full Bangla, alphabet appears to have developed by 12th.

Bankimchandra Chattopadhyay or **Chatterjee** (1838–1894): one of the earliest and greatest novelists in Bangla, also an essayist who wrote on a variety of subjects. He came to Calcutta to study law in Presidency College; in 1858 he appeared for the B.A. examination and obtained the highest aggregate marks. (He and his classmate Jodunath Basu were the first graduates of Calcutta University. He was appointed Deputy Magistrate and spent 33 years serving the British. After starting his career as novelist with a work in English, *Rajmohan's Wife* (1864), he wrote all his other novels in Bangla. Among these are *Durgesh-nandini* (1865) *Kapal-kundala* (1866), *Bish-briksha* (1873), *Krishnakantar-uil* (1878), *Rajsingha* (1882), *Anandamath* (1884); the last named contains the celebrated 'Vandemataram' song. The monthly magazine *Bangadarshan* founded by him carried his essays, most of which were later collected in the three volumes *Lok-rahasya* (1874), *Vijnan-rahasya* (1875) and *Vividha prabandha* (1887). In his *Krishna-charitra* (1886) he discussed the historicity of the life of Shri Krishna while in *Dharmatattva* (1888) he presented his concept of religion. Thus, not only was he a pioneering novelist; he also took the lead in intellectual debate through his prose writings.

Bansi Hansraj (b. 1742): poet in Hindi; author of *Sneha-sagar Viraha-vilas, Ramachandrika, Barahmasa*. His patron was the ruler of Panna (M.P).

Bar-git (Asamiya): a form innovated by Shankaradeva, these are lyrics set to classical melodies and tend to be devotional in purpose. The more popular ones are those which deal with the pranks of the child Krishna. Shankaradeva is said to have composed 'twelve score' bar-git songs but only about 40 have survived.

Bara-anvah (*c*1650; Panjabi) of Abdullah: verse work which treats 12 topics of Islam in 9000 couplets.

Bara-mah (Panjabi): poetic form giving account of twelve months of the year. The poet describes the pangs of divine separation in each month; for the twelfth, he relates the ultimate union with god.

Bara-mahi git (Asamiya): probably originated as songs of lonely wives of boatmen engaged in riverborne trade; later acquired spiritual meanings in the devotional Vaishnav context.

Barah-masa (Hindi): poetic form which follows the monthly cycle of the year and tells of separation of a woman from her lover. The oldest known barah-masa in Hindi is *Chandayan* of Mulla Daud (14th).

Baraha-mahinah (Sindhi): form of poetry which contains stanzas named after the twelve months of the year. Sindhi poets introduced a new element to this traditional form by describing various aspects of human love according to seven days of the week ('hafto') or to the days ('dinhan') or the nights ('ratyeon') of the month.

Baraha-masa (Maithili): popular seasonal song featuring love-lorn women whose husbands or lovers have gone abroad. Four months of 'chaturmasya' were excluded; these covered the rainy season, when no long journeys were possible. Vidyapati composed the earliest barahamasa songs in Maithili. Rajasthani poetry had a form similar in content and purpose to this. The oldest available example in Rajasthani is *Neminath chatuspadika* of Vinayacandra Suri; composed in chaupai form, it describes the feeling of separation experienced by the heroine Rajmati.

Barahatha Aso (16th) poet in Rajasthani from near Barmer, later settled at Nathusara village of the Bikaner region. Among his works are *Rawala Mala ro guna*, the heroic deeds of Megharaja; *Rava Chandrasena ra rupaka,* the virtues of Chandrasena; *Umade Bhatiyani ra kavitta*, on the queen of Rava Maladeva committing sati.

Baramasi (Gujarati): poems depicting the moods of a hero or heroine, generally in separation, as he or she reacts to each of the twelve months in a year. Such verses are often found inside a long poem.

Barsalpur-gad Vijay (*c*1712; Hindi) by unknown author: a kavya in Dingal which tells of the prowess of Sujansingh, ruler of Bikaner.

Barvay (Hindi): a verse metre consisting of four feet; also known as 'dhruva' and 'kuvanga'. Like the doha, it cannot accommodate an expansive subject matter. Rahim and Tulsidas were the two earliest users of this metre; later Rahim wrote *Barvay nayika bhed* and Tulsi wrote *Barvay Ramayana.*

Barvay Nayika-bhed (*c*1600; Hindi) of Abdur Rahim: kavya work in Avadhi.

Barvay Ramayana (*c*1612; Hindi) of Tulsidas: a condensed *Ramayana* story in Avadhi composed in 'barvay' metre.

Basavanna (Basaveshwara) (*c*1106–1167): sant-poet in Kannada and social reformer; founded the Virashaiva sect, which discarded the caste-system and gave up orthodox rituals. He also established a religious centre called 'Anubhavamandapa' in Kalyan, where scholars and sants met for communion. Basavanna was for a time minister to king Bijjala of Kalyan, thus wielded political authority for some time also. He composed poems in the vachana form and all his vachanas contain the name of Kudalasangama, his chosen god.

Basava-purana (early 15th; Kannada) of Bhima Kavi: a version of the Telugu biography of Basavanna, *Basava-puranamu* by Palkuriki Somanatha. This work was composed in shatpadi metre.

Basava-puranamu (13th/14th; Telugu) of Palakuriki Somanatha: a biography of Basavanna, written in the popular dvipadi metre. The author was a Lingayat teacher.

Basavaraja-devare ragale (13th; Kannada) of Harihara: verse biography of Basavanna. This is his earliest known biography, and only the first half of Harihara's work is extant.

Basavo-daharanam (earlier 13th; Telugu) of Palakuriki Somanatha: a formal innovation, combining vrittas of Sanskrit and ragadas of desi Telugu.

Basudev Ghosh (mid-16th): poet in Bangla; a direct follower of Shri

Chaitanya and composed many songs on him; also composed a few on the Radha-Krishna theme.

Bat-samgraha (*c*1766; Hindi): a collection of 105 popular tales in prose from Rajasthan; includes many romantic stories.

Bata-gamani (Maithili): type of Tirahuti love song which portrays the nayika while she is going to meet her lover. Vidyapati is its most famous exponent.

Baul: mendicant singer of Bengal.

Bavan akkhari (Panjabi): a medieval poetical form in which the 52 letters of the Sanskrit alphabet are explicated by way of moral advice. In actual practice, all 52 letters were seldom explicated.

Bayt (Sindhi): verse form based on couplets; the oldest genre of Sindhi poetry.

'Bedil' [Qadir Baksh (1814–72)]: poet in Sindhi, who has also written in Urdu, Farsi and Hindi. His two main works in Sindhi are *Bahadat-namo* and *Surud-namo.*

Benjamin Baily (1791–1871): Christian missionary who translated the Bible into Malayalam and had it printed at Kottayam in 1824. His more valuable work was as lexicographer; he produced *A Dictionary of High and Colloquial Malayalam* and *English* (1846) and *English and Malayalam Dictionary* (1849). After spending 33 years in India, he returned home in 1850.

Beschi [Constantices Beschi (1680–1746)]: an Italian Jesuit, who came originally to Goa in 1708, later moved to Tamilnadu and became a Tamil scholar; composed many works in Tamil, the most famous of which is *Tempavani*, a Christian purana.

Bhabani-nath (17th): court-poet of Jagatmanikya of Tripura; composed a narrative poem in Bangla on *Adhyatma Ramayana*.

Bhadravahu (?C): surmised author of *Uvasaggahara-stotra*, which eulogises Parshwanatha and is said to be the earliest of Jain hymns in Prakrit. An author with the same name is said to have composed *Kalpasutra.*

Bhagavad Gita (?C; Sanskrit): belongs to Bhishma-parvan in *Mahabharata* Consisting of 750 verses divided into 18 chapters, it is in the form of a conversation between Krishna and Arjuna on the battlefield of Kurukshetra, being reported by Sanjaya to the blind king

Dhritarashtra. As a philosophic discourse, it defends rightful action as against contemplative withdrawal; as a religious document it is central to the worship of Krishna as Vishnu. Perhaps the most widely revered sacred book of the Hindus, it continues to influence Hindu thought even today.

Tr. C. Wilkins, London, 1785; E. Arnold, London, 1885; C. Isherwood & S. Radhakrishnan, London, 1948.

Bhagavadajjuka (?4th; Sanskrit): attributed to Bodhayan; farce named after its two main characters, the yogin Bhagavan and the courtesan Ajjuka. It is the earliest known example of a prahasana.

Bhagavan Singh (1842–1902): poet in Panjabi who received court patronage in Nabha and Patiala. Most of his works deal with local events and immediate surroundings. Among them are *Pacchiye da kal* (1868), *Jiuna mod* (1894) *Chauttiye di agga* (1899). He also wrote poems re-telling qissa tales like Hir-Ranjha, Suhni-Mahiwal and Mirza-Sahiban.

Bhagavat (Oriya): name of a metre of nine letters to the line, innovated by Jagannatha Dasa in his rendering of *Bhagavatapuranam*.

Bhagavat-purana (?9th/10th; Sanskrit) of unknown authorship: also known as *Srimadbhagvata* or simply as *Bhagavata*. Consisting of nearly 18,000 verses divided into 12 'skandha' (sections), it deals chiefly with the early life and sports of Krishna; important to literature because many literary works are based on some story or another about the young Krishna. Quite remarkably, there is no mention of Radha or Radhika in this work. According to some scholars, the text was originally composed in South India; its 10th skandha is especially popular with Vaishnavs.

Tr. M.N. Dutta, Calcutta, 1895.

Bhagavatam (15th; Malayalam) ascribed to Rama Panicker: prose rendering of *Bhagavata*.

Bhagavatam (late 16th; Malayalam) of Ezhuttacan: verse rendering of *Bhagavata*. Ezhuttacan is said to have worked only on the first nine skandhas; his disciples completed the work after his death.

Bhagavritti (?C; Sanskrit): lost commentary on *Ashtadhyayi*, but extensively quoted by Purushottamadeva and other grammarians of East India of 12th and later centuries. Authorship has been attributed by some scholars to Bhartrihari, by others to Vimalamati.

Bhagirath Kavi (late 16th): poet of Mithila; probably brother of the king Mahesh Thakur.

Bhagvata (12th): scholar of Sanskrit: author of *Bhagvata-lamkara*, a work on rhetoric. A Jain by faith, he probably belonged to Anahilapatana in Gujarat.

Bhagvata (14th): scholar of Sanskrit: author of *Kavya-nushasana*, a work on poetics. He refers in the work to the earlier Bhagvata.

Bhaimarathi (?C; Sanskrit) of unknown authorship: a lost prose kavya, mentioned by Patanjali in his *Mahabhashya*.

Bhairavananda-natakam (*c*1390; Sanskrit): a play probably written by Manika, a Maithil scholar invited to the court of Nepalese king Jayasthiti-malla (r. 1380–94); was performed during the marriage celebrations of his son Dharma-malla. It is a secular work, dealing with the romance between a prince, Bhairava, and Madanavati, a celestial dancer cursed by a rishi to be reborn as a human being.

Bhaktacharan Dasa (1729–1823): poet in Oriya; wrote philosophical works like *Mathura-mangala* and *Manah shiksha* which expound Vaishnav faith. Among his popular works are *Gopa-mangal, Manabodha-chautisa* and *Kalakalevara-chautisa*. Originally called Bairagicharan Pattanayak, after initiation he was named Bhaktacharan; travelled to many sacred places of the country; established several matths in Orissa.

Bhakta-mal (*c*1600; Hindi) of Nabhajidas: verse work narrating the lives of 200 sants. Priyadas wrote a commentary in Hindi on it in 1712.

Bhakta'mal (18th; Bangla) of Laldas: a biographical encyclopaedia, based on the poem in Hindi by Nabhaji and the commentary on it by Priyadas.

Bhakta-namavali (1614; Hindi) of Dhruvadas: verse work which tells of 16 important bhaktas, of whom Nabhadas is one.

Bhakta-rasa-bodhini (*c*1712; Hindi) of Priyadas: a commentary on *Bhaktamal* of Nabhajidas.

Bhakti-pradipa (c1500; Asamiya) of Shankaradeva: an exposition of bhakti in the form of a dialogue between Krishna and Arjuna.

Bhakti-pradipa (16th; Asamiya) of Madhavadeva: collection of translations from Vishnupuri Sanyasi's

Bhakti-ratnavali, Ramcharan Thakur's *Bhakti-ratnakar* and Narottam Thakur's *Bhakti-premavali*.

Bhakti-rasamrita-sindhu (mid-17th; Sanskrit) of Rupa Goswami: a work in which bhakti has been analysed on the basis of rasa.

Bhakti-ratnakar (18th; Bangla) of Narahari Chakrabarti: an encyclopaedia of Vaishnav lore.

Bhakti-vijaya (1762; Marathi) of Mahipati Bua Tahrawadkar: a prose work giving life-stories of sants and other devotees. Because of its simple and sweet language, it is very popular in rural areas.

Bhakti-viveka (*c*1610; Sanskrit) of Bhattadeva: work treats the nature of bhakti with appropriate citations from Sanskrit sources.

Bhalan (1434–1514): poet in Gujarathi from Patan; rendered 10th skandha of *Bhagavata* into series of lyrics; also abridged Banabhatta's *Kadambari* in verse. He is credited with having developed the narrative akhyana form by adapting puranic stories. Among his works are *Bhiladi-samvad, Jalandhar-akhyan, Nalakhyan, Durvasa-akhyan, Rambalcharit, Har-samvad*, etc.

Bhallata-shataka (*c*900; Sanskrit) of Bhallata: sequence of 108 verses of varied metres, in which the poet reflects on ways of the world. These verses have been quoted by Abhinavagupta, Kshemendra and other eminent scholars; some were included in the anthologies *Sarangadhara-paddhati* and *Sadukti-karnamrita*. According to *Rajatarangini* Bhallata belonged to the court of Shankaravarman, king of Kashmir (r. 883–902).

Bhamaha (mid-6th): Kashmiri scholar of Sanskrit; author of *Kavyalamkara*. He is considered to be the founder of alamkara theory; he was the first to propose a theory of poetics other than what had been proposed in *Natyashastra*.

Bhamini-vilasa (mid-17th; Sanskrit) of Jagannatha: poem in four sections, 'Anyokti' (101 verses), 'Shringara' (102), 'Karuna' (19) and 'Shanta' (31). Notably elegant in form and sophisticated in pictorial fancy, the verses deal with various matters but are mainly didactic or erotic.

Tr. S. Iyer, Bombay, 1894; H.D. Sharma, Poona, 1938.

Bhana (Sanskrit): play in one act with only one character speaking a monologue; generally satirical in purpose and aimed at popular enjoyment.

Bhana Das (17th): sant poet in Gujarati; contemporary of Akha. Among his poetical works are *Hastamalak, Prahlad-akhyan, Ajagarvadhut samvad, Nrisingh-ji ni hamchi*, etc.

Bhanita (Bangla): the last couplet (of an 8 or 14 line poem) which mentions the poet's real or assumed name.

Bhanu-datta or **Bhanukara** (*c*1475): scholar of Sanskrit from Mithila; wrote on poetics. Of his two best-known works, *Rasa-manjari* deals with nayaka and nayika characteristics, *Rasa-tarangini* with bhava and rasa; an anthology, *Rasa-parijata*, contains about 1000 verses written by him and by his father Ganapati.

Bhanumati-parinayamu (17th; Telugu) of Reduri Rangaraju: poem in four 'aswas' (sections) describing the marriage of Bhanumati to Sahadeva, the fourth Pandava. Bhanumati was a cousin of Krishna.

Bhaona (Asamiya): a kind of play in Sanskrit specially composed for a drama-festival initiated by rulers of Assam. In these plays, while the dialogue and other speeches were in Sanskrit, occasionally there were songs in Asamiya.

Bharani (Tamil): a type of song which celebrates achievements in battle. The form was probably known in the Sangam period, but it became popular with *Kalingattu bharani* which celebrates the victory of Pandyan king Kulottunga I over the northern Kalingas in 1105.

Bharat-bahubali Rasu (*c*1185; Gujarati) of Shalibhadra Suri: describes the rivalry between Bharat and Bahubali, sons of 'adi tirthankar' Rishabha-deva. Ultimately Babubali renounces worldly life. The giant image at Shravanbelgela is one of Bahubali.

Bharatchandra Raye Gunakar (*c*1712–60): one of Bengal's greatest poets. He was born in a brahman family of Bhursat area of South Rahr. After an early marriage, he left home without completing his studies; came to a village near Hooghly and lived here for some years reading Sanskrit and Farsi; earliest poems, including two on Satyanarain, were composed here. Family fortunes having declined, he decided to seek a living elsewhere; went to Chandarnagar, where he found employment with the local agent of the French government who subsequently introduced him to Raja Krishnachandra Raye of Krishnagar. Bharatchandra was made the court-poet, granted salary and lands; settled at Mulajore on the Hooghly river for the rest of his life. Apart from his great work *Annarda'mangal*, he also wrote *Rasa'manjari*; many Vaishnav songs; several humorous poems with odd features (for example one poem employs four languages: Sanskrit, Bangla, Farsi and Hindustani); some Sanskrit verse including *Naga'sataka*, a poem in 8 stanzas. He was working on a Sanskrit play with Bangla songs, based on the puranic story of Chandi killing the buffalo demon, when he died.

Bharat-gatha (?15th; Malayalam) of unkonwn author: long poem based on *Mahabharata*, composed in gatha style. At one time it was suggested that the poet is the same as the author of *Krishna-gatha*; now it has been established that *Bharat-gatha* is the work of an inferior poet.

Bharat-mala (late 14th; Malayalam) of Shankara Paniker: condensed version of *Mahabharata*; perhaps the earliest major work in Malayalam based on *Mahabharata*.

Bharata (?C): generally accepted as author of *Natyashastra*, and dated as earlier than AD 4th/5th. This work in Sanskrit being the earliest extant treatise on dramaturgy, the author is sometimes referred to as Adi-Bharata; also called Bharata Muni because, according to legend the work is of divine inspiration. *Gitalamkara*, a work on music, is also attributed to him.

Bharata Champu (?11th; Sanskrit) of Ananta Bhatta: a condensation of *Mahabharata* in 1000 shlokas and divided into four sections. As in champu style, it uses prose as well as verse; but the prose is as ornate as the verse.

Bharata-manjari (*c*1037; Sanskrit) of Kshemendra: long poem based on *Mahabharata* which summarises the story in about 500 stanzas. The poet has also rearranged the sequence at places.

Bharata-vakya: term for the concluding verse of a Sanskrit play; so called because it used to be recited by the 'bharatas' (actors). It generally offers a prayer to the gods and solicits benediction for the spectators. Though most playwrights have used the term, it is not found in Bharata's *Natyashastra*.

Bharata-venba (?7th; Tamil) of Perundevanar: an earlier poet of the same name had rendered *Mahabharata* into Tamil for the first time probably also in 9th. This work is partly in verse, partly in prose; latter is full of Sanskrit expressions.

Apart from 'venba', the poet has also used 'asiriyam' and 'viruttam' metres. The work has survived in an incomplete recension.

Bharataka-dvatrimshika (?C; Sanskrit) of unknown authorship: a collection of 32 tales which ridicule the Bharatakas, who were probably Shaiva mendicants. The work seems to be of Jain origin and is designed to deride brahmans. There are vernacular verses interspersed in the text, suggesting that it is the Sanskrit version of a vernacular work.

Bharatam (9th; Tamil) of Perundevanar: an early adaptation of *Mahabharata*, done during the reign of Nandivarman III (*c*826–49). Only a part of this work is extant.

Bharatam (?14th/15th; Tamil) of Villupputturar: an adaptation of *Mahabharata* considered a great poem in Tamil. Consisting of 4351 verses, it deals with only the first ten parvas. The work was commissioned by Varapati Atkondan, Kongar chieftain of Vakkapahai.

Bharatam (late 16th; Malayalam) of Ezhuttacan: a re-telling of *Mahabharata* in verse.

'Bharatendu' Harishchandra (1850–85): pioneering writer in Hindi. In poetry he followed the Ritikal phase and sought to change the purpose of poetry by relating it to contemporary life, especially to the common man's feelings. In prose, he chose a simple, popular form of expression in preference to the Sanskritised form being used by some writers; he edited several magazines and established a group of writers who helped to propagate modern Hindi prose. In drama, he not only wrote plays but also helped to stage them and himself acted in several. Considering his short life, his literary output was substantial—18 plays, 12 collections of verse, 13 books related to history, about 45 essays on a wide variety of subjects. The title 'Bharatendu' was conferred upon him by an admiring public and he became better known by this name than his own.

Bharatesh-vaibhava (late 16th; Kannada) of Ratnakaravarni: long poem in praise of Bharatesha or Bharata, elder son of the first tirthankara. The work is in 'sangatya' metre and runs to about 10,000 verses.

Bharateshwar Bahubali ghora (*c*1170; Rajasthani) of Vajrasena Suri: small poem (of 48 verses) describing the battle between two brothers, Bharata and Bahubali. It is said to be the oldest known literary work in Rajasthani.

Bharateswar-Bahubali ras (*c*1185; Apabhramsh) of Shalibhadra Suri: ras poem dealing with the story of Bharat and Bahubali. The work is in 203 verses, composed in an Apabhramsh much influenced by Old Rajasthani and Old Gujarati; it employs chaupai, ras, doha, trutak and other metres. The work is also known as *Bharateshcharitra*.

Bharati Parva (1640; Marathi) of Mukteshwar: a rendering of five parvas of *Mahabharata* in 14,687 ovi verses.

Bharavi (?mid-6th): poet in Sanskrit; author of one of the five major mahakavyas, *Kiratarjuniya*. He is mentioned along with Kalidasa in the Aihole inscription of Chalukya king Pulakesin II, dated A.D. 634. He is also mentioned by Dandin in *Avantisundari-katha* as a friend of Dandin's great-grandfather Damodara.

Bhartrihari (?C): poet in Sanskrit; author of three sequences of one hundred lyrics each, *Niti-shataka*, *Vairagya-shataka* and *Shringara-shataka*. Some scholars identify him with Bhartrihari, author of *Vakyapadiya*.

Bhartrihari (d. 651): grammarian of Sanskrit; author of *Vakyapadiya*. He is also supposed to have written *Mahabhashya-dipika*, a commentary on *Mahabhashya* of Patanjali. His death around A.D. 651 was recorded by the Chinese traveller, I-tsing. Some scholars identify him with Bhatti, author of *Ravanavadha*.

Bharud (Marathi): a narrative form in semi-prose, occasionally practised by Eknath.

Bhasa (?C): oldest known playwright in Sanskrit. Although he is mentioned by Kalidasa, Banabhatta and Rajasekhara, the existence of his works were unknown until the manuscripts of 13 plays were discovered in 1910–11 by Ganapati Shastri in Trivandrum. Controversy continues about the real authorship of these works. Also, there is no general agreement about Bhasa's date, and he has been placed in different periods from 5th to 11th. His works are *Dyuta vakyam, Karnabharam, Dyuta-Ghatotkacham, Urubhangam, Madhyama-vyayogam, Pancharatram, Abhishek anatalakam, Balacharitam, Avimarakam, Pratime-natakam, Pratijna-Yaugandharayanam, Swapna-Vasavaddattam* and *Charudattam*.

Bhasagita-samgraha (Maithili):

term used for manuscript collections of Maithili lyrics, consisting mainly of poems by Vidyapati. Among the better known such collections are the Tarauni manuscript, Nepal manuscript, Ramabhadrapura manuscript, Raj Library manuscript.

Bhasha Bhagavad-gita (*c*1400; Malayalam) of Madhav Paniker: first ever translation of *Bhagvad Gita* into a modern Indian language, done sometime between 1350 and 1450. The work is particularly important to Malayalam because it uses a fairly modern form of the language.

Bhasha-bhushan (*c*1650; Hindi) of Jaswantsingh: work on poetics. It contains dohas which offer an explanation and also provide examples of an alamkar in the same doha; hence very useful for students.

Bhasha-Kautaliyam (late 11th/early 12th; Malayalam) of unkonwn author: the earliest extant prose work in Malayalam, being a translation and commentary on *Arthashastra*. The language contains a great deal of Tamil and the intermixture with Malayalam shows no regulated order; perhaps it was close to contemporary speech. It is the oldest translation of *Arthashastra* into any other Indian language.

Bhasha Naishadha Champu (18th; Malayalam) of Mazhamangalam Narayanan Nambutiri: work in Manipravala retelling the story of Nala. It uses a fully developed form of Manipravala and is said to be the finest literary work in this language.

Bhasha-Ramayana Champu (15th; Malayalam) of Poonam Nambutiri: a work in Manipravala retelling the *Ramayan* story. With it champu works in Malayalam began using puranic material for their stories; previously it only used to eulogise the heroine.

Bhashya (Sanskrit): general term for a learned commentary on some well-known text. The most respected example is the *Mahabhashya* of Patanjali where he has commented on the *Ashtadhyayi* of Panini.

Bhaskara Kavi (*c*1300): poet in Telugu; is supposed to have produced the first Telugu adaptation of *Ramayana*. The work is dedicated to one Sahini Marana, a brahman cavalry officer, who declared himself king of his region after the fall of the Orugallu kingdom. Nothing is known about the poet's life or his other works. He has sometimes been identified as Mantri Bhaskara, grandfather of the eminent poet Tikkana.

Bhaskara Ramayanamu (*c*1350; Telugu): named after Bhaskara Kavi, but actually includes the work of four others. This retelling of *Ramayana* was sponsored by the local brahman ruler, one Sahini Marana. When he wanted the work's completion to be expedited, Bhaskara Kavi sought the collaboration of his son Mallikarjuna Bhattu, of his disciple and the ruler's son Kumar Rudradeva, and of two friends, Hulkki Bhaskarudu and Ayyalaryudu. Out of 6081 verses in the work, 4064 were composed by father and son.

Bhaskarabhatta Borikar (early 14th): poet in Marathi from Bori village in Marathawada; joined the Mahanubhav sect, but, unlike the others, wrote longer poems. His two major works are *Shishu-palavadha*, a Krishna-bhakti poem in ovi metre consisting of 1037 verses, and *Uddhava'gita*, which condenses the 11th skandha of *Bhagavata* into 827 ovis.

Bhatima (Asamiya): name for a kavya style innovated by Shankaradeva, mainly for the purpose of eulogy. Madhavadeva later composed a work entitled *Bhatima* in honour of Shankaradeva.

Bhatta Avatra (15th): scholar of Sanskrit and poet in Kashmiri: belonged to the court of Zainul Abidin; author of *Jaina-vilasa*, long poem in Kashmiri on his patron.

Bhatta-Deva (1558–1638): earliest known writer of prose in Asamiya. Out of the feeling that religious texts adapted from Sanskrit originals into Asamiya verse remained confined to the elite, he rendered *Bhagavata* and *Bhagavad Gita* into prose, respectively *Katha Bhagavat* (1596) and *Katha Gita* (1598). This did not necessarily become more popular, but Bhattadeva showed the way of using prose as an alternative medium to verse. His other works include *Bhakti-viveka, Sarana-samgraha, Prasanga mala, Katha-ratnavali, Bhakti-sara* and *Guru-rasavali.* His full name was Baikunthanath Bhagavat Bhattacharya; was also given the popular title of 'Kaviratna'.

Bhatta Gopal (?15th): scholar of Sanskrit poetics: wrote *Sahitya-chudamani*, a commentary on the *Kavyaprakash* of Mammata. According to some scholars, he also wrote *Rasika-ranjani*, a commentary on the *Rasamanjari* of Bhanudatta; also *Rasa tarangini*, a commentary on the *Shringar-tilaka* of Rudrata.

Bhatta-kalanka (17th): scholar and grammarian of Kannada; author of *Karnataka Shabdanushasanam.*

Bhatta-narayana (?8th/9th): playwright in Sanskrit; author of *Venisamhara.* An unreliable tradition identifies him as one of the five brahmans of Kanyakubja (Kanauj) brought to Bengal by king Adisura.

Bhattanayaka (?9th/10th): scholar of Sanskrit poetics. From references made by others, it appears he wrote *Hridaya-darpana*, a work on poetics, also *Bhukti-vada*, an interpretation of the 'rasa-sutra' of Bharata. Both these works are lost. He may be the same Bhattanayaka whom Kalhana mentions as being a contemporary of Shankaravarman, son and successor of Avantivarman, king of Kashmir.

Bhatta Tauta (late 10th): Scholar of Sanskrit, acknowledged by Abhinavagupta as his teacher. He may have written a work on poetics, *Kavya-kautaka*, now lost; Abhinavagupta's commentary on it, *Vivarana* is also lost.

Bhattara-Harichandra (?5th/6th) poet in Sanskrit; may have composed a romantic kavya entitled *Malati*. He is mentioned by Banabhatta in an introductory verse of *Harsha-charita*. He may be the same as the Harichandra who is quoted and praised in *Sadukti-karnamrita*; quoted also in other anthologies.

Bhatti (mid 6th): poet in Sanskrit; author of *Ravana-vadha*, which is also known as *Bhatti-kavya*. Some scholars identify him with Bhartrihari, author of *Vakyapadiya*.

Bhatti-kavya (5th/6th; Sanskrit) of Bhatti: a work designed to teach principles of grammar and rhetoric through kavya. Originally entitled *Ravanavadha*, it deals with the *Ramayan* story in 22 sections up to the return of Rama from Lanka and his coronation.

Bhattoji Dikshita (*c*1575–*c*1625): grammarian of Sanskrit; author of *Siddhanta-kaumudi Shabda-kaustubha, Bala-manorama, Prauda-manorama* and other commentaries. Born a South Indian, he lived at Varanasi and established a school of grammarians there.

Bhattumurti (early 16th): poet in Telugu; may have belonged to the Ashta-diggaja group; author of *Vasu-charitra* and *Harischandra-Nalopakhyanamu*. He was also known as Ramaraja Bhushana.

Bhausaheb-anchi-bakhar (*c*1760; Marathi): an important narrative of the 3rd Battle of Panipat (1761) fought between the Marathas and Ahmad Shah Abdali. It is generally accepted that this bakhar was written soon after the event; authorship has been ascribed to Krishnaji Shamrao, who may have witnessed the battle.

Bhava (Sanskrit): term in poetics for emotion or feeling as the basis of rasa. There are two kinds — 'sthayi' (permanent or principal) and 'sanchari' or 'vyabhichari' (transient or accessory).

Bhava-bhavana (*c*1110; Prakrit) of Maladhari Hemchandra Suri. Consisting of 531 gathas, the work deals with the question of re-birth.

Bhava-chintaratna (*c*1530; Kannada) of Gubbi Mallanarya: hagiographical poem about three eminent Virshaiva scholars, Sivalekamanchanna, Shripati Pandit and Mallikarjun Pandit. It is an early effort at writing 'charit-kavya' in a language other than Sanskrit.

Bhava-kavya (Marathi): term for the lyric poem; became popular in modern Marathi literature.

Bhava-vairagya-shataka (?C; Prakrit) of unknown authorship: an anthology of verses on worldly sufferings and how Jainism is the sole means of release.

Tr. L.P. Tessitori, in *GSAI* : 22 and 24.

Bhava-prakasha (12th or 14th; Sanskrit) of Sharadatanaya: a work on dramaturgy in ten chapters called 'adhikara'. It is particularly valuable for the indication it gives of the opinions of other scholars whose works have not survived. The author, son of Bhatta Gopala and grandson of Krishna, was a native of North India. This work is also known as *Bhava-prakashika* and *Bhava-prakashana*.

Bhava-samudra (early 16th; Oriya) of Balarama Dasa: long poem of 750 stanzas. According to legend, Balarama, then a comparatively unknown poet, once tried to occupy a seat in the main car during the Ratha-jatra (car festival) at Puri, but was beaten up and thrown off the car in public view. He ran to the secluded sea-beach and poured out his anger, shame and frustration in this poem. The title of the work aptly means 'sea of emotion'; in it he challenges and belittles Jagannatha, but ultimately forgives him and confirms his devotion.

Bhavabhuti (late 7th/early 8th): playwright in Sanskrit. Born to a brahman family in Padmapura

(probably in Vidarbha); moved to Padmavati and won the patronage of king Yashovarman of Kanauj (r. 725–52). His real name was Shrikantha but he was called 'Bhavabhuti' by fellow scholars after a poem in praise of goddess Parvati written by him. Of the three plays he is known by, *Mahavir-charit* and *Uttara-Rama-charit* deal with the story of Rama; but Malati Madhava is based on an imaginary love story.
R.D. Karmakar, *Bhavabhuti* (1963).

Bhavana sandhi-prakaran (?13th; Apabhramsh) of Jaidev Muni: a short didactic work in six 'kadvak' sections, each containing ten verses.

Bhavartha-dipika (1290; Marathi) of Jnaneshwar: a commentary on *Bhagavad Gita*. The work, which came to be known as *Jnaneshwari*, consists of 9000 ovi stanzas. It was probably completed in Banaras and first read out to scholars there.

Bhavartha Ramayana (*c*1590; Marathi) of Eknath: a re-telling of *Ramayana*, consisting of 20,000 ovi verses.

Bhavisayatta Kaha (late 10th; Apabhramsh) of Dhanayala (or Dhanapala): a long poem which uses folk-tale materials in order to glorify the 'panchami-vrata'. The story tells of Bhavisayatta, the son born to Dhanapati and Kamalshri, a couple who live in Gajapur (Hastinapur). On account of a quarrel with his wife, Dhanapati marries again, Sundari, and a son Bandhudatta is born to them. The two step-brothers set out for Kanchan dvip from where they hope to bring back much wealth. During this, Bhavisayatta has to suffer a lot because of the traitrous acts of Bandhudatta. After their return, Bhavisayatta is rewarded and Bandhudatta punished. Subsequently, Bhavisayatta marries a princess named Sumitra and is nominated heir to the throne of Podampur. After leading a peaceful life, he hands over the kingdom to his son and retires to the forest.

Bhikhari-das (mid-18th): poet of the riti tradition in Hindi. His patron was Hindupatsingh, brother of Pratapsingh, ruler of Pratapgarh. Among his works are *Rasa-sarangsha, Chhandornav-pingal* (1742), *Kavya-nirnay* (1743), *Shringar-nirnay* (1750), *Nam-prakash* (dictionary), Vishnu-puran-bhasha, Chhanda-prakash, Shatranj-shatika, Amar-prakash.

Bhim (*c*1400): poet in Gujarati; author of *Sadayavatsa charita*, a work which depicts the nine rasas. Of three available manuscripts, one dates back to 1430, hence is of great value from the linguistic point of view.

Bhim (16th): poet in Gujarati; author of *Bhim gita* (or *Rasa gita* or *Uddhava gita*), a work which re-tells the 10th skandha of *Bhagavata* in 135 stanzas.

Bhima-charita (16th; Asamiya) of Ramasaraswati: work deals with Bhima's period of service as cow-herd under Shiva; depicts local rural life with humour.

Bhima Dhibara (17th): poet in Oriya; author of *Kapata-pasha*. The work, in 10 sections each in a different metre, re-tells the aftermath of the dice-game in *Mahabharata*. As the poet's surname indicates, he was a fisherman by caste.

Bhima Kavi (14th) poet in Kannada; best known for his *Basavapurana*, probably the first work in the language composed entirely in 'bhamini shatpadi'. metre. It is a free rendering of the Telugu *Basavapurana* of Palkuriki Somnatha. Two more works sometimes attibuted to Bhima Kavi, *Bhimakavishwara-ragale* and *Bhringidandaka*, have never been found.

Bhima Kavi Vemulavada (*c*1150) poet in Telugu who is known only as a legend. No work of his has been found but he is supposed to have written four kavyas — *Raghava Pandaviyam, Satakanantha Ramayanam, Nrisimhapuranam,* and *Haravilasam.*

Bhishma Antarvedi (early 17th): poet in Hindi and scholar; translated *Bhagavata* into doha and chaupai verses.

Bhoja (943–1022): scholar of Sanskrit; author of *Saraswati-kanthabharana and Shringara-prakasa*. He is referred to also as Bhoja-raja, ruler of Dhara. Among his other works are *Samarangana-sutradhara*, on architecture and iconography; *Yukti-kalpataru*, on ethics; *Tattva-prakasha*, on religious and philosophical topics; *Raja-martanda*, a commentary on *Yoga-sutra*; a *Ramayana* champu.

Bhoja-prabandha (?C; Sanskrit) of Vallala: a prose work which may be classified with tales. It purports to describe the court of king Bhoja of Dhara, especially in relation to many poets attached to the court. The work has no historical value because it disregards chronology and brings together eminent literary figures like Kalidas, Bhavabhuti, Dandin and Mogha. It was obviously popular because several versions of the text are extant; it has also been printed in several editions.

Bhojo (1785–1850): poet in Gujarati. He was an illiterate peasant, but his poems and songs condemning social inequities became well-known as "Bhoja Bhagat Na chabkha".

Bhojpuri: a speech derived from Magadhi Apabhramsh; spoken in West Bihar and areas around Banaras.

Bholanath Sarabhai Divetia (1822–86): poet in Gujarati and social reformer; author of *Ishwar prarthanamala*, a collection of prayer songs.

Bharamar-git (Hindi): a convention of poetic composition in Brajbhasa wherein the gopis of Braj address the 'bhramar' (bee) in order to communicate with Uddhav. Poems following this convention have been composed by Brajbhasa poets from Surdas to Jagannath-das.

Bhubaneswar Vachaspati Mishra (early 18th): scholar who composed Asamiya version of *Brahmanda-purana* under the patronage of Kachar king Tamradhvaja, during 1706–08.

Bhupati (mid-18th): poet of the riti tradition in Hindi; author of *Satsai, Kanthabhusan, Rasa-ratnakar*. He was the ruler of Amethi (in Uttar Pradesh) and his real name was Gurudattsingh.

Bhupati Pandit (17th): poet in Oriya; author of *Prema-panchamrita*. He was a Saraswat brahman from Uttarakhand who came on a pilgrimage to Puri and stayed on at the court of the ruler of Orissa.

Bhupatindra-malla (18th): poet in Maithili of Nepal; belonged to the Bhatgaon ruling family. He is represented in anthologies like *Prakirnagitani*, while some of his poems appear in *Gitamala*; also wrote plays.

Bhushan (*c*1613–1712): poet in Hindi from Tikwanpur (M.P). He was given the title of 'Kavi Bhushan' by Rudra Solanki, ruler of Chitrakot. From this he came to be known as 'Bhushan'; his real name remains unknown. Apart from Rudra, he was also honoured by Shivaji Maharaj as well as by Chhatrasal, ruler of Panna. He generally composed panegyrics, in works like *Shivaraj Bhushan, Shiva Bhavani, Chhatrasal-dasak*. The language he used was Brajbhasha, but he drew words freely from Sanskrit, Arabic, Farsi.

Bhuvana-vijayamu: name of the literary meet organised periodically during the reign of Vijayanagar ruler Krishnadeva Raya (r. 1509–30). At its sittings, eight seats were placed in eight directions and these were occupied by eight eminent poets.

Biah'git (Maithili): type of folk song.

Bichitra Ramayana (early 18th; Oriya) of Biswanath Khuntia: the most popular of the *Ramayana* adaptations in Oriya. The reason must be the simple language and popular metres chosen by the poet. Unlike other *Ramayana* poets in Oriya, Biswanath used the Southern recension as his model and not the Bengal recension. At the end of each long section of the work, the poet has identified himself as 'Bisi'; from this the work is also known as "Bisi Ramayana".

Bidambana (Hindi): used for the English term 'irony'.

Bihari: collective name given by G.A. Grierson to three speeches of the Bihar region—Maithili, Magadhi and Bhojpuri. 'Bihari' emerged from the western form of Magadhi Apabhramsh.

Biharilal or **Bihari** (1560–1663): poet in Hindi at the court of Raja Jaisingh of Amber; composed mainly in Brajbhasha; best-known work is his collection of 700 verses, *Bihari-satsai* (*c*1660). On the strength of this work alone he has enjoyed a popularity among Hindi readers second only to that of Tulsidas.

Bihar-satsai (1630; Hindi): of Biharilal. A collection of 700 'doha' verses. Though there is no narrative sequence or any other structural unity, the work has always been praised for its aesthetic effect.

Bihayi (Dogri): a type of folksong sung on occasions connected with conception, birth and post-birth rites.

Bihu-git (Asamiya): songs expressing the spirit of Bihu, a festival of Assam which celebrates the change of seasons, especially the advent of spring; usually composed in couplets.

Bihula-lakhindara (15th; Asamiya) of Mankara: series of love-songs featuring Bihula and Lakshmindar.

Bijhre Ahir ri bat (*c*1790; Hindi) of unknown author: a prose romance in Dingal: tells of the affection and loyalty of Bijhro Akir for his sister Nanand.

Bijoy Gupta (?15th): poet in Bangla: author of a Manasa-mangal poem known as *Padmapuran*. The poet was a native of Goila-Phullasri village of Barisal district (now in Bangladesh).

Bilhana (*c*1100): poet in Sanskrit of Kashmir; author of *Vikramankadeva-charitra* and *Chaurapanchasika*. Born in village Konamukha (now Khumnoh) near Pravarapura; appears to have travelled to Mathura, Brindavan, Kanauj, Prayag, Varanasi, Dahala (Bundelkhand) and Gujarat. He finally settled at Kalyan in the court of Chalukya king Vikramaditya VI Tribhuvanamalla (1076–1127); composed *Vikramankadeva-charitra* in his honour and received the title 'Vidyapati'; subsequently, may have had to leave the area because he had offended the king on some account.

Bilva-mangala see Lilasuka.

Bimba (Hindi): equivalent of the English term 'image'. From this, 'bimba-vad' stands for imagism.

Birasimha (16th): poet in Oriya, also known as Buddha (here meaning Buddhist); composed many chautisa poems. The best known of this is *Birasimha chautisa* which describes a mystic cult of body-worship.

Birhare (Panjabi): a type of folk-song which expressed the feelings of women separated from their husbands or lovers. These were composed by women, especially by young women, and sung in social gatherings. The form was so popular earlier that Guru Arjan Dev adapted it for at least three shabads. Its popularity has declined since then and little effort has gone into preserving them.

Bishnu Dasa (*c*1575–1625): poet in Oriya. His major work, *Premalochana*, marks the transition in Oriya literature from simple puranic style of kavya composition (as in his own *Sabitri-charitra*) to the more ornate style of riti kavyas that would remain in vogue for the next 200 years. He also wrote several chautisa poems—*Sumukhi Chautisa, Barsha-bhavana chautisa*, etc.

Bishnu Pal (mid-17th): poet in Bangla; author of a Manasa-mangal poem, composed in the dialect of North-West Bengal. He was probably a native of that region.

Biya-nam (Asamiya): marriage-songs, regarded as indispensable in various wedding rituals.

Bobbili-katha (?C; Telugu): a popular historical ballad which deals with the political feud between the Bobbili chief and the Vijayanagar king, culminating in a day's battle. A French adventurer named Bussey got involved on the Vijayanagar side and attacked Bobbili on 24 January 1757.

Bodha (late 18th): poet in Hindi; belonged to Rajapur village in Banda district of Madhya Pradesh; his patron was the ruler of Panna. Originally named Buddhisen, he was nicknamed Bodha by the ruler. When separated from his beloved courtesan Subhan, he composed *Viraha'varis*. Another work ascribed to him in *Ishq-nama*.

Bodhayana (?C): poet in Sanskrit; lived sometime between A.D. 1st and 4th. The play *Bhagavadajjuka* is ascribed to him.

Boli (Urdu): used to mean any composition which could be spoken (bolna).

Bon-git (Asamiya): originally forest-dweller's songs; generally, folksongs celebrating the beauty of mountains, rivers, jungles, etc.

Brahma-bharata (?C; Sanskrit) of unknown author: an incomplete work on dramaturgy, of which the six available chapters deal with abhinaya of the 'marga' (classical) tradition. It does not refer to 'desi' tradition nor mention any earlier work. This may be the same as the work *Brahmanatyashastra* cited by Damodaragupta in his *Kuttanimata*.

Brahma-git (Maithili): type of devotional song associated with a whole range of rural deities in North Bihar. Brahma is a village god.

Brahmana (Veda): generic name for a class of works, consisting of utterances and discussions of priests about sacrifice. These are in prose, with occasional verses of two kinds—'gatha' (songs in general) and 'narasamsi' (songs in praise of heroes). Each of the vedas contains one or more brahmanas; thus 'Aitareya-brahmana' and 'Kausitaki-brahmana' belong to *Rig-veda*.

Brahmanda-Bhugola (late 15th/early 16th; Oriya) of Balarama Dasa: a geography of the universe.

Brahmanda-purana (?C; Sanskrit): one of maha-puranas relating to the god Brahma; deals with the origin of the universe as told by him.

Brahmanda-puranam gadyam (late 14th; Malayalam) of unknown author: early prose work in which several chapters of *Brahamanada-purana* have been retold. The language used here is that employed by Nambiars in recitation and known as 'Nambiantmish'; from it later emerged modern Malayalam prose.

Brahmanda-puranam kilippattu (16th/17th; Malayalam) of disputed authorship: some scholars ascribe this to Ezhuttacan, others to Karunakaran, a disciple of Ezhuttacan.

Brahmasiva (mid-12th): scholar and poet in Kannada; author of *Samaya-parikshe*, a work which criticises other religious faiths. Born into a Shaiva brahman family, he later became a Jain.

Brahmi: name of an ancient Indian script. The oldest specimens have been found Piparawa in Basti district of Madhya Pradesh and at Badli in Ajmer district of Rajasthan. It appears to have been in use from 5th century B.C. to about A.D. 350; thereafter it divided to produce a Northern style and a Southern style, from both of which other styles developed.

Brahmon-Roman Kyathalik sambad (1743; Bangla) of Dom Antonio de Rozario: early prose work in the form of a dialogue between a brahman and a catholic. The author was a native Christian convert.

Brajabuli: an artificial literary language created in 15th by the Maithili poet Vidyapati in which a large portion of Bangla Vaishnav lyrics were written. The language is a mixture of M. Bangla and M. Marathi with some W. Hindi and Apabhramsh forms; began being used in Bengal towards end-15th and continued till 17th. Oldest known specimens are the lyrics by Yashoraj Khan in *Krishna-mangal*, and the compositions of a court-poet of king Dhanamanikya of Tripura.

Brajanath Badajena (1730–95): the most versatile of writers in Oriya, he experimented successfully with several styles and forms; author of *Chatura'vinoda, Ambika-vilasa, Samara'taranga,* etc. He came from a prosperous family with high cultural attainments; he and his three brothers, all accomplished in literature and other arts, were officials under the raja of Dhenkanal. In spite of his many accomplishments, Brajanath had a chequered career during which he served under many rulers and left each because of violent disagreements.

Braja-vilas (*c*1770; Hindi) of Brajbasi-das: long poem in praise of

Krishna. The poet belonged to Brindavan; he also translated *Prabodha chandroday* from Sanskrit into Hindi.

Brajangana kavya (1861; Bangla) of Maikel Madhusudhan Datta: a series of poems (which are like odes of European literature) dealing with Radha as a love-lorn woman. The religious and mystical connotation of Radha's relationship with Krishna is absent here.

Brajbhasha: also known as Braji or Braj Hindi; a form of Western Hindi, which probably emerged in 10th out of Sauraseni Apabhramsh. However, the earliest literary composition is found in 16th and the first well-known poet of Braja is Surdas. Other poets who have composed in this language are Nandadas, Tulsidas, Bihari, Matiram, Bhushan, Dev, Bharatendu and Ratnakar. It was used mainly for composing verse and it occupied an important position in medieval Hindi literature. The best Brajbhasha is spoken around Mathura, Agra, Aligarh and Dholpur.

Brata-katha (Oriya): votive tales in prose dating back to 13th/14th. Among the better known ones are 'Somanatha bratakatha', 'Nagalachauthi (Naga-chaturthi) katha', and those relating to the young girl Tapoi. The latter is associated with the 'Khudkuri upabas', a festive fast observed by unmarried girls in Orissa.

Brihad-harivamsha-purana (late 8th; Prakrit) of Jinasena: also known as *Harivamsha-purana*, this work is a Jaina adaptation of *Mahabharata* in 66 sargas wherein changes have been made to propagate Jainism. Thus, Kauravas are converted to Jainism; Pandavas became ascetics and attained nirvana; Gautama is a disciple of Mahavira.

Brihaddeshi (5th/7th; Sanskrit) of Matanga: a work on music, of which only six chapters are available. Though the title suggests it dealt only with regional music, the extant portions include discussion of classical principles like 'sruti' and 'swara'. Matanga mentions Bharata but differs from him in several places; may have lived not very long after Bharata; is referred to by Abhinavagupta and Sharngadeva. He is said to have introduced the prabandha form called Harivilasa and the dance form Zakkini. According to one tradition Dattila and Kohala were his sons.

Brihaddevata (?C; Sanskrit) ascribed to Shaunaka: a matrical work which lists a large number of gods worshipped in different hymns on

Rig-veda; also contains myths and legends relating to these devatas. It is one of the earliest narrative works in Indian literature.

Brihat-katha (?C; Prakrit) of Gunadhya: a lost but highly influential work. It is generally believed that it was written in Paisachi Prakrit prose somewhere in western Dakhan (probably in Pratisthan city of Andhra Pradesh) sometime during 1st to 3rd centuries A.D. The original appears to have been a voluminous story or series of tales. It has been partially preserved in three Sanskrit versions — *Brihatkatha-manjari* of Kshemendra, *Brihatkatha-lokasamgraha* of Budhaswamin, and *Kathasarit-sagara* of Somadeva. There is also a Tamil version, *Perunkkottai*. The main story concerns prince Naravahanadatta, his travels and numerous romances, fetching as many as 26 brides, the most beautiful of whom is princess Madanamanjuka. Despite the royal hero and heroine, the work portrays various strata of middle class Indian society.

Brihat-katha-manjari (11th; Sanskrit) of Kshemendra: represents the north-western version in which *Brihatkatha* was preserved. Consisting of over 7000 verses divided into 18 sections called 'lambhaka', it narrates the adventures of Naravahanadatta, son of king Udayana, and how he won princess Madanamanjuka as his bride and the land of Vidyadharas as his empire. According to scholars, Kshemendra has reduced factual details, enlarged erotic matters and prolonged religious portions.

Brihatkatha-shlokasamgraha (8th/9th; Sanskrit) of Budhaswamin: represents the version in which *Brihatkatha* was preserved in Nepal. Consisting of 4539 stanzas in 28 sections, the work is available in incomplete form. Nothing is known about the author.

Brindavan-das (mid-16th): poet in Bangla; author of *Chaitanya-mangal*. A grand-nephew of Shrinivas Pandit, Chaitanya's elderly neighbour and one of two earliest followers, Brindavan became a disciple of Nityananda, a close follower of Chaitanya. The work was done at the instance of Nityananda, who, along with Advaitacharya and other followers, provided the material.

Brishbhan Kunwari (1728–47): woman poet of Krishna-bhakti in Hindi; author of *Bhakti-virudavali, Auranga-chandrika, Dara-lila*. She was a wife of the ruler of Orchha.

Bronson [Miles Bronson (1812–83)]: Christian missionary who worked in Assam and published an Asamiya-English dictionary in 1867. This is based on 14,000 words from spoken Asamiya.

Brown [(Charles Philip Brown (1798–1884)] scholar of Telugu. Born to English parents at Calcutta, he was sent away to England after his father's death; returned in 1817 to live mainly in Madras Presidency; worked for East India Company until his retirement in 1855. He developed a deep and abiding interest in Telugu; discovered the works of Vemana, got them published, also translated them into English; got pubished many prabandha manuscripts along with annotations; produced an English-Telugu and a Telugu-English dictionary, which were published in 1852–53; earlier, had published a grammar of Telugu in English. On returning to England after retirement, for sometime he was professor of Telugu at London University.

Buddha-charita (?1st; Sanskrit) of Ashwaghosha: a kavya on the life and acts of Gautam Buddha, perhaps the earliest extant kavya in Sanskrit. Originally it may have comprised 28 sections, but only parts of I and XIV and the whole of II-XII are available. There are Chinese and Tibetan translations of the text.

Tr. Cowell, *SBE*, 1893; Johnston, Lahore, 1935–36.

Buddha-datta (?5th): Bouddha scholar, a contemporary of Buddhaghosha; author of *Abhidhammavatara, Vinaya-vinicchaya, Uttara-vinicchya, Ruparupa-vibhaga, Madhurattha-vilasini*, all treatises in Pali on aspects of Buddhism. He was a native of Uragapur (Uraiyur), then capital of the Chola kingdom, near the river Kaveri: later lived in the Mahavihara of Sri Lanka.

Buddha-ghosha (?5th): Bouddha scholar and author in Pali; wrote *Nanodaya*, and *Visuddhi-magga*, both dealing with Buddhist philosophy, and commentaries on all three pitakas. A biographical account is to be found in Mahavamsha, chapter 37, which was probably incorporated in 13th by Dhammakitti. Born to a brahman family of Magadha, he converted to Buddhism with a desire to write commentaries on *Tipitaka*; went to the Mahavihara of Anuradhapura in Sri Lanka, during the reign of Mahanaman (earlier 5th), for theological studies. There he translated the entire atthakathas from Sinhala into Pali. He returned eventually to Magadha—perhaps by way of Burma, or made a separate visit there. Besides preaching Buddhism in Burma, he translated Kacchayana's grammar of Pali into

Burmese and wrote a commentary on it; is also said to have introduced Manusmriti to Burma.

Buddhaghos-uppatti (14th; Pali): also known as *Maha-Buddhaghosa Nidanavatthu*. Attributed to Mahamangala, who may be the same as the grammarian Mangala, the work purports to be a biographical account of Buddhaghosha, but the events narrated in it are very similar to those in *Milindapanha* and *Mahavastu*.

Buddha-ppiya (12th): author of *Pajjamadhu*. He may be the same as Buddhappiya Dipankara, author of *Rupasiddhi* or *Padarupasiddhi*, a grammatical work on Pali.

Buddha Rakkhit (12th): writer in Pali; author of *Jinalankar*, a work containing 250 poems on the life of Gautam Buddha.

Buddha-vamsha (?C; Pali) work in verse telling of the 40 Buddhas who were supposed to have preceded Gautam Buddha; part of *Khuddhanikaya*.

'Bulbul' [Lakhimanjooh Koul (1812–24)]: poet in Kashmiri, known mainly for his *Samnama* which is an adaptation of Firdousi's epic narrative in Farsi, *Shahnama*. Bulbul's other works like *Radhasuyamvar*, *Nal-va-daman* and *Sikandarnama* have not yet been published.

Bulhey Shah (1680–1758/9): Sufi poet in Panjabi. His real name was Abdulla and he was born in Pandoke village of Kasur tehsil, Lahore district (now in Pakistan). He wrote poetry in a variety of forms and many of his verses are available in manuscripts at the Panjab University library.

Buranji (Asamiya): originally a Tai (dialect from which the Ahoms derived their language) word meaning 'storehouse of knowledge for the ignorant', it was adopted to describe the prose chronicles of Ahom kings who brought with them the practice of recording important events of the time. From the advent of the Ahoms to Assam in 13th to late 16th, the records were kept in Tai; subsequently chroniclers began using Asamiya and these records continue unbroken until the occupation of Assam by the British in 1826. These chronicles have been divided into three broad categories: (1) chronicles of Kamrup kings prior to the establishment of the Ahom kingdom in 1228; these mix tradition and legend with the accounts. (2) chronicles of Ahom kings, from 1228 to termination of their rule in 1826; these are more authentic and mutually corroborative; (3) chronicles of adjoining kingdoms or countries with whom the Ahoms had diplomatic relations; this includes *Badshah buranji*, which deals with 17th century Mughals.

Burhan-ud-din Janum (d. 1583): poet in Dakhni; author of *Jannatul-baqa*. He was the son of Shamsul-ushaq.

C

Cachhari (Apabhramsha): as derived from the Apabhramsha work *Cachhari* of Jinadatta Suri, this became a term for compositions that could be sung to the accompaniment of informal dancing.

Cachhari (late 12th; Apabhramsha) of Jinadatta Suri: a work in eulogy, of the poet's preceptor, Jinavallabha Suri. It is in 47 verses, meant to be sung. The work is also called *Dharma-rasayana*, and there is a commentary on it by Jinapala.

Carey [William Carey (1761–1834)]: British missionary and versatile scholar of Indian languages; best remembered as the first translator of the Bible into Bangla and one of the pioneers of Bangla literary prose. Though based at the Baptist Mission in Serampore (then a Dutch enclave), he was closely associated with Fort William College, especially in planning the Indian language teaching programme there. Between 1801–1825, he prepared and published the grammars of six Indian languages (Bangla in 1801; Marathi, 1805; Sanskrit, 1806; Panjabi, 1812; Telugu, 1814; Kannada, 1817) and two dictionaries (Marathi, 1810; Bangla, 1815). His *Bangla to English Dictionary* (1815–25) is one of the earliest lexicographical works in Bangla; he also compiled 'Universal Dictionary of the Oriental Languages' which covered 13 languages, but more than half of this manuscript was destroyed in a fire. Two other books prepared by him are *Kathopakathan*, a series of dialogues in various styles of Bangla, and *Itihasmala*, a collection of stories and anecdotes.

Chada laihui (?C; Manipuri) a book which reccords the names of kings of Manipur from the time of Nongda Lairen Pakhangba. The record includes details of their parentage and information about important events of their reign. It supplements *Cheitharol kumbaba*, the royal chronicle of Manipur.

Chaita or **chaitabara** (Maithili): class of songs meant to convey the emotion of love in the month of Chaitra (March–April).

Chaitanya (1486–1533) or Shri Chaitanya: founder of a large Vaishnav movement of East India, who came to be regarded as an avatar in his later life. Born at Nabadvip, his parents were Jagannath Misra and Sachi Debi; distinguished himself even quite young as a grammarian and rhetorician. Known as Nimai Pandit after his initiation by Ishwar Puri at Gaya, he developed a small circle of followers, and started the ritual of samkirtan. After renouncing householder's life in 1509, travelled to various parts of India, and made Puri his final home.

Chaitanya Bhagavat (mid-16th; Bangla) of Brindavandas: common name of the work *Chaitanya-mangal*. A long narrative poem divided into 3 kanda and 52 adhyay. The popular title, *Ch-mangal*, suggests that it was meant to be chanted and sung like the traditional poems on puranic themes; the given name, *Ch-bhagavat*, indicates that it became connected with Chaitanya worship. The material was obtained from close followers of Chaitanya, hence has documentary value. The work was begun while Chaitanya was alive and completed after his death, but makes no reference to the latter event. It presents an entirely human picture of Chaitanya and was a popular success from the beginning. The poem also contains descriptions of social conditions in Bangla in late 16th.

Chaitanya-chandrodaya (1579; Sanskrit) of Kavikarnapura: drama in ten acts on the main incidents in Shri Chaitanya's life; probably modelled on Krishnamishra's *Probodha-chandrodaya*. The author's real name was Paramanand Sen; Shri Chaitanya gave him the title of 'Karnapura', hence the name Kavikarnapura.

Chaitanya-chandrodaya-kaumudi (?C; Bangla) of Premadas (real name Purushottam Mishra): an adaptation in Bangla verse of the Sanskrit drama *Chaitanya-chandrodaya* by Paramananda Sen.

Chaitanya-charitamrita (1542; Sanskrit) of Paramananda Sen: a long biographical poem on Shri Chaitanya.

Chaitanya-charitamrita (*c*1580; Bangla) of Krishnadas Kaviraj: most important of the Chaitanya biographies in Bangla because it incorporates the rhetorical and philosophical theories of Shri Chaitanya and Vaishnav faith propounded by Damodar Swarup and accepted by Rup Sanatan, and other Vaishnav leaders at Brindavan. The work is thus not merely a biography but also a compendium of the Vaishnav faith in its mystic as well as philosophic aspects. As a biography it outlines Chaitanya's early life (Brindavandas has already written about this) but treats the last 18 years in great detail; it also gives an account of Chaitanya's extensive travels.

Chaitanya-charitamrita (late 16th; Sanskrit) of Kavikarnapura: long poem of about 2000 verses in 20 sections on the life and acts of Shri Chaitanya.

Chaitanya-mangal of Brindavandas: work is better known as *Chaitanya Bhagavat*.

Chaitanya-mangal (late 16th; Bangla) of Lochandas: a Chaitanya biography based largely on the Sanskrit poem by Murari Gupta. The work begins like a purana but otherwise the traditional narrative manner is used. It is full of lyrical passages, thus maintained its popularity among the masses longer than any other biographical poem on Chaitanya.

Chaitanya-mangal (late 16th; Bangla) of Jayananda: biographical poem on Shri Chaitanya, the only work in which his death is mentioned. The introductory part mentions several previous biographers, of whom only Brindavan is known. The work is aimed at common people, not to devoted Vaishnavs; gives additional information about Chaitanya and his ancestors, which may not all be authentic. Also, Jayananda incorporates into his work long puranic tales such as those about Dhruva, Jadabharat, Indradyumna and others.

Chaitanya-samhita (?C; Bangla) of Bhagirath Bandhu: work follows the tradition of agama or tantric texts in its presentation as a story told by Shiva to his spouse.

Chaitanya-vilasa (16th; Oriya) of Madhava Dasa: a short poetical work in ten sections dealing with the life of Shri Chaitanya. The poet probably came into contact with the sant when the latter came to Puri.

Chakradhar (late 13th): founder of the Mahanubhava panth, whose utterances collected by a disciple constitute one of the earliest available works in Marathi, while other compositions by his followers form the beginnings of Marathi literature.

Chalisa (Hindi): a work consisting of 40 poems. Thus, *Hanuman-chalisa.*

Chamarasa (15th): poet in Kannada; lived during the reign (1419–

46) of Praudhadeva Raya and was honoured by him. He is the author of *Prabhulingalile*, an allegorical poem with Allama Prabhu as the central character.

Chamatkara (Sanskrit): term in poetics for the supernatural and inexplicable joy produced by a literary compositions.

Champu (Sanskrit): a kavya-form which uses verse as well as prose. Older critics like Bhamaha, Dandin, Vamana, etc., do not mention it at all; later critics like Vishwanath mention only its mixture of verse and prose and have not specified any other literary feature. Possibly, it was not regarded highly in Sanskrit but gained ground in the more modern languages. Thus, in Malayalam, about 200 champu works are extant. The earlier champus were composed in Manipravalam; the verse followed the rules of Sanskrit prosody, but the prose portions followed Dravidian metres. It is said that champus were first composed in Kerala to meet the needs of Chakyars who wanted some literary pieces for 'kuttu' performances.

Champu Ramayana (11th; Sanskrit): champu work based on the Valmiki *Ramayana*. Bhojaraj composed up to Kishkindya kanda; Lakshman Bhatt extended it to Yuddha kanda; Venkatraj completed the work by composing Uttar kanda.

Chand Bardai or **Bardoi** (late 12th): popularly regarded as the first major poet of Hindi and author of *Prithviraj raso*. But there is much controversy about his dates and authorship, even about whether he ever existed. According to tradition, he belonged to Lahore and rose to be the court poet of Prithviraj Chauhan, last Hindu ruler (d. 1195) of Dilli (Delhi); of Chand's ten sons, one named Jalhan helped the poet to complete *Prithviraj raso*.

Chand-Kunwari-ri bat (1765; Hindi) of Pratapsingh: kavya which tells of the romance between Chand, a prince of Amravati, and Kunwari, daughter of a leading merchant of that place.

Chanda (?C): grammarian of Prakrit and author of *Prakrita-lakshana*. Another work of the same title is attributed to Panini.

Chanda Jha (1831–1907): scholar of Maithili and versatile author. His major work is the *Maithilibhash Ramayana* (1886); translated Vidyapati's *Purushapariksha* into Maithili prose and verse, with a long introduction in Hindi (1889);

tried his hand at drama in *Ahalyacharitra-nataka*, a traditional play of the 'kirtaniya' type. His devotional poems on Shiva, known as "Maheshavani", were published posthumously in 1912; another collection of his poems is *Chanda padyavali* (1936).

Chandan (late 18th): a poet of the riti convention in Hindi; author of *Keshari-prakash, Chanda-satsai, Pathik-bodh, Patrika-bodh, Tatva-samgraha, Krishna-kavya, Prajna-vilas*. He belonged to Shahjahanpur (Uttar Pradesh) and was the ward of Keshari Singh, ruler of Goud.

Chandan-Malayagiri-ki bat (1740; Hindi) of Bhadrasen: kavya which tells of the romance between Chandan and Malayagiri.

Chandarbhan (mid-17th): scholar of Panjabi and poet in Farsi, whose poetical name was 'Barahman'; composed mostly Sufi poems and tracts. He belonged to Lahore.

Chandayan (*c*1370; Hindi) of Maulana Daud: long poem in early Avadhi; tells of the romance between Lorik or Lor or Laur, a hero of the Ahir caste, and his wife Chanda. The work, of Sufi inspiration, is mentioned by Badauni, the historian of Akbar's court. Manuscript fragments dating from mid-16th have been found, where the Perso-Arabic script has been used for transcribing Avadhi. The story was popular enough to be translated into Magahi, Maithili and Bangla. A rendering into Bangla was particularly popular among East Bengal Muslims.

Chandi-das: this 'bhanita' has been used by several poets in about 1200 poems in Bangla from around 1400 to 1600. Three are generally distinguished from the others—Badu Chandidas, Dvija Chandidas, Dina Chandidas; all wrote poems of Krishna-bhakti.

Badu Chandidas, author of *Shri Krishna-kirtan*, probably belonged to an era preceding Shri Chaitanya. The work, a ballad drawing largely upon *Gita-Gobinda* of Jayadev, sets the Radha-Krishna episode in a rural setting.

Dvija (or Dviju) Chandidas was probably a contemporary of Shri Chaitanya and his work was much appreciated by the sant. Dina (or Dinu) Chandidas belonged to a post-Chaitanya era. The well-known legend of Chandidas' love for and companionship with a low-caste woman (named Ramatara, Rami or Tara) probably relates to yet another and later Chandidas.

Despite the uncertain identity of these poets, the name Chandidas is often mentioned without any epithet and taken to represent a high point of Vaishnav lyricism in Bangla poetry.

Chandi-di var (17th; Panjabi) of Guru Govind Singh: poem in praise of the goddess Chandi. It describes a battle between the goddess and demons, and praises anybody on either side who shows real courage and skill in warfare.

Chandi-mangal (Bangla) a kind of mangal-kavya associated with the religious vows of women folk in Bengal and featuring the goddess Chandi, who is not the same as the one that appears in *Markandaya-purana*; she is more of a forest goddess indigenous to Bengal. The theme of these long poems relate to the problem of introducing the worship of this goddess on earth. Two cycles of stories are used for this purpose—that of Kalketu the hunter, and of Dhanapati the merchant. Manik Datta (end-15th) is supposed to be the first poet to have composed in this form; among 16th poets are Madhavacharya and Mukundaram Chakrabarti. Older works in this form began with the account of a dream in which the goddess appeared to the poet and commanded him to write the poem; this was later replaced by an autobiographical account by the poet.

Chandi-mangal (1579; Bangla) of Madhavacharya or Divija Madhav. The poet mentions that in his time a ruler named Akbar was master of Bengal: this is the first ever reference to a Mughal ruler in Bangla literature. The poem is a comparatively short work; it does not contain the introduction story of Shiva and Sati. All manuscripts of the poem, none older than 1759, came from remote East Bengal, mainly Chatgaon.

Chandi-mangal (1589; Bangla) of Mukundaram Chakrabarti. The work is also known as *Kavikankan Chandi* or *Chandi-kavya*; representative in nature and substantial in bulk, it superseded all earlier works in this form, forestalled later attempts, and served as a model for other mangal compositions. The preface includes an autobiographical account, which hereafter replaced the dream episode that generally prefaced such works. The poem is in three parts; the first deals with the puranic story of Shiva, of Sati and of Parvati; the second is the 'Akhati (fowler) khanda'; the third is the 'Vanik (merchant) khanda'. The first may have been composed originally as 'Shivayana' poem, when the poet was still living in his ancestral home. Though the subject-matter of the poem is mythological in origin and religious in character, Mukundaram has managed to incorporate a large measure of the contemporary social life and atmosphere. A vein of humour keeps the long work from being pedestrian. Though the poet was a good Hindu, his description of Muslim settlers shows intimate knowledge, understanding and sympathy. The work is a narrative poem to be chanted and sung; it contains very few lyrics.

Chandi-mangal (?C; Bangla) of Manik Datta: one such work is mentioned by Mukundaram as the inspiration for his own *Ch-mangal*. But this is some work other than the one extant in a late 18th manuscript from North Bengal, which shows features that can be dated later than Mukundaram; hence there was a second and later Manik Datta who composed a *Ch-mangal* incorporating the earlier work. The 'original' Manik Datta may have introduced the ritual song of Chandi in Southwest Bengal.

Chandi-purana (15th; Oriya) of Sarala Dasa: a long poem; the first work in the language to glorify the goddess Durga.

Chandi-shataka (7th; Sanskrit) of Banabhatta: a verse-sequence of 102 stanzas in sragdhara metre, praising the goddess Chandi.

Chandra-vyakarana (?7th; Sanskrit) of Chandragomin a work of grammar, apparently intended as an abridgement and simplification of *Ashtadhayi*. Instead of the original eight chapters, this has six; instead of 3981 aphorisms, this has 3100; the portion dealing with Vedic grammar and accents has been omitted.

Chandrabadan-wa mahiyar (?C; Urdu) of Muqumi: a masnavi work.

Chandragomin (?7th): Bouddha scholar of Sanskrit probably from Bengal; author of *Chandra-vyakarana*. He is also credited with the authorship of *Lokananda*, a play; *Nyayasiddhya-loka*, a philosophical work; *Aryataradevi stotra-mukutika-mala*, a collection of hymns.

Chandralekha (17th; Prakrit) of Rudradas: a sattaka play celebrating the marriage of Manaveda and Chandralekha.

Chandraloka (?C; Sanskrit) of Jayadeva (not the poet of Gita-Govinda): a work on poetics in ten chapters called 'mayukha', consisting of about 350 verses.

Chandranath Basu or **Bose** (1844–1910): literary critic and writer of prose in Bangla. He wanted to write in English (his critique of *Krishnakanter uil* was published in *Calcutta Review*) but was inspired by Bankimchandra to write in Bangla; he wrote many essays and articles in Bangla on religion, philosophy and literature.

Chandra-prabha Puran (*c*1190; Kannada) of Aggal: a champu kavya about the eighth tirthankar. This work is based on the Sanskrit *Chandraprabha-purana* of Vir Nandi. It is also known as *Aggal Lilavati*.

Chandrasakhi (1643–1733): composer and singer of bhajans in Rajasthani. Originally known as Chandra, when younger he had served as a thanedar at Motha village near Dacha in Bundelkhand (Uttar Pradesh); later he gave up a worldly life and settled in Brindavan, where he was initiated in the Radhavallabha faith. He travelled in Rajasthan and Malwa, singing bhajans written by him; late in life he moved back to Dacha. His bhajans are so popular in Rajasthan that few people realise he did not belong to Rajasthan.

Chandrashekhar Mukhopadhyay or **Mukherjee** (1849–1922): prose writer in Bangla who became well-known only after he wrote the poem *Udbhranta prem* (1875) on his wife's sudden death. For some time he was editor of the monthly *Upasana*; his articles appeared in important journals of the time.

Chandrashekhar Simha (mid-17th): poet in Maithili from Nepal; brother-in-law and minister for war of Jagatprakash-malla. He seems to have used a number of pen-names (viz., Chandra, Sekhara, Shekharasimha, etc.) and this has made it difficult to identify poems composed by him.

Chandrayana (Rajasthani): a metre of four padas, widely used by medieval poets, but seldom as the only metre in a poem.

Chandrotsavam (?15th; Malayalam) of unknown author: a kavya work in 5 sargas, consisting of 579 quatrains. It tells of a gandharva whose beloved, a kinnar woman, bids him to fetch a particular flower of unusual fragrance. This mission brings him to earth to a place called Chikkilappali (in central Kerala), where he finds that the fragrance is emitted not by a flower but by a lamp lit by the courtesan Medini Vennilavu during Chandrostsavam. The gandharva stays on for a time to witness the festival, then returns to his beloved and gives her an account of all he has heard and seen.

Chappa (*c*1650; Gujarati) of Akho: a collection of 756 six-line poems that is a classic of Gujarati literature. It consists of 45 sections ('anga') of unequal length; unity is provided by the intimate tone in which the poet addresses the listener or reader. Most of the poems chastise or make fun of pseudo-spiritual behaviour.

Chappaya (Rajasthani): a metrical form often used by bards in their anegyrics and eulogistic poetry. This metre is also known as 'kavitta'.

Charairongba (1672–1709). Manipuri king and poet in Manipuri, who was a patron of literature and other arts. He composed a long poem, Leirol, which describes all the varieties of beautiful flowers of his kingdom.

Charana (Rajasthani): a caste of bards who kept genealogies, maintained historical and family records, and composed poems in eulogy of their patrons. The beginnings of 'charana' poetry go back to the 10th century.

Charit-punthi (Asamiya): biographies, often in verse, of Vaishnav masters. These also contained pictures of religious life of Assam, records of current customs and manners, and accounts of religious institutions.

Charitropakhyan (*c*1720; Panjabi): the longest part of Guru Govind Singh's *Dasam Granth.* It is a collection of about 400 tales known to early 18th India.

Chariya-pitaka (?C; Pali): fifteenth part of Khuddanikaya. It contains 35 *Jataka* stories composed in verse arranged in three vargas, and sets forth the 'Paramitas' acquired by the Buddha in his past lives as Bodhisattva.

Charya-giti see *Charyapad* below.

Charyapad (*c*1050–1200) or Charya-giti : earliest available relics of Old Bangla, discovered in a manuscript in Nepal in 1916 by Haraprasad Shastri. The material consists of 47 mystic songs relating to the secret doctrine of a religious practice which may be pre-Aryan in origin. In each song the melody is indicated at the top and the poet is named in the last couplet; the songs usually consist of 10 verse lines, except three which have 14. Fourteen names that have been accepted as names of poets are Lui, Bhusuku, Kanha, Kamali, Dombi, Santi, Saraha, Ajadeva, Darika, Bhadi, Tadaka, Kankana, Jayanandi, Dhama. Three of the songs are anonymous; at least four were written by disciples on the masters named as authors. These poets were known as 'Siddhacharya' and at least two generations of poets are represented here, possibly four.

These represent the only connected and copious specimens of the earlier literary productions in a New Indo-Aryan speech; the language carries the definite stamp of Bangla, idiom and syntax, while the contents show that the poets were thoroughly acquainted with Bangla life and settings. However, the charya poems have also been claimed by Asamiya, Marathi and Oriya as belonging to their ancestory.

Chatur-bhani (?4th/6th; Sanskrit): collection of four one-act bhana type of plays; closely similar to one another and to *Mrichhakatika* in spirit and atmosphere. The separate titles and ascribed authors are "Ubhayabhisarik" of Vararuchi, "Padmaprabritaka" of Shudraka, "Dhurtavitasamvada" of Ishwardatta and "Padatadilaka" of Syamalika. The action is set in imperial capitals like Ujjayini or Kusumapura; the plays present amusing pictures of the lives, adventures and scandals of rogues and rakes who lived in such cities. Both in literary style and in character portrayal, these plays occupy a unique place in Sanskrit literature.

Chaturbhuj-das (mid-16th): poet in Hindi, one of the Ashtachhap group; son of Kumbhandas and disciple of Vitthaldas. He composed *Dvadas-yash, Bhakti-pratap* and *Hitajuko-mangal.*

Chatura Chaturbhuj (late 16th): poet of Mithila whose padas in Maithili are included in most of the important manuscript collections of verse. One of his Sanskrit verses is included in the Sanskrit anthology *Vidyakarsahasrakam.*

Chaturdaspadi kabitavali (1866; Bangla) of Maikel Madhusudhan Datta: a collection of 102 sonnets in Bangla written by the poet during his stay in Versailles (France). Many of these sonnets are on European subjects, but among the best are those dealing with the river in his village, Bangla rituals and festivals, his mothertongue, etc.

Chaturmukha (?7th): an early poet in Apabhramsh whose works have not yet been recovered. He has been praised for his choice of words and credited with popularizing the 'paddhadiya' metre.

Chatur-vinoda (*c*1770; Oriya) of Brajanath Badajena: prose work composed in early life by the author and meant for a courtly audience. The frame story is the romance between the local prince and the pretty daughter of a rich merchant. She permits him to visit her secretly at night, but a religious vow forbids her to make love and enjoins her to keep a vigil. The prince shares the vigil with her and tells her stories to pass the time. These stories are presented in four groups called 'vinoda' (entertainment) — *Hasa-vinoda, Rasa-vinoda, Niti-vinoda, Priti-vinoda* — each of which contains several stories within the main story. The form is not new, but the style is very close to common speech and the stories are full of suspense; a nearly modern work.

Chatuva (Telugu): an occasional poem inspired by events, episodes, persons and objects. Such poems are judged by their spontaneity.

Chaubis avatar (17th; Panjabi) of Guru Govind Singh: a part of *Dasam granth* and it describes in verse 24 avatars of Vishnu. Their names are 1. Maccha; 2. Kaccha; 3. 4. Nara-Narayan; 5. Mohini; 6. Baraha; 7. Narsingh; 8. Bavan; 9. Parasram; 10. Brahma; 11. Rudra; 12. Jalandhar; 13. Bishan; 14. Seshasayi; 15. Arhattadev; 16. Man Raja; 17. Dhanatar; 18. Surya; 19. Chandrama; 20. Ram; 21. Krishna; 22. Nara (Arjun); 23. Buddha; 24. Nihkalanki (Kalki).

Chaubisi (Rajasthani): as with 'baisi', 'pachisi', 'battisi', this is a poem containing 24 stanzas. This number found particular favour with Jain poets.

Chaupai (Hindi): verse-form, consisting of four lines; found also in Gujarati, Maithili, Rajasthani with slight variations. The best-known user of chaupai verse in Hindi is Tulsidas in *Ramcharitmanas.*

Chaupanna *Mahapurusha-chariyam* (?868; Prakrit) of Srilanka: prose work with alternating verses containing 10,800 shlokas; gives biographical accounts of 54 excellent persons or 'Salakapurushas' of the Jain tradition. There are other works of this nature, but this is the earliest of its kind. Its language is Maharashtri Prakrit.

Chaura-panchashika (*c*1000; Sanskrit) of Bilhana: erotic poem in 50 stanzas, dealing with secret love and the liveliness of woman in various amorous situations. The work is available in three recensions. In the South Indian recension it appears as part of a longer poem entitled *Bilhana-kavya.*

Tr. E. Arnold, London, 1896, S.N. Tadpatrikar, Pune, 1966 (rpt); Barbara S. Miller, New York, 1971.

Chaurasi Vaishnavan-ki varta (?C; Hindi): prose work attributed to Gokulnath, son of Vitthalnath and grandson of Vallabhacharya, founder of the Pushti community. It tells of his disciples. There is little agreement among scholars about the validity of these accounts, but they give valuable evidence of the social, religious, and economic life of the time.

Chautisa (Oriya): a poetic composition in 34 stanzas, each stanza beginning with a consonant of the Oriya alphabet from 'ka' to 'kha'. The form probably came from Sanskrit and may be found in other Indian languages, but Oriya cultivated it the most. Essentially a lyrical form, it is long enough to be used for narration; themes are quite varied, but the most popular is the lamentation of separated lovers who can be Radha and Krishna or the poet and his beloved. The earliest extant example is the *Kalasa-chautisa* of Baccha Dasa.

Chavundaraya (900–84): warrior and man of letters in Kannada; author of *Trishasti-lakshana mahapurana* (978), more popularly known as *Chavundaraya-purana*. Until the discovery of *Vaddaradhane*, this was considered the first great prose work in Kannada. Chavundaraya was also responsible for the installation of the Gomateswara image at Sravanabelgola.

Cheitharol Kumbaba (?C; Manipuri): a record of the kings of Manipur from the time of Nongda Lairen Pakhangba (A.D. 33–54); written in the Meitei script. There are several versions of this record but the one preserved in the royal palace at Maniput is considered to be the most authentic.

Cheluvamde (early 18th): woman poet in Kannada; author of *Varandi kalyan, Venkatachal-mahatmya, Lalipragalu, Mahatmyatike.* She was the chief queen of Mysore ruler Doddakrishna Raja.

Chemakura Venkata Kavi (17th): poet in Telugu. Attached to the court of Thanjavur ruler Raghunatha Nayaka, Chemakura is believed to have accompanied the king on military campaigns as well. He wrote Vijayavilasam, a description of Arjun's amorous adventures when in exile, and *Sarangadhara charitra*, which tells the love story of prince Sarangadhara and the courtesan Chitrangi. The poet's full name was Chemakura Venkataraju.

Chenna'basava (mid-12th): Virshaiva sant poet in Kannada; composed vachanas. Among his vachana-collections are *Shatsthal-vachan, Karan-hasuge, Misrarpan, Mantra'gaunya, Kalajnan* and *Rudrabharat*. He was Basaveshwar's nephew and disciple; helped him to organise the Anubhava-mandapa.

Cheraman Perumal (early 9th): Chera king and Shaiva devotee, also poet in Tamil; composed four devotional works, chief of which is *Tirukkailaya nanaula*. This is included in the 11th *Tirumurai*. Sundarar was a close associate of his.

Cheriyachi-varnanam (?C; Malayalam) of unknown author: a champu work about the beautiful maiden Cheriyachi.

Cherusseri Namputiri (15th): earliest known author in Malayalam; composed *Krishna-gatha* or *Krishnappattu*. He may have been the court-poet of Udayvarman king of Kollanulal (r. 1446–73) who is acknowledged at the beginning of the work.

Chhabi (Asamiya): a popular verse metre.

Chhand (Sanskrit): generally means rhythm; in particular instances, it is the term for metre. Prosody or the study of metre is known as 'Chhanda-shastra'.

Chhand chand varnan-ki mahima (*c*1580; Hindi) of Gang Kavi: a short work in Khariboli prose.

Chhandah-sutra (?C; Sanskrit) ascribed to Pingala: work on prosody, dealing mainly with classical metres. Some metres are named after attributes of the beloved woman; thus, 'Chanchalakshika' (one with restless eyes), 'Tanu-madhya' (one with slender waist), 'Charuhasini' (one with sweet smile). Some are named after animals; thus, 'Asvalalita' (gait of the horse), 'Sardulavikridita' (the tiger's play). Some are named from plant-life; thus, 'Manjari' (cluster), 'Mala' (garland).

Chhandobudhi (late 10th; Kannada) of Nagavarma: work on poetics. Perhaps the earliest in Kannada. It is in verse and divided into six aswas (sections); at the end of each section there is a prose summary.

Chhandovichiti (?C:) remains disputed whether this is the title of a work or it denotes metrics as a branch of study. As the title it has been ascribed to a lost work by Dandin; to *Chhandasutra* of Pingala; to a work by Sarangadeva. Possibly the work or term refers to a composition in Prakrit.

Chappa (*c*1650; Gujarati) of Akho: a collection of six-line poems that is a classic of Gujarati literature. Divided into 45 unequal 'anga' (sections), the work gains its unity from the intimate tone in which the poet addresses the listener.

Chhappaya (Hindi): six-line metrical form; widely used in long poems of heroic sentiment ('virgatha'). But Tulsidas and Nabhadas have also used it effectively in devotional poems.

Chhara (Bangla): short poems, aphoristic or satirical; sometimes merely funny.

Chhatra-prakas (1707; Hindi) of Lal Kavi: verse biography of Raja Hindi Chhatrasal of Bundelkhand (who fought the Mughals).

Chhedluvadu Mallanna (16th): poet in Telugu from Chhedalvada, near Gudluru (Andhra Pradesh). Of his two known works, Rukmangad-charitramu, has not been recovered and is known only from reference by others. The other, *Vipranarayan-charitramu*, is a prabandha-kavya which tells the life-story of Tondam Dippodi, an alwar from outside Tamilnadu.

Chhumma Sampradaya (?C; Kashmiri): a recently discovered work of unknown authorship and date, which contains 74 verses. Their subject matter and language belong to the age of *Mahanaya-prakasha*.

Chihala (?1495–1570): poet in Rajasthani; probably from Sekhawat region of Jaipur. Several works are assigned to him but the best known are *Pancha-saheli-gita* and *Bawani*. The first describes the feelings of women during separation from their husbands, followed by reunion. Five women are featured, one from each caste of a gardener, a betel seller, a cloth printer, a wine brewer and a goldsmith. The women use diction relevant to the profession each represents. *Bawani* discusses ethics and practical living.

Chihna-yatra (*c*1468; Asamiya) of Shankaradeva: precursor of the ankiya-nat, presents a dramatic action on stage with dance, song and music; perhaps the first such enactment in any Indo-Aryan language. The author himself played a role at the first performance.

Chikkadeva-vamshavali (early 18th; Kannada) of Tirumalarya: prose work dealing with the family history of Chikkadevaraja Wodeyer, ruler of Mysore. The work is important mainly because it used prose at a time when prose was not favoured as a literary medium; may have brought about a revival of prose writing in Kannada.

Chikkadevaraja (1645–1704): a distinguished Wodeyar of Mysore; not only an able administrator but also a generous patron of poets and scholars; himself a writer in Kannada. He appears to have been much influenced by his friend Tirumalraya, who later became his court poet. Perhaps assisted by him, Chikkadeva wrote *Gita-Gopala*, a collection of songs reminiscent of *Gita Govinda*, and *Chikkadevaraya binnapa*, a collection of prose prayers addressed to the god Narayan of Yadugiri (also called Melkote) near Mysore city.

Chinnaya Suri Paravastu (1806–62): scholar of Telugu, grammarian and prose writer; was the first professor of Telugu, Madras University. Among his many works, the best known are *Netichandrika*, a book of Telugu prose which seeks to teach the language through stories, and *Balavyakaranam*, a book of Telugu grammar written in *Ashtadhyayi* style with 10 chapters and 465 aphorisms.

Chintalapudi Ellanarya (1510–60) poet in Telugu whose patron was Vijayanagar king Krishnadeva Raya; author of *Radha-Madhavamu* and *Tarkabrahma-rajiyamu*.

Chintamani Tripathi (1600–1680/85): poet in Hindi; from Tikavpur village near Kanpur, Uttar Pradesh. He is said to have pioneered riti poetry. Among his works are *Kavya-kalpataru* (1650), a treatise on poetry; *Kavya-viveka, Kavya-prakash*, both collections of verse; *Ras-manjari*, on erotic sentiment; *Chhand-vichar*, on prosody; *Shringar-manjari*, a translation of the Sanskrit *Rasa-manjari*.

Chiplunkar, K.S.: see Krishna Shastri Chiplunkar.

Chiru-kappiyam (Tamil): term for poetical works that are judged as less than mahakavyas. Tamil critisism did not use Sanskrit based terms until about 12th when *Dandiyalamkaram* was written on the model of Dandin's *Kavyadarsha*. In it, a distinction was made between 'perund-kappiyam' (mahakavya) and 'kappiyam' (kavya); later 'chiru-kappiyam' came to be used for inferior kavya works. The examples of such works in Tamil sometimes given are *Udayankumara-kavyam, Nagakumara-kavyam, Yasodhar-kavyam, Chulamani* and *Nilkesi*. All these are works which propagate the Jain faith.

Chirupanarru-ppadai (?C: Tamil) of Nattattanar: third idyll of *Pattuppattu*. It extols the chieftain Nalliyakkodan; also describes cities and villages and the life led by the people there.

Chitalai Sattanar (?C): Bouddha monk and poet in Tamil; author of *Manimekalai*.

Chitra kavya (Sanskrit): poem which suggests a picture or some peculiarity or variety. Sanskrit criticism regards this as the lowest form of poetry.

Chitravali (*c*1620; Hindi) of Usman: verse work of Sufi inspiration in Brajbhasha; tells of the triangular romance involving Sujankumar, a prince of Nepal, Kevalavati, princess of Sagargarh, and Chitravali, princess of Rupnagar. The story is entirely imaginary. The work begins with eulogy of Ishwar and Muhammad, of the four khalifas, of emperor Jahangir, Shah Nizam Chisti, and Guru Baba Haji. No other Sufi work of romance ever used such a beginning. Usman is thus considered the last of the liberal Sufi poets.

Chitta-utthana (1732; Bangla) of Hayat Muhammad: work of a Bangla Muslim poet; adapted from a Farsi rendering of the Sanskrit *Hitopadesha.*

Chittukkavi (Tamil): epistles in verse, a form which appeared in Tamilnadu during 17th. Examples are *Virali-vidudutu, Kulappa Nayakkan-kadal, Varuna Kulatillan-matal.*

Chokha (Chokhamela) (14th): sant poet in Marathi. An outcaste by birth, he belonged to Mangalvedhe, near Pandharpur; came under the influence of Namdev and became a devotee of Vitthala although he was not allowed to enter the temple; composed about 450 abhangas.

Chor dhara (16th; Asamiya) of Madhavdeva: an ankiya nat based on the story of the child Krishna's stealing milk and butter.

Chudamani-das (mid-16th) poet in Bangla; author of *Gauranga-vijay.*

Chulamani (late 9th; Tamil) of Tolamoli Tevar: one of the minor 'kappiyam', notable for its use of the viruttam metre. The 'payiram' (introduction) to the work states it was presented for the first time at the court of Pandyan ruler Sendan (also known as Avani Chulamani Maravarman); possibly the work was named after this king. The poem tells a Jain version of the story of Krishna; is based on *Shri puranam* of Gunabhadrachariar.

Chula-vamsa (?C; Pali): a supplement to Mahavamsa. It deals with Sri Lankan kings from Sirimeghavanna, son of Mahasena, to Sirivikkama-rajasimha. According to Sri Lankan tradition, the work was commenced by Thera Dhammakitti who came from Burma to Sri Lanka at the time of king Parakramabahu II (13th). Parts of the work appear to have been composed by different persons at different periods.
Tr. Geiger & Mrs. R. Rickmers, 1939.

Chunadi (late 12th; Apabhramsh) of Bhattarak Vinayachandra Muni: a short work consisting of 31 poems. It offers moral and religious advice in simple language to householders.

Churnika (Marathi): term for a certain rhetorical and rhythmic strain of prose style occasionally used by akhyana writers of 17th and 18th, to embellish their works. Ananda Tanaya was probably the first akhyana writer to employ this device.

Crepar Xastrer Orth-bhed: see *Kripar Sastrer Artha bhed.*

D

Dabir [(Mirza Salamat Ali (1803–75)]: poet in Urdu: especially famous for his marsiya works. Born in Delhi, he came to Lakhnau at an early age and grew up here to become the leading poet at the Nawab of Awadh's court. He composed about 3000 marsiyas and was as popular in his time as Anis.

Dadu Dayal (1544–1603): mystic and sant poet in Hindi, in the tradition of Kabir; composed mainly doha verses. Born at Ahmadabad (Gujarat), he lived mostly in Amber (near Jaipur in Rajasthan) and died there. Although his own language was Rajasthani, his works are found recorded in Brajbhasha or in a mixture of Brajbhasha and old Khariboli which came to be known as 'Sadhukada boli' (as in the case of Kabir).

Dadoba Pandurang (1814–1881): scholar of Marathi; wrote the first grammar of the language while he was still a student. He also wrote in Marathi grammars of Sanskrit and Farsi. Among his other works are *Shishubodh, Yashoda-Pandurangi*, and an autobiography.

Daggupalli Duggayya (early 15th): poet in Telugu; author of *Nasiketopakhyanamul* and *Kanchipura-mahatmyamu*. Only the first is extant; it is a kavya work which uses an upanishadic story.

Dagh [Nawab Mirza Ibrahim (1831–1905)]: poet in Urdu; son of Nawab Shamsuddin Ahmad of Jhirka Ferozpur, who was executed by the British in 1835 on the charge of causing the murder of William Fraser, Resident of Delhi. Dagh served in the Rampur court for 24 years before moving to Haidarabad in 1888 and was appointed court poet in 1891. His works are *Gulzar-i-Dagh* (1878), *Masnavi Fariyad-i-Dagh* (1882), *Aftab-i-Dagh* (1885), *Mahtab-i-Dagh* (1883), and *Yadgar-i-Dagh* (1905).

Dah Majlis (1732; Urdu) of Fazli: a translation of Mulla Husain Nazir's work in Farsi *Rauzat-ush-shohada*. It is an account of the massacre of Muhammad Husain and his companions at the field of Karbala. The language provides example of an early stage of Urdu, but the diction is heavily influenced by Farsi and Arabic. The work is also known as *Karbal katha*. A copy of its manuscript was discovered in a library in Germany and a modern, properly edited text was published from this.

Dahasu (Sindhi): a folk-poetry form, in which a couplet or stanza containing ten synonyms refers to the beauty of the beloved or other comparisons expressing admiration.

Daityari Thakur (early 16th): scholar of Sanskrit, wrote in Asamiya; author of *Guru-charit*, a verse biography of Shankaradeva. To this he appended a brief account of Madhavadeva's life. Daityari was the son of Ramcharan Thakur who wrote *Shankara-charit*.

Dak-bhanita (Asamiya): also known as 'Dakar bachan' or 'Dak mahapurushear bachan'; a collection of aphorisms attributed to Dak, a wise man. Similar sayings are also available in Bangla. While Bangla tradition regards him as a milkmaid's son, in Assam he is regarded as a potter's son and has seven brothers. His home is supposed to be in Lehi-dangora village near Barpeta in Kamrup district. The material was transmitted orally for generations. The oldest manuscript belongs to 18th.

Dakarnava (?C; Sanskrit/Prakrit): a Buddhist work on tantra. According to some scholars, a portion of the work is in Sauraseni Apabhramsh; according to Haraprasad Shastri, the language is Old Bangla.

Dakhni: the speech of the South (Dakhan) as opposed to Hindustani, the speech of the North. It developed as a literary language in 15th from northern dialects carried by North Indian Muslims when they invaded the southern and western parts of India. Literature in Dakhni developed at various centres: Gujarat, Bidar, Golkonda, Bijapur, Aurangabad. The Qutb Shahi kings of Golkonda (1590–1697) were great patrons of Dakhni. In the first half of 18th, after Aurangzeb had conquered the whole of Muslim Deccan, Dakhni got merged into Urdu, the speech favoured by Muslims in cities like Delhi, Lakhnau, etc.

Dalel-prakash (1791: Hindi) of Than Kavi: a work which honours the poets' patron, Dalelsingh. The poet belonged to Raebareli; wrote in the riti convention.

Dalpat Vijay (late 17th): poet in Hindi; author of the vir-gatha kavya *Ghumman raso*.

Dalpat-vilasa (16th; Rajasthani) of

unknown author: an incomplete prose work. It deals with the first 13–14 years of the life of Dalpatsingh (born 1564) and was probably written between 1597 and 1605. Apart from its historical and linguistic importance, the work offers rich cultural material relating to the time.

Dalpatirai (18th): poet in Hindi; author of *Alamkar-ratnakar,* written in collaboration with Bansidhar probably in 1735. He belonged to Ahmadabad (Gujarat) but settled finally in Udaipur (Rajasthan) and served in the court of Maharaja Jagatsingh.

Dalpatram (1820–98): writer in Gujarati who also composed sometimes in Brij; belonged to the Swaminarayana sect. He collaborated with James Forbes in the establishment of the Gujarati Vernacular Society and was its first assistant secretary; started the periodical *Buddhi-prakash* in 1850 and was its editor till 1878. Though his early work was in prose (mainly essays), he is better remembered and loved as a poet. Among his other works are *Lakshmi-natak* (1851), a play based on a Greek original; *Dalpat-pingal* (1855) a book on metres; *Kavyadohan*, in two parts (1860–62), an anthology of medieval Gujarati poetry.

Damini-charitra (18th; Bangla) of Saruf: a secular verse tale; the author was probably a Muslim.

Damodar (16th): poet in Panjabi, from Jhang. He composed, during the reign of Akbar, a qissa in 1000 stanzas on the Heer-Ranjha story. Written in Lehnda, a western dialect of Panjabi, this work probably introduced the Heer legend to Panjabi culture. Damodar is also credited with having initiated the qissa tradition in Panjabi literature.

Damodar Pandit (14th): poet in Marathi; one of the early Mahanubhava writers; author of *Vachha-harana* (1316), a poem based on an episode in the life of Shri Krishna as given in the 10th skandha of *Brahamandapurana*. It is a relatively short poem of about 500 verses in ovi metre. This and six other such poems by early Mahanubhava poets are known as 'Sati kavya'.

Damodara (17th): also known as Chatura Damodara; authority on music, wrote *Sangita-darpana*. He was attached to the court of either Jahangir or Shahjahan. Son of Lakshmidhara, he is supposed to be a descendent of Chatura Kallinatha, who wrote a famous commentary on *Sangita-ratnakara* of Sarangadeva.

Damodara-gupta (9th/1th): Kashmiri writer in Sanskrit, author of *Kuttanimata*.

Dana'keli-kaumudi (late 16th; Sanskrit) of Rupa Goswami: one-act play of the bhanita type.

Danda-vritta (Oriya): term used for the material liberties taken by Sarala Dasa and Balaram Dasa in their verse compositions when they departed from the customary 14-letter line. The term can be said to mean 'free verse'.

Dandi (early 8th): scholar of Sanskrit; author of *Kavyadarsha*, a work on poetics, also of the prose-romance *Dashakumara-charita*. He belonged to South India and was probably associated with the Pallava royal court at Kanchipuram.

Dandi-ramayana (16th; Oriya) of Balaram Dasa: a retelling of the *Ramayana* story using the dandi metre. The poet has departed in many places from Valmiki, introduced many episodes drawn from puranas, described all the holy places of Orissa. Because of the emphasis given to Jagamohan (Jagannath), the work is also known as 'Jagamohan Ramayana'.

Dara Sikandar nama (*c*1670; Bangla) of Alaol: an adaptation of the Farsi work of Nizami, *Iskandarnamah*; work was done at the behest of Majlis Navaraj, a minister of the Arakan court.

Dard [Khwaja Mir (1717–85)]: poet in Urdu; regarded as one of the main creators of the ghazal form. He used colloquial language and short metrical units; apart from the themes of love, he also wrote on concepts of mystical experience. His works have been collected in *Diwan-e-Dard, Nala-e-Dard, Dard-e-dil* and *Bardat-e-Dard.*

Dariyai [Kazi Mahmud (d. 1435)]: Sufi sant poet of Gujarat. He was revered so highly that it was said that a strong sea would get calmed if one remembered him; hence the name. He used to compose short poems in a form that came to be called 'zikri' (probably from zikr, meaning description); their subject-matter was love, divine as well as human.

Darpa-dalana (11th; Sanskrit) of Kshemendra: poem in seven sections which denounces vanity arising out of pride in lineage, wealth, learning, beauty, valour, charity and penance.

Darya-i-latafat (1802; Farsi) of Insha: a scholarly work of great importance dealing with Urdu grammar and poetics; written in verse and published from Murshidabad in 1848. It was translated into Urdu by Pandit Dattatreya Qaifi and published from Aurangabad in 1935. In this work Insha has discussed in detail the roots of Urdu words, the rules of their pronunciation, and epigrams in Urdu. He has also analysed the various forms of Urdu spoken in different regions and in various situations, the language used by women, the common and archaic words, the influence of other speeches on Urdu. He has indicated the notable differences between the Urdu of Lakhnau and that of Delhi. The work is in two parts. According to some scholars, Insha wrote only the first part which deals with linguistic history and grammar; the second part was written by Mirza Muhammad Ahsan 'Qatil'.

Dasha-bodha (17th; Marathi) of Ramdas: philosophical work divided into ten 'books'. The first seven appear to have been written at one stretch, tracing the life of a householder from youth to old age, and suggest a somewhat passive and negative outlook upon life. But the last three books, written piecemeal, exhort people to a more active and constructive life in fulfilling their duties. The idea of 'duty towards the nation' is stated here for the first time in Marathi writings and inspired Shivaji particularly.

Dashakumara-charita (early 8th; Sanskrit) of Dandin: prose romance, dealing with the adventures of Rajavahana and seven other imaginary princes. The deeds of two princes are described in the 'purva-pithika' (introductory portion); account of prince Vishruta's deeds is completed in the 'uttara-pithika' (concluding portion). The introduction and conclusion portions are generally regarded as later additions to the work.

Tr. P.W. Jacob & rev. C. Rylands, London, 1928; A.W. Ryder, Chicago, 1927. Tr. M.R. Kale, Bombay, 1925.

Dasham granth (1718; Panjabi) attributed to Guru Govind Singh: sacred book of the Sikhs, second in importance only to the *Granth Sahib*. The work runs to 1428 pages and contains the following: 1. Jap; 2. Akal ustat; 3. Bachittar natak; 4. Chandi charittar (in two parts); 5. Chandi di var; 6. Gyan prabodh; 7. Chaubis avatar; 8. Brahmavatar; 9. Rudra avatar; 10. Shabad hazare; 11. Swaya; 12. Khalsa mahima; 13. Shastarnam mala; 14. Charitropakhyan; 15. Zafar nama; 16. Hakaitan. Authorship of the work is still controverted. The Guru had employed

52 poets in his court and whatever they wrote or translated they attributed it to the name of the Guru.

Dasharathi shatakamu (late 17th; Telugu) of Bhakta Ramdasu: a series of 100 lyrics on Shri Rama.

Dasha-rupaka also **Dasharupa** (late 10th; Sanskrit) of Dhananjaya: work on dramaturgy, which derives its name from the ten 'rupakas' (primary forms of drama) recognised by *Natyashastra*. The text is in four parts. The first consists of basic definitions; the second defines the hero, heroine and other dramatis peronae; the third defines and illustrates the rupakas; the fourth discusses rasa.
Tr. G. Haas, New York, 1912, Tr. J.K. Shastri, 1927..

Dasharathi Raye (1806–57): poet in Bangla, known especially as 'panchalikar'. He began his career as a kaviyal and is said to have had an affair with Akshya Bayatini, a woman kaviyal. Around 1835 he changed his line and began composing panchali narratives which he sang, enacted and explained. He generally used stories of Krishna, Rama, Shiva and Shakti; also dealt with events in contemporary society. He became widely popular and very successful in this professsion and remained an abiding influence on panchali composers who came after.

Dashavadhan Thakur: the name of at least two poets of Mithila, one of whom was a contemporary of Vidyapati; the other came later.

Dashavatara-charita (1066; Sanskrit) of Kshemendra: a work which describes and extols the ten incarnations of Vishnu in ten separate sections. In the ninth, Buddha has been represented as the personification of Krishna.

Dashavatara-gitam (?C; Maithili): manuscript collection of devotional padas, generally about the ten avatars of Vishnu, mainly by Jagajjyoti, Bhupatindra, Jagatprakasha, Chandraprakasha and Ranajita.

Dasopant (1551–1615): poet in Marathi and prolific writer; said to have composed about 5 lakh lines of verse. He wrote two commentaries on the *Gita—Gitarnava* (about 150,000 couplets in ovi metre) and *Gitartha-chandrika* (about 9000 couplets); some other works are *Grantharaj, Prabhodaya, Panchikaran pasodi.*

Dastan (Urdu): a long prose narrative, not necessarily about the same central character; several stories could also be linked together. The form was developed in Arab countries where the 'dastan-go' (storyteller) had made it into a profession that was honoured by kings and nobles. In India, the form was encouraged by the courts at Delhi, Lakhnau and Rampur. Most dastan works in Urdu are translated from Panjabi and Arabi, also from Sanskrit; the form lent itself to stylistic demonstration.

Dastan Amir Hamza (?C; Farsi) of Faizi: written for the entertainment of Emperor Akbar, this is a series of inter-locking prose tales featuring Amir Hamza.

Dastan-e-Tilism-e-Hoshruba (1800–25; Urdu) of Ahmad Husain Qamar: a massive prose work in seven books concerning the deeds of Amir Hamza, a humble, dutiful and brave warrior on behalf of goodness. He attacks the magic city of Tilism Hoshruba and, after overcoming many hurdles, conquers it by defeating the forces of evil led by Afrasiyab.

Datha-vamsa (early 4th; Prakrit) of Dhammakitti: poem in five sargas, in a variety of metres. According to the author, the poem was originally composed in Sinhala by several poets, later rendered by him into Magadhi Prakrit. The poem contains valuable information about the tooth-relic and Sri Lankan history. It is also known under the title *Dalada-vamsa.*
Tr. B.C. Law, Lahore, 1910.

Dattilam (?C; Sanskrit) of Dattilacharya or Dattila: treatise on music and dancing. Dattila is mentioned in *Natyashastra* as one of the immediate disciples of Bharata, hence lived earlier than 4th/5th. According to one tradition, he was the son of Matanga.

Daulat Qazi (early 17th): leading poet in Bangla of 17th, who lived in Chatgaon and was attached to the Arakan court; his patron was Ashraf Khan, a commander of king Srisudharma (1622–38). Apart from the narrative poem in two parts, *Lor-Chandrani/Sati Mayana*, Daulat composed a number of baramasiya songs. He was conversant with classical Sanskrit poetry and more recent Vaishnav lyrics.

Daulatram (late 18th): author in Hindi, translated the *Padmapurana* of Ravisenacharya into Khariboli prose. He belonged to Baswa village in Madhya Pradesh.

Davavaita (Rajasthani): a metrical composition in praise of somebody. The term consists of two Arabi words—'dua' (prayer) and 'baita' (a kind of metre).

Dayaldas (early 17th): poet in Hindi; from Mewar (Rajasthan); author of *Rana-raso* (a history of Mewar), *Raso-ka ang* and *Akal-ko ang*, all works in Dingal.

Dayaldas Sindhayach (*c*1798–1891): poet in Rajasthani, chronicler and statesman. He belonged to a charan family of Kubia village in Bikaner district, and is regarded as the last great charan chronicler of Bikaner. Among his works are *Bikaner-re-Rathoran-ri khyat* (also known as *Dayaldas-ri-khyat*), *Arakhyand-kalpadruma, Deshadarpana, Parwar-vamsapradip.*

Dayaram (1777–1853): devotional poet of Gujarat, who wrote mainly in Gujarati and Brajshasha. Born at Chandod in South Gujarat, he became a disciple of a Pushti sect scholar named Ichhasanakar Bhatta; at his guru's bidding Dayaram travelled to many places and learnt languages like Marathi, Panjabi, Sindhi, and Urdu so well that he could write poems in these languages. *Prema-rasgita* and *Prema-pariksha*, both in Gujarati, are his two major collections of Krishna-bhakti poems. He also wrote some long narrative poems on *Mahabharata* episodes like *Rukmani-virah, Ajamilakhyana, Okha-haran.* Among his prose treatises, *Rasika-vallabh* and *Bhakti-poshan*, are in Gujarati; *Rasik-ranjan* and *Bhakti-ranjan* are in Braj.

De Tassy [Garcin de Tassy (1794–1878)]: Frenchman who was one of the earliest Western scholars of Urdu language and literature. His major work is *Tarikh-e-adabiyat-e-Hindvi wa Hindustani* (1839), later published in French as *Histoire de la Hindouie et hindoustanie*, (1870–71).

Deha-vicarar Git (16th; Asamiya) of Shankaradeva: series of poems on the transitoriness of the body. These correspond to the dehatter git poems in Bangla. The name was later used as a term for this kind of poem.

Dehlavi: for some time, this was the name given to Urdu in the region around Dehli (modern Delhi).

Delarama-kathasara (?C; Sanskrit) of Bhatta Ahladaka: poetical work in 13 sections. Apparently the Sanskrit version of a story contained in Muslim works, it tells how two young brothers are driven away from home, pass through ups and downs of fortune, get separated from each other, and are finally re-united. The title derives from the name of the courtesan Delaram, who deceives the elder brother.

Derozio [Henry Louis Vivian Derozio 1809–31): the first Indian poet in English; lived his short life in Calcutta where, as a teacher in Hindu College, he became the leading spirit of 'Young Bengal'. His long poem, *The Fakir of Jungheera* (1828) won him immediate recognition, first by way of an editorial post in *The Indian Gazette*, then appointment as professor of history and English Literature in Hindu College. He composed a number of sonnets and lyrics that were published in periodicals.

Deshi (Sanskrit): a term signifying the popular or local as opposed to the classical and universal (= margi). Used earlier in discussions of music, dance and drama, it came to be used in literature as well. In some contexts 'deshi' can mean that which is not found in Sanskrit.

Deshi Nama-mala (*c*1150; Prakrit) of Hemachandra: a specialised dictionary which gives deshi works (i.e., not to be traced to Sanskrit), together with quotations illustrating their use.

Desopadesha (late 11th; Sanskrit) of Kshemendra: poetical work in eight sections. These deal respectively with the villain, the miser, the prostitute, the old procuress, the voluptuary, the foreign student (especially from Gauda), the passionate fellow, and the depraved Shaiva teacher.

Deula-tola Suango (?C; Oriya) of Bipra Nilambara: short verse narrative which tells the story of the construction of the Jagannath temple at Puri. Its literary merit is not high, but as a literary document it is unique because it embodies the Buddhist-Hindu compromise which characterised life in Orissa at the time.

Deva (1673–1767): poet of the riti convention in Hindi. He was from Etawa and among his patrons at various times were Azamshah (son of Aurangzeb), Bhabanidatta Vaishya, Kusalsingh Segar of Etawa, Raja Bhogilal and Akbar Ali Khan of Pihani. He travelled quite a lot in search of patrons and obtained wide experience of places and people; everywhere he particularly observed women and wrote exciting descriptions of them. He is said to have written at least 52 works, of which 29 are listed in *Hindi Navaratna.* Among these are *Bhava vilas, Sukhsagar-tarang, Jati-vilas, Rasa-vilas, Prema-chandrika, Shabda-rasayan, Niti-shatak, Vairagya-shatak.*

Deva chandra (1770–1841): poet in Kannada from Kanakagiri; was attached to the court of Mysore ruler Krishnaraja Wodeyar III. He wrote *Pujyapada charitre*, a long poem in sangatya metre narrating the life of Jaina saint Pujyapada; *Ramkathavatara*, a champu work which tells the *Ramayana* story in the Jaina tradition. He is also author of the prose work *Rajavalikathe* (1838), a genealogical account of Mysore's royal family, biographies of some kings and poets of an earlier period, and stories of religious significance to Jains.

Devaram: collective title for the Shaiva hymns in Tamil composed and sung by three Nayanamar sants, Sambandar, Vukkarasar and Sundarar. Their collection was organised by Rajaraja Chola Abayakulashekaran (11th).

Deva-sen: (early 10th): Jain poet and scholar; composed his *Avakachar* in doha form in a langunge that is some popular Apabhramsh. As a companion to this work, Mayilla Dhval prepared a Prakrit version in dohas and called it *Davyasahavpayas*. Both works have been found in the same manuscript.

Devaki'nandan (late 18th to early 19th): poet of the riti convention in Hindi; author of *Shringar-charita* (1784), *Sarafraj-chandrika* and *Avadhut-bhushan* (1800).

Devar-dasimayya (mid-11th): poet in Kannada, composed vachanas in the name of his god named Ramnath. He was an early propagator of Virshaiva faith; preceded Basava. About 150 of his vachanas have been recovered.

Devare-Nayakde-ri bat (1790; Hindi) by unknown author: prose work which tells of the romance between prince Devaro and princess Nayakde.

Devi Chandragupta (11th; Sanskrit) attributed to Vishakhadeva (who may be the same as Vishakadatta, author of *Mudra-rakshasa*): lost play, quoted by Ramachandra, and Gunachandra, cited by Abhinavagupta and Rajashekhara. From the latter's *Kavyamimamsa*, it appears that the plot is based on the rescue by prince Chandragupta, in the guise of a woman, of princess Dhruvadevi, who was abducted by a Saka prince.

Devi-mahatmyam (15th; Malayalam) of unknown author: early prose work.

Devi-shataka (late 9th; Sanskrit) of Anandavardhana: poem of 100 verses in honour of the goddess Parvati.

Dhadhi Bahadara-ri Nisaniyan (16th; Rajasthani): memorial verses known as 'nisani' composed by the Muslim bard Dhadhi Bahadara; later these compositions came to be known as *Viramayana.*

Dhahil (mid-12th): poet in Apabhramsh, author of *Paumsiri-chariu.*

Dhal (Gujarati): a class of poetical composition (songs as well as poems) which was identified by the populariy of a particular poem or song. Thus, 'Vinchhia ni dhal', meant compositions that imitated a particular song or poem about 'vinchhia'. These were deshi or popular songs, and the term is also used for a particular variety of folk-songs in Rajasthani.

Dhamali (Bangla): a kind of song innovated by Lochandas, derived from women's recitals; written in popular metre and inelegant diction, reflecting the supposedly low taste of women; themes were almost exclusively the love affair of Krishna and the cowherd maidens. Lochandas adopted this style even for some of his songs of Shri Caitanya.

Dhamma-kitti (13th/14th): Bouddha scholar, wrote in Pali; author of *Datha-vamsa, Saddhamma-samgahu; Balavatara* generally ascribed to him. He is also said to have added chapter 37 of *Mahavamsa* and begun the composition of *Chulavagga.* According to Sri Lankan tradition, he came from Burma to Sri Lanka during the reign of Parakrambahu II (13th).

Dhamma-pada (?C; Pali): a part of *Khudda nikaya.* A metrical work of 423 verses divided into 26 sections called 'vagga', it contains the main teachings of Buddhism and is the most well-known of Buddhist canonical works. There are versions of it in Sanskrit; parts of a Prakrit version; also a Chinese version.

Tr. M. Muller, *SBE,* 1875; J. Gray, London, 1881; A.J. Symonds, Chicago, 1902; P.L. Vaidya, Bombay, 1934. An edition with Roman text, English translations and introduction with Pali index, by S. Radhakrishnan, London, 1950.

Dhammapada-attha-katha (?5C; Pali) of Buddhaghosa: commentary on *Dhammapada.* It explains the stanzas and illustrates with tales drawn from the four Nikayas, *Vinaya, Udana, Jataka* and the author's own works.

Dhamma-pala (?C): Bouddha scholar, author in Pali of many original works as well as of commentaries. Among his extant works are *Paramattha-tipani, Mahatika, Netti-pakaranassa*; among his commentaries are on *Petavatthu, Theragatha, Chariyapitaka.* Originally from Padaratittha on the southern coast, he appears to have studied at the Mahavihara of Anuradhapura in Sri Lanka. He may be a contemporary of Buddhaghosa; may or may not have been the Dhamma-pala mentioned by Hiuen Sang as his preceptor at Nalanda. According to Hiuen Sang, Dhamma-pala was born in Kanchi, then capital city of Tamilnadu.

Dhananjaya (late 10th): authority on Sanskrit dramaturgy, wrote *Dasha-rupaka*; not the same Dhananjaya who composed *Raghava-pandaviya.* He calls himself son of Vishnu; has also been identified with Dhanika, author of the commentary *Avaloka*, but some scholars believe they were brothers. He appears to have enjoyed the patronage of Munja, Paramar king of Malwa who ruled in the last quarter of 10th.

Dhananjaya Bhanja (1611–1701): Poet in Oriya whose works adopted the traditional form of Sanskrit kavya. Among these works are *Ichhabati, Ananga-rekha, Tripura-mohini, Madana-manjari, Raghunath-vilasa.* He belonged to the royal family of Ghumusar and ruled for 65 years; besides being a poet himself, he was a great patron of art and culture.

Dhananjaya Laibu Ningba (early 19th; Manipuri) of Pukhrambam Ananda: a work of prose fiction written in ancient Meitei script; was transliterated into modern Manipuri and published only in 1968. The story tells of the travails of Dhananjay, younger brother of Puma Deva, king of Iswa. Driven out of the kingdom by the elder brother, Dhananjay and his family suffered many hardships but remained devoted to the gods. Ultimately the gods rescue him and his family.

Dhana-pala (Dhanayala) (late 10th) a Swetambara Jain, author of Apabhramsh works *Rishabha-panchasika, Pailachhi, Bhavisayatta-katha*, and Sanskrit prose work *Tilaka-manjari*; latter was composed under patronage of Munja Vakpatiraja, ruler at Dhara. Among poets who preceded him, Dhanapala mentions Sripalitta, author of *Tarangavati*, and Rudra, author of *Trailokya sundari-katha*. He also mentions Banabhatta.

Dhanapala (13th): Jain poet and author of *Tilaksundari-kathasar*, a summary in Old Hindi of the *Tilak-manjari* of Dhanapal (10th/11th).

Dhandi Alamkaram (mid-12th;

Tamil) of Dhandi: work on poetics, known earlier as *Ani athikaram*. It mainly defines and illustrates figures of speech.

Dhaneswhara (late 11th): poet in Prakrit; composed *Surasundari-charita*. He was a disciple of Jineshwar Suri and of Buddhisagara.

Dhaneshwara (*c*1750; Marathi) of Madhva Muni: a character-sketch and narrative in verse. It is the first secular story in Marathi literature, centred in a miser's love of money.

Dhanika (late 10th): scholar of Sanskrit dramaturgy; wrote *Avaloka*, a commentary on *Dasharupaka* of Dhananjaya. In *Avaloka*, he mentions that he also wrote a work on poetics, *Kavya-nirnaya*. Because his father's name was Vishnu and because he was a minister of the Paramar king Utpaladeva, he has been identified with Dhananjaya or as Dhananjaya's brother.

Dharanidhara Mishra (late 16th): poet in Oriya; one of the earliest translators of *Gita Govinda* into Oriya. In his version, Dharanidhara recast the material of 12 sargas of the original into 16 chhandas composed in various Oriya metres. His was the most popular of about half a dozen translations available at the time. That it was produced early is sometimes cited as evidence in favour of the notion that Jayadev was a native of Orissa.

Dharmadas (late 15th): sant-poet in Hindi; composed mainly in Brajbhasha; author of *Sukh-nidhan*. He was a younger contemporary of Kabir's and is said to have collected the verses of Kabir; became the leader of the Kabirpanthi sect, which was formed after Kabir's death.

Dharma-katha (Prakrit): a narrative form in which tales, fables and anecdotes, not necessarily related to one another, are told in order to emphasize moral and ethical principles. It was developed particularly by Jain authors. Among the earliest such works are *Tarangavati-kaha*, *Malayavati* and *Magadhasena*, none of which is extant. The oldest available examples are *Tarangalola* of Nemichandra, *Vasudevahindi* of Sangadasa, *Samaraichha-kava* of Haribhadra.

Dharma-mangal (*c*1650; Bangla) of Ruparam Chakrabarti: oldest extant poem in this tradition. Written under the patronage of Ganesh Raye, brahman chief of Edal village, north of the Damodar. The popularity of the poem is indicated by the numerous manuscripts that are available.

Dharma-mangal (*c*1710; Bangla) of Ghanaram Chakrabarti: regarded by some scholars as the best work in this form.

Dharma-mangal kavya (Bangla): a mangal-kavya form devoted to the glorification of a regional (and male) deity named Dharma, worshipped mainly by low-caste Hindus. The form was practised mainly in South-west Bengal (the 'Rahr' area) and has pre-Aryan origins. The narratives deal with the heroic exploits of Lausen, son of a dispossessed feudal chief named Karnasen; with the blessings of Dharma, and the help of Kalu Dom, Lausen conquers the kingdom of Kamrup and marries a princess of Kalinga; after a long and peaceful reign he hands over the kingdom to his son Chitrasen and goes to heaven. The legendary Mayura Bhatta is said to have composed the first dharma-mangal poem.

Dharma Pariksha (*c*980; Sanskrit) of Harisena: composed earlier than a Sanskrit work of the same title by Amitagati, it records a still earlier work in gatha form by Jayaram. The story tells of two friends, Manovaga (a Jaina) and Pavanabega (a brahman), who travel to Pataliputra, where Manovaga challenges learned brahmans to a debate and defeats them. Manovaga discusses various flaws in sacred texts of the brahmans and convinces Pavanabega of the superiority of the Jain faith. Consequently, Pavanabega becomes a Jain householder.

Dharma Pariksha (*c*1015; Sanskrit) of Amitagati: narrative work, based on an earlier Prakrit text, which seeks to demolish the credibility of brahmanical and Bouddha beliefs and, instead, promote the Jain faith. A special feature of this text is the author's dwelling on numerous amorous adventures of puranic characters. The author was a Digambara monk.

Dharma parikshe (late 14th; Sanskrit) of Vrittavilas: a champu work in ten aswas; tells the same story as Harisena's *Dharma pariksha* (see above).

Dharma-puran (Bangla): ritualistic treatises in verse relating to Dharma worship. These begin with cosmogony; the myths of creation are different from those in the Sanskritic tradition, but have definite affinity with the cosmogynic hymn of *Rig-Veda* (10.129). The second section narrates the activities of Dharma in search of human worshippers. The third section narrates the story of Ramai Pandit, the priest of king Harischandra who worshipped Dharma. The fourth and final section contains verses and poems used in the worship of Dharma; these are known as 'gajan' (from garjana, shout), because the initial ritual was a loud supplication to Dharma to wake up and listen to the appeal of his devotees. The whole ritual was called 'Baramoti' (from *dvaramuktika*, opening of the door).

Dharmamrita (*c*1100; Kannada) of Nayesen: champu work in which 14 eminent followers of the Jain faith have been eulogised. These were ordinary people, and this was the first 'Jaina puran' written for common folk.

Dharmashram-abhyudaya (?C; Sanskrit) of Harichandra (or Harischandra): long poem in 21 cantos on the life of the 15th tirthankara, Dharmanatha. The work is modelled on *Shishupalavadha*.

Dharmavardhana (1643–1726): poet in Rajasthani; disciple of Jain monk Vijayaharsha of Kharatara-gachha. He was a scholar and commanded several languages, viz., Sanskrit, Prakrit, Apabhramsh, Rajasthani, etc. His *Shrenik-chaupai, Amarsen Vayarsen-chaupai* and *Surasundari ras* are poetical works based on Jain stories; he also wrote many shorter works, including songs in Dingal in praise of Shivaji.

Dharmopadesha-mala vivarana (*c*850; Prakrit) of Jayasimha Suri: work in gatha metre containing 156 narratives presented in 98 gathas. The stories are invariably didactic, but much cultural information is also made available in these stories; in between the stories the author has inserted Sanskrit and Prakrit quotations.

Dharnidas (b.1616) sant-poet in Hindi, from Chapra district in Bihar; composed *Prem-prakash* and *Satya-prakash* in Bhojpuri.

Dhenu-mahatmyamu (*c*1660; Telugu) of Kameshwara Kavi: prose work in glorification of the cow.

Dhiro (1753–1825): poet in Gujarati; wrote short poems on philosophical subjects. These have been collected *in Swarup, Jnanakako, Prashnottar-malika, Atma-jnana* and *Jnana-batrishi*.

Dhola Marva-ni chaupahi (?C); a presumed work in Dingal, ascribed to Hararaj and composed perhaps around 1560. Four copies of a version in Hindi (or Rajasthani) done in dohas and entitled *Dhole-Marura duha* were subsequently discovered in Bikaner.

Dhole'maru-ra duha (?C): Hindi version in dohas of the presumed work *Dhola-Marva-ni chaupahi*; see above. It tells of the romance between prince Dhola (or Salha) of Nalabhgarh and princess Marav of Marwar.

Dhoyi (12th/13th): also known as Dhoi or Dhoyika; poet in Sanskrit; author of *Pavana-duta*. He belonged to the court of Lakshman Sen, king of Bengal, and may have belonged to the weaver caste. Other verses by him, not to be found in *Pavana-duta*, have been included in anthologies like *Sadukti-karnamrita, Subhashita-muktavali* and *Sarangadhara-paddhati*.

Dhruva-das (1575–1643): a bhakti poet in Hindi. He was born in Deoband (Saharanpur district, Uttar Pradesh) but settled in Brindavan after being initiated into the Radhavallabh sect. He is said to have composed 42 works; among these are *Jivadasha-lila, Brindavan-sat-lila, Hitshringar-lila*, and *Rasananda-lila*. He also wrote some prose; his *Siddhanta-vichar lila* is a prime example of effective Brajbhasa prose.

Dhurjati (*c*1480–1540): poet in Telugu; one of the Ashta-Diggaja group. A Shaiva especially devoted to the deity of Kalahasti, his major work *Shrikalahasti-mahatmya*, describes the greatness of this particular place and its presiding deity. His other work, *Shrikalahastiswara shalaka*, is among the more popular 'shataka' works in Telugu literature.

Dhurt-akhyayana (8th; Prakrit) of Haribhadra: a satirical work unique in Indian literature. Five rogues (four men, one woman) narrate their personal experiences; the fantastic and absurd personal story of each is confirmed by the others who cite parallel stories from itihasa and purana sources; thus puranic legends are satirised.

Dhurta-samagama (late 15th/early 16th; Sanskrit) of Jyotishwara: unusual play of the prahasana type, concerning a number of rogues. The religious mendicant Vishwanagara and his disciple Durachara quarrel over the ownership of Anangasena, a beautiful courtesan; they refer the dispute to a brahman, Asajjati, who decrees that she should remain in his care until the real owner is decided; while he is debating, his vidushaka seeks to appropriate her, and this leads to further complications. The author later adapted this work in Maithili; see *Maithili Dhurttasamagama*.
Ed. S. Bhattacharya, Calcutta, 1874.

Dhurta-vita-sambada (?C; Sanskrit) of Ishwaradatta: one-act monologue play, like a bhana; gives an amusing picture of the adventures, scandal and gossip of rogues. Other plays of this type are *Ubhayabhisarika* of Vararuchi, *Padma-prabhritaka* of Shudraka, and *Pada-tadilaka* of Shyamalika.

Dhvani (Sanskrit): an important literary concept which forms a turning point in the history of Sanskrit poetics. According to this theory 'dhvani' is the essence of poetry while 'vyanjana' is the means of its propagation. Anandavardhana expounded this theory in his *Dhvanyaloka.*

Dhvanikara (?9th): literary theorist in Sanskrit; presumed author of the 'karika' portion of *Dhvanyaloka*. Some scholars have also suggested his name to be Sahridaya.

Dhvanyaloka (?C; Sanskrit) ascribed to Anandavardhana: work on poetics which asserts, contrary to traditional views, that 'dhvani' (suggested sense) was the essence of kavya. It also critically examines the concepts of rasa, alamkara, riti, guna and dosa. According to some scholars, the 'karika' portions are the work of Dhanikara and only the 'vritti' thereon is the work of Anandavardhana.

Dibakara Dasa (?C): wrote the first biography in Oriya, *Jagannatha-charitamrita*, which deals with the life and works of Jagannath Dasa who rendered *Bhagavathapuranam* into Oriya. Dibakara also produced a Sanskrit version of the biography.

Dilli (Delhi) **College**: founded in 1825; gave instruction in Urdu on literature, mathematics, history and some Western sciences. Within it was established the Dehli Vernacular Translation Society, the purpose of which was the translation into Urdu of major books relating to various areas of knowledge.

Dina or **Dinu Chandidas** (17th): relatively the most inferior of the poets in Bangla who signed themselves 'Chandidas'; a pedestrian but prolific poet, he composed three-fourths of the current corpus of Chandidas poems: lived after 1600.

Dinabandhu Gupta (1830–74): playwright in Bangla. Born in a village in Nadia district he was educated in Calcutta and found employment in the postal service. He began his literary career by writing poetry but later turned to the theatre and became famous with his very first play, *Nil-darpan* (1860). His other plays are *Nabin tapaswini* (1863), *Pagla burho* (1866),

Sadhabar ekadasi (1866), *Lilabati* (1867), *Jamai barik* (1872), and *Kamale kamini* (1873).

Dinakrishna Dasa (1650–1710): poet-scholar of Krishna-bhakti in Oriya; author of *Rasaka-llola, Artatrana-chautisa*, and perhaps ten other works. He seems to have been poor and contracted leprosy in middle age, but his devotion remained undiminished.

Dindayal Giri (1802–65): poet in Hindi and devotee of Krishna. He was a Dashnami ascetic and lived in Kashi. His works are *Anurag bag, Vairagya dinesh, Drishtanta tarangini, Anyoktimala* and *Anyokti kalpadrum*.

Dingal: literary form of Rajasthani speech; also regarded as an early form of literary Hindi.

Dinnaga, also called Dhirnag and Virnag (6th/7th): playwright in Sanskrit, author of *Kundamala*. The play deals with Rama's story from the rejection of Sita to their reunion. There are resemblances to and differences with Bhavabhuti's *Uttara Ramacharit*. The manuscript of the play was discovered only in 1923 and published that year from Madras.

Dipa-vamsa (?C; Pali) of unknown authorship: a chronicle of the island of Sri Lanka. It is the earliest historical work in Pali and appears to date back approxmately to a period between A.D. 4th and 5th. Composed in verse, with occasional prose passages, it gives an account of the colonisation of the island by Vijaya, a prince of Bengal; also tells of the introduction of Buddhism to Sri Lanka during the reign of Devanampiya Tissa through Mahinda at the instance of Moggaliputa Tissa.

Divya-prabandham (early 10th; Tamil) of Nathamuni: anthology of hymns by Alvar sants, containing about 4000 compositions. Nathamuni edited and compiled them into four books, like the Vedas; each has a separate title also. Many commentaries were written on this anthology, all in Manipravala style; only the commentary of Periya Achhan Pillai is now available for all the 4000 hymns.

Divya-vadana (4th; Sanskrit): a collection of Buddhist parables relating to the life of Gautam Buddha and also drawing upon his earlier lives and the lives of Bodhisattvas. The present text, divided into 38 sections, contains the writings of authors from different periods, probably ranging from 1st century B.C. to A.D. 4th century. The tales are mainly in prose, occasionally relieved by gatha songs and poems. A bulk of the material was borrowed from previous collections.

Diwan (Urdu): usually a collection of 'ghazal' compositions of the same poet; but other forms of poetry could also be included. Thus *Diwan-e-Ghalib* contains four qasida, one masnavi, one sehra, 16 qatawe and 16 rubai poems, apart from 231 ghazals.

Diuha (Rajasthani): variant of the 'doha' metre which originated in Apabhramsh. It has been practised in Rajasthani from about 12th. Some older poets who used this metre were Thakkara Pheru, Asaita, Alha Charana, Vyas Shridhara, Bhima and Gadana Shivadasa.

Dnyaneshwar see Jnaneshwar.

Dnyaneshwari see Jnaneshwari or Bhavartha-Dipika.

Dogri: main language of a region consisting of the whole of Jammu, parts of Himachal Pradesh and of undivided Panjab. It is spoken by about 1 million persons who are known as Dogra. Derived from Shauraseni Prakrit, it was a separate speech by 12th. A.D. But the earliest known literary work in Dogri is a late 18th translation of a Farsi text. Dogri writing has grown only in 20th.

Doha (Hindi): a verse-form which came into Hindi from Apabhramsh. The 4th act of Kalidas' *Vikramorvashiya* contains some fairly pure samples of doha in Apabhramsh.

Doha-kosha: collection of didatic and directive couplets and guartrains composed by Buddhist Siddhas either in Apabhramsh or in Sanskrit. Collections of only three masters are extant—Tilo, Saraha, Kanha—these being the names of some of the *Charyapad* poets.

Doha-vali (*c*1583; Hindi) of Tulsidas: a collection of 573 dohas on ethical and devotional matters, contemporary affairs, autobiographical experiences, etc.

Dohra or **Dohira** (Panjabi): a form of verse, often conveying Sufi sentiment.

Dosha (Sanskrit): literary 'fault' or 'flaw'. In Sanskrit poetics, anything which detracts from the charm of literary compositions is a 'dosha'. Like all other literary concepts in Sanskrit tradition, 'dosha' has been defined, analysed and classified from 2nd Century (Bharata) onwards.

Draupadi-vastraharan (*c*1740; Marathi) of Amrit Raya: long poem on a *Mahabharata* episode.

Drishtanta path (late 13th; Marathi) of Chakradhar: a compilation of the philosophic principles propagated by the founder of the Mahanubhav sect. The work is specially important as example of early prose in Marathi.

Dugagunta Narayana (*c*1500): poet in Telugu; adapted *Panchatantra* into Telugu verse.

Duggupalli Duggayya (early 15th): poet in Telugu; author of *Nasiketop-akhyanamu* and *Kanchipura-mahatmyamu*, of which only the first is extant. It is a kavya based on an upanishadic story. The work was dedicated to Gangayya, son of Chandluri Anantamatye, the chief minister of Udaygiri ruler Prabhu Basavabhupal.

Durga-mangal (early 17th; Bangla) of Bhahaniprasad Raye: kavya work based on puranic story of Chandi. But it also includes an account of Durga worship conducted by Rama.

Durga-simha (mid-11th): poet in Kannada; author of a champu work entitled *Panchatantra*. He claimed that after Gunadhya wrote *Brihatkatha* in Paisachi Prakrit, Vasubhag Bhatt selected five episodes from it to compose his *Panchatantra* in Sanskrit; Durgasimha's work is a Kannada version of this. There are variations between this *Panchatantra* and the one composed by Vishnu Sharma; the main difference is the leaning towards Jain faith in Durgasimha's work.

Durgavar Kayastha (late 15th): composer in Asamiya of lyrics and narrative verse set to tunes; author of *Beula-upakhyan* and *Giti Ramayan*.

Durvasa-yatra (*c*1730; Marathi) of Amrit Raya: long poem on a *Mahabharata* episode.

Duta-ghatotkaca (?C; Sanskrit) of Bhasa: one-act play of the 'vyayoga' type, based on a *Mahabharata* episode.

Duta-nagad (13th; Sanskrit) of Subhatt: play dealing with Angad's visit as messenger to Ravan's court. It was probably first performed in Anhilapattan at the court of Chalukya ruler Tribhunpal sometime in 1242.

Duta-vakya (?C; Sanskrit) of Bhasa: one-act play of the 'vyayoga' type, based on a *Mahabharata* episode, where Krishna makes his last bid to avert the final clash between the Kauravs and the Pandavs.

Duta-vakyam (?14th; Malayalam) prose drama composed by an unknown author from Kerala. Tamil forms can be found in the prose used, but the sentence structure is Sanskritic. The story deals with Krishna's last mission to the Kaurav court, in *Mahabharatha*, before war breaks out.

Dvija (Dviju) Chandidas (early 16th): the most important of the poets in Bangla who signed themselves 'Chandidas'; probably a younger contemporary of Shri Chaitanya who was very fond of the poems by this Chandidas. He is regarded as the author of the few poems on which the fame and popularity of 'Chandidas', mainly rests.

Dvijadev [Maharaja Mansingh Dvijadev (1820–70)]: poet in Hindi, belongs to the last phase of Ritikal, author of *Shringar-latika* and *Shringar-batisi*. Adopted by his uncle Bhaktawar Singh, ruler of Ayodhya in Uttar Pradesh, he succeeded the uncle and ruled from 1855–70. Besides writing poetry, he encouraged poets like Lachhiram, Jagannath, Chandi Datt, Baldev, Thakurprasad, etc., and gave them place in his court.

Dvipada (Telugu): a prosodic form of two lines which was made popular by Pulkurki Somana in his works *Basavapuranam* and *Panditaradhya-charitra*.

Dvitiya Rajatarangini (mid-15th; Sanskrit) of Jonaraja: a continuation of *Rajatarangini* of Kalhana. Intended as bringing the history down to the time of the author's patron, Sultan Zainul Abedin, the work was left incomplete on account of Jonaraja's death in 1459.

Dvyasraya-kavya (12th; Sanskrit and Prakrit): same as *Kumarapala-charita* of Hemachandra Suri.

E

Eiham (Urdu): a form of verse based on words of double meaning.

Ekadasi mahatam (13th/14th; Panjabi): a recently discovered manuscript in prose, of the pre-Nanak period. It may be regarded as the earliest known specimen of Panjabi preserved in writing. The writing is in Sarada script.

Ekakkhara-kosa (16th; Pali) of Saddhammakitti Thera of Burma: dictionary of monosyllabic words compiled in verse. Some scholars (viz., Geiger) believe the work was compiled in 1465.

Ekavali (*c*1300; Sanskrit) of Vidhyadhara: work on poetics. It comprises eight 'unmesha' (chapters) but much of the material is derived from previous scholars. A distinguishing feature of the work is that all the poetical examples given here were all composed by the author. Many of the examples eulogise Utkal ruler Narasimha Deva (r. 1282–1307), who was the author's patron.

Ekavali-parinaya (?C; Maithili) of Badrinath Jha: a mahakavya on Sanskrit model, based on episode drawn from sixth skandha of *Devibhagavatam*. Ekavali is the princess who was abducted by the asur Kalketu; Ekavira, son of king Turvasu, challenges the asur and defeats him; Ekavali is rescued and marries Ekavira.

Ekeyi ki boley sabhyata (1860; Bangla) of Maikel Madhusudhan Datta: a prahasan in two acts making fun of undue imitation of Western manners. The title translates as "Is this called civilization?".

Eknath (1548–99): poet in Marathi and social reformer; composed *Eknathi Bhagavat* and other works. Born into a brahman family, he became a disciple of Janardan Swami of Daulatabad (near modern Aurangabad). At the master's behest he composed a short work, *Chatushloki Bhagavat*, before undertaking the much greater work which came to be known as *Eknathi Bhagavat*. After this he composed a number of poems based on *Mahabharata* and *Ramayana* episodes, which became more popular than his philosophical works. He also revised *Jnaneshwari* and produced a simpler version in more contemporary Marathi; this version is now read more widely than the original work by Jnaneshwar.

Eknathi Bhagavat (*c*1580; Marathi) of Eknath: an exposition of the eleventh 'skandha' of *Bhagavatpurana* consisting of 18,000 ovis. To the Warkari sect this work is second in importance only to Jnaneshwari.

Elhana (15th/16th): poet in Marathi; nothing definite is known about his life or time, except that he belonged to the Mahanubhava sect. He wrote *Ashtanayika-viraha*.

Errana or Errapragada (*c*1280–1350): third of the 'kavitraya' poets in Telugu; was the first poet of the Reddi kings of Andhra. He completed the Telugu rendering of the better part of Vanaparva in *Mahabharata* left incomplete by Nannaya, whose language and style he tried to maintain. He is said to have composed a Telugu *Ramayana* which is lost; rendered *Harivamsha* into Telugu; initiated the prabandha genre in his *Nrisimha-puranam*. Like Nannaya and Tikkana, he also belonged to Rajahmundry.

Errapragada see Errana.

Ettuttokai (?C; Tamil): anthology of eight collections of shorter poems by representative poets of the Third Sangam age. The separate titles of each are *Narrinai, Kuruntogai, Ainkurunuru, Kalittogai, Ahananuru, Padirruppattu*, *Purananuru* and *Paripadal*. The first five are aham literature; the next two puram; the last is only extant 'isai' work. Altogether there are 2372 poems. Some of these anthologies have valuable colophons which identify the 'tinai' (authors) and 'turai' (occasions) of the poems. Generally there are two occasions for their composition: either a natural literary desire to present romantic situations in poetic language, or an expression of gratitude by the poets for a favour received or expected. A third possible occasion is prayer to divinity and description of nature.

Etuka (Malayalam): a poetical device based on sound, with the second letter of each pada being the same. This alamkar is also known as 'dvitiyaksharpras'.

Ezhuttacan (late 16th): poet in Malayalam; a major author who inducted bhakti into the cultural life of Kerala through literature; important also because he created a suitable literary medium by incorporating the essential features of Manipravalam into the simpler texture of Malayalam of his time. He is credited with many works, among which are Malayalam versions of *Adhyatma Ramayana*, *Mahabharata* and the first nine sections of *Bhagavatpurana*. His many followers looked upon him as a guru; towards the end of his life, he established a 'gurumadhom' (order of preceptors) at Chittoor, where his disciples studied and taught.

F

Fakirmohan Senapati (1843–1918): the first major novelist in Oriya; author of *Chha man atth guntha* (1902), *Manu* (1913), *Lachhma* (1914), and *Prayaschitta* (1915). All his novels portray the depressed and deprived classes of Oriya society. He also wrote poems, stories, essays and was a translator. Though educated only upto primary level, he learnt Sanskrit as well as English.

Fallon [S. W. Fallon (1817–80)]: Englishman who compiled dictionaries that would be useful to British administrators in India. Thus, his *The English-Hindustani Law and Commercial Dictionary* (1858) lists words and phrases used in civil, criminal, revenue and mercantile affairs. In an essay entitled 'What is Urdu (Hindustani)?' appended to this dictionary, he criticised Urdu for deriving words and expressions from Farsi and Arabi instead of from spoken Hindi. His other work, *New Hindustani English Dictionary* (1875–79), gave importance to colloquial words and to language used by women. He entered the Bengal Educational Service in 1837, retired in 1875, and resided for a while in Delhi before returning to England.

Farid see Baba Farid.

Farid Ghulam (1845–1901): Sufi poet in Panjabi from Lehndi village, now in Pakistan. Named Khurshid Alam at birth, he was a scholar of Arabi and Farsi. He used mainly the 'kafi' form in his poetry; composed about 272 kafis and these were very popular in West Panjab. His other works are *Diwan-i-Faridi* and *Asrar-i-Faridi.*

Farid-ud-din Ganj-shakar (d.1244): sant-poet in Hindi; lived in Multan and Pakpattan. From two poems by him included in *Adi-Grantha*, he may be regarded as a precursor of Kabir. These poems are among the oldest compositions available in Hindi.

Fasana-e-ajayeb (1824; Urdu) of Mirza Rajab Ali Beg 'Sarur': a novel portraying Lakhnau society of the early 19th. This work began a new age in Urdu fiction; though heavily influenced by Farsi and Arabi, its language is simple and easy to read.

Fasana-e-azad (1878; Urdu) of Ratananath Sarsar: a novel which portrays the decadent society of Lakhnau in mid-19th. Its hero, Azad, falls in love with Husn Ara, a nobleman's daughter. War having broken out between Russia and Turkey, Husn Ara stipulates that she will marry Azad only if he goes to fight on behalf of Turkey and returns victorious. He does so and wins the maiden. The work runs to 4000 pages and was published in four volumes.

Fasana-e-mubtala (1888; Urdu) of Nazir Ahmad: a novel depicting Muslim society in an urban setting. Though the city is not named, it is Delhi.

Fateh-bhushan (1773; Hindi) of Ratan Kavi: treatise on poetics. The work is named after the poet's patron, Fatehsahi, ruler of Srinagar in Garhwal district (Uttar Pradesh); whenever the poet needed to give illustrations, he composed verses in praise of his patron. Born in 1741, Ratan Kavi also belonged to Srinagar and wrote in the riti convention of Hindi poetry.

Fatehnama Nizam Shah (17th; Urdu) of Hasan Shawqi: heroic poem in Dakhni describing the battle of Talikota (1565) in which the five Muslim states of Dakhan combined to crush the Hindu kingdom of Vijayanagar.

Fayiz [Sadruddin Muhammad Khan (d. 1739)]: poet in Urdu and a scholar of Farsi; composed mainly in the ghazal and masnavi forms. He was the first North Indian poet to have his poems collected in a diwan; *Diwan-e-Fayiz* (1720) contains 33 ghazals, 6 masnavi and a few qasida.

Fazal Shah Sayyad (1828–96): poet in Panjabi, best known for his qissa tales in verse, especially Sohni-Mahiwal. He belonged to Lahore district and was taught Farsi as well as English. At the early age of fifteen he produced the poetical work *Tuhfaye Fazl*; subsequently wrote *Sohni-Mahiwal* (1849), *Sassi-Punnu* (1863), *Heer-Ranjha* (1867), *Laila-Majnu* (1871) and *Yusuf-Zulekha* (1885). He adapted the 'masnavi' form for composing these works; the Panjabi used by him is so heavily interlaced with Farsi words that modern Panjabis cannot read him easily.

Fazil Shah 'Sayyad', (1836–1900): poet in Sindhi from Hyderabad (Sindh); scholar of Arabi, Farsi, and of Islamic theology. He belongs to the Farsi school of Sindhi poetry and did compose some poems in Farsi; but the bulk of his verses was composed in Sindhi. These have been collected in *Diwan Fazil*. He also wrote *Mizanal shair*, a treatise in Sindhi on Farsi poetic forms and prosody. He compiled *Chunda kafiyun*, a selection of 'kafi' poems by well- known Sindhi poets; wrote an introduction to the work and notes on these poets.

Fazli [Fazle Ali Khan (early 18th)]: prose writer in Urdu; translated *Rauzat-ush-shohada* of Mulla Husain Waiz from Farsi into Urdu as *Karbal katha*. He began the work in 1732 and went on revising the text till 1758.

Firoz (16th): poet in Urdu from Bidar, now in Karnataka. He was a disciple of the well-known Sufi scholar and poet, Maqdumji Sheikh Muhammad. Possibly, once when invited by Sultan Ibrahim Qutbshah of Golkonda, Maqdum sent Firoz in his place, thus giving him the opportunity to establish himself. Other Dakhni poets like Wajahi and Nishati acknowledged the supremacy of Firoz.

Forbes [Alexander Kinloch Forbes (1821–65)]: Englishman who initiated various kinds of research in Gujarati language, literature and history. His two-volume *Rasmala* (1856) is a history of Gujarat in English. He helped to found institutions like the Gujarat Vernacular Society in Ahmedabad (1848), Andrews Library in Surat (1850) and Gujarati Sabha in Bombay (1865); the latter was re-named Forbes Gujarati Sabha in his memory. He came to India in 1843 and joined the civil service of Bombay Presidency.

Fort William College: founded by the East India Company at Calcutta in 1800 for the purpose of training its officials. The college is important in the history of Indian literature because it developed methods and prepared books for the teaching of Hindi and Urdu to non-native speakers.

G

Gada-yuddha (*c*1000 Kannada) of Ranna: champu kavya based on the *Mahabharata* episode in which Bhima and Duryodhan engage in a mace-duel on the 18th day of the battle of Kurukshetra. The work, also known as *Sahasa Bhimavijayam* was composed probably during the reign of Chalukya king Tailapa II (r. 973–97); the poem also celebrates the exploits of his son, prince Satyasraya. It has such a dramatic quality that some scholars have suggested that it might originally have been written as a play and later transformed.

Gadadhar Bhatta (b. 1533): a Krishna-bhakti poet in Hindi, also a scholar of Sanskrit; belonged to the Gaudiya sect. Only fragments of his verse are extant.

Gadadhar Das (mid-17th): poet in Bangla: younger brother of Kashiram Das; was living in Kataka (Cuttack) in Orissa when he composed *Jagannatha-mangal*.

Gadana Kesodas (between 1553–1663): poet in Rajasthani, associated with the court of Jodhpur ruler Gajasimha. Among his works are *Gajaguna rupaka bandha*, about 1000 verses in praise of Gajasimha; *Rava Amarasimhara duha*, historical poem about Amarasimha Rathor of Agra; *Chhanda Mahadevji*, 23 stanzas in honour of Shiva; *Chhanda Shri Goraknathji ra*, devotional poem in praise of Gorakhnath. He also wrote five sorathas on Bundi ruler Ratnasimha Hada.

Gadya (Sanskrit): the word literally means 'what is to be spoken clearly'; as a term it is used to mean prose statements as distinct from verse compositions. In Sanskrit the earliest samples of prose are to be found in the brahmanas.

Gadya-chintamani (? C; Sanskrit) of Odayayadeva (alias Vadibhasimha): prose work dealing with the legend of Jivaka or Jivandhara. It is modelled on *Kadambari*.

Gaja-simha (?14th): poet of Mithila; may have been a contemporary of Vidyapati; some of his poems are found in *Rajatarangini*.

Gajendra-moksha (mid-17th; Marathi) of Vaman Pandit: a long narrative poem.

Gamdhani [Shah Ali Muhammad (d. 1563)] poet in Urdu from Gujarat; called 'Gamdhani' because he was a 'dhani' (rich person) of the 'gaon/gam' (village). His masnavi poem *Jawahar-asrar-alla* is a Sufi work; it also shows the stage to which Urdu had developed in Gujarat at the time.

Ganaka-charitra (18th; Asamiya) of Dhananjaya: kavya work which presents Hanuman as an astrologer who confounds Ravan by wrong predictions.

Ganda-vyuha (?C; Sanskrit) by unknown author: a narrative of religious purpose, perhaps the earliest of its kind. It narrates the wanderings of the youth Sudhana who, on the advice of Bodhisattva Manjusri, travels all over India in quest of the highest knowledge. He seeks instruction from many people including the mother and wife of Gautam Buddha, Maya and Gopa, and ultimately attains perfect knowledge with the grace of Manjusri through Bodhisattva Samantabhadra. The text corresponds to one of the Chinese translations of *Avatamsa*; no *Avatamsa* or *Buddhavatamsaka-sutra* has been received in Sanskrit.

Gandha-vamsa (?C; Pali) of Nandapannacharya: work containing accounts of many works in Pali and their authors; also includes anonymous works. The authors are divided into two groups: those living in Lanka (Sri Lanka) and those in Jambu (India). The work was composed in Burma and is mainly in prose.

Gang (1538-*c*1625): poet in Hindi of Akbar's time; generally composed on shringar and vir themes. On account of his independent nature, he never found a raja or nawab to act as patron; his verses appear in many anthologies, but there is no separate volume of poetry in his name. The only full text written by him is *Chhand chhand varnan-ki mahima*, a work in Khariboli prose.

Ganga-dasa (13th?): poet and scholar of Sanskrit; author of *Chhandomanjari*, also of *Achyuta-charita*, *Kamsari-shataka* (or *Gopala-shataka*), and *Dinesha-shataka*. He was either a Bengali or an Oriya.

Ganga Devi (14th): woman poet in Sanskrit. One of the few women poets at least one full composition by whom is available. She was the queen of Vijayanagar prince Vira Kampana who ruled at Kanchi. Her kavya work *Madhura-vijaya* recounts events concerning her husband who fought Turki invaders and reconquered Madurai.

Ganga-mangal (late 16th; Bangla) of Madhav: narrative poem on the descent of Ganga to earth. The poet seems to have been a follower of Shri Chaitanya.

Ganga-natak (late 18th; Hindi) of Kushal Mishra (b1769): the author was a poet of Ram bhakti from Agra.

Ganga-prarthana (late 18th; Marathi) of Moropant: a series of devotional lyrics.

Gangotpatti ragade (early 13th; Telugu) of Palakuriki Somanatha: a text on music.

Gaonli-galpa (Oriya): term for folk-tales and other stories emanating from rural life.

Garbi (Gujarati): a kind of lyrical poem which is sung to the accompaniment of dance. The poems were usually composed in praise of a Mother Goddess; later these also depicted Shri Krishna's sport with maidens who tended cows.

Garib-das (b. 1717) sant-poet in Hindi; deeply devoted to Kabir; composed some 7000 verses, of which only 1800 are available. He belonged to Churani village in Rohtak district (Panjab); founded the Garibdasi sect.

Garibulla (early 18th): poet in Bangla. Only two poems of his are known—one, a version of Amir Hamza's *Jangnama*; the other, a version of *Yusuf-Zulekha* based on the Farsi poem of Nuruddin Jami. He belonged to the Bhursut region (on the southern stretch of Damodar river) where a literary centre for Bengali Muslims of the time had developed. The Bangla used by him was full of Apbhramsha, Farsi and Hindi words.

Gatha (Pali/Prakrit): originally meant a speech or verse or song; has been used with various meanings in different contexts. The general meaning of 'verse' was true in Pali and Prakrit, but a particular metrical form, called 'gatha', emerged in due course. Hala's *Gathasaptashati* is an anthology of Prakrit poems in gatha metre, which is also known as 'arya' metre.

Gatha-kosa (*c*1100; Prakrit) of Munichandra Suri: a collection of didactic verses. The same title is also used for *Gatha-saptashati*.

Gatha-lakshana (?C; Prakrit) of Nanditamsa: work in poetics, mainly discusses varieties of gatha.

Gatha-sahashri (1630; Sanskrit/Prakrit) of Samayasundara: anthology of verses by earlier poets.

Gatha-saptashati (1st/3rd; Prakrit) of Hala: an anthology of 700 verses in arya metre. It is the most celebrated of Prakrit anthologies. Unique because it has no didactic intent; deals instead with natural scenery, cycle of seasons, aspirations of common people, etc. The influence of folk literature is evident and the erotic sentiment predominates. Several recensions are available, some containing more than 700 verses. No poets are named in the anthology, but a commentator has tried to identify them and the verses appear to have been culled from different works. The anthology is ascribed to a Satavahana king of Pratisthanapura (Paithan) in Dakhan. These verses may have led to the composition of lyrics in Sanskrit; *Aryasaptati* of Govardhan appears to have been modelled on this anthology.

Tr. Radhagovinda Basak, Calcutta, 1971.

Gauda-vaha (700/725; Prakrit) of Vakpatiraja: kavya work of 1209 verses in arya metre. The work is mainly an eulogy of king Yashovarman of Kanauj in the form of a biographical account; also gives an account of why the poet composed it. But the killing of the king of Gauda, as suggested by the title, does not occur in the extant text; either the text has been preserved in a truncated form, or the poet never completed the work. The story element is scanty; much space is devoted to highly ornate description.

Gaulana or Gavalana (Marathi): word means female cowherd. The devotees of Shri Krishna identified themselves as his cowherd companions, male as well as female, and wrote songs depicting this relationship. These came to be known as 'gaulana' and they date back to 13th. Eknath wrote a large number of these songs, which became very popular.

Gaura-chandrika (Bangla): Songs about Gauranga (Shri Chaitanya) sung by kirtan-singers before they proceed to sing any aspect of the lila of Krishna. The Gauranga devotees believe the life and activities of Gauranga are a clue to the mystery of Krishna's lila. Subsequently, the term "gaura chandrika" came to mean a prefatory statement.

Gauranga-vijaya (*c*1550; Bangla) of Chudamanidas: a biography of Shri Chaitanya which contains some valuable information about the early life of Chaitanya and Nityananda. The poet was a disciple of Nityananda.

Gaurcharan (1814–90): poet and song writer in Oriya as well as singer. A Vaishnav by faith, he was a devotee of Shri Chaitanya. His songs were first collected as *Gaurkrishna bhajan shatak* (1926) by his son Harikrishna Mishra; this contained only 100 lyrics. A later and larger collection *Gaurcharan gitabali* (1951) was further enlarged to include 276 songs and published as *Gaurcharan padyabali*.

Gavari Bai (1758–1808): woman poet in Rajasthani; composed about 600 padas devoted to Giridhara Gopala. Born into a Nagara brahman family of Dungarpur, she was married as a child of five or six and widowed soon after; received some education, then became a composer as well as singer of devotional songs.

Gazala (Rajasthani): an old poetical form, used to describe a place or ceremony or other important event. For example, *Ghanerva ri gazala* by Manchha Kavi (18th), *Chittoda ri gazala* (18th), *Udaipur ri gazala* (1811).

Ghananand (1696–1740): poet in Hindi and singer. A kayastha by birth, he served as a munshi under Muhammad Shah, ruler of Delhi; fell in love with a courtesan named Sujan who spurned him, where upon he went to Brindavan and became a Vaishnav. Many of his poems are addressed to 'Sujan', who may be regarded as the beloved at a romantic level and Krishna at a devotional level. Among his works are *Ghanananda kavitta, Kripakand nibandh, Viyog-beli, Prema-patrika, Virah-lila, Sujan-sagar*. He composed mainly in Brajbhasa.

Ghanaram Chakrabarti (early 18th): poet in Bangla; author of the best-known Dharma-mangal kavya in the language. He belonged to Krishnapur village of Bardhaman district (West Bengal); from his eulogy of the then Bardhaman ruler Kirtichandra, it is inferred that the poet had obtained court patronage.

Ghanashyam (early 18th): versatile writer in Prakrit and Sanskrit from Maharashtra. He is said to have authored 109 works, 64 in Sanskrit, 20 in Prakrit and 20 in local languages. The more important among these are *Venkatesha-charita*, a long poem about Venkateshwara of Tirupati; *Abodhakara* and *Kalidushana*, both poems; *Prachhanda-rahudaya, Damaruka, Madana sanjivana* and *Ananda-sundari*, all plays.

Ghatakarpara kavya (?C; Sanskrit) attributed to a poet called Ghatakarpara: lyric in 22 stanzas. Reversing the situation of Meghaduta, here a young wife, at the advent of the rainy season, sends a message through a cloud to her absent husband. Some scholars have suggested that Kalidas may have composed this poem. At the end, the poet offers to carry water in a 'ghatakarpara' (broken jar) for anyone who can surpass him in yamaka and anuprasha. The poem derives its title from this. The poet is traditionally included among the 'nava-ratna' of the court of king Vikramaditya.

Ghavvasi (17th): poet in Urdu, associated with the Qutbshahi court of Golkonda. His two works are *Saiful Muluk-o-Badiuzzaman* (1624), based on the Alif-Laila qissa, and *Tutinama*, based on the Farsi translation of *Hitopadesha* done by Ziauddin, Garvasi eliminated Arabi and Farsi words as far as possible, thus making his language more accessible to common people.

Ghazal (Urdu): the most popular poetical form in Urdu. It consists of at least five and not more than fifteen verses (sher). The opening verse is called 'matla' and the final verse 'maqta'; in the latter the poet places his 'takhallus' (pseudonym). Each ghazal is written in a parrticular 'bahr' (metre). The form came into Urdu from Farsi where it originated in 10th or 11th; inside India it was developed in Dakhani during 16th and 17th before it came north and was established firmly, especially by the Urdu poets of Delhi and Lakhnau.

Ghulam Ali (17th): poet in Urdu, associated with the court of Golkonda ruler Tanashah Abul Hasan. At his patron's instance, Ghulam Ali rendered Jayasi's *Padumavat* from Hindi into Urdu (in 1680). This was a departure from the more common practice of rendering Farsi works into Urdu.

Ghulam Qadir Sami (d.1780): poet in Urdu from Aurangabad (now in Maharashtra). His ancestors probably came here during Aurangazeb's Dakhan campaign. He is best-known for his masnavi work *Sarva-o-Shamshad*, which is derived from a Farsi source.

Ghunucha-kavya (16th; Asamiya) of Shridhar Kandali: deals with the story of Krishna's visit to the house of Ghunucha, daughter of king Indradyumna; based on episode from *Jagannath-purana* but given local colour and humorous treatment.

Gilchrist [John Borthwick Gilchrist (1759–1848)]: eminent English scholar of Urdu. He came to India in 1782 to join a military medical corps; began to learn Urdu and spent 1787–94 in Ghazipur district of Uttar Pradesh. Here he prepared and subsequently published *An English-Hindustani Dictionary* (1786–90), *A Grammar of the Hindoostanee Language* (1796), and *The Oriental Linguist* (1798). When the East India Company decided to set up a training institution for its young recruits in Calcutta, Gilchrist was summoned to teach Urdu. The institution known initially as the Oriental Seminary (or Gilkrist ka madarsa), was enlarged within a year to become Fort William College; Gilchrist served here until 1804. During this period he produced a number of books, among which are *The Stranger's East India Guide to the Hindoostanee or Grand Popular Language of India, The Hindoostani Manual or Casket of India, Nastaliq-e-Hindoe, The Hindu Roman Orthoepical Ultimatum, The Oriental Fabulist*.

Girdhar Kaviraya or Giridhar Kaviraj (late 18th): poet in Hindi. His simple kundaliyan verses on moral themes were very popular among rural people. He composed in Brajbhasa, but mixed with Kharibоli and Avadhi; may have lived in an Avadhi-speaking region.

Girija-kalyan (*c*1200; Kannada) of Harihar: a champu work based on *Shaiva-puran*, with the marriage of Shiva and Parvati (Girija) as the main story.

Girishchandra Ghosh (1844–1912): playwright in Bangla, also leading actor and successful director of plays. His creative work was of several kinds. One, he dramatized some novels of Bankimchandra. Two, he wrote plays on puranic themes, like *Abhimanyu vadh* (1881) or *Nala-Damyanti* (1887). Three, plays about saints and sages, like *Chaitanya-lila* (1886) or *Bilvamangal* (1888). Four, plays on social issues, like *Prafulla* (1889) or *Balidan* (1905). Five, historical plays that aroused nationalist fervour, like *Salam* (1904) or *Sirajuddaula* (1906).

Girnar inscription (A.D. 150; Sanskrit) of Mahakshatrapa Rudradamana I, Saka ruler (r.130–150) of North-West Dakhan. Inscribed on a rock at Girnar near Junagad in Kathiawar and celebrating an event of about A.D. 150, it provides one of the earliest samples of elaborate prose composition in Sanskrit.

Git-alamkara (?C; Sanskrit) attributed to Bharata: work on music, dealing with 15 different topics in 15 chapters. The editors claim it is earlier than *Natyashastra*.

Git-arnava (17th; Marathi) of Dasopant: commentary on the *Gita* consisting of over one lakh ovis.

Gita-govinda (*c*1200; Sanskrit) of Jayadeva: a dramatic poem, which mingles devotion with erotic appeal in presenting the romance between Krishna and Radha. By practically creating the character of Radha, the poet gave a wholly new focus to the story. The form of the work is equally unprecedented; divided into 12 'sargas', it contains 24 'prabandhas' of unequal length and loosely linked by the theme.

Tr. William Jones, London, 1807; E. Arnold, London, 1875; George Keyt, 1947; Barbara Miller, 1973.

Gita-govinda (late 18th; Marathi) of Ratipati Bhagat: a rendering of the Sanskrit work of Jayadeva.

Gita-govinda-bhasa (*c*1698; Maithili) of Jitamitra-malla: manuscript anthology which contains Jayadeva's *Gita-Govinda* in Sanskrit followed by Maithili padas composed in the same manner by Jagatchandra, Chandrasekhar Simha, Jagatprakash and Jagajjyoti.

Gita-panchakam (mid-17th; Maithili) of Jagatprakasha. The title is used both for a collection of this poet's songs in Maithili and Sanskrit, and also for his elegy on Chandrasekhar consisting of 56 padas.

Gitavali (*c*1570; Hindi) of Tulsidas: a collection of 329 verses in Brajbhasha presented in seven sections. All the verses relate to Rama and were perhaps composed by the poet to counter the profusion of Krishna-bhakti poetry around him. The poet deals mainly with Rama's beauty and glory.

Giti Ramayana (late 15th; Asamiya) of Durgavara: a retelling of the *Ramayana* story in songs. The poet does not appear to be familiar with Valmiki's work and has drawn instead on Madhav Kandali's Asamiya version of *Ramayana*.

Goalari (Maithili): a type of Tirahuti love song which deals with the youthful pranks of Krishna in the company of gopis. Nandipati was a great composer of such songs in Maithili.

Gobinda-chandra (16th; Oriya) of Yashovanta Dasa: a narrative poem generally sung by Natha mendicants. The story is about a prince of Bengal named Gobindachandra who renounced royal comforts and family life at the persuasion of his mother Mukta Debi. His spiritual guide was Hadipa, a scavenger, who taught him that worldly pleasure was worthless.

Gobinda-daser Kadcha (15th/16th; Bangla) of Gobindadas Karmakar: a journal or daily account in verse, supposedly written by the author when he accompanied Shri Chaitanya on his travels to South India. The journal records an almost daily account over a two-year period. Modern scholars have questioned the authenticity of this text and doubted the existence of Gobindadas.

Gokulnath (b. 1458): author in Hindi; son of Vitthalnath; wrote two works in Brajbhasa prose, *Chaurasi Vaishnavon-ki varta* and *Dosau'bavan Vaishnavon-ki varta.*

Gokulnath (late 18th/early 19th): writer in Hindi and scholar; author of works on poetics like *Chetachandrika, Amarkosh-bhasha, Kavimukha-mandan*. He also wrote devotional works like *Govinda-sukhadvihar, Radha-Krishna-vilas*; compiled a reference volume, *Radha-nakhashikha Namaratna-mala*; translated *Adhyatma Ramayana* into Hindi as *Sita Ram-gunarnav*. In collaboration with his sons Gopinath and Manidev, and under the patronage of Uditnarayan Singh, ruler of Kashi, he rendered *Mahabharata* and *Harivamsha* into Hindi between 1776 and 1827.

Gona Buddha Reddi (13th): a tributary prince under Pratap Rudra of the Kakatiya dynasty; composed the earliest Telugu version of *Ramayana*, known as the *Ranganatha Ramayana.*

Gonardiya (?C): presumably a grammarian of some authority; mentioned several times in *Mahabhashya*. According to some sholars, it was a name assumed by Patanjali, who belonged to a place called Gonarda.

Gonasuru Narayanaguru (late 18th): poet in Telugu at the court of Vijayaraghunatha, ruler at Pudukkotai; translated the Sanskrit work *Rasamanjari* of Bhaskara Mishra into Telugu verse.

Gonika-putra (?C): presumably an ancient grammarian; mentioned by Patanjali in *Mahabhashya*.

Gopal Ata (1547–1611): poet and playwright in Asamiya from Nazira village in Upper Assam; later settled in Bhavanipur, now in Barpeta district. He was one of the disciples of Madhavadeva and promoted the Vaishnav faith all his life. He wrote two plays with religious themes: *Janmayatra* and its sequel *Nandotsava*, and *Gopi-Uddhav samvad*; also composed some devotional lyrics.

Gopal Das (1815–88): poet in Hindi from Rajasthan; author of *Lavarasa, Sikharvamsotpatti* and *Krishna-vilas*. For composing verse, he developed a Brajbhasa idiom based on spoken Rajasthani.

Gopal-vijay (16th; Bangla) of Kavishekhar: long narrative poem on Krishna's exploits, especially amorous ones, as cowherd.

Gopalcharan Dvija (late 16th): poet in Asamiya and Vaishnav scholar; contemporary of Koch king scholar Raghudeva (r. 1584–96). A follower of Damodardeva, he ran a 'tol' for students of Sanskrit at Baranagar in Kamrup district. He rendered *Harivamsha* and *Bhagavatapuranam* (Books 3 and 8) into verse, and Shankaradeva's *Bhaktiratnakara* into prose.

Gopalkrishna Pattanayak (1784–1862): Vaishnav poet in Oriya from Paralakhimundi; for some time served the Gajapati Maharaja as record-writer. As poet he initially composed chaupadis on earthly love; later took up the theme of divine love as between Radha and Krishna. His padavali remained widely popular for a long time.

Gopanna [Kancharla Gopanna alias Bhadrachala Ramadas (1620–80)]: devotional poet in Telugu; his songs known as 'Ramadasu kirtanalu' continue to be very popular with common people. He was a nephew of Akkanna and Madanna, famous dewans of Golkonda; through their influence, he was appointed tahsildar of Bhadrachalam. When he used public funds to repair a Rama temple, he was charged with misappropriation and imprisoned for 12 years. According to tradition, Shri Rama appeared in person and paid the required amount to secure his release. He is supposed to have composed some kavya works on Rama, but these are lost. The other poems devoted to Rama were collected in *Dasharathi Shatakam*.

Gopibhasa (18th; Oriya) of Danai Dasa: the only known kavya work of this poet who has been assigned to many periods between 15th and 16th. The poem deals with what the gopis recall of their dalliance with Krishna after he has left Gokula for Mathura. Consisting of 3610 two-line verses, the kavya has 32 sections.

Gopichander Gan (early 18th; Bangla): of Durlabh Mallik: verse narrative about Manikchand and his marriage with Moynamati.

Gopichandrer Panchali (1734; Bangla) of Krishnachohan Sharma: a verse chronicle about the early history of Kachar, a region of Assam. It also traces the genealogy of the then Kachar king Gopichandra Narayan and describes the life in

Kachar valley during this king's reign.

Gopiram Wangkhei (1730–90): writer in Manipuri, also painter and sculptor. He wrote *Chingthangkhomba thougallal*, a book of etiquette for the gentry, and *Govinda nirupon*, an account of Manipuri ruler Bhagyachandra's exile to Assam and return.

Gora-Badal-ki bat (1824; Hindi) by unknown author: prose tale of Rajput heroism. It is based on a verse romance composed by Jatmal around 1623.

Gorakhnath (*c*940–1030): foremost propagator of the Nath sect. He composed both verse and prose in early Hindi. Among numerous works attributed to him are *Sabadi-pada, Sishya-darsan, Pranasankati*, *Narve-bodh*, *Abhayamatrajog*, *Pandraha-tithi*, *Saptavar*, *Machindra-Gorakh-bodh*, *Romavali*, *Jnan-chautisi* and *Panchamatra*. He was the disciple of Matsyendranath (also known as Machhindranath) and is said to have influenced Kabir.

Goraksha-vijaya (early 15th; Maithili) of Vidyapati an early specimen of what would develop into the kirtaniya drama of Mithila. It has Sanskrit as well as Prakrit speeches and stage directions, but the invocation, dance-songs, lyrics and other speeches are all in Maithili. The play was composed at the behest of king Shivasimha; it depicts the traditional story of Matsyendranath, the preceptor of Gorakhnath.

Goshthi (Panjabi): a form of prose composition, dealing with theological subjects. Its authors were yogis, fakirs and siddhas. Their work is known as 'Goshthi sahitya'. Guru Nanak's *Sidh-goshthi* is the first example of such writing in Panjabi.

Gourahari Parichha (1794–1893): Vaishnav poet in Oriya and Bangla; also an excellent veena player. He composed a *chaupadi* in Oriya depicting the love of Radha and Krishna; *Ashtakal-seva* in Bangla, describing the duties of a 'duti' (messenger from Radha to Krishna); translated *Gita-Govinda* into Oriya as *Bhasha sangita-vinoda*.

Gourna (15th): poet in Telugu; author of *Navanatha-charit, Harischandropakhyanmu* and *Lakshandipika*. The first is about the lives of nine siddhas; the second is the earliest separate kavya work about Raja Harischandra. Both were written in the local dvipada metre.

Govardhana (*c*1200): poet in Sanskrit; author of *Arya-saptashati*; belonged to the court of Lakshman Sen, ruler of Bengal (*c*1185–1205). Jayadeva mentions him in *Gita-Govinda* as a poet who cannot be matched in erotic composition.

Govind Singh, Guru (1666–1708) tenth and last Sikh guru; poet in Hindi and Panjabi; scholar of Sanskrit and Farsi. Among his literary works, *Dasham granth, Govind gita* and *Prem prabodh* are highly regarded. He composed poetry mainly in Brajbhasa; of his Panjabi compositions, we know only of *Chandi-di var* and *Chandika-puran*. He had many important Sanskrit and Farsi texts translated into 'bhasa'; he gathered more than 50 poets in his court.

Govinda Mishra (*c*1580–1650): poet in Asamiya who rendered the entire *Bhagavad Gita* into Asamiya using prevailing metres like 'pada, duladi' and 'chaki'. This work is known as *Pada Gita* or *Mishra Gita*. Another work of his is a metrical rendering of Bhattadeva's *Bhakti-viveka* from Sanskrit into Asamiya. The poet has left no details about his life in his writings. His family probably belonged to Kamrup district in West Assam.

Govinda Pillai [P. Govinda Pillai (1829–1907)]: prose writer in Malayalam from Thiruvanathapuram; was a school teacher before he joined the royal court; later became a lawyer. His great contribution was a history of the Malayalam language, entitled *Malayalam bhasha charitram*.

Govinda Thakur (*c*1450/1500): scholar of Sanskrit from Mithila; wrote a commentary in *Kavya-prakash* entitled *Kavyaprakash-pradip*, which is commonly referred to as Pradip.

Govinda Vaidya (17th): poet in Kannada; associated with the then royal court of Mysore. He wrote *Kanthiravana-rasaraja-vijaya* (1648) in praise of his patron. More than its poetic qualities, the work is valued because its subject matter is contemporary history. The poem gives an account of how the king, Kanthiravanarasaraya repulsed Ranadulla Khan's invasion of Karnataka.

Govinda-das (later 17th): poet in Maithili, perhaps the greatest after Vidyapati; one of several Maithili poets claimed by Bengal. A contemporary of king Sundar Thakur (r.1663–71), he is said to have written a long poem entitled *Krishna-lila* but this may be the name given to a series of Radha-Krishna padas composed by him. All his brothers —Gangadas, Haridas, Ramdas— were also writers.

Govinda-das Kabiraj 1535–1613): Younger brother of Ramchandra Kabiraj. Like his brother, he was a Shakta who became a Vaishnav under the influence of Srinivas Acharya. Apart from Brajabuli poems, also wrote a Sanskrit play on the love-episodes of Radha and Krishna; this work is known only from references. Regarded as the first Vaishnav poet of his time, he was given the title of 'Kabiraj' by Jiva Goswami.

Govinda-lilamrita (late 16th; Sanskrit) of Krishnadas Kaviraj: long poem on Radha-Krishna theme. The author lived in Bengal.

Govinda-prabhu-charit (*c*1290; Marathi) of Mahim Bhatt: prose biography of Shri Govinda Prabhu, based on hundreds of stories about him collected by the author by travelling throughout Vidarbha and neighbouring areas. The work is also known as *Riddhipur-charit*.

Govindaram Nungangbam (18th): Manipuri writer who was among those largely responsible for the growth of Manipuri literature in 18th. He knew Sanskrit and Bangla and translated from Bangla into Manipuri. His major work is *Takhel ngamba*, a contemporary biography of Manipur ruler Garibiniwaz.

Grantha Saheb: see *Adi Grantha*.

Grantha-raj (*c*1750; Hindi) of Gadan Gopinath: a work in Dingal in praise of Gajasingha, ruler of Bikaner.

Grierson [George Abraham Grierson (1831–1941)]: perhaps the most famous English scholar of his time of Indo-European languages. Best known for the monumental project organized by him—*The Linguistic Survey of India*, published in 19 volumes between 1903 and 1928, containing over 8000 pages. Grierson won prizes in Sanskrit and Hindi even while he was a student of Trinity College (Dublin). He qualified for the ICS and came to Bengal in October, 1873; became inspector of schools in Bihar and, while spending several years in Madhubani, took special interest in Mithila; appointed Additional Commissioner of Patna and Opium Agent of Bihar in 1898. In the same year he was asked to organise the Linguistic Survey project and worked on this for the next 30 years; retired from ICS in 1902 but continued to work in the project. Among his many works are *Bihar Peasant Life* (1885), *The Modern*

Vernacular Literature of Hindustan (1889), *The Pisaca Language of North-Western India* (1906), *A Dictionary of the Kashmiri Language* (1916–32).

Gujarati: main language of Gujarat state in West India, it is spoken by about 45 million persons. The speakers are also known as Gujarati. Descended from Gurjara Apbhramsha, the immediate ancestory of Gujarati was a dialect prevalent in Marwar (Rajasthan) where a nomadic tribe called 'Gurjara' established its rule between 6th and 8th century. It evolved from dialect to language by 10th; Gujarati separated from Rajasthani, by 15th. The script is a modified form of Devanagari.

Gujari: the form of Urdu as it developed in Gujarat following Muslim conquest of the region.

Gul Muhammad 'Gul' (1811–58): poet in Sindhi; disciple of Pir Pagaro Ali Gohar Shah the first (1815–46) who was a well-known Sufi-sant and poet. Gul was the first poet in Sindhi to collect all his ghazal poems in a diwan. This work, *Diwan Gul* (1855), was published from Bombay a few months before he set out on Haj; he died on this trip.

Gul-e-bakavali: a qissa story in Urdu probably derived from Farsi. It concerns 'gul', a magic flower with healing properties, belonging to Bakavali the fairy. A prince named Taj-al-Maluk comes looking for it so that his blind father, Zain-al-Maluk, can get back his eyesight. While stealing the flower, he sees Bakavali asleep in the garden and falls in love with her. After many other adventures, Bakavali is burnt alive but is reborn as a human and gets married to Taj.

Gulal Saheb (1693–1743): sant-poet in Hindi; his compositions in the barahmasa, hindol, holi, basant, rekhte, mangal and arati forms show the influence of Kabir. He belonged to Basahari village in Ghazipur district (Uttar Pradesh).

Gulrez (1846; Kashmiri) of Maqbool: a masnavi work which became extraordinarily popular when it was published as a book in the 1930s; dozens of reprints appeared subsequently. The original was in Farsi composed by Ziauddin Nakshab (d. 1350).

Gulshan-i-ishq (*c*1670; Urdu) of Nusrati: romantic poem in Dakhni on the love between Manohar and Madhumalati.

Gulzar-e-iram (1778; Urdu) of Mir Hasan: a masnavi work which praises Faizabad and criticises Lakhnau, but its language is replete with aphorisms typical of Lakhnavi Urdu.

Gulzar-e-nasim (1838; Urdu) of Dayashankar 'Nasim' : a masnavi work, which tells the weil-known story of Gul-e-Bakavali.

Guman Mishra (mid-18th): poet of Krishna-bhakti in Hindi; composed *Krishna-chandrika*. He belonged to Panna (Madhya Pradesh) and was a ward of Akbar Ali Khan ruler of Pihani. He also translated the Sanskrit *Naishada-charit* of Sriharsha into Brajbhasha prose

Guna (Sanskrit): a term meaning certain merits of composition by which the literary worth of the work is to be judged. In XVI:96 of *Natyashastra*, Bharata enumerated ten 'guna' and these have generally been accepted as such by later authorities. The gunas are 'shlesha', 'prasada', 'samata', 'samadhi', 'madhurya', 'ojas', 'saukumarya', 'arthavyakti', 'udara' and 'kanti'.

Gunabhiram Barua (1837–94): prose writer in Asamiya, also playwright. He wrote *Ramnavami* (1857), a play; *Anandaram Dhekial Phukan* (1880), a biography; *Asam Buranji* (1884), a history of Assam. He also edited *Asam-Bandhu*, an Asamiya monthly published from Calcutta.

Gunachandra (late 11th): Jain scholar, wrote in Prakrit; author of *Mahavira-chariya*. There is another work with the same title (by Devendragani), also other authors with the same name. This Gunachandra was the pupil of Sumativachaka; his patron was Prasannachandra Suri, a pupil of Jinachandra Suri.

Gunachandra (mid-12th): scholar of Sanskrit; pupil of Hemachandra; joint author with Ramachandra of *Natya-darpana*.

Gunadhya (?4th): author of the lost *Brihat-katha*. According to one tradition, he was born at Pratisthana and became a favourite of the Satvahana king of his time; lost a wager with the grammarian Sarvavarman and abjured the use of Sanskrit thereafter; retired to the Vindhya forests and wrote *Brihat-katha* in Paisachi Prakrit. According to another tradition, he belonged to Mathura and enjoyed the patronage of king Madana of Ujjayini; composed in Paisachi on the advice of sage Pulastya.

Gunakudi Masthan [Sultan Abdul Qadir Labbai (1788–1835)]: Muslim ascetic and devotional poet in Tamil. Also known as Masthan

Sahib, he renounced the world in 1805 and wandered all over Tamilnadu, often living in a cave. He composed 1011 devotional songs, most of which are to be found in the collection *Masthan Sahib padalgal.*

Gunaraj Khan: see Maladhar Bosu.

Gunavarma (*c*900): poet in Kannada, whose works have not been recovered. From references made by others it is inferred that he is the author of two champu-kavyas, *Shudrak* and *Harivamsha.*

Gunavira-panditar (?C): a Jain scholar of Tamil; author of *Neminadham* and *Vachanandimalal,* both treatises in Tamil.

Gundert [Hermann Gundert (1814–93)]: German scholar of Malayalam. He learnt, many other Indian languages during his missionary work in South India from 1836 to 1859. Of his 21 works in Malayalam, the more important are *Kerlappazhama* (1836), *Kerlolpatti* (1843), *Gundert vyakaranam* (1868), and *Gundert nighantu* (1872). The latter, a Malayalam-English dictionary, is the first such reference work for Malayalam. He also began two periodicals, *Rajyasamacharam* (1841) and *Paschimodayam* (1847).

Gurmukhi: script adapted in 16th by the Sikh gurus for writing down the scriptures; hence the name, which means 'from the mouth of the Guru'. It has been used thereafter as the script for Panjabi.

Gurney [A.K. Gurney (1845–1907)]: American who wrote some books in Asamiya. He came to India in 1874 and joined the Baptist Mission at Sibsagar. He was associated with the journal *Orunoday* and edited it until 1883. Of his two novels, *Elokesi beshyar katha* (1877) is translated from the original Bangla novel with the same title; *Kaminikantar charitra* (1877) tells of a Bengali youth who became a Christian.

Guru-charita (1540; Marathi): of Nrisimha Saraswati; a history in verse of the god Dattatreya worshipped mainly in Maharashtra. It has little literary merit but acquired the status of a gospel; regarded as sacred also by the Varkari sect though it originated as a Mahanubhava work.

Guru-dakshina (16th; Malayalam) of unknown author: narrative poem based on *Bhagavatapurana* episode in which the sage Sandipani, tutor of Balaram and Krishna, stipulates as his reward as tutor that his dead son be retrieved from Yama.

Guru-kavya (Panjabi): term mainly refers to verse composed by six Sikh gurus. But the verses of Baba Farid, Kabir and other sants have also been given this status.

Guru-shabad (Panjabi): term for verses by gurus and sants that offer moral advice. It is the same as 'guru-vani'.

Guru-sobha (*c*1710; Panjabi) of Senapati, one of the court-poets of Guru Govind Singh: the work is a verse-biography of the guru. Its language is predominantly Brajbhasha which has been much influenced by Khariboli.

Guru-vilas (1718; Panjabi): the work of three poets, Bhai Mani Singh, Bhai Kuhar (Keyar) Singh and Bhai Sukkha Singh, of whom the latter two probably compiled what the first had composed. It is a biography of Guru Govind Singh and is associated with the sixth 'padshahi' in order to distinguish it from another work with the same title (see below).

Guru-vilas (1797; Panjabi) of Bhai Sukkha Singh of Keshavgarh: a verse biography of Guru Govind Singh. It includes a description of the tenth 'padshahi' and the work is identified thereby.

Gurudas, Bhai (1551–1637): poet in Panjabi; son of Ishar Das, younger brother of Amardas, the third guru. He preached Sikhism and also transcribed parts of *Granth Sahib* at the behest of Guru Arjan Dev. Besides being a poet of high order, he was also a theologian and elucidator of Sikh philosophy. He composed 556 kavitta and swayya verses in Brajbhasha and 39 verses in Panjabi.

Gurupratap Suraj (1843; Panjabi) of Bhai Santokh Singh: a lengthy verse-narrative telling the life-stories of the nine Sikh gurus who came after Nanak Dev. It is a sequel to this poet's earlier work on the first guru's life *Sri Guru Nanak Prakash* (1823). The language of the work is Brajbhasha, written in Gurmukhi script; consists of 51,829 couplets and took the poet ten years to complete.

Gwal (1792–1867): poet in Hindi; belonged to Brindavan. He is said to have written about 50 works, of whom the important ones are *Rasarang, Alamkar-bhram bhanjan, Kavi-darpan, Prastar-prakash, Rasikanand* and *Krishna-shatak.*

H

Habba Khotun (1551–1606): popular woman poet in Kashmiri, famous for her love lyrics. Originally named Zun (Moonlight), she was a talented singer also. Unhappily married to an ordinary villager, she drew the attention of Yusuf Shah Chak, ruler of Kashmir, who got her divorced and married her. Her new name was Hubb (Love). After Akbar conquered Kashmir in 1586, Yusuf Shah was banished, never to return. Habba Khotun spent the rest of her life like a recluse.

Habibullah Hubbi [Khwaja Habibullah Naushehri (1555–1617)]: poet and song-writer in Kashmiri, also scholar of Farsi. He was a contemporary of Habba Khotun; it is said he began composing in Kashmiri after a 'kalam' of hers was sung to him. His poems and songs have been collected in *Diwan Hubbi*.

Hadibadeya dharma (*c*1680; Kannada) of Honamma: poetical work propagating the virtue of wifely service to the husband. While extolling society's need of this traditional virtue, in this work she has also challenged society to allow the exercise of women's rights.

Hafiz Barkhurdar (*c*1675): poet in Panjabi, author of four qissas: *Yusuf Zulaikha, Sassi Punnu, Mirza Sahiban*, and *Kissa Khetri*. There have been other poets in Panjabi bearing this name.

Hafiz Hamid Thikrai (1832–79): poet in Sindhi; composed poetry also in Arabi and Farsi. His ghazals and qasidas in Sindhi have been collected in the volume *Armaghan-e-Hamid*. He was specially known for writing 'khutba' addresses that were read out during Friday prayers. He became blind at the age of three on account of small-pox, but this did not deter him from learning Arabi and Farsi in boyhood.

Hafta-dinh-ratyu-mahina (Sindhi): terms for love-poetry which describes the condition of the lover of the beloved over weeks ('hafta'), days ('dinh'), nights ('ratyu') or months ('mahina').

Haidari [Saiyad Haidar Baksh (d.1823)]: prose writer in Urdu. Born in Delhi and educated in Banaras, he was employed by Fort William College in Calcutta. Here, he wrote *Qissa Laila-Majnu, Tota kahani, Arayise mahfil, Tarikhe nadari, Gul-e-magfarat, Gulzar-e-danish, Qisse Maharo Mah*; these include original works as well as translations from Farsi. His *Gulshan-e-Hind* is a history of Urdu poets.

Hajv (Urdu): a poetic form whose main element is satire. Generally it criticizes a person, a governing order, a particular situation or object.

Hakikat Raye (d. 1734): Hindu martyr, entombed alive by a Muslim governor of Panjab. He became the subject of long poems, the earliest of which is one by Agra Sethi in 1790, entitled *Hakikat Raye-di var*. It consists of 213 verses, each of four lines, and is notable for its musical quality.

Hala (?C): poet in Prakrit, compiler of and contributor to *Gatha-saptashati*. He is usually identified as a Satvahana king of Pratishthanpura (Paithan) in Dakhan. Opinion on his dates vary from 1st to 2nd century.

Hala Jhalan-ra-kundaliyan (1600; Hindi) of Barahatha Isardas: heroic tale in 50 kundaliya verses written in Dingal, about the battle between Jhala Rayasimha, thakur of Halawada, and Hala Jaraji, thakur of Dhrola. The oldest available manuscript of the poem is from 1641.

Halasya-mahatmyamu (mid-18th; Telugu) of Nanjaraju: prose work written under the patronage of Mysore rulers.

Halbe [Lakshmanshastri Moreshwar Halbe (1831–1904)]: novelist in Marathi and scholar of Sanskrit from Wai village in Satara district of Maharashtra; later moved to Bombay and became associated with social reform activities, especially widow remarriages. Of his two novels, *Muktamala* (1861) and *Ratnaprabha* (1866), the first was a pioneering effort at writing romantic fiction in Marathi and it was widely read.

Halhed [Nathaniel Brassey Halhed (1751–1830)]: British scholar of Farsi and Bangla; came to Calcutta in 1773 as a writer of East India Company. At the instance of Warren Hastings, governor-general, he prepared the work published as *Gentoo Law* in 1774–76. Its basis was a Sanskrit work *Vivadarnavasetu*, compiled by Hindu pandits and then translated into Farsi; Halhed translated the Farsi version into English. He is better known for his *A Grammar of the Bengali Language* (1778), which is one of the earliest attempts to study Bangla in a scientific way. For its printing, Bangla types were cut for the first time in the history of printing.

Hali [Altaf Husain (1837–1914)]: pioneering prose writer in Urdu; author of *Yadgar-e-Ghalib, Hayat-e-Sadi, Mukadamma-e-Shair-o-Shairi*. He belonged to Panipat; came to Delhi and became one of Ghalib's pupils; later lived in Lahore and translated English books into Urdu. He also wrote some poetry.

Hamd (Urdu): a poem in praise of god; another term for such poems is 'munazat'.

Hammir Mahakavya (*c*1400; Apabhramsh) of Jaichandra: a work in praise of Hammir. Hammir was a particularly brave ruler of the Chauhan clan from Ranthambor, who was killed in a battle with Alauddin Khalji in 1300. His deeds have been praised in many other poems as well. This poet was a Jain and enjoyed the patronage of Gwalior ruler Viramdeva.

Hammir raso (?1350; Apabhramsh) of Sarangadhar: a work describing the battle between Hammir and Alauddin Khalji. The original work has never been found; the copy from which it was first printed is regarded as composed by many hands.

Hammir raso (1728; Hindi) of Jodhraj: verse work which includes occasional prose passages when the author is presenting a vachanika, vartik or varta.

Hammirayana (15th; Rajasthani) of Bhandau Vyas: a long poem narrating the battles between Chauhan prince Hammir of Ranthambor and Alauddin Khalji of Delhi. Composed maily in chaupais, it is also known as *Rai Hammirade chaupai*.

Hans-jawahir (late 18th; Hindi) of Kasim Shah: verse work in Brajbhasa. The poet (b. 1731) was from Barabanki (Uttar Pradesh) and subscribed to Sufi thought.

Hansauli (*c*1371; Gujarati) of Asait Nayak: long poem which tells the same story as *Hansraj-Vachharaj chaupai*.

Hansraj-Vachharaj chaupai (*c*1355; Gujarati) of Vijayabhadra: long tale in verse of the winning of the beautiful but man-hating Hansauli by king Naravahan-datta. Two sons, Hansa and Vachha, are born to them; they are later persecuted by a stepmother and banished from the kingdom.

Hanuman-charit (1639; Hindi) of Rayemalla Pandey: verse work in praise of Hanuman. It is modelled on *Ramcharitmanas* of Tulsidas.

Hanuman-natak (?C; Sanskrit) by unknown author: two versions are available. The West India version entitled *Hanumannatak* was edited by Damodar Mishra; consists of 14 acts and 548 verses. The East India version entitled *Mahanatak* was edited by Madhusudan Mishra; consists of nine acts and 720 verses. Though largely derived from previous works, it is important as a source. Anandavardhan quoted many instances from it in *Dhvanyaloka*.

Hanuman-natak (1623; Panjabi) of Hridayram Bhalla: also known as *Ram-git* in Panjab. Based on a Sanskrit work of the same title, it is partly a translation, partly a free rendering and partly sequence of verses on the same theme. Though the language is Panjabi, it is heavily laden with Sanskrit words.

Hanuman-natak (Hindi): two versions based on the same Sanskrit original. One was produced by Balbhadra Misra of Orccha in 1543; the other was produced by a Rambhakta poet of the riti period.

Haracharita-chintamani (?C Sanskrit) of Jayadratha: a very large but incomplete work in verse describing the various myths and legends relating to Hara (Shiva). It is more like a purana or a 'mahatmya' than like a kavya. Many of the legends are associated with places of pilgrimage in Kashmir, hence the poet may have been a Kashmiri.

Hara-Gauri Samvad (?14th; Asamiya) of Hema Saraswati: long poem in pada form which deals with the marriage of Shiva and Parvati.

Hara-Gauri vivaha (*c*1630; Maithili) ascribed to Jagajjyotirmalla, king of Nepal (r.1613–37): play about the marriage of Shiva (Hara) to Gauri (Parvati). The dialogue is mainly in verse, with occasional prose passages; there are many songs. Stage directions are in Sanskrit. The text was first published only in 1970.

Harakanta Sadar-aminar Atmajiboni (*c*1900; Asamiya) of Harkanta Barua: the first autobiography in Asamiya, but published 60 years after the author's death. Harakanta Barua (1815–1901) was a government official under the British and he maintained a record of the private as well official events of his life. The first two parts of the work covering the author's life upto 1856, are in narrative form; the third part, upto 1890, is in the form of a daily journal.

Hara Parvati-ri veli (early 17th; Rajasthani) of Kishana: poetical work in 382 verses, written in Dingal, telling the story of Parvati's tapasya, her marriage with Shiva, the birth of their son Kartikeya, and his victory over asuras. Some doubt remains about the identity of the poet. He is either Adha Krishna or Vithu Kishana, both of whom lived during the same period and both obtained the patronage of Bikaner ruler Rayasimha.

Harapati (?15th): poet and scholar of Mithila; most probably one of the sons of Vidyapati and the author of a popular work in astrology. *Vyavahara-dipika*. It was believed in Nepal that this son and not Vidyapati composed *Goraksha-vijaya*.

Hara Vali (17th; Oriya) of Ramachandra Pattanayaka: verse-novel, illustrates a new literary form which began in Oriya in the early 17th. Its hero is an ordinary householder's son and the heroine is a farmer's daughter.

Hara-vijaya (*c*850; Sanskrit) of Ratnakara: mahakavya in 50 sections. It deals with the destruction by Shiva of the demon Andhaka.

Hara-vilasamu (*c*1500; Telugu) of Srinathudu: poetical work which tells all the traditional stories about Shiva's greatness.

Hari Raye (mid-17th): author in Hindi, wrote mainly in prose; a disciple of Vallabhacharya. Among his works are *Shri Yamunaji-ke nam*, *Shri Acharya Mahaprabhu-ke swarup*, *Shri Mahaprabhu-ke devadas niji-varta*.

Hari-charitra (?C; Mithila) of Manabodha: see *Krishna-janma*.

Hari-katha a form of story-telling in Andhra. The tellers are called Haridasu. While telling the story (generally puranic), the Haridasu acts it a little and also plays a musical instrument. The form is also found with local variations, in Kannada and Tamil.

Hari-vamsha (?C; Sanskrit) of unknown authorship: a supplement to *Mahabharata* consisting of three parts (i) "Harivamsha-parvan", which contains an account of creation, mythological narratives, genealogy of the lunar dynasty in which Krishna was born; (ii) "Vishnu-purana", which deals with Krishna, the god Vishnu become mortal; (iii) "Bhavishya-purana", which is a loose collection of puranic texts.

Hari-vamsa (9th; Apabhramsh) of Dhavala: an adaptation of the Sanskrit *Harivamsha*, in which the original stories have been given a Jain colouring. Thus, the descendants of Dhritarashtra and Karna are shown to have become Jains in order to expiate the sins of their ancestors; the five Pandavs, instead of going to heaven, become ascetics and attain nirvana. There is another Apabhramsh work with this title composed by Raidhu.

Hari-vams-a-purana (8th/9th Apabhramsha) of Swayambhu: a work based on Mahabharatha but focussing mainly on Krishna.

Hari-vamshamu (14th; Telugu) of Errana: the first rendering of *Harivamshamu* into Telugu. In this work the author believed he had perfected the prabandha form and called himself 'Prabandha Parameshwara'.

Haribhadra Suri (8th): scholar and logician from Chittor in Rajasthan; wrote in Prakrit as well as Sanskrit. Born into a brahman family, he later converted to the Jain faith when, according to tradition, he was bested in debate by a Jain nun named Yakini Mahattara. After initiation he travelled to other places in Rajasthan, Gujarat and probably North India. He wrote on a variety of subjects and is said to have composed over 100 works; among these, the best known are *Samaraiccha kaha* and *Dhurtakhyana*.

Haribhadra Suri (12th): author in Prakrit from Anahillapatan (mod. Patan) in Gujarat; contemporary of Chalukya king Kumarapala. He undertook to compose verse biographies of all the tirthankars; is reported to have completed 24. Of these only four are extant, *Ajitanatha-charita, Chandraprabhacharita, Mallinatha-charita* and *Neminatha-charita;* the first three are in Prakrit, the last in Apabhramsh.

Haribrahma Harihara (earlier 14th): poet of Mithila; author of at least one poem (no.108) in *Prakrita Paingala*; according to some scholars, he compiled or revised the whole anthology. This particular poem is in nearly modern Maithili and praises Chandeshwar Thakur, ancestor of Vidyapati. The poet is the father of Ravikar, a late 14th commentator on *Prakrita Paingala.*

Hari chandra (*c*900): poet and scholar of Sanskrit; author of

Jivandhara-champu. He was probably a Digambara Jain; had the title of 'Sravastiputra'. He is mentioned by Rajasekhara in *Karpuramanjari*. He may or may not be the same as the author of *Dharmasram-abhyudaya*.

Harihar (*c*1200): Virshaiva poet in Kannada; author of *Pampa-shataka, Raksha-shataka, Mudigeya-ashtak, Girijakalyan* and 102 short verse biographies of eminent devotees of Shiva. He revived the Prakrit metre raghala (ragale) for the purpose of writing these biographies. His influence on other poets in Kannada is so great that a particular direction of Kannada poetry is known as 'Harihar-marga'.

Harihar Vipra (?C): poet in the court of a king of Kamatpura. He along with another poet, Kaviratna Saraswati, rendered *Mahabharata* episodes into Asamiya.

Harilila shodas kala (mid-16th; Gujarati) of Vishnudas Bhim: a poetical work in praise of Krishna, based on *Shrimad Bhagavata*.

Harinath Majumdar (1833–96): writer in Bangla from Kumarkhali village (now in Bangladesh). While working as a primary school teacher in his village, he began *Grambarta prakashika*, a monthly journal which published local news and articles of local interest. Among his 18 books are a prose narrative, three collections of verse, two musical drama scripts and the novel *Chitta-chapala* (1876). He also composed devotional songs that became quite popular.

Hariram Vyas (late 16th): poet of Krishna-bhakti in Hindi; founder of the Harivyasi sect and guru of Madhukar, ruler of Orchha. His verses have been collected in *Vyas-ki vani*.

Harischandra Kavya (*c*1200; Kannada) of Raghavanka: poetical work based on the story of Raja Harischandra. Written in 'vardhaka shatpadi' metre, it has 14 'sandhis' comprising about 750 stanzas altogether.

Harischandra-Nalopakhyana (mid-16th; Telugu) of Bhattumurti: the work can be read in two ways; one tells the story of Harishcandra and Saibya, the other of Nala and Damyanti.

Harisena or Harishena (mid-4th): court-poet of Gupta emperor Samudragupta; is believed to have composed the Allahabad Inscription.

Harsevak Mishra (mid-18th): poet in Hindi; author of *Kamrup-ki* *katha*. He was attached to the court at Orchha.

Harsha-charita (*c*640; Sanskrit) of Banabhatta: prose composition of the akhyayika type in eight chapters. In the introductonry portion, the author gives some autobiographical information, also refers to earlier poets and dramatists. The rest deals with the deeds of Harsha's father Prabhakaravardhana, the expedition of Harsha's brother Rajyavardhana against the Hunas, and with the main events of the reign of Harsha.

Tr. E.B. Cowell & F.W. Thomas, London, 1907.

Harshavardhana (7th): playwright in Sanskrit; author of *Ratnavali, Priyadarshika* and *Nagananda*. He is generally identified with Harsha, king of Thaneshwar and Kanyakubja (r. 606–48).

Haryaksha-masa samarotsavam (late 16th; Malayalam) of Nilakanthan: narrative poem about a military exercise sponsored by the rulers of Venad, Quilon and Kayamkulam, and involving 4000 men.

Hasan Shawqi (mid-17th): poet in Dakhni from Bijapur; received the patronage of Muhammad Adil Shah (1626–56); author of *Fatehnama Nizam Shah*.

Hasham Shah (*c*1750–*c*1840): poet in Panjabi who also composed in Hindi and Farsi. In Panjabi he became popular as the author of qissa works on Sohni-Mahiwal, Sassi-Punnu, Shirin-Farhad and Hir-Ranjha; in Hindi wrote *Jnanprakash, Chintaheer, Rajniti*; in Farsi *Diwan Hasham, Masnavi Hasham, Chahar bahar Hasham*. Pleased with his work, Maharaja Ranjit Singh made several land grants to him.

Hathigumpha inscription (1st century B.C.) of king Kharavela: regarded as the earliest indigenous literary expression of Orissa. The inscription is in Prakrit.

Hatim [Sheikh Zahuruddin (1691–1787) also known as Shah Hatim]: poet in Urdu. A professional soldier, who lived a carefree life when young; later gave up all material comforts and became a darvesh; lived at a place under the Lal Qila walls and this was frequented by famous poets of the time. Because of his influence over them, he is said to have established what came to be known as the 'Delhi school' of Urdu literature. He composed in all forms of Urdu verse; his voluminous 'kuliyat' was lost during Nadir

Shah's invasion of Delhi. A selection from it, made by him and named *Diwanzada*, was published almost 100 years later.

Hayagriva-vadha (?5th; Sanskrit) of Mentha: a lost play, the first verse of which is quoted by Rajsekhara in *Kavyamimamsa* and by Kshemendra in *Suvritta-tilaka*. The author is also called Bhartrimentha or Hastipaka; according to Kalhana, he enjoyed the patronage of king Matrigupta (5th).

Hayat Mamud (early 18th): earliest known Muslim poet in Bangla; a native of Rangpur in North Bengal. Among his works are *Maharam-parva* (1723), a jangnama; a *Hitajnan-vani* (1753), an Islamic theological treatise also known as *Hetu-jijnasa; Ambiya-vani* (1758), exposition of the message of the prophets.

Helvankatte Giriyamma (*c*1750): woman poet in Kannada. She wrote *Chandrahasan-kathe*, *Sita-kalyan*, *Uddalak-kathe* and some devotional songs.

Hema Saraswati (?13th): regarded as the earliest writer in Asamiya. He was a poet in the court of a king of Kamatpura in West Assam. Among his works are *Prahlad-charit, Hara-Gauri samvad*.

Hema-chandra (1088–1172): poet and scholar of Sanskrit as well as Prakrit; author of the kavya work *Kumarapala-charita*, the philosophical works *Pramana-mimamsa* and *Abhida-chintamani*, the grammatical work *Shabdanushasana*. Born at Dhunduka or Dhanduka (near Ahmedabad), became a Jain monk in later life; composed a Jain work, *Trishasti-shataka-purusha-charita*. On *Shabdanushasana* he himself wrote two glosses, *Laghu-vritti* and *Brihad-vritti*, also a commentary, *Brihan-nyasa*. He is regarded as a major literary figure of his time who elevated the Jain faith to a dominant place in Gujarat by winning over kings.

Hemadri (13th): an administrator under the Yadava ruler Shiromani Ramdev Rao of Deogiri. He encouraged Sanskrit learning and himself composed works in Sanskrit like *Chaturvarga chintamani*, an exposition of the caste system, and *Lekhana-kalpataru*, a manual of writing.

Hema-kumara-charitra of Somaprabha: same as *Kumarapala-pratibodha*.

Hemaratan Suri (1579–1623): poet in Rajasthani; at least 12 poetical works have been assigned to him. Among these are *Abhayakumara* *chaupai* (1579), *Mahipala chaupai* (1579), *Gora Badala Padmini chaupai* (1588), etc.

Hemchandra Bandopadhyay (1838–1903): poet in Bangla. Born in Gulita village of Hugli district in Bengal; attended Hindu college in Calcutta; served as a munsif for some time before stating private practice as a vakil. Among his poetical works are *Chinta taranggini, Birbahu kavya, Kavitavali, Asha-kanan, Chayamayi, Britta-samhar, Dasha mahavidya, Chitta vikas.*

Hemchandra Barua (1835–96): prose writer in Asamiya. the first of the great modern writers in that language. He not only wrote prose but also helped to stabilise the form through his textbooks, grammars and dictionaries. Among his works are *Asamiya vyakarana* (1856), a grammar; *Adipath* and *Pathmala*, textbooks which offer models for prose-writing; *Asamiya bhashar padhasaliya abhidhan*, a school dictionary; *Asamiya Hemakosha*, the first etymological dictionary of the language; *Bahire rang-chang bhitare kova bhaturi*, a prose satire; *Kaniyar kirtan* (1861), a farce.

Hindi: the language (or some variety of it) spoken in the states of Bihar, Uttar Pradesh, Haryana, Himachal Pradesh, Rajasthan, and Madhya Pradesh. The predominant language of North India, it has about 437 million speakers, a larger number than any other Modern Indian language. Hindi literature of earlier times includes works composed in dialects like Brajbhasa and Awadhi and others, but in due course Khariboli (the dialect once spoken in and around Delhi) became the standard medium of literary expression. Hindi is written in the Devanagari script.

Hir Damodar (late 16th; Panjabi) of Damodar: a qissa work on the Hir-Ranjha story but with a happy ending. Composed in davayya metre, its language is simple and unadorned, based on Lahanda (West Panjabi) speech. It is the first known qissa-kavya in Panjabi.

Hir-Ranjha: Hir and Ranjha are the hero and heroine of a tragic love story in the folk literature of Panjab. Among well-known works on the story are those by Damodar, Muqbil, Waris Shah.

Hita Harivams (1502–55): poet of Krishna-bhakti in Hindi. His verses have been collected as *Hita chaurasi*; also composed a Sanskrit work, *Radhasudhanidhi*. He belonged to Bad village in Mathura district (Uttar Pradesh) and founded the Radhavallabh sect.

Hita-brindavan Das (b. 1708): poet of Krishna-bhakti in Hindi. His verses have been collected in *Chachaji-ki vani*. He composed in Brajbhasa and his padas are said to have numbered over four lakh.

Hita-tarangini (1540; Hindi) of Kriparam: long poem on the theme of 'Nayika-bhed'. It is the first of four such works composed during the Bhakti period of Hindi literature, the others being *Sahitya-lahari* by Surdas, *Rasa-manjari* of Nandadas, *Barvay nayika-bhed* of Rahim.

Hitopadesha (?C; Sanskrit) of Narayana: title of the Bengal version of *Panchatantra*. It consists of four books in place of original five; also contains many additions and alterations. The author's patron was one Dhavalachandra; lived some time between 900 and 1373. The lower date is derived from a manuscript found in Nepal.

Tr. C. Wilkins, London, 1787; M.S. Apte, Poona, 1957; M.R. Kale, Delhi, 1967.

Honaji Bala (1754–1844): poet in Marathi, especially popular for his lavani compositions on stories of Krishna. He also wrote five powada, of which three are on Peshwa Bajirao II. The poet was a milk-seller (gwala) by caste.

Honamma or Sanchiya Honamma (late 17th): woman poet in Kannada; employed under Yalandur Devajammani, queen of Chikkadevaraja Wodyar of Mysore. The prefix to her name suggests she was betel-leaf-bag (=sanchi) bearer of the queen. Though a maid-servant by occupation, she claimed Alasingaraya, the court poet, as her guru. At his instance, the king asked Devájammani to ask Honnamma to write something in Kannada. She wrote *Hadibadeya dharma*, which discusses the essential qualities of an ideal wife. The work, in sangatya metre, has 479 stanzas spread over nine sections.

Hukmi-chand (late 18th): poet in Hindi; composed dohas and chappays in Dingal. These were very popular among common people in Rajasthan. His patron was Pratapsingh, ruler of Jaipur.

Hullaki Bhaskara (13th): poet in Telugu who composed a version of *Ramayana* in Telugu. The work is dedicated to Sahinimara, a cavalry commander, son of Buddhiraju who was the patron of Ranganatha.

Husaini [Mir Bahadur Ali (late 18th/early 19th)]: prose writer in Urdu employed by Fort William College of Calcutta. Not much is known about his life. He rendered Mir Hasan's masnavi *Sahrul bayan* into Urdu prose, and named it *Nasre benazir*; condensed Gilchrist's grammar of Hindustani as *Risalaye Gilchrist*; translated Shahabuddin Talish's *Tarikh-e-asam* from Farsi into Urdu. Husaini's best-known work is *Akhlake Hindi*, which is based on Mufti Tajuddin's rendering of *Hitopadesha* into Farsi.

I

Ibne Nishati (mid-17th): poet in Urdu from Golkonda; received the patronage of Abdullah Qutb Shah (1625–74); author of *Phulban*, a masnavi work.

Ibrahim Adil Shah II (1580–1626): ruler of Bijapur and patron of the arts. He built a garden city near his capital and called it "Nauraspur" (city of the nine rasas); author of *Naurasnama*.

Icchabati (late 17th; Oriya) of Dhananjay Bhanja: poetical work dealing with the earthly life of gandharva Kalavat and apsara Kalavati, both of whom had been exiled from swarga under a curse. The first five 'chhand' (sections) were composed by the poet; the rest were translated from *Chaurapanchasika* of Bilhana.

Ihamgoi (Urdu): a term in poetics for the device which 'creates delusion'. In practice it means using words which have an immediate and popular meaning as well as a remote and obscure meaning. Such use creates the delusion.

Ilampuranar (10th): Jain scholar of Tamil, who wrote the pioneering commentary on *Tolkappiyam*; was known thereafter as 'Uraiyasiriyar' (the commentator). His is the only commentary which has survived in complete form.

Ilango Adigal (late 2nd): princely author of the Tamil classic *Silappadikaram*. Internal evidence gleaned from the work suggests that he was the second son of a Chera prince; renounced material life and became an ascetic; story of the poem was narrated to him by Sattanar. While it is generally accepted that he was a Jain, in this poem he is equally respectful of all creed.

Imam Baksh (1778–1863): poet in Urdu. Born in Pasianwala village of Sialkot district (now in Pakistan) and educated in Lahore, he used to earn a living as a carpenter and also by teaching Quran Sharif to children. His most famous work is *Shah Bahram Husn Baro* which is based on a foreign story; other verse romances composed by him are *Laila-Majnu, Malikzada Shahpari,*

Gul-Sanovar, Gulbadan, Chandarbadan Mahiyar. Most of his works derive from Farsi masnavi works. Perhaps because of the un-Indian nature of his material, interest in his work has remained confined to specialists.

Inder Sabha (1852; Urdu) of Agha Hasan Amanat: loosely termed a play, it is a combination of drama, poetry, dance and song presented within an ancedotal framework. Amanat's creation was the first of its kind; later it became more of a style of presentation than a drama text. The style began in Lakhnau but spread to other parts of the country. Amanat's original version contained only two prose dialogues but was replete with 31 ghazal, 9 thumri, 4 holi, 15 git, 2 chaubola and 5 chhand songs. A flimsy story line brings the earthly prince Gulfram into Raja Indra's heavenly darbar; he gets into trouble, is punished, then reprieved. Gulfram dresses, speaks and behaves like a prince of Avadh, while Indar is presented like an Irani or Mughal emperor but is said to be the ruler of 'Simhal dvip'. Later in 20th, the commercial Farsi stage took over the tradition and introduced many new features conducive to popular taste.

Indra (?C): presumed authority on grammar, probably referred to by Panini in his use of the term 'Pracham'. He is supposed to have founded the Aindra school of grammar.

Indravati (*c*1740; Hindi) of Nur Muhammad: kavya work on the romance between prince Rajkunwar and princess Indravati.

Insha [Insha Allah (*c*1764–1818)]: poet in Urdu; son of Masha Allah. The poet was born in Murshidabad; later lived in Delhi and Lakhnau; studied Arabi, Farsi, Hindi and some other Indian languages. Among his works are *Urdu ghazalo ka diwan, Diwan-e-rekhti, Divan-e-farsi, Divan-e-benukt, Farsi masnavi benukt, Masnavi ashikana, Farsi masnavi shairo-braj*. He was one of the earliest writers of Hindi prose and his *Rani Ketaki ki kahan*i is an example of early Hindi prose. He also wrote the first grammar of Urdu entitled *Daraya-e-latafat*.

Iramnatakam (18th; Tamil) of Arunachalakkvarirayar: a sequence of songs relating to the *Ramayana* story.

Irattiyar (mid-15th): a name which identifies two poets who lived together in mutual assistance. One of them was blind, the other lame, but together they travelled to many places in Tamilnadu. They innovated the 'kalambakam' style of verse-composition which uses a variety of Tamil metres. Their main works are *Tiruvamatturakkalambakam, Tillaikkalambakam,* and *Ekambar natrula.*

Irayimman Thampi (1782–1856): poet in Malayalam. He was related to the Travancore royal family and became the court-poet of Maharaja Swati Tirunal. He is the author of three atthakathas: *Kichaka-vadham, Uttara-swayamvaram, Dakshayagam*; also wrote many songs.

Isardas (1538/1559–1618): bhakti poet in Hindi; author of many works in Dingal among which are *Hari-rasa, Bal-lila, Garuda-puran, Sabha-parva, Halajhlara, Kundaliyan, Guna-agam, Rasa-kailash.* The poet was born in Jodhpur but lived nearly 40 years in Jamnagar.

Ishwarchandra Gupta (1812–59): poet in Bangla, scholar and journalist. His name is associated mainly with the journal *Samvad-prabhakara*; he also edited *Pashandapidan* and *Samvad-sadhuranjan.* Much of his poetry was published in journals and collected only after his death in *Ishwar Gupta kavitavalir sarasamgraha* in eight volumes, edited by Ramchandra Gupta (1862–64). Among his prose works are *Prabodha prabhakara* (1857), *Hitaprabhakara* (1861), *Bodhenduvikasha* (1863). He also collected the kirtans of Ramprasad Sen in his *Kalikirtan* (1883), and wrote *Rayagunakar Bharatchandra Rayer jivanvrittanta* (1855), a biography of Bharatchandra Raye.

Isi'dasi (?C): a Bouddha nun (Theri) whose compositions are included in *Therigatha.*

Ismail Mohammad Merathi (1844–1917): poet in Urdu from Merat. Though he had obtained a diploma from Roorki Engineering College, he became a school teacher of Farsi; retired from service in 1899. His *Kulliyat-e-Ismail* was published in 1910; a more complete collection, *Hayat-o-Kulliyat-e-Ismail* appeared in 1939.

Itivuttaka (?C; Pali): fourth part of *Khuddanikaya.* The title means "Thus spoke the Buddha", and the work is supposed to represent the utterances of Buddha; consists of 110 suttas in prose and verse.
Tr. K.H. Meare, Columbia U., 1908.

Iyalpa: title of the third collection of Vaishnav hymns in Tamil by Alvar sants. Containing 1000 poems, it is the work of three Alvars.

J

Jadumani Mahapatra (*c*1780–1886): poet in Oriya; became popular for his devotional poems and songs as well as witty and satirical statements. He composed two longer poems in the ornate riti style, *Prabandha purnachandra* and *Raghaba bilasa*.

Jaduram Barua (1801–69): lexicographer in Asamiya; said to have compiled a dictionary of the language in 1839, which subsequently served as the basis of *Assamese-English Dictionary* (1867) by Miles Bronson.

Jafar Zatal (mid-18th): poet in Urdu; wrote biting satire in a language full of distorted Arabi and Farsi words, along with a mixture of words from various Indian dialects. It is said that a sarcastic couplet he wrote about the enthronement of Mughal king Farrukhsiyar cost him his life.

Jaga-gan (end-18th; Bangla) of Rabiram Das. The work is a lengthy chhara which relates the oppresive activities of the East India Company's 'ijaradar' Devi Singh and the protection he received from the English Collector of Rangpur. The poet was a Rajvamshi.

Jagadanand (mid-17th): bhakti poet in Hindi; author of *Braja-parikrama*. He also wrote *Upakhyayan sahit Dasam skandha*, a summary of the 10th chapter of *Bhagavatapurana*.

Jagajjyoti-malla (early 17th): poet who belonged to the Nepalese royal family in Bhatgaon; mainly composed devotional songs in Maithili and wrote copiously on music in Sanskrit. Songs composed by him are to be found in notable anthologies like *Dashavatara-gitam, Prakirna-gitam, Gita-panchasika, Gita-samgraha*. He also wrote several plays.

Jagamohan Ramayana (16th; Oriya) of Balaram Dasa: an adaptation of the *Ramayana* story. The work ranks with Sarala Dasa's *Mahabharata* as two great influences upon Oriya language and literature. It is also known as *Dandi Ramayan*, after the colloquial style used by the poet.

Jaganik (late 12th): a bhat poet in Hindi, who is said to have composed the original *Alha-khand.* He belonged to the court of Kalinjar ruler Parmal.

Jaganmohan Lala (1838–1913): writer in Oriya from Mahanga village in Kataka district of Orissa; served the British government of India for some time and rose to be Deputy Collector. He wrote *Bhrama-bhangana* (1868), a long poem based on the English work *The Hermit* by Parnell; two plays, *Babaji* (1877) and *Sati* (1886); a collection of historical essays, *Odisa-vijaya*. He built a permanent stage in his village and named it 'Radhakanta Rangamancha'.

Jagannath (*c*1650): poet and scholar of Sanskrit; author of *Rasagangadhara.* Born a South Indian brahman, he appears to have settled in the north and obtained the title of 'Pandita-raja' from the Mughal emperor Shah-jahan. Among his other works are *Chitra-mimamsa*, on poetics; *Bhamini-vilasa,* an erotic poem of didactic intention; eulogies of Asaf Khan, brother of Nur-jahan *(Asapha-vilasa),* of Jagatsimha king of Udaipur *(Jagadabharana)*, and of Prana-narayana, king of Kamarupa (Pranabharana). His grammatical work *Manorama-kucha-mardini* is directed against *Praudha-manorama*, the commentary by Bhattoji Diksita on *Siddhanta-Kaumudi*. Jagannath is the last great authority on Sanskrit poetics.

Jagannath Bhagavat (15th/16th; Oriya): The popular name of *Bhagavatapurana* rendered into Oriya by Jagannath Dasa. It is not a literal rendering of the Sanskrit original; also, it includes matter from other puranas as well.

Jagannatha Dasa (15th/16th): second in importance only to Balarama Dasa among the Pancha-sakha poets in Oriya. A brahman and learned in Sanskrit, of almost the same age as Shri Chaitanya, the poet and the sant became life-long friends. Like Chaitanya in Bengal, Jagannath Dasa in Orissa became the subject of the earliest biographies in the local language. His own major work is the *Bhagavatapurana* in Oriya; also composed *Artha-koili*, a theological interpretation of *Keshava-koili* of Markanda Dasa, and *Tulabhina*, a metaphysical discourse. Chaitanya used to call him "Ati-bada" (excessively great), from which his followers named themselves the Atibadi sect; he never married and spent his life in yogic practices.

Jagannath Das (mid-18th): scholar of Sanskrit and poet in Kannada; belonged to the Haridas sect. Among his works, *Harikatha-mritasar* is the most important; an exposition of Madhva philosophy, it was composed in 'bhamini shatpadi' metre and consists of about 988 stanzas. Another work, *Tattva suvvali*, is a collection of tripadi stanzas meant for the teaching of Madhva philosophy; of its reported 1200 stanzas, only about 600 are extant.

Jagannath Narayana Deva (early 18th): poet in Oriya; ruler of Paralakhemundi state in Orissa; able warrior, statesman and scholar, he was also a talented muscian. He composed *Brindavana-vihara* in Oriya. In Sanskrit he wrote expository texts like *Sangita narayana Sangita-Kaumudi*, and *Alankara-Chandrika.*

Jagannath-mangal (1643; Bangla) of Gobardhan Das: also known as *Jagat-mangal*, the work is a narrative poem in eulogy of the deity Jagannath at Puri in Orissa.

Jagannath vijaya (c1180; Kannada) of Rudra Bhatta: champu work based on the story of Krishna from his birth to the slaying of Banasur.

Jagatprakasha-malla (mid-17th): poet in Maithili who belonged to the Nepalese ruling family of Bhatgaon; was often called by his pen-name 'Prakasha'. Some of his devotional poems have been collected as *Padya samychhaya, Gita panchaka, Nanaranga gitani, Nanartha devadevi-gitam.* He encouraged other poets among whom are Chandrasekhara, Jagatchandra, Vamshamani Jha, etc.

Jahangir-jasha chandrika (*c*1590; Hindi) of Keshavdas: kavya work in praise of Mughal emperor Jahangir.

Jaichand-prakash (*c*1168; Hindi) of Bhatta Kedar: poetical work in praise of Raja Jaichand. The text has not yet been found.

Jaiguner-Punthi (1797; Bangla) of Saiyad Hamza: a jangnama of Hanifa.

Jaimayank-jasha Chandrika (*c*1183; Hindi) of Madhukar: another work in praise of Raja Jaichand, the text of which remains untraced.

Jaimini-bharata (late 16th; Kannada) of Lakshmisha: a free rendering in condensed form of the Sanskrit original. The poem composed in 'shatpadi' metre, consists of 1906 stanzas in 34 sections. Shri

Krishna is the hero of the poem which has also been called *Krishna-charitramrita*.

Jaimini-bharatamu (18th; Telugu) of Sanmuk Venkatkrishnan Naykudu: prose work based on the poetical rendering in Telugu by Pillamri Virbhadradu of the Sanskrit *Jaimini-Bharat*.

Jaimini-puran bhasa (1748; Hindi) of Surajram Pandit: collection of puranic tales retold in doha or chaupai form.

Jaina-charita (15th; Kashmiri) of Yodhabhatta: biography of the author's patron, Zainul Abidin. The work is not extant. This author also wrote a play in praise of his patron entitled *Jaina-prakasha*, but this too is lost.

Jaina Mahabharata: popular title of *Pandava-purana*, a work in Prakrit by Subhachandra.

Jaina purana (Apabhramsha): general term for a class of Jain religious works composed in Apabhramsha. These are modelled on Sanskrit puranas and their purpose is to propagate Jainism.

Jaina Rajatarangini (late 15th; Sanskrit) of Srivara: a continuation of Kalhana's *Rajatarangini*, covering the period 1459–86.

Jaina-vilasa (15th; Kashmiri) of Bhatta Avatara: long poem on the author's patron, Zainul Abidin. The work is not extant.

Jakkana (14th): poet in Telugu; author of *Vikramanka-charitramu*. The work deals with a historical person but the poet has attributed superhuman powers to him, thus reducing the value of the poem as history.

Jalal [Saiyad Zamin Ali Lakhnavi (1833–1909)]: poet in Urdu and scholar from Rampur. He came to Lakhnau for study; became a disciple by turns of Hilal, Rashk and Bark; the latter two being disciples of Nasikh. Jalal also came under the influence of Nasikh. His poems have been collected in four diwan volumes — *Shahide-shaukh-tabwa, Karishmajane-sukhan, Mazmunhaye-dilkash, Nazm-e-rangi*. He also wrote a book on the use of Urdu proverbs, *Sarmaya-e-zaban-e-Urdu*, and two dictionaries, *Tanquihullugat* and *Gushan-e-faiz*. He also wrote books on grammar, poetics and history-writing.

Jalal-Gahani-ri bat (1696; Hindi) by unknown author: kavya work telling of the romance between Jalal and Gahani.

Jalhana (*c*1250): poet in Sanskrit; compiled *Subhasita-muktavali* or *Sukti-muktavali*. According to Kalhana, he also composed the poem *Somapala-vilasa* in honour of his patron Somapala; but he may not be the same as the poet who composed *Mugdhopadesha*.

Jambavati-vijaya (?C; Sanskrit) ascribed to Panini: a lost kavya cited by one Rajashekhara in Jahlana's *Sukti-muktavali*. A fragment is to be found in Ramayukta's commentary on *Namalinganushasana*. From the title it may be inferred that the work dealt with Krishna's winning Jambavati in the underworld as his bride.

Jambhala-datta (?C): author of a version of *Vetala-panchavimshati*; his dates and personal history are unknown.

Jambu-chariya (9th/10th; Prakrit) of Gunapala: poem of about 600 verses featuring the lives of Jambuswami, a disciple of Mahavira and head of the Jain community in 5th century B.C. His story appears along with other stories in some earlier works like *Vasudevahindi*. Here Gunapala is the first poet to devote an independent work to the story.

Jambu-dvipa-pannatti (?C; Prakrit): the sixth 'uvarga'. The work describes Jambudvipa, the central continent, and gives the mythical geography in Jain tradition.

Jambuswami-charita (*c*1210; Gujarati) of Bharama Suri: raasu work on the life of Jambuswami who is regarded by Jain tradition as the last 'kevali'.

Jambuswami-chariu (1020; Apabhramsha) of Vir: kavya work on the life of Jambuswami (see above also). The poet has mainly followed Gunapala's work on the same subject but changed some of the subsidiary stories.

Jan Saheb [Mir Yar Ali Khan (1810–86)]: poet in Urdu. Born at Farrukhabad in Uttar Pradesh, he was taken as an infant to Lakhnau; grew up there and lived through the 1857 Revolt: tried his luck at making a living in Delhi and in Bhopal; finally settled in Rampur. He wrote poetry in rekhti, i.e., the language spoken by women among themselves. The poems are often so candid as to be obscene, but they also reflect the position of women, thus are significant as social history.

Janabai (?C): woman poet in Marathi; belonged to a shudra community. Orphaned as a child, she was given shelter by Namdev. Though illiterate, she learnt to express herself under the influence of the sant. A devotee of the god Vitthal, she wrote most of her abhangs about him. She composed about 450 poems altogether; in these she always refers to herself as 'Namayachi Jani Dasi'.

Janaka-harana (?6th; Sanskrit) of Kumaradasa: mahakavya on the *Ramayana* story of which only 20 sections are available. According to a Sinhalese commentary, the original work consisted of 25 sections and dealt with events up to the re-installation of Rama as king. The poet is also known as Kumarabhatta or Bhattakumara; one tradition makes him a friend of Kalidasa. According to Sri Lankan tradition he ruled the island (*c*517–26).

Janaki-mangal (*c*1583; Hindi) of Tulsidas: kavya work which describes Rama's marriage to Sita (Janaki), also the marriages of his three brothers.

Janamsakhi (Panjabi): the name given to old biographies of Guru Nanak. There are many such, with variations. Four main traditions have been accepted—1. 'Puratan janamsakhi'—though the first published text (1926) is based on two manuscripts, many other manuscripts from the same tradition also exist. The oldest copy is probably of 1588. 2. 'Meharban Janamsakhi'—attributed to one Meharban and discovered only in 1940; earlier parts written before 1645, later parts written by his sons completed by 1650. 3. 'Bala janamsakhi'—attributed to Bhai Bala, a close companion of the Guru. Though popular among Sikhs, it is not a reliable version. The oldest copy bears the date 1658. 4. 'Mani Singh janamsakhi'—the latest of the traditions, beginning with Bhai Mani Singh, a comtemporary of Guru Govind Singh.

Janardan Swami (16th): sant-poet in Marathi; belonged to the Varkari sect and was the guru of Eknath. He composed some verses also in Hindi.

Jangi khawar (Kashmiri): masnavi work, a translation of the Farsi epic *Khawarnama* of Ibn-e- Hissam (15th/16th). The translation was begun by Syed Amir Shah Kreri (1846–1905) and completed by his son Qabul Shah (1869–1930). The story is not based on any historical episode and its main purpose was to propagate Islam.

Jangnama (Bangla): narrative poems in the manner of *Mahabharata*, describing either the conquest and conversion of Iran by Hazrat Muhammad's followers or the cruel fate of the brothers Hasan and Husain, grandsons of the Prophet. The form was practised mainly by 17th century Muslim poets of Bengal, especially in Chatgaon and Srihatta; among these poets are Mohammad Khan, Nasarullah Khan, Hayat Muhammad, Mansur, etc.

Jangnama (Panjabi): term derived from Farsi (meaning description of battle) came into Panjabi literature in mid-19th with the composition of Shah Muhammad's poem on the Sikh-English battles of 1846–47. Previous to this, long narrative poems on battle-themes in Panjabi were known as var; but these included other matters as well while 'jangnama' describes only the battle.

Janna (early 13th): poet in Kannada. As law-officer, minister and poet, he became a leading light in the court of Hoysala king Narasimha. At first Janna used to compose verses for stone inscription; later he wrote *Yasodhar-charite, Anantanath-purana* and *Anubhav mukur* (also known as *Smara-tantra*).

Jannatul-baqa (*c*1575; Urdu) of Burhanuddin Janum: work of 1610 verses in Dakhni which shows Gujarati influences.

Japuji (*c*1605; Panjabi) of Guru Nanak; his most popular though philosophical work, composed towards the end of his life. When Guru Arjun Dev was compiling *Adi Granth*, he placed this poem first. It consists of 38 'pohri' (stanzas), with a 'mool mantra' at the beginning and a 'saloka' at the end. It offers an outline of Sikh philosophy as elaborated in *Adi Granth*.

Jasahara-chariu (10th; Apabhramsha) of Pupphayanta: an account in verse of the king Yashodhara who converted to Jain faith after certain events.

Jaswant Singh Rathor (1626–78): poet in Hindi and scholar of Vedanta. Rajput chief from Jodhpur, he fought many battles for Mughal emperor Shah Jahan but fell out with Aurangzeb. He translated *Prabodha-chandrodaya* from Sanskrit into Brajbhasa prose and verse; this has been regarded as the first play in this dialect. He is also said to have translated *Bhasha-bhushana*, a Sanskrit work on rhetoric, into Brajbhasa. He wrote many books on Vedanta, such as

Siddhanta-bodh, Ananda-vilas, Anubhav prakash, etc.

Jataka (?C; Pali): a part of *Khudda-nikaya*; collection of stories about the previous births of Buddha as Bodhisattva. Each story in its present form is divided into five parts: (i) 'Paccuppanna-vatthu' or present facts, stating the occasion on which Buddha narrated the story: (ii) 'Atita-vatthu' or past facts, prose narration of one of the lives of Bodhisattva; (iii) 'Gatha' or verses, occurring in both the above parts, more often in the latter; (iv) 'Veyyakarana' or brief exposition, wherein each word of a gatha is explained; (v) 'Samodhara' or exposition, wherein Buddha identifies the distinguished personages mentioned in the second part. According to a later mode of division, the contents are divided into 22 sections called 'nipatas'; each succeeding nipata contains a lesser number of stories but a larger number of gathas than the preceeding one.
Tr. various hands and ed. Cowell & Rouse, Cambridge, 1895. Index by Rouse, *JPTS*, 1890.

Jataka-mala (3rd/4th; Sanskrit) of Arya Sura: work in prose and verse, rendering 34 selected stories from the Pali *Jataka* and *Charyapitaka*, illustrating the perfections of a Bodhisattva. The Chinese traveller I-tsing mentions this text and some of the frescoes of Ajanta suggest that it was in existence at the time.
Tr. J.S. Speyer, Oxford, 1895.

Jatakattha-vannana: the proper title of the work usually known as *Jataka*, the original form of which is not known. As the title indicates, it is an exposition of the *Jataka* stories. It is supposed to have been composed by a Sri Lankan monk, who collected material from an older commentary called *Jatakattha-katha*.

Jatra (Bengali): a form of popular drama enacted on an open stage without any curtain in front.

Javan [Mirza Kazim Ali Javan (late 18th/early 19th)]: prose-writer in Urdu originally from Delhi, later moved to Lakhnau. Brought to Fort William College in 1800, he was commissioned to translate Kalidas' *Shakuntala* into Urdu; he did so, from a Brajbhasa version by Nivaj, which Lallu Lal used to read out to him. Javan also wrote *Barah-masa*, a masnavi which describes each month's Muslim as well as Hindu festivals; *Tarikh-e-Farishta*, a history of the Bahmani kings of Dakhan.

Jawahir-ul-asrar (*c*1570; Urdu) of

Shah Ali Mohammad Jan Gamdhani: collection of poems.

Jayadeva (*c*1200): poet in Sanskrit; author of *Gita-Govinda*. His native village Kendubilva has been identified by Bengali scholars as the Kenduli on the Ajay river in Birbhum district of West Bengal; but he is also claimed by Mithila (in Bihar) and Orissa. He lived during the reign of Lakshman'sena, the last independent Hindu king of Bengal. His other works are not known, but fragments of these have been found in a Sanskrit anthology, *Sadukti'-karnamrita*, compiled in Bengal about 1205.

Jayagounda (1716–48): wrote on poetics in Kannada; author of *Kannada Kuvalayananda* and *Rasamanjari*, both rendered from Sanskrit originals.

Jayananda (early 16th): poet in Bangla; author of *Chaitanya-mangal*. He belonged to South-west Bengal and his work was known only to that region. His father was a disciple of Gadadhar Pandit, one of the closest followers of Chaitanya.

Jayanarayan Ghosal, Raja (1752–1821): zamindar of Bhukailas near Calcutta; associated with social, religious and educational activities in Calcutta; later settled in Banaras. He translated into Bangla the 'Kashi-kanda' section of *Padma-purana* and added to it a description of the Banaras of his time.

Jayasi [Malik Muhammad Jayasi (1477–1542)]: Sufi poet in Hindi, so named because he belonged to Jayas village near Amethi in Uttar Pradesh. A disciple of Mohd. Shaikh Burhan of Kalpi, he was also influenced by Syed Ashrif Makhdum Sahib, a fakir who spent the latter part of his life in Jayas. He is said to have written 24 works but only six are available. These are *Kaharanama, Maslanama, Akhravat, Akhiri-kalam, Chitra-rekha* and *Padmavat*. The last named is the poet's most outstanding work.

Jayasthiti-malla (r. 1380–94): Nepalese king who invited a number of Maithili scholars and poets to his court and encouraged the writing and performance of drama. A four-act play in Sanskrit on *Ramayana*, the earliest drama composed in Nepal, was performed at the birthday ceremony of the king's son Dharma-malla. Another Sanskrit play associated with his reign is *Bhairavananda natakam*.

Jaymati kumarir git (?C; Asamiya): akhyana-git depicting the self-sacrifice of princess Jaymati to save her husband prince Gadadhar from the executioner of king Ratnadhvaja Simha alias Ghulikpha (1679–81) who had ordered the killing or disabling of all princes of royal blood who might claim the throne. Jaymati managed to send Gadadhar away secretly to the Naga hills but was herself arrested and tortured to death.

Jhula Sanyon (1575–1646): sant poet in Rajasthani from Idar state in Gujarat. His family received many state awards, including the village Kubaba where his descendants are said to be residing even now. He was a Krishna-bhakti poet, as seen in his two works, *Naga-damana* and *Rukmini-harana*.

Jhulana (Rajasthani): a popular metre of 16th and 17th centuries in Rajasthan. It was extensively used by poets such as Sandu Malo (1523–1623) and Durasa Adha (1538–1651).

Jina-charita (late 13th; Pali) of Medhamkara: poetical work of about 500 verses dealing with the life of Buddha. The work is based chiefly on *Jataka-nidananidhi* and bears the influence of *Buddha-charita* of Ashwaghosa, also of Kalidasa.

Tr. C. Duroiselle, Rangoon, 1960.

Jinadatta chariu (*c*1220; Apabhramsha) of Pandit Lakhu or Lakkhan: biographical account of Jinadatta in 11 'sandhi' sections.

Jinadatta Suri (1075–1154): Jain scholar and poet in Prakrit/Apabhramsha. He wrote *Upadesha-rasayana-rasa*, a didactic poem in Prakrit; Kalaswarupakulakam, another didactic poem in 32 verses in Apabhramsha; *Cachhari*, a poem in Prakrit written in honour of his teacher Jinavallabha Suri. The poet was a contemporary of Hemachandra.

Jina-dharma-pratibodha of Somaprabha: same as *Kumarapala-pratibodha*.

Jina-harsha (17th/18th): name of at least two Jain poets who may have been contemporaries and composed in Gujarati/Rajasthani. Among their works are more than 30 'rasa'-kavya poems such as *Shukaraja rasa, Shripal Raj-no rasa, Jambuswami rasa*, etc; many narrative poems such as *Vidyavilas chaupai, Mrigaputra chaupai, Matsyendra chaupai*, etc; about 400 short poems in various traditional forms like 'stavana', 'sajjhaya', 'saleke', etc.

Jina-prabha Suri (14th): Jain sant poet in Sanskrit; author of *Chatur-*

vimshati-Jinastuti which deals with the lives of 24 Jinas. Among his other works are the long poem *Dvyashraya kavya* on the life of Shrenika; a commentary on *Vidagdha-mukha-mandana* by Dharmadasa; another commentary on *Bhayahara-stotra* by Manatunga. It is believed he visited the court of Muhammad-bin-Tughlaq in Delhi in 1328 and was duly honoured there.

Jinasena (late 8th): poet in Sanskrit; author of Harivamsha-purana, a work based on *Mahabharata*. As mentioned by the poet in his concluding verses, the poem was completed in A.D. 783.

Jinasena (9th): poet in Sanskrit who was a contemporary and friend of Rashtrakuta king Amoghavarsha. He wrote *Adi-purana*, which deals with the life of Rishabha, the first tirthankara; *Parshvabhyudaya*, about the 23rd, Parshvanatha.

Jinendra-buddhi (early 8th): Bouddha grammarian of Sanskrit from Bengal; author of the earliest known commentary on *Kashika* of Jayaditya and Vamana. This work, *Kashika-vivarana-panchika*, is also known as *Kashika-nyasa* or more briefly, *Panchika* or *Nyasa*.

Jineshwara Suri (11th): Jain writer of stories in Prakrit; author of *Kahanya-kosha*, also called *Kathanka-kosha* or *Kathakosha-prakarana*, a collection of religious stories.

Jiva Goswamin (late 16th): Bangla Vaisnav poet and scholar of Sanskrit; brother of Rupa Goswamin and Sanatan Goswamin; settled in Bridavan. Among his kavya works in Sanskrit are *Gopala-champu, Samkalpa-kalpadruma, Madhava-Nahotsava* and *Gopala-birudavali*; also composed many works on theology, philosophy, aesthetics and ritual, all associated with matters of Vaishnav faith.

Jivadevacharya (15th/16th): poet and playwright in Sanskrit. Also known as Bhiyidevacharya, he was a minister and guru of Orissa ruler Prataprudra Deva. He wrote *Bhakti-bhagvata*, a mahakavya work based on the tenth book of *Shrimad Bhagavat; Bhakti-vaibhava*, an allegorical play; *Utsahavati*, another play drawing upon a *Mahabharata* episode.

Jivaka-chintamani (late 9th/early 10th; Tamil) of Tiruttakka Tevar: one of the five major kappiyam, this is a long poem about the prince Jivaka, edifying love and religiosity. Probably modelled on the Sanskrit *Kshatra-churamani*, the work introduced the kavya form of Sanskrit to Tamil literature, which was adopted later by authors like Kamban and Sekkilar. It also employed the viruttam metre for the first time in a work of this nature; similies and phrasing used here would be imitated by many later poets. Divided into 13 'ilambakam' (sections specially devised here), the work consists of 3147 verses. There are many commentaries on it, the best of which is one by Nachhinarkkiniyar.

Jivan Jha (1848–1912): playwright in Maithili from Mandar village in Madhubani district; went to Banaras for higher studies and worked for the rest of his life as treasury officer in the Ramnagar state. His plays are *Sundar-samyoga* (1904), *Maithili-sattaka* (1906), *Narmada-sagar-sattaka* (1906), *Punarjanma* or *Samavati-punarijanm* (1920). He introduced changes in the plot structure of Maithili plays, also in their stage presentation.

Jivani (Hindi): term for biography, also found in other Indian languages.

Jnana-dip (1619; Hindi) of Shaikh Navi: kavya work of Sufi inspiration. It tells of the romance between king Jnandip and queen Devjani. The work is in Brajbhasa.

Jnana-das (mid-16C): poet in Bangla; contemporary of Gobinda-das and Balaram-das; disciple of Nityanand. He occupies an important place in Vaishnav padavali literature of the period following Shri Chaitanya's departure. He composed in Bangla as well as in Brajbuli.

Jnanappana (?17th; Malayalam) of Poontanam: a philosophical poem, of 360 lines, occasioned by the loss of the poet's only child.

Jnana-ratnavali (early 18th; Panjabi) of Mani Singh: an important version of the original janamsakhi.

Jnana-sambandhar: also known as Tiru 'jnana' sambandhar; see Sambandhar.

Jnana-vimal Suri (1638–1726): poet in Gujarati and scholar of Sanskrit. He composed many 'rasa' poems such as *Jambu-rasa* (1682), *Chand-Kevali-rasa* (1714), *Rohini rasa* (1720), etc. He also wrote several 'balavabodha' works in prose.

Jnaneshwar (Dnyaneshwar) (1271–93): sant poet and earliest major author in Marathi. Born at Alandi (near Pune), he completed writing *Bhavartha-dipika* at a relatively young age; went to Banaras with this work and engaged in learned discussions there with scholars and priests. On his return, he propagated his ideas of equality and drew a growing number of followers; adopted the god Vitthal (a form of Vishnu), whose temple is at Pandharpur, as his personal deity. The annual pilgrimage to Pandharpur was instituted by him, and the custom continues today. He also composed a number of devotional songs and prayers, and another philosophical work, *Amritanubhava*. After writing this he believed he had completed his life's mission and took 'samadhi' at Alandi, his birthplace. He is supposed to have been only 22 years old then.

Jnaneshwari (Dnyaneshwari): The popular name of Jnaneshwar's great work, *Bhavartha-dipika*.

Jodhraj (late 17th/early 18th): poet in Hindi; author of *Hammir-raso*. Though he was a Ritikal poet, Jodhraj wrote a considerable amount of 'vir-rasa' exemplifying verse. His patron was Raja Chandraman, the local chief of Nivagarh or Nimrana near Alwar in Rajasthan.

Joga (Maithili): class of songs sung to the bridegroom or lover in order to bind him to the bride or beloved.

Jonaraja (15th): scholar of Sanskrit from Kashmir, also poet. He wrote the first continuation of Kalhana's *Rajatarangini*, bringing the account down to his own time, but could not complete it. He also wrote commentaries on Kiratarjuniya of Bhavani, Prithviraja-vijaya of Jayanaka, and Shrikantha-charita of Mankhaka.

Joygopal Tarkalankar (1775–1846): scholar of Sanskrit from Bengal, whose abiding interest was in ridding Bangla of gross rusticity as well as of Perso-Arabic influence. For this purpose he revised famous works in Bangla like the *Krittibas Ramayan*, the *Kashiram Mahabharata* and Mukundaram's *Chandi*; these were published from Serampore where he worked under William Carey. Among his other works are *Shikshasara* (1818), for the education of children; *Bilwamangal*, a collection of shlokas in Sanskrit (along with their Bangla translation); *Patrer dhara* (1821), on letter writing; *Persian and Bengali Dictionary* (1838); *Bengali Dictionary* (1838). He also edited the journal *Samachar darpan* from 1818 to 1823.

Jur-at [Sheikh Qalandar Baksh; real name Yahya Oman (d. 1810)]: poet in Urdu; born in Delhi but moved to Bareli while still a boy and served Nawab Hafiz Rahmat Khan; later moved to Faizabad, finally to Lakhnau in 1800 and joined the court of Nawab Suleman Shikoh. Though not well-educated, Jurat was an unusually talented poet. One diwan collection is available containing many ghazals, stray verses and two marsiya poems. He wrote two masnavi works, of which *Husno-ishk* is better known; this tells of the romance between Khwaja Hasan and a prostitute named Bakshi.

Jyotipant Mahabhagavat (d. 1788): poet in Marathi; fought in the 3rd Battle of Panipat. He wrote a verse commentary on *Shrimad Bhagavat* using mainly abhang and ovi metres; also wrote many short poems. He was a devotee of Vitthal; had vowed to build one thousand temples to his god and is said to have built about 750 before he died.

Jyotirindranath Thakur (1849–1925): playwright in Bangla: and a man of many parts; an older brother of Rabindranath. He was a good actor and opened a theatre at his home in Patthuriaghata; his plays were written mainly for enactment here. These are *Kinchit jalajog* (1872), *Purubikram natak* (1874), *Sarojini ba chitorakraman natak* (1875), *Eman karma ar korbo na* (1877; revised as *Alik babu*, 1900), *Ashrumati* (1879), *Manmoi* (1880), *Swapnamoi natak* (1882), *Hitey biparit* (1896), *Basanta lila* (1900), *Dhyanbhanga* (1900).

Jyotishwar Thakur (*c*1280–1340): earliest writer of Maithili, generally called 'Kavi-sekhar'; describes himself in one of his works as 'Kavisekhara-acharya'. A Vedic priest, scholar and musician, he knew many languages and was a high official in the court of Karnat king Harisimha Deva (*c*1296–1324); his patron was Ganeswar, one of the king's ministers. He was probably a contemporary of Vidyapati's grandfather, Dhireswar Thakur. He composed in Sanskrit (the plays *Panchasayaka, Dhurttasamagama*) as well as in Maithili (the prose encyclopaedia, *Varnaratnakara*); his fame rests on the latter, but he also prepared an abbreviated Maithili version of *Dhurtta-samagama*. His place in the history of Maithili literature was unknown until the discovery of the manuscript of *Varna-ratnakara* in Nepal during 1885–90 by Pandit Haraparsad Shastri.

K

Kabbigara Kava (*c*1200; Kannada) of Andayya: a champu work in 272 stanzas. It tells the story of king Karuvilla who fights with Shiva in order to rescue Chandra, a follower of the king abducted by Shiva. On being cursed by Shiva, the king is separated from his wife Ichegarthi and becomes ruler of another kingdom. Eventually, when an apsara reveals his past to him, he is released from the curse and is reunited with his wife. The poet called the work "Kavanegellam"; he was probably in the court of a Kadamba king. He declared that while all his predecessors made excessive use of Sanskrit words, he had composed this poem as a 'Kabbigara kava' (one who composed a poem in pure Kannada). According to some scholars, Andayya has celebrated here the victory of Kadamba king Kamdeva over Hoysala king Vir Ballala; historical events tally in many places with episodes in the narrative.

Kabi Karna (17th): poet in Oriya; not much is known about his life and this was probably an assumed name. He composed 16 'pala' poems which describe how the local deity Satyanarayan (a Hindu version of the Muslim Satyapir) comes to the rescue of people in times of distress. The works are known collectively as "Sholopala", though each "pala" tells a different story. Kabi Karna introduced the pala form into Oriya from Bangla; the poems use a large number of Bangla words as well.

Kabir (Kabir) Das (*c*1399–*c*1518): sant-poet in Hindi and source of inspiration of the Kabirpanthi sect; traditionally credited with an abnormally long life. According to legend he was born to a brahman widow of Kashi who abandoned the infant near a pond in Lahartara; was picked up by a Muslim weaver named Niru. He and his wife Nimi had no children and brought Kabir up as their own son. Though Kabir married when he came of age (wife's name Loi, who bore him a son Kamal and daughter Kamali), Kabir adopted Ramanand as his guru and preached his own unique faith in and around Kashi even while he practised his profession as weaver. He probably spoke Bhojpuri at home, but his compositions later became available in a mixed language popularly known as 'Saddukada boli' (speech of holy persons). He himself called his speech 'Purabi', but it contains elements of Farsi, Panjabi, Rajasthani, Khariboli, Avadhi and Brajbhasa. He has been credited with a large number of works, all in verse, among which *Bijak* is considered authentic, also the large number of poems included in *Adi-Granth*. His poems are generally doha compositions, and his padas are set for singing in different ragas. He condemned all social discrimination, especially by creed or caste, and had a following which consisted of Hindus as well as Muslims. When he died, in Magahar village, Hindus wanted to claim his body for cremation and Muslims claimed it for burial. According to legend, when the shroud was removed, only some flowers were found.

Kabir granthavali (Hindi): the authenticated collection of Kabir's poems, first published in 1930 by Nagari Pracharini Sabha, edited by Shyamsundar Das. This is based on the manuscript which was compiled in 1504 by one Malookdas some years before the death of Kabir. The collection is in three parts: (i) 409 'sakhi' (couplets) in doha metre, grouped under 59 captions; (ii) 403 'pada' composed in different ragas; (iii) 7 'ramainis' of various types, mostly descriptive in content. In the 'parishishta' (appendix), the editor has reproduced verses from *Adi Granth* that are not to be found in the *Granthavali*; this contains 192 sakhi and 222 pada poems.

Kachhayana (?C): grammarian of Pali; author of *Kachhayana-vyakarana* or *Kachhayana-gandha*. Other grammar works attributed to him are *Mahanirutti-gandha, Chulla-nirutti-gandha, Vannaniti-gandha* and *Susandhikappa*. According to Buddhist tradition, he is the same as Mahakachhayana, a disciple of Buddha; according to others, he is the same as Katyayana (3rd century B.C.), author of *Vartika-sutra*; some others place him later than Buddhaghosa (?5th) but earlier than 12th century.

Kachhayana-gandha (?C; Pali) of Kachhayana: the earliest of extant Pali grammatical works. It is also known as *Kachhayana-vyakarana* and is based on earlier works of the Kacchayana school like *Sandhi-kappa* and *Katantra-vyakarana*; author also appears to have utilised *Kashika*, a 7th century commentary on *Ashtadhyayi*. The work is in eight sections and contains about 687 rules. According to some sources, the rules are by Kachhayana, the commentary by Samghanandan, the illustrations by Brahmadatta.

Ed. & trans. F. Mason, *Bib. Ind.*, 1868; S.C. Vidyabhusan, Calcutta, 1901.

Kadam Rao aur Padam (15th; Urdu) of 'Nizami': masnavi poem written in early Dakhni. Beginning with praise to divinity, the work also pays homage to the local ruler Nizam Shah Bahmani. This is probably the first known work in Urdu to contain eulogy of a contemporary ruler. The language used has more words from Hindi than from Arabi or Farsi; also, the influence of Apabhramsha is quite strong.

Kadambari (*c*640; Sanskrit) of Banabhatta: prose romance of the katha type. It narrates the love story of Chandrapida and Kadambari in their present as well as past lives; parallel to this runs the love story of Pundarika and Mahashweta. The introductory portion contains some autobiographical account by the author.

Ed. and Tran. J.N. Chakravarti & P.L. Vaidya, Poona, 1959. Trans. C.M. Ridding, London, 1896; M.R. Kale, Bombay, 1926.

Kadambari (*c*1480; Gujarati) of Bhalan: a verse rendering of the well-known Sanskrit work which is in prose. Balan was so successful that his translation is often regarded as an original work. In it he pioneered the 'akhyana' form in Gujarati literature.

Kadambari-kathasara (10th; Sanskrit) of Abhinanda: a verse summary in eight sections of Banabhatta's prose romance *Kadambari*. Son of Jayantabhatta, the author lived in Kashmir.

Kadaryar or **Qadaryar** [Kadar Baksh 'Kadaryar' (1805/06–50)]: poet in Panjabi. Born into a Jat peasant family of Gujranwala (now in Pakistan), he did not receive much education. Apart from qissa poems like *Puran Bhagat, Raja Rasal, Sohini-Mahiwal, Siharfi Harisingh Nalua*, he also wrote some religious books. By introducing Hindu heroes into the qissa form (which traditionally had Muslim protagonists), he made an innovation which was taken up by some later Hindu poets.

Kadvak (Apabhramsha): term for the sections of a long poem in Apabhramsha.

Kafi (Gujarati): a distinctive form of poetry established by the poet Dhira in late 18th century. In these poems a 'mukhabandha' or opening statement in two lines is followed by three or four stanzas of three lines each which illustrate or substantiate the initial proposition.

Kafi (Panjabi): short poem of six stanzas, generally on attributes of divinity, sometimes on various Sufi beliefs.

Kafiyan (Panjabi): verse in couplet form, generally spoken. As composed by the Sufi sant Bulhe Shah, it grew into the first successful example of Sufi literature in Panjabi.

Kahakoshu (late 11th; Apabhramsha) of Shrichandra: a compendium of stories in verse. It has 53 'sandhi' (chapters) each containing on an average 20 'kadvak' each of which are of 10 to 15 lines. The poet was a Digambara Jain monk.

Kahani (Hindi): short piece of fiction in prose telling a story.

Kahini (Bangla): same as 'kahani' in Hindi.

Kaina baramahi'git (Asamiya): another variety of akhyana'git, dealing with lovelorn women. Among these are *'Chikan Sariyaharar git'*, *'Dubala Santir git'*, *'Jayadhan Baniyar git'*, *'Phulkonwar-ar git'*.

Kakka (Gujarati): a form of didactic poems in which the first letter of each stanza is a letter of the Devanagari alphabhet, and the entire alphabet is covered in sequential order.

Kalahastiswara-mahatmyamu (mid-16th; Telugu) of Dhurjati: kavya work based on *Srikalahastipuranam*. In it Shiva appears in the form of a 'jangam' (devotee of Shiva) and tells Narayanvan ruler Vir Nrisimha Yadav about the significance of Shrikalahasti.

Kalakacharya-kathanaka (10th; Prakrit) of unknown authorship: a work in prose and verse, narrates the initiation of prince Kalaka into Jainism and his elevation to headship of his sect.
Ed.& trans. H. Jacobi, ZDMG, 1880.

Kalakeya vadha (late 17th; Malayalam) of Kottayah Tampuran; Kathakali play in 11 scenes, concluding with Arjuna's killing the asura Kalakeya. Arjuna is visiting devaloka at this time and rescues apsaras like Urvashi who were being carried off by asuras. This play is in two parts, the first part ending with scene 4; the fifth scene is usually omitted.

Kalamekam (late 15th): poet in Tamil. According to tradition he was a brahman serving in the kitchen of the Ranganatha temple at Shrirangam; he fell in love with a devdasi of the Shiva temple in nearby Tiruvanaikka and became a Shaiva because of her. He composed many satirical poems criticising rich people and this made him quite popular. Among his works are *Tiruvanaikkaula, Chettirmadal, Kadal vilasam*; the last is not extant.

Kalampakam (Tamil): the word means a garland made of different flowers; as a literary term it is used for works featured by a variety of forms and content. The first work of this kind was *Nandikkalampakam*; the poet's name is not known but he was a contemporary of Pallava king Nandivarman III.

Kala-nidhi (b.1712): poet of Rambhakti in Hindi; began a translation of Valmiki *Ramayan* into Hindi but completed only three kandas. Among his many works are *Shringarrasa-madhuri, Ramayana suchanika, Navsai, Samasya-purti, Vritta-chandrika*; the last is a treatise on rhyme and metre. His patron was Rao Buddhisingh of Bundi.

Kalapurnodayamu (1550; Telugu) of Pingali Suranna: the earliest known 'prabandha' kavya work in Telugu centred in an original lovestory; for this it used to be condemned as an 'artificial jewel'. The story involves the courtesan Kalabhashini and her lover Manikandhar; describes the various stages of their love relationship. It does not follow any 'shringar-shastra' model but tells the story in a natural setting.

Kalasa (Oriya): also known as 'asabari' in Oriya and 'payar' in Bangla, it is a metre with 14 letters to the line; effectively used in Oriya first by Sarala Dasa, then by Balarama Dasa.

Kalasa-chautisa (12th/13th; Oriya) of Bachha Dasa (or Vatsa Dasa): the earliest extant example of the chautisa form. Seemingly a panegyric to Shiva, it has satirical overtones because the story is about the marriage of decrepit old Shiva to beautiful young Uma. When Shiva first appears as the bridegroom, Uma's mother protests and Uma herself is unwilling. Nothing is known about the author, and there is much controversy about when the work was composed. It is regarded as earlier than Sarala Dasa's *Mahabharata* because there is a reference to it at one place in this work.

Kalavali-narppadu (?C; Tamil) of Poygaiyar: poem in 40 quartrains, describing the battle of Kalumalam and praising the Chola king Kochenkannan who defeated the Chera king Kanaikkal Irumporai in this battle. There are grim descriptions of the battlefield in this poem.

Kala-vilasa (11th; Sanskrit) of Kshemendra: poetical work in ten sections. It is in the form of instructions given by Muladeva to one Chandragupta on various forms a deceit practised by people in different walks of life.

Kalhana (12th): poet and scholar from Kashmir; author of Rajatarangini in Sanskrit. He was the son of a senior court-official under Kashmir ruler Harsha (r. 1049–1101); could have also joined the king's service but chose to live apart and retain his independence in order to write an account of the kings of Kashmir. Rajatarangini was written in 1148–50, during the reign (1127–59) of Raja Jaisingh.

Kali-kirtan (mid-18th; Bangla) of Ramprasad Sen: songs in praise of the goddess Kali. There is no narrative in these lyrics but aspects of the devi's divinity are singled out for worshipful praise.

Kalicharan Upakhyan (18th; Bangla) of Krishnamohan Sharma: a narrative dealing with the life of one Kalicharan Sharma, a brahman by birth who lost caste when he became a trader. He amassed much wealth, took many wives, and was ultimately drowned in the Barak river while returning from a business trip. The work tells us of economic activities of the Kachar valley, also of customs and superstitions of the people who lived there.

Kalidas Trivedi (late 17th): poet in Hindi; is believed to have gone with Aurangzeb on the latter's Golkonda campaign. Among works ascribed to him are *Radha-Madhav milan budh-vinod, Vadhu-vinod* or *Barvadhu-vinod, Janjira-bandh, Kalidas-hajara.*

Kalidasa (?5th): India's greatest poet and playwright; wrote in Sanskrit. He composed two mahakavyas, *Raghuvamsha* and *Kumara-sambhava;* two khanda-kavyas, *Meghaduta* and *Ritu-samhara;* and three plays, *Vikramorvashiya, Malavikagnimitra,* and *Abhijnan-Shakuntala*. Very little is known about his life and his dates are uncertain. According to tradition, he was one of the nine jewels (nava-ratna) at the court of a king who bore the title Vikramaditya; but there were several kings in Central India who had this title. Possibly, the relevant one was the Gupta king Chandragupta II (*c*375–415); or he may have been Kumaragupta I (415–453). It is generally accepted that

Kalidasa lived during the so-called 'golden age' of ancient Indian culture.

Kalika-mangal (Bangla): a type of religious narrative honouring the goddess Kalika (Kali). The story is about how the handsome prince Sundara won the beautiful princess Vidya. Originally a love-story based on Sanskrit works such as *Chaurapanchasika*, the pre-marital meetings of Sundara and Vidya were illicit in nature; to make this acceptable to 16th/17th century society in Bengal, poets introduced the character of Kali, the goddess by whose grace Sundara overcomes all obstacles and marries Vidya.

Kalika-mangal (*c*1670; Bangla) of Krishnaram Das; according to Pranram Chakrabarti, a later poet who used the same story for his poem, Krishnaram's work is the first 'kalika-mangal' kavya in the language.

Kalinga'ttupparani (early 12th; Tamil): of Jayakontar: long poem describing the victorious battle of Kulottonga's general Karunakara Tondaiman, against Anantavarman Choda Ganga, which resulted in the Chola conquest of Kalinga. Though conventional in language and hyperbolic in its eulogies, it is one of the few historical poems in Tamil; as a 'parani', the first and the best of its kind Jayakontar was a court poet of Kulottonga I; a native of Dipankundi village, he also wrote a short poem on his native place.

Kaliprasanna Singha (1840–70): prose writer in Bangla. His work *Hutom pyanchar naksa* (1862) is perhaps the earliest narrative in Bangla dealing with a contemporary subject. Also, he translated *Mahabharata* into simple Bangla prose during 1860–66. He belonged to a rich family and used his wealth in the service of literature. Thus, he was among the earliest to felicitate the poet Maikel Madhusudan; on the other hand, when Rev. Long was fined Rs.1000 for Nildarpan, Kaliprasanna paid this fine. Within his short life, he made a name for himself as a man of letters.

Kalittogai (?C; Tamil) of Nallanduvanar: one of the *Ettuttogai* collections. Consisting of 150 longer love poems, it dwells on the theme of love but there are also many moral maxims. The poets represented here are Perunkadungo, Kapilar, Marudan Ilanganar, Chola Nattutiran, and Nallanduvanar; the last named is said to have compiled this anthology and written an invocation to Shiva for it.

Kalladam (10th/11th; Tamil) of Kalladanar: a poetical work which describes the divine sport of Shiva; also celebrates the glories of Madurai. It consists of 100 'ahavarpa' stanzas in agaval metre. Kalladanar is also the name of a Sangam poet.

Kalladanar or **Kalladar**: several poets in Tamil have had this name. The earliest is a Sangam poet. Another, the author of *Kalladam*, probably belongs to 9th or 10th; he may be the same as one Kallada Deva Nayanar whose poems were included in *Tirukkannappar Maram.* A third Kalladar, grammarian and commentator on *Tolkp*, probably belongs to 13th or 14th.

Kalpa-sutra (?C; Pali) of Bhadrabahu: a Jain work on right behaviour. It combines three texts to make one volume 'Jinacharitra', biographies of Jinas; 'Theravali', list of schools, their branches and institutional heads; 'Samachari', rules for ascetics. According to tradition, these three texts, not contained in the tradition, were added later by Devardhi.
Tr. H. Jacobi, *SBE*, 1894.

Kaluve Vira-raju (late 17th): poet and scholar, also military commander and minister under Mysore ruler Chikkadeva Raya. He knew many languages; composed in Sanskrit, Kannada and Telugu. In the latter language his most important contribution is a prose rendering of *Mahabharata*.

Kalyana saugandhika (late 17th; Malayalam) of Kottayah Tampuran: Kathakali play in five scenes which show how Bhima located the saugandhika flower and brought it back for Draupadi.

Kalyan-malla (16th): poet in Sanskrit; author of *Anangaranga*, a work on erotics which is said to have been composed for Lad Khan, son of Ahmad Khan, a Lodi ruler of Avadh.

Kama-dahanam (late 15th; Malayalam) of unknown author: a re-telling of Kalidasa's *Kumarasambhavam.*

Kamasutra (?3rd; Sanskrit) ascribed to Vatsyayana: earliest extant work in erotics. Consisting of 1250 verses, it is divided section-wise into seven 'ladikarana', 14 'prakarana' and 36 'adhyaya'. The work enumerates the 64 'kala' (arts) particularly to be learnt by women; it also describes in detail the life of a 'nagaraka' (man about town).
Tr. R.W. Burton, London, 1883; K.R. Iyengar, Lahore, 1921.

Kamba Ramayanam (?12th; Tamil) of Kamban: an adaptation of *Ramayana* in six kandas, upto Rama's return to Ayodhya and coronation. Composed in 'viruttam' metre, the work runs to about 12,000 verses of four lines each. Kamban has generally followed Valmiki's story, but departed from it wherever he felt the need to do so and added episodes of his own creation. The most important departure is that Rama is regarded throughout as an 'avatar'; in fact, the work was originally designated *Ramavataram*. Later it also came to be known as *Ramakathai*.

Kamban (?12th): poet in Tamil; according to some scholars, the greatest in this language; adapted *Ramayana* in to Tamil and made an original poem based on Valmiki's work. Very little is known about his life, hence many unverifiable details have been proposed. Born probably in Tiruvalundur village near Mayavaram, he probably died in Nattarasankottai in Ramnad district; may have belonged to the Uvachar community; was probably befriended and helped by Sadaiyappa Mudaliar, a philanthropist of Velala; he is said to have been associated with the court of Chola king Kulottonga II, later with Kakatiya prince Prataparudra I. He appears to have had difficulty in getting his *Ramayana* accepted by the Vaishnavs of Srirangam; to please them he wrote *Saraswati andadi,* also *Salagopar andadi.* But his continuing fame rests on *Kamba Ramayanam.* His popular name is a contraction of Ekamban or Ekambaran.

Kameshwara Kavi (1623–70): poet and scholar in Telugu; author of *Dhenu-mahatmyamu* and *Satyabhama-santvanamu.*

Kamsa-narayana (?C): last of the Oinivar kings of Mithila; a lyric poet in Mithila himself and a patron of poets like Govinda, Kashinath, Ramanath, Sridhar.

Kamsa-narayana Padavali (?C; Mithila): of verse anthology containing the padas of 27 poets, including Vidyapati.

Kamsa-vadha (?C; Sanskrit): a play mentioned by Patanjali in his *Mahabhashya*, but never recovered. No authorship has yet been attributed.

Kamsa-vaho (mid-18th; Prakrit) of Ramapanivada: a kavya work consisting of 233 verses in four 'sarga', written partly in 'matra-vritta' metre and partly in 'varna-vritta' metre. In addition to the slaying of Kamsa, the poet gives a biography of Shri Krishna in the fourth sarga.

The work is modelled on Magha's *Shishupal-vadha* and there are various similarities between the poems. The language is mainly Maharashtri Prakrit but the poet has also used Shauraseni.

Kana Haridatta (?12th/13th): poet in Bangla; supposed to be the earliest composer of Manasa-mangal poems. 'Kana' in his name refers to some eye-defect.

Kanaka-das (16th): poet and songwriter in Kannada. Nothing definite is known about his life. But it is believed he was born in Barh village of Dharwar district in North Karnataka and was a devotee of the god Adikeshav of Kaginell village. He became a professional soldier; after some battle he gave up this profession, distributed all his belongings among the poor, and went away to Vijayanagar in search of a spiritual guide; found Vyasatirtha. He composed hundreds of verses for songs; also wrote *Haribhaktisar, Ramdhyan-charitre, Nalacharitre, Mohantarangine.*

Kanaka-manjari (late 17th; Hindi) of Kashiram: a verse romance which narrates the unsuccessful wooing of Kanakamanjari, wife of Dhandhir Sah, by the prince of Ratnapur when her husband had gone abroad. The poet (b. 1663) enjoyed the patronage of Nizamat Khan, a subehdar under Aurangzeb.

Kanakamara Muni (11th): poet in Apabhramsha; author of *Karakanda-chariu*. He was the pupil of Mangaladeva or Buddha Mangaladeva; his patron was a minister of king Vijayapala, ruler perhaps of Bundelkhand.

Kanchi-Kaveri (?C; Oriya) of Maguni Dasa: romantic poem with a seeming historical background, giving an account of king Purushottam Deva and princess Padmavati.

Kanchi-kaveri (late 17th; Oriya) of Purushottama Dasa: long narrative poem describing the conquest of Kanchi (in 1st century A.D.) by Gajapati king Purushottama Deva. The work celebrates the supremacy of the god Jagannath who is the real monarch of Orissa and whose power is made manifest through his agents, the Gajapati rulers. In naming the poem after a place (Kanchi) and a river (Kaveri), the poet breaks significantly with the tradition of naming kavyas after the main characters.

Kanda-puranam (late 11th/early 12th; Tamil) of Kachiyappa Sivachariar: an elaborate verse work of 10,346 stanzas in seven kandas about the god Murugan. It is based on *Srikalahastipuranam* but the poet has introduced original material at many places. According to some scholars Kachiyappa wrote the first six kandas and the seventh was written by Koneriyappa Mudaliar, probably a disciple of Kachiyappa.

Kandarpa-chudamani (1577; Sanskrit) of Virabhadra: verse work on erotics. As stated by the author, it is an amplified exposition of *Kamasutra*.

Kandikai (Tamil): term for short commentary on an important text.

Kanhad-de prabandh (*c*1450; Gujarathi) of Padmanabh: historical 'vir-charit' kavya about Kanha (Krishnadev Chauhan), ruler of Jalor. When Alauddin Khalji invaded Gujarat, Krishnadev beat back the attack the first time; a subsequent attack by Alauddin's commander Alaf Khan was also resisted; but the third attack, led by Alauddin, succeeded. The poem describes the heroism of Krishnadev and his son Viramdev. To the historical episode the poet has added the story of an imaginary romance between Viramdev and Firoza, the daughter of Alauddin. The text of the work, preserved almost in the original, is an invaluable document for the study of a Modern Indian Language emerging out of Apabhramsha. Also, the historical material is fairly reliable.

Kanhapa (?C): perhaps the most eminent among the 84 siddhas, He is said to have authored about 80 texts of Apabhramsha. Among these are *Kanhapada gitika* and *Dohakosh*. He was born into a brahman family of Karnataka, hence came to be called 'Karnapa'; because he was dark-skinned he was called 'Krishnapa' or 'Kanhapa'.

Kanhopatra (15th): woman poet in Marathi from Mangalved village, near Bidar. Her mother Shyama was a prostitute. Repelled by the realities of her mother's life, Kanhopatra withdrew from society and lived in Pandharpur. Here she wrote many ovi poems devoted to Vitthal and spent the rest of her life in group singing and dancing at this temple. Twenty three of her verses have been included in the well-known anthology of Marathi sant poetry, *Sakal sant-gatha*.

Kankanti Paparaju (18th): poet and dramatist in Telugu; author of an *Uttara-Ramayana* in champu style; also of a drama, *Vishnumaya-vilasa*.

Kankhowa (16th; Asamiya) of Shridhar Kandali: two long poems in 'dulari' verse about two small incidents on the child Krishna's life. In the first, one evening Jashoda is trying to put the child to sleep and he resists; then she tells him the story of demon Kankhowa, an ear-eater. In the second, on the following morning Jashoda tries to wake the child up, telling him that all the other cowherd boys have gone to the fields. Both poems are written in the form of lullabies, and mothers in Assam sing them even today.

Kannada (or Canarese, also Kanarese in British usage): main language of the state of Karnataka (earlier called Mysore) in South India, spoken by about 44 million persons. The speakers are known as Kannadigas. Kannada belongs to the Dravidian family of languages and is closest to Tamil; but its script is nearest to that of Telugu. The antiquity of the language is proved by its presence in old inscriptions dating back to 5th century A.D.

Kannada Bhagavat (16th; Kannada) of disputed authorship: verse rendering of *Bhagavatapuranam* in bhamini-shatpadi metre, running to about 12 thousand verses. Some scholars hold it was written by one Chatu Vitthalnath, others that it was a group effort involving five sages of which Vitthalnath was one. The others were Nityatmanath, Vidyanath, Sadanandayogi and Nirvannath. Vitthalnath was responsible for putting their work together.

Kannada Bhagavat Gita (*c*1650; Kannada) of Nagaras: verse rendering of *Bhagavat Gita* in 'bhamini-shatpadi' metre. This is the first Kannada version of *Bhagavat Gita*.

Kannada Kuvalayanand (*c*1750; Kannada) of Jayagounda: verse work on poetics written in shatpadi metre. In it the author made a conscious departure from Sanskrit models in the style and structure of his treatise.

Kannassa Ramayanam (late 14th/early 15th; Malayalam): a retelling of *Ramayana*, mainly by Rama Panikker. It is the major work in the *Kannassan Pattukkul* canon.

Kannassan Pattukkal (14th/15th; Malayalam): a collection of poems composed by a family of poets.

Kannassan poets (Malayalam): also known as the Niranam poets, they were a group of three—Madhava Panikker, Sankara Panikker, Rama Panikker—of which possibly the first two were brothers and the third a nephew. They belonged to the late 14th/early 15th; took the name 'Kannassan' from an ancestor called Karunesan; lived first at Niranam village in Tiruvilla taluka of the Travancore region, then at Malayinkinzh in South Kerala near Tiruvananthapuram. Rama Panikker is the most eminent poet in the group; his main works are *Ramayana, Bhagavata, Shivaratri mahatmya*, and *Bharata*.

Kanti (early 12th): the first woman poet of Kannada. However, there is much dispute about whether she existed at all.

Kantthir Banarasaraj Vijay (*c*1650; Kannada) of Govinda Vaidya: a vir-kavya written in raso style about Mysore ruler Kanthir Banarasaraj Wodyer. Composed in sangatya metre, it is the first historical poem in Kannada. Some scholars hold that it was written not by Govinda but by Bharatikanj; according to another opinion, Bharatikanj was the first reciter of the poem.

Kanuparti Abbayamatya (mid-18th) poet in Telugu: author of two prabandha works, *Aniruddha-charitramu* and *Kaviraj-manoranjanamu*. The latter is also known as *Pururavas-charitramu*.

Kapilar (?C): poet in Tamil; one of the four great poets of the Third Sangam (the others being Nakkirar, Paranar, Auvaiyar), perhaps the greatest of them all. His poems are included in all the Third Sangam anthologies; he was a specialist in the 'kurinjittinai' variety of aham poetry.

Kapphin-abhyudaya (*c*870; Sanskrit) of Shivaswamin: a kavya work in 20 'sarga'. It tells the story of Kapphina, a king of South India, who invades the kingdom of Shravasti, then ruled by Prasenjit; subsequently, Kapphina is converted to Buddhism through a miracle. Shivaswamin, son of Arkaswamin, was a court-poet of Kashmir ruler Avantivarman (r. 855–84).

Kappiyam (Tamil): term of a long poem. There are five major kappiyam in the language; *Chintamani, Silappadikaram, Manimekalai, Valaiyapati, Kundalakesi*.

Karaikkal Ammiyar (5th): Shaiva woman sant-poet in Tamil, whose work forms the 11th book of *Tirumurai*. It consists of three poems that amount to 143 verses; the first and most important poem of 100 verses in venba metre states the essence of Advaita philosophy. She was born to a deeply religious merchant family of the coastal town of Karaikkal. Given the name of Punitvati, she was married in due course to a young merchant named

Paramadatta. According to legend, one day he discovered by chance that she had miraculous powers; frightened at this, he left Karaikkal and, after conducting successful trade elsewhere, settled in Madurai and married again. A daughter was born to him and he named her Punitvati after his first wife. Afterwards, when he met the first Punitvati, he prostrated himself before her. At this, she decided to give up her life.

Karakanda-chariu (*c*1060; Apabhramsha) of Kanakamara Muni: poem in ten sections. The main story is about king Dadhivahana of Champa who installed his son Karakanda on the throne and became an ascetic; later Karakanda also took to asceticism. Among subsidiary stories is the one of Naravahanadatta and Madanamanjusa found in *Brihatkatha*.
Tr. H.L. Jain, Berar, 1934.

Karanidana (1693–1783): poet in Rajasthani; belonged to Mewar and settled in Jodhpur where he won the patronage of Maharaja Abhayasimha. His *Suraj-prakash* is an account of the rulers of Mewar up to Abhayasimha; *Vidad shinagar* is a condensation of the same work. Pleased with the poem, the king nominated him court-poet and donated a village to him. But the next ruler, Bakhatsimha, was hostile to him and confiscated the village. He went away to Kishangarh and lived there for the rest of his life.

Karbal-katha (1732; Urdu) of Fazl Ali Fazli: prose rendering of the famous Farsi text *Rozatul sohda* which is read out during Muharram. It used to be regretted that those who did not know Farsi were denied the merit to be earned by listening to this text with understanding. Whereupon Fazli undertook to produce a prose version in simple Urdu. It is one of the earliest texts in Urdu written in North India; in it the language of Delhi was put to literary use for the first time.

Karika (Sanskrit): term for any metrical composition on a topic or doctrine; often used for a short exposition of topics or doctrines that have been stated earlier in a 'sutra'.

Karna-bhara (?C; Sanskrit) of Bhasa: one-act play based on a *Mahabharata* episode relating to Karna.

Karna-sundari (early 12th; Sanskrit) of Bilhana: play in four acts. It was composed in the honour of Karnadeva Trailokyamalla, Chalukya king of Anhilvad (r. 1064–94), whose marriage with a princess is elaborated as a romantic story.

Karnamritam (late 16th; Malayalam) of Poontanam: a re-telling in 160 quatrains of the first ten sections of *Bhagavatapurana.*

Karnaparya (mid-11th): poet in Kannada. He was mentioned by Durgasingh, author of *Panchatantra*, but the work cited, *Malati-Madhav* (by Karnaparya), has not been recovered.

Karnarappadu (?C Tamil) of unknown authorship: work containing 40 stanzas on the rainy season; main theme is the patient suffering of the lady love at home waiting for the return of her beloved.

Karnataka Bharata Kathamanjari (15th; Kannada) of Kumaravyasa: a retelling of the first ten 'parva' of *Mahabharata*. Also known as Kumaravyasa bharata or Gaduginu bharata (because the author was from Gadag), the work includes some episodes drawn from Pampa's re-telling of *Mahabharata*. There are also a few episodes that may have been invented by the poet or taken from some folk tradition.

Karnataka Bhasha-bhushan (*c*1150; Sanskrit) of Nagavarma II: a grammar of Kannada. The 1150 principles and explanations are in Sanskrit, the examples are drawn from earlier literary works in Kannada.

Karnataka Kadambari (10th; Kannada) of Nagavarma I: a rendering of the Sanskrit *Kadambari* adopted to the champu style.

Karnataka Panchatantram (1030; Kannada) of Durgasimha: a rendering of Vasubhaga's *Panchatantra* in champu form. This is the first translation of this Sanskrit text into any modern Indian language. Vishnusharma's *Panchatantra* was translated into Kannada only in the 19th century.

Karnataka shabdanushasan (*c*1600; Kannada) of Bhatta Akalanka: a grammar of Kannada written on the model of *Ashtadhyayi*.

Karnesh (mid-16th): poet in Hindi and scholar; composed *Karnavaran* and *Shruti-bhusan*. He also wrote a treatise on poetics, *Bhup-bhusan*.

Karpura-manjari (*c*900; Prakrit) of Rajashekhara: play of the 'sattaka' type, often cited as a model for comedies. A love intrigue, it shows how king Chandpala overcomes the objections of his elderly queen Vibhramalekha in order to marry her young cousin Karpuramanjari. Prakrit of various kinds is used in the play—Avanti; Shauraseni; mixed Shauraseni and Maharashtri.

Kartika Tirunal Ramavarma (1724–98): Travancore ruler who encouraged Kathakali and himself composed a number of attakathas. He founded the Kottaram Kathakali Yogam, a palace troupe, and effected many reforms in costume and in acting. He was also responsible for making Kathakali performances a permanent feature of the festivals of the Shri Padmanabhaswami temple at Tiruvanathapuram. In Sanskrit he wrote *Balarama-bharata* which deals with the techniques of classical dance. He succeeded his maternal uncle, Marttandavarma, to the throne in 1758 and ruled until his death.

Kashi-khandamu (*c*1450; Telugu) of Srinathudu: kavya work in praise of the holy city of Kashi.

Kashika-vritti (?6th/7th; Sanskrit) partly of Jayaditya, partly of Vamana: a famous commentary on *Astadhyayi*. The first five books are regarded as Jayaditya's work, the rest as Vamana's.
Tr. L. Renou & Y. Ojihara, Paris, 1960.

Kashiram Das (late 16th/early 17th): poet in Bangla; generally regarded as author of the Bangla *Mahabharata*. Actually, he translated only the first four parvan and the work came to be known as *Pandava-vijaya* or *Bharat panchali*. The remaining parvan were rendered anonymously by sons, nephews and other poets; the latter also made additions to the original story. Kashiram came from a kayastha family of Singi village in Bardhaman district of West Bengal. His work was mainly responsible for making *Mahabharata* known to the common people in Bengal.

Kashmiri: main language of the Kashmir valley and some surrounding areas in the northern-most state of Jammu & Kashmir. Its speakers are also known as Kashmiri. Kashmiri probably originated in a Dardic branch of the Indo-Iranian family of languages but became so overlaid with Sanskrit that it came to be regarded as an Indo-Aryan language which emerged around 1200 A.D. It used to be written in the Sharada script but this was displaced in early 16th century by the Perso-Arabic script.

Kasida (Qasida) (Urdu): poems written in praise of a king or great sage of rich person of some substance.

Kassapa (?C): Bouddha theologian; author of *Moha-vichhedani* or *Vimati-chhedani*. According to *Gandhavamsa*, also wrote *Anagatavamsa* and *Buddhavamsa*. He belonged to Chola country.

Katantra (?1st; Sanskrit) of Sarvavarman: a grammatical work, which appears to be an abridgement of *Astadhyayi*. Originally comprising four books, it omits many rules of Panini, modifies many others and wholly omits the Vedic portion. The work appears with supplements in the Tibetan translation, also in Durgasimha's commentary. It was held in very high esteem in Kashmir and in Bengal, and deeply influenced the Pali grammar of Kachhayana as well as the Dravidian grammarians. Sarvavarman was probably a protege of a Satvahanan king of the Ist century A.D. According to legend, the author had a wager with Gunadhya, and wrote this simplified grammar in order to teach the ignorant king Sanskrit in six months. The work is also known as *Kaumara* or *Katapa*, which acknowledges the belief that it was written with Shiva's divine blessing.

Katav (Marathi): a quick-moving verse metre, suited to narratives; innovated by Amrit Raya in early 18th.

Katha (Sanskrit): along with 'akhyayika', this term is used for prose narratives in general. The two terms were differentiated in *Amarakosha* where it is said that while 'katha' is wholly invented, 'akhyayika' has some historical basis. Bana confirmed this when he designated his *Harshacharita* as an akhyayika and *Kadambari* as a katha.

Katha (Hindi): term for prose fiction, borrowed from Sanskrit, Prakrit and Apabhramsha where it was used with the same meaning.

Katha Ahamani or **Katha Ahadanavani** (1470; Rajasthani) of Delhaji: a narrative poem in various metres and meant to be sung in different ragas. It deals with Abhimanyu, one of the heroic characters of *Mahabharata*.

Katha Banasur (Banasur-katha) (?15th; Kashmiri) of Bhattavar: a narrative poem describing the Usha-Aniruddha romance derived from *Harivamsha*, presented within the broader setting of Shri Krishna's slaying of the demon Bana. This is the earliest extant 'paband' or 'kavya-paband' in Kashmiri; earlier ones have been lost. The poet belonged to the court of Zainal Abidin.

Katha Bhagavata (1596; Asamiya) of Bhattadeva: prose rendering of *Bhagavatapurana*.

Katha Gita (1598; Asamiya) of Bhattadeva: prose rendering of *Bhagavat Gita*. It is said that the author undertook this work at the behest of his guru Damodar and wrote it mainly for the benefit of women and shudras. He has simplified many philosophic ideas and explained others; he has employed similes drawn from common experience; where necessary he has used Sanskrit words as well as words from Asamiya speech. After Shankardeva, Bhattadeva was the first to use Asamiya prose for literary purpose.

Katha Gurucharita (late 17th/ early 18th; Asamiya) of unknown authorship: a hagiographical work in prose, dealing with the lives of ten or eleven Vaishnav preachers. The main attention is on Shankaradeva and Madhavadeva; others are dealt with cursorily.

Katha-kautuka (1550; Sanskrit) of Shrivara: poetical work in 15 sections. It is a Sanskrit version of the well-known story of Yusuf and Zuleikha as told by Mulla Jami. The work was composed for the benefit of Muhammad Shah, the poet's patron. The author belonged to Kashmir for a time and served in the court of Zainul Abedin.
Tr. C.H. Tawney, London, 1895.

Katha-mahodadhi (1448; Prakrit/Sanskrit) of Somachandra: a work partly in Prakrit prose, partly in Prakrit and Sanskrit verse. It contains 157 moral and religious narratives relating to the Jain faith. Many of the stories are based on *Karpuraprakara* or *Suktavali* of Harisenu.

Katha-Ramayan (18th; Asamiya) of Raghunatha Mahanta: prose version of *Ramayana* wherein several kanda are considerably abridged.

Katha-ratnakara (17th; Sanskrit/Prakrit) of Hemavijaya: a work, mainly in prose, which seeks to introduce and teach the Jain doctrine. It consists of 258 tales, fables and anecdotes, mostly about fools, rogues and artful women, many of which resemble stories of the Sanskrit *Panchatantra*. These are arranged in 10 sections ('taranga') and composed in prose, interspersed with verses in Sanskrit, Maharashtri Prakrit, Apabhramsha., Old Hindi and Old Gujarati.
Tr. J. Hertel, Munich, 1920.

Katha-ratnakosha or **Kaharayanakosa** (1100; Prakrit) of Gunachandra Gani: collection of popular stories in prose as well verse upholding Jain doctrine.

Katha-sarit-sagara (*c*1075; Sanskrit) of Somadeva: the most famous version of *Brihatkatha.* It contains about 24,000 verses in 18 books divided into 124 'taranga' (sections), and is the earliest large collection of stories extant in the world. It is the source of many tales in *The Thousand and One Nights* collection, through which story-ideas were transmitted not only to writers in Persia and Turkey but also further west to Boccacio, Chaucer, La Fontaine and others.

Tr. C.H. Tawney, *Bib. Ind.,* 1880–87; rept. in 10 vols., London, 1924–28.

Katha-vatthu (?C; Pali): fifth section of *Abhidhamma-pitaka* containing, as the title suggests, 'subjects of discourse'. Sri Lanka tradition has ascribed authorship to Moggaliputta Tissa (3rd century B.C), but modern scholars believe that the core of the work originated much earlier and assumed its present form as a result of later additions. The work now has 23 sections, each containing a number of questions and answers. All the questions are direccted against the Buddha and Buddhism; the answers attempt to defend the Buddha and glorify Buddhism.

Tr. S.Z. Aung and Mrs. R. Davids, *PTS*, 1915.

Kathakali: the unique dance-drama form of Kerala, which has a bearing on literature because a literary text ('attakatha') invariably supports the dance performance. Evolving from previous forms like Koodiyattam, Krishnattam and Ramanatham, it reached full development in 17th century and continues till the present day. Two singers, accompanied by four instrumentalists, introduce each sequence; the songs are translated into hand-gestures and body-movements by dancers, who are invariably men.

Kathakosha (Prakrit): collection of stories illustrating Jain doctrine, compiled from time to time by Jain monks for the benefit of adherents. These were composed mainly in Prakrit and Apabhramsha, but also in Sanskrit, Kannada, Tamil, Gujarati and Hindi.

Kathakosha-prakarana or **Kahanayakosh** (1050; Prakrit) of Jineswar Suri: collection of 30 Prakrit gathas, explained in Sanskrit, whose purpose was to show that liberation (moksha) from life may be obtained.

Kathanak (Sanskrit): term for the arrangement by which, in any story-based literary work, the material is presented in a particular sequence and with logical relation in happenings between cause and effect. 'Plot' would probably be the nearest term to 'kathanak' in western poetics.

Kathanor (late 18th): a Christian convert from Kerala and chief disciple of Malpan. He accompanied Malpan on an arduous journey to Rome and wrote a prose account of it in Malayalam, *Vartamana pustakam.* His full name was Paramakkal Thoma Kathanor.

Kathopakathan (1801; Bangla) of William Carey: also known as 'Dialogues' or 'Colloquies', it was prepared as a textbook for teaching/learning Bangla. It depicts the variety in the daily life of Bengalis of the time; it uses Bangla proverbs and sayings; the language is close to what is spoken among Bengalis. On many accounts it is an invaluable book.

Katyayna (?C): grammarian of Sanskrit; author of the supplementary rules to *Ashtadhyayi* known as 'Vartika-sutra'. His other name appears to have been Vararuchi; lived sometime between 500 and 350 B.C. somewhere in South India. Another Katyayna (mentioned by Yajnayvalkya) was one of the 20 original writers of smriti; lived sometime between A.D. 4th and 6th century.

Kaumara or **Kaumara-vyakarana**: another title for *Katantra.*

Kaumudi-mahotsava (?7th; Sanskrit) of Vijaya, a woman playwright. The play is set in Magadha, at the time when the king Sundaravarman is killed in battle against his adopted son Chandasena who has conspired with the Lichhavis to seize power. The real son, Kalyanavarman still a child, is taken away to a safe place by some ministers. Some years later the people of Magadh revolt against the tyranny of Chandasena and Kalyanavarman is set up as king. Meanwhile he has fallen in love with princess Kirtimati, daughter of Surasena king Kirtisena. Their marriage is celebrated after Kalyanvarman has been installed as king.

Kaveri-mahatmyam (1794; Malayalam) of Suppu Menon: long poem on the river Kaveri.

Kavi-chandra Dvija (early 18th) poet in Asamiya; commissioned by Ahom king Shiva Simha (r. 1714–44) and his queen Ambika Devi to translate *Dharma-Purana.* Kavichandra did a selective rendering and introduced into the work many episodes from other puranas.

Kavi-kankana Chandi (*c*1580; Bangla): of Mukundaram Chakrabarti, who was awarded the title of 'Kavikankana'. Also known as *Chandi-kavya*, this is a long poem which glorifies devi Chandi or Durga. It also gives a vivid picture of life in 16th century Bengal. The main importance of the poem lies in the evidence it provides of Bangla advancing from its middle to the modern phase.

Kavi-kanthabharana (11th; Sanskrit) of Kshemendra: work on poetics.

Tr. Suryakanta in his *Ksemendra Studies*, Poona, 1954.

Kavi-karnapura (*c*1560): Bengali poet in Sanskrit; author of the verse works *Chaitanya-charanamrita-kavya, Krishnahnika-kaumudi, Ananda-Brindavana champu*, and one play, *Chaitanya-chandrodaya*. He was born near Naihati (West Bengal) a few years before the death of Shri Caitanya in 1533; his father Shivananda was a disciple of Chaitanya. The poet's real name was Paramananda Sen; he was given the title 'Kavikarnapura'.

Kavikarna-rasayanumu (mid-16th; Telugu) of Nrisimha Kavi: prabandha work in six sections.

Kavikul-kanthavaran (*c*1750; Hindi) of Dulah: work in the riti convention. The poet was a grandson of Kalidas Trivedi, son of Udaynath Trivedi.

Kavi-mala (1655; Hindi) of Tulsi (not to be confused with Tulsidas): a compilation drawn from the works of 75 poets from about 1443 to 1653.

Kavindra (16th): poet in Bangla: a translator of *Mahabharata* whose very brief version is known as *Pandava-vijay* or *Vijay-Pandav katha*. The work was commissioned by Paragal Khan and Chuti Khan, two Muslim governors of Chatgaon.

Kavi-priya (1601; Hindi) of Keshavdas: treatise on poetics, which is said to have turned the direction of Hindi poetry from 'bhakti' towards 'riti'.

Kavi-putra (?C): mentioned as a dramatist by Kalidasa in the prologue to *Malavikagnimitra*.

Kavi-rahasya (?10th; Sanskrit) of Halayudha: a grammatical poem. The work illustrates the modes of formation of the present tense, but also serves as an eulogy of Rashtrakuta ruler Krishna III (r. 940–56).

Kavi-shekhar (16th): pen-name of Devakinandan Simha, poet in Bangla and scholar of Sanskrit. He wrote in Sanskrit *Gopala-charit*, a long poem, and *Gopinath-vijay*, a play, neither of which is extant. His best known work in Bangla is *Gopala-vijay*, based on the Krishna story. He also wrote a number of songs on the same theme and these have been collected as *Gopala-kirtanamrit.*

Kavi-shekhar (18th): poet of Assam who rendered the Vishnu parvan of *Harivamsha* into Asamiya under the patronage of princess Premada, consort of prince Charu Simha, son of king Rajeswar Simha (r. 1751–69).

Kaviraja or **Kavirajasuri**: (late 12th) scholar and poet in Sanskrit from North Karnataka. His own name was Madhavabhatta; the title 'Kaviraja' was bestowed upon him by a local ruler, Kamadeva of Jayantipura (r. 1182–97). His *Raghavapandiya* is the earliest known kavya work in which two stories are told by the same words and lines. He also wrote *Parijata-harana*, based on an episode from *Bhagavata-puranam.*

Kaviraja-marga (*c*850; Kannada) of Shrivijay: work on poetics, also the earliest extant text in the language. At one time its authorship was attributed to Rashtrakuta king Nripatunga Amoghavarsha (r. 814–866), but further research has established that one of his courtiers, Shrivijay, is the author. Written on the model of Dandi's *Kavyadarsha*, this work deals, apart from literary principles, with the Kannada language, Pingal literature, geographical boundaries of Karnataka, etc. Also, most remarkably, it mentions 'dhvani' theory though *Dhvanyaloka* was written more or less at the same time in far away Kashmir.

Kaviranjan Vidyapati (17th): a native of Srikhanda in Bardhaman district of Bengal whose poems in Brajabuli won him the title of 'Chhoto' (lesser) Vidyapati.

Kavisara-ppakarana of Dhammananda: see *Kavisara-tika-nissaya*; also known as *Kavisara-prakaranam.*

Kavi-sara-tika-nissaya (?C; Pali) of Dhammananda: work on metrics. Composed at Hamsavati, the work is a commentary on *Vuttodaya.*

Kavitta (Hindi): a verse metre, widely used most effectively by 'saguna-bhakti' poets at one time.

Kavitta ratnakar (1649; Hindi) of Senapati: a kavya work in five 'tarang' (waves)—namely, 'Shlesh varnan', 'Shringar varnan', 'Ritu varnan', 'Ramayan varnan', and 'Ram rasayan'.

Kavivag bandana (*c*1270; Telugu): treatise on prosody ascribed to Tikkana Yajvi.

Kavya (Sanskrit): general term for

poetry and poetical works. According to one definition, what a 'kavi' (poet) creates is kavya.

Kavya-darsha (early 8th; Sanskrit) of Dandin: work on poetics. It comprises only three chapters, dealing with (i) definition and divisions of kavya, the two 'marga' styles and the ten 'guna' elements; (ii) definition of 'alamkara' and description of 35 of them; (iii) detailed treatment of 'shabdalamkara' (figures based on sound).
Tr. S.K. Belvalkar, Poona, 1924.

Kavyalamkara (7th/8th; Sanskrit) of Bhamaha: work on poetics, which emphasises alamkara (poetical embellishment) as the essential element of kavya. Divided into six chapters, it offers, for the first time in the history of literary theory in Sanskrit, a definite scheme of poetics systematically elaborated and authoritatively established. The work is also known as *Bhamahalamkara*.

Kavyalamkara (?9th; Sanskrit) of Rudrata: work on poetics; consists of 16 chapters and 734 'karika'. Rudrata, also known as Satananda, claims in the work he was the son of Bhatta Vamukha. He probably belonged to Kashmir and lived during 825–900. Some scholars identify him also as Rudrabhatta.

Kavyalamkara-samgraha or Kavyalamkara-sara-samgraha (8th/9th; Sanskrit) of Udbhata: work on poetics. Divided into six 'varga' and consisting of 75 'karika', it deals with 41 alamkara in the treatment of which the author closely follows Bhamaha, but has certain independent views. Some of the illustrative verses were later ascribed to Udbhata himself.

Kavyalamkara-sutra-vritti (8th/9th; Sanskrit) of Vamana: work on poetics, which emphasises 'riti' (arrangement of words) as the essence of poetry. The work is divided into five 'adhikarana', which are sub-divided into 'adhyaya'. It is notable among the early works because it gives a thoughtfully discussed and carefully outlined scheme of poetics. The author, probably from Kashmir, is believed to have been a minister of king Jayapida of Kashmir (r. 779–813).
Tr. G. Jha, Allahabad, 1920.

Kavya-mimamsa (*c*1000; Sanskrit) of Rajshekhara: work on poetics. The extant work, consisting of 18 chapters, appears to be only the first part of a projected larger work; this part deals with 'kavi-rahasya'.

Kavya-nirnay (1746; Hindi) of Bhikhari Das: an early work on poetics in Hindi, next only to Keshav

Das's *Kavipriya* among scholarly works of the Riti-kal period.

Kavya-nushasana (*c*1150; Sanskrit) of Hemachandra: work on poetics, written in the form of sutra and vritti. It covers all topics in poetics and also refers briefly to dramaturgy.

Kavyanushasana (13th; Sanskrit) of Vagbhata: work on poetics, written in the form of sutra and a running commentary. It consists of five chapters and deals in brief with most topics in poetics. There is another work bearing the same title and several other authors with the same name.

Kavya-prakasha (*c*1100; Sanskrit) of Mammata: work on poetics, of which a small portion of the final chapter was left incomplete by the author and was completed later by one Alata or Alaka. Consisting of 10 chapters, it attempts a synthesis of the principles of different doctrines in poetics and finally establishes the principles of 'dhvani'. The work was so highly esteemed that as many as 70 commentaries are known to have been written, chief among which are those by Ruyyaka, Vishwanatha and Nagoji. Tr. G. Jha, Allahabad, 1925.

Kavya-sar (*c*1550; Kannada) of Vidyanand: a compilation of about 1000 verses from various poets, arranged in 45 chapters. Many poets otherwise unknown as well as many works never recovered have been quoted here, making it a valuable document of literary history. It was compiled during the reign of Vijayanagar king Krishnadeva Raya.

Kavya-shastra (Sanskrit): formal study of literature, in which literary principles are formulated and the rules of literary evaluation enunciated. The western term 'poetics' is a fairly close equivalent.

Kavya-valokan (*c*1150; Kannada) of Nagavarma II: work of grammar which draws upon existing literature for its examples.

'Kayem' Chandpuri [Sheik Muhammad (d. 1832)]: poet in Urdu from Chandpur who assumed the name 'Kayem' for composing poetry. Among his more successful works are his ghazal and masnavi compositions.

Kayyarunilai (Tamil): literally means 'helpless state of grief'. This is an ancient poetical form which expresses the grief of relations at the death of a person. An example from Sangam literature is Avvaiyar's *Purunanuru*.

Kayyata (12th): grammarian of

Sanskrit from Kashmir, known for his *Pradipa*, a commentary on *Mahabhashya*. The commentary is also known as *Kaiyatadipa* or *Bhashyapradipa*; it marks further development of the Paninian school. Kayyata, also known as Kaiyata or Kajjata, was according to some scholars the younger brother of Mammata.

Kekavali (late 18th; Marathi) of Moropant: a poetical work in the form of an anguished invocation to god; composed when he was quite old, this is probably Moropant's last work. The title means 'cry of a peacock'.

Keli-kallol (*c*1690; Hindi) of Mohan: verse work in praise of Krishna. The poet was from Mathura and generally wrote Krishna-bhakti poems.

Keralavarma [Kottayam Keralavarma (1645–96)]: poet in Malayalam, also statesman and soldier; better known as Vira Keralavarma. He translated *Ramayana* into Malayalam. His other works are *Patalaramayanam, Banayuddham, Vairagyachandrodayam, Bhishmopadesham*, etc.

Keralavarma Ramayanam (*c*1685; Malayalam) of Keralvarma: a partial rendering of the Valmiki *Ramayana* into simple Malayalam. Keralvarma's work ended with 'Sundarakanda'; some other poet added to it his own rendering of 'Yuddha kanda'.

Keralavarma Valiya Koil Tampuran (1845—1914): poet in Sanskrit and Malayalam, translator from Sanskrit and English into Malayalam, prose-writer in Malayalam. He married into the Travancore royal family and was encouraged to pursue literary and educational activities; later he was charged with treason and imprisoned; released in 1885. He is the author of about 50 poetical works, of which 30 are in Sanskrit. Six of his works in Malayalam are 'attakathas'. An outstanding original work is *Mayura sandesha* (1864), which is modelled on *Meghaduta*. He wrote several textbooks, setting examples of modern Malayalam prose. His *Mahacharitra samgraham* (1895) is a collection of 107 biographical sketches, of which 40 were by him.

Kesabraj Harichandan (late 17th/early 18th): poet in Oriya, also painter. He ruled (1697–1715) over Surangi, an area now in northern Andhra Pradesh, and was a contemporary of Upendra Bhanja. His kavya work *Rasasindhu-sulakhy-*

ana (1710) compares favourably with Upendra's works.

Kesauji [Godaro Kesauji (1573–1679)]: poet and composer of songs in Rajasthani. He belonged to Madiyo village, near Nekha town in Bikaner. He became a disciple of Vilhoji, a poet and social reformer of the region. Among his many compositions are *Katha bal-lila, Katha Udai Atali ka, Katha Sainsai Jokhani ki*, etc.

Keshav-das (1555–1617): poet in Hindi and scholar: son of Kashinath and brother of Balabhadra Mishra; attached to the court of Orchha ruler Ramsingh. Apparently he enjoyed the esteem of Akbar, because he once got exempted a fine of one crore rupees imposed by the emperor; also is supposed to have been paid one lakh by Birbal as reward for a poem. More than his own verse, he is important because his discussions of poetry formulated the poetics on which the riti convention developed in Hindi poetry. Among his works are *Vijnan Gita, Ratan bavani, Jahangir rasa'-chandrika, Virsinghdeva-charit, Rasika-priya, Kavi-priya, Rama-chandrika.* His language is Brajbhasa, with a large admixture of Bundelkhandi speech.

Keshava-koili (14th/15th; Oriya) of Marakanda Dasa: long poem describing the grief of Yashoda when Krishna leaves Brindavan for Mathura. The work combines chautisa and koili patterns. The sentiments of an ageing mother are expressed in simple, everyday speech, with allusions to the everyday habits and customs of Oriya homes.

Keshiraja (end-13th/early 14th): grammarian of Kannada; author of *Shabdamani-darpan.* Other works assigned to him but not yet recovered are *Cholapalak-charitra, Chitramale, Subhadra-haran, Prabodhachandra*, etc. He has said at one place that his father Mallikarjuna had compiled *Sukti-sudharnava*, the earliest known anthology of Kannada poetry.

Keshub Chunder Sen [Kesavchandra Sen (1838–84)]: writer in English and Bangla; better known as leader of the Brahmo Samaj movement. He initiated the publication of *Bamatosini* (1863), a magazine for women, *Sulabhsamachar* (1870–), a weekly for general readers), and *Balak-bandhu* (1878), a magazine for boys.

Ketakadas: see Kshemananda.

Ketana (13th): poet and scholar in Telugu. Contemporary of Tikkana, his full name was Mulaghatik Ketana. All three of his major works are innovations in Telugu. Thus he rendered Dandi's *Dashakumaracharita* into Telugu as a champu work. His *Andhrabhashabhushanamu* is the first grammar of the language to be written in Telugu. His *Vijnaneswariyamu* is a Telugu rendering of Yajnavalkya's reflections along with a translation of the sage's commentary *Mitakshari*.

Keyurbahu-charitramu (13th; Telugu) of Manchanna: a poetical rendering of the Sanskrit work *Viddhasala-bhanjika*.

Khagania (early 17th): woman poet in Hindi; renowned for her 'paheliyan' compositions. She belonged to Unnao (midway between Kanpur and Lakhnau).

Khaliq bari (early 14th): attributed to Amir Khusro: a rhymed vocabulary list of Farsi and Arabi words with their Hindi (Hindvi) equivalents. The authorship of Amir Khusro has been controverted.

Khanda-kavya (Sanskrit): term for a poem of medium length (as compared to a mahakavya) dealing with a particular aspect of life or a significant episode. The term was first used by Vishwanath in *Sahityadarpan*; he probably based it on Abhinavagupta's use of 'khanda-katha' in *Dhvanyalokalochan*.

Khari-boli: the Hindi spoken at one time in Delhi, Meerut and surrounding areas; now practically the same as standard Hindi. It is used more often as a synonym for Hindi prose as written from about 1800 onwards.

Kharoshti: the name of an ancient script which was used in many parts of India. The extant samples date from 4th B.C. to 3rd A.D.

Khatmal baisi (1730; Hindi) of Ali Muhib Khan 'Pritam': said to be the first humorous work in the language. It was composed in 22 different metres.

Khawar-nama (1649; Urdu) of Rustumi: long poem in Dakhni giving the story of Ali, son-in-law of Hazrat Muhammad.

Kheur (Bangla): a form of ribald songs.

K.C. Khilnani [Kauromal Chandanmal Khilnani (1844–1916)]: prose-writer in Sindhi, scholar and educationist; wrote over 50 books, many of which are textbooks on various subjects. He translated Harsha's play in Sanskrit *Ratnavali*; wrote *Pako pahu*, a plea for women's education; biographies of women, *Arya nari charitra*; of devout people, *Bhagata jivinyu*; of Jaidev, *Santa Jaideva jo jivan charitra*. He was the first Sindhi writer to translate Bangla short stories into English.

Khrista purana (1614; Marathi) of Father Thomas Stephens: long poem in 11,032 verses, written in response to a directive (from a conference of bishops in Goa in 1579) that books should be written in local languages for facilitating the propagation of Christianity. The poem is in two parts, the first narrating the history of the Jews, the second narrating the life of Jesus Christ. The author (1549–1619) came to Goa in 1579 and learnt Marathi as well as Konkani; the narrative style of the work shows the influence of Maharashtri sant poets, particularly Jnanadev. This is the first printed book in Marathi, though the script used is Roman; subsequent editions followed in 1649 and 1654.

Khuddaka-nikaya (?C; Pali) Fifth and last 'nikaya' (collection) of *Sutta-pitaka*; sometimes included in *Abhidhamma-pitaka*. The work appears to be a miscellany, comprising some small tracts and large treatises of the Pali canon. These parts must have originated at different periods and in different sects and were later collected into one work. The major portion is in verse; parts are in mixed verse and prose. Important Buddhist kavya works in Pali like *Jataka, Theragatha, Therigatha* etc., are included here. According to Sri Lankan tradition, it comprises 16 works; according to Buddhaghosa, the number is 15; according to Burmese tradition, four more treatises including *Milindapaha* are included.
Tr. Mrs. Rhys Davis, *PTS*, 1931.

Khumman Raso (early 12th; Hindi) attributed to Dalpat Vijay: vir-kavya in Dingal. It gives an account of Chittor rulers Raval Suman II (r. 813–43) to Rana Pratapsingh (16th) and their brave deeds. The text has grown and altered over the centuries. No earlier redaction than a 17th century one is available but the original is generally considered to be an older work than *Prithviraj raso*.

Khush-nama (*c*1490; Urdu) of Shamsul-ushaq: work in Dakhni portraying a girl of 17 who renounces the world and adopts the Sufi path of divine love. In a related following work, *Khush-naqz*, the girl asks mystical questions and the poet answers them.

Khyata (Rajasthani): name for historical prose works. These began to be written from the beginning of 17th century. They are also known by such names as 'vat', 'vigat', 'vamshavali', 'pidhiyavali', 'tattavali', 'hal', 'yad', 'vachanika', 'dadavait', etc.

Kichaka-vadha (?10th; Sanskrit) of Nitivarman: a 'yamaka' kavya, based on a *Mahabharata* episode. The work is in 177 verses, arranged in five sections and yamaka is used in all sections except the third (where the author has employed 'shlesa'). He lived before 11th, probably in some eastern region.

Killippattu (Malayalam): literally 'parrot song'; a style of verse composition on puranic themes. The introductory invocation is always addressed to the sacred parrot of goddess Saraswati.

Kiratarjuniya (early 7th; Sanskrit) of Bharavi: kavya work based on a *Mahabharata* episode. The poet has made some modifications in the original story.

Kirloskar [Balvant Pandurang Kirloskar (1843–83)]: early playwright in Marathi; also fine actor and director. While working as a school teacher in Belgaum, he wrote a play on the life of Shankaracharya entitled *Shankar-digvijaya* but this was hardly noticed. Only after he came to Pune and wrote *Shakuntala* (1880) did he innovate the 'sangit natak' (musical play) form, which became very popular; of his two other plays, *Saubhadra* has an original plot, but *Ramarajya-viyoga* (1882) is based on a *Ramayana* episode.

Kirmira vadha (late 17th; Malayalam) of Kottayath Tampuran: Kathakali play in 13 scenes, concluding with Bhima's killing the demon Kirmira, whose sister Simhika had been disfigured by Sahadeva when she tried to abduct Draupadi. Earlier, Simhika's brother Shardula had attacked Arjuna and was killed by him.

Kirtan (Bangla): a style of singing. Vaishnav lyrics in Bengal, whether in Bangla or Brajabuli, were essentially songs; the second couplet, often containing a shorter verse line, is the refrain; the poet's name occurs in the last line. The peculiar musical style in which these songs are sung is known as kirtan and was developed by Narottam Das towards end-16th. Two lighter styles of kirtan developed in 17th; these absorbed much from folk music.

Kirtana: term used in many Indian languages for religious songs.

Kirtana-ghosa (*c*1550; Asamiya) collection of 'kirtana' poems composed by Shankaradeva and collected at the behest of Madhavadeva.

Kirtaniya (Maithili): form of drama which began with the introduction of Maithili songs in Sanskrit plays and eluminated in lyrical drama predominantly in Mithila, used mainly to propagate Vaishnav faith. The 'ankiya-nat' of Assam and the Maithili drama of Nepal were developments related to kirtaniya.

Kirtti-kaumudi (13th; Sanskrit) of Someshwara: kavya work based on the life and deeds of Vastupala.

Kirtti-lata (late 14th; Maithili) of Vidyapati: narrative poem in Maithili Avahatta on how Virasimha and Kirttisimha (in whose praise the poem was composed) regained the kingdom of Mithila from the Muslim conqueror Asalana. This work of 800 lines uses doha, chaupai, canda and some obsolete Apabhramsha and Prakrit metres; also has some prose passages which offer fine specimens of early Maithili prose. It is divided into four 'pallavas' (leafy branches) or chapters; the framework is a dialogue between a 'bhringa' (bee) and his wife. This is probably Vidyapati's first work.

Kirtti-pataka (early 15th; Maithili) of Vidyapati: eulogy of king Shivasimha, composed in Maithili Avahatta. The manuscript was discovered, along with that of *Kirttilata*, in Nepal by Haraprasad Shastri; but the text is very corrupt and it is difficult to reconstruct any connected sequence. At least two different story-lines have got mixed up in the same manuscript. One appears to deal with the love affairs of one Arjuna Raya, a prince; the other describes the battle between Maharaja Shivasimha and a sultan.

Kisanaji-ro vyanvalo (early 16th; Rajasthani) of Padma Bhagat: popularly known as "Vyanvalo" or "Vivahalo", this narrative poem deals with the episode of Shri Krishna's marriage with Rukmini. The work is also known as *Rukmini-mangal* or *Bada Rukmini-mangal.*

Kisanji (1767–1831): poet in Hindi; attached to the court of Maharana Bhimsingh of Mewar. He generally composed in Dingal. Among his works are *Bhim-vilas* (in praise of his patron) and *Raghuvar-jasa-prakas.*

Kissaye Mahar Afroz va Dilbar (?C; Urdu) of Isvhi Khan: probably a story about Delhi; originally composed in the language of Delhi. The extant manuscript is obviously a copy but bears no date; nor does it indicate the date of composition of the original.

Kittikunju Tankachi (1820–1908): woman poet in Malayalam; composed mainly 'kilippattu', 'tiruvatira' and 'kuratti' songs, also three 'attakatha' works. Born in Vilavahkoda taluka to the poet and composer Irayimman Tampi, Lakshmi Pillai (as she was originally called) was taken as an infant to Tiruvananthapuram; lived there for the rest of her life.

Kizhkkanakku (Tamil): term for a literary piece, short in length.

Kobi (Bangla): a style of poetry which developed towards end-18th and remained popular, especially in the Calcutta area, for a half-century. The kobi compositions were almost always sung by two contesting parties; the first singer would put a question in song; the second would reply and also put his own question; the singer who was unable to reply lost the contest. The theme was generally mythological. Musical instruments permitted as accompaniment were the 'dhol' (small drum) and the 'kamsi' (bell-metal plate). In general use, the word 'kobi' in Bangla means poet.

Kobir ladai (Bangla): literary contest of poets; a corrupted form of poetical contests, where rival poets would seek to pour ridicule upon one another in impromptu, often indecent, verses.

Kobiyal (Bangla): composers of 'kobi' poems, who also sang their own compositions. These were lyrics mainly on the Radha-Krishna theme, but with secular emphasis. These composers flourished during 1780–1830, singing to audiences in Calcutta and its suburbs. The lyrics were of no literary value and have not been preserved. Some of the popular kobiyals were Horu Thakur (1738–1812), Nitai Boiragi (1751–1821), Ram Bosu (1786–1826).

Kochhuni Tampuran (1828–1926): playwright in Malayalam; belonged to a royal family of Kochi. His play *Kalyani* drew attention to outstanding social problems of the time; among other plays are *Uma-vivaham, Madhur-mangalam, Panchali-swayamvaram.* He also wrote poetical works *Goshrisaditya charitam, Pandavodayam, Vanchisvamsam.*

Kodiya-viraham (late 16th; Malayalam) of Mazhamangalam: champu work on a non-puranic theme. It tells of a kshatriya youth Sangitaketu who visits the Pooram *charitam, Pandavodayam, Vanchis-vamsam.*

Kodiya-viraham (late 16th; Malayalam) of Mazhamangalam: champu work on a non-puranic theme. It tells of a kshatriya youth Sangitaketu who visits the Pooram festival at Trichur, where he meets and falls in love with the maiden Shringara-chandrika; they spend some time together as lovers, are then separated by circumstances but are finally reunited in wedlock. This is largely a work of fiction and it has provided opportunity to the poet for portraying contemporary society.

Kohala (?C): authority on music, who wrote in Sanskrit; author of the lost treatises, *Kohala-rahasya* and *Sangitameru*; a fragment of his *Taladhyaya* is extant. He appears to be an immediate disciple of Bharata, and seems to have improved upon *Natya-shastra* in details of classification; cited by later scholars, especially Abhinavagupta, and by commentators on Sharangadeva.

Kohala-rahasya (?C; Sanskrit) of Kohala: treatise on music of which only the 13th chapter has been recovered.

Koili kavya (Oriya): like the duta-kavya convention in Sanskrit poetry, this is an Oriya convention in which poems are addressed to the koili (cuckoo). The earliest example in Oriya literature is also the most famous, *Keshava-koili* of Markanda Dasa.

Koka-sandesham (*c*1400; Malayalam) of unknown poet: a sandesha-kavya in Manipravala, not all of which has been recovered. In it, the hero falls into a swoon; on recovering, he recounts to his beloved a dream in which a spirit took him to South Malabar, from where he sent a message to her through a chakravaka bird.

Konkani: spoken by about 4 million persons, is the main language of Konkan, an area lying along the west coast of India, partly in Maharashtra and partly in Goa. It probably had a Dravidian origin but this has been almost completely overlaid by Sanskrit elements, making modern Konkani an Indo-Aryan language. Though spoken from 10th onwards it was developed as a literary language only in 16th by Christian missionaries.

Konthoujam Labango Singh (1750–1820): writer in Manipuri, also scholar of Sanskrit, attached to the court of Maharaja Bhagyachandra (r. 1763–98). His major work is for Malayalam prose renderings of Sanskrit drama; along with translated texts, there was also elaborate instructions to the actors as well as expository material. The form is said to have derived from earlier forms like Mudiyettu, Tirayattam and Kolan Tullal.

Kooth (Malayalam): the recital accompanying the action of Koodiyattam. The text for both were in Sanskrit but the commentary was often in Malayalam.

Korad Ramchandra Shastri (1816–1900): poet in Telugu and Sanskrit; also wrote a play, *Manjari-Madhuriyamu*, which is probably the first original play in Telugu. Among his other works in Telugu are *Kumarodayamu, Shringar-sudharnavamu, Ramachandra vijayamu*. He translated works in Sanskrit like *Unmatta Raghava, Venisamhara, Uttara Ramacharit*, into Telugu; also wrote prose works in Telugu such as *Rathangdutamu, Nayepradipamu, Parasuram vijayamu*, and helped the development of Telugu prose.

Korada (Panjabi): a popular metrical form.

Koreshi Magan Thakur (17th): Muslim poet of Bengal; author of the Bangla work *Chandravati*, a romance based on Avadhi sources.

Koti Brahmanda-sundari (*c*1700; Oriya) of Upendra Bhanja: regarded as his supreme creation because it demonstrates all his skills as a poet. This original kavya tells the story of Koti Brahmandasundari, daughter of Champa ruler Vishwanandak, and her romance with Pushyaketu, son of Pataliputra ruler Diptasagar, culminating in marriage. Among the more notable reflections of the poet's own times is the picture of administration and state activities, along with his comments on them.

Kottayattu Tampuran (17th): poet in Malayalam, who is credited with establishing the literary credentials of attakatha texts meant for Kathakali performance. He wrote four such texts based on *Mahabharata* episodes—*Baka-vadham, Kalyan-saugandhikam, Kalakeya-vadham, Kirmir-vadham*. He belonged to a minor royal family of north Kerala.

Kovur Kizhar (1 A.D.): poet in Tamil. He was probably a peasant; 16 of his poems have been found in various anthologies. He obtained the patronage of Chola king Nalarkillil and helped to bring about peace between him and another king Nedudkillil.

Krama-dipika (Malayalam): term for treatises giving direction for the performance of Koodiyattam. These works are largely in prose, interspersed with poetry, and use a great deal of folk vocabulary to facilitate popular understanding.

Kramadishwara (13th): grammarian of Sanskrit; author of *Samkshiptasara*, the last chapter of which deals with Prakrit grammar. He was a native of Purvagrama in south Rahr (West Bengal); son of Chakrapani, grandson of Sripati; styled himself 'Vadindra-Chakrachudamani'.

Kridabiramamu (15th; Telugu): of disputed authorship. Some scholars attributed it to one Vallabharaya of Vinukonda, others to Shrinatha. The work is a 'veedhi' play in which a native of Orugallu, Govinda Mancharan Sarma, who has been abroad on business, returns home and goes around the city with his friend Tittibha Setti to see the famous sights. They end up in the house of a prostitute. The work reflects the life of the people of the time in a part of Andhra Pradesh.

Kripa-nivas (b. 1786): poet in Hindi; author of *Bharana-pachisi, Samay-prabandh, Madhuri-prakash, Janaki-sahasranam, Lagan-pachisi*. He was from Ayodhya and an adherent of Ram-bhakti.

Kripar shasterer artha-bheda (1743; Bangla) of Manoel da Assumpcaon: first published in Roman characters from Lisbon, entitled *Crepar Xastrer Orth-bhed*. The work is the translation of a catechism of the Catholic faith, written in Bangla of the Dhaka dialect; provides specimen of early Bangla prose. It was later transcribed into more standard Bangla. The author was a Portuguese priest, who also wrote a Bangla grammar and compiled a Bangla-Portuguese vocabulary list.

Krishna Lal (late 18th): poet in Panjabi: rendered *Mahabharata* into Hindvi verse in 1748.

Krishna Pillai (1827–1900): poet in Tamil. Born into a peasant family, he was appointed by Bishop Caldwell in the Sayarpuram school near Tirunelveli to teach Tamil; when he was about 30 years old, he converted to Christianity and was named Henry Alfred Krishna Pillai. Thereafter he wrote *Irattchaniyayattirikam*, which is a verse rendering of Bunyan's *The Pilgrim's Progress*. His other writings are also meant to propagate Christianity among Tamil readers.

Krishna Singh (1739–1788): poet in Oriya and scholar of Sanskrit; best known for his literal rendering of *Mahabharata* into Oriya. He was born into the Gharakot raj family of Ganjam district; chose to hand over all administrative duties to a suitable person and devoted himself wholly to the pursuits of religion and literature. He was a Vaishnav.

Krishna-chandrika (*c*1750; Hindi) of Guman Mishra: treatise on Krishna literature, composed in Brajbhasa.

Krishna-charana Pattanayaka (?C): poet in Oriya; composed a *Mahabharata*, also *Vamana-purana* and *Kalki-purana*.

Krishna-das (b. 1496): poet in Hindi; one of the Ashtachhap group and a disciple of Vallabhacharya; author of *Bhramar-git, Prema'tatvanirupan, Jugalman-charit*. He was born a shudra.

Krishna-das (late 18th): a poet of Krishna-bhakti in Hindi; author of *Madhurya-lahari*. He belonged to Mirzapur (Uttar Pradesh).

Krishnadas Kaviraj (early 16th): poet in Bangla; author of *Chaitanya-charitamrita*, which has been for long a source book of Bengali Vaishnav thought and creed. He belonged to Jhamtapur village, in Bardhaman district; brahman by birth, he became a Vaishnav and, after much hardship, settled in Brindavan; wrote his work on Shri Chaitanya when he was over eighty years old. He also composed a long poem in Sanskrit on the Radha-Krishna story, *Govinda-lilamrita.*

Krishnadas Sharma (16th): poet in Konkani; said to have belonged to Kelosi, then a centre for Saraswat brahmans in Goa. Krishnadas used to read and explain the puranas; translated some of them, also long stories from *Ramayana* and *Mahabharata*, into Konkani prose. These were transliterated in Roman by missionaries and preserved in the public library of Braga (Portugal). The Goan scholar Panduranga Pisurlekar found them there and identified their author as Krishnadas Shama.

Krishnadeva Raya: Vijayanagar king who ruled from 1509 to 1530. He was a scholar of Sanskrit, Telugu and Kannada; composed verse in all three languages; author of *Amuktamalyada*, a work in Telugu. He was a great patron of literature; used to organise a literary assembly known as 'Bhuvan-vijaya'; the 'Ashta-diggaja' group of poets was attached to his court.

Krishna-gatha (15th; Malayalam) of Cherusseri: long poem on the Krishna story as found in *Bhagavathapuranam.* It is perhaps the first work entirely in Malayalam where the poet has consciously avoided Tamil and Sanskrit traditions in his diction and metre. Though the theme is puranic, the setting is Kerala; this and the simple language made the poem extremely popular. The popularity of the poem gave the name 'gatha' to the metre employed here. The work is also known as *Krishnappattu.*

Krishna-giti (?C; Malayalam) of Manaveda Raja: a dance-drama, supposed to have been composed under the influence of *Gita-Govinda.*

Krishna'hari Das (early 18th): poet in Bangla; author of long poem on the tradition of Muslim pirs. He belonged to North Bengal.

Krishna'hari Das (end-18th): poet in Bangla; author of a short ballad on how the ryots of an area in North Bengal appealed successfully to the British district collector against the appointment of a zamindar's manager; probably a contemporarry account.

Krishna-janma (*c*1780; Maithili) of Manabodha: long poem in a language which shows the link between the Old Maithili of Vidyapati and modern Maithili. The title is misleading because the work deals also with Krishna's childhood, including the slaying of Kamsa. Unlike Vidyapati's songs on the love of Radha and Krishna, this is a devotional poem based mainly on *Harivamsha* and *Bhagavata-Purana*; also unlike the Vidyapati tradition of songs set to melodies, this is a narrative poem. In some manuscripts, it is titled *Haricharitra.*

Krishna-karnamrita (?9th/15th; Sanskrit) of Lilasuka or Bilvamangala: long devotional poem. The work exists in two recensions; the southern and western manuscripts present a text in three 'aswasa' (sections) of more than 100 verses in each; the eastern or Bengal text contains just one aswasa of 112 verses.

Krishna-keli-mala (mid-18th; Maithili) of Nandipati: kirtaniya play dealing with some events in the life of Shri Krishna.

Krishna-krida (1535; Gujarati) of Keshavdas Rare Kayastha: long poem based on the 10th 'skandha' of *Bhagavata-purana.* It has 3041 stanzas in 40 sections; 107 of the stanzas are in Sanskrit.

Krishna-kumari (1861; Bangla) of Maikel Madhusudhan; historical play dealing with Udaipur ruler Bhimsingh's daughter, Krishnakumari, and her two suitors, Jaisingh and Mansingh. It is the earliest known historical play in Bangla, also the first play in that language with a tragic ending. The story is drawn from Tod's *Annals*.

Krishna Lal (late 18th): poet in Panjabi; rendered *Mahabharata* into Hindvi verse in 1978.

Krishna-Lila' Sukha (13th): Vaishnav poet in Sanskrit and Prakrit, grammarian of Sanskrit; also known as Lilasukha or Bilvamangal. He probably belonged to Kerala but travelled all over the country; stories connect him to other parts of India like Andhra, Bengal, Orissa. His most famous work is the Sanskrit *Krishna-karnamrita*, a collection of poems on Shri Krishna; it is available in a South Indian recension and a Bangla one. He also wrote *Govindabhisheka* in Prakrit, a poetical work which illustrates the rules of Vararuchi's Prakrit grammar, *Prakrita-prakasha*. His works on Sanskrit grammar are *Purushakara, Daiva, Subantasamrajya* and Tinantasamrajya. He also wrote some hymns devoted to Krishna, Shiva, Durga and Ganapati.

Krishna-mangal (16th; Bangla) of Yashoraj Khan (real name Damodar Sen): narrative poem on the Krishna legend; no extant manuscript; existence of the work is known from a quotation in a late-17th century work on Vaishnav rhetoric. This quotation consists of four narrative lines and a short lyric poem, the last couplet of which contains the poet's name and mentions his patron Husain Shah. Yashoraj Khan is presumed to have been an officer of Sultan Husain Shah. The material may be regarded as one of the earliest specimens of modern Bangla lyric poetry and one of the two oldest specimens of Brajabuli songs.

Krishna-vijaya (late 18th; Marathi) of Moropant: a retelling of the Krishna story in verse.

Krishnakamal Goswami (1810–88): writer and producer of jatra plays in Bangla; also a renowned singer of Vaishnav lyrics. Born in Bhajanghat village near Nabadvip town in southern Bengal, he travelled to various places in search of a livelihood before settling in Dhaka. Most of his jatra plays were first performed here. These are *Swapnabilas, Dibyonmad* (popularly known as 'Rai-unmadini'), *Bichitra-bilas, Bharat-milan* and *Gandharva-milan*.

Krishnam-acharyulu (14th): poet in Telugu who innovated 'vachana' composition in this language. He belonged to Simhachal and was probably a later contemporary of Kakatiya king Prataparudra II (r. 1295–1326).

Krishnamohan Sharma (18th): poet in Bangla and a chronicler of Kachar, an area in lower Assam. He composed *Gopichandrer panchali* (1734) and *Kalicharan upakhyan* (1748); in both the subjects belong to Assam though the language is Bangla.

Krishnamurthi Shastri (1790–1840): scholar of Sanskrit and Telugu, also poet. He belonged to Gollepalam village in East Godavari district of Andhra Pradesh; obtained patronage of a zamindar of Ramchandrapuram. While returning from a pilgrimage to Rameshwaram, he was invited to spend some time in Kalahasti and stayed here for 17 years. Among his works in Sanskrit are the long poem *Yakshollasamu,* the play *Madanabhyudayamu*, a *Ramayana* story *Kankana-bandhama*; among his Telugu works are *Sarvakamada parinayamu, Venkatachal mahatmyu, Strinitisastramu.* In collaboration with either Manda Narahari or Kamayya, he translated *Ramcharitmanas* into Telugu; a special feature of the translation was the way he adapted Hindi verse forms like doha and chaupai into Telugu.

Krishnaram Das (late 17th): poet in Bangla. He was born (probably 1656) into a kayastha family of Nimta (or Nimtita) village about four miles north of Calcutta. Of his three well-known poetical works, *Kalikamangal* (?1676) is in praise of Devi and also tells the Vidya-Sundar story; *Shashthi-mangal* narrates a ritual; *Raye-mangal* features a tiger-divinity.

Krishnashastri Chiplunkar (1824–78): versatile writer in Marathi; wrote on poetics, justice, religion and economics; was a teacher, journalist and editor at various times; also translated from English and Sanskrit. Among his works are *Sanskrit bhasha ka samskshipta vyakaran, Arabi bhasha ki saras evam adbhut kahaniya, Sakretiz ka caritra, Arthasastra paribhasha, Padya-ratnavali.*

Krishnattam: a dance-drama form of Kerala which was a precursor of Kathakali. It is supposed to have been innovated by Manaveda Raja who, presumably influenced by *Gita-Govinda*, set his own work *Krishna-giti* to a dance form which came to be called Krishnattam. The songs were in Sanskrit, thus could not appeal to the people; the form also lacked music and not at all the rasas were exhibited.

Krishnavatar-lila (?C; Kashmiri) by anonymous poet. Also known as *Krishnavatar-charit*, this is the earliest known poem of Krishna-bhakti in the language. It is written in the form of 'vatsum', a folk form of Kashmiri poetry.

Krittibas Ojha Mukhati (15th): the first great poet of Bangla; possibly the first and certainly the most popular poet to adapt *Ramayana* into Bengali. Also known as Krittibas Pandit, he was a kulin brahman descendant of Narasimha (courtier of a king Danuja) who came from East Bengal and settled at Phuliya on the east bank of the Hooghly. A birth date as early as 1398 has sometimes been claimed for him, but probably belongs to mid-15th because he was first acknowledged by a Pathan sultan whose court he visited as a young man. His famous work was originally known as *Ramkathakavya* or *Shri Ram Panchali*; subsequently it was named *Krittibas Ramayana* after him.

Krittibas Ramayana (mid-15th; Bangla) of Krittibas Ojha: the earliest and most popular Bangla adaptation of *Ramayana*. A penalty of the popularity was that each important gayen modified the text to suit his own purpose and added various short tales at will. The numerous available manuscript copies belong mostly to late 18th and early 19th, the oldest to end-17th. The work was printed for the first time at the Mission Press in Serampore in 1802.

K.S. Advani [Kewalram Salamatrai Advani (1809–76)]: prose-writer in Sindhi. He engaged in the study of literature and religions after retirement from service with the local government (Muslim upto 1843; then British) and wrote three books during 1864–70. These are *Gula,* which contains short essays on different subjects; *Sukhiri*, tales and anecdotes bearing moral lessons; *Gulu-Shakar*, a collection of Sindhi proverbs and sayings. They were published only in 1905. The first two works provide good specimens of early Sindhi prose; the author also took care to use Sindhi vocabulary rather than Farsi.

Kshemananda or **Kshamananda**: mid-17th: poet in Bangla; author of a Manasa-mangal kavya, which became more widely known in Bengal than any other Manasa-mangal work. Kshemananda's poem is not original in any respect but it uses all previous versions and presents them in a simple but sincere tone. Born into a kayastha family of southern Rahr, he adopted the name of Ketakadas. This has given rise to the speculation that there were two different poets in Bangla, one called Kshemananda, the other Ketakadas.

Kshemendra (11th): Kashmiri scholar and poet in Sanskrit; author of a number of works not all of which have yet been discovered. He wrote *Auchityavichara-charcha* and *Kavi-kanthavarana*, two works on poetics; *Suvritti-tilaka*, work on prosody; *Bharata-manjari* (on *Mahabharata*), *Ramayana-majari* (on *Ramayana*), and *Brihatkatha-manjari* (version of *Brihatkatha*), poetical works. Among his satirical and didactic works are *Charu-charya, Darpa-dalana, Kala-vilasa, Narma-mala, Samaya-matrika* and *Sevya-sevakopadesha*. He was a pupil of Abhinavagupta's; Shaiva by faith in his earlier life, he later became a Vaishnav.

Kshemishwara (9th/10th): playwright in Sanskrit; author of *Chandakausika* and *Naishadhananda*. A verse in the prologue to the former play states that it was composed at the behest of king Mahipala. This ruler has been identified with Mahipala Bhuvanaikamalla of Kanauj (9th/10th) rather than with Mahipala of Bengal.

Kshetrayya (*c*1600–60): poet in Telugu; sometimes referred as the 'Andhra Vidyapati' because his verses lend themselves easily to be sung to the accompaniment of dance. It is said that he composed 4000 verses altogether, but only about 350 have been recovered. Born in Nubba village of Krishna district in Andhra Pradesh, he lived for a long time in Thanjavur where he was the court-poet of local ruler Raghunath Naikudu.

Kshiraswamin (late 3rd): scholar of Sanskrit; author of *Amarakoshodghatana*. Scholars have differed on whether he was a Kashmiri of 8th century or lived somewhere in Central India in late 11th. Other works attributed to him are *Arya-vritti, Nipatavyayopasarga* and *Kshira-tarangani*, the latter being a commentary on *Dhatupatha* of Panini.

Kuchelavrittam (*c*1750; Malayalam) of Ramapurathu Varier: the most popular 'boat-song' in the language, composed while the poet accompanied Maharaja Martand Varma on a river voyage of three or four days. This work of 700 lines begins with an invocation to the deity of the Vaikom temple, offers a tribute to the king, then describes Tiruvananthapuram.

Kuhar Singh or **Keyar Singh**: earlier 18th: poet in Panjabi from Lahore. He was present in Lahore when Bhai Mani Singh, author of *Guruvilas*, was imprisoned there in 1738. Bhai Mani Singh recited his poem to fellow-prisoners. This was overheard by a Turki sentry, who repeated it to Kuhar Singh. The latter wrote it down in the form of a manuscript in 1741.

Kulapati Mishra (late 17th): poet of the riti convention in Hindi; author of *Rasa-rahasya* (1670), *Drona-parva* (1680) *Yukti-tarangini* (1686), *Nakha-shikha, Samgramsar* (1676), all composed around 1667-86). The first work, on poetics, is particularly renowned. He was from Agra and married a sister of Biharilal's wife.

Kulashekhara (late 8th): sant-poet in Tamil and one of the 12 Alvars; author of *Perumal Tirumoli.* It is said he was born a prince of Kerala; gave up his throne and came to Srirangam where he joined workers who were then building the Ranganatha temple.

Kulashekhara Varman (?C): playwright in Sanskrit from Kerala, who probably came from a royal family. The plays are *Tapati samvarana* and *Subhadra-Dhananjaya.* He is said to have made innovations in the staging of plays. For example, the Vidushaka could speak in Malayalam even though the play was in Sanskrit.

Kulottungan Pillaitamizh (12th; Tamil) of Ottakuttar: kavya work narrating the brave deeds of Chola king Kulottunga II. The work also mentions his ancestors and contemporary kings in Sri Lanka, Java, Sumatra and North India. The historical validity of the information given here has been confirmed by stone inscriptions and other sources.

Kumar Guruparar (17th): poet in Tamil. Shaiva by faith, he mainly wrote accounts of the glory of places where famous temples are situated; thus, *Meenakshiyamme pillaitamil* relates to the Meenakshi temple in Madurai. Among his other works are *Kayilei kalambakam, Tiruvarur nanmanimalai, Chidambar mummanikkobai.* He had travelled in North India and is believed to have set up a mutth in Banaras; learnt Hindi in order to propagate Shaiva faith. Occasionally he has used Hindi words in his Tamil lines.

Kumar Valmiki (late 15th/early 16th): poet in Kannada. Originally named Narahari, he was born in a brahman household of Tokhe village in Bijapur district of Karnataka. His two works are *Tokhe Ramayana* and *Eravan kalag*. The former is the earliest known adaptation of the Valmiki *Ramayana* in Kannada. For this the poet came to be known as 'kumar' (=young) Valmiki.

Kumar Vyasa (mid-15th): the title of Kannada poet Naranappa, who rendered the Vedavyas *Mahabharata* into Kannada verse, using the bhamine shatpadi metre. The work came to be known as *Karnata Bharatakatha'manjavi* or *Kannada Bharata*. The poet belonged to Koilwad village in Dharwar district; his original name was Viranarayaner.

Kumara-dasa (?C): poet in Sanskrit. Also known as Kumarabhatta, Natha Kumara, Kumaradatta and Bhatta Kumara, he has not yet been clearly identified. According to Sanskrit tradition, he is the author of the kavya work *Janaki-haran*, which has been cited by later Sanskrit poets and critics; some scholars regard him as a friend and contemporary of Kalidasa. According to Simhala tradition, he was a Sri Lankan king named Kumaradhatusena (r. 517–26).

Kumara-sambhava (?5th; Sanskrit) of Kalidasa: a unique poem which has no precedence. It narrates how Shiva and Uma (Parvati) came to be married, so that a son (name Kumara or Kartikeya) could be born to them who would rescue the gods from the persecution of demons. No specific source has been determined; several puranas tell of the marriage between Shiva and Parvati; in *Mahabharata*, when Mahisasura attacks Shiva, the latter invokes the help of his son Skanda who overpowers the demon. If not the story, the manner of presentation resembles portions of *Ramayana*; also the title appears in a *Ramayana* sloka in Balakanda. All extant manuscripts of the work consist of 17 sarga; but only the first eight are generally regarded as Kalidasa's work and of his early career. Mallinath's famous commentary also deals only with eight sarga. Yet the title-episode, the birth of Kumara, does not take place until the 10th sarga. While sarga 1–8 are composed in an unprecedented style, ninth sarga onwards the style is reminiscent of Kalidasa's other works. Hence the speculation that either he left the work incomplete or that his own remaining sarga have been lost; in either case, other poets composed the later sarga.

Tr. R Griffith London, 1879; S.R. Sehgal, Delhi, 1966;

Kumarsambhavamu (*c*1125; Telugu) of Nannechodudu: the first kavya work in the language which propagates Shaiva faith. It is not a translation of Kalidasa's *Kumarasambhava* but an independent work based on stories about Shiva known mainly in South India. Unlike Kalidasa's poem, this one begins with the birth of Sati as well as of Ganesh; concludes with Kumara's victorious battle over Taraka. This work set the formal model for later prabandha kavyas in Telugu.

Kumara-harana kavya (16th; Asamiya) of Ananta Kandali: kavya work on the story of Usha and Aniruddha.

Kumara-haranam (17th; Malayalam) of Poontanam: narrative poem based on *Mahabharata* episode of Arjun and Krishna recovering the lost children of a brahman.

Kumaralata (between A.D. 150 and 200): Bouddha philosopher and prose-writer in Sanskrit from Takshashila. His *Drishtanta-pankti*, a series of parables, is an early gadya-kavya in Sanskrit.

Kumarapala-charita (*c*1150; Sanskrit/Prakrit) of Hemachandra Suri. It is also known as *Dvyashraya-kavya* because it is in two parts, the first containing 20 sarga in Sanskrit, the second 9 in Prakrit; there are also several Apabhramsha verses in both parts. The work is an account of the Chalukya rulers of Anhilvad (in Gujarat) down to the career of king Kumarapala, and includes his encounter with king Mallikarjuna of Konkan. It was composed for the purpose of illustrating rules of the author's grammar, *Siddha-Hemachandra-shabdanushasana*.

Kumarapala-pratibodha (1185; Prakrit) of Somaprabha: also known as *Jinadharma-pratibodha* and *Hemakumara-charita*. The work gives an account of the initiation of king Kumarapala to Jainism by Hemachandra. Composed 11 years after this king's death, it offers valuable information on its time and society; describes Gujarat and its capital; briefly mentions Chalukya kings. The work is in five sections called 'prastava'; some sections are written in Sanskrit and Apabhramsha.

Tr. L. Alsdorf, Hamburg, 1928.

Kumaresh Shatakam (18th; Tamil) of Gurupad Dasar: a sequence of 100 poems in praise of god Kartikeya. Each poem also discusses an ethical principle or matter of social conduct.

Kumari Molla (late 16th): woman

poet in Telugu; belonged to the potter caste; author of *Ramayanumu*.

Kumaravyas-Bharat (15th; Kannada) Kumar Vyas: composed in shatpadi metre, the work covers only the first ten parvan.

Kumbha or **Kumbhakarna** (*c*1440): ruler of Mewar at Chittor, who was also a scholar of music; author of *Sangitaraja*. He also wrote a commentary on Sanskrit on *Gita-Govinda*.

Kumbhan-das (b. 1550): poet in Hindi; one of the Ashtachhap group. He was called to Sikri by Akbar and had much honour bestowed upon him. Only a few fragments of his verse are extant.

Kumudendu Ramayana (*c*1275; Kannada) adaptation of *Ramayana* by Kumudendu, Jain poet. The work is not as successful nor as well-known as *Pampa Ramayana*.

Kunchan Nambiar (b. 1705): poet in Malayalam, humorist and satirist, said to have innovated the Tullal form. Born in Killikurisimangalam, he went further south after growing up and became a court poet of Ambalappuzha Raja. He composed 40–45 Tullal works; also wrote other forms of Malayalam verse.

Kundakunda (?C): Jain scholar, so named after his native place Kondakunda, in South India. He is said to have written, in Pali, over 80 'pahuda' (prabhrita, Sanskrit) works, of which the best-known is *Panchatthiya-sara*. His own name was Padmanandi, but he has also been called Elacharya, Gridhrapichha, Vakragriva. He was a pupil of Bhadrabahu, and has been variously assigned to 1st, 3rd or 5th century.

Kundalakesi (?C; Tamil) of unknown authorship: one of the pancha-kappiyam; available only in fragments, and derives its stature from being cited or quoted in many commentaries. Scholars have inferred that it is a Buddhist work, comparable to *Manimekalai*. The story is about Kundalakesi, a vaishya girl who kills her husband, who had planned to kill her; thereafter, in repentance, she became a Bouddha nun and went about meeting Jain teachers whom she invariably defeated in debate.

Kundaliya (Hindi): a metrical form of 24 'matra', presented in six-line stanzas; the first two lines comprise a doha; the remaining four are in rela metre.

Kundaliya Ramayana (early 17th; Hindi) of Agradas: the popular title of his *Hitopadesh upakhyayan bavani*, which was composed in kundaliya metre. But the work does not relate to *Ramayana*.

Kundamala (before 5th; Sanskrit) ascribed by some to Dinnaga, an early Bouddha logician; a play in six acts, dealing with the *Ramayana* story after Rama's coronation. Neither the date of the work nor its authorship has been established. Other authors to whom the work has been ascribed are Dhiranaga, Viranaga, Ravinaga, Nagayya.

Tr. J. Shastri & S.D. Bhanot, Lahore, 1935; A.C. Woolner, London, 1935.

Kuntaka (10th/11th): author of *Vakrokti-jivita*. He was probably from Kashmir; lived sometime between 10th and 11th centuries. He is sometimes referred to in alamkara literature as 'Vakrokti-jivitakara'. He came immediately after Anandavardhana and was an elder contemporary of Abhinavagupta.

Kunvarasi Sankhalo (18th; Rajasthani) of anonymous authorship: prose narrative, interspersed with over 150 doha verses. The hero, Kunavarsi Sankhalo, is mentioned in several historical works; belonged to Jangalu village, near Bikaner. The story features his marriage with Bharamal, the blind daughter of the Kharala Rajputs, and his subsequent battles with them.

Kunvarbai-nun Namerun (1683; Gujarati) of Premanand: akhyana work featuring Kunvarbai's father, Narasimha, who is a devotee of Shri Krishna. He cannot pay the appropriate dowry ('namerun') on her first pregnancy; he prays to Krishna and eventually is saved by him. Among other poets in Gujarati who have written on the same theme before Premanand are Vishnudas, Krishnadas, Govind and Vishanath Jain. While his predecessors emphasised the devotional elements in the story, Premanand portrayed it as reflection of contemporary family life in Gujarat.

Kural: see Tirukkural.

Kuravanzhi (Tamil): a form of ancient drama; also known as 'Kurattippattu'.

Kurigami [Prakash Ram Kurigami (1819–88)]: poet in Kashmiri, also known as Devakar Prakash Bhat or Prakash Bhat. His identity has been established only recently. He is the author of *Akanandun, Krishnavatar lila, Ramavatar charit* and *Lav-Kush charit*; the first two works have not yet been recovered.

Kurinchi-ppattu (?C; Tamil) of

Kapilar: the eighth idyll of *Pattuppattu.* This long poem is supposed to have been composed by Kapilar in order to acquaint the Aryan king Pirahattan with the charms of the Tamil language. It contains beautiful descriptions of mountain scenery; also brings out the social conditions in Tamilnadu; emphasises that qualities of modesty and chastity are the most valuable ornaments for women.

Kurrala-kkurvanchi (18th; Tamil) of Tirikudrasappan: verse narrative. In it a hill-tribe woman appears before a love-struck heroine and tells the latter about the nature of her affliction, also how to cure herself.

Kurun-ttogai (?C; Tamil): one of the *Ettutogar* collections; an anthology of 402 short lyrics on love by 204 poets. These are aham poems, varying in length from eight to four lines. It was compiled under the patronage of the chieftain Purikko.

Kushal Labh (*c*1520–90): poet in Rajasthani or Old Gujarati; lived much of his life in Jaisalmer (Rajasthan); author of *Madhavanal Kamakandla chaupai* and *Dhola Maruri Chaupai.* Among other works assigned to him are *Tejsar ras, Aga-udatta chaupai, Stambhan Parsvanath stavan, Jina-palit Jinarakshit sandhi gatha*, etc. He was a Jain by faith.

Kusumavali (early 13th; Kannada) of Dev Kavi: champu kavya narrating the adventures of Kandarpa and how he won Kusumavali, the daughter of Chakravakpur ruler Chandrodaya. Kandarpa was the son obtained by Vimalpuri ruler Vishwambhar after he had organised a 'putrakameshti' yajna.

Kuta Gita (Marathi): riddle-like songs that express some metaphysical concept, especially in the Advaita Vedanta tradition. All leading sant-poets like Jnaneshwar, Namdev, Eknath, Muktabai, etc., composed 'Kuta Gita' songs.

Kutban or **Qutban** (b. 1493): Sufi poet in Hindi; author of *Mrigvati.* He was a disciple of Shaikh Burhan of the Chisti following, and a ward of Jainpur ruler Badshah Husain Shah.

Kuttani-mata (*c*800; Sanskrit) of Damodaragupta: a work which created a new genre. In it, a courtesan who is losing her elientele, seeks the advice of an older harlot. The latter gives instruction on how to win and keep a rich young man; she also tells erotic stories in the process. Kalhana mentions Damodaragupta as a poet and minister in the who is losing her elientele, seeks the advice of an older harlot. The latter gives instruction on how to win and keep a rich young man; she also tells erotic stories in the process. Kalhana mentions Damodaragupta as a poet and minister in the court of Jayapida, ruler of Kashmir (779–813).

Kuttikunju Tankachi (1820–1908): woman poet in Malayalam; composed mainly 'kilippattee', 'tiruvatird' and 'kuratte' songs, also three 'attackatha' works. Her original name was Lakshmi Pillai; lived most of her life in Tiruvananthapuram.

Kuttu (Tamil): term means 'dance'. The Tamil classic, *Silappadikaran*, has described eleven kinds of dance—'kodukotit adal', 'pandarangkkuttu', 'alliya tokkudi', 'malladal', 'tudikkuttu', 'kudaikkutu', 'kudakkuttu', 'pedikkuttu', 'marakkalkkuttu', 'pavaikuttu' and 'kadaiyakkuttu'. Each of these is associated with a dance performed by an ancient god before slaying a demon (asur). Some other dances described in Sangam age works are 'rettuv varikkuttu', a group dance of hunters; 'kallilkuttu', a dance of women at skanda temples; 'allikkuttu', a dance which celebrates a royal victory in battle; 'velankkuttu', a dance performed by a person who is under Skanda's influence.

Kutub-shatak (1573; Hindi) by unknown author: a Sufi work which tells of the romance between Kutub, son of Ferozeshah Tughlak, and Kisori Sahiba.

Kuvalaya-mala (*c*779; Prakrit) of Uddayotana: collection of edifying tales, like *Samaraichha-kaha*, upholding Jaina principles. The work is composed mainly in Jain Maharastri, but it also uses Paisachi and Apabhramsha, passing sometimes from high-flown Prakrit to conversational prose in Apabhramsha which was probably quite close to popular speech.

Kuvalayananda (late 16th; Sanskrit) of Appayya Dikshita: a rhetorical work. It incorporates all 'karika' from chapter 5 (dealing with 'arthalamkara') of Jayadeva's *Chandraloka* and adds a running commentary in prose.

L

Labanyabati (*c*1700; Oriya) of Upendra Bhanja: work which is most typical of the kavyas of this poet. It tells of a heavenly couple, reborn on earth for some misdemeanour, as Chandrabhanu, prince of Karnataka, and Labanyabati, princess of Simhala. The work is in 48 sections, each set to a particular musical mode—'basanta', 'ramkeli', 'chokhi', etc.

Lado (Sindhi): a kind of folk-song sung by women on happy occasions like marriage, birth of a male child, sacred thread ceremony, etc.

Lagani (Maithili): a variety of folk tales in verse sung by village women while they grind corn early in the morning. The name is also used for another kind of song in Maithili, comprising four to five stanzas of melancholy tone.

Laghari [Hamal Faqir Laghari (1815–79)]: poet in Sindhi, known mainly for his parodies. He also composed a Hir-Ranjha poem which is mainly a dialogue between Hir and her mother.

Laghusiddhanta-kaumudi (?C; Sanskrit) of Varadaraja: a primer of grammar based on *Siddhanta-kaumudi* of Bhattoji Dikshita. The work is popularly known as *Laghu-kaumudi*.

Tr. J.R. Ballantyne, Banaras, 1867.

Laithak leikharon (?C; Manipuri): book of genesis of the Meitei community; probably composed no earlier than 17th.

Lakhsmipati [Lakshminatha Gosain (*c*1787–1872)]: devotional poet in Maithili from Parasarma village, in Bhagalpur district of Bihar. He gave up a householder's life for some time and travelled as a devotee to many shrines in Mithila and Nepal; returned to settle in Benagam village. He wrote hymns to Radha, Krishna or Shiva in Maithili as well as Hindi; used the name 'Lakshmipati' in the bhanita.

Lakhu-lakkhan (early 13th): poet in Apabhramsha; author of *Jinadatta-chariu* and *Anubaye ramanpaiu*. These were written nearly 40 years apart. It is presumed the poet wrote other works during this interval but these works have not yet been recovered.

Lakkana Dandesha (early 15th): poet in Kannada; senior official of Vijayanagar king Prauda Devaraya. He wrote the voluminous *Shiva-tattvachintamani* which is like an encyclopaedia of Virshaiva faith.

Lakshan sar-sangrahamu (16th; Telugu) of Peddana: work on poetics about 'lakshana'. While other scholars give examples of lakshana from the work of other poets, Peddana has composed his own examples here.

Lakshana (Sanskrit): term in poetics; denotes a function by which a word expresses a sense other than its primary sense.

Lakshman Kavi Enugu (18th): poet in Telugu and Sanskrit. He composed *Suryashatak* in Sanskrit. Among his Telugu works are *Rameshwar-mahatmyamu, Ganga-mahatmyamu, Subhashita-ratnavali, Vishweshwarodaharanamu,* etc.

Lakshman Kavi Pendiyari (17th): scholar of Telugu: compiled *Andhra nama samgraha*, which is a classified listing of desaj (i.e., non-Sanskrit) words in Telugu. There is also an appendix listing words that have more than one meaning. Subsequently, a scholar of 18th century named Adiyamu Surakavi added many words to the existing list and prepared his *Andhra-nama-seshamu.*

Lakshman Singh, Raja (1826–96): prose writer in Hindi; a notable figure of the pre-Bharatendu era. He was an advocate of 'pure' Hindi and eschewed even popularly understood words from Arabic and Panjabi. In 1861 he began publishing the magazine *Praja-hitaishi* from Agra; through it he sought to propagate his ideal Hindi. 'Raja' was a title conferred on him at the Delhi Durbar of 1870; earlier he had served as tahsildar of Etawa, then deputy collector of Banda.

Lakshmana Gani (12th): poet in Prakrit, author of the 'charita-kavya' *Supasanaha-chariya*. He was a disciple of Hemchandra Suri.

Lakshmansen Padmavati-katha (*c*1459; Hindi) of Damou Kavi: kavya work which tells of Lakshmansen and Padmini of Chittor.

Lakshmi-mangal (late 17th; Bangla) of Krishnaram Das: narrative poem based on a folk-tale.

Lakshmidhara (early 12th): of many authors bearing this name, the best-known wrote *Kritya-kalpataru*, a famous smriti digest, and influenced early smriti writers in Mithila, Bengal, and North India in general. According to him, he was the son of Bhatta Hridayadhara and wrote the above work at the command of Govindachandra, the Gahadwal or Rathore king of Kanauj (r.1114–56).

Lakshmisha (mid-16th): poet in Kannada; author of *Jaimini-bharat*. Not much is known about his life. He probably lived in a place named Devanuru or Surpur which had a Lakshmiraman temple. It is surmised that he belonged to the Bhagawat sect.

Lal (Kashmiri): a secular lyric form; brief song set to music stating a single mood and expressing human love.

Lal Chandra (late 18th): singer and poet in Bangla; generally associated with his brother Nandalal. He is said to have adapted Vaishnav lyrics into love songs about mundane lovers.

Laldas (earlier 16th): poet in Hindi; author of *Hari-charit* and *Bhagavat dasham skandha bhasha*. He was from Raebareli and adhered to Krishna-bhakti. Of two other poets bearing this name, Laldas (mid-17th) founded the Laldasi sect, while Laldas (latter 17c) a poet of Ram-bhakti, wrote *Awadh-vilas*.

Lal Dasji (1540–1648): bhakti poet in Rajasthani. Born to a poor Muslim family in Dholidup village near Alwar, he moved later to Nagla village and settled there. He remained a householder while preaching his faith; his disciples included Muslims as well Hindus. He left behind a sect known as 'Lalpanth'. About 700 sakhis, 600 padas and a work called *Chitavani* are ascribed to him but much of this was composed by his followers. The language was Mewati, which was spoken in that region. His faith is basically that of a Vaishnav.

Lal Ded (1335–1383/86): the popular name of Lalla Didi, a Shaiva woman-sant who is the earliest poet in modern Kashmiri. Born during the rule of Udyayan Deva, the last Hindu king of Kashmir, she had an unhappy married life and became a sanyasin, moving around the countryside and singing her poems on Shiva. It is said that she met Shah Hamdani, the first great Sufi sant and preacher in Kashmir, and that she was converted to Islam by this contact. She remains equally popular among Kashmiri Muslims (who call her

Lall Arifa) and Hindus (who call her Lalla Yogeswari).

Lal Kavi (b.1658): poet in Hindi. His real name was Gorelal Purohit and he belonged to Mai village in Bundelkhand. He received the patronage of Raja Chhatrasal and wrote *Chhatra-prakash* in praise of his patron; also wrote *Chhatrasal-shatak, Chhatrakirti, Chhatra-chanda*, etc. with the same purpose.

Lalan Fakir or Lalanshah (*c*1775–1891): mendicant singer and composer in Bangla, who sang of the Navi as well as of devis and devatas with equal fervour. Born of Bengali parents in Bhanra village in Kushtia district (now in Bangladesh), he fell ill during a pilgrimage and was abandoned by Hindu fellow-pilgrims. A Muslim family nursed him back to health; he married a Momin Muslim woman and lived with her in the ashram he built in Senuria village. Most of his songs are lost.

Lalita (Marathi): an old form of drama in Maharashtra, generally staged during festivals. A more specific variety is the kind staged on the last evening of Navaratra.

Lalita'madhava (*c*1550; Sanskrit) of Rupa Goswamin: a play in ten acts that depict Krishna's 'lila' at Brindavan and his life in Mathura and Dwaraka.

Lalita'vistara (?C; Sanskrit) of unknown authorship: an 'avadana' work in prose, mixed with long metrical passages. It gives a detailed account ofthe 'lila' of Buddha. Apart from being important for the religious history of Buddhism, it also offers glimpses of social conditions in India during early centuries of this millenium.
Tr. P.L. Vaidya, Calcutta, 1881–86.

Lalitalalam (*c*1680; Hindi) of Matiram: work in poetics dealing with alamkar. It depends mainly on the works of Jayadev and Appaya Dikshita but it has also drawn upon Mammata and Vishwanath.

Lalitya-kala (*c*1773; Hindi) of Datta: work in the riti convention. The poets patron was Sumansingh, ruler of Charkhari.

Lallu Lal (1763–1825): prose writer in Hindi; author of *Premsagar* and other works. Born to a Gujarati brahman family of Agod, he became proficient in Urdu, Kharibaoli, Hindi and Brajbhasa. Appointed by Fort William College of Calcutta to write books in Hindi, he helped to develop Kharibaoli prose.

Lalu Lakkhan (early 13th): poet in Apabhramsha who settled in Bilrampur village of Etah district in Uttar Pradesh. Only two of his works are extant, *Jnadatta-chariu* and *Anuvaya/ratrana-pariyu*, which were composed 38 years apart. It is therefore believed he wrote other works but these have been lost.

Latak melak (12th; Sanskrit) of Sankhadhar: a farce in two acts which bring together a number of rogues ('dhurta-sammelan').

Lav-Kus-dian paurian (*c*1650; Panjabi) of Jasodanandan: poem in 88 stanzas of the battle between Rama's army and Lava and Kusha. The work also reflects contemporary village life in Panjab.

Lavani (Marathi): songs of earthly love, often used in tamasha performances. It came into prominence in 18th century. Among famous lavani composers of the Peshwa period were Honaji Bala, Prabhakar, Saganbhau, Parashuram, etc.

Lavanya'samaya (1465–1534): poet in Gujarati. Among his works are *Siddhanta- chatuspadi, Goutamprichha-chaupai, Vimala-prabandha, Surapriya Keval-no rasau, Devaraj Vachharaj chaupai*. He was a major Jain poet of his time.

Lebedeff [full name, Gerasim Lebedeff]: a Russian who opened a 'Bangla Theatre' in central Calcutta and staged a Bangla musical play on 27 November 1795; performance repeated on 21 March 1796. These are the first ever stage-performances of a play in Bangla. The play was a free adaptation of the European farce, *The Disguises* (probably by Chapman), done by Lebedeff in collaboration with his Bengali teacher Goloknath Das; songs from Bharatchandra's *Vidyasundar* were incorporated and comic interludes added. The play was performed by an entirely Indian cast, both male and female.

Leiron (*c*1700; Manipuri) of Charairongba: poetical work describing a variety of flowers. It is the first work of Manipuri literature bearing the name of the writer. The writer was a chieftain who ruled over ten other chiefs.

Lekhan-kalpataru (13th; Sanskrit) of Hemadri: treatise on letter-writing. It uses verse as well as prose. The author was a high official of a Yadav ruler.

Likhanavali (*c*1420; Sanskrit) of Vidyapati: manual of letter-writing, composed at the behest of Puraditya, a jagirdar of North Mithila.

The model letters frequently mention a date equivalent to 1417–18.

Lila (Oriya): a kind of folk-drama featuring gods and goddesses. Apart from Ram-lila and Krishna-lila, there are Bharat-lila and Gopalila, also Radhaprema-lila.

Lila-tilakam (14th; Sanskrit) of unknown author: treatise on Malayalam grammar and rhetoric. The work is divided into eight sections called 'silpam'; the first three deal with the history of the language and grammar; the rest discuss literary principles. The author has pointed out the basic differences between 'Aryabhasha' (Sanskrit), 'Cholabhasha' (Tamil) and 'Keralbhasa' (Malayalam), and claimed that the latter is an independent language; has devoted a lot of space to Manipravalam and recommended that there should be no Tamil usage in it. The work was discovered only in 1908.

Lila-charitra (1286; Marathi) of Mahendra Bhat: a biography of Chakradhara, founder of the Mahanubhava sect. This the earliest known biographical work in the language; contains over 100 stories ('lila') about the subject. After Chakradhara's death, Mahendra Bhat travelled for about five years collecting these stories.

Lilasukha or Bilvamangala (?C): also known as Krishna Lilasukha; devotional poet in Sanskrit, author of *Krishna-karnamrita*. He mentions in the work that his parents were Damodara and Niti; has been assigned to different periods from 9th to 15th century. According to some scholars, there were three Bilvamangalas, of which Lilasukha was the first; probably belonged to Kerala.

Lilavati (?C; Prakrit) of Kutuhala: a kavya work. It deals with the romance between king Satvahana and princess Lilavati of Simhaladvipa. There are no formal divisions, as in *Gaudavaha*, but is less pedantic and more racy in narration.

Lilavati (*c*1200; Kannada) of Nemichandra: champu kavya in 14 aswas. It tells of Kandarpa Dev, son of Kadamba king Chudamani and queen Padmavati. After a dream he had one night about a young woman, Kandarpa set out with his friend Makarand (son of minister Gunagandha) to look for her. She was Lilavati, daughter of Raja Shringara-shekhar of Kusumpur. She too had dreamt of a young man and sent out people in search of him. Ultimately they meet and marry.

Lilabati Prabandha (*c*1200; Kannada) of Nemichandra: champu work based on the Sanskrit *Vasavadatta* of Subandhu.

Lochan Das (1523–89): poet in Bangla who was a disciple of Narahari Sarkar Thakur, a close associate of Shri Chaitanya. Lochan wrote *Chaitanya' mangal*, a verse biography in four parts consisting of about 1,000 lines in all; this could be set to tune in different specified ragas and raginis and sung to the public. He also wrote a large number of padas on the Brindavan lila of Krishna and about Shri Chaitanya.

Lochana Kavi (late 17th): poet and music scholar of Mithila; compiled the anthology *Ragatarangini*. Also known as Lochan Pandit, he enjoyed the patronage of king Narapati Mishra (r.1673–90). He was the first to define and describe comprehensively the Maithili ragas and raginis on the basis of chahnda. It was claimed at one time that he was a Bengali.

Lochana or Kavyaloka-lochana (*c*1000; Sanskrit) of Abhinavagupta: a commentary on *Dhvanyaloka* and an authoritative exposition of the dhvani theory in Sanskrit poetics.

Lokahitavadi (1823–92): prose writer in Marathi, whose real name was Sardar Gopal Harideshmukh. After retiring from service as a judge of the small causes court, he devoted himself to social service. He wrote 32 books on various subjects and is regarded as one of the makers of modern Marathi prose.

Lol (Kashmiri): brief song set to music, stating a single mood and expressing human love.

Lollata or Bhatta Lollata (?C): scholar of Sanskrit from Kashmir; wrote the earliest known commentary on *Natyasastras*, but it is not extant. Some of Lollata's opinions have been quoted by Abhinavagupta.

Lor chandrani sati Moyna (early 17th; Bangla) of Daulat Kazi: a panchali work in two parts with different titles. Only the first part was completed by Daulat Kazi; Alaol composed the second part many years later. The first part tells of Lor, ruler of Gohari and husband of Moyna (or Moynamati), who falls in love with the beautiful princess of Mohara, Chandrani, and goes to live with her after killing her husband in a duel. In the second part, Moyna rejects the offer of Chatan, a rich young man, and sends a brahman to search for her husband. He is found and returns home to Moyna, along with Chandrani.

Lutfullah Quadiri (1611–79): sant poet in Sindhi; belonged to the Quadiri sect of Sufis. His philosophic work *Sindhi risalo* contains ever 300 bayts in Sindhi; written between 1667–72, this is the earliest known work composed entirely in Sindhi verse. He also wrote a treatise in Panjabi, *Minhajiu marfat*, in which there is reference to another work of his entitled *Tuhafat-ul-salikin*. The latter has not yet been recovered.

M

Ma'bap-nama (late 17th; Urdu) of Husain Zawqi; poetical work in Dakhni, in praise of the Sufi sant Sheikh Abdul Qadir Jilani.

Macdonell [Arthur Anthony Macdonnell (1854–1930)]: scholar of Sanskrit. Born at Muzaffarpur in North Bihar to British parents, he studied in Germany and England; succeeded Monier Williams as Boden Professor of Sanskrit and Keeper of Indian Institute at Oxford; retired in 1926 but continued in honorary positions of distinction. His scholarly work was mostly in the area of Vedic. Among his works are editions of *Sarvanukramani* (1886) and *Brihaddevata* (1904); *Vedic Mythology* (1897), *Vedic Grammar* (1910); in collaboration with A.B. Keith, *A Vedic Index of Names* and *Subjects* (1912); *History of Sanskrit Literature* (1900), *India's Past* (1927).

Madah (Sindhi): term for a poem or song in praise of some paigambar or darvesh or nabi. The word is derived from 'madha' in Arabic which means praise or glorification.

Madala panji or the Drum Chronicle: chronicle in Oriya prose of the Jagannath temple at Puri, so called because of the drum-like shape assumed by the palm-leaf manuscripts when bound together with string. The chronicle is in two parts. One part describes the various ceremonies at the shrine which are followed in every detail even today; the other part describes the ruling dynasties and individual rulers of Orissa; all of whom seem to have accepted Jagannatha as the divine source of the sanction of their kingship. The chronicle is supposed to have been started by Chodaganga Deva of 12th/13th century, the first king of the Ganga dynasty. There is much controversy today about the date when the chronicle began. The record of events after 12th century usually corroborates other historical evidence, hence the traditional belief that it began in 12th century may be accepted. The material has no literary value, while its historical value has been reduced by interpolations and fantasies.

Madan-shatak (*c*1670; Hindi) of

Dama Kavi: kavya work telling of the romance between Madankumar and Champakamal.

Madantilak (early 11th; Kannada) of Chandra-raj: champu work on erotics. The author was a contemporary of Chalukya king Jaisingh (r.1012–42).

Madana mahotsava (*c*1550; Sanskrit) of Jiva Goswami: poem in ten 'ullasa' (sections). Its theme is Krishna's consecration of Radha as the queen of Brindavan; also describes the related festivities.

Madaygiri Mallanna (15th/16th): poet in Telugu; author of *Rajashekhar-charitramu*, a kavya-work based on an imaginary story.

Maddu Palani (18th): woman poet in Telugu; courtesan in the court of Pratapasimha (r. 1740–62); author of *Radhika santvanam*, also known as *Iladeviyam*. This is her only work; sometimes she is wrongly credited with *Saptapadulu*. An able poet herself, she helped other artists with gifts of land or gold. She was a disciple of the Vaishnav teacher, Tatadharya.

Madhab-sulochana (18th; Asamiya) of Kaviraj Chakrabarti: kavya work adapted from *Padmavathipuranam*.

Madhaodas Dadhawadiyo (1553–1621): poet in Rajasthani from Jodhpur state. Among his available works are *Ramarasau*, a condensed re-telling of the *Ramayana* story; *Nisani Gajamorkha*, a devotional work based on the Gajendramoksha episode in *Bhagvata-purana; Hadamana-gita*, a long prayer to Hanumana.

Madhav: name assumed by more than one 16th century poet in Bangla who composed a 'Krishna-mangal' poem. According to *Gour-Ganesh dipika* and *Chaitanya-charitamrit* the notable poet was one Madhavacharya, a son-in-law of Nityananda Prabhu. According to *Prema-vilas*, he is Madhav Mishra (or Acharya), son of Kalidas Mishra, nephew of Vishnupriya, disciple of Advaitacharya. From the text it appears 'Madhav' was a disciple of Shri Chaitanya.

Madhava Kandali (14th): first great poet in Asamiya; was attached to the court of Kachar ruler Mahamanikya. A scholar of Sanskrit, he translated the Valmiki *Ramayana* into Asamiya verse. This is the earliest translation of *Ramayana* into a Modern Indian language. As in other such translations, Madhava Kandali incorporated contemporary customs and other local colour into the work. He innovated a rich literary diction drawing upon Sanskrit as well as Asamiya.

Madhava Paniker (late 14th): poet in Malayalam; one of the Kannassan trio. His rendering of *Bhagavath Gita* into Malayalam was probably the first translation into any Modern Indian language. He condensed the original 700 shlokas into 328 couplets without omitting a single important idea.

Madhava deva (1498–1595): poet in Asamiya; also preacher, scholar, playwright and singer. A Shakta by birth, he became a Vaishnav and disciple of Shankaradeva after being defeated by him in debate; remained unmarried all his life in order to serve his guru. *Namaghosha* is his greatest creation. Among his other works are translations into Asamiya of *Ramayana* (Adi-kanda) and *Bhakti-ratnavali*; the long poem *Rajasurya kavya* based on a *Mahabharata* episode; a number of 'ankiya-nat' plays—*Chorodhara, Pimpara guchuva, Kotora khelova, Bhushan herova, Bhumi lutiva*. All these plays present incidents about the child Krishna. Towards the end of his life Madhavadeva came into conflict with East Koch king Raghudeva and was briefly imprisoned; later was released with honour and given shelter at Kochbehar by Lakshminarayan, ruler of West Koch kingdom.

Madhavanal prabandh dogdhabandh (*c*1527; Hindi) of Ganapati: probably the earliest kavya work telling the story of Madhavanal and Kamakandala. Madhavanal is a youthful musician and scholar who travels through many lands and charms women everywhere. In Kamavatipura he sees the dancing girl Kamakandala perform and is much impressed; when he gives her a present as mark of his appreciation, the king is offended and expels him from the country. After spending one night with the girl, Madhavanala goes to Ujjain and inscribes his story on the walls of Mahakal temple. King Vikramaditya traces him and hears about the girl. He meets her and proposes marriage; when she refuses, he tells her Madhavanal is dead. She faints and dies; on hearing this news Madhavanal also dies. Vikramaditya does penance for having caused these deaths. The couple is restored to life and the king has them married. The work contains 2565 couplets in eight sections; its language is Old Rajasthani or Maru-Gurjar.

Madhavanal Kamakandala (*c*1580; Hindi) of Alam: kavya work telling of the romance between Madhavanal, a musician, and Kamakandala, a dancer.

Madhavanalkamakanla-charitra (*c*1559; Hindi) of Vachak Kusha'-Labh of Jaisalmer: a kavya work in Dingal.

[Madhavaswami] Ramayana (1707; Marathi) of Madhava Swami of Thanjavur: exists in two versions, 'shloka-baddha' and 'ovi-baddha'. The latter consists of 18,975 ovi verses.

Madhumalati (*c*1544; Hindi) of Manjhan: kavya work of Sufi inspiration; only an incomplete text is extant. It tells of the romance between prince Manohar of Kanesar and princess Madhumalati; composed in Avadhi.

Madhu malati (early 18th; Bangla) of Saiyad Hamza: romantic poem based on a popular folk-tale.

Madhura-mangal (late 18th; Oriya) of Charandasa: kavya work based on events in the life of Krishna. The work derives its title from Madhura (Mathura) being liberated by Krishna's slaying of Kamsa.

Madhuryalahari (1796; Hindi) of Krishnadas: poetical work in praise of Krishna.

Madhvamuni (late 17th/early 18th): also called Madhva munishwara and Madhvanatha; sant-poet in Marathi. Even as a little boy he became a devotee of Shri Krishna and developed into an excellent Haridasa (kirtan-singer); in due course he began composing lyrics about Radha and Krishna.

Madhyama-vyayoga (?C; Sanskrit) of Bhasa: one-act play on a *Mahabharata* episode. It deals with the love of Hidimba for Bhima, their marriage, the birth of their son Ghatotkacha and their parting.
Tr. E.P. Jamier, Mysore, 1921.

Maduraikkanchi (?C; Tamil) of Mangudi Marudanar: the sixth and longest (782 lines) idyll of *Pattuppattu*. It celebrates the ancient city of Madurai, also the Pandyan king Nedunchezhiyan, hero of the Talaiyankanam battle. The poem seeks to persuade the king to desist from further warfare by impressing upon him the magnitude of his martial achievements, also the futility of war.

Maffei, Father [Agneld F. Saverio Maffei (1844–99)]: grammarian and lexicographer of Konkani; was a member of the first Italian mission that came to Mangalore. He wrote *Konkani Grammar* (1882); compiled *English-Konkani Dictionary* (1883) and *Konkani-English*

Dictionary (1885). His pamphlet *Ranantlo tallo*, now lost, argued in favour of developing the Konkani language.

Magha (7th/8th): poet in Sanskrit; author of *Shishupala-vadha*. He mentions at the end of this work that his grandfather was minister of a king named Varmala; some scholars identify this king as Varmalata, dated 625 according to an inscription. Magha is mentioned by 8th/9th century rhetoricians like Vamana and Anandavardhana.

Mahabhagavatamu (mid-15th; Telugu) of Potana: a free and enlarged rendering of *Bhagavat-purana*. Potana composed the bulk of this work, but portions are said to have been written by his disciples Veligandala Naraya, Ganganarya and Erchuri Singanna.

Mahamangala (?C): scholar in Pali; author of *Buddhaghosuppatti*, a work which gives some biographical account of Buddhaghosha. He may be the same as Mangala, the grammarian of Pali.

Maha-nataka (?C; Sanskrit) of unknown author; very large work almost wholly in verse, dealing with the *Ramayana* story. It has little resemblance to any nataka form. A loose narrative composition, which incorporates verses from most of the known and some probably now forgotten dramas of the time, it may have been originally written as a regular kavya. Because one verse in one recension ascribes the work to the mythical Hanumat, the work is also called *Hanuman-nataka*.

Maha-purana (9th; Sanskrit) of Jinasena. The full title of the work is *Trishasti-lakshana-mahapurana samgraha*; narrates the lives of the 63 eminent persons in Jain tradition. Consisting of 76 parvan and divided into two parts, Adi-purana and Uttara-purana, the work is also a Jaina encyclopaedia dealing with a variety of subjects. The work, left unfinished at the author's death, was completed by his disciple Gunabhadra.

Mahavamsa (? 6th; Pali) of Mahanaman: a refined and enlarged version of *Dipavamsa*. The original work narrated events upto Mahinda's visit to Sri Lanka; later, events down to the reign of Mahasena (A.D. 4C). Though not consistently reliable, it contains valuable information on the history and geography of Sri Lanka; also gives information on the history of Buddism and mentions many Pali works.

Mahavastu (?1st; Sanskrit): an

'avadana' work. Although its main subject is 'vinaya' it contains the life-story of the Buddhas as well as some narratives of the *Jataka* type.

Mahabharata (?C; Sanskrit) of Vyasa: the so-called national epic of India, classified as an 'itihasa-purana' work, which also contains *Bhagavad Gita*. The longest poem known to world civilization at present, it consists of 100,000 verses, spread over 18 books (parva). It was probably composed and the text continuously inflated by various hands between 400 B.C. and A.D. 200. The original or core poem is attributed to Vyasa, known also as Vedavyasa because he is believed to have compiled the vedas as well.

Editions: (1) Calcutta edition, 5 volumes, 1834–39; edited by pandits attached to the Education Committee; first ever printed version. (2) Bombay edition, 1863; ed. Atmaram Khadilkar, first printed in Pothi form. (3) Kumbhakonam edition, 23 volumes, 1906–14; ed. T.R. Krishnacharya and T.R. Vyasacharya; printed in Kumbhakonam and entitled *Sriman'Mahabharatam* (4) The Southern Recension, 18 volumes, Madras, 1931–36; ed. P.S.S. Shastri. (5) Critical Edition, 19 volumes, Pune, 1933–66; general editor V.S. Sukthankar; published by Bhandarkar Oriental Research Insitute, Pune; only text, without critical apparatus, published in two volumes, 1973. Translations: (1) K.M. Ganguli, 18 volumes; ed. P.C. Roy and based on the Calcutta edition; Calcutta, 1883–96; 2nd Edition, 11 volumes, 1919–35; reprinted in 12 volumes, Delhi, n.d. (2) Manmathanath Dutta, six volumes; Calcutta, 1895–1905. (3) J.A.B. Van Buitenen; three volumes so far; Chicago, 1974-; based on Critical Edition.

Mahabharatan Killippattu (16th; Malayalam) of Ezhuttachan: a condensed rendering of *Mahabharata*.

Mahabharatamu (*c*1030; Telugu) of Nannaya: earliest extant literary work in the language. An adaptation of *Mahabharata* in champu form, it was probably undertaken at the behest of the poet's patron, king Rajaraja Narendra. For some reason not known to history, he wrote only two parvan, 'Adi' and 'Sabha', and only a part of Vana-parva. The work remained incomplete for two centuries until Tikkana (13th) rendered the remaining 15 books. The work was really completed only when Erranna (14th) rendered the latter part of Vana-parva left unfinished by Nannaya. These three poets who contributed to the Telugu *Mahabharata* are specially esteemed as the 'Kavi-traya' of Telugu literature.

Mahabharatamu (*c*1730; Telugu) of Viraraju: a verse retelling of *Mahabharata*, done under the patronage of Mysore rulers.

Mahabhashya (?2 B.C.; Sanskrit) of Patanjali: the oldest extant commentary on *Ashtadhyayi* of Panini. Patanjali comments on 1228 rules of Panini in the same order as in original work; the commentary is divided into parts called 'ahnika', of which there are 85 altogether.

Mahabodhi-vamsa (10th/11th; Pali) of Upatissa: prose work on the history of the Bodhi tree. It gives an account of the Bodhi-tree of Anuradhapura, the attainment of 'bodhi' by Ananda, the Buddha's 'mahaparinirvana', the first three Buddhist councils, Mahindra's visit to Sri Lanka and other exploits, etc. The author has derived his material from *Dipavamsa, Mahavamsa* and other sources. According to some scholars, the author lived in the 4th century.

Mahadaisa (1228–1303): female disciple of Chakdradhara and the first woman poet in Marathi. She composed in 'dhwala' metre and her songs have come to be called dhwalas, especially those that constitute the work *Rukmini swayamvar*. She also wrote *Matruku Rukmini* in a narrative form. In the work *Shri Chakradhar nirupit Shrikrishna charitra*, she recorded all the answers given by Chakradhara to her queries about Shri Krishna's life. Originally called Rupai, she was named Mahadaisa by Chakradhara; later this name was sanskritised to Mahadamba.

Mahadeva Dasa (? 17th): poet in Oriya. A prolific composer, he produced numerous works on puranic themes. Among these are *Markandeya-purana, Vishnukeshari-purana, Padma-purana, Karttika-mahatmya, Vaisakha-mahatmya, Ashada-mahatmya, Dvadasi-mahatmya, Niladri-mahatmya.*

Mahadeviakka see Akka Mahadevi.

Mahanay-prakash (?13th; Kashmiri) of Sitikanta Acharya: the earliest known work in Kashmiri; contains 94 four-line stanzas or 'vak'. These verses deal abstractly with Shaiva Tantric philosophy as current in Kashmir as a popular faith. The language is full of Sanskrit words and expressions; the original ms is written in Sharada script. In the history of Kashmiri language and literature, these verses have the same position as *Charyagiti* verses in the history of Bangla or Marathi or Asamiya.

Mahanubhava panth: a reform sect within the Hindu fold which rose in Maharashtra towards end-13th. They chose Krishna and Dattatreya as their special objects of devotion and used Marathi for preaching their ideas, thus marking the beginnings of Marathi literature. Their founder was Harpaldev alias Chakdradhara who organised the sect from about 1263 to 1271. The early compositions of Mahanubhava teachers during 13th/14th century were mainly in prose; later when the sect lost favour with the people, they began to write in a cipher alphabet; these became a kind of underground literature which remained undiscovered until modern times. Other than the prose works, seven long poems in ovi metre are attributed to Mahanubhava authors; *Vachha-haran, Rukminiswayamvara, Shishupal-vadha, Uddhava-Gita, Jnanaprabodha, Sahyadri-varnan, Ridahipur-varnan.*

Mahapurusa-charita (868; Prakrit) of Silacharya: prose work dealing with the lives of great men.

Maharamparva (1723; Bangla) of Hayat Muhammad: a jangnama.

Maharasta-Puran (18th; Bangla) of Gangaram: in spite of the pretentious title, the work is a small poem of less than 200 lines describing one of the worst raids in West Bengal led by the Maratha chief Bhaskar Pandit. The first section concludes with the defeat and death of Bhaskar; it is not known whether the story was continued to other sections. The author was a contemporary if not actually an eye-witness, thus the work has importance as a historical document even if its literary value is low. The manuscript was discovered only in 1900 by Kedarnath Mazumdar.

Mahavira-charita (late 7th/early 8th; Sanskrit) of Bhavabhuti: a play in seven acts which dramatises Rama's story upto the time of his departure to the forest.
Tr. J. Pickford, London, 1871.

Mahavira-chariya (1082; Prakrit) of Gunachandra: verse account of Mahavira's life, half of which is devoted to his earlier births. The work was composed in Maharashtri Prakrit prose and verse, with a few Apabhramsha passages, yet the grammar is remarkably regular. From this it is deduced that the work is that of a scholar.

Mahesh Thakur (mid-16th): scholar and poet of Mithila. He founded a new dynasty in 1557, abdicated in 1569, thereafter lived like a hermit and is said to have composed hymns on Ganga and Tara in Mithila.

Maheshavani (Maithili): a type of song about Maheshwar or Shiva, frequently addressed to Menaka (called Mana in Mithila), the mother of Gauri. The songs relate to the marriage of Shiva and Gauri.

Maheshwara Suri (early 14th): Jain scholar and poet in Apabhramsha; author of *Sanjama-manjari*. He was a disciple of Hemahamsa Suri and probably a contemporary of Hemachandra.

Mahima Bhatta (?10th): scholar of poetics in Sanskrit; author of *Vyaktiviveka*. He is said to have also written *Tattvokti-kosha*, but it has not been recovered.

Mahinath Thakur (1559/71–1590/93): successor to king Mahesh Thakur of the Khandva dynasty. He is important to Maithili literature because in the courts of Mahinath and his brother Narapati, the Maithili lyric regained its glory. He was himself interested in composition in the local language.

Mahindra Bhat or Mhai Bhat (late 13th/early 14th): of Maharashtra, a leading disciple of Chakradhara. He collected the master's sayings and teachings in *Acharya-sutra* and *Siddhanta-sutra*; also wrote an account of his life, *Lila-charitra*.

Mahipati Baba (1715–90): devotional writer in Marathi. He was born in Tahrabad village of Ahmadnagar district and his parents belonged to the Varkari sect. His first work, *Bhakti-vijaya* (1762), based on Nabhadas's *Bhakta-mal*, was about the lives of sants. Works which followed were *Sant-lilamrit* (1767), *Bhakta-lilamrit* (1774), *Sant-vijay (1789)*. The last is a voluminous work, consisting of 40,628 ovi verses. All these writings record the lives of nearly all the sants from Mukundaraj to Ramdas. Mahipati was born into a kulkarni family of hereditary accountants; after coming of age, he served the local Muslim ruler in this capacity but resigned when he was ill-treated by a palace-servant; became a wandering sadhu for some time.

Mahipatram Ruparam Nilkanth (1829–91): prose-writer in Gujarati, also educationist, and social reformer. His *Inglandani musaphari* (1864) is one of the earliest travelogues in the language. He wrote a social novel, *Sasuvahuni ladai* (1866), and two historical novels, *Vanaraja charado* and *Sadharo jesanga*. He also wrote two biographies, *Karsandasa Mulajinum charitra* (1878) and *Mahetajinum* *charitra* (1893). His *Bhavai-samgraha* is a valuable collection of 'bhavai' folk-songs.

Mahiravan-vadh (16th; Asamiya): of Ananta Kandali: kavya work dealing with Ravan's solicitation of his brother Mahiravan to fight Rama. It was composed by the poet under an assumed name, 'Shri Chandra Bharati'.

Mahmud Gami (*c*1805–55): poet in Kashmiri. Not much is known about his life but from internal evidence it appears he knew Arabi and Farsi and drew upon Iranian sources for his own works. He wrote in Kashmiri verse the stories of Laila-Majnu, Yusuf-Zuleikha, Shirin-Khusro, Harun-al-Rashid, etc. Among his shorter masnavi works are *Mansur-nama, Mahmud Ghaznavi, Yak hikayat, Pahalnama, Sheikh Sannan*.

Mahumahaviaa (?C; Prakrit): probably on poetics. This is a lost work, attributed to Vakpatiraja by Anandavardhan in *Dhvanyaloka*.

Maikel Madhusudan Datta (1824–73): poet and playwright in Bangla: whose works illustrate how the impact of Western literature could be absorbed creatively by an Indian writer. His early ambition was to write in English (he became a Christian and, in his two marriages, both wives were European women living in India) and he composed *Captive Ladie* (1849), a long narrative poem. Subsequently he began writing in Bangla, starting with the play *Sharmistha* (1858), followed by *Ekeyi ki boley sabhyata* (1860), *Burosaliker gharey ron* (1860), *Padmavati* (1860), *Krishnakumari* (1860). He also wrote his first epic poem in blank verse, *Tillottama sambhab kavya* (1860), during this extraordinarily productive phase, and followed up next year with his masterpiece, *Meghnadbadh kavya* (1861). Before going abroad in 1862, he published two more books of verse, *Brajangana* (1861) and *Birangana* (1862); some sonnets he wrote while in Europe were later collected in *Chaturdaspadi kavitavali* (1866). During his last few years, spent in poverty and ill-health, he did some translations from French and Greek, into Bangla.

Maimansingh gitika (Bangla): collection of ten ballads selected and edited by Dineshchandra Sen for publication by Calcutta University in 1923. They belong to the oral tradition of Maimansingh district (now in Bangladesh) and were composed probably no earlier than 18th century. Persistently secular in tone, the poems present narratives that often end in tragedy. Women characters predominate in most stories.

Mairavan charitra (16th; Telugu) of Madayya Kavi: kavya work which narrates how Hanuman rescues Rama and Lakshman by killing Mairavan.

Maithili: language spoken in Mithila region, consisting of some ten districts in northern Bihar, a state in East India. Maithili is also spoken in some parts of Nepal. Descended from Magadhi Apabhramsha, it developed as a separate speech 10th century onwards. It used to be written in Tirhuta modified from a Gupta script; subsequently it has adopted Nagari for writing. The word 'Maithil' is used to describe those who belong to Mithila and (generally) speak Maithili.

Maithili (Mythili): another name for Sita, because she was the daughter (foundling) of king Janaka of Mithila. The name thus means 'daughter of Mithila'.

(Maithili) Dhurtta-samagam (early 14th; Mithila) of Jyotishwar Thakur: a farce adapted by the author from his own Sanskrit original. The manuscript was first disccovered in 1957 by Dr. Jayadev Misra. According to him it is the first example of what developed into the kirtaniya drama of Mithila. Maithili is used here not only for the songs but also for the speech of superior characters; the play also breaks decisively with tradition by having the protagonist, Vishwanagara, a sanyasi, assume the role of a love-lorn hero. It is practically a new play in Maithili, not just an adaptation of the Sanskrit original.

Maktul Hosen (1645; Bangla) of Mohammad Khan: the oldest jangnama in the language. It deals with the death of Husain, a grandson of Hazrat Muhammad.

Maladhar Bosu 'Gunaraj Khan' (late 15th): poet in Bangla; author of *Shrikrishna-vijay*. A rich kayastha from Kulingram village, then a centre of Vaishnav culture, he was probably a revenue officer of the state and attended the sultan's court for some time. The title 'Gunaraj Khan' was awarded by the sultan Ruknuddin Barbak Shah.

Malaippadukadam (?C; Tamil) of Perunkausikanar: the tenth idyll of *Pattupputtu*. A long poem of about 600 lines in akaval metre, it extols the chieftain Nannan, and the mountainous countryside he ruled. The poem describes nature; also presents a critical account of the art presents a critical account of the art of dancing as well as the details of musical instruments along with the artists' way of life.

Malati Madhava (late 7th/early 8th; Sanskrit) of Bhavabhuti: a ten-act play of the 'prakarana' type. It tells of the romance between the young student Madhava and Malati, a minister's daughter, and how they are finally united, after many difficulties, through the intervention of Kamandaki, a Bouddha nun.
Tr. M.R. Kale, Delhi, 1967.

Malavikagnimitram (?5th; Sanskrit) of Kalidasa: play in five acts. It tells how king Agnimitra falls in love with the disguised Malavika; this angers the youngest queen Iravati, who insults the king; the oldest queen Dharini hides Malavika. Finally, Dharini consents to the marriage, Iravati is appeased.
Tr. C.H. Tawney, Calcutta, 1875.

Malayalam: main language of the state of Kerala in South India; is spoken by about 35 million persons. The term 'Malayalam' was originally used to denote the land and only later came to mean the language. The origin of the language remains a matter of controversy. But it is generally accepted that Malayalam belongs to the Dravidian family and was, in its early phase, much under the influence of Tamil; emerged as an independent language from about 10th century. For writing, the Vattezhuttu script was used in the earliest stages; subsequently modified with addition of some letters from Brahmi and some from 'Grantha' to produce the present script which is being used from about 13th century.

Malik Muhammad Jayasi (mid-16th): renowned poet in early Hindi; belonged (like Kutban and Manjhan) to the Sufi tradition and composed in Avadhi; author of *Padumavat*.

Mallana: See Chedluvadu Mallana, Madaygari Mallana, Nandi Mallana, Pavuluri Mallana; all Telugu writers.

Mallanaga: another name of Vatsyayana, the author of *Kamasutra*.

Mallika Maruta (mid-17th; Sanskrit) of Uddandin or Uddandanatha: a play in ten acts. Modelled on *Malati Madhava*, it tells of the romance between Mallika, daughter of a Vidyadhar king, and Maruta, a Kuntala prince; a subplot shows the romance between the prince's friend Kalakantha and the princess' maid Ramayintika. The author was patronised by Manavikrama, zamorin of Kozhikode (Calicut).

Mallinatha (late 14th/early 15th): scholar of Sanskrit; wrote commentaries on the poetical works of Kalidasa, Bharavi, Bhatti, Magha, Sriharsa; also on some works on poetics, especially *Ekavali* of Vidyadhara. Original works attibuted to him are *Udarakavya, Raghuviracharita-kavya, Vaidya-kalpataru* and *Vaidya-ratnamala*, but some of these may have been written by other persons of the same name. Father of another erudite scholar, Kumaraswamin, this Mallinatha may have been a Tailangi brahman.

Mallinatha-charita (? 12th; Prakrit) of Haribhadra: verse biography of Mallinath, the 19th tirthankar.

Mallinatha-purana (*c*1100; Kannada) of Nagachandra, who was also known as Abhinava Pampa: chanpu-work dealing with the lives of Mallinatha, the 19th tirthankar.

Malpan (late 18th): a Christian convert of Kerala who studied Latin and Portuguese; also wrote several prose works in Malayalam, the best known of which is *Vedatarkkam*. He undertook an arduous voyage to Rome, accompanied by his disciple Kathanor. His full name was Kaziyatti Ouseph Malpan.

Malukdas (1574–1682): sant poet in Hindi from a village near Ilahabad. His poetry belonged to the 'Nirgun bhakti' school. Among his works are *Gyanbodh, Gyanparochi, Bhakti-vivek, Bhakta-bachhavali, Ratankhan, Braj-lila*, etc.

Mamankoddharanam (late 17th; Malayalam) of Katancheri Nambudiri: a poem describing the Mamankam festival of Kozhikode (Calicut) which was celebrated every 12 years. Katancheri was a court-poet and the poem can also be read as a panegyric to Zamorin power. The last Mamankam was held probably in 1754; before the next one could be organised in 1766, Haidar Ali over ran Kozhikode and unseated the Zamorin.

Mammata (late 11th/early 12th): Kashmiri scholar of Sanskrit; author of the whole or part of *Kavyaprakasha*, also of *Shabdavyaparaparichaya*. In the first work, he reviews the earlier doctrines of different schools of poetics, then establishes the doctrines of the Dhvani school.

Mamulnar (1st cent A.D.): poet in Tamil, a member of the Third Sangam. Thirty-one of his poems were collected in the Sangam anthologies. These provide much information about kings, reigns, forts and battles.

Man Kavi [Man Singh (late 17th)]: poet in Hindi; author of *Rajvilas*, a battle-account. Though nothing is known about his life, it is surmised he was related to the Mewar ruling family. The poem eulogises the Maharana and his bravery.

Mana (Maithili): class of poems somewhat like dramatic lyrics, dealing with the heroine's annoyance with her lover. Umapati is its greatest exponent.

Manabodh or Manabodh Jha (early 18th): poet in Maithili; credited with having pioneered the 'prabandha-kavya' in Maithili and provided an alternative to the lyric tradition ongoing since Vidyapati. His only known work is *Krishnajanma*; Grierson was the first to edit the text but he published it as *Harivamsa*.

Manaka (15th; Kashmiri) of Utthasoma: treatise on music.

Manakkudvar (17th): scholar of Tamil; wrote a commentary on *Tirukkural*. Nothing is known about his life or other works.

Manasa-mangal (Bangla): a kind of mangalkavya featuring Manasa, the serpent goddess. The story common to all these works is that of Manasa winning over as her devotee Chand Sadagar, a wealthy merchant of high social status who was earlier a staunch devotee of Shiva.

Manasa-mangal (late 15th; Bangla) of Bijoy Gupta: also known as *Padma-purana* (Manasa is also called Padma because she was born in a lotus pond), this is the earliest known text in the Manasamangal tradition. Bijoy Gupta wrote during the reign of Husain Shah, hence belongs to the second half of 15th century.

Manasa-mangal (16th; Bangla) of Narayandev: oldest Manasamangal poem among those that can be dated, but no manuscripts older than 18th century. This work probably introduced the form in North-East Bengal.

Manasa-mangal (17th; Bangla) of Ketakadas: the most popular poem on this theme. Its simple style and diction, without being cheap or vulgar, appealed to the masses and ensured its popularity. Following Mukundaram, Ketakadas began his work with an autobiographical account.

Manasa-vijay (1495; Bangla) of Bipradas: the oldest known and most complete homogeneous narrative poem in Bangla on a non-puranic theme. In the opening section, the poet describes the poem as a panchali. The story of Manasa is presented here in a form that is really old and not to be found in other or later works.

Manasar Bhasan (17th; Bangla): a treatment of the Behula legend, done jointly by Ketakadas and Kshemananda.

Manasollasa (1129; Sanskrit) of Someshwara: treatise in verse on kingship. The work consists of 100 sections divided into five 'vimsati' (twenties) and deals with the means of acquiring a kingdom, methods of establishing it, royal enjoyment, games and sports, etc. About 2500 verses are devoted to music and musical instruments, and discusses new forms of music like the 'prabandha'. The author was a Chalukya ruler.

Manay-prakash (?13th; Kashmiri) of Sitikanta Acharya: the earliest known work in Kashmiri which contains 94 four-line stanzas or 'vak'. These verses deal abstractly with Shaiva Tantric philosophy as current in Kashmir as a popular faith. The language is full of Sanskrit words and expressions; the original manuscript is written in Sharda script. In the history of Kashmiri language, these verses have the same position as *Charyagiti* verses in the history of Bangla or Maithili or Asamiya.

Manchana (13th/14th): poet in Telugu and Shaiva preacher. His best-known work is the prabandha-kavya *Keyurbahu-charitramu*, which is based on Rajashekhara's play in Sanskrit, *Viddhasalabhanjika*.

Mandakranta (Sanskrit): name of a verse metre.

Mandan (late 17th): poet in Hindi of the riti convention; author of *Rasa-ratnavali, Rasa-vilas, Janak-pachisi, Janakiyi-ko vyah*, *Nayan-pachisa*. He belonged to Jaitpur village in Bundelkhand (Uttar Pradesh).

Mangal-kavya (Bangla): a form which developed in Bengal probably as early as 13th century. The works in this form were composed to recognise and propagate indigenous deities, mainly goddesses. The form is that of a long narrative poem, often of a voluminous nature, where the main theme is the struggle of a god or goddess to establish himself or herself by bestowing benefits on chosen human beings and persecuting those who defy this new authority.

Mangala-kavya (Rajasthani): poems celebrating a marriage, viz., *Rukmani-mangal*.

Mangala-shloka (Malayalam): poem written in praise of a person and presented to him on some auspicious occasion.

Mangarasa (late 14th): lexicographer in Kannada; compiled *Mangaraja nighantu.*

Mangarasa (early 16th): poet in Kannada; belonged to a Jain royal family of Kallahalli, near modern Hunsur. At least six works are attributed to him. *Jayarupa kavya*, containing 16 sections and 1037 stanzas, written in parivardhini shatpadi metre, tells the story of Jayarupa derived probably from Jinasena's *Mahapuran; Supa-shastra*, a work on cookery written in vardhaka shatpadi, contains six chapters and over 350 stanzas; *Samyaktva kaumudi* includes several stories that uphold the greatness of Jain faith; *Prabhanjanacharite; Sripala charite; Nemijinesha sangati.*

Mani Singh, Bhai (1669–1739): early writer of prose in Panjabi: author of *Sikhon-di bhagatmala* and *Janamsakhi Guru Nanak Devji*, a biography of Guru Nanak. The latter is the most important janamsakhi work in Panjabi.

Manikkavachakar (8th/9th): sant-poet in Tamil, one of the four great Nayanamars; composed the 8th 'tirumurai' which is in two parts, *Tiruvachakam* and *Tirukkovaiyar*. His real name is not yet known; his birthplace has been identified as Vathavur village, south of Madurai. From this he has also been called Vathavurar; acquired the name Manikkavachakar because of the gem-like quality of his language. He was a contemporary of one of the Pandya kings, Varaguna II or Arimardhana; may have become a minister at court before he renounced wordly life. He is said to have visited the temples at Tiruvadamarudur, Tiruvarur and other places before settling down at Chidambaram; died here probably at the age of 32.

Manikoanr (?9th; Asamiya): popular narrative poem, named after the eldest son of Kamrup ruler Sankaladev. He died young and the poem was composed in lamentation. It is the oldest known such work in the language.

Manikram Gangopadhyay (late 18th): poet in Bangla; author of a Dharma-mangal work as well as Shitala-mangal work.

Manikyachandra Suri or **Manikyasundarsuri** (late 14th/early 15th): prose-writer in Gujarati; author of *Prithvichandra-charit* and

Neminathkumar-charit. His unpublished works in Gujarati are 'Satarbedi sat prakar katha', 'Vichar sar stvan', 'Parshwanath stavan', 'Chaknaputra-kathanak'.

Manimekalai (?C; Tamil) of Sittalai Sattanar: long narrative poem, a sequel to *Silappadikaram*. It tells of young and pretty Manimekalai, the daughter of Kovalan and Matavi; after Kovalan's death Matavi abandons her profession as dancer and takes the vow of austerity. Manimekalai does the same but Matavi's mother wants the girl to lead a normal life and encourages the local prince Utayakumaran to court Manimekalai. The girl is drawn towards him, yet wants to practise austerities, eventually becomes a Bouddha nun. Like *Silappadikaram*., this also is composed in 'achiriyam' metre; consists of the same 30 sections (over 4800 lines); frequently uses the same imagery, phrases and sentiments. But it cannot compare in literary excellence with the earlier work.

Manipravala (Malayalam): a highly Sanskritized style in old Malayalam, described by *Lilatilakam* as a necklace strung with the jewels ('mani') of Malayalam and the coral ('pravala') of Sanskrit. Originally the medium was used for exposition and commentary; later, for literary composition, especially champu. Apart from many champu works, many 'stotra' and 'muktaka' compositions are available; only one kavya work, *Chandrotsavam*, is extant. The use of Manipravala was particularly encouraged by the Zamorin's court.

Manipuri: spoken by about 1.7 million persons, it is the main language of Manipur, one of the seven newly formed states in North East India. The speakers are also known as Manipuri. Manipuri belongs to the Tibeto-Burman language-group and it evolved out of Mei-tei, the speech of the ruling class of ancient Manipur. It had a script of its own but, under the influence of Bengali Vaishnavism, chose to adopt the Bangla. script from mid-18th century.

Maniram Barua (1806–58), also known as Maniram Devan; prose-writer in Asamiya, author of *Buranji Viveka'ratna* (1838), manuscript of which only the second part has been found so far. He took part in the 1857 Revolt, was captured and executed in 1858. Subsequently a ballad entitled *Maniram Devanar git* was composed in his honour; a play with the same title has been written by Provin Phukan.

Maniram Mishra (late 18th): poet in Hindi of the riti convention; author of *Chanda-chhapani*. He also composed *Ananda-mangal*, a prose translation of the tenth skandha of *Shrimad Bhagavat*.

Manjhan (1513–93): Sufi poet in Hindi; a disciple of Sheikh Muhammad Ghaus and a contemporary of the poet Qutban. He is known mainly as the author of *Madhumati*, a long poem in Awadhi, written during the regime of Salimshah Suri, son of Shershah Suri.

Mankar (late 15th): composer in Asamiya of lyrics set to tune; author of *Padma-purana*, a work devoted to the snake-goddess Manasa (also known as Padma).

Mankhak (12th): poet in Sanskrit; was attached to court of a Kashmir ruler Jaisingh (r. 1128–49). His only extant work is *Shrikanttha charit*, a long poem in 25 'sarga' describing the combat between the god Shankar and the asur Tripur.

Manlagan (late 17th; Urdu) of Qazi Muhammad Bahre: a poetical work in Dakhni.

Manmohan Basu or Bose (1831–1912): playwright and song-composer in Bangla. Under the influence of Ishwar Gupta he maintained his interest in kavigan; his songs were collected in *Manmohan Gitavali* (1887) for which he wrote a preface giving the history of this type of song and the techniques of how it was sung. Most of his plays were on puranic themes, viz., *Ramabhisheka* (1867), *Sati* (1873), *Harischandra* (1875), *Partha-parajaya* (1881), etc. These were more like jatras than like modern drama.

Manoel da Assumpsam (18th): Portuguese missionary who wrote the first Bangla grammar. He served as the rector of an Augustinian mission near Dhaka. His first work, *Krepar shastre orthobed* (written 1734; published 1743 from Lisbon) was produced as a bi-lingual book; both the Portuguese text and the Bangla translation were printed in Roman. The second work, *Vacabulario em Idioma Bengalla e Portugez* (1743), is the Bangla grammar published along with a Bangla-Portuguese lexicon.

Manohar Kavi (early 17th): a Kachhwaha Rajput prince, who lived in Akbar's court and composed verses in Hindi and Farsi.

Manorama-charita (1080; Prakrit) of Vardhamana: a religious romance.

Mansimha (*c*1752; Bangla): of Bharatchandra Raye; the third part of his *Annada-mangal*. It is a semi-historical story of Raja Mansingh of Amber coming to Bengal to quell the rebellion of Pralapaditya of Jashor, a Bengali findatory chief.

Mansukhram Tripathi (1840–1907): Gujarati prose-writer.

Mantra-vilasam (?C; Malayalam): early prose work, in attaprakara form of unknown authorship.

Manu-bhashya (9th; Sanskrit) of Medhatithi: the oldest extant commentary on *Manu-smriti*. The author was the son of one Viraswamin; probably belonged to South India.

Manu-charitramu (*c*1540; Telugu) of Allasani Peddana: the first full-fledged 'prabandha-kavya' in the language. Its story is derived from *Markandeya-purana*, featuring the inordinately handsome, learned and pious brahman named Arunaspad Pravara. The apsara Varudhini falls in love with him but he does not respond. This situation is exploited by a gandharva whose advances had been rejected by Varudhini earlier.

Maqbul Shah Kralavari (1820–76): poet in Kashmiri; wrote in a variety of forms and on different themes. His most famous work is the masnavi *Gulrez* (1850), story of which derives from a Farsi source. Among his other works are *Grisnama* (1852), a satire on the peasantry; *Pirnama*, in which he attacks the priests; *Baharnama*, a short descriptive poem.

Maqta (Urdu): the last line of a ghazal or the penultimate line of a qasida, in which the poet mentions his 'poetical name' (taqallas).

Marannai (13th): poet in Telugu; composed the Telugu version of *Markandeya-purana*.

Marasi-e-anis (*c*1860; Urdu) of Mir Babbar Ali 'Anis' of Lakhnau: collection of his marsiya poems. Anis' contribution to this form was that he made the poems more descriptive than was conventional.

Marathi: main language of the state of Maharashtra in West India, it is spoken by about 70 million persons. Descended from Maharashtri Prakrit and Maharastri Apabhramsha, it became an independent language by 11th cent. A.D. Written in the Modi script until 18th century, it adopted Nagari thereafter.

Marathi inscriptions: earliest (983) available is the sentence inscribed in Marathi (also in Kannada) at the foot of the Gomateshwara statue in Sravanbelgola near Mysore. Six more have been dated between 979–1270. The Pandharpur inscription of 1273, assigned to the reign of Raja Shiromani Ramdevrao, Yadav ruler of Deogiri, indicates a well-developed language.

Marga (Sanskrit): term in musicology, but also used in poetics. When used to denote classical music, the term derives from the root 'mrig' (to seek); thus, the music which Brahma obtained after seeking. In a more general sense, marga is the path shown by the sages; hence, a mode which conforms to rules laid down in authoritative texts.

Mari hakikat (*c*1866; Gujarati) of Narmad: an early autobiography in Gujarati, but published only in 1933.

Markanda Dasa (15th): poet in Oriya, probably lived and wrote during the same time as Sarala Dasa or a little earlier. His *Keshab koili* is the earliest extant example of koili lyrics in Oriya literature. Composed in chautisa style, it tells of Yashoda's lamentation on Krishna's leaving home.

Markandeya Dasa (?C): scholar of Orissa; author of the Prakrit grammar *Prakrita-sarvaswa*. In this work is quoted a couplet illustrating 'Odra Vibhasa', which may be regarded as the forerunner of modern Oriya.

Markandeya-purana (?C; Sanskrit): one of the major puranas, relevant to literature because it contains many legends and narratives that resemble legends told in *Mahabharata*.

Tr. F.E. Pargiter, *Bib. Ind.*, 1904.

Marsiya (Urdu): elegy on the martyrdom of the Prophet's grandson Hussain and his companions, which is recited every year at the anniversary of their death.

Marthanda-mahatmyam (18th; Malayalam) of unknown authorship: poem in eulogy of Marthanda Varma, ruler of Travancore.

Masnavi (Urdu): a verse-form used for elegiac poems as well as for narrating historical events. Its distinguishing feature is that in it each verse is linked to the next, thus forming a chain of connections. Generally it is a poem of some length.

Masnavi Sahrul-bayan (1785; Urdu) of Mir Hasan: the most famous masnavi work in the language. It tells the love-story of prince Benazir and princess Badr-e-Munir. Benazir was such a handsome youth that a fairy abducts him. He is given a grand palace to live in and a magic horse which can take him anywhere. One day he sees the beautiful princess Badremunir in a garden and falls in love with her. Her friend and the wazir's daughter Najmunnisa helps them to meet secretly. On hearing about this the fairy gets very angry and casts Benazir into a deep and dark well in a desert. But Badremunir rescues him with the help of Ferozeshah, the son of the king of jinns. The lovers are reunited and they marry.

Masud (1173–1265): also known as Sheikh Farid. A Muslim ascetic of Panjab, he wrote some poems and about 200 couplets in the local language to please and instruct his newly converted (to Islam) Jat and Rajput followers.

Mathura-mangala (*c*1800; Oriya) of Bhaktacharan Dasa: long poem telling the story of Shri Krishna's departure from Mathura and the slaying of Kamsa. The work became very popular even within the poet's lifetime.

Matiram (b.1617): poet in Hindi and scholar; brother of Bhushan; author of *Rasa-raj, Lalit-lalam, Sahitya-sar, Lakshan-shringar*. He also composed dohas which were collected as *Matiram Satsai*. His patron was Raja Bhavsingh of Bundi in Rajasthan.

Matla (Urdu): The preliminary verse in a ghazal or qasida in which the two lines are linked by apparent reiteration.

Matricheta (?1st A.D.): poet in Sanskrit; at one time wrongly identified with Ashwaghosha. He was a brahman ascetic and belonged to Kusumapura (in modern Bihar); later converted to Bouddha faith. He composed 101 hymns to Buddha, some of which were translated into Tibetan, Chinese and Japanese within a couple of centuries after his death; thus he is known as Makhol in Tibetan and Mashiriseita in Japanese. The finest of these hymns, *Shatapanchastka-strota*, contains 150 verses divided into 13 sections.

Matrigupta (?1st A.D.): poet in Sanskrit; associated with the court of Kashmir ruler Vikramaditya Harshavardhana. Kalhana's *Rajatarangini* mentions Matrigupta and gives an account of his friendship with the king. It is believed he succeeded Harshadeva as ruler. No work of his is extant.

Matsya-purana (?C; Sanskrit): one of the major puranas, which conforms in a large measure to the traditional definition of puranas. It relates the legend of the flood during which Vishnu assumes the form of a fish and rescues only Manu of all mankind.

Matta-vilasa (*c*600; Sanskrit) of Mahendra Vikramavarman: a one-act play of the 'prahasana' type. It portrays the drunken revelries of a Shaiva mendicant, his bearing a human skull as alms-bowl, his dalliance with a wench, his scuffle with a Bouddha monk, and so on. The author was a Pallava king who ruled in Kanchi around A.D. 600. This play and another, *Bhagavadajjukiya* ascribed to Bodhayana, is mentioned in the Mamandur inscription of 610.

Mattinachurukkam (11th; Tamil) of Pukazhenti: poem in 71 stanzas describing the beauty of women.

Matul-hosen (1645; Bangla) of Mohamad Khan of Chatgaon: the oldest jangnama poem in Bangla; written at the instance of the poet's murshid, Pir Shah Sultan; deals with the death of Husein.

Maujajjo (Sindhi): a poetical form which eulogises a prophet or holy man of Islam by describing some miraculous event in his life. It is different from 'munakibo' wherein the subject is the same but the event described is normal and ordinary.

Max Mueller [Friedrich Max Mueller (1823–1900)]: great German linguist and scholar of Sanskrit; devoted his whole life to the study of ancient Indian texts but never actually came to India. His work on Indian literature was a translation of *Hitopadesha* published in 1844. Commissioned by East India Company in 1847 to collate and edit *Rig-veda*, he completed this work in six large volumes during 1849–74. His translation of *Meghaduta* was published in 1847. Between 1876 and 1900 he edited the unique series, *The Sacred Books of the East*, in 51 volumes. Among his other works are *History of Ancient Sanskrit Literature* (1859), *The Origin and Growth of Religion* (1878), *India: What Can It Teach Us* (1883).

Mayan Bhatt or Mayan Bambh (late 15th): poet in Rajasthani; mainly composed amorous verses. Some of these have been collected as *Mayana kutuhal*; his work has also been referred to by others as *Mayana chhand* or *Mayana ras* but no manuscript of this has been recovered as yet.

Mayura (?7th): poet in Sanskrit; author of *Surya-shataka*. It is said that he was afflicted by leprosy and wrote these poems on the god Surya in order to cure himself. He was a contemporary of Bana Bhatta and may have been associated with emperor Harsha's court.

Mayurabhatta (?C): poet in Bangla; supposed to be the earliest composer of Dharma-mangal poems.

Mayuraja (?C): playwright in Sanskrit; author of the lost work *Udatta'Raghava*. According to some scholars he was a Chedi king with his capital at Mahismati. His verses are quoted in *Suktimuktavali* of Jalhana.

Mazhamangalam Nambutri (*c*1525–93): poet in Malayalam; also composed in Sanskrit. He belonged to the Mazhamangalam family of Trichur; originally called Narayanan, he was the son of another poet named Shankaran. His four works in Sanskrit are *Mazhamangalam bhanam, Smartta prayashchitta vimashini, Rasakrida kavyam* and *Uttara Ramayana champu*. Among his works in Malayalam are *Bhasha Naishadham, Rajartnavaliyam, Kotiyaviraham, Banayuddham*, etc.

Mazhar Jan-e-janan Mirza (1701–81): poet in Urdu; also composed in Farsi. Born as Shamsuddin Habibullah at Agra, he became a well-known sufi when quite young. He is credited with having reformed Urdu poetry and restored its simplicity of expression in conveying sublime thoughts. But no collection of his Urdu poems is extant. His poems in Farsi were collected as *Diwan-e-Mazhar*; he also prepared a selection of verses from great Persian poets entitled *Kharita-e-Jawahir*.

Medhankara (late 13th): Jain scholar and poet in Pali; author of *Jinacharita*. He is said to have lived in Sri Lanka during the reign of king Bhuvaneka Bahu I (r. 1277–88).

Medini-kosha (14th; Sanskrit) of Medinikara: a lexicon which gives the gender and meaning of words. It also features words having the same meaning as well as words having two meanings. The real title of the work is *Anekartha-shabdakosha*.

Meenakshiammai Pillai Tamil (early 7th; Tamil) of Kumarguruparar: poetical work in the 'pillai tamil' form which deals with the god Shiva's consort Meenakshi devi, narrating various episodes featuring her drawn from puranas. It is regarded as the finest example of literary work in this particular form. According to legend, when the poet first recited it in the court of king Tirumalai Nayak at Madurai, the goddess appeared in the form of a six-year old girl, daughter of the temple priest and seated herself in the lap of the king.

Meenakshisundaram Pillai, Mahavidwan (1815–76): poet in Tamil and scholar from Advatoor, near Tiruchirappalli. He composed nearly 50 works, which include 16 puranas, 9 pillai-tamils, 11 antadis, 2 kalambakams, 4 malais, and one each of a kovai, lilai, venba, kalippu. Among his works are *Woriyur puranam, Seerkazhi kovai, Kashi rahasyam*, etc.

Megha-duta (?5th; Sanskrit) of Kalidasa: a love poem, among the most popular in Sanskrit literature, as evidenced by the existence of about 50 commentaries. It gave a name to the form 'sandesh-kavya'. The poem tells of a Yaksha who has been banished to Ramgiri in central India for a year as punishment for some misdemeanour; he pines for his beloved left behind in Alaka; when the monsoon is about to begin, he addresses a cloud to send news about himself to his beloved. The poem is in two parts, 'Purva-megha' and 'Uttar-megha'. In the first part, the Yaksha details the route to be followed by the cloud; in the second part, he describes Alaka and gives the message to be conveyed by the cloud.

Tr. H.H. Wilson, 2nd edition, 1943; G.H. Rooke, London, 1935; R.D. Karmarkar, Poona, 1947; Franklin & Eleanor Edgerton, Ann Arbor, Michigan, 1964; Leonard Nathan, Berkeley, 1976.

Meharban [Sodhi Meharban (*c*1558–1618)]: poet as well as prose-writer in Panjabi. Originally named Manohardas, son of Prithvichand, the older brother of Guru Arjan Dev, Meharban is believed to have composed his earlier poetry under the pseudonym of 'Nanak'. His best-known work is *Janamsakhi Guru Nanak Dev*; from the manuscript it appears this was a much larger text, consisting of five books. Only 288 of the original 575 'goshtian' are extant. Meharban also wrote *Var Piran ki, Sukamani sansharnama*, and *Rambali onkar vada*. Along with his son Sodhi Hariji, he founded the Meharbania sect.

Mentha (?1st A.D.): poet in Sanskrit; associated with Kashmiri king Matrigupta; author of the long poem *Hayagriva-vadha*. References to Mentha are to be found in many later texts.

Merajul ashiqin (*c*1398; Urdu) of Banda Nawaz Gesu Daraz: the first available treatise in Dakhni; a prose work devoted to mystic interpretation of life and ethics. The title means 'the ascent of lovers'.

Merumantira-puranam (?C; Tamil) of Vammanacharyar: long poem in 1406 stanzas; tells the story of two Jain brothers and expounds Jain beliefs.

Meyuppatu (Tamil): general term for 'acting', it literally means bodily efforts by which a person conveys some inner feeling.

Mhaimbhat (13th): prose-writer in Marathi; belonged to the Mahanubhava sect. He compiled the earliest known prose work in the language, *Lila-charitra*, which is an anecdotal biography of Chakradhara. A similar work, *Riddhipura-charitra*, was compiled by him.

Miguel de Almeida (1607–83): Jesuit priest; author of *Onvillancho mallo*, a religious treatise written in Konkani. This work provides a rare example of early Konkani prose.

Milindapanho (1st/2nd; Prakrit) of unknown authorship: extant work is a Pali translation done in Sri Lanka of a lost work originally in Sanskrit or Prakrit. It is in the form of questions asked by Milinda (or Menander or Menandros, a Greek ruler) about certain aspects of Buddhism, and the answers given by Thera Nagasena. Milinda ruled over some Greek territory in North-West India sometime in 1st century B.C.; nothing is known of Nagasena. The work is generally placed between A.D. 100 and 200. It consists of seven parts, of which portions of the first part and whole of the second and third parts are considered authentic.

Tr. T.W. Rhys Davids, *SBE*, 1800, 1894.

Mir (1722/23–1810): poet in Urdu; first great master of the ghazal form; also composed love narrative in the masnavi form.

Mir Amman Dehalvi (18th/19th): Urdu writer from Delhi; belonged to a family which had been associated with Mughal rulers from the time of Humayun. When the city was sacked by Ahmadshah Durrani, and the family lands confiscated, Mir Amman moved for some time to Azimabad (Patna), then to Calcutta. Here he was appointed to Fort William College and commissioned to translate *Qissa Chahar Darves* from Farsi into Urdu. This translation, entitled *Bag-o-bahar*, became justly famous and popular. He also translated *Anbar saheli* from Farsi into Urdu as *Ganj-e-khubi* but this was not as successful as the earlier work.

Mir Dard (1719–85): poet in Urdu, whose verses are mainly mystical in content.

Mir Hasan [Mir Ghulam Hasan (1736–86)]: poet in Urdu; famous as the composer of masnavis, especially his longest, *Sahrul-bayan*, which is the love story of prince Benazir and his beloved Badr-e-Munir.

Mir Hasan Ali (1824–1909): poet in Sindhi; son of the ruler of Sindh, Mir Nasir Khan; after the annexation of Sindh, remained in house detention until 1862. He is best known for the work *Sindhjo Shahnamo*, an account of the kings of Sindh, based on Firdausi's *Shahnama* in Farsi.

Mir Khaliq (1774–1814): poet in Urdu; real name Mir Musathasin; father of the poet Anis and a disciple of the poet Mushafi. He was an exponent of the marsiya and contributed to the development of this form in Urdu.

Mir Musharraf Husain (1848–1912): Muslim novelist in Bangla; author of the three-volume *Bishad sindhu* on which his reputation mainly rests. His other novels, *Ratnavali* (1869), *Udasi pathik maner katha* (1891) and *Ghazi Minchar dastani* (1896) are romantic narratives full of events. He also wrote two plays, *Basantkumari* (1872) and *Jamidar-darpan* (1873).

Mir Taqi Mir [Mir Muhammad Taqi (1724–1810)]: poet in Urdu from Agra; among the greatest ghazal composers; gave the form a new direction by using everyday speech in poetry. His works have been collected in six diwans; he also has a diwan of poems in Farsi. Apart from ghazals, he composed well-known marsiya works, viz., *Akhgar namah, Shewla-e-ishk, Jash-e-ishk*, etc. His prose work in Farsi, *Nukatul-shaora*, is an account of Urdu poetry.

Mira or **Miran** (*c*1498–1546): woman sant-poet of Rajasthan, popularly known as Mirabai; renowned singer and devotee of Giridhar (Shri Krishna). Born in Medta and daughter of Rao Ratansingh, she was married off to Bhojraj, son of Rana Sanga of Mewar; disclaimed this marriage on the plea that she was already wedded to Krishna; widowed seven years after the marriage, she had to face persistent criticism and hostility from her in-laws; ultimately left for Brindavan, from where she went to Dwaraka. Her compositions have been collected in four volumes: *Narsiji-ka mayera, Gita Govind-ki tika, Raga Govind* and *Raga Soratha-ke pad*. She composed in the Marwari form of Rajasthani speech, but her songs have been preserved in Brajbhasa.

Miranbai-ki padavali (16th; Hindi): collection of padas composed by Mira or Miran. Only three of more than two dozen such collections are based on available manuscripts. These are *Miran mandakini* (Agra, 1930) ed. Narottam Swami; *Miran smriti grantha* (Calcutta, 1950) published by Bangiya Parishad; some 55 padas included by Udaysingh Bhatnagar in his *Rajasthan mein hindi hastalikhit granthon ki khoj*.

Mirza-Sahiban: the hero and heroine of a popular folk story of Panjab; among qissa works based on it are those by Pilu (in early 16th) and by Hafiz Barkhurdar.

Mitravinda-Govinda (late 17th; Kannada) of Singarayya: the earliest known play in the language. Though the writer has not indicated this, it is an adaptation of the Sanskrit play *Ratnavali*, Singarayya was a contemporary of Mysore ruler Chikkadevaraya (r. 1672–1704).

Mitravinda-parinayamu (early 18th; Telugu) of Venkatachalapati: prabandha in six sections. The author was a court poet of Vijayaranga Chokkantha.

Miyen Inat jo kalam (Sindhi): the first definite edition of the works of Shah Inat, a 17th century poet in Sindhi. It contains 469 'bayt' and 42 'wai' under 22 suruds or modes of singing. Though the poet was a Sufi, these poems or songs are about local folk-tales, traders, weavers, and other aspects of ordinary life.

Mobed Rustom Peshotan (17th): poet in Gujarati; the first Parsi to make a name as a poet in Gujarati. All his four known works—*Jarathostra nameh, Swabaksh nameh, Viraf nameh, Aspandayar nameh*—are hagiographical poems about Parsi sants.

Moggallayana-vyakarana (?C; Pali) of Moggallana; a grammatical work, also called *Sadda-lakkhana*. It was written with the help of *Chandra-vyakarana* and *Ashtadhyayi*. According to some scholars, it is more extensive and of a higher standard than Kachhayana's grammar. The author himself wrote a commentary on the work later.

Mohamudgara (?C; Sanskrit) ascribed to Shankaracarya: a verse composition, lyrical in form and didactic in content. It points out common human frailties and seeks to inculcate the correct attitude to life.

Mohan-tarangini (*c*1550; Kannada) of Kanakadasa: long poem in sangatya metre, re-telling several episodes about Krishna drawn from *Mahabharata* and *Bhagavatapurana.*

Moharaj-parajay (13th; Sanskrit) of Yashah Pal, symbolic play, which was first performed on a Mahavira birth anniversary. It has five acts; among the episodes enacted is the initiation of Chalukya king Kumarpal into Jain faith by Hemachandra. The playwright was a Jain from Gujarat.

Moirang Ninghthoural Lambuba (?C; Manipuri): a prose chronicle of the kings of Moirang, written in Meitei script. The date or period of composition is uncertain; it appears to have been written by pandits of the royal court over many years.

Molla Ramayanamu (16th; Telugu): a condensed version of *Ramayana* by Atukuri Molla, the earliest woman poet in Telugu. Of all versions of *Ramayana* in Telugu available at the time, this became the most popular and was referred to by the poets' name.

Momin [Hakim Momin Khan (1800–51)]: poet in Urdu from Kashmir. He was also interested in medicine and astrology. He composed six masnavi poems, of which three are better-known: *Shikayat-e-sitam, Qissa-e-gam, Kause-sami.*

Moomal-Rano: tragic couple of a popular romance in Sindhi literature.

Morang poets: Morang is the Maithili speaking area of Nepal which at one time was the kingdom of a dynasty which patronised Maithil poets like Lachminarayan, Gopinath, Viranarayan, Dhireswar, Bhisma Kavi, Gangadhar. These came to be known as the Morang poets.

Moropant (1729–94): poet in Marathi, whose great work is a version of *Mahabharata* in arya metre. Born into a brahman family of Panhala (near Kolhapur), he became proficient in Sanskrit at an early age and began giving discourses on religious as well as secular topics. A jagirdar of Baramati, Babaji Naik, heard of his fame and offered him employment. Moropant spent the rest of his life in Baramati. He composed several long poems on puranic subjects, viz., *Krishna-vijaya, Mantra-bhagvata*; also wrote devotional lyrics which have been collected in his *Samasya-ratnamala, Kekavali, Ganga-prarthana.* Moropant is also known as Mayura Pandit to scholars.

Moyanamotir gan (17th; Bangla) of Bhavanidas: poetical work featuring Gopichandra and his mother Moyanamoti, whose story was popularised by the Natha sect. The poet probably belonged to Tripura.

Mricchakatika (?C; Sanskrit) of Shudraka: a play in ten acts, which is unique because it does not deal with royal life. The main plot tells the love story of the impoverished but large-hearted brahman Charudatta and the rich courtesan Vasantasena; the sub-plot tells of the dethroning of the bad king Palaka. It is essentially a social drama, depicting a plebian world.

Tr. A.W. Ryder, HOS, 1905; M.R. Kale, Bombay, 1924; R.P. Oliver, Illinois, 1938.

Mrigavati (1501/1603; Hindi) of Kutban: romance of Sufi inspiration composed in Avadhi. It tells of princess Mrigavati of Kanchanpur and the prince of Chandragiri, son of Ganapati Dev. The prince wins her after overcoming many difficulties.

Mrigavati-charita (17th; Asamiya) of Rama Dvija: romance which tells of the love of a prince for a princess; resembles the Hindi kavya *Mrigavati.*

Mrityunjay Kavi (*c*1800): poet in Telugu; belonged to Komargiri village of Godavari district in Andhra Pradesh. Among his works are *Gharatmaja parinayemu*, a 'dvyarthi' kavya which describes the marriage of Sita as well as of Parvati; *Nirostthaya Nalacharitramu*, a chitrakavya; *Brihannaridiyamu*, a puran kavya.

Mrityunjoy Vidyalankar (d. 1819): early prose-writer in Bangla, who assisted William Carey at Fort William College. He wrote *Batris simhasan* (1802) and *Hitopadesh* (1808), both translations of Sanskrit story books; *Rajavali* (1808), which appears to have been adapted from a contemporary Sanskrit work based on Mughal chronicles; *Prabodhchandrika* (1833), which contains translations as well as original writing. His writing represents the 'Pandit' style (Sanskrit based) of Bangla prose as distinct from the 'Munshi' style (Farsi based) of Ramram Bosu. He also wrote *Vedantachandrika* (1817), which is a protest against the Vedantism advocated by Rammohan Roy.

Muamlambd (Urdu): a poetical

form in which the 'ashik' (lover) seeks to attain the level of his 'mashuk' (beloved). He abandons his sense of prestige, engages in conversation with her, and expresses a somewhat inferior form of love for her. The poet Juruant is said to have innovated this form.

Mubarak [Saiyad Mubarak Ali Bilgrami (b.1583)]: poet in Hindi. He composed a hundred dohas each for ten features of the human body. Only a portion of these have been recovered as *Alak-shatak aur Til-shatak*.

Muddupalni (18th): woman poet in Telugu, associated with the court of Raja Pratapsingh; author of *Radhika santwanamu*. This kavya-work deals with the three-cornered romance between Krishna, Radha, and Ila. There are excesses of erotic description in the poem but it probably catered to the popular taste of its time.

Mudra-manjusha (1823; Kannada) of Kempunarayan; prose-work which elaborates upon the story summarised at the beginning of the Sanskrit play *Mudra Rakshasa*. The most notable feature of the work is its language, which shows modern Kannada emerging out of old Kannada.

Mudra Rakshasa (?4th/5th; Sanskrit) of Vishakhadatta: a play in seven acts which is unique because it deals with a political theme. The main plot tells of how Rakshasa, the faithful minister of the Nandas, was won over through astute diplomacy, by Chanakya, minister of king Chandragupta.
Tr. K.H. Dhruva, Pune, 1923.

Mugdhabodha (*c*1300; Sanskrit) of Vopadeva: a grammar for beginners. It partly adopts the method of Katantra, partly the system of *Ashtadhyayi*, but omits the Vedic portion of the latter. The work was particularly popular in Bengal, which leads some scholars to believe that the author was a Bengali.

Mugdhopadesha (?C; Sanskrit) of Jalhana: a didatic poem in 66 verses. The work warns against the wiles of harlots and asserts that no harlot is capable of love. The author is not the same as the compiler of *Suktimuktavali*.

Muhabara (Hindi): term for statements that have gained the status of idioms.

Muhaidin-puranam (?C; Tamil) of Vannakkalanji Pulavar (Muhammad Ibrahim): work on tenets of Islam.

Muhammad Zaman, Khwaja (1713–74): Sufi sant poet in Sindhi. After his studies and travel, he settled in Lawari village, which in course of time became known as Lawari Sharif because of his reputation. Very little of his poetry has been preserved, but his philosophic thoughts and preaching are to be found in *Fatah-al-Fazi* (in Arabi) and *Sharah abyat sindhi* (verses in Sindhi, explanations in Arabi).

Muhanota Nainasi (1610–70): prose writer in Rajasthani: served the Jodhpur ruling family as warrior and minister. His *Marawar-ra pargana-ri vigata* is a historical survey of the different parganas of the then Jodhpur state. In the other work, *Nainasi rikhyata*, he had planned to write a history of all important Rajput dynasties, ruling clans and sub-clans of Rajasthan as well as of adjoining regions like Gujarat, Bundelkhand and Malwa upto 1660. This work could not be completed because Nainasi committed suicide when charged with misdemeanour by his patron, Maharaja Jaswant Singh of Jodhpur.

Muka panchashati (?C; Sanskrit) of Muka Kavi: a religious poem of 500 stanzas in praise of the goddess Kamakshi of Kanchi. The poet was called Muka because he probably had a speech impairment. Very little is known about the poet who may have been a contemporary of Shankaracharya.

Mukkudarpallu (14th/15th; Tamil) of unknown authorship: a dramatic poem which eventually glorifies Mukkudal Algar, the local deity of Mukkudal, a place where the rivers Sittraru and Kodandaram meet the river Tamraparni. As in other 'pallu' works, here too we get a lively picture of peasant life. It tells of the peasant Alagukkunduban who has two wives, Mukkudar, a devotee of Vishnu, and Marudur, a devotee of Shiva. The two wives quarrel over favours shown by the husband, blame each others' chosen deities, but ultimately make up and join in the praise of Algar.

Mukta'bai (d.1290): woman poet in Marathi. She was the younger sister of sant Jnaneshwar. Abhangs composed by her are widely sung.

Muktaka (Sanskrit/Prakrit/Apabhramsha): a complete poem in a single stanza. The form was popular in all old Indian languages.

Muktanand (1761–1830): poet in Gujarati, who is also known as a representative voice of the Swaminarayan sect. His original name was Mukunda Das; he became the chief disciple of Ramananda, the famous sant of Saurashtra; later he took initiation from Swami Sahajananda. His well-known works are *Mukunda-bavani, Udhvav-gita* and *Sati-gita*; among others are *Dharmamrita, Premlila, Ramlila,* etc.

Mukteshwar (1608–60): poet in Marathi; composed a version of *Ramayana* early in life, then a version of *Mahabharata*. Only four parvan of the latter are now available and these are considered to represent work superior to the former. He is said to have written many smaller poems and other miscellaneous pieces, including an exposition of *Bhagavata-purana*, but none of these has survived. He was the son of Eknath's daughter.

Mukundaraj (13th): philosopher and poet in Marathi. According to some scholars, he preceded Jnaneshwar. Two of his works, *Viveksindhu* and *Paramrita*, deal with Shankara's vedanta; he also composed *Pavana-vijaya, Mula-stambha, Panchakirana*. It is sometimes held that he belonged to a schism founded by Gorakhnath.

Mukundaram Chakrabarti 'Kavikankan' (late 16th): poet in Bangla; author of *Chandi-mangal*. Born to a brahman family of Damunya village in Bardhaman district of West Bengal, Mukundaram had to leave his ancestral home when this and lands were confiscated by Afghan chiefs; he migrated to Adada village in Midnapore district where the local brahman chief Bankura Raye gave him and his family shelter. Mukundaram was appointed tutor and companion to the chief's youngest son, Raghunath Raye, during whose regime (1573–1603) he wrote the poem.

Mulasutra: collective name of four ancient texts in Maharashtri Prakrit. These are: (1) *Uttarajjayan* (*'Uttaradhyayan'*); (2) *Avassaya* or *Avassaga* (from 'Avasyak'); (3) *Dasvepaliya* of Sajjambhav (Swayambhuva); (4) *Pindunijjutta* of Bhadrabahu.

Mulaghatika Ketana (*c*1200–60): poet and scholar in Telugu; rendered the Sanskrit work *Dashakumara-charita* into Telugu verse and dedicated it to Tikkanna; also composed a Telugu grammar, *Andhrabhasha-bhushanamu*.

Mulla Ahmad (15th): scholar and poet in Farsi from Kashmir; translator in the court of Zainul Abidin; rendered *Rajataranagini* into Farsi; also adapted *Mahabharata* into Farsi.

Mulla Wajhi (early 17th): poet in Urdu; author of the masnavi *Qutab mushatari* (1609) and of *Sabras* (1634), a prose allegory on Sufism, both composed in Dakhni.

Mullaippattu (?C; Tamil) of Napputanar: the fifth idyll of *Pattuppattu* It portrays the feelings of an ideal wife waiting for her husband's return from a military expedition. The work is supposed to have been composed in praise of the Pandya king Nedunchezian. The author was a gold merchant of Kavirippumpattinam.

Munaziro (Sindhi): a form of folk-poetry in which two sides (ideas or view points or attitudes) are taken up and each tries to overcome the other in argument. The form is basically meant to entertain by making fun of each other.

Muni Kankamar (mid-11th): poet in Apabhramsha. He was born a brahman but later became a Digambar Jain; on his travels reached a city called Asaiyan; here he wrote the biographical work *Karakandu-chariu*. The work was probably sponsored but the poet does not give the sponsor's name nor does he mention any detail of his own life.

Munidatta (?C): scholar of Bengal; wrote a commentary in Bangla on the *Charya* songs.

Muojajjo (Sindhi): a poetical form which eulogises a prophet or holy man of Islam by describing some miraculous event in his life.

Muppina Shadakshari (early 16th): poet in Kannada of Virashaiva faith; composed 74 'kaivalya' poems faith collected as *Shiva-ashataka* and *Shiva-yogashtaka*.

Muqaddama-al-sawat (*c*1700; Sindhi) of Abu-al-Hasan: a treatise in verse on 'namaz'. Also known as *Abul-al-Hasan ji Sindhi*, it is considered to be the first ever Sindhi book written in a Perso-Arabic script. The script was devised by Maulvi Abu-al-Hasan and it was taken up by other maulvis, until it became the standard form for writing in Sindhi.

Muqbal (18th): Muslim poet in Panjabi; author of *Jangnama Imam Husain* which tells of the battle of Karbala. According to biographical information provided in this worrk, his full name was Shahjahan Muqbal and he was blind. He also composed a Hir-Ranjha qissa and *Machhah Muqbal*, an account of the miracles in the life of Abdul Qadar Jilani, Sufi sant and leader of the Qadri sect.

Murali-vilas (early 17th; Bangla) of Rajballabh: a biography of Shri Chaitanya.

Murari (early 8th): playwright in Sanskrit; author of *Anargha-Raghava*, a play in six acts. In its prologue he has made a critical reference to Bhavabhuti.

Murari Gupta (early 16th): scholar of Sanskrit from Bengal; one of Shri Chaitanya's oldest followers, who wrote his first biography in Sanskrit. The work is a narrative poem, known as the 'kadacha' of Murari Gupta, and it became the source for all later biographers. He also wrote a few lyrics in Bangla on the Radha-Krishna theme.

Musaddas (Urdu): verse-form consisting of six lines. There is no stipulated metre or subject and the poem can be of any length. Perhaps the best known example is Hali's *Madd-o-jajra-e-Islam* which depicts the rise and fall of Muslims; it is now known as *Musaddas-e-Hali*.

Mushafi (1750–1824): a versatile man of Urdu letters of the Lakhnau school; knew many languages; wrote a grammatical treatise on Urdu, also an early novel, *Rani Ketaki-ki kahani*, using pure Hindi words. Besides composing lyrics and romances, he also compiled several tazkiras.

Mushaira (Urdu): gathering of poets where each recites from his latest work. The custom originated in Iran. Associated mainly with Urdu poets in India, it probably became popular after Mughal emperor Aurangzeb banned recitation of poetry in the royal court. Whereupon, princes and nobles began to hold such gatherings at their homes.

Muttollayiram (?5th; Tamil) of unknown author: collection of verses in venba metre on the Chera, Chola and Pandya kings. The original work consisted of 900 verses to each king, thus totalling 2700. Of these, 109 were reproduced in *Purattirattu*, one in Ilampuranar's commentary on *Tolkappiyam* and a few in Perasiriyar's commentarry on *Seyyul'iyal*; only these have been recovered. All the major *Tolkappiyam* commentators refer to this work, hence it must have been well-known and much respected at one time.

Muvarula (12th; Tamil) of Ottakkatur: Common title of three poetical works in 'ula' form. In this form, the hero, after watching a cavalcade of men, horses and elephants, reflects upon the various moods of women ranging from girlhood to mature young women.

N

Naat (Kashmiri): poetry written in love and praise of Nabi Muhammad; a specific form of qasida, with models provided by the Quran 2Sharif itself. The form was introduced to Kashmiri poetry by the 14th century sant-poet Sheik Nuruddin.

Nabhadas (1570–*c*1662): poet of Ram-bhakti in Hindi from Gwalior; composed *Bhakta-mal* in Avadhi and *Ramashtayam* in Brajbhasha. Born blind and abandoned as a five-year-old in a forest by poverty-stricken parents, the poet was rescued by Agradas and reared as his son.

Nabi-vamsha (Bangla): a form of religious narrative poetry composed by Muslim poets of Bengal, on Hindu models like *Harivamshapuranam*; deals with stories of Nabi Muhammad and earlier prophets.

Nabinchandra Sen (1847–1909): poet in Bangla from Noapara village in Chatgaon district of undivided Bengal. He served in civil administration under the British but also wrote the famous patriotic poem 'Palasir juddho' (The battle of Palasi) in 1875. Among his poetical works are *Raibatak* (1887), *Kurukshetra* (1891), *Prabhas* (1896). He also wrote the travelogue *Prabaser patra* (1892), the novel *Bhanumati* (1900), and the five volume autobiography *Amar jibon* (1908–14).

Nabo-babu-bilas (1823; Bangla) of Bhabanicharan Bandopadhyay: satirical prose work, perhaps the first of its kind in Bangla. It describes the life-style of the new (*nabo*) elite (*babu*) of 19th century Calcutta. The satire reflects the anguish of conservatives at the social irresponsibility and moral depravity exhibited by the upcoming 'babu' class. Though coarse in parts, the work is redeemed by humour and hilarity.

Nachana Soma (*c*1335–1377): poet in Telugu, attached to the court of Bukkaraja; author of *Uttara-Harivamshamu*. He was a great admirer of Tikkanna and a follower of the Hari-Har cult.

Nachari (Maithili): type of song that is a direct prayer to Shiva. The name derives from Shiva's aspect as dancer.

Nachhinarkkiniyar (13th/14th): scholar of Tamil from Madurai; author of commentaries on *Tolkappiyam, Pattupputtu, Jivaka-chintamani*, part of *Kurunttogai*, etc. Though he is the last of a succession of great commentators, he was the first to comment on both literary and grammatical elements of a text. His own prose also provided a model of clear diction and sophisticated syntax.

Naduvath Achhan Namdudiri (1841–1912) poet in Malayalam: associated with the 'pure Malayalam' school of literary composition sponsored by the Kodungallur royal family. He was called Naduvathu Achhan (father) to distinguish him from his son, also a poet, known as Naduvathu Mahan (son). His works are *Ambopadesham*, a poem upholding virtuous women; *Bhagavaddutu nataka*, a play on Shri Krishna's mediation between the Pandavs and the Kauravs; *Shringeri-yatra* and *Ashtamatiit-yatra*, accounts of pilgrimage; Bhagavadstuti, hymns in praise of divinity; *Balyudhbhavam.*

Nagachandra (11th): poet in Kannada; became famous as 'Abhinava Pampa' after he had composed *Ramachandra-charita purana*, popularly known as *Pampa Ramayana*. This is the first *Ramayana* in the language belonging to the Jain tradition. The poet also wrote *Mallinatha purana*. Little is known of his life and there is much controversy about his dates.

Nagakumara kaviyam (Tamil) of unknown date and authorship: a lost work, known only by references, but included among the five minor 'kappiyam' of the language.

Nagananda (?7th; Sanskrit) of Shriharsha: drama in five acts, based on a Bouddha legend. It tells of Vidyadhar prince Jimutvahana who falls in love with Siddha princess Malayavati and marries her; one day, out of pity for the serpents being killed by Garuda, offers himself and is devoured by Garuda; later is restored to life by Gauri's blessing, and lives happily ever after with Malayavati.

Tr. P. Boyd, London, 1872; H. Wartham, London & New York, 1911.

Naga-shataka (mid-18th; Sanskrit) of Bharatchandra Raye: poem in eight stanzas written as an appeal to his patron when Ramdev Nag, an agent of the local chief attempted to oust him from lands granted to him by Raja Krishnachandra of Nadia.

Nagari'das (b.1699): poet in Hindi and scholar; said to have authored 73 works. Among these are *Bhajasar, Ramacharit-mala, Vairagyaballari, Jugalbhakti-vinod.*

Nagarjuna (2 A.D.) important Bouddha philosopher, who has been credited with composing in Sanskrit 'lekha' (epistles), 'stotra'' (lyrics) and 'parikatha' (tracts) which gave literary treatment to philosophical ideas. His followers like Matricheta and Aryasurya carried on this tradition.

Nagavarma (late 10th): poet in Kannada. It is said that he won the patronage of Parmar king Bhoja by reading out his compositions in the royal court. Of two works attributed him, *Chhandobudhi* is the first work in Kannada which discusses Pingal. As for *Karnataka Kadambari*, this is a champu kavya which condenses Bana's prose work in Sanskrit.

Nagavarma (mid-12th): scholar of poetics in Kannada, also grammarian. A Jain by faith, he was associated with the court of Chalukya king Jagadekamalla. Among his works are *Shabdasmriti, Bhashabhushana, Kavyavalokan, Chhandovichiti-vyutpatti-sadhak.*

Nagesh (early 17th): poet in Marathi; also known as Nagakavi, Nagajoshi, Nagendra, Nagesha Joshi Bhingarkar. He belonged to Bhingar village and was a 'grama-joshi' by occupation. Among his works are *Chandravali-varnana, Sitaswayamvar, Rukmini-swayamvar, Rasa-manjari, Sharada-vinoda, Arya-tika.*

Nagesh Bhatta or Nagoji Bhatta (18th): scholar of Sanskrit, author of several works on dharma, yoga, alamkara and vyakarana; also wrote commentaries on *Ramayana* of Valmiki, *Adhyatma-Ramayana, Saptashati, Gita-Govinda, Sudhalahari*, etc. Born to a Maharashtri brahman family settled in Banaras, his grandfather was Bhattoji Dikshita, his parents Shiva Bhatta and Sati; his patron was Ramasimha, a local prince of Shringaverapura (modern Singarur, near Allahabad city).

Naharar git (early 17th; Asamiya): earliest extant ballad in the language, recovered only in parts. The work deals with the career of one Nahar Chetia, lover of a palace-maid who became the third wife of king Chukhampha alias Khor Raja (1552–1603).

Nahush (1814; Hindi) of Gopal Chandra: a play on the puranic character Nahush; written in 1814 and published in *Kavi-vachan-sudha*. Some scholars regard this as the first proper play in Hindi. The playwright, better known as Giridhardas the poet, was the father of Bharatendu Harishchandra.

Naidradam (17th; Tamil) of Adivirraman: translation of the Sanskrit *Naishada-charit* by Shriharsha.

Naima Saab (1800–80): poet in Kashmiri, disciple of Soch Malyari; composed mainly 'vatsun' poems. He lived near his relative, younger contemporary and poet Shams Faqir (1843–1904). Naima earned a living by working in a shawl-embroidery workshop.

Naishadha-champu or **Naishadham** (15th/16th Malayalam) of Mazhamangalam: this poet's most important work. Though based on the story of Nala, the work re-tells it in a free and original manner.

Naishadha-charita (?12th; Sanskrit) of Shriharsha: (not the same as the playwright) a kavya work in 22 sections based on the Nala-Damayanti story, narrated upto the point where their marriage takes place and Kali arrives in Nala's capital. The poem has traditionally been praised for it's 'pada-lalitya' (elegance of diction); many modern scholars find it in bad taste and flawed by artificiality.

Tr. K.K. Handiqui, Lahore, 1934.

Naishada-parijatiyamu (late 17th Telugu) of Krishnadhvari: a 'dvyarthi' kavya work which is superior to similar efforts by Suranna and Bhattumurti.

Najabat (mid-18th): poet in Panjabi, author of *Var Nadarshah*. This var work is a notable contribution to Panjabi literature, regarded as second in importance only to Guru Gobind Singh's *Chandi-di var*.

Naji [Sayed Muhammad Shakir (d.1754)]: poet in Urdu; used to work for Wazir Umdatulmulk Amir Khan, a poet at the court of Muhammad Shah. He fought in battle against the invader Nadir Shah and was an eye-witness to the sack of Delhi, of which he later wrote an account. His complete works have not yet been recovered.

Nakar (1516–69): poet in Gujarati. It is said that he wrote akhyanas on behalf of a brahman friend. He was himself a merchant from Vadodara (Baroda); because he was not well-read in the puranas (which are in Sanskrit) he made use of stories he had heard. Among his many works are *Harischandrakhyan, Chandrahasakhyan, Dhruvakhyan, Nalakhyan, Okha-haran, Lav-Kusakhyan, Shiva-vivah, Vyadh-Mrigi samvad, Bhilni-ke baramas.*

Nakha-shikha (Sanskrit): poetic convention which requires a detailed and appreciative dipiction of the female form. The description begins with the feet or toe-nails (hence 'nakha') and concludes with the head or hair (hence 'shikha').

Nakkirar (?2nd): poet in Tamil and scholar; contributor to *Kurunttogai.* His commentary on *Kalaviyal* provided the core around which later commentaries (7th/8th) were written. He belonged to Madurai; was a brahman who made a living by making bangles out of conchshells. He was apparently an extremely righteous and uncompromising person, who led a rebellious but frustrated life.

Nakkirar (12th): scholar of Tamil; wrote a critical commentary on *Ahapporul* which is regarded as the earliest extant prose work in Tamil (if the prose portions of *Silappadikaram* are not taken into account).

Nala-champu (*c*900; Sanskrit) of Trivikrama Bhatta: also known as *Damayanti-katha*, it is the earliest known champu kavya. The work narrates a part of the Nala-Damayanti story in seven sections; it is full of stylistic affectations.

Nala-charitram (late 17th/early 18th; Malayalam) of Unnayi Varier: the most famous attakatha of Kerala. Based on the Nala-Damayanti story, it is in four parts, each of which can be performed all night. This poet was the first to adopt the story for Kathakali performance.

Nala-charitramu (Telugu): of five published and four unpublished works on this theme in Telugu, the one composed around 1630 by Raghunath Nayakudu is supposed to have the best literary quality, while the one composed around 1690 by Chakrapuri Raghavacharya became the most popular.

Nala-charitre (*c*1300; Kannada) of Chaundarasa: champu work on Nala's story. There are no 'sarga' or 'ashwas' divisions in this poem of 810 verses, which has also been regarded as a 'khanda-kavya'.

Nala-charitre (1550; Kannada) of Kanakadasa: long poem on the same subject, composed in bhamini-shatpadi metre.

Nala Damyanti-swayamvara (mid-17th; Marathi) of Raghunath

Pandit: long poem on the Nala-Dhamayanti story based on the Sanskrit work *Naishadh-charitra by* Shri Harshra. Raghunath has condensed the story and told it in 254 shlokas.

Naladiyar (6th/7th; Tamil): anthology of 400 quatrains composed by different Jain ascetics. The arrangement and subject matter is almost the same as *Tirukkuaral*; the purpose is didactic. The work has three sections—'Arattuppal', 'Porutpal' and 'Kammattuppal—and is divided into 40 sections, each containing 10 verses.

Nalakhyan (*c*1680; Gujarati) of Premananda; the finest of several akhyana works composed by this poet.

Nala-venba (12th/13th; Tamil) of Puhalendi Pulvar: retelling of the Nala-Damayanti story in venba metre. Though the poet is supposed to have also composed *Rathina-surukam* (a work which describes an ideal woman) and *Senjikkalambakkam* (in praise of a chieftain of Korrandai), his fame, especially as an exponent of venba, rests on this work.

Nalayirappirapantam or **Nalayiar Divyaprabandham** (10th; Tamil): collection of 4000 hymns by 12 Alwar poets spread over 300 years (from late 6th to end 9th) and collected by Nathamunigal or Shri Natha-muni (910–90). The sant-poets included are 1. Poygai Alwar from Kanchi (7th); 2. Bhootha Alwar from Thirukadalmallai (same); 3. Peyalwar from Mylapore (same); 4. Thirumalisai Alwar from Thirumalisai of Thonda Nadu (same); 5. Thondaradipodi Alwar from Mandangudi of Thanjavur district; original name Vipra Narayana (same); 6. Kulasekhara Alwar from Kongu Nadu; a Chera king (early 9th); 7. Thirupan Alwar from Uraiyur; low caste bard (date unknown); 8. Thirumangai Alwar from Thirukuraiyaloor of Chola Nadu; probably a robber chieftain at one time (8th); 9. Perialwar from Srivilliputhur; real name Vishnu Chithan; a brahman priest (early 8th); 10. Andal; adopted daughter of Perialwar; associated with Srirangam temple; 11. Nammalwar from Alar Thirunagari; real name Sadagopan (9th); 12. Madura Kavi Alwar; disciple of Nammalwar. A brahman, Nathemunigal first heard the 'padigam' of Madurakavi; next discovered Nammalwar; went on to collect the others. The largest number of hymns are from Nammalwar and Thirumangai Alwar. This collection represents the first clear expression of bhakti doctrine in any Indian language literature.

Nallappillai (?C): poet in Tamil; added about 10,000 stanzas to Villupputturur's *Bharatam*.

Nalodaya (?C; Sanskrit) of undecided authorship: a yamaka kavya ascribed at one time to Kalidasa by some scholars; by others to Ravideva; by yet others to Vasudeva. Tr. W. Yates, Calcutta, 1844.

Namaghosha (16th; Asamiya) of Madhav Kandali: a prayer book or devotional handbook of the followers of the Ekasarana sect. It contains 1000 verses, of which a little over one half are translated from puranic texts. As indicated by its title, the work consists of the names and praise of the Supreme Being. It is also known as 'Hajari ghosha', from 'hajar' meaning thousand and 'ghosha' being the refrain of a song.

Namalinganushasana (?4th; Sanskrit) of Amarasimha: a standard lexicon, popularly known as *Amarakosha*. The work is arranged in three books, entitled 'Swaradi-kanda', 'Bhumyadi-kanda' and 'Samanya-kanda'; there is also an appendix on homonyms, indeclinables and genders.

Nambi Andar Nambi (10th/11th): Shaiva poet in Tamil, who compiled the 11 collections of hymns known as *Tirumurai*. His own verses are to be found in the 11th collection. He also wrote *Tiruttondar tiruandadi*, which enlarges upon the *Tiruttondattogai* of Sundarar. He was born in Tirunaraiyur village of South Arcot district; became a devotee of Pallappillaiyar, for whom there was a temple in that village. Later, he discovered the Tevaram hymns in the Nataraja temple of Chidambaram and, at the behest of Chola king Rajaraja I, compiled these into the first seven *Tirumurai*.

Namdev (1270–1350): sant-poet in Marathi; composed about 2000 'abhanga' poems on a variety of subjects. He was born into a tailor caste at Narasi-Vamani village of Satara district; the family moved to Pandharpur where Namdev became an ardent devotee of Vitthala; was initiated into the Varkari sect by Visobha Khechar, a grocer by caste. He met Jnanadeva at Alandi in 1291 and accompanied him on a pilgrimage of North India during which he travelled through Gujarat and Rajasthan to Panjab; wrote an account of this, *Tirthavaliche abhanga*. After Jnaneswar attained 'samadhi' in 1296, Namdev again left for North India; remained in

Panjab for over 20 years; probably died there and his ashes were brought back to Pandharpur. He composed 236 padas in Marathi and 102 in Hindi; the latter have been collected in *Namdev padavali*; of his Marathi padas, 61 were included in *Guru Granth Sahib*. He wrote many autobiographical abangas, which tell us about the major events of his life; also wrote a poetical account of the life of Jnanadeva. Most of his devotional poems are addressed to Vitthala.

Nammalvar (9th): one of the 12 Alvars, whose hymns are to be found in *Divya prabandham*. Nearly half the poems of this anthology are attributed to him (1296 out of 4000). Not much is known about his life except that he was born in Thirukkuruhur (now named Alvar Thirunagari) village on the bank of Tamiraparani river; may have been the son of a local chieftain belonging to the non-brahman Vellala community. Other names by which he was known are Maran, Sadagopan, Parankusan.

Nammayasundari-katha (12th; Prakrit) of Mahendra Suri: a work containing 1117 verses and occasional prose lines, composed in Maharashtri Prakrit. It tells the life-history of Nammayasundari, who passed through numerous ordeals in her previous births but invariably came out enhanced in purity because of her steadfast loyalty to her husband. The work deals mainly with purity of conduct as required by Jain tradition; is based, according to the author, on the teachings of his mentor, Shanti Suri.

Nanapanchami kahao (early 11th; Prakrit) of Maheshwar Suri: didactic work in 2000 verses spread over ten unequal sections and written in Ardhamagadhi Prakrit. It tells ten stories about observing the vow of 'panchami' and the gains, material as well as spiritual, obtained by those who observe the vow.

Nana'raga-gita'samgraha (Mithila): the title of several manuscript collections of Mithila poems, found in Nepal libraries.

Nanartha-deva'devi-gitani (*c*1660; Mithila) of Jagatprakasha'malla: a manuscript anthology of 1660 miscellaneous padas in the Maithili manner of Vidyapati.

Nanak Dev, **Guru** (1469–1538): founder of the Sikh sect; composed about 50,000 lines of verse in Old Hindi, Braj and the speech of Dehli, mixed occasionally with Panjabi. With him, Panjabi literature may be said to have made a fresh start. A tentative chronology of his literary output shows three periods: the first (1489–98) containing youthful and revolutionary verse directed chiefly against rituals and false piety; the second (1498–1521) reflects his missionary travels; the third (1521–39) is the crowning period of philosophic composition, containing *Japji* and other major works. Among other works generally ascribed to him are *Siddha-goshthi, Rag Asavari, asa-di-var, Bara mah, Sohle, Pahare, Banjare, Alauhania, Ashtapadia, Rekhta*.

Nanak Yusuf (1783–1853): sant-poet in Sindhi, whose life and poetry was governed by the influence of Sachal Sarmast. He belonged to Agras village in Larkhana district; returned here after his travels to pass the rest of his life in meditation.

Nanak-vijay (*c*1840; Panjabi) of Santaren: a biography of Guru Nanak in about 24,382 verses, divided into 20 sections and 324 chapters. The work is known more for its devotional ardour than for literary quality. Its language is mainly Braj.

Nandadas (1533–86): poet in Hindi; one of the Ashtachhap group, second in importance only to Surdas. Among his 16 works are *Ram-panchadhyayi, Bhramar-git, Nasiket-puran, Rukmini-mangal, Dasham-skandha masa*. He also composed a number of 'manjari' works, such as *Rasa-manjari, Anekartha-manjari, Man-manjari, Virah-manjari* and *Rup-manjari*.

Nandalal: see Lalcandra.

Nandashankar Tuljashankar Mehta (1835–1905): novelist in Gujarati; and social reformer; author of *Karana ghelo*. Educated only upto matriculation, he chose to be a school teacher and eventually became the principal of a teachers' training college; later joined the civil service and served in many princely states of Gujarat; retired as dewan of Kutch.

Nandi (Sanskrit): term in dramaturgy for one of the preliminaries of a dramatic performance; in it, the gods and high-born mortals are eulogised along with benediction sought for actors and spectators.

Nandi Mallana (early 15th): poet in Telugu who used to compose jointly with another poet, Ghanta Singanna. They wrote *Prabodhachandṛodayamu*, a prose rendering of the play in Sanskrit by Krishna Mishra. Their *Varaha-puranamu* is a collection of Varahavatar episodes drawn from Sanskrit sources.

Nandikeshwara or **Nandin** the name of many authors in many disciplines. Among those relevant to literature and language are the ones-cited by Vatsayayana as an authority on 'kama-shashtra'; by Bhatta Upala in his commentary on *Brihatsamhita*; by Kshiraswamin as an authority on grammar in his commentary *Kshiratarangini* on *Amarakosha*; by Sayana in *Dhatuvritti;* by Vishwanatha Vaidya in *Koshakalapataru* as a lexicographer; by Rayamukta in his commentary on *Amarakosha*. The last named is said to have authored works on music and dance like *Taladhyaya* and *Talalakshanam.*

Nandikkalambagam (late 9th; Tamil) by unknown author: poem on Pallava king Nandivarman III (r. 825–50). It mentions his victory in 2the battle of Tellaru (835), after which he was called Tellarerinda Nandivarman. This is the earliest known work in 'kalambagam' form.

Nandiram Thadomal Mirani 'Sewhani' (1819–75): prose-writer in Sindhi; pioneer in establishing the Arabi-Sindhi alphabet and standardising the Arabi-Sindhi script. He was the first writer to translate the Persian work *Tarikha masumi* (a history of Sindh, written by Masoom Shah) into Sindhi, using the standardised script; won praise for this and was appointed translator of the Education department. Among his other works are *Babnamo* (1853; primer of Sindhi); *Isapjun akaniyun* (1854; Aesop's fables in Sindhi); *Lekhe ji pirha* (1856; book on arithmetic); *Jabro muqabalo* (1856; book on algebra); *Dharati nirvaru* (1855; book on world geography); *Sansari nirvar* (1861; book on nature study); etc. Most of these are translations from English or Urdu.

Nanjunda (early 16th): poet in Kannada. Born into a noble family of Jains, he appears to have adopted the Virshaiva faith when he grew up. His great work is *Ramanathacharite* or *Kumara Rama sangatya*, which uses a historical theme and is set just before the rise of Vijayanagar.

Nannaya Bhatta (11th): first poet in Telugu whose works are extant; family priest of king Rajaraja Narendra. The poet's home was near Vengi-nadu, the area between the Krishna and the Godavari where the best Telugu is supposed to be spoken. He is credited with having reformed Telugu for literary use in emulation of Sanskrit, thus pioneering the 'marga' tradition in Telugu literature. He freely borrowed Sanskrit words and expressions, also liberally used 'marga' metres along with 'desi' metres. Apart from composing *Andhra Mahabhataram*, a Telugu rendering of *Mahabharata*, Nannaya is said to have written *Chamundika vilas, Andhra shabda chintamani, Indra-vijayam,* and *Lakshana-saram.*

Nannichoda (12th): poet in Telugu; author of the long narrative poem, *Kumarasambhava*, based on Sanskrit versions by Kalidas and Udbhata. The poet was the son of Choda Belli, a Chola ruler of Pakanadu, of which Nellore district was then a part. An ardent Shaiva, he dedicated his work to Jangama Mallikarjuna Dena, a renowned Shaiva sage of the period. In the work he does not mention any poet in Telugu prior to him, but refers to Valmiki and Vyasa, also to Kalidas and Udbhata. This poem was discovered only in 20th century

Nannul (12th; Tamil) of Pavananti Muni: a work on grammar which remained in use even during the British period and was included in school and college curricula. It served as a reference work for Caldwell and was the first Tamil work on grammar to be translated into English. According to its prologue, it discusses all five branches of grammar but only the sections on 'eluthi' (phonology) and 'chol' (morphology) are extant. Nannul is particularly important because it recognises that changes took place in Tamil after *Tolkappiyam* was written and revises grammatical principles accordingly. The work was studied so often that there are 44 commentaries on it.

Naothinkhong phambal kaba (?17th; Manipuri): a work which combines history, legend and myth to tell of the accession of Meitei king Naothingkhong, preceded by the conflict between the Meiteis and the Langmais.

Narada-samrit (1730; Asamiya) of Bhubaneswar Vachaspati: metrical adaptation of *Naradiya-puran*, undertaken at the instance of Chandraprabha, widow of king Tamradhvaj of Kachar.

Naradiya-shiksha (?C; Sanskrit): attributed to Narada, the work deals with music of Saman generally as well as chanted at sacrifces. It is in two parts, each consisting of 'khanda' divisions. The work represents the earliest extant record of musical divisions and terminology; also provides a link between Vedic and post-Vedic music.

Narahari (early 16th): poet in Bangla; the guru of Lochandas and composer of Vaishnav lyrics. Some of these, in later manuscripts, appear with the signature of Chandidas.

Narahari (1611–63): poet in Gujarati, who translated works of religious philosophy from Sanskrit and also composed reflective poems of his own. Among his translations are *Vasisthasar Gita, Bhagavad Gita, Bhakti-manjari*; among his original works *Prabodh-manjari, Harililamrit, Jnan Gita, Santanalakshano.*

Narahari Bandijan (b.1505): poet in Hindi; author of *Rukmini-mangal, Chappay-niti, Kavitta-samgraha*. He was from Asani village in Fatehpur district of Uttar Pradesh; won the esteem of Akbar.

Narahari Chakrabarti (*c*1700): Vaishnav scholar of Nadia (Bengal), whose *Bhakti-ratnakar* (in, Sanskrit) was widely used as a source book. His other name was Ghanashyam Chakrabarti; he lived for some time in Brindavan and served as a cook in Govindji's temple founded by Rup Goswami. His other works, also in Sanskrit, are *Gaur-charit-chintamani, Narottambilas, Braja-parikrama Chhandasamudra, Lila-samudra.*

Narahari Sarkar (16th): poet in Bangla and close associate of Shri Chaitanya. He used to write pada verses about Krishna but, after coming under Shri Chaitanya's influence, wrote only about the latter. He also preached a brand of Vaishnav faith centred in Chaitanya and known as Gaurangavad.

Narakasura Vadha (late 18th; Malayalam) of Karthika Tirunal: Kathakali play in eight scenes, concluding with the killing of Narakasura by Krishna.

Narasiji ro mahero (15th or 16th; Rajasthani) of Ratansah: an account of the life and works of Narsingh Maheta, the famous sant-poet of Gujarat. Of many works on this subject in Gujarati and Rajasthani, Ratansah's is perhaps the earliest and most famous. ('Mahero' is a custom according to which a married girl's relatives are expected to give suitable presents on the occasion of the marriage of her children). As told here, Narasiji's daughter Nani Bai was married into a family of Anjar in Gujarat; when her daughter's marriage is to be held, she sends word to her father that he should come to attend only if he can perform the mahero. Undeterred, he turns up empty-handed in the belief Shri Krishna will come to his help. This is fulfilled when Krishna appears as Nani Bai's brother and performs mahero.

Narayandev (16th): poet in Bangla; author of the oldest known *Manasamangal* poem known as *Padma-puran*. He belonged to North-east Bengal but his ancestors came from West Bengal to settle by the Brahmaputra. Possibly this family introduced poetry about the goddess Manasa to North-east Bengal. Narayan, whose full name was Ramnarayan, often added the prefix 'Sukavi' (good poet) to his name, which led to his being known later as 'Sukavi-Narayan'.

Narayana (between 900 and 1400): prepared a Bangla version of *Hitopadesha*.

Narayana (after 14th): author of *Nigudarth padabodhini*, a commentary on *Mahabharata*.

Narayana (15th): was the village-chief of Dubagunth village in Nellore district of Tamilnadu. He translated the Sanskrit *Panchatantra* into Telugu; his version is the earliest known in Telugu.

Narayana (mid-16th): wrote the Sanskrit work on prosody, *Vritta-ratnakara* (1545).

Narayana (17th): composed *Swahasudha-champu* in Sanskrit.

Narayana Bhatta (*c*1000): poet and scholar in Telugu; a contemporary of Nannaya Bhatta who has acknowledged help from him in his poetical labours. Narayana's eminence as poet and scholar is mentioned in the Nandimapudi inscription.

Narayana Bhattatiri (*c* (1560–1666): scholar and devotional poet in Sanskrit, also grammarian, from Kerala. His *Prakriya-sarvaswam*, on Sanskrit grammar, was used all over India; for *Narayaniyam* he composed 1036 verses in praise of Shri Krishna of the Guruvayur temple; in *Manameyodayam* he discourses on the means and objects of knowledge. He is said to have written more than 50 books.

Narayaniyam (*c*1585; Sanskrit) of Narayana Bhattatiri: devotional poem written in the form of a colloquy addressed to the deity of the Guruvayur temple. The work summarises the main episodes of *Shrimad Bhagavat* in 1036 verses divided into 100 sections called 'dashaka' (decades). The poet has claimed that the work is 'dvedha narayaniyam', that is, in two ways the book is 'Narayaniyam' (written on Narayan by Narayan).

Narma-gadya (Gujarati): collection of the prose-writings and speeches of Gujarat's famous writer

Narmada Shankar. The first edition or Book I (published in 1865) contains a variety of pieces written during the period of 1850–65. Book II (published 1886) consists of a history of Surat in the first part, and the author's autobiography (Mavihakikat) as the second part. In 1874 he was asked by the Education Department to prepare a school edition of his prose-writings; this became *Sarkari Narmagadya* (1874).

Narma-mala (11th; Sanskrit) of Kshemendra: a satirical work, directed against wicked persons, especially kayasthas who held high offices and oppressed the people.

Narmad [Narmadashankar Dave (1833–86)]: pioneer of Gujarati prose and generally a leading figure in the making of modern Gujarati literature. Poet, playwright, critic, Narmad was a versatile writer and also participated actively in social reform. Among his major prose works are *Narma-kosh, Narmagadya* and *Mari hakikat*, the last named being his autobiography.

Narottam-Das (mid-16th): poet of Krishna-bhakti in Hindi; author of *Sudama-charitra*, a work which made him popular. His other work, *Dhruva-charitra*, has not survived.

Narottam Das (late 16th): Vaishnav poet in Bangla, preacher and mystic. A kayastha, he was trained in religious faith at Brindavan by Lokenath, a disciple of Advaitacharya. He developed and standardised the kirtan style of singing Vaishnav lyrics. Besides prayer poems and songs, he composed a few short treatises on Vaishnav devotion and practice, of which the most important is *Premabhakti-chandrika.*

Narottam-vilas (early 18th; Bangla) of Narahari Chakrabarti: a verse biography of Narottam, apostle of Shri Chaitanya.

Narrinai (?C; Tamil): one of the *Ettuttogai* collections, compiled at the instance of Pandya king Maran Vazhudi. It consists of 400 love lyrics in ahaval metre by 175 poets. There is an invocation to Tirumal by Bharatam Padiya Perundevanar.

Narsi Mehta [Narsingh Mehta (1414–80)]: poet in Gujarati, bhakta and social reformer; composed many bhajans that are popular even today (viz., 'Vaishnav jana to tene re kahiye'). Among his longer works are *Kunwarbai-nu nameru, Shringarmala, Ras-sahasrapadi, Sudama-charitra, Govinda gaman, Harmala, Shamal Shah-no vivah*.

Nasiketopakhyan (1803; Hindi) of

Sadal Mishra: a work in Khariboli prose recounting a puranic tale. It is particularly significant in the history of Hindi literature because the author has made use of everyday language instead of stylised Brajbhasha.

Nasikh [Sheikh Imam Baksh (1757–1838)]: poet in Urdu; probably born in Faizabad but lived much of his life in Lakhnau. A physically large and strong person, he practised two hobbies of writing poetry and wrestling. Unusual among poets in Urdu, he adopted no 'ustad'; but he had many followers and is generally regarded as the pioneer of a literary movement. Of his three 'diwan' collections, *Daftar-e-pareshan* is the most famous; also wrote a masnavi, *Nazm-e-Siraj*.

Nasim Lakhnavi [Dayasankar Koul (1811–43)]: poet in Urdu. A Kashmiri brahman born in Lakhnau, he is famous for having composed *Gulzar-e-Nasim*, a masnavi poem based on the Gul-Bakavali story. The work became the subject of a widely-read critical controversy in the pages of the newspaper *Awadhpatra* between Brajnarain 'Chakbast' and Abdul Halim 'Sharar'.

Natak (Sanskrit): term for drama, used in many other Indian languages as well.

Nataka-chandrika (16th; Sanskrit) of Rupa Goswamin: a work on dramaturgy, illustrated mostly from Vaishnav works. It is in eight sections dealing with various topics. In composing it, the author says, he has rejected *Sahitya-darpana* because it opposes the views of Bharata Muni.

Natakalakshana-ratnakosha (?C; Sanskrit) of Sagaranandin: work which brings together a number of views of different authorities on 18 important topics of dramatugy. It is valuable not only for this collection of views, but also because it cites a large number of dramatic and dramaturgic works. There is no certainty about its date; the author may have lived any time between the first quarter of 10th and end of 13th century.

Tr. V. Raghavan, jointly with M. Dillon and M. Fowler, Philadelphia, 1960.

Natha Panth (Sampradaya): this North Indian sect is important to literature because the language in which its adherents wrote prose or poetry upto 15th century is regarded as the precursor of Hindi and Panjabi. The founder was Adinath (or Shiva himself). He had two disciples, Matsyendranath and

Jalandharnath. The former had four disciples, Gorakshanath, Charpatnath, Rewanath and Meenanath. Of them all, Gorakshanath is probably the best known. He lived sometime between 10th and 12th century and preached successfully in Panjab and Rajputana.

Nathamuni (*c*824–924): an acharya of Tamilnadu who compiled the *Divya prabandham* anthology. He had to travel all over Tamilnadu in order to collect the 'prabandham' (hymns), which he edited and compiled; also set them to music.

Nathan Brown (1807–86): American missionary who learnt Asamiya and was the first editor of the journal-cum-newspaper *Orunodai* (1846–54). He began a translation of the New Testament into Asamiya in 1838 and had it published in 1848; was the first president of the Baptist Association of Assam when it was established in 1851; started a number of Asamiya-medium schools and initiated the writing of Asamiya textbooks. When the American Board of the mission disapproved of the teaching programme, he resigned from his missionary duties and returned home in February 1855.

Natika (Sanskrit): according to *Natyashastra* 'drishya-kavya' is of two kinds, 'rupaka' and 'upa-rupaka'. 'Natika' is the more important variety of the latter.

Natya (Sanskrit): term denoting drama, or imitation of a condition.

Natya-darpana (12th; Sanskrit) jointly of Ramachandra and Gunachandra: work on dramaturgy. It consists of four sections called 'viveka'; mentions twelve varieties of rupaka and a number of upa-rupaka.

Natya shastra (Sanskrit): dramaturgy.

Natya-shastra (?C; Sanskrit): also known as *Bharat-natyashastra* ascribed to Bharata Muni; the earliest extant treatise on literature in India, especially on dramaturgy. In 36 or 37 adhyay, consisting of 6000 shloka, it discusses the subject ranging from the origin of drama to the construction of a theatre. It is more like a reference-volume than a continuous exposition; about one-tenth of it is in prose. Though the language is Old Sanskrit, it is remarkably simple and easy to understand. There is only one known commentary to this text, *Abhinavbharati* by Abhinavgupta.

Natyashastra-samgraha (?17th; Sanskrit): a collection of texts on dramaturgy, compiled by Utaka Govindachar at the behest of the Maratha kings of Thanjavur. The work is in two parts; the first part is based entirely on the seventh chapter of *Sangita-ratnakara* of Sarangadeva; the second draws mainly from *Sangita-muktavali* of Devendra, *Shringara-sekhara* of Bhallata, *Sangita- darpana* of Damodara, and *Sangita-makaranda* of Vedasuri.

English and Tamil trans. of Marathi version by K.V. Shastri, A.K.M. Row Sahib and G.N. Rao, Tanjore, 1953.

Naurasnama (*c*1620; Urdu) of Ibrahim Adil Shah II, ruler of Bijapur; a work on music in Dakhni. It has a preface in Farsi by two Indian scholars.

Nau-tarz-e-murassa (1798; Urdu) of Mir Ata Husain 'Tahseen': a retelling of 'Qissa chahar darvesh' in a new kind of prose which mixes Arabi and Farsi with Urdu. Because of this work, its author came to be known as 'Murassa-rakam'.

Navalram [Navalram Lakshmisankar Pandaya (1836–88)]: leading critic in Gujarati; also a poet, playwright, translator and essayist. His *Bal-lagna battrisi* and *Bal garabavali* are poetical works; *Bhatanubhopalu* and *Virmati* are plays; *Vyutpatti-path* and *Nibandha-riti* are essays; *Premanand-krita 'Kunwar Bainu Mameru'* was edited by him. His critical essays have been collected in the four-volume *Naval granthavali*. For some years he edited the journal *Gujaratsala patra*.

Navaratna-satik (*c*1490; Hindi) of Vitthalnath: an account of the Vallabhachari sect, written in Brajbhasa prose.

Navasahasanka-charita (1005; Sanskrit) of Padmagupta, alias Parimala: a narrative poem written in honour of the poet's patron, Sindhuraja (also known as Navasahasanka), Paramara ruler of Dhara. Of its 18 'sarga', 12 are devoted to the Paramara genealogy. The rest tell of the marriage of Sindhuraja with Shashiprabha, daughter of Naga king Samkhapala. For this the king has to invade Nagaloka, kill the demon Vajrakusha and fetch the golden lotus.

Nayachandra (15th): poet and playwright in Prakrit and Apabhramsha; wrote the long poem *Hammira-kavya* and the sattaka play *Rambha-manjari*. He was a Jain monk from Krishnagaccha.

Nayaka (Sanskrit): literally means 'leader'. As a literary term, it indicates the hero (protagonist) of a play or story.

Nayakumara-chariu or **Nagakumara-charitam** (10th; Apabhramsha) of Pupphadanta (Pushpadanta): a biographical account in verse of prince Nagakumara of Magadha. The story begins with king Jayandhara of Kanakapura (Magadha), his queen Vishalanetra and son Shridhara. Jayandhara happens to see a picture of princess Prithvidevi of Girinagar, falls in love and marries her. The son born to them undergoes many experiences and wanders all over Bharatadesha helping people in distress. The work basically upholds the Jain faith; it also provides much information about ancient Indian customs and manners, also of geography.

Nayanandi (11th): scholar of Apabhramsha. Two of his works have been recovered, *Sudarshan-chariu* and *Sakal-vidhi-vidhan kavya*.

Nayanmar: the general name for 63 Shaiva sants of Tamilnadu who, from about 6th century A.D., contributed substantially to Tamil literature through the songs and poems composed by them. These compositions have been collected in 12 books called *Tirumurai*. The first seven books have the collective name of *Devaram*; included here are works of three great Nayanmars, Sambandar, Appar and Sundarar. The fourth great Nayanmar, Manikkavachagar, contributed two more books. The last book, *Periyapuranam* of Sekkilar, tells of the lives and legends associated with all 63 Nayanmars.

Nayasena or **Nayasen Muni** (12th): poet in Kannada; author of the champu work *Dharmamrita* which expounds principles of Jain faith by telling the stories of 14 Jain sages. Nayasen's great contribution was to write on such subjects in a language simple enough to reach the common people.

Nayasundar [also known as Vachak Nayasundar (16th/17th)]: poet in Gujarati, composer of 'ras' works and 'stavan' poems. Among these are *Yashodharni-rup chaupai, Roopkunwar ras, Surasundari ras, Nala-Damayanti ras, Atmapratibodh stavan, Shantinath stavan, Sthulibhadra stavan*, etc.

Nayasundari (?C; Prakrit): a sattaka type play. The author is supposed to have been a Jain author of the time of Akbar.

Nazim [Abdul Ahad; also known as Waiz Shah Nur-ud-Din (1807–65)]: poet in Kashmiri; composed a number of naat, ghazal and masnavi works.

Nazim [Nawab Yusuf Ali Khan

(early 19th)]: poet in Urdu, also composed in Farsi; belonged to a noble family of Rampur. He used to seek literary advice first from Momin, and then later from Ghalib; exchanged some letters with the latter that have been published. In his own work as well as in the patronage he extended, he upheld the reputation of Rampur as a centre of culture.

Nazir Ahmad (1826–1912): prose-writer in Urdu and first major novelist of the language. Among his many works are *Marat-ul-urus, Banat-ul-nayash, Tobah tulansuh, Ibn-ul-vakt*, etc. He was also a skilful translator and rendered many English books into Urdu. He rose in life from being a teacher to a deputy collector and was thereafter referred to as 'Dipti (Deputy) Nazir'.

Nazir Akbarabadi (1740–1830): poet in Urdu; wrote on themes of every day life in a simple and lucid manner, thus giving Urdu poetry a democratic outlook; author of *Banjara-nama* and *Admi-nama*. Though born in Delhi, he moved with his parents to Akbarabad (Agra) when he was about 20 years old.

Nazm (Urdu): general term for verse, as opposed to 'nasr' which is the term for prose. However, a 'ghazal' is not regarded as 'nazm'; while a ghazal is brief, a nazm tends to be expansive.

Nedunalvadai (?C; Tamil) of Nakkirar: the seventh idyll of *Patitupputtu*, celebrates the Pandyan king Nedunchezhyan. As indicated by the title ('The tedious but favourable cold north wind'), the poem contains a fine description of winter.

Nemichandra (*c*1200): poet in Kannada and scholar, Jain by faith; author of *Lilavati* and *Neminathpuran*. He wrote the latter under the patronage of Padmanabh, the chief minister of Hoysala king Virballal.

Neminadam (11th; Tamil) of Gunavira Panditar: A work on orthography and morphology.

Neminatha-chariu (*c*1159; Apabhramsha) of Haribhadra: long poem in 'radda' metre about the tirthankar Neminath. The work is modelled on Sanskrit kavya in its greater concern for manner than for matter; also there are deliberate digressions in which the poet displays his skills.

Neminatha chatushpadika (13th; Gujarati) of Vijayasen Suri: the earliest known 'baramasya' work in the language. It tells of Neminath, how Rajul feels romantically drawn to him, finally she takes 'diksha' from him.

Neminatha chaupai (12th; Apabhramsha) of Vinayachandra Suri: a short work of 40 verses featuring the story about Neminath, the 12th tirthankar. He was to have married Rajmati or Rajul but for some reason he turned back from the ceremony and went away to Girnar hill for doing tapasya. Rajul is much aggrieved and dies 12 months later. Her feelings in each month from Shravan to Ashad have been depicted in the form of a 'baramasya' which may have set the model for similar work later in modern Indian languages.

Neminatha phagu (*c*1349; Gujarati) of Rajasekhara: long poem about Jain tirthankar Neminath. It tells of how he turned away from worldly life on the eve of his marriage with the beautiful Rajimati; later she also renounced the world. Other works with the same title are by Jayasekhara Suri (late 14th), Samudhara (*c*1450), and Dhandavaghani.

Neminatha puran (*c*1200; Kannada) of Nemichandra: kavya work dealing with Harivamsa as well as Kuruvamsa but with Sri Krishna in main focus.

Nidana-katha (?C; Pali) a narrative of beginnings, prefacing the *Jataka* commentary *Jataka-attavannana*. It consists of three sections—'durenidana' (remote past), 'aviderenidana' (not very remote past), 'santikenidana' (present).

Nidhu Babu [Ramnidhi Gupta (1741–1839)]: poet in Bangla and song-writer; said to be the first English-knowing poet of Bengal. He spent nearly half his life in Chiran village of Chapra district in Bihar working as a clerk in an East India Company agency house; learnt English here, also Sanskrit and probably Russian. While at Chapra, he learnt to sing the Hindustani 'tappa' from a Muslim ustad. On his return to Calcutta in 1794, he began a music school where he taught songs composed by him and set to the tappa style; he also innovated the 'akhadai' style based on classical forms. His four-line poems, meant for singing, are the earliest secular lyrics of the language. These were collected in *Gitaratna* (1837). The 'tappa' style originated by him later came to be known as 'Nidhu Babur tappa'.

Nighantu (Sanskrit): glossaries of obscure words occurring in Vedic hymns; compiled by descendants of ancient sages for easier understanding of transmitted texts. These were ascribed at one time to Yashka.

Nihalchand 'Lahori', Munshi (18th/19th): prose-writer in Urdu. Though he belonged to Panjab, he was educated in Delhi and found employment at Calcutta in Fort William College. His translation into Urdu of Izzatulla's Farsi work, published as *Mazhabe-ishk* (1803), became very popular as an Indian version of the Gul-Bakavali story.

Nijabat (?C): poet in Panjabi; composed a var on the invasion of India by Nadir Shah.

Nijaguna Shiva yogi (16th): poet in Kannada. It is said about him that he was a king somewhere before he got fed up and became a Virshaiva ascetic. His poetical works, mostly religious or reflective, are *Kaivalya paddhati, Paramanubhav bodhe, Paramartha gite, Anubhav-sar* and *Arubathumuvar tripadi.* He also wrote in prose *Paramartha prakasike* and *Vivek-chintamani.*

Nilakantha Dikshita (17th): poet and scholar in Sanskrit from Kerala; younger brother of Appayya Dikshita. A Shaiva by faith, he wrote *Nilakantha-vijaya champu, Shivalilarnava, Gangavatarana*, all works in praise of Shiva. He also wrote *Nalacharitra-nataka*, a play in seven acts, and *Kalyana-saugandhika*, an one-act vyayoga play.

Nilakesi (?C; Tamil) of unknown date and authorship: one of the five minor kappiyam. It is a Jain work and appears to be a counter to the Bouddha *Kundalakesi.* The poem tells of the young woman Nilakesi, the human embodiment of a spirit (Plaiyanur Nili), who tries to disturb the penance of Munichandra, a Jain ascetic. She fails, then becomes his disciple, then goes about preaching Jain faith and defeating in debate Bouddha preachers, among whom is Kundalakesi.

Nilamba (Nilambika) (*c*1200): woman devotional poet in Kannada; Virshaiva by faith, she was married to Basaveshwara. Her 'stotra' compositions have been collected as *Nilamman-stotra, Nilambika-panchasiti* and *Nilamman-trividhi.* The poetical works *Prasad- sampadane* and *Kalajnan* have also been ascribed to her.

Nilambara Dasa (15th): scholar and poet in Oriya; composed Oriya versions of the Jaimini *Mahabharata* and of *Padmapurana.*

Nilasundari parinayamu (*c*1725; Telugu) of Kuchimanchi Timmakavi. Composed in popular Telugu, without the use of any 'tatsama' words, this romance came to be known as "Nil-Peydil katha" or "Lachhimagani katha". It tells of a

Yadav chief in Mithila named Kumbhak. His daughter Nila happened to hear of Nanda's son Shri Krishna and fell in love with him. Once when an enraged bull was causing havoc in his locality Kumbhak announced that he would marry of his daughter to the person who succeeded in taming this bull. On hearing of this Nila became most worried and began suffering the woe of separation from her imagined beloved. However, Shri Krishna tames the bull and marries Nila.

Nilakantha (*c*1650/1700): scholar of Sanskrit; wrote a famous commentary on *Mahabharata*. His ancestors came from Kopal village in Maharashtra to settle in Kashi. Apart from the *Mahabharata* commentary, he also wrote *Mantra Ramayan* and *Mantra Bhagavat*.

Niranavrittam (Malayalam): a metre innovated by the Panikkar family of poets (the Kannassan poets) and named after their place of residence, Niranam.

Niranjan Madhav (1703–90): scholar of Sanskrit and writer in Marathi. He wrote *Subhadrachampu* in Marathi on the model of Sanskrit champu kavya. Among his other poetical works are *Vrittavatamsa, Vrittamuktavali; Vrittaratnamala; Jnaneswar-vijay* and *Niroshthaye Raghava* are biographical works; *Chidbodh Ramayan* and *Adhyatma Ramayan* are commentaries.

Nirant (1779–1843): devotional poet in Gujarati; wrote numerous poems in 'var', 'tithi' and 'mahina' forms.

Nirayavaliyao (?C; Pali): the eighth 'uvanga'. It narrates how the ten half-brothers of the king of Champa, Kuniya or Ajatshatru, were killed by their grandfather, Chedaga of Veshali, and how they were reborn in various hells.

Nirukta (?6th/7th; Sanskrit) of Yashka: commentary on the nighantus. At one time, the nighantus themselves were ascribed to Yashka. The only *Vedanga Nirukta* work that has been preserved, it is in three sections (as are the nighantus).

Ed. and Tr. L. Sarup, 6 volumes, 1920–29.

Nirvachanottar Ramayanamu (*c*1260; Telugu) ascribed to Tikkana: relates the story of Uttarakanda of the Valmiki *Ramayana*. In Tikkana's time, neither *Mahabharata* nor *Ramayana* had been fully rendered into Telugu. He helped to complete the task by composing this work.

Nirvana Lilavati katha (*c*1030; Prakrit) of Jineshwar Suri: long verse narrative of about 18,000 couplets, the original of which is lost. An abridged translation into Sanskrit was done by Jinaratna Suri under the title *Lilavati-kathasara*; this has 21 sections containing 5350 stanzas. According to the latter text, the story deals with Rajgiri ruler Sangharaja and his queen Lilavati. They ask their Jain teacher Vijayasena to tell them about their previous lives. After hearing the account, both Sangharaja and Lilavati decide to give up worldly life and become asectics; eventually they attain 'nirvana'.

Nishani (Hindi): a verse metre of Dingal, of which the two more popular varieties are 'Shuddha nishani' and 'Garbat nishani'. The work *Khumman raso* uses both these varieties.

Nishani (Panjabi): one of the metres on which 'var' poems were composed. Guru Gobind Singh's *Chandi di var* was composed in this metre.

Nishatul Ishaq (end-14th; Urdu) of Abdulla Husaini: work is a Dakhni translation of Sheikh Abdul Qadir Jilani's work of the same title in Farsi.

Nishkulananda (1766–1848): devotional poet in Gujarati. Born into a 'suthar' (carpenter) caste, his original name was Lalji Suthar; he obtained initiation from Sahajanand Swami and joined the Swaminarayan sect. About 20 books and 3000 verses are ascribed to him. Among the books are *Purushottam prakash, Yama-danda, Bhakta-chintamani, Dhirajakhyan*, etc.

Nispatti (Sanskrit): term in poetics, especially when used as in the phrase 'rasa-nispatti', meaning the realisation of rasa. Nispatti has been variously explained as arising out of 'utpatti' (production), 'anumiti' (inference), 'bhukti' (enjoyment), or 'abhivyakti' (manifestation or revelation).

Niti-kalpataru (11th; Sanskrit) of Kshemendra: didactic work in verse, in 138 sections, giving instructions on worldly wisdom and polity.

Niti-shastra (*c*1180; Telugu/Sanskrit) of Pratap Rudra: work on worldly wisdom and statecraft, composed in both languages. The author, a Kakatiya prince of Warangal (1140–1196), was a follower of the Virashaiva faith.

Niti-shataka (?C; Sanskrit) of Bhartrihari: sequence of 100 poems which seek to inculcate worldly wisdom, and incidentally denounce material pleasure.

Tr. C.H. Tawney, *IA*, 1876; B.H. Wortham, London, 1886; J.M. Kennedy, London, 1913; C.W. Gurner, Calcutta, 1927.

Nityananda Acharya (late 17th): poet in Bangla in the court of Ramkrishna of Santol, the first zamindar of North Bengal to appear as a patron of Bangla poetry; at his instance, Nityananda wrote a *Ramayana* poem based on the *Adbhuta Ramayana* and later came to be known as Adbhutacharya.

Nityananda Ghosh (late 17th): poet in Bangla; author of a short *Mahabharata* poem, parts of which were included in the *Pandav-vijay* compilation ascribed to Kashiram Das.

Niyama (Sanskrit): term in philosophy and in grammar, also used in poetics to denote a convention.

Nondinatakam (Tamil): a dramatic form patronised by the Palaikar chiefs of Tirunelveli district in 17th/18th. There being no evidence of any drama in Tamilnadu during the medieval period, it is surmised that this form probably derives from the ancient 'varikkattu' in which a single actor enacted various parts. In nondinatakam, there is one protagonist and an antagonist who, between them, perform the whole story.

Noornama (14th/15th; Kashmiri) a collection of the verses of Noor-ud-Din Wali (1377–1441), popularly known as Nand Rishi, the patron-saint of Kashmir. The title of this work had been used earlier for a 'rishi-nama' (books on the Muslim Rishi order of Kashmir) compiled by Baba Kamal of Chari Sharif around 1840. The modern compiler, Muhammad Amin Kamil, has used Baba Kamal's text and other sources to produce the present work published in 1965. It runs to 304 pages and contains 275 'shruk'.

Nrisimha-purana (18th; Oriya) of Pitambara Dasa: a wholly original work because it does not derive from any Sanskrit purana. The well-known story of Hiranyakshipu and Prahlada and Nrisimhavatar has been told in Oriya by Mahadeva Dasa and other poets. Pitamabara Dasa's story is about two brothers Nrisimha and Shesha, incarnations of the god Vishnu and his serpent Ananta, who are reborn on earth as sons of a pious brahman king of Badrika named Krishnavallabha, in order to fight and kill two demon brothers, Mura and Daruna.

Nrisimha ultimately truimphs and wins the hand of Lakshmi, beautiful daughter of Varuna, king of the seas. Apart from the originality of conception, the work is remarkable for the effective narration, character delineation and practical wisdom.

Nritta (Sanskrit): term in dramaturgy for dance based on 'tala' and 'laya'.

Nritya (Sanskrit): term in dramaturgy for representation by gestures of an emotion which is expressed by words.

Nund Rishi (1377–1438): Sufi sant and poet in Kashmiri. Though a follower of Islam, he was revered all over Kashmir by Hindus as well. His poetry, mainly in the form of 'shruk' verses, is full of allusions to Hindu purana and shastra. After his son and daughter died when they were still children, Nund Rishi withdrew from life for 12 years and lived in a cave. On emerging, he wrote a long verse narrative, *Buddha-charita*, which has not been recovered. His shruk compositions have recently been collected under the title *Noornama*. He innovated the nazm in Kashmiri poetry and was one of the founders of the Muslim Rishi order of Kashmir. Among many epithets used as reference to him are Sheikh-ul-Alam, Sheikh Noor-ud-Din, Alamdari Kashmir, Shams-ul-Aarifin, Kashur Wazkhan, etc.

Nur Muhammad (mid-18th): a Sufi poet in Hindi; author of *Indravati* and *Anurag-bansuri*. He belonged to Jaunpur (Uttar Pradesh) but later moved to Bhadon village, in Azamgarh district. He had studied Hindi poetry more widely than any other Sufi poet; was also a scholar of Farsi.

Nuri-Jamtamachi: principal characters of a famous love-story in Sindhi literature. Nuri was the beautiful daughter of a fisherman, while Jamatmachi was the ruler of Samabans, who fell in love with her. He married her and brought her back into his palace where she experienced a lot of hostility from the other queens. But she won them over with her humility and gentleness.

Nusrati [Muhammad Nusrat (d.1683)]: poet in Urdu from Bijapur (now in Karnataka), regarded as the finest poet produced by the Adil Shahi regime. His fame rests on three masnavi works: *Gulshan-i-ishq*, which tells of the romance between Kunwar Manohar and Madhumalati; *Ali-nama*, an account in verse of ten years, 1656–66, in the reign of Sultan Ali Adil Shah; and *Tarikh-e-sikandare*. He also left behind a collection of ghazals, *Guldasta-i-ishq*, and one of qasidas. Not much is known about his life; according to one surmise, he was a Hindu brahman who wrote under a Muslim pen-name.

O

Okhana (Rajasthani): Corrupt form of the Sanskrit term 'upakhyana', meaning a secondary episode or story. Generally, the story is associated with a proverb or saying.

Ommen Koshy (1825–99): prose-writer in Malayalam. He was a foreign Christian missionary who learnt Malayalam for the purpose of propagating his religion in Kerala. A collection of his articles, published under the title *Pulleli Kunchu* (1882), is sometimes regarded as the first novel in the language. He also wrote *Kannittoupadesham*, a didactic work, and *Paradeshi moksha yatra*, a Malayalam translation of Bunyan's *The Pilgrim's Progress*.

Oriya: main language of the state of Orissa in East India, it is spoken by about 32 milliion people. Its speakers are also known as Oriya. Oriya belongs to the eastern group of Indo-Aryan languages. Descended from Magadhi Prakrit through Magadhi Apabhramsha; it emerged in 9th/10th Century. A.D. as a separate language. Its script originated in Brahmi, then developed to the present form by modifying the so-called Gupta and Proto-Bengali scripts.

[Oriya] Bhagavat (mid-16th), of Jagannatha Dasa: the poet is said to have started writing this in Oriya for the benefit of his illiterate and widowed mother. While the work was in progress, he used to recite it within the precincts of the Jagannatha temple. That is how he attracted the notice of Shri Chaitanya. Jagannatha Dasa created the most mellifluous and lucid diction possible at the time in Oriya and also innovated a new metre of nine letters which later came to be known as the Bhagavat metre in Oriya. The work is not a translation of *Bhagavata-purana* and many episodes have been incorporated from other puranas.

[Oriya] Harivamsha (16th) of Achyutananda Dasa: the major work of this prolific writer. It is esteemed nearly as highly as the Jagannatha Bhagavata by the common people.

[Oriya] Mahabharata (15th) of Sarala Dasa: the most popular of the four or five versions of *Mahabharata* in Oriya. The poet abridged the original story in 700 verses and thus brought it within easy reach of the common people who could not understand the Sanskrit original. The work is thoroughly steeped in local atmosphere and reflects the contemporary socio-economic conditions in Orissa. Not only are the original epic characters changed into peasant personalities; the order of events has also been changed at places and some new episodes added. Thus, this is not a translation but a re-telling of the main events.

[Oriya] Ramayana (mid-16th), of Balaram Dasa: see Balarama Ramayana.

Ottakkuttar (11th/12th): poet in Tamil; author of Muvarula and *Takkaygapparani*. Two inferior works, *Arumbailtollayiram* and *Itti Elupades* have been ascribed him, but these may be forgeries. Born into a weaver community of Tiruverumbur village near Tiruchi, his original name was Kuttan; an ardent Shaiva, he won favour with the Cholas and was court-poet of four Chola kings from Kulattongan I to Rajaraja II. He is said to have been a rival of Kamban and wrote "Uttara Kandam" in competition; is also said to have quarrelled with Puhalendi and Auviyar. He lived an inordinately long time, and many stories, often unfavourable, are told of him.

Ottan tullal (Malayalam): the more popular of the three forms of 'tullal' performance innovated by Kunchan Nambiar. It generally uses the more rapid metres like taranggini, ardhakeka, vaktra, etc. Most of his compositions are in this form. In it the dancer-narrator has green coloured make-up and wears a crown.

Ovi (Marathi): a verse-metre which sounds like rhythmic prose; often employed in narrative poems. It came into use from about mid-14th century.

Oyarattu Chandu Menon (1847–1900): novelist in Malayalam; best known as author of *Indulekha* (1889), generally regarded as the first novel in Malayalam; also wrote *Sharada*.

P

P.B. Godbole [Parashuram Ballal Godbole (1799–1874)]: lexicographer and translator of Sanskrit drama into Marathi, but best known as the compiler of *Navanita* (1854) which consists of selected extracts from the work of classical Marathi poets. His own works in Marathi are *Vritta darpana* (1860), a commentary on Moropant's *Kekavali*. He was one of the editors of *Panditi kosha* (1829), a dictionary prepared by Sanskrit scholars for the govt. His translations of Sanskrit plays into Marathi were widely read because he used a simple, colloquial Marathi.

Pada (Sanskrit): one-fourth of a shloka or a metrical stanza; generally, a line of verse.

Padakalpataru (*c*1770; Bangla): of Gokulananda Sen,who later took the name of Vaishnav Das: an anthology of 3101 Vaishnav padas composed in Bangla, Brajabuli and Sanskrit. Most of the poems feature Radha-Krishna episodes; some are about Shri Chaitanya and came to be known as 'gaura-chandrika'. The poets represented are Jnanadas (182 padas), Balaramdas (136), Jayadev, Brindavandas, Rai Ramananda, Madhav Ghosh, Basudev Ghosh, Lochandas, Narottamdas and Radhamohan Thakur. The original title of the collection may have been "Gitakalpataru".

Padarupasiddhi (?C; Pali) of Buddhappiya Dipankara: a grammatical work in seven chapters, written in the manner of Kachhayana's work.

Padalipta Suri or **Palitta Suri** (1st/2nd): poet in Prakrit/Apabhramsha, author of the lost work, (*Taramgavai kaha Tarangarati katha* in Sanskrit). There are many legends about his life and deeds. Most probably he was a Jain monk of Koshala; went to Pratisthan (mod. Paithan in Maharashtra), then the seat of Satavahan rule and a centre of Prakrit literature; overcame initial opposition to join the literary circle of Hala Satavahan and won an eminent position there.

Padam or **Bharatanatya Padam** (Tamil): lyrical compositions sung as accompaniment to dance, especially in order to support the abhinaya.

Padavali (Oriya/Bangla): the word, meaning musical composition, occurs for the first time in *Gita Govinda*. But 16th century onwards, first in Bengal, then in Orissa, it came to mean Vaishnav lyrics. The works of many Vaishnav poets in Bangla and Oriya have been collected as their 'padavali'.

Padavali (15th; Mithila) of Vidyapati: the poet's fame rests on about 900 or so padas that have been collected here. They were collected from MSS found in Mithila and Nepal, from various collections of Vaishnav songs, and from orally transmitted sources. Love songs outnumber the devotional and occasional songs in this collection. Though the influence of Jayadev is apparent, the range of emotions depicted by Vidyapati is much greater. While the love songs refer only to the Radha-Krishna relationship, the devotional songs are in praise of Krishna, Shiva, Durga and Ganga; of these again, the songs about Shiva are the most important.

Padikkasup Pulavar (16th): poet in Tamil from Kalandai in Thondaimandalam. He composed three 'sadhagam' (one hundred songs) works. *Thondaimandala sadhagam* covers the entire Pallava kingdom while *Pullirukku veloor sadhagam* and *Thandaliyar sadhagam* related to well-known holy places with ancient Shiva temples. About 30 other songs of his are to be found in the collection *Thanippadal thirattu*.

Padinenkizhkkanakku (Tamil): all but one are collections of short poems by the same writer. Some have been assigned to the Third Sangam, but most belong to a later date. The most famous of these works is *Tirukkural*.

Padirruppattu (2nd BC/2nd AD; Tamil): one of the *Ettuttogai* collections, consisting of ten groups of ten poems each, each group by one of ten poets. The first and the last have been lost. All the poems are in praise of Chera kings. The work provides a wealth of historical facts about these kings, and also gives a picture of the political condition of Tamilnadu about 2000 years ago. Each 'ten' mentions fabulous gifts received by the poets from their patrons. Among the poets represented are Kapilar, Paranar and the woman poet Kakkaippadiniyar.

Padmapuran (probably end-15th; Bangla) of Vijaygupta: poetical work dealing with the goddess Manasa also known as Padma. It became very popular but there is no definite evidence about its time of composition.

Padma-purana (?C; Sanskrit): a purana work of unusually large size. Extant in two recensions, it upholds the cult of Vishnu. The older recension has survived in a Bangla MSS and is in five 'khanda' (parts): 'Srishti', 'Bhumi', 'Swarga', 'Patala', 'Uttara'. These parts are probably centuries apart in their times of composition; the latest portions are later than *Bhagavat-purana*.

Padma-purana (17th; Asamiya) of Sukavi Narayandeva: a verse narrative, interspersed with songs, and dealing with the worship of Padma (or Manasa), the snake-goddess. Two earlier poets, Mankar and Durgavara, had also written on the same theme but not at such length. Narayandeva's work includes what his predecessors wrote about and adds much more, especially the conflict between Padma and Chandradhar, the merchant-prince of Champaknagar. Written on the puranic model, the work has many digressions. It offers a view of Assamese society of the time, its customs, ceremonies and life in general.

Padmabati (1651; Bangla) of Alaol: an adaptation of the Avadhi romance by Jayasi, written at the instance of Magan Thakur. Alaol abridged and revised the story to make it into a panchali, and added some new episodes.

Padmagupta (11th): poet in Sanskrit; also known as Parimala or Parimala Kalidasa. He was the son of Mriganka Gupta (or Datta), court-poet of Paramara king Sindhuraja (also known as Navasahasanka or Munja), ruler of Dhara. He wrote *Navasahasanka-charita* to honour the king. He is said to have another poem, now lost, on the theme of Tailanga king Baspa's campaign against Chalukya king Mularaja of Gujarat. The poet was an ardent admirer of Kalidasa and imitated him; hence he is sometimes called 'Parimala Kalidasa'.

Padmakar Bhatta (1753–1833): poet of the riti convention in Hindi; son of Sanskrit scholar and poet, Mohanlal Bhatta; belonged to a Tailanga brahman family. He travelled widely in search of patronage and was handsomely rewarded by many patrons. Among his works are *Himmat Bahadur virudavali* (in praise of Himmat Bahadur, a commander of the Nawab of Avadh); *Jagat-vinod* (in praise of prince Jagatsingh of Jaipur); *Padmavaran* (work on poetics, composed in dohas); *Ghangaur-varnan* (description of the fair at Ghangaur near Udaipur); Prabodh-pachasa; Ganga-lahari; Ram-rasayan.

Padmanabha (mid-15th): poet in Gujarati; author of *Kanhade prabandha*. A Nagara brahman from Visnagar, he obtained the patronage of Jalor ruler Akheraj.

Padmaraj puran (early 15th; Kannada) of Padmanank: poetical work dealing mainly with Padmaras, author of *Dikshabodh*, and generally with the poet's ancestors.

Padmavat or **Padumavat** (*c*1530; Hindi) of Malik Muhammad Jayasi: kavya work which is a detailed allegorical treatment in Sufi manner of the story of Chittor queen Padmini. She was the daughter of Simhala ruler Gandharvasen. The ruling prince of Chittor, Ratansen, hears about her beauty from the parrot Hiraman and determines to win her; leaves behind his existing queen, Nagmati, and travels to Simhala. Overcoming many difficulties on the way; attacks the Simhala fort, captures Padmavati and brings her back to Chittor. The Simhala ruler seeks the help of Delhi sultan Alauddin to recover Padmavati. Alauddin lays siege to Chittor for many years, manages to capture Ratansen, but Padmavati manages to get him released. Finally Ratansen is killed in a battle with Kumhal ruler Devpal; both his queens immolate themselves on his pyre. The work is written in Avadhi, but the poet has used, where necessary, words from Sanskrit, Prakrit, Apabhramsha, Farsi, Arabi, and from various speeches heard around Jayas. Thereby he has added to the richness of Hindi.

Padmini-charit (*c*1650; Hindi) of Lalchand or Lakshoday. This kavya work tells of Padmini and Ratnasen, but the story is somewhat different from that of *Padmavati*. The poet belonged to Mewar.

Padya (Sanskrit): kavya composition in metre.

Padyavali (16th; Sanskrit) of Rupa Goswamin: anthology of devotional poetry, containing 386 verses representing more than 125 poets. The poems relate to Krishna-bhakti and are arranged to exemplify the general features of bhakti as a rasa.

Pahare (Panjabi): a poetical form based on a unit of time called 'pahir' (one-eighth part of a day or night).

Paheli (Hindi): a riddle or a concealed statement about a person, event or thing.

Pahuda-doha (*c*1000; Apabhramsha) of Ramasimha Muni: a collection of poems dealing mainly with metaphysical issues. 'Pahuda' probably means a gift. Of 222 poems in the collection, 12 are in Prakrit and three in Sanskrit; all but 16 are in doha form.

Paiyalachhi-namamala (*c*970; Prakrit) of Dhanapala: the earliest available work on Prakrit lexicography, listing about 1000 words. It is said to have been composed by Dhanapala in order to teach his sister the meaning and usage of Prakrit words.

Pajjamadhu (*c*1100; Prakrit) of Buddhappiya: a shataka series of verses. The work describes and praises the Buddha's appearance and wisdom; concludes with praise of the 'samgha' and 'nirvana'.

Palakuriki Somanatha (*c*1200/1240): Shaiva poet in Telugu, who also composed in Kannada and Sanskrit. A crusader of Virashaiva faith, he was also a literary rebel in the sense that he opposed the marga tradition of Nannaya. The desi movement initiated by him aimed at freeing Original Telugu from its dependence on Sanskrit. He also innovated literary genres in Telugu like 'gadya', 'ragade' 'shataka', 'udaharana'. Among his works are *Shila-sampadane*, a prose work explaining 64 Virashaiva principles; *Someshwar-shataka*, also known as *Somaradhya-shataka; Pancha-ratna; Sadguru ragale; Chennabasava-strotrad ragale; Shranau-basava ragale*.

Palanativira-charita (*c*1400; Telugu) of Shrinathudu: poetical work dealing with an event in local Andhra history. The event concerns domestic strife between two sets of cousins belonging to the Haihaya rulers of Palanadu. The poet has portrayed this strife on the lines of *Mahabharata*. The poem, composed in dvipadi metre, was meant to be sung. It was not a popular form before Shrinathudu's time, but his work made it so.

Pali: an old Indian language widely used from about 5th century B.C to 1st century A.D. There is no certainty about its area of origin but it seems to have developed in 'Madhyadesha'. It was the language in which the sayings of Gautam Buddha were preserved. There may have been variants of the language in other regions, from which the various Prakrits developed. Pali is thus a link between Sanskrit and the Prakrits.

Palliyeluchhi (Tamil): a poetical form in which the poet praises his king or patron by way of awakening him from sleep. Each complete poem generally consists of ten shorter poems in 'enchir achiriya viruttam' metre.

Pallu (Tamil): an old dramatic form of Tamilnadu. It is said to have evolved out of the ancient 'ulattippattu' form of songs which were sung by the wives of peasants. The typical story tells of a peasant with two wives, the quarrel between them, how one takes the side of the husband but the other does not when the local zamindar intervenes; finally, amity between the wives is restored. In its developed form, 'pallu' became a song-based dramatic form.

Pamay Dhorandhar-ri bat (1790; Hindi) by unknown author: prose work which tells of the romance between Raja Dhorandhar and Pamay, the granddaughter of Kanjoi.

Pampa (10th): the first great poet of Kannada; came to acquire titles such as 'Kavitagunarnav', 'Prasannagambhir vachan-rachana-chatur', 'Sukaviranmana-manosottamhans'. Of his two major works, *Adipuran*, is a champu work honouring Vrishabhanath, the first tirthankar, while *Vikramarjun-vijay* (also known as Pampa Bharata) is based on *Mahabharata.*

Pampa Bharata: see *Vikramarjun vijay*.

Pampa Ramayana or **Ramchandra-charitra puran** (late 11th; Kannada) of Nagachandra, who called himself Abhinav Pampa: a kavya work based not on the Sanskrit *Ramayana* of Valmiki but on the Prakrit *Pauma-chariu* of Vimal Suri. Some of the main differences are that Rama cannot kill Ravan because that would violate the principle of 'ahimsa', hence Lakshman has to do the job; Ravan abducts Sita under the influence of Kamadeva and later repents this deed; Rama and Lakshman have many wives; and so on.

Pana (Malayalam): a ritual performed in connection with worship of the goddess Kali in Kerala. Prayers sung at the ritual are called 'panattottam' or 'panappattu'. Some of these are considered the earliest specimens of poetry in Malayalam.

Panch saheli (1642; Hindi) by unknown author: a work comprising 65 dohas which described the pangs of separation of five women who are friends.

Pancha kappiyam: five long poems in Tamil, often mentioned together as the five 'major epics', though they are not of the same period. Of these the oldest are *Silappadikaram* and *Manimekkelai*. The third, *Jivaka-chintamani*, belongs to 10th century. The other two, *Valaiyapati* and *Kundalakesi*, are extant only in fragments. There are also the five so-called 'minor epics': *Chulamani*, *Perunkathai*, *Nilakesi*, *Yasodara-kapiyam* and *Nagakumara-kapiyam*.

Pancha-ratra (?C; Sanskrit) of Bhasa: play in three acts; uses a *Mahabharata* situation and some characters to tell a different story. Towards the end of the Pandavas' 12-year exile, Drona effects a truce between them and the Kauravas. Duryodhana, portrayed here as a noble king, agrees to end the dispute and share the kingdom on the condition that the Pandavas are discovered within five days (or nights). The play has a happy ending.

Pancha-sakha: five great poets of Orissa, all friends or followers of Shri Chaitanya, who became known as a group. The poets are Achyutananda Dasa, Ananta Dasa, Balarama Dasa, Jagannatha Dasa and Yasobanta Dasa. They were contemporaries of Maharaj Prataprudra Dev (r.1495–1540) and was much honoured by him. Following the example of Sarala Dasa, they abjured the use of Sanskrit and composed in Oriya for the benefit of fellow-Oriyas. Their presence is generally acknowledged by the period being called the 'Panchasakha yuga'.

Panchatantra (?C; Sanskrit) ascribed to Vishnusharma: the only work of fables in the language, it has been transmitted to the rest of the world more widely than any other Indian work. Rendered into Pahlavi as early as mid-6th, it travelled west as well as east outside India through Farsi and Arabi versions; over 200 versions are known to exist in 50 languages. The original work is lost; came down in three recensions, of which two again were lost; from one lost recension were derived the Kashmiri version, *Tantrakhyayika*, and two Jain versions; from the other lost recension came the South Indian *Panchatantra*, the Nepal version and the *Hitopadesha* of Bengal. *Tantrakhyayika* is the earliest and nearest to the original. The work is in five parts: 'Mitrabheda' (separation of friends); 'Mitra-prapti' (acquiring friends), 'Sandhi-vigraha' (peace and war), 'Labdhansa' (loss of what is acquired); 'Aparikshitakaritva' (rash action). The main body of the text is in prose but the author has at places quoted verses from *Ramayana, Mahabharata* and other ancient works, to illustrate some point.

Tr. A.W. Ryder, Chicago, 1925; C. Rajan, 1950.

Panchatantra (earlier 11th; Kannada) of Durgasingh: a champu work based not on Vishnusharma's *Panchatantra* but on Vasubhag Bhatt's *Pancha-tantra*. The original of the latter is not extant but Durgasingh's translation made it known. Vasubhag Bhatt selected five episodes from Gunadhya's *Brihadkatha* (composed in Paisachi Prakrit) and put them under the title *Panchatantra*. Durgasingh translated this work into Kannada, which is thus very different from the Sanskrit *Pancha-tantra* of Vishnusharma or its various versions.

Panchatantra kilippattu (18th; Malayalam) of Kunchan Nambiar: a verse adaptation into the 'kilipattu' form of the Sanskrit original. As in other works by this author, the language is aimed at the common man's understanding. Parts of the work are meant to be sung.

Panchali (Bangla): narrative song which may have originated as accompaniment to a puppet show. The song was long enough to be sung or chanted on successive days. It generally extolled local deities or puranic gods.

Panchali parinayamu (16th; Tamil) of Kakmani Murthikavi: a kavya work in five sections, narrating the story of Draupadi from her birth to her marriage with the Pandava brothers.

Pandav Yasendu Chandrika (1835: Rajasthani) of Swarupdas: a retelling of the *Mahabharata* story in about 3000 shlokas. The poet used a mixture of Pingal, Dingal and Sanskrit in order to reach out to a wider audience.

Pandava-charita (*c*1200; Prakrit) of Devapriya Suri: an adaptation of *Mahabharata*. The work is in 18 sarga, in which each parvan of *Mahabharata* is condensed and remodelled to propagate Jainism.

Pandava pratap (*c*1700; Marathi) of Shridhar: a long narrative poem based on *Mahabharata*, but includes ideas and events from many other Sanskrit works. It is in 64 sections and consists of 13,397 original stanzas.

Pandava-purana: Of three works under this title, one composed by Subhachandra in Prakrit and dated about 1550 is a retelling of the *Mahabharatha* story; it is also known as *jaina Mahabharata*. Another work with this title in Prakrit is a long poem in 18 'sarga' composed by Vadichandra. A third work, by Yashakirti, is a long poem in Apabhramsha.

Pandava-vijaya (?16th; Bangla) of Kavindra: a brief version of *Mahabharata* in verse, also known as *Vijay-Pandavkatha*. The work was sponsored by the Muslim general Paragal Khan, a deputy of Husain Shah in Chatgaon.

Pandava-vijaya (17th; Bangla) ascribed to Kashiram Das: earliest known *Mahabharata* poem in the language. Only the first four parvan were written by Kashiram during first decade of 17th century; next two or three parvan by his nephew Nandaram; rest taken from the works of Nityananda Ghosh (who wrote towards end of 17th) and of others. The work is thus a compilation. Its first book was printed for the first time in 1802–04 at the Serampore Mission Press.

Pandikkasuppulvar (1686–1723): poet in Tamil; author of *Tonte-mantal satakam*, a series of 100 poems set in his native village of Tontemantalam in Northern Tamil nadu. The work is particularly important for the picture it draws of life lived in that time and place.

Pandikkovai (7th; Tamil) of unknown author: the earliest poem in 'kovai' form in the language. It has been gleaned from stanzas quoted in several commentaries; quoted specially to illustrate 'aham' situations. The poem deals with Pandyan king Nedumaran, a contemporary of Sambandar.

Pandurang Dadoba (1814–82): grammarian of Marathi and social activist; author of *Marathi bhashesch vyakarana* (1836), the only grammar of its time based on scientific study of the language. He began writing it when he was still a school student; later it became a standard textbook prescribed for schools. He also wrote *Yashoda-Pandurangi* (1865), thus named to commemorate his parents Pandurang and Yashoda; this work is a prose commentary on Moropant's *Kekavali*. His autobiography, *Atmacharitra ani athavani*, published many years after his death, gives a picture of contemporary life in Bombay.

Panini (4th or 6th/7th B.C.): the most famous grammarian of Sanskrit; author of *Ashtadhyayi*. Two kavyas *Patala-vijaya* and *Jambavati-vijaya* are also attributed to him, also some verses preserved in anthologies. There is some doubt whether the grammarian and the poet are identical; dating has varied him, also some verses preserved in anthologies. There is some doubt whether the grammarian and the poet are identical; dating has varied from 4th to 6th/7th B.C. Patanjali calls him Dakshi-putra, thus his mother was one Dakshi. He has been referred to in later literature as Salaturya; thus he belonged to Salatara, identified with the present Lahaur in the Yusufzai valley.

Panjabi (earlier spelt as Punjabi): main language of the British Indian province of Punjab. Its speakers, also known as Panjabis numbering about and 95 million, are now to be found in the modern Indian state of Panjab, also in parts of Haryana and Himachal Pradesh as well as in Pakistan. Derived from Shauraseni Apabhramsha, Panjabi emerged around A.D. 1200. For writing it uses the Gurumukhi script, which developed out of Brahmi.

Panthoibi khongul (?C; Manipuri): prose narrative, the original of which was believed to have been composed in ancient Meitei language in first half of 8th century. A.D. Recent opinion, however, places the original sometime in late 17th. The story concerns the girl Panthoibi, who is married against her wishes to one Khaba Khoinucha, though she is already in love with Nongpok Nigthou. She continues to meet him even after her marriage. Eventually they elope and settle down in Nongmaijing. Apart from this romance, the story tells of the beginnings of Manipuri dance, various features of Manipuri marriage, introduction of agriculture to Manipur, etc. It is thus a valuable document on old Manipuri culture. The work was translated into modern Manipuri, transcribed in Bangla script and published in 1963.

Paparaju [Kankati Paparaju (mid-18th)]: poet in Telugu from Nellore, close friend of Pushpagiri Timmana; author of *Uttar-Ramayanamu*. It is said he was commanded in a dream by Madan-gopal (Vishnu) to compose this work.

Paramal Raso: see *Alha Khand*.

Paramananda Sen (mid-16th): given the title 'Kavi-Karnapur'; youngest son of a Chaitanya follower and author of several works in Sanskrit relating to Chaitanya. Among these are a play, *Chaitanya-chandrodaya* (1538), and a long poem, *Chaitanya-charitamrita* (1542).

Paramartha (Panjabi): a form of prose.

Paramartha Guruvin Kathai (1740; Tamil) of Father Veschi:

and Muthan. The stories, left by the author in MS form, were printed only in 1822 by Muttieswami Pillai of Pondicherry.

Parameshwar Das (16th): poet in Bangla; oldest known poet to compose a *Mahabharata* poem in Bangla. Later given the title 'Kavindra', he was the court-poet of Paragal Khan, at whose behest the work was undertaken. MSS going back to mid-17th have been recovered from all parts of Bengal, thus proving the popularity of the poem. Practically nothing is known of the poet's life. According to some scholars, his real name was Shrikar Nandi.

Parani (Tamil): particular kind of literary composition which eulogises a warrior who has killed a thousand male elephants on the battle-field.

Paranjoti Munivar (1650–1725): Shaiva poet in Tamil from Vedaranyam town in Thanjavur district. His two known works are *Vedaranya-puranam*, which extols Shiva, and *Tiruvilaiyadal-puranam*, which is in praise of Shri Sundaresha of Madurai.

Parasbhag (early 18th; Panjabi) of Addan Shah: prose translation of *Kimiyae-sadat* in Farsi of Imam Ghazali, the great Muslim scholar. The translation is so successful that it has often been regarded as an original work. In eight chapters it discusses Vedanta, Sufi beliefs, customs, political and administrative issues with examples.

Parasuram (1754–1844): poet in Marathi; composed mainly powada and lavani poems. He belonged to Bavi village near Nasik and was a tailor by caste; became a devotee of Vitthal in childhood.

Parch (Panjabi): a form of prose.

Paribhasha (Sanskrit): originally meant a speech or discourse found in *Bhagavata-purana*; more generally, means an explanation. Among special meanings, it is used to mean terminology or technical terms.

Parichai (Rajasthani): a short biographical poem on a sant, written by his disciples or their followers. These works are valued more as information than as literature.

Parijatapaharanamu (*c*1520; Telugu) of Nandi Timmanna: a prabandha work based on the story of the tiff between Shri Krishna and Satyabhama over the parijata flower he presented to Rukmini. In order to mollify Satyabhama, Krishna had to steal the parijat tree from

Nandanvan (the garden of the gods) and plant it in his courtyard. It is said that the poet wrote this when he had to intercede in a quarrel between Vijayanagar ruler Krishnadeva Raya and his wife.

Parijata-harana (?C; Sanskrit) of Umapati Upadhyaya: a semi-dramatic work dealing with Krishna's exploit of carrying off Indra's parijata tree; contains songs in Maithili. The author belonged to Mithila and lived during the second part of the reign of Hariharadeva.
Tr. G.Grierson, *JBORS*, 1917.

Parijata-harana (*c*1650; Maithili): of Umapati: a play in 'kirtaniya' style which set the model for several generations. The author has named himself in the play as kavi Pandita Mukhya Umapati Upadhyay; his biography remains a matter of controversy.

Parijata-harana Nata (?16th; Asamiya) of Shankaradeva: a play written during the author's last 14 years' stay at Patbausi. The full title of the work is "Naraka-vadha parijata-harana lila-yatra"; it includes two episodes, the killing of Naraka and the stealing of the parijata tree from Indra's garden.

Parijata-haranam (15th; Malayalam) of Tharakal Varier: champu work in Maniprvalam dealing with the quarrel between Sachi and Satyabhama in which their respective husbands, Indra and Krishna, also get involved.

Parimala (16th; Oriya) of Narasimha Sena: an 'akhyaika' poem, probably the longest literary work of the time. It tells of princess Parimala of Kanchi, who is betrothed as a child to prince Makaraketu of Dharmavati. When she grows up, she falls in love with the gandharva Chitraratha and visits him every night, even after she is married to Makaraketu. After many supernatural events, they are properly united as husband and wife. The character of Parimala is somewhat unusual, inasmuch as she keeps both her lovers satisfied. This double relationship gives the poet a lot of scope to create erotic scenes.

Parimelalagar (late 13th): scholar of Tamil and Sanskrit; wrote a commentary on *Tirukkural* which has been considered the best ever written on this work. The scholar was a Vaishnav priest at the Ulagalandar Perumal temple in Kanchi; earlier he lived in Okkur, near Madurai. He is said to have written commentaries also on *Paripadal* and on *Tirumurugattrupadai*.

Paripadal (?C; Tamil): one of the

Ettuttogai collections. 'Paripadal' is a generic term for certain longer verse compositions set to music. Apparently the First Sangam produced numerous paripadals, the Second 70 and the Third 30. The present collection is from the Third Sangam; out of the original 30, only 24 (by 13 poets) have survived. These relate to (a) the city of Madurai; (b) the river Vaigai which flows by Madurai; (c) the god Murugan of Tirupparankunram, a hill to the south of Madurai; (d) the god Tirumal on the Alagar hills to the west of Madurai. Thus, all of them relate to this city. For 22 of the poems, the names of poets concerned are known, also of those who set the poems to music.

Parmal raso (?C; Hindi) of unknown authorship: two parts of the work have been published by the Nagari Pracharini Sabha; these tell of the prowess of Parmal (Paramardidev) and Jaichand. The work is different in every way from *Alhakhand.*

Parmanand also known as Nandaram (1791–1879): poet in Kashmiri; generally composed on philosophic and religious themes. Among his works are *Radha-swayamvar, Sudama-charit, Siva-lagna,* etc. Because of his mastery of other languages, his Kashmiri was often mixed with Sanskrit, Farsi, Panjabi and Hindustani.

Parmananddas (1493–1584): a bhakti poet in Hindi; one of the Ashtachhap group; author of *Dhruva-charitra* and *Dan-lila*. His other verses have been collected as *Parmanand-sagar*.

Parnar (1st/2nd): poet in Tamil; friend of Kapilar, famous poet and member of the Third Sangam. At least 82 poems by Parnar are to be found in ancient anthologies. Apart from reflecting various human emotions, these poems also mention contemporary kings and events and living conditions.

Parswanath purana (*c*1225; Kannada) of Parswa Pandit: a champu work dealing with the life of the 23rd tirthankar, Parswanath. This is the earliest known work on Parswanath in Kannada. The poet was attached to the court of Raja Kartavirya.

Parvati-mangal (*c*1583; Hindi) of Tulsidas: long poem describing the marriage of Shiva and Parvati.

Pasanaha-chariu (10th/11th; Apabhramsha) of Padmakirti: biography of Parswa, the 23rd tirthankar. The work has 18 'sandhi', containing about 3300 shlokas. The first seven sandhis tell of the nine previous lives of Parswa; the 8th sandhi describes his present birth. The next four sandhis narrate an imaginary episode about his valour.

Pasupuleti Rangajamma (mid-17th): woman poet in Telugu; won the patronage of Nayaka ruler Vijayaraghava; composed two prabandha works, *Nannarudasa-vilasamu* and *Usha-parinayamu*.

Patala-vijaya (?4th B.C.; Sanskrit) ascribed to Panini: lost work cited by Namisadhu in his commentary on *Kavyalamkara* of Rudrata. It was a mahakavya dealing with Krishna's descent into the lower world for winning Jambavati as his bride; provides evidence that kavya composition was already in existence in 4th century B.C.

Patanjali (?2nd B.C.): grammarian of Sanskrit; author of *Mahabhashya*. Some scholars regard him as the same as the author of *Yoga-sutra*. He appears to have been a contemporary of the Sunga king Pushyamitra and was greatly honoured by the king; may have gone with the court when Pushyamitra shifted his capital from Pataliputra to Saket in ancient Ayodhya.

Pathinen-kizhkanakku (Tamil): the collective title for 18 'small works' (i.e. consisting of four-line poems) that were composed during late 6th and early 7th, often considered a 'dark age' coming after the Third Sangam. All the works are didactic in nature; included among them are *Tirukkural* and *Naladiyar*.

Patra (Sanskrit): participant in the action of a novel, story or play; a character.

Patra-kaumudi (?C; Sanskrit) ascribed to Vararuchi: manual of letter-writing; also discusses how letters are to be carried to persons concerned.

Pattappattu (*c*1670; Malayalam) by unknown author: long poem narrating the changing fortunes of the ruling dynasty of Kochi from about 1645 to 1670.

Patti (Panjabi): a poetical form practised in medieval Panjabi literature. In it, the initial letters of each line in a poem followed an alphabetical order. The 'patti' form may have derived from the 'siharfi' of Farsi.

Pattinappalai (?C; Tamil) of Rudran Kannanar: the ninth idyll of *Pattuppattu*. The work celebrates the Chola king Karikala; presents an elaborate picture of Puhar or Kaviripppupattinam, a great seaport which was the Chola capital and also a centre for international trade. The title means 'a port and separation'; the hero has to choose between love and battle, and finally decides to remain with his beloved.

Pattinattar or **Pattinattuppillaiyar** (10th): Shaiva ascetic and poet in Tamil; born in Tiruvenkadu (hence called Tiruvenkadar when he was a boy) near Kavirippumpattinam (where the Kaveri flows into the sea), hence was also named Pattinattupillai. He composed two kinds of verse; one religious and philosophical, of the kind included in *Tirumurai*; the other more earthy and pessimistic, employing popular language, as in *Arutpulambal*.

Pattu (Malayalam): literally means song, but it was developed into a poetic form which used Malayalam as well as Tamil. According to *Lilatilakam*, the vocabulary should be such as can be written in Tamil; the metre should be from Tamil but never from Sanskrit; hence 'pattu' was conceived on the lines of Chentamil epic poetry. The earliest extant sample in Malayalam is *Ramacharitam*, composed probably in 12th. In view of the importance assigned to this form in *Lilatilakam* and the quotations given therein, there must have been many works in the pattu form. But only fragments of some works have survived, such as *Anchutampuram pattu*, *Ulakudaya Perumal pattu*, etc.

Pattuppattu (2nd B.C./2nd A.D.; Tamil): anthology of ten long poems ranging from 782 to 103 lines, representing the work of eight poets who are named. Eight of the poems are dedicated to Tamil kings of the second half of 1st century A.D. Their separate titles are *Tirumuraigarruppadai, Porunararruppadai, Sirupanarruppaddai, Perumbanarruppadai, Mullaippattu, Maduraikkanchi, Nedunalvadai, Kurinjippattu, Pattinappalai, Malaipadukadam*. The first, composed by Nakkirar, is like an invocation meant for the whole anthology; it invokes the god Murugan and instructs a devotee about this deity. The second, third and fourth poems advise minstrels and actors on likely patrons who might rescue them from destitution.

Pauma-chariu (8th; Apabhramsha) of Swayambhu: a kavya work in the Jain tradition dealing with the *Ramayana* story. There are many drastic differences from the Valmiki *Ramayana*. Thus, Ravan is a great-souled ('mahatma') being devoted to Jina; Sita is his daughter who is abandoned in the forest because of the prediction that she will cause trouble; Lakshman kills Ravan, not

Rama, and for this act Lakshman has to go to 'narak'; in the end both Rama and Sita adopt Jain faith. The work is in five 'kanda'—Vidyadhar, Ayodhya, Sundar, Yuddha and Uttar; left unfinished at his death by the poet, his son Tribhuvan completed the work.

Pauma-chariya (?4th; Prakrit) of Vimala Suri: a long poem based on *Ramayana*. The work is in arya metre and consists of 118 sections, some called 'uddesa', some 'parva'. The author has affected many innovations to further the Jain viewpoint. Thus there are many variations from the story as told by Valmiki.

Paumasiri-chariu (?11th; Prakrit/Apabhramsha) of Dhahila; a narrative poem dealing with the story of Padmashri. Dhanasena, a merchant of Vasantpur, had a daughter named Dhanashri and two sons, Dhanadatta and Dhanavaha, whose wives were, respectively, Yashomati and Yashoda. Dhanashri became a widow early in life and devoted herself to religious works. Because she spent money freely, her sisters-in-law became jealous and complained against her. But Dhanashri tricked them and caused them to quarrel; later brought about their reconciliation. She is reborn in her next life as Padmashri, daughter of the merchant Shankha of Hastinapur. She passes through many ordeals before attaining salvation at her death.

Pavanaduta (12th/13th; Sanskrit) of Dhoyi: a duta-kavya which tells of the gandharva maiden Kuvalayavati, living on the Malaya hills, who fell in love with king Lakshmansena of Bengal when he was campaigning in South India; with the advent of spring, she pines away in separation and proposes to send a message to him, through Pavana (the wind) blowing in the north-easterly direction. The poem consists of 100 verses; there is a four-verse epilogue. This is the earliest available poem written on the model of Kalidas' *Meghaduta*. The poet has also been named as Dhuyi or Dhoyika; he was a contemporary of Jayadev.

Pavananthi (?C): Jain scholar; author of *Nannul*, a popular Tamil grammar, based on his study of Ilampurananar's commentary of *Tolkappiyam*. The work was undertaken at the request of Siya Ganga Amarabharanan, king of Kolar.

Pavuluri Mallanna (*c*1060–1070): scholar of Telugu; translated a Shakta treatise on mathematics, *Ganita-sara* by Mahaviracharya into Telugu verse.

Payar (Bangla): the characteristic Bangla verse-line, which evolved out of the chaupai by about end-13th.

Payiram (Tamil): the introduction to a prose work.

Payyannur pattu (?12th/Malayalam): one of the earliest known examples of Malayalam literary composition. It is a narrative song of folk origin found in the Cananore area in 1834 by the German missionary Hermann Gundert. The story tells of Nilakesi Chettichhi of Peroor who had several husbands but no child. She renounces domestic life and goes away to Kachhil. There she marries the merchant Nampuchetty and has a son by him. Soon after his birth, during a feast Nilakesi's brothers arrive there unexpectedly. A fight breaks out and the brothers are killed. Nilakesi goes away again, leaving behind her husband and their son, Nampusari Aran. The boy grows up and sets out in a ship with merchandise; visits many lands and returns to Kachhil with gold. A female ascetic meets him and invites him to a feast conducted by women. At this point the MS breaks off and the story remains incomplete.

Peddanna [Allasani Peddanna (*c*1470–1535)]: poet in Telugu; much honoured by Vijayanagar ruler Krishnadeva Raya, who appointed the poet his minister for some time and gave him the title of 'Andhra Kavitapitamaha'. Only two of Peddanna's works have been recovered, *Lakshansara-samgrahamu* and *Manu-charitramu*; a third, *Harikatha-saramu*, is known only by reference.

Perashiriyar (13th/14th): scholar of Tamil; wrote a commentary on *Tolkappiyam*. Only the third part of this work, dealing with poetics, is extant. His own prose was quite influential as a model for later writers of Tamil prose.

Periya-puranam (mid-12th; Tamil) of Chekkilar; collection of life-stories and legends of the 63 Shaiva sants of Tamilnadu. The work, of 72 cantos in 4286 stanzas, was composed during the reign of Kulottunga II (1133–1150); is regarded as analogous to *Raghuvamsha* of Kalidasa as a hagiological work. Also known as *Tiruttondar-puranam*, it completes what was began by Sundarar in *Tiruttondat-togai*, and carried further by Nambi Andar Nambi in *Tiruttondar tiru andai*. Composed in viruttam metre and written in a simple style, it combines religious fervour with literary aptness in a manner that is unique in Tamil literature. After the poet's time, the work was often referred to as the 12th *Tirumurai.*

Periyatirumoli (?C; Tamil) of Tirumangai Alvar: collective title of the second 1000 Vaishnav hymns.

Periyalvar (7th/8th): sant-poet in Tamil; one of the 12 Alvars. In his hymns, he regards divinity as mother, nurse, devotee and lady-love. A brahman from Srivilliputtur, he was the foster-father of Andal. It is said that he first won renown by defeating in debate a number of learned men in the court of Pandyan king Ballabh-deva. Of his two extant works, *Tiruppalandu* is in praise of the divine; *Periyalvar tirumouli* tells of the child Krishna. He contributed 473 songs to the Alwar Pasuram collection *Nalayira divya prabandham.*

Perumpanarruppadai (?C; Tamil) of Uruttirankannanar; the fourth idyll of *Pattupattu*. The poem is in praise of the ruler of Kanchi, Tondaiman Ilantiraiyan.

Perun kadai or **Perunkathai** (6th/7th; Tamil) of Kongu Velir: a verse adaptation of the lost prose work, *Brihat-katha.* It is a long poem telling the story of Udayana king of Kausambi, and his winning of Vasavadatta, daughter of the king of Ujjayini. The narrative is full of descriptions and details of institutions, customs and manners of the author's own time. The author was from Vijayamangalam; was probably a Jain; may have been a prince. The poem in achaval metre is a rare instance of a southern work on a northern theme. Available only in an incomple recension. (the beginning and the end are missing) it is regarded as one of the major literary works in Tamil.

Phagu (Gujarati): lyrical poem describing the festival of spring and its erotic influence on lovers.

Phagua (Maithili): type of song associated with the festival of Holi.

Phataka (Marathi): verse-form innovated by Ananta Phandi; particularly effective for satirical statement.

Phulban (1655; Urdu) of Ibne Nishati: a masnavi of about 3500 lines. At the end of the work, the author gives an account of the more important poets of his time.

Pillai Tamil (Tamil): a literary form in which a man (or woman's) life, from the third month after birth to the 21th month, is described in terms of ten acts performed by the infant. Though this form is mentioned in *Tolkappiyam*, its first notable exponent in literature is Periya Alvar (7th/8th).

Pillapperumal Iyengar (17th): Vaishnav poet in Tamil from Tirumankai village. All his works are in praise of Vishnu in local form and of holy places where there are Vishnu temples. Thus his *Tiruvarankattu-antati* and *Tiruvarankattu-malai* glorify Tiruvarankam; *Chirankanaya-karuchal* honours the deity of Shrirangam; *Alakat antati* honours the deity of Tirnmalirun-cholai; *Nurrettu tirupati antati* consists of 108 verses in praise of 108 sacred placed celebrated by the Alvars.

Pilu (late 16th/early 17th): poet in Panjabi about whom very little is known. It is said that he was born into a Jat Muslim family of Tarantaran village of Amritsar district. A Mirza-Sahiban qissa work is attributed to him; its language is close to what is spoken in the Amritsar-Jalandhar area.

Pinavirabhadrudu [Pillalamari Pinavirabhadrudu (late 15th)]: poet in Telugu from Pillalamari village, near Hyderabad city; later associated with the court of Vijayanagar ruler Saluva Narasimharaya (r. 1485–93). Of his two extant works, *Shringar-Shakuntalamu* is an adaptation of the Shakuntala story in four 'aswas' and with emphasis on Shringar aspects; *Jaimini-bharatamu* focuses on the Aswamedh parva of *Mahabharata*.

Pingal: a form of Brajbhasha which bore the influence of Shauraseni Apabhramsha and was used by poets in Rajasthan for works dealing with heroism, devotion, moral duty, etc. This language was challenged by other poets in Rajasthan who chose another form of the language carrying the influence of Gurjar Apabhramsha; the latter came to be known as Dingal.

Pingal shiromani (*c*1580; Rajasthani) of Vachak Kushal Labh: a work on Rajasthani poetics, prepared by the author while tutoring Jaisalmer prince Har Raj. The first four chapters deal with Rajasthani metres (viz. 'varnik', 'matrik', 'sankar', 'dandak') and their derivations; the seventh chapter contains the earliest work on lexicography known in Rajasthani.

Pingala (?1st B.C.): scholar of prosody who laid down the rules for 'chhanda' (metre) in his *Pingala-chhanda-sutra*. His concepts were incorporated in *Natyasastras*, hence it is presumed he preceded Bharata.

Pingala chhanda-sutra (?1st B.C.; Sanskrit) of Pingala: work on metre which discusses their origin and development in Vedic and classical Sanskrit. A section on Prakrit was added to the work later, perhaps by the author himself, but the main focus is on Sanskrit. Many of the metres named and described by Pingala are not to be found in classical 'kavya' works; hence the inference that there was a period during the transition from Vedic to Sanskrit when these metres were tried out but later dropped.

Pingalandai (11th; Tamil) of Pingalar, son of Divakarar: a lexicon.

Pingali Suranna (early 17th): poet in Telugu; author of a number of works in a rather learned and artificial style; among his works is *Kalapurnodaya*.

Pirdan Lalas (1663–1736): sant poet in Rajasthani; belonged to the Lalas sub-caste of Charan, a caste which traditionally composed and sang poems in praise of royal patrons. Pirdan however wrote mainly to express his devotion to gods and goddesses. Among his works are *Narain-neh, Parameshwar-purna, Hinglaj-rasau, Alakh-aradh, Ajampa-jap, Jnan-charit, Patig-pahar*.

Pitambar (early 16th): poet in Bangla; for some time at the court of Vishwasimha, ruler of Kamata in Kochbehar. At the behest of the ruler's eldest son Samarasimha, Pitambar rendered stories from *Markandeya-purana* into Bangla verse in 1530; later composed *Nala Damayanti-charitra*, (1544).

Pitambar Kavi (late 16th): poet in Asamiya from Kamata or Kamatipura in Kamrup district; possibly a senior contemporary of Shankaradeva. His *Usha-parinaya kavya* (1533) won him a reputation and he was commissioned by Koch Behar prince Samarasimha to render *Bhagavata purana* into Asamiya; he did Books I and X.

Platts [John Thomson Platts (1830–19094)]: British scholar of Urdu. Born in Calcutta, he was sent away for schooling to England; returned to take up the job of Mathematics teacher in Banaras. He taught also in Madhya Pradesh and served there as inspector of schools until his retirement due to ill health in 1872. After going home to England, he published *A Grammar of Hindustani* or *Urdu Language* (1874). This was followed by his being appointed Farsi teacher at Oxford University, where he compiled a *Dictionary of Urdu, Classical Hindi or English* (1884).

Poi (Oriya): term for verse-stanza; probably derived from the Sanskrit 'pada'. A poem of eight verses would be called an 'aathpoi'.

Ponna (10th): poet in Kannada; a contemporary of Pampa and Ranna; also composed in Sanskrit, and was awarded the title of 'Ubaya Kavichakravarti' by Rashtrakuta king Krishna III. Among his Kannada works are *Shantipuran*, a champu kavya in 12 'aswas' about the 16th tirthankar Shantinath; *Bhuvanaikaramabhyuday*, which tells of the prowess of local chief Shankargand (who was given the title of Bhuvanaikaram), a vassal of Krishna III. Because of Ponna's preference for Sanskrit-based words, his Kannada is not easy to understand.

Ponnikanti Telenganarya (*c*1578): poet in Telugu; author of *Yayati-charitra*.

Poonam Namputiri (16th): poet in Malayalam, who established the champu form in this language; he also refined the use of Manipraval for literary composition. His best-known work is *Bhasha Ramayan champu*; also composed other champu works like *Bharatam, Kama-dahanam, Parijata-haranam*. He is mentioned in a contemporary kavya work *Chandratsaram*.

Poontanam (17th): sant-poet in Malayalam, devoted to Krishna; author of *Jnanappana, Kumaraharana-pana, Bhasha karnamrutam*.

Poreiton Khunthokpa (?10th; Manipuri) of unknown authorship: a narrative in prose and verse describing how a horde of immigrants left their original homes under the leadership of Poreiton, wandered to many places, then settled in Manipur around 33 A.D.

Porunararruppadai (?C; Tamil) of Mutattamakkanniyar: the second idyll of *Pattuppattu*. The work is in praise of the wisdom and martial glory of the Chola king Karikalan. The poet tells an itinerant poet how well he was treated and rewarded by this king; advises the other poet to find such a benevolent patron.

Potana Bammera (15th): bhakti poet in Telugu; initially a Shaiva, later became a devotee of Vishnu. He is best known as author of *Mahabhagavatamu* which is said to be as popular in Telugu speaking areas as Tulsidas's *Ramcharitmanas* in Hindi-speaking areas. Among his other works are *Bhoginidandakamu, Narayan-shatakamu* and *Virabhadra-vijayakamu*. Potana belonged to a peasant family of Orugullu village. According to some scholars, he was an associate of the poet Srinadhudu.

Potana charitramu (?C; Telugu) of Vanamamalai Varadarharyulu, also known as Abhinava Potana: an account of the life of Potana which uses historical facts as well as legends about the poet.

Powada (Marathi): a form of heroic poetry which emerged during late 17th century. Those who composed and sung them were known as 'sahirs'; professional powada-singers later formed a guild or caste known as Gondhalis. The first famous powada is by Agnidas on the episode of Afzal Khan's meeting with Shivaji; the second by Tulsidas on the capture of Simhagad fort by Tanaji. The early powadas were often composed by eye-witnesses of the great events celebrated in them.

Poygai Alvar (6th): sant-poet in Tamil from Vehka village near Kanchipuram; author of *Mudal tiruvandadi* which consists of 100 poems in 'andadi' metre. He is counted among the 63 Alvars and was probably the earliest poet to compose in andadi.

Prabandha (Sanskrit): originally meant a literary composition, especially one with a poetic structure. The meaning of the term has undergone changes over time, also as it passed into other Indian languages.

Prabandha (Telugu): a literary form which emerged during the first half of 16th. It resembles the Sanskrit kavya, but embodies in itself the excellence of 'shravya' (or poetic), 'drishya' (or dramatic) and 'madhura' (or lyrical) elements. As a literary type it was orgininal to Telugu literature and was innovated by Allasani Peddana in a work like *Manu-charitramu.*

Prabandha (Malayalam): term for arrangement of connected narratives (for recital) of selected stories with verse and prose sequences taken from Sanskrit texts. Two important samples that have survived are *Ramayana-prabandha* and *Bharata-prabandha*. These were compiled by bards known as Chakyars.

Prabandha-chintamani (*c*1420; Sanskrit) of Merutunga: prose work interspersed with occasional verses. Divided into five 'prakasha', each containing several 'prabandha', it relates the legend of Vikramaditya and Shalivahana and many other stories.

Prabhandha-kosha (1348; Sanskrit) of Rajashekhara Suri: prose work consisting of 24 accounts relating to seven rulers (including Laksmanasena), four lay persons, ten Jain teachers (including Hemachandra), and four poets (including Sriharsha).

Prabandha-purnachandra (18th; Oriya) of Yadumani Mahapatra: an ornate kavya which narrates the episode of Krishna's marriage to Rukmini using much word-play and metrical variations. The work is a favourite with itinerant pala singers of Orissa.

Prabhakar (1769–1843): poet in Marathi, well-known for his lavani compositions. Thirteen such works have been recovered, of which two are on Peshwa Bajirao II.

Prabhavati Pradyumna (*c* 1550; Telugu): a prabandha work which draws upon *Harivamsha* and tells of the romance between Prabhavati and Pradyumna with the swan named Suchimukhi acting as the go-between. A special feature of the work is that it is written in the form of a drama.

Prabhulinga leele (15th; Kannada) of Chamarasa: an allegorical account in verse of the life and spiritual achievements of Allama Mahaprabhu. It consists of 25 'gati' (movement) covering about 1100 stanzas composed in bhamini shatpadi metre. The poet has used the life of Allama to propound Virshaiva principles.

Prabodha-chandrika (1833; Bangla) of Mrityunjay Vidyalamkar: an introduction to the study of Sanskrit, written at the behest of William Carey.

Prabodha-chandrodaya (late 11th; Sanskrit) of Krishnamishra: allegorical play in six acts. It defends the Advaita form of Vaishnav doctrine; the characters are all abstractions, viz.'Viveka' (conscience), 'Moha' (delusion) etc. The work refers to one Gopala, presumably a ruler, at whose command the play is stated to have been written to celebrate the victory of his friend, king Kirtivarman, over the Chedi ruler Karna.
Tr. J. Taylor, Bombay, 1886.

Prabodha-chandrodaya (*c*1480; Telugu) of Ghanta Singaya; an adaptation in champu form of the Sanskrit drama by Krishnamishra.

Prahasana (Sanskrit): comic drama, generally of one act, in which the plot is the dramatist's own invention.

Prahlad (?C): scholar of Farsi from Panjab; rendered the Farsi version of Urs, as executed under Dara Sikoh, into Dehlavi prose.

Prahlada-bhakti-vijayamu (*c*1800; Telugu) of Tyagaraja; a dramatic composition, with songs.

Prahlada-charita (14th; Asamiya) of Hema Saraswati: short kavya work based on the puranic episode. Sometimes regarded as the first literary work in Asamiya, it does not have much poetic quality.

Prakash Bhatta (early 15th): poet in Kashmiri, contemporary of Sultan Zainul Abidin (*c*1420–72). He was well versed in Sanskrit as well as in Farsi, but composed three popular works in Kashmiri—*Ramavatar-charit, Lav Kush-charit*, and *Shiva-lagna*.

Prakasharama (late 18th): poet in Kashmiri; a contemporary of Raja Sukhajivana Malla, a Hindu governor of Kashmir under the Afghans. He adapted *Ramayana* into Kashmiri.

Prakirna-bhasa-gitani (mid-17th; Maithili) of Jagajjyotimalla and Jagatprakasamalla: collection of devotional padas.

Prakirna-gitani (?C; Maithili): anthology of six sets of secular padas by four poets of Nepal—Jagajjyoti, Bhupatindra, Jagatprakasha, Ranjita.

Prakrit: generally, a term for the 'natural' or 'common' speech of ancient times, as different from Sanskrit which was 'refined'. More specifically (and used in the plural), it meant the Middle Indo-Aryan languages of the period ranging from 500 B.C. to A.D. 1000. The earliest stage in this period was represented by Pali and Ardhamagadhi. The middle stage is represented by Maharashtri, Shauraseni, Magadhi, Paisachi. The third and final stage is represented by Apabhramsha.

Prakrita-lakshana (?C; Prakrit) attributed to Panini: a grammatical work.

Prakrita-lakshana (?C; Prakrit) of Chanda: a work dealing with Prakrit dialects like Maharashtri, Adhamagadhi, Jaina Maharashtri and Jaina Shauraseni.

Prakrita-paingala (?14th; Prakrit) of unknown authorship: a manual of Prakrit and Apabhramsha metres. The work analyses about 40 metres in some detail and illustrates each metre with many examples drawn from existing Prakrit and Apabhramsha texts. The work was written in Avahatta, interspersed with many other Apabhramshas. The language of some of the verses quoted as examples is very close to newly emerging Indo-Aryan languages.

Prakrita-prakasha (?C; Prakrit) attributed by some to Vararuchi,

who is also identified as Katyayana: a grammatical work.
Tr. E.B.Cowell, London, 1868.

Prasanna Raghava (13th; Sanskrit) of Jayadeva (not the author of *Gita Govinda*): play in seven acts, which appears to be modelled on earlier plays, esp. *Vikramorvashiya* of Kalidasa. Though based on the *Ramayana* story, some changes have been effected; in the first act, Bana and Ravan are shown as Sita's suitors and ridiculed; in the last act, a pair of vidyadharas describe the battle and the restoration of Sita.

Prastavana (Sanskrit): term in dramaturgy for the prologue in which the actors converse with the stage-manager about the plot or their own roles.

Pratap Singh Sahi (early 19th): scholar-critic of Hindi from Bundelkhand. Of many works ascribed to him, only two are available, *Kavyavilas* and *Vyangartha-kaumudi*; in the first he refers to another work of his entitled *Rasa-chandrika*.

Pratapa-charita (16th; Telugu) of Ekamranatha: prose account of the life of 14th century Kakatiya ruler, Pratapa Rudra II.

Pratapamalla (1639–89): poet in Maithili of Nepal; belonged to the royal family of Kantipura (Kathmandu). Among his collections of verse are *Gitam-Pratapamalliyam, Gita-Govindam, Pratapamallyasa, Pratapamalla-virochita gitam.*

Prataparudra Deva (r. 1497–1539): Gajapati king of Kataka (in Orissa) and scholar of Sanskrit; author of *Saraswati-vilasa* and other works. He also composed a work on erotic games and other amusements entitled *Kautuka-chudamani.*

Pratapaditya-charita (1801; Bangla) of Ramrama Bosu; a prose-text prepared at Fort William College and printed at Serampore Mission Press. It presents the popular stories about Jasohar ruler Pratapaditya and also makes use of references to him in Mughal records.

Pratiharendruraj [Bhattenduraj (mid-10th)]: scholar of Sanskrit from Konkan region on the west coast; has acknowledged the tutelage of Mukul Bhatta; has been acknowledged as 'guru' by Abhinavagupta. He wrote the commentary *Laghuvritti* on Udbhata's *Kavyalankara-samgraha*, making references to Bhamaha, Dandin, Vamana, Rudrata and Anandavardhan.

Pratijna-Yaugandharayana (?C: Sanskrit) of Bhasa: play in four acts based on Udayana's story in *Brihatkatha*. While out on a hunting trip, Udayana is tricked into being captured by his enemy, Pradyota Mahasena; Mahasena's daughter Vasavadatta takes music lessons from the captured prince; they fall in love and, helped by his minister Yaugandhanarayana, Udayana elopes with the princess.

Pratinayaka (Sanskrit): one who opposes the 'nayaka' (hero or protagonist); hence, the antagonist. Generally he is depicted as possessing bad qualities and defects of character.

Pratikraman balavabodha (14th; Gujarati) of Tarunaprabha Suri: early prose work.

Pratimamana-lakshana (?C; Sanskrit) of unknown authorship: manual of measurement of images and icons. There is a separate work, *Pratima-lakshana*, dealing with Buddhist images and icons.

Tr. J.N. Banerji in appendix to his *Development of Hindu Iconography*, 2nd edn., Calcutta, 1956.

Pratima-nataka (?C; Sanskrit) of Bhasa: play in five acts based on a *Ramayana* story. It centres chiefly on the characters of Bharata and Kaikeyi; besides presenting them in a new light, the author has created some other new situations as well.

Pratisakhya (Sanskrit): generic name for textbooks accompanying every 'samhita' recension. These contain instructions about how a samhita is to be recited. Apart from the fact that they helped to preserve the Vedic texts intact, they are also valuable for the history of grammatical studies in India, which probably commenced with these works.

Pravarasena (?7th): poet in Prakrit; author of *Setubandha*. Some scholars identify him with king Pravarasena II of Kashmir, others with Pravarasena II, Vakataka king. He is mentioned in *Harshacharita* of Banabhatta (7th).

Prema bhakti-chandrika (late 16th; Bangla) of Narottam Das: a treatise in verse on Vaishnav devotion.

Prema-panchamrita (17th/18th; Oriya): of Bhupati Pandita: long poem in bhagvata metre, deals with the Krishna story. An unpretentious kavya which describes the raslila episodes, it is the most elegant and restrained of all such works in Oriya.

Prema-sudha nidhi (*c*1700; Oriya)

of Upendra Bhanja: a romantic poem in shankarabharana metre. In it there is a letter of the young hero to his royal sweetheart which has been a perennial favourite with educated young men in Orissa.

Prema-tarangini (*c*1580; Hindi) of Lakshminarayan: a work in praise of Krishna.

Prema-vilas (early 17th; Bangla) of Nityananda Das: a biography of Shri Chaitanya.

Prema-vinod (*c*1700; Hindi) of Chatra Kunwari Bai: the author was a woman poet of Krishna-bhakti.

Premanand (1636–1714): poet and story writer in Gujarati: belonged to Vadodara. He used to recite his stories while beating a rhythm on a copper 'gagar' (water-pot); from this he came to be called 'Mana bhatt' or 'Gagariya bhatt'. Among 35 akhyana narratives in verse composed by him, the most popular were *Nalakhyan, Okha-haran, Mameru.*

Premanand 'Prema-sakhi' (1779–1845): a bhakti poet in Gujarati associated with Swaminarayan community. His major work *Baramasi* is regarded as one of the greatest 'barahmasa' works in Gujarati. He was also a competent musician.

Pritam Das (1720–96): bhakti poet in Gujarati from Bavla village near Ahmedabad city; belonged to the Barot caste; was probably blind from birth. He composed in many of the contemporary poetic forms of Gujarati like 'mahina', 'tithi', 'var', 'kavako,' etc; also composed 'sakhiya' in Hindi. Among his works are *Jnan-prakash, Saras-Gita, Ekadashi-skandha, Brahma-lila, Guru-mahima, Bhakta-namavali, Shri Krishna-ashtak.*

Prithvichandra-charita (15th; Gujarati) of Manikyasundar Suri: prose romance dealing with the story of king Prithvichandra of Paithana and princess Ratnamanjari of Ayodhya. The narrative, composed in short rhythmic sentences, is a remarkable achievement of Gujarati prose.

Prithviraj raso (*c*1190; Hindi): of Chand Bardai; most famous of the Rajput romances. The story is mainly of Prithviraj's winning of Samyukta (Sanyogita), daughter of Kanauj ruler Jaychand, followed by Jaychand's pact with Muhammad Ghuri, Turki sultan of Afghanistan, to bring about the ruin of Prithviraj. Prithviraj Chauhan was the last Hindu ruler of Delhi (d. 1195) and his career is eulogised in the work; the poet was a bard attached to his court. The language of the work may be called Old Hindi, but it is an admixture of Old Hindi, Old Rajasthani and Shauraseni Apabhramsha in varying degrees.

Prithviraj Rathor (1549–1600): poet in Hindi, also a feudal chief. Son of Bikaner ruler Rao Kalyanmal he is mentioned in *Bhaktamal* and was honoured by Mughal emperor Akbar. His best work is *Beli Krishan Rukmini-ri*; among his other works are *Dasham Bhagavatra duha, Gangalahari, Basaderaut* and *Dasharath-raut*. He was also known as 'Pithal' in literary circles of his time.

Prithviraja-vijaya (?late 12th; Sanskrit) of unknown authorship: fragmentary and unfinished long poem, dealing with the victories of Chahumand (Chauhana?) king Prithviraj of Ajmer and Delhi, who fought with Shahabuddin Ghori and fell in 1191. The work gives a dependable genealogy and account of Prithviraj's ancestors starting with Vasudev; also provides a history of Rajasthan from mid-8th to end-12th century. It may have been composed between 1178 and 1193; the author may have been Jayanka, a Kashmiri poet who appears in the poem.

Priyadarshika (?7th; Sanskrit) of Shriharsha: four-act play of the natika type. Priyadarshika, daughter of king Dridhavarman, is brought through strange circumstances into the household of the king of Vatsa and, under the assumed name of Aranyika, is made an attendant of queen Vasavaddatta; the king falls in love with her; the enraged queen throws her into prison. Later the queen comes to know that the girl is a relative of hers; she arranges to get Aranyika married to the king.

Tr. Nariman, Jackon & Ogden, New York, 1923.

Puhupavati (*c*1673; Hindi) of Duhkaharan'das: long poem narrating the romance between princess Puhupavati and prince Rajkumar.

Pukazhenti (11th): poet in Tamil who popularised *Mahabharata* in Tamilnadu through simple adaptations of single episodes. He also composed other works like *Rattinachurukkam* and *Kalampakam*.

Punyasrav champu (*c*1330; Kannada) of Nagaraj: appears to be the translation of a Sanskrit work. Apart from instructions on ritual, it tells 52 separate stories presented in 12 'adhikar' (sections).

Puram (Tamil): a broad category of poems of the Third Sangam period, as classified in *Tolkappiyam*. These are 'exterior' poems, mostly relating to man's social behaviour. These poems describe five types of geographical tracts and their distinctive features, analogous to five regions of Tamilnadu. These are 'kurinichi' (mountainous region), 'mullai' (forest region), 'marutam' (agricultural region), 'neytal' (coastal region), and 'palai' (desert region).

Purana (Sanskrit): generic term (meaning 'old traditional story') for ancient narratives which purport to tell the history of the gods (as distinct from 'itihasa', which tells the history of heroic men). According to *Vishnu Purana*, Krishna Dvaipayana Vyasa compiled a puranic samhita, and communicated it to a pupil, Suta (also known as Romaharshana). Suta had working under him six scholars, Sumati, Agnivarchas, Maitreya, Samsapayana, Akritavarta and Savarani, who in due course expanded the purana samhita into 18 puranas. These are known as the 'maha-purana' and they have been classified in three groups. Thus, *Brahma-P, Brahmanda-P, Brahma-vaivarta-P, Markandeya-P, Bhavisya-P* and *Vamana-P*, relate to Brahma; *Vishnu-P, Bhagavata-P, Naradiya-P, Garuda-P, Padma-P* and *Varaha-P* relate to Vishnu; *Siva-P, Linga-P, Skanda-P, Agni-P, Matsya-P* and *Kurma-P* relate to Shiva. Each purana is supposed to be characterised by 'pancha-lakshana' (five topics), these being 'sarga' (creation), 'prati-sarga' (re-creation), 'vamsa' (genealogy of gods and sages), 'manvantara' (periods of the Manus), and 'vamsanu-charita' (history of the solar and lunar race of kings); but many puranas deal with many other topics or with very different matters. Puranic literature appears to have originated before 5th or 4th century B.C.; extant puranas probably came into being before A.D. 7. They were very popular because shudras and womenfolk (who were debarred from vedic study and observance of vedic rites) were allowed to listen to puranas and also perform vratas and other puranic rites. They are important to later literature because many poems and plays are based on puranic legends.

Purananuru (?C; Tamil): one of the *Ettuttogai* anthologies; a collection of 400 poems on war and statecraft by some 500 poets. It is the counter-part of the *Ahananuru* collection which deals with love. This is the most popular and historically the most valuable of the eight anthologies of the Sangam period. Much of Sangam political and social history has been derived from these poems, which were written by a very wide cross-section of contemporary society.

Purandardasa (1484–1564): the most eminent sant-poet of Karnataka; composed poems as well as songs in Kannada, and these are generally called 'kirtan'. He was a devotee of Vishnu in the form of Vitthaldev of Pandharpur. It is said he composed nearly five lakh songs during his lifetime but only about 1000 have been recovered.

Purapporul-venbamalai (9th/10th; Tamil) of Iyanar Itanar: earliest available work on Tamil prosody, especially important for its exposition of the theme of 'puram'. Following an earlier work that is no longer extant *Panniru padalam*, the theme is divided into 12 'tinai'. These generally relate to situations of war. The tinai are further explained by a verse in 'venba' metre. These verses were all composed by the author.

Purathirattu (15th; Tamil) compiled by unknown person: an anthology of nearly ten centuries of Tamil poetry from the earliest times to 12th century (i.e. from Sangam period to Kamban's *Ramayana*). The 1570 long and short poems chosen are all on worldly themes. The anthology was so popular that it has been recovered almost intact. However, many of the works from which poems were selected are now lost. Among these are the *Muttollayiram* and *Thahadoor yathirai* of the Sangam period; *Perumporul vilakkam, Valayapati* and *Kundalakesi* from 9th/10th; and so on.

Purusha'pariksha (late 14th; Sanskrit) of Vidyapati of Mithila: collection of 44 tales, in prose and verse, on the question of what constitutes manly virtues. Through these stories, the work illustrates qualities such as charity, piety, learning, truthfulness, etc; some of the stories refer to historical personages and incidents. Composed at the behest of king Shivasimha, it is planned like the *Panchatantra* but has human characters. It was intended to be a manual for administrators.

Tr.as *Text of Man* by G.A.Grierson, 1935, in Vol.33 of New Series of the Oriental Translation Fund.

Purushottama Dasa (*c*1550–1600): poet in Oriya, author of *Kanchi-Kaveri*. A cowherd by caste, he lived in Puri where he served as keeper of accounts in the general store of the Jagannath temple. Apart from *Kanchi-Kaveri* which is considered a pioneering literary work, he also wrote *Ganga-mahatmya*. Other works ascribed to him are *Mriganist-uti, Dutia-osa* and *Gundicha bije*.

Purusottam'deva (12th): Bangla scholar of Sanskrit at the court of king Lakshmansena of Bengal; wrote the 'Bhasa-vritti' commentary on *Ashtadhyayi*. He or another Purushottam compiled several lexicons like *Haravali* and grammatical works like *Ganavritti*.

Purvaranga (Sanskrit): that which happens before the play. This preliminary action propitiates the deities and sets the play in motion; it also introduces the play and the playwright.

Pushpadanta or **Pupphayanta** (mid-10th): most important poet in Apabhramsha; author of *Mahapuranu, Jasahara-chariu, Nayakumara-chariu*. Son of poor parents Keshava and Mughadevi, he had to wander far from home in search of a living. He came to Manyakheta, where the Rashtrakuta king Krishnaraja III was ruler. Here the king's minister, Bharata, offered him patronage, which enabled him to compose the above-mentioned works.

Pushpadanta-purana (early 13th; Kannada) of Gunavarma II: a work dealing with the ninth Jain tirthankar, Pushpadanta.

Puttamittiranar (?C): scholar of Tamil; wrote an elaborate work on the five-fold divisions of Tamil grammar. In this he diverged from the rules and conventions of Tamil grammar and freely adopted the rules of Sanskrit grammar. This was not acceptable to the learned, hence the work fell into oblivion.

Puzhalendi (13th): poet in Tamil, known from the early poetical work *Nalavenba* that has been ascribed to him. This poem re-tells the Nala story of *Mahabharata* in 424 'venba' verses.

Pyarichand Mitra (1813–83): prose writer in Bangla under the pseudonym of 'Tekchand Thakur', His most famous work is *Alaler gharer dulal* (1858), a satirical portrait of Bangla society of his time. His great contribution to Bangla literature was the innovation of a prose capable of handling the lighter sides of life.

Q

Qadar Yar (18th): poet in Panjabi; narrated the exploits of the illustrious Sikh general, Har Singh Nalwa. He is also credited with the authorship of the qissa *Puran Bhagat*.

Qalaq [Khwaja Asadullah (d. 1879)]: poet in Urdu; son of Khwaja Bahadur Husain, nephew and disciple of Khwaja Wazir of Lakhnau. Because of his close association with Nawab Wajid Ali Shah of Avadh, he was arrested in 1856 and taken to Calcutta along with the nawab; was released after seven months and came back to Lakhnau. Known mainly for his masnavi poems, Qalaq wrote *Qalaqnama* and *Tilism-e-ulfat*. Among his other works are *Wasokhte Qalaq, Diwan Mazher-e-Ishq* and *Safar Ashob*. The latter, a collection of 'musaddas' poems, contains an account of his imprisonment and journey to Calcutta.

Qasida (Urdu): originally a poem in praise of a religious leader, king or important person; later it widened its scope to include poems on natural beauty, moral value, changes of fortune in human life, etc. The form has a long history in Urdu because some of the Dakhani sultans who were poets, like Quli Qutub Shah (1569–1611), tried their hand at composing qasida.

Qazi Qadan (1463–1531): regarded as the first poet of Sindhi on the basis of only seven poems recorded in a Farsi MS *Bayan-al-arfin* by Mohammad Raza in 1628. Subsequently, 112 more poems of his were discovered by Pandit Raja Ram Shastri in an old MS called 'Santon ki vani' preserved in a village mutth in Haryana. All these poems show him to have been a Sufi mystic.

Qissa (Panjabi): originally an Arabi term meaning 'story', it refers to a verse-narrative telling the tragic story of two young people who love each other beyond discretion. The earliest extant work in this form is *Heer* written by Damodar in late 16th, but the form probably dates back to 10th or 11th century.

Qissa-i-Bahramwa Gul-andam (1670; Urdu) of Taki: this prose work, in Dakhni, is an adaptation of the Persian poet Nizami's *Haft paikar*.

Qissa-e-mehar Afrozo-dilvar (?18th; Urdu) by unknown author: a dastan work the MS of which was discovered only in 1966 in a private library in Gwalior. Scholars have suggested that it was written some time in 18th century by one Nawab Isur Khan who was mainly a Hindi writer.

Quli Qutb Shah, Sultan (b.1566; r.1580–1611): ruler of Golkonda; champion of the ghazal and a patron of poets in general; author of *Qulliyat*, a compilation of nearly one lakh verses. His work is full of local colour and includes many poems on Indian fruits, vegetables, birds, customs and festivals. He adapted many Farsi words and constructions into Urdu, and used Hindi epithets in praise of god. While a young prince, he fell in love with Bhagamati (or Bhagyamati), a Hindu girl. In spite of the opposition of his father, he married her, made her his queen and built in her honour a new city named 'Bhagya-nagar'; later this was changed to 'Haidarabad', when she was given the Muslim name of Haidar Begam.

Qutb Mushtari (*c*1609; Urdu) of Mulla Wajhi: a poem which treats of the romance between prince Quli Qutb Shah and the girl Bhagmati who later became his queen.

R

Radha Krishna-rasakalpavalli (17th; Bangla); anthology of Vaishnav lyrics compiled by Ramgopal Das.

Radhamohan (end-18th): poet in Bangla; author of a short ballad which realistically records the plight of forced labour when Warren Hastings built the trunk road from Salkia to Chandalgarh in Bengal.

Radhika-swantwanamu (18th; Telugu) of Muddu Palani or Muddupalni: a long poem in four 'aswas' in which the erotic element predominates. The story tells of Radha and her ward Ila, how Radha got Krishna married to Ila and then experiences 'viraha'—whereupon Krishna seeks to console her. At places the explicit eroticism of the poem has been found excessive by male readers and scholars; the poet was a woman. The authenticity of the work was questioned at one time; later, it was banned by the British government on moral grounds.

Radif (Urdu): literally means the person who sits behind the rider on a horse. In Urdu poetry it refers to the phrase which follows the 'kafiya' in a line of verse.

Raga (Sanskrit): term in musicology. That which pleases (ranjayati) the minds of listeners is called a raga. Though six ragas are supposed to be basic, treatises describe many more.

Raga gita-samgraha (late 17th; Maithili) of Lochana: as yet unrecovered, this work is mentioned by the author in his *Ragatarangini*.

Raga-mala: the title of several MS collections found in Nepal libraries. Some contain Sanskrit padas of Jayadeva and Maithili padas of Vidyapati.

Raga-nirupana (?C; Sanskrit) attributed to Narada: a metrical description of 140 ragas.

Raga-tarangini (1685; Maithili) of Lochana: anthology containing the lyrics of 39 poets, including Vidyapati. The work was meant to be more an aid to learning music than a literary work. It is particularly valuable because it has preserved the verses of many unknown poets.

Raga-vibodha (1609; Sanskrit) of Somananda: work on music. Composed in verse, it explains the theory of musical sounds and describes the different types of vina and the mode of using them; also classifies the ragas into 'janaka' (primary) and 'janya' (derivative), and states a number of melodies developed from the ragas. The author was a Telugu brahman, probably of Rajahmahendry, probably a practising musician as well as a scholar and poet.

Ragale (Kannada): a well-known verse-metre of Kannada in use from about 10th onwards. It was really established by Harihara who was the first to employ the metre for an entire work.

Raghava Pandaviya (1130; Sanskrit) of Dhananjaya (not the author of *Dasharupaka*): long poem in 18 sections. Each verse applies equally to *Mahabharata* and *Ramayana*, hence the work is also known as a 'dvisamdhana-kavya' (poem with double meaning). The poet, who may also have been called Shrutakirti, was a Digambara Jain, and probably composed between 1123 and 1140.

Raghava Pandaviyamu (*c*1545; Telugu) of Pingali Suranna: the first 'dvyaitarthi' (with two meanings) kavya in Telugu. Each verse contains two meanings, one pertaining to *Ramayana*, the other to *Mahabharata*.

Raghavanka (late 12th): Virshaiva poet in Kannada; nephew of Harihar and also tutored by him. If Harihar established the 'ragale' metre in Kannada poetry, Raghavanka did the same for the 'shatpadi' metre. His works are *Somnath-charite, Viresh-charit, Siddha Ram-puran, Harishchandra-charitra, Sarava-charitra* and *Harihar-mahatva*.

Raghavanka charitra (1650; Kannada) of Chikkananjesh or Siddha Nanjesh: biographical account of the 12th century poet Raghavanka.

Raghu Arakhita (16th): poet in Oriya and devotee of Shri Jagannath of the Puri temple. He was born to rich parents and married early; lost all his wealth and had to leave his ancestral home; became a Vaishnav sanyasi, went to Puri, lived like a destitute (hence 'arakhita'). Eventually re-united with his wife and they lived in a monastery devoting themselves to Jagannath. Among his compositions are *Shakuntala-chautisa, Jnana-ude chautisa, Gochar-*

sidhi gita, and a number of lyrics on the Radha-Krishna theme.

Raghu Pandit (16th): Bangla scholar and bhakta; author of *Krishnaprematarangini*; a professional reciter of *Shrimad Bhagavat*, he was known as Bhagavatacharya.

Raghunath (b.1740): poet in Hindi from Chaura village, near Kashi; became associated with the court of local chieftain Bariband Singh. Among works of his that are available, *Rasikmohan* deals with figures of speech, accompanied by illustrative verses that are generally erotic; *Kavyakaladhar*, an exhaustive classification of emotions and sentiments, heroes and heroines; *Jagat Mohan* describes the daily schedule of Shri Krishna; *Ishka-mahotsava*, a sequence of erotic verses. While the first three works are in Brajbhasha, the last was composed in Khariboli.

Raghunath Das (early 16th): Bengali bhakta; author of a short biographical poem in Sanskrit on Shri Chaitanya. Sole heir to a large estate, Raghunath renounced his life as householder in order to live as a mendicant in Puri, serving Chaitanya during the last ten or twelve years of Chaitanya's life. Hence this poem is regarded as an authentic record of the later life of Chaitanya.

Raghunath Das (18th): poet of Krishna-bhakti in Gujarati. He composed 'garbi' poems on Krishnalila, verses on Holi, poems related to Krishna's departure from Gokul to Mathura, and so on.

Raghunath Mahanta (18th): prose writer in Asamiya; came from a family believed to have been initiated into Vaishnav faith by Shankaradeva himself. Only three of his works have survived: *Shatrunjay*, which relates the heroic exploits of monkey-king Bali; *Adbhuta Ramayana*, which is different from the Asamiya version of the Sanskrit work of the same name; *Katha Ramayana*, which seems to derive from the *Ramayana* of Madhav Kandali.

Raghunatha Nayaka (1575–1630): poet and scholar in Telugu and Sanskrit; belonged to the royal family of Thanjavur and was a great patron of art and literature. He wrote two treatises on music in Sanskrit and invented a 'vina' which is named 'Raghunatha Vina' after him. Among his poetical works in Telugu are *Parijatapaharana kavya, Valmiki-charitram, Nala-charitram, Raghunatha Ramayanam, Savitri.*

Raghunath Pandit (mid-17th): poet in Marathi; composed long narrative poems like *Nala Damayanti-swayamvara*. He is perhaps better known as an associate of Sahaji and Shivaji. Born at Thanjavur where Sahaji was a jahgirdar; when Shivaji founded his kingdom, he invited Raghunath to join his council of eight ministers.

Raghunath Parichha (1802–72): poet in Oriya from Lahuri village near Parlakhemundi. Among his works are *Gopinath-ballabh natak kabya, Lakhana chandrodaya* and *Raghunath-vilas kabya*. The first of these has been regarded by some scholars as the first Oriya drama.

Raghunath-rupak gitan ro (Rajasthani; 1806) of Manchh or Manasaram Kuwara: work on the prosody of Rajasthani git (songs and lyrics). All the illustrations are drawn from the story of *Ramayana*. Manasaram (1766–1840) was honoured by Maharaja Narsingh of Jodhpur and was granted a village named Unta-vadia as reward.

Raghunathraj Harichandra (17th): poet in Oriya; belonged to the royal family of Banapur, an area to the west of Chilka lake. The family patronised poetry and other arts; Raghunath thus came to know many famous poets of the time. He himself wrote a number of 'chaupadi' love lyrics and some longer poems in the 'chautisa' form. Apart from works like *Chandramukhi chautisa* and *Kalakantha chautisahe*, also wrote *Lilabati*, a kavya work.

Raghuraj Singh (1723–79): ruler of Rewa; poet in Hindi and bhakta; author of *Rama-swayamvar, Rukmini-parinay, Anandambunidhi*.

Raghuvamsha (15th; Sanskrit) of Kalidasa: long poem in 19 sections, dealing with deeds of the Ikshvaku kings from Dilip to Agnivarna. Raghu of the title is the son of Dilip; Raghu conquers the whole of Bharatvarsha but also becomes famous for his charitable deeds. Three 'sarga' are devoted to the swayamvara of Indumati, her being won by Aja, then Aja's lamentation at her death. The tenth to fifteenth 'sarga' are devoted to Ram. The final sarga draws a poignant picture of the lecherons king Agnivarna.

Tr. H.H. Wilson, .Ed. and Tr.G.R. Nandargi-kar, Bombay, 1897; K.M. Joglekar, NSP, 1916.

Raghuvar jas prakash (1824; Rajasthani) of Adha Kisna: work on Rajasthani prosody; of its five chapters, the fourth deals with Dingal lyrics. The author was honoured by Maharana Bhim Singh of Mewar, who granted him freehold jagir of Sisoda village. He helped Colonel Tod in the collection of MS, and other documents.

Rahasya-manjari (16th; Oriya) of Debadurlava Dasa: a kavya work on the Radha-Krishna story, which also projects Vaishnav philosophy. The work is in 24 'chhanda' and in different metres; through various situations the poet demonstrates that Radha's love for Shri Krishna is superior to that of Rukmini of the gopis. Apart from following the main Vaishnav tradition, the poet has also made use of prevailing folk elements in order to present Radha and Krishna as characters in a social enviornment.

Rahim [Mirza Abdur Rahim Khan-e-khana ibne Bairam (1556–1627)]: poet in Hindi, scholar of Arabi, Farsi, Sanskrit and Turki; musician. Son of Bairam Khan, Mughal emperor Akbar's guardian and tutor, Rahim was brought up by Akbar as his own son and educated in accordance with the emperor's new ideals; was elevated to high positions in Akbar's court; in older age, underwent much hardship caused by Jahangir. Among his many works are *Madanashtaka*, a sequence of eight poems depicting the love gopis bore for Shri Krishna; *Nagar shobha,* a collection of 142 verses describing 70 different kinds of heroines on the basis of their caste and place of origin; *Barvai nayika-bhed*, in 116 couplets in Avadhi depicting different kinds of heroes and heroines; *Barvai-samgrah*, in 105 couplets dealing with spiritual love; *Rahim dohavali*, consisting of about 300 couplets dealing with Hindu scriptures, deities, festivals etc. *Rahim-satsai*, a work in 700 dohas of which 400 have been lost. Besides these, he wrote many stray verses in a variety of forms—pada, savaiya, ghanaakshari, chhappaya. He used all the various 'literary' forms of contemporary Hindi like Brajbhasha, Avadhi and Khariboli, but freely drew words from Sanskrit and older languages like Arabi, Farsi, Sanskrit.

Raidhu (15th): poet in Prakrit and Apabhramsha from Gwalior; received patronage from the Tomar ruler Dungarasimha and his son Kirtisimha as well as from another ruler Rudrapratap Chauhan. A devoted Jain and prolific writer, he is particularly important because the Apabhramsha used by him marks the transition between Middle I-A and New I-A languages. Among his extant compositions are puranic works like *Harivamsha-purana, Parswapurana, Mahapurana* and *Adipurana*; narrative poems *Anathami-katha, Samyak sammotta kaumudikaha* etc.; biographical poems *Sukosala-charita, Nagheshwar-*

charita, Dhanyakumar-charita, etc; doctrinal works *Siddhanta-sara* and *Vratasara*; collection of hymns *Sohamthudi*; jaimala poem sequences *Dashalakshana-jaimale*, *Sodash karana-jaimale*; one muktaka poem, *Anupreksha*.

Raja Rasalu (early 19th; Panjabi) of Qadar Yar: long poem concerning Raja Rasalu, the brother of folk-tale hero Puran Bhagat, and his false romance with Rani Kokila. There is no authenticated text of the whole work but it became very popular through oral presentation.

Rajab Ali Baig 'Sarur' (1823–60): writer in Urdu from Lakhnau; a friend of Mirza Ghalib who wrote the introduction for two of his works. His best known work is the romance *Fasana-e-ajayeb*.

Rajabali (1808; Bangla) of Mrityunjay Vidyalankar: prose work giving an account of kings who ruled India before the advent of the British. Since the author has derived many names from *Mahabharata, Ramayana*, and other puranic sources, the work has little value as history. Even the introductory chapter which gives the physical geography of India relies mainly on puranas.

Rajagopala-vilasamu (late 17th; Telugu) of Chengalvakala Kavi: a long poem about Krishna and his eight wives representing eight types of nayikas. The author was a poet in the court of Thanjavur ruler Vijayaraghava Nayaka.

Rajaraja Narendra: Eastern Chalukya ruler (1022–63) whose capital was at Rajahmahendry. He commisioned Nannaya to render *Mahabharata* into Telugu because of his 'Bharata-shravanasakti' (passionate desire to listen to the story of the Bharatas), which may have derived from his consciousness of belonging to the line of descent from the Kauravas. He also may have deemed such an undertaking necessary as a Vedic countermeasure to the spreading Jain influence of the period.

Rajaratnavaliyam (late 16th; Malayalam) of Mazhamangalam: champu work. While most champus are based on puranic themes, this one centres on a historical king of Kochi, Rama Varma (r. 1565–95), and his alleged love for Mandarmala, a celestial nymph.

Rajashekhara (*c*855–930): playwright and literary critic, probably from Maharashtra or Madhyadesha. He wrote the play *Karpuramanjari* in Prakrit, the work on poetics *Kavyamimamsa* in Sanskrit. Some more plays *Viddhasala-bhanjika, Bala-Ramayana* and *Bala-Bharata* all in Sanskrit, have been ascribed to him; other works *Shatprabhandha* (six compositions), *Haravilasa* (kavya), and *Bhuvana-kosha* (geography) are not extant. From his own account we learn he was the preceptor of king Mahendrapala of Kanauj; the king's son Mahipala was his patron.

Rajashekhara-charitramu (*c*1515; Telugu) of Madayyagari Mallana: a work in prabandha form.

Rajashekhara-vilas (*c*1660; Kannada) of Shadakshar Dev: champu work in 14 'aswas'. The poet was a Virashaiva.

Rajashekhara-vilasamu (18th; Telugu) of Kuchimanchi Timmakavi; a kavya work in three 'aswas' glorifying Shiva.

Rajasthani: name given to a group of languages known earlier as 'Maru-bhasha' or 'Maru-vani', and spoken in the state of Rajasthan (earlier known as Rajputana) in Western India by about 40 lakh persons. Descended either from Shauraseni Prakrit or from Ahira Apabhramsha, it emerged by about 13th. Main speeches of the region constituting Rajasthani are Marwari (of Western Rajasthan), Jaipuri (east), Mewati (north) and Malwi (south).

Rajaraj Varma (1812–45): attakkatha writer in Malayalam; was given the title of 'Vidwan' by Maharaja Swati Tirunal. He belonged to the Kilimanur ruling family and was for some time their court poet. He wrote scripts for, produced and acted in kathakali performances. His stories were generally unconventional; for example Ravan is the hero of *Ravanavijayam attakkatha*.

Rajasuya (late 18th; Malayalam) of Karthika Tirunal: kathakali play in nine scenes, concluding with the killing of Shishupala by Krishna in the hall where Yudhisthir's rajasuya yajna is being performed. Tirunal is author of the South Kerala version of the text: the other, known as the Malabar version, was composed by Elayedeth Namboodiri.

Rajatarangini (*c*1150; Sanskrit) of Kalhana: historical account in verse of the kings of Kashmir. Consisiting of eight sections, it deals in the earlier part with legendary rulers and draws upon earlier sources, especially *Nilamata-purana*. The latter part deals with historical kings upto mid-12th. The work is particularly valuable for the political and social history of Kashmir, also for its topography. The author, son of Champaka who was a minister (1089–1101), mentions Jayasimha (r.1127–59) as the reigning monarch.

Tr. M.A. Stein, Westminster, 1900; R.S. Pandit, Allahabad, 1935.

Rajavali Kathe (1838; Kannada) of Devachandra: work mainly in prose, telling of kings, poets and the Jain faith. The poet (1779–1841) was associated with Mysore ruler Krishnaraja Wodeyar III and the work is dedicated to him. It also traces the genealogy of the Wodeyar family.

Rajavali-pataka (?C; Sanskrit) of Priyabhatta and Suka: a continuation of *Rajatarangini*, consisting of about 1000 verses. It deals with the kings of Kashmir till about 1586 when Akbar annexed that area.

Rajavamshavali (Asamiya): dynastic chronicle in verse, a form introduced by the non-Ahom kings of Western Assam. Notable works in this genre are "Darrang Rajavamshavali" (1798) by Suryakari Dairajnya, "Koch Rajvams" (1802) by Ratikanta Dvija, etc.

Raje (early 18th): Muslim poet of Krishna-bhakti in Gujarati; belonged to Kervada village near Bharoch in Gujarat. Among his compositions are *Rasa-panchadhyayi, Gokul-lila, Viraha-gita* etc.

Rajendra-karnapura (*c*1100; Sanskrit) of Shambhu: a work of 75 verses in varied metres in praise of king Harshadeva of Kashmir (r. 1089–1101). The poet was a protege of the king.

Rajiyai-ra soratha (*c*1820; Rajasthani) of Kriparam Khidiya; work consisting of didactic poems addressed to his personal attendant. The poem became quite popular and many interpolations took place after the poet (1743–1833) passed away. Thus, of 500 verses printed in some editions, only about 160 belong to the original work.

Rajjab (1567–?1689): sant-poet in Rajasthani; along with Sundardas, leading disciple of Dadu. He was born to a Pathan soldier father at Sanganer (near Jaipur). When he was going for his marriage to Ajmer, he stopped on the way to pay respects to Dadu; the sant impressed him so much that Rajjab decided on the spot to renounce worldly life. He soon developed a following himself and is mentioned in their works by 16th century sant writers such as Raghodas, Jangopal, Ramcharandas, etc. His two works, *Rajjab-vani* and *Sarvangi*, consist of poetical statements of various sants, including those by himself in a variety of metres like sakhi, pada, chhappay, tribhangi, soratha, chaupai, arilla, sawaiya and kavitta.

Rajnarayan Bosu (1826–99): essayist in Bangla, who was a strong advocate for using the mother-tongue in education. His writings are to be found in *Dharmatatva dipika* (1866), *Atmiyasabhar brittanta* (1867), *Sekal ar ekal* (1874), *Hindu athoba Presidency kalejer brittanta* (1876), *Bangla bhasha-o-sahitya bishayak baktrita* (1878), *Atmacharit* (1901).

Rajrupak (1749; Hindi) of Virbhan: a heroic poem in Dingal describing the battle between Jodhpur ruler Abhaysingh and Sarbuland Khah, subedar at Ahmedabad.

Rakshastagdi-chi Bakhar (?C; Marathi): prose account of the battle near Rakshastagdi (also known as the battle of Talikota) which led to the destruction of Vijayanagar. It was originally written in Kannada by Ramji Tirumal in 1565; he was attached to the Vijayanagar court and saw the actual battle. Besides describing the action, it also discusses the political situation prior to the battle. The work was subsequently translated into Marathi so effectively that it is often regarded as a work of original Marathi.

Ram Joshi (1762–1812): poet and composer in Marathi. In his youth he composed lavanis for tamasha; later came under the influence of Moropant and wrote on serious subjects using metres more often employed in lavani composition. He may be credited with popularising the aryas of Moropant; he also showed that the lavani form, generally associated with vulgarity, can be used for better purposes.

Ram rasau (*c*1595; Rajasthani) of Madhodas Dadhawadia: narrative poem on Shri Ram's life from his birth to his enthronement. The work consists of 1034 verses in a variety of metres. While following the Valmiki *Ramayana*, the poet has also been influenced by *Adhyatma Ramayana, Ananda Ramayana, Vichitra Ramayana* and other texts.

Rama Panikar (early 15th): the most eminent of the Kannassan poets in Malayalam; composed *Ramayanam, Bharatam, Bhagavatam, Shivaratri-mahatyam*, of which the first is the most outstanding. The importance of his work lies in his having brought the literary culture of Kerala into closer contact with Sanskrit literature.

Rama Panivada (18th): poet and scholar in Sanskrit and Prakrit from Kerala. He was born into a Nambiar family of Killikurisai village, in South Malabar, where his father was a priest in the Shiva temple. He won recognition from several Kerala kings and remained associated with royal courts. Among his many works in Sanskrit are the long poems *Raghaviya* and *Vishnu-vilasa*; the plays *Sita-Raghava, Chandrikavithi, Lilavati, Madanaketu-charita*; the hymns *Mukunda-shataka, Surya-shataka, Ambaranadi-stotra*; the champu work *Bhagata-champu*; a work on prosody, *Vritta-matrika*; a work on 'tala', *Talaprastara-kavya*. Of his few works in Prakrit, *Kamsavaho* and *Ushaniruddham* are poems; he also wrote a composition on Vararuchi's *Prakita-prakasha*.

Ramabhadra Dikshita (17th): poet and playwright in Sanskrit from Kandramanikyam village, near Kumbakonam, in Tamilnadu. A devotee of Shri Rama, he received the patronage of Thanjavur ruler Shahji. Among his many works are *Ramashtaprasha*, a hymn in 116 verses in 'shardulvikridita' metre; *Janaki-parinaya*, a seven-act play on the *Ramayana* theme but using two sets of characters to create comic confusion; *Shringara-tilaka* also known as *Ayyabhana*, a one-act play featuring the erotic feelings of Bhujangashekhara; *Patanjalicharitra*, a verse biography of Patanjali. The author was popularly known as 'Ayya Dikshita'.

Ramabhadramba (early 17th): woman poet in Sanskrit and queen of Thanjavur ruler Raghunatha Nayaka; wrote the kavya work *Raghunathabhudaya* which deals with the exploits of her husband. The poet apparently knew as many as eight languages.

Ramabhyudayamu (*c*1550; Telugu) of Ramabhadra Kavi; a condensation of the *Ramayana* story in verse, concluding with Rama's coronation.

Rama-bibha (15th/16th; Oriya) of Arjuna Dasa: first long poem in the language. In form it is a sequence of lyrics on the sentiment of love, with some comic interludes. The story, derived from *Ramayana*, begins with Vishwamitra's requesting Shri Rama to protect the sages from demons; ends with Rama's return to Ayodhya after his marriage with Sita.

Rama-charita (?9th; Sanskrit) of Abhinanda: poem in about 40 sections based on the *Ramayana* story. The poet has introduced changes to glorify Rama's character. He is also called Abhinanda Gauda because he belonged to Bengal; was the son of Satananda; appears to have been a protege of Devapala, king of Bengal in 9th century.

Rama-charitam (late 12th/early 13th; Malayalam): the oldest work in pattu form discovered so far; also the earliest extant work that can be claimed by Malayalam. The subject relates to the Yuddha-kanda of *Ramayana* and the work may have been composed to exhort soldiers to battle. It has been conjectured that the author was a prince, probably Vira Rama Varma who ruled in Travancore 1195–1208.

Rama-vijaya (*c*1700; Marathi) of Shridhar Nazarekar (1658–1730): an adptation of the *Ramayana* story composed in 9147 ori stanzas. The poet drew his material from 19 previous *Ramayana* texts and occasionally added episodes from other sources as well.

Ramachandra (12th): playwright and scholar in Sanskrit; pupil of Jain scholar Hemachandra. In collaboration with fellow-student Gunachandra, he wrote *Natyadarpana*, an important treatise on dramaturgy. Among the plays he wrote are *Nala-vilasa, Yadava-bhyudaya, Rohini-Mriganka, Nirbhay Bhima*, etc.

Ramachandra charita purana: see *Pampa Ramayana*.

Ramachandrika (1601; Hindi) of Keshavdas: a re-telling of the *Ramayana* story in chaste and scholarly language for the delectation of learned readers, as opposed to the 'rural' language in which Tulsidas composed *Ramacharitmanas*. The work is also known as 'Ramchandra-chandrika'.

Ramacharitmanas (1574; Hindi) of Tulsidas: the great work of this poet, also his most popular work. It tells the *Ramayana* story in seven kandas and about 10,000 padas, using doha as well as chaupai forms; the language is Avadhi. Before composing this, Tulsidas studied a number of earlier works, of which the main are *Adhyatma Ramayana, Valmiki Ramayana, Hanuman-natak, Prasanna Raghav* and *Shrimad Bhagavat*; the first of these appears to have influenced him the most. While Rama has been deified, all the other characters have been portrayed as ideals of what each represents in the story. Besides telling the story, the poet has dealt with many philosophic and religious issues.

Ramai Pandit: character of a Dharma-puran work, who appears in the third section of such works. According to the story, Ramai was the son of an unpopular brahman sage; after his father's death, Ramai was declared an outcast and denied initiation; he was redeemed by Dharma through the sage Markandeya, and later became the priest of King Harishchandra.

Rama-kathai or Ramavataram: see *Kamba Ramayanam*.

Rama-katha-ppattu (15th; Malayalam) of Ayyippilli Asan; a pattu work based on *Ramayana*; associated with festivals at Shri Padmanabhaswamy temple. It consists of 3163 songs composed in 279 metres. These used to be sung to the accompaniment of a musical instrument called 'chandravalayam'. Though the work does not have high literary value, it is important because it is the earliest known attempt in Malayalam to re-tell *Ramayana* in colloquial language.

Ramananda Rati (late 18th): poet in Bangla); author of a Chandimangal work, 1766; also a *Ramayana* poem, 1762.

Ramanataka Kirtanaigal (18th; Tamil) of Arunachala Kavirayar: a work which narrates the *Ramayana* in an operatic form. It contains 268 'vriddha' (literary compositions to be sung), 167 'kirtana', 59 'kania' (two-line pieces of folk song), and other kinds of musical pieces. This work was a great innovation in Tamil; because of its extent and elaborate structure, it is seldom presented in its full form.

Ramanattan (Malayalam): form of dance-drama; represents the stage following Krishnattam in the evolution of kathakali. The songs are in Malayalam, the linking narratives in Manipravala shlokas. Kottarakara Tampuran is credited with having innovated the form.

Ramanattam (17th; Malayalam) of Kottarakara Tamburan: the first full-fledged attakatha accompanying a kathakali performance of *Ramayana*. The work is divided into eight parts so that each would be sufficient for a whole night's performance. The parts are 'Putrakamesthi', 'Sita swayamvaram', 'Vischinna-bhisekham', 'Kharavadham', 'Balivadham', 'Torana yuddham', 'Sethubandham' and 'Yuddham'.

Ramapala-charita, also known as **Ramacharita** (11th; Sanskrit) of Sandhyakara Nandi: a kavya work in about 200 verses which simultaneously relates the story of Rama as well as of Ramapala, king of Bengal. The poet belonged to Pundravardhana in North Bengal; wrote this poem during the reign of Madanapala.

Ramaraja'bhushana (*c*1510–80): poet in Telugu associated with the court of Vijayanagar ruler Ramaraja. His real name was Prabhandhankam Bhattu Murti. Of his three extant works, *Kavyalankara-sangrahamu* is on poetics; *Vasucharitramu* is a 'prabhandha-kavya' based on a minor episode in *Mahabharata* concerning Vasu Maharaja and Girika; *Harishchandra-Nalopakhyamu* is a kavya in which each verse can be interpreted as relating either to the Harischandra or to the Nala story.

Ramarasamrita Sindhu (17th; Oriya) of Kahanu Dasa: a kavya work on the *Ramayana* story in 108 sections of 108 verses each.

Ramasaraswati (16th): poet in Asamiya); contemporary and disciple of Shankaradeva. At the behest of Koch king Naranarayandeva and his brother Shukladhvaja, he rendered into Asamiya parvas of *Mahabharata*. He also composed 15 akhyana poems based on *Mahabharata* and puranas. Some of these are *Hansakaki, Shiva-rahasya, Pushpaharan-parva, Bhima-charitra, Panchali-bibaha*, etc. These akhyanas, though not written for that purpose, helped to consolidate Vaishnav influence in the north-eastern regions.

Ram-ashwamedh (*c*1782; Hindi) of Madhusudandas: a Ram-bhakta poet from Mathura. The work retells the story of Rama on the model of *Ramacharitmanas.*

Ramashwamedham (?C; Kannada) of Muddana: prose narrative which tells how Shri Rama's ashwamedha is halted by Lava and Kusha, which leads ultimately to his reunion with Sita. The poet's real name is Nandalike Lakshminarayana. For narrating this work he invents a poet named Muddana who tells the story to his young wife Manorama in order to while away a dull and rainy afternoon. This framework gives the work a particular distinction; it also gives freedom to the poet sometimes to describe places, persons, seasons, etc., sometimes to record fond exchanges between husband and wife.

Ramavatar-charita (late 19th; Kashmiri) of Prakash Ram: an adaptation of *Ramayana*, with a sequel entitled *Lava Kusha-charita*. The work is of 1786 stanzas, some in the two-line Farsi hazaj metre and the rest in the four-line accented metre of Kashmiri. The work was so popular that it circulated widely all over Kashmir in hand-written copies. It was first printed only in 1910 in the Perso-Arabic script.

Rama-vijaya (*c*1700; Marathi) of Shridhar Nazarekar (1658–1730): adaptation of the *Ramayana* story, composed in 9147 ovi stanzas.

Ramayana of Valmiki (Sanskrit): the other national 'epic' of India, classified as a 'mahakavya' and regarded as the 'adi-kavya' (first poem) of the nation. Editions: (1) Earliest were two partial editions: ed. William Carey and Joshua Marshman, Serampore, 1806–10; ed. Augustus Schlegel, Bonn, 1829–38. (2) Bengal or Eastern recension; ed, Gaspare Gorresion, 5 vols, Parigi, 1843–50. (3) Kumbhakonam edition, representing a South Indian text: ed. T.R. Krishnacharya and T.S. Vyasacharya, 3 vols; Kumbhakonam and Bombay, 1911–13. (4) Lahore edition or Northwestern recension: ed. Pandits Bhagvad Dutta, Rama Labhya, Viswabandhu Shastri; Lahore, 1923–49; pub. D.A.V. College Research Dept. (5) Critical edition; gen. ed. P.L. Vaidya, 9 vols, Baroda, 1960–74; pub. Oriental Institute. Translations: (1) Ralph T.H. Griffith, 5 vols, London, 1870-74; verse (2) Manmathanath Dutta, 7 vols, Calcutta, 1891–94; prose. (3) Makhanlal Sen, 3 vols., London, 1959.

Ramayana-champu (?C; Sanskrit) ascribed to Bhoja: work based on first five books of the *Ramayana* story. The sixth ('Yuddha-kanda') was composed by Lakshmana Bhatta (?C). Some MSS contain a seventh book ('Uttara-kanda') by Venkataraja (?C).

Ramayana-champu (mid-16th; Malayalam) of Punam: a re-telling of *Ramayana* through the kind of selective narrative which Chakyars used for temple recitals. The work consists of over 2000 verse stanzas and 150 prose sequences, each devoted to a major episode. A special feature of the work is its humour and occasional satire.

Ramayana-katha (16th; Asamiya) of Madhava Kandali: verse rendering of *Ramayana*, done under the patronage of Varahi King Mahamanikya.

Ramayana maha-natak (*c*1610; Hindi) of Pranchandra Chauhan: a re-telling of the *Ramayana* story in the form of dialogues. There is no other element of drama in this work.

Ramayana-manjari (11th; Sanskrit): of Kshemendra: an abridged version of the *Ramayana* story in verse. The original 'kanda' titles are retained in each section, but the contents have been recast considerably.

Ramayanam (15th; Malayalam):

of Rama Panikar: an adaptation of *Ramayana*, the most outstanding of this poet's several works.

Ramayanamu (late 16th; Telugu) of Kummari Molla: a version of *Ramayana* known for its beautiful descriptions.

Rambhamanjari (15th; Prakrit): of Nayachandra: incomplete sattaka play of which only three acts have been recovered. It celebrates the wedding of king Jaitrachandra of Varanasi with Rambhamanjari, daughter of king Madanavarman of Gujarat.

Ramchandra (1821–80): prose writer in Urdu, who contributed substantially to the development of Urdu prose. Born and educated in Delhi, he joined Delhi College as teacher and helped to establish the vernacular translation society. He bought out the monthly journal *Favaid-e-nazirin* in 1876, later started the weekly *Qiran-ur-sadain*. In these he published not only translations but also original articles. He was among the earliest in Urdu to write serious articles on subjects of social significance.

Ramchandra Kaviraj (16th): scholar and poet in Bangla, author of *Smarana-darpana*; from an affuent family, his mother's father Yashoraj Khan was an officer of Husain Shah. Originally a Shakti worshipper, Ramchandra became a Vaishnav under the influence of Shrinivas Acharya and composed many Vaishnav lyrics.

Ramchandra Khan (mid-16th): poet in Bangla; an administrative officer under Husain Shah. He wrote a complete *Mahabharata* poem in Bangla around 1532. Earlier, as military governor of the lower Gangetic region, he helped Shri Chaitanya to cross over from Bengal into Orissa.

Ramcharan Thakur (1520–1600): of Assam; nephew of Madhavadeva; composed a 'charit punthi' of Shankaradeva and Madhavadeva; also wrote a play, *Kamsa-vadh.*

Ramdas or Samartha Ramdas or Swami Ramdas (1608–82): sant poet in Marathi and spiritual leader. It is believed that Shivaji derived his concept of 'Ramrajya' from the poem "Anandavana bhuvan" by Ramdas. Born Narayan Thorat in Jamb village of Jalna district (Maharashtra), he ran away from home while a boy and lived like an ascetic at Takli, near Nasik, for 12 years, studying the scriptures and seeking enlightenment. He experienced a mystical vision of Shri Rama and began calling himself

Ramdas thereafter. From 1632 onwards he travelled all over India and acquired other languages like Hindi and Urdu. His most famous work *Dasabodha*, consisting of 7751 stanzas, is in the form of a dialogue between the guru and his disciple. Other works by him are *Atmaram, Manache-shloka* or *Manobodhana*, *Karunashtake*. He composed innumerable padas, more than 700 of which have been collected in *Shri Samarthanchi gatha*; others are in *Dasavishramadharma*.

Ramdasu [Bhakta Ramdasu (late 17th)]: poet of Ram-bhakti from Bhadradi, near Hyderabad. While working as a minor state official, he used state funds to build a Rama temple in Bhadradi; for this he was imprisoned for 12 years. Only two of his works are extant—*Dasarathi shatakamu*, which consists of 100 poems in praise of Rama; *Ramdasu-kirtanalu*, songs written while he was in prison.

Rameshwar Bhattacharya (b. 1677): poet in Bangla; author of *Shivayana*, one of the very few Shaiva works in Bangla of this period. Rameshwar was born in Jadupur village in the Ghatal area of Midnapore district. During the rebellion of Shobha Singh, he was driven out of his village and took refuge in Karnagarh, also in Midnapore, where he received the patronage of the local zamindar Ram Singha. Under the direction of zamindar's son Yasovant Singha, Rameshwar completed this work in 1750.

Ramgati Nyayaratna (1831–94): prose writer in Bangla and educationist. He served in the education department of Bengal government and retired as headmaster of Hooghli Normal School. As author of *Bangla Bhasha-o-Bangla sahitya bishayak prastab*, he wrote the first history of Bangla literature. Among his other works are *Ramabali* (1862), *Ramabali-natak* (1869), *Bharatbarsher samasta itihas* (1879), *Ramcharita* (1882), *Bastubichar* (1884).

Ramkamal Sen (1783–1844): Bangla educationist, notable among whose various contributions was *A Dictionary in English and Bengali* (1817–34) in two volumes.

Ramkrishna Kavi Tenali (*c*1505–1575): poet in Telugu, also scholar of Sanskrit. According to tradition he was one of the 'Ashtadiggaja' poets, but scholars no longer accept this; he is known now as a 'vikatkavi' about whom there are many funny stories. In earlier life he was a Shaiva named Ramlinga; later he became a Vaishnav and called himself Ramkrishna. Among his works are *Panduranga-mahatyamu, Udbhataradhya-charitramu, Ghatakachal-mahathyamu*; most of these are place-descriptions.

Ramlala nahachhu (*c*1586; Hindi) of Tulsidas; a poem which relates to pre-wedding rituals, during which the bridegroom has a haircut and is shaved, his nails are manicured, etc. The poem is meant to be sung on such occasions. In it, 'Ram' stands for the bridegroom, 'Kausalya' for his mother, 'Dasrath' for his father, and so on.

Rammohan Roy, Raja (?1774–1833): apart from his other fame, was an early writer of Bangla prose. His translations of two Vedanta treatises and of the Upanishads, as also his polemical tracts advocating social and religious reform make him the first writer of Bangla prose outside of text books. He also wrote some devotional songs and translated *Bhagavat Gita* in Bangla verse.

Ramnarayan Chakrabarti Kaviraj (earlier 18th): poet in Asamiya, most outstanding in his period; court-poet of several Ashom kings. During the reign of Rudra Simha (1696–1714), he adapted *Gita Govinda* into Asamiya; rewrote *Shakuntala* in kavya form. At the behest of Shiva Simha (1714–44) and his queen Pramatheswari, he made a long poem out of the Sankhasura-vadha episode from *Brahma Vivarta-purana*. He is also said to have rendered into Asamiya the Madhava-Sulochana episode from an appendix to *Padmapurana*. His *Gita Govinda* is profusely illustrated on every page; probably, the work of Dilip and Dosai, two famous painters of the Ahom court.

Ramnarayan 'Tarkaratna' (1822–86): playwright in Bangla, whose most famous play *Kulin Kulasarvaswa* (1854), criticises the 'kulin' system. His other social drama, *Nava-natak* (1866), shows the evils of mutiple marriages. He also wrote farces like *Jeman karma temani phal* (1865), *Chakshudan* (1869) and *Ubhaya-sankat* (1869); plays on puranic themes, *Rukmini-haran* (1871), *Kamsa-vadh* (1875), *Dharma-vijay* (1875); translated several Sanskrit plays into Bangla.

Ramnidhi Gupta (1742–1849): better known as Nidhi Babu, a writer of love-songs. One of the leading sponsors of akhdai music, he introduced the tappa variety of song from Hindi into Bangla.

Ramprasad (late 18th): composer in Bangla; a name associated with a number of very popular devotional songs about Kali, later known as Ramprasadi songs. These songs are appeals to the goddess, made as if by a wayward but repentant child; the combination of pure devotion and homely affection made them very popular. Despite lack of poetic quality, these songs were held in high esteem perhaps in reaction against the over-emphasis on Vaishnav songs in Bengal until then. The older songs of this kind were probably composed by Ramprasad, a brahman and a younger contemporary of Ramprasad Sen Kaviranjan, a vaishya; this Ramprasad belonged to Calcutta and was reputed as a composer of kabi songs.

Ramprasad Niranjani (mid-18th): prose writer in Hindi who was associated with the court of Patiala. In 1741 he wrote *Bhasha Yoga Vashistha* in refined Khariboli. The composition of this work at this date refutes the view that Khariboli prose was developed in Fort William College at Calcutta after 1800.

Ramprasad Sen 'Kaviranjan' (d. 1775): poet in Bangla; to be distinguished from his younger contemporary, also Ramprasad; belonged to Kumarhatta, about 25 miles above Calcutta on the Hooghly. He composed a Vidya-Sundar poem in 1760 or 1770, which shows the influence of Bharatchandra. His other works include *Kali-kirtan* and the fragmentary *Krishna-kirtan*; both poems were written in the new panchali style that had developed from the older kirtan tradition.

Rampurattu Varier (18th): poet in Malayalam. It is said that during a river-journey undertaken by Travancore ruler, Martanda Varma, he heard a 'vanchippattu' song composed and sung by Rampurattu; the king was so impressed that he bestowed large money gifts on the poet. His best known work is *Kuchel vrittam vanchi ppattu*.

Ramraj'bhushanudu (mid-16th): poet in Telugu, also scholar of Sanskrit. His real name was Prabandhank Bhattumurti, but he was awarded the title of 'Ramrajbhushanudu' by the last Vijayangar king Ramrayalu. Of his three extant works, *Vasucharitramu* and *Harischandra-Nalopakhyam* are kavya works, while *Narasabhupaliyamu* is a philosophical work.

Ramram Basu or **Bose** (1757–1813): a pioneer of Bangla prose writing, he was associated at first with the Baptist Mission at Serampore, esp. with William Carey. When the Fort William College was founded at Calcutta in 1800, Carey brought him here to teach Bangla.

Ramram is the author of *Pratapaditya-charitra* (1801), the biography of a 16th century Bengali chieftain; this is the first major prose work, in Bangla. His other work, *Lipimala* (1802), is a collection of essays and short narratives written in the form of letters. The latter was particularly designed to help East India Company officials to learn Bangla.

Ramshankar Raye (1838–1917): playwright in Oriya, perhaps the first in the language. Before beginning his career as a playwright, he edited a monthly magazine *Vikul madhupa*, wrote a long poem "Prema-ratri", began two novels ("Saudamini" and "Unmadini") which he did not finish. His first play *Kanchi Kaveri* (1882) adopted the structure of Western drama and used blank verse. He wrote 10 plays altogether, two dance dramas and two farces.

Ranajitmalla (1722–72): a poet of Nepal who belonged to the Bhatgaon ruling family; represented in anthologies like *Prakirna-gitani*. He compiled a treatise on music entitled *Sangita-chudamani*; also wrote several plays in prose.

Ranamalla chhanda (1408/1411; Gujarati/Rajasthani) of Shridhar Vyas; a historical poem in 70 verses describing the battle between Ranamall Rathore of Idat and Zafar Khan, the Tughlak governor of Gujarat, which took place in 1398–99. Though a short work, it is important because it was written soon after the event and is remarkably faithful to history. The language used is Maru-Gurjar (or Old Gujarati/W. Rajasthani) which bears the influence of Apabhramsha or Avahatta.

Ranchhodbhai Udayaram (1837–1923): playwright in Gujarati and drama producer; regarded as the father of Gujarati theatre. He formed a theatre-group, with the idea of trying to reform 'bhavai' performances by eliminating the vulgar and obscene elements. This group performed his plays *Harishchandra* and *Nala-Damyanti*; soon after some friends in Bombay got together to produce his *Lalita-duhkhadarsak*; in due course his group known as the Gujarati Natak Mandali got accepted as the leading theatre-group. Apart from translations of Sanskrit plays based on puranic themes, he also wrote ten original plays like *Balasur-mardan, Madalasa ane Ritudhvaja, Vantthela virahana Kunda dritya, Vairano vanse-vasyo varso.*

Ranchhodji Amarji Divan (b.1824): writer in Gujarati and

Braj, scholar of Farsi. He belonged to Junagad where he was much honoured as a politician and military commander. He wrote a history of Sorath, *Tavarikhe-sorath*, in Farsi. Among his Gujarati works are *Chandipatra-garba, Jalandhar-akhyan, Sombar-mahatmya*, etc; among his works in Braj are *Sankhachud-akhyan, Daksha yajnabhanga, Kalakhanj-akhyan*, etc. He wrote more in Braj than in Gujarati.

Rangajamma (17th): woman poet in Telugu; attached to the court of last Nayaka king of Thanjavur, Vijayaraghava. She was also the king's beloved and was publicly acknowledged by him. Among works ascribed to her are *Mannarudas-vilasamu, Yajna-ganamu, Usha-parinayamu.*

Rangalal Bandopadhyay (1827–87): poet and novelist in Bangla. Born in Bankulia village of Bardhaman district of Bengal; graduated from Hooghly College and joined government service. Among his works are *Ritu-samhar, Bangla kabita bishayak prabhandha, Bhekmushiker juddho, Padmini-upakhyan, Karmadebi.* He also contributed numerous articles to two periodicals, *Samvad-sagar* and *Samvad-prabhakar*.

Ranganatha Nayaka (r.1600–31): Thanjavur ruler who extended patronage to Telugu writers after the fall of Vijayanagar. A poet himself, he composed in both Telugu and Sanskrit; author of *Achyutabhyudayamu, Nala-charitramu, Valmiki-charitramu.*

Ranganatha Ramayana (early/late 13th; Telugu): the earliest known *Ramayana* in Telugu, composed either around 1240 or during 1290–95. The poet, Gona Buddha Reddy, also known as Buddha Natha or Buddha Raja, was probably a prince and wrote at the instance of his father, Vithal Nath. The work is a fairly close rendering of the Valmiki *Ramayana*, done in dvipadi metre and simple language. 'Yuddha kanda' covers almost half the space; there is no 'Uttara kanda', so the story ends with Shri Rama's coronation.

Rangin [Saadat Yar Khan 'Rangin' (1755–1835)]: poet in Urdu, friend of Insha. When he once sought the tutelage of the poet Mir, Mir refused him saying Rangin was a wealthy person, hence was incapable of appreciating art. Among Rangin's works are *Masnavi Dilpajir, Ijad-e-Rangin* (a masnavi), *Chardiwan, Masnavi Mazhar-ul-ajaib, Majalis-e-Rangin.* He also wrote

Farasnama which is a work on the diseases of horses.

Rani Ketaki-ki Kahani ya Udaybhan charit (*c*1800; Hindi): of Isha Alla Khan: early prose work. In his prose the author made conscious effort to avoid all foreign languages (Arabi, Farsi, Turki) and local speech (Braj, Avadhi, Bhakha) in order to produce a very chaste Hindi. The story tells of the romance between Udaykhan, son of Raja Surajbhan, and Ketaki, daughter of Raja Jagatprakash.

Rani Mahadevi (early 12th): woman poet in Kannada. She was a contemporary of Akka Mahadevi and also composed vachana poems. She was the wife of 'vachanakar' Mollige Marayya and wrote vachanas as rejoinders to what her husband composed.

Ranna (late 10th): poet in Kannada, ranked along with Pampa and Ponna as the three jewels ('ratnatraya') of Kannada literature. He was educated at the ashram in Sravanvelgola; attached for sometime to the court of Chamundaraya, later he obtained the patronage of king Tailap and his son. Three of his extant works are *Ajitnatha-puran, Gada-yuddha* (also known as "Sahas Bhim yuddha") and *Rannakanda*. Two other works, *Parasuram-charit and Chakreswar-charit* are ascribed him but these have never been recovered.

Rannakanda (*c*990; Kannada) of Ranna: a lexicon in verse, of which only 12 sections are extant; derives its name from being composed in 'kanda' metre.

Ras (Panjabi): a popular form of folk-drama in Panjab. Its popularity is believed to have delayed the developement of formal literary drama in Panjabi. Generally it presented Krishna as one of the characters; thus it filled some religious need as well.

Raspanchadhyayi: five chapters of *Bhagavata-purana* are known by this term. These chapters describe Shri Krishna dancing with gopis on the full-moon night of Sharad. This situation has been used by many Hindi poets to compose what came to be known as 'ras panchadhyayi kavya'. Among these poets were Surdas, Nandadas, Rahim, Hariram Vyas, Nawalsingh, etc.

Raspanchadhyayi (*c*1538; Hindi): of Nandadas: a kavya in Brajbhasha which describes Krishna's 'ras-lila' on the model of what is given in *Bhagavata-purana*.

Ras sahashrapadi (15th; Gujarati)

of Narsi Mehta: poem based on the 'panchadhyayi' of *Bhagavata-purana*. Though the title claims one thousand, there are only 113 padas in the poem. The poet describes the 'ras-lila' as if he were watching it himself.

Rasa (Sanskrit): term in poetics for the inexplicable inward delight experienced by a qualified person ('sahridaya') on witnessing a dramatic performance or in reading or listening to a practical composition. Eight rasas are generally recognised—'sringara' (erotic), 'vira' (heroic), 'raudra' (furious), 'bibhatsa' (disgusting), 'hasya'(comic), 'adbhuta' (marvellous), 'karuna' (pathetic) and 'bhayanaka' (terrible). A ninth rasa, 'santa' (quietistic), is accepted by some scholars. In the Vaishnav literature of Bengal from 15th century onwards, 'bhakti' came to be regarded as a rasa also.

Rasa (Maithili): like 'goalari', the rasa is a class of love songs in Mithila dealing with Krishna's 'rasa-lila'. Saheb Ramdas is the most successful composer of such songs.

Rasa Khan (1560–1633): poet in Hindi; He was a Pathan sardar of Delhi; became a favoured disciple of Vitthalnath and devoted himself to Krishna-bhakti. His use of simple and common Brajbhasa is particularly remarkable.

Rasaka (Prakrit): also called 'Rasa' or 'Rasabandha', it was a popular dance associated with religious festivals. The song accompanying the dance, composed in Prakrit, was also called a rasa or rasaka.

Rasagangadhara (late 17th: Sanskrit) of Jagannatha: work on poetics, written in the form of 'sutra' and 'vritti'. It appears to have consisted of five chapters originally; only the first and part of the second have survived. The first chapter deals with a definition of kavya; its four degrees of achievement ('uttamottama'; 'uttama'; 'madhyama'; 'adhama'); rasa; bhava; guna. The second chapter deals with divisions of dhvani; discusses abhidha and lakshana; followed by treatment of upama and other poetic figures.

Rasa'kallola (17th; Oriya) of Dinakrishna Dasa: a kavya work dealing with the Radha-Krishna story; every line begins with the consonant 'ka'. This is a simpler and less ornate work than any of Upendra Bhanja's, but the poet's conception of love does not rise much above the physical plane.

Rasaleen [Nabi Sheikh 'Rasaleen'; real name Sayyid Ghulam Nabi

(1689–1750)]: poet in Hindi from Bilgram in Hardoi district of U.P.; also noted marksman and soldier who joined the army of Nawab Safdarjung and died in battle near Agra. His best-known poetical work *Arg-darpan* consists of 180 dohas which depict the physical charms of a 'nayika'; the other work, *Ras-prabandh*, portrays 'rasa' in 155 dohas.

Rasalu-kokila (?C; Hindi): the title of a qissa based on the lives of the hero Rasalu and the heroine Kokila or Kaulan.

Rasamanjari (*c*1550; Sanskrit) of Bhanumishra or Bhanudatta or Bhanu Kavi: verse work which discusses 'shringar-rasa' in the limited context of lovers in a particular situation.

Rasamanjari (*c*1745; Bangla) of Bharatchandra Raye: an erotico-historical work based on a Sanskrit text.

Rasamanjarini varta (*c*1550; Gujarati) of Bacharaj: a prabhandha kavya of about 600 lines using metres such as doha, chaupai and chhappaye. It is based on the traditional story of Premavati; the erotic element predominates.

Rasa'nidhi (late 17th): poet in Hindi; author of *Ratan-hajara*, which he composed in imitation of *Bihari-satsai*; at places he has retained Bihari's lines. Some other verses of his have been collected as *Arilla aur Manjho*. In his dohas he tried to incorporate attitudes and devices of Farsi poetry. The poet was a wealthy landlord of Barouni in Datia state; his real name was Prithvisingh.

Rasaratna (1616; Hindi) of Puhkar Kavi: long poem telling of the romance between Surasen and Rambhavati; composed in several metres. The poet was imprisoned for some reason by Jahangir, but released when he composed this poem.

Rasaratnakar (*c*1600; Kannada) of Salva: work in poetics which follows the tradition of Kannada scholars like Nagavarma and Kaviram rather than that of Sanskrit critics.

Rasatarangini (*c*1550; Sanskrit): of Bhanumishra or Bhanudatta or Bhanu Kavi'; a prose work which discusses 'rasa' in eight 'taranga' sections.

Rasavahini (early 14th; Prakrit) of Vedeha: a verse work consisting of 103 stories, perhaps modelled on the shataka form in Sanskrit. The first 40 relate to Jambudvipa (India) and the rest to Lanka; offers much information on the social conditions of the time in these two countries.

Rasika (Sanskrit): one who is able to appreciate a poem or play because he can experience the rasa presented in the poem or play. The term came into vogue along with the doctrine of 'rasa'. Anandavardhana used the term 'sahridya' more often for rasika though in the same sense. In a modern context, rasika would mean a critic of literary or any other art who enjoys that work of art.

Rasika-mangala (*c*1652; Bangla) of Gopijanaballabha Das; a biography of Shri Chaitanya.

Rasikajanamanobhiramu (18th; Telugu) of Kuchimanchi Timmakavi; kavya work telling of the Gandharva maiden Shyama and her romance with king Ritudhvaj.

Rasikapriya (1591; Hindi) of Keshavdas: a work which discusses and describes married love.

Raso (Hindi): a kavya-form in Old Hindi or Dingal, which gives an account of some king, of his prowess in battle and of his romances. Example: *Prithviraj-raso*. See also *Rasu*.

Raso or **Rasau** (Rajasthani): originally meant a circular dance accompanied by music, performed by a male dancer along with a specified number of women dancers, who sang as they danced. Each raso had a different song. Over the course of time, the dancing was discontinued but the song or musical text continued to be recited. This developed into a literary form. Early examples of it are *Upadesh-rasayan* (1143) by Jinadutta Suri, *Bharateshwar-Bahubali raso* (1184) by Shalibhadra Suri, *Jeevadaya raso* (1200) by Asigu.

Rasu (Gujarati): term for long narrative poems, a form which developed during the Gurjari Apabhramsha phase; themes were mythological or historical. Judging from works known and/or extant, historical rasus outnumber mythological rasus. See also *Raso*.

Rasul-bijay (Bangla): a form of religious narrative poetry by Bengali Muslims, following Hindu models such as *Pandav-vijay*. Poems in this form deal with stories of Muhammad and earlier prophets. A work of this kind in 1654 by Saiyad Sultan of Chatgaon included some Hindu gods and avatars.

Ratan-bavani (*c*1590; Hindi) of Keshavadas: long poem in praise of

Ratan Singh, elder brother of the poet's patron Indrajit Singh. The work is in chhappay verses.

Ratan-wa-Padam (late 17th; Urdu) of Wali Vellori: a Dakhni version of the *Padumavat* of Jayasi.

Ratanu Virbhan (1688–1735): poet in Hindi from Ghadoi village of Jodhpur state. His *Raj-rupak* describes the battle between Jodhpur ruler Abhaysingh and Mughal subedar Sarbuland Khan.

Ratirahasya (?12th; Sanskrit) work on erotics ascribed to Kokkoka: believed to have been composed before 13th century. Kokkoka followed Vatsyayan in some respects but also refers to works by authors such as Nandikeshwara and Gonikaputra.

Tr. R. Schmidt, Berlin, 1903; A. Comfort, London, 1964.

Ratikanta Dvija (18th; Asamiya): poet and scholar of Assam who with three others—Nandeswar Dvija, Narrottam Dvija, Khargeshwar Dvija—produced a complete Asamiya version of *Brahmavaivarta Purana* under the patronage of the Koch prince Hayanarayan of Darrang. The work was completed around 1717.

Ratipati Bhagat (late 18th): poet in Maithili; rendered *Gita Govinda* of Jayadeva into Maithili. In the work he first explains his purpose, then translates all the major prabandhas from Jayadeva's poem.

Ratnakara (mid-9th): poet of Sanskrit from Kashmir; composed *Hara-vijaya* and *Vakrokti-panchasika*. He appears to have lived during the reign of Kashmir kings Chippata Jayapida (832–44) and Avantivarman (r. 855–84). His father's name was Amritabhanu.

Ratnakaravarni (16th): poet in Kannada, used to be called the 'Kannada-kokil' of his age; was attached to the court of Karkal ruler Bhairav. His greatest work is *Bharatesh-vaibhav*, which deals with the son of the first tirthankar; among his other works are *Trilok-shatak, Aparajiteshwar-shatak, Annan-padagalu.*

Ratnamala vyakarana (17th; Sanskrit): of Purushottam Thakur: a work of grammar. The author was from Assam.

Ratnavali (?2nd; Sanskrit): metrical work in the form of an epistle addressed to an unnamed king. It has been called 'raja-parikatha' and consists of 77 verses. The work contains the essence of Buddhist doctrine. It is generally attributed to

Nagarjuna and the person addressed is identified by some scholars as a Satavahana king.
Ed. & trs. G. Tucci, *JRAS*, 1934.

Ratnavali (early 7th; Sanskrit) of Shriharsha: 'natika' type play in four acts. It tells how king Udayana married Ratnavali, daughter of the king of Sri Lanka, despite mishaps and obstacles, with the help of his clever minister, Yaugandharayana.

Ratneshwara (1654–1714): poet in Gujarati from Dabhol; rendered *Bhagavat Gita* into Gujarati around 1690; also translated parts of *Mahabharata* in verse; wrote a number of didactic poems as well as devotional lyrics.

Rau Jehatsi-ra chanda (*c*1550; Hindi) of Sujo: long poem in Dingal describing the battle between Babar and Rao Jaitsingh of Bikaner.

Ravanarjuniya, also known as *Arjunaravaniya* (?C; Sanskrit): of Bhaumaka: a grammatical poem in 27 sections, which imitates *Bhatti-kavya*. While relating the story of Ravana's fight with Kartaviryarjuna, it illustrates the rules of Panini in the same order as in *Ashtadhyayi*. The author, also called Bhatta Bhima, Bhima or Bhauma, appears to have lived before 11th century.

Ravanavadha (?C; Sanskrit) of Bhattiswamy: also known as *Bhatti-kavya*, this poetic work which gives a summary of the *Ramayana* story, was really written to explain certain rules of Panini's grammar and illustrate some features of rhetoric. It is thus a 'shastra-kavya', though it bears all essential features of a mahakavya. Bhatti is said to have lived during the reign of Dharasena (6th), the ruler of Saurashtra, but he may have lived much earlier.

Ravanavaho: same as Setubandha.

Ravanodbhava (late 18th; Malayalam) of Kallaikulangara Raghava Pisharoty: Kathakali play which tells of the rise of Ravana.

Ravidas (late 14th/early 15th): also called Raidas, sant-poet in Hindi, from Kashi; disciple of Ramanand and founder of the Raidas sect; a tanner by caste. Some of his verses were included in *Adi-Granth*; others have been collected in *Ravidas-ki vani* and *Ravidas-ke pada*.

Raya Pasenaijja (?C; Pali): the second 'uvanga'. It contains a story, told in the puranic manner, of the pilgrimage of god Suriyabha to Mahavir; also there is an important dialogue between king Paesi and the monk Kesi, which concludes with the king's conversion to Jainism.

Rayadhu (15th): poet in Apabhramsha; also composed in Sanskrit and Prakrit, but his writings are larger in volume than that of any other writer in Apabhramsha. He is said to have composed 25 works, of which the best-known are *Sukausal charit, Savomatinath-charit* and *Balbhadra-puran*. Rayadhu belonged to Gwalior (M.P); was a contemporary of Dungarsingh of the Tomar dynasty and his son Kirtisingh.

Rayaraghunatha Tondaman (late 18th): ruler at Pudukottai (r. 1769–89): poet in Telugu; author of *Parvati-parinayamu*.

Rayavachakamu (?1600; Telugu) of unknown authorship: prose biography of Vijayanagar king Krishnadeva Raya. In the text it is stated that the work was submitted by an unknown person to Vishwanatha Nayakudu, ruler at Madurai. The work is a good example of early prose literature in Telugu.

Raye-mangal (Bangla): a mangalkavya form associated with Sundarban in deltaic Bengal. It glorifies the presiding deity of the region, Dakshin Raye (lord or master of the south), whose icon is a soldier carrying a gun and riding a full-size 'Royal Bengal tiger'. During the annual worship, the traditional story is narrated with musical accompaniment. The story deals with the boatmaker Ratai Baulya of Bardaha who is commissioned by a merchant to build some boats. Accompanied by his six brothers and only son, Ratai goes into a forest to fell trees and collect wood. They happen to cut down the tree where Dakshin Raye resided. The deity is enraged and he orders the killing of Ratai's all six brothers. They are duly killed by tigers. The grief-stricken Ratai decides to commit suicide and asks his son to return home. He is told by a voice from the sky that the brothers will be restored to life if Ratai offers to sacrifice his son. Ratai does so. The deity is propitiated and restores all of them to life. The rest of the narrative follows the 'Chandi-mangal' line. The raye-mangal narratives date back probably to early 17th. Among variations there is one (used by the poet Rudradev) in which there is a terrible fight between Dakshin Raye and Bada Ghazi Khan, a Muslim, who vied with each other for territorial supremacy in Sundarban.

Raye-mangal (1686; Bangla) of Krishnaram Das: regarded as the finest of the raye-mangal poems in Bangla.

Raye Shekhar (16th): poet in Bangla of the post-Chaitanya era. There are at least two or more poets who composed Vaishnav lyrics in the name of Shekhar, so there is controversy about each.

R.C. Dutt or **Romeshchandra Datta** (1848–1909): novelist in Bangla, historian in English, and nationalist; was president of the Indian National Congress in 1899. Earlier, he went to England for higher studies and qualified for the ICS in 1871; served till 1897 and took voluntary retirement. At one time he wanted to write novels in English but was advised to write in Bangla by Bankimchandra; wrote *Bangabijeta* (1874), *Madhavikankan* (1877; trans. by him into English as *The Slave Girl of Agra*, pub. 1909), *Maharashtra jibanprabhat* (1878) and *Rajput jibansandhya* (1879). His varied writings in English began with the autobiographical *Three Years in Europe* (1877; trans. by him into Bangla as *Iyuropey tin vatsar*, pub. (1873); *Peasantry in Bengal* (1875); *Economic History of India* (1899), *Famines of India* (1900); *A History of Civilization in Ancient India* (1899), condensed and translated *Ramayana* and *Mahabharata* into English as *Great Epics of Ancient India* (1890) and selections from old Indian poetry as *Lays of Ancient India* (1894).

Rekhta: another name for Urdu as it developed in North India.

Rekhti (Urdu): a form of verse, probably peculiar to Urdu poetry, in which the poet assumes the voice of a woman and expresses her feelings. More specifically, this form is used to give unrestrained expression of woman's sexual fantasies. It originated in Dakhan and the first poet who wrote such poems was probably Lutfi; later, the poet Hashmi consolidated the form. The best rekhti-composer of his time was Golkonda ruler Muhammad Quli Qutb Shah.

Revantagiri rasu (*c*1230; Gujarati) of Vijaysena Suri: long poem narrating Vastupala's pilgrimage to Girnar. There are fine descriptions of the Gir forest; also useful information about temples in this region. The author was a Jain.

Riddhipur-varnan (?C): see *Sahyadri-varnan.*

Rishabha-panchasika (late 10th; Prakrit) of Dhanapala: a sequence of 50 verses in honour of Rishabha, the first tirthankar. The first 20 narrate various events in his life; the rest is eulogy.

Risi-nama (?C; Kashmiri) also called *Nur-nama*: a collection of verses and sayings of Sheikh Nuruddin or Nanda Risi. A large portion of this collection may be spurious.

Riti (Sanskrit): term in poetics for a particular mode of composition ('visishta padarachana') or arrangement of words in a literary work. Of three ritis that have been named—'Vaidarbhi' (of Vidarbha, in Central India),'Gaudi' (of Gauda, in East India), 'Panchali' (of Panchal, in North India)—the first is supposed to be the best.

Riti-kavya a: convention of Hindi poetry. The term 'riti' belongs to Sanskrit poetics; as applied in Hindi it meant poetry which celebrates erotic sentiments in a classical or learned manner. Poets in Hindi of the Riti mode are said to belong to a period called 'Ritikal' of Hindi literature during the 17th century.

Ritthanemi-chariu (?C; Apabhramsha) of Swayambhu: a kavya work which features Shri Krishna while giving a condensed Jain version of *Mahabharata* in four 'kanda'.

Ritu'samhara (?C; Sanskrit): lyric poem describing the six seasons as seen through a lover's eye. Some scholars believe this is an early work by Kalidasa; others believe it was composed by an inferior poet who also bore the same name or associated the great poet's name with the work in order to gain it prestige. Ed. & Tr. V.R. Nerurkar, Bombay, 1916. Tr. M.R. Kale, Delhi, 1967.

Rohal (*c*1734–1804): sant poet in Sindhi from a village near Amarkot town. He travelled for some years in Rajasthan before setling down in a place called Rohidi in Northern Sindh. Only some stray verses of his in Sindhi have been recovered. He composed also in Farsi and Hindi; among his Hindi works are *Adhbhut-granth, Man-prabodh, Sarvajnan* and *Agam-varta*.

Rubai (Urdu): term for a four-line verse. It derives from the Arabi word 'rubaya' meaning one-fourth. While a quatrain (also of four lines) is a stanza, 'rubai' is a complete poem by itself.

Ruchinath Kandali (*c*1710–70): poet in Asamiya, probably associated with the court of Ahom king Rajeswara Simha (r. 1751–60). Of the four verse-renderings of *Markandeya Chandi* into Asamiya, Ruchinath did the second one. In order to complete the story of Chandi, the poet incorporated into his work material from *Kalika-purana, Vamana-purana* and *Brahmavaivarta-purana.* Before undertaking to translate *Markandeya Chandi*, he had rendered *Kalika-purana* into Asamiya verse. The latter has not yet been found.

Rudra Sudhanidhi (16th; Oriya) of Abadhuta Narayana Swami: an elaborate prose work, among the earliest in the language. It tells of the childless king Ananga Padmakar who prays to Shiva for a child. Shiva is pleased and decides to send one of his 'gana' (follower) to earth as the king's son. In order to test the ganas, Shiva asks Parvati to create the beautiful maiden Trailokyasundari and all the ganas are captivated by her. When Shiva commands the gana Abhinava Chaitanya to go down to earth as a human being, he begs to be spared. Shiva is moved and promises that, after serving his time, Abhinava would return to heaven. Accordingly he is born to king Ananga Padmakar as his son and is named Rudra Sudhanidhi; Trailokyasundari is also reborn on earth and named Aridya Mrityusanjivani Karani. The rest of the story is an account of how Sudhanidhi won Karani despite the yogi Kamananda who also falls in love with Karani. Though written in prose, the language is richly poetic. It is one of the most original literary works of its time.

Rudrabhatta (?10th): scholar of Sanskrit; author of *Shringar-tilaka*. This work, devoted partly to poetics and partly to erotics, follows Rudrata's *Kavyalamkara* so closely in its literary principles that Rudrabhatta and Rudrata are sometimes regarded to be same person. However, there is another and later scholar of Sanskrit named Rudrabhatta who is credited with the work *Rasakalika*; this deals in detail with rasa.

Rudrabhatta (late 12th): poet in Kannada; author of *Jagannatha-vijaya*. After the upheavals caused in mid-12th Karnataka by the Virshaiva movement, the Hoysala rulers, esp. Virabhallala II (r. 1173–1220), brought about a more liberal climate for the encouragement of art and literature. Some poets like Rudrabhatta were able to uphold Vaishnav beliefs again. He lived in Dwarasamudra (mod. Hassan district) and belonged to the 'Smarta Bhagavata' tradition.

Rudradasa (?17th): playwright in Prakrit; author of *Chandralekha*. The Zamorin of Kozhikode was his patron.

Rudrakavi [Kandukuri Rudrakavi (*c*1480–1560)]: poet in Telugu. There seems to have been at least three poets in Telugu by the name of Rudrakavi from a Vishwabrahma family of Kandukuru, a place in Prakasham district of A.P. The first Rudrakavi wrote some stray verses in Telugu and Sanskrit but no substantial work; the second Rudrakavi was one of the 'Ashtadiggaja' poets in the court of Vijayanagar ruler Krishnadeva Raya (r. 1509–30); the third Rudrakavi had his verses quoted by grammarians but left behind no work. The second poet, truly called Kandukuri Rudrakavi, wrote several works of which three are extant: *Sugriva vijayamu*, the oldest available, Yakshagana text in Telugu; *Nirankushopakhyanamu*, a 'prabhandha' kavya in four sections dealing with the redemptions of a fallen youth by divine intervention; *Janardan-ashtakamu*, eight separate verses addressed to Shri Janardan, the deity of Kandukuri.

Rudrata (*c*900): literary critic in Sanskrit: author of *Kavyalamkar*. He belonged to Kashmir and advocated the 'alamkar' school of poetics; may have been a contemporary of Anandavardhan.

Rukmangada-charita (late 18th; Malayalam) of Mandavapali Ittiraricha Menon: Kathakali play in three scenes showing how the pious king Rukmangada's devotion to Vishnu is tested by the heavenly enchantress Mohini.

Rukmini-bibha (16th; Oriya) of Karttika Dasa: poetical work in ten sections re-telling the story of the marriage of Shri Krishna with Rukmini, daughter of the king of Vidarbha. A pioneering work of poetry in Oriya, it also depicts contemporary social norms in matters such as marriage, courtship, chivalry, etc.

Rukmini-haran (*c*1650; Marathi) of Samraj: kavya work in 1140 verses on Sanskrit model; contains occasional references to contemporary life.

Rukmini-haran nat (16th; Asamiya) of Shankaradeva: the longest of his ankiya-nat works. Based on puranic sources, it emphasises the devotional element.

Rukmini-mangal (*c*1500; Rajasthani) of Padam Bhagat: a narrative poem in about 265 verses, also known as *Kishanji no vyjayalo*. Though the story is drawn from *Bhagavata-purana*, the poem is generally secular in spirit.

Rukmini Parinaya (early 13th; Sanskrit) of Vatsaraj: a three-act play featuring Shri Krishna, Shishupal and Rukmini.

Rukmini-swayamvara (*c*1290; Marathi): long poem on an episode in the life of Shri Krishna, composed by a Mahanubhava author. It was first read out in the court of Yadav king Ramdev Rao.

Rukmini-swayamvara (late 18th; Malayalam) of Aswati Tirunal Tampuran: Kathakali play in five scenes showing how Krishna carries off Rukmini from her swyamvara in order to marry her.

Rupa Bhavani (1625–1720): woman mystic poet in Kashmiri.

Rupa Goswamin (16th): perhaps the greatest of the six goswamins of Brindavan who were directly associated with Shri Chaitanya; also poet and scholar of Sanskrit. Apart from several tracts of Vaishnav faith, wrote three plays, *Danakeli-kaumudi, Vidagdha-madhava* and *Lalita-Madhava*; composed two long poems, *Hamsa-duta* and *Uddhava-sandesha*, also hymns and songs; compiled the anthology *Padyavali*. Born into a South Indian brahman family that had settled in Bengal, he was a resident of Ramkeli village, and son of one Kumara. For a time he served the Muslim ruler of Bengal who honoured him with the title of 'Davir Khas'. The influence of Chaitanya turned him into a devout Vaishnav; after Chaitanya's death, went to Brindavan and lived there for the rest of his life.

Rupak (Sanskrit): kind of drama.

Rupak (Sanskrit): literary device based on similarity.

Rupaka kavya (Apabhramsha): allegorical poetry in which the whole story is told through metaphors and symbols. It was particularly popular with Jain poets.

Ruparam Chakrabarti (mid-17th): poet in Bangla; author of the most popular Dharmamangal poem in the language. A native of Srirampur village in South-West Bengal, quite near the home of Mukundaram Chakrabarti, Ruparam is alleged to have fallen in love with and married a very low caste (Hadi) girl, and was compelled to leave home. He migrated northwards, crossing the Damodar, and was finally given shelter by Ganesh Raye, brahman chief of Edal village.

Rupchandkunwar ras (16th; Gujarati) of Nayesundar: narrative poem telling of the romance between Rupchand of Ujjayin, a merchant's son, and Sohag, the daughter of Gunasen, also a resident of

Ujjayin but subservient to the ruler of Kanauj. The poet was a Jain.

Ruyyaka (?12th): Kashmiri scholar of Sanskrit; author of a number of works. Thus *Alamkara-manjari, Alamkaranusarini, Alamkara-sarvasva, Alamkara-vartika, Harsh-acharita-vartika, Nataka-mimamsa, Shrikantha-stava*; also wrote commentaries on Mammata's *Kavya-prakash* and Mahimabhatta's *Vyakti-viveka.*

S

Sabalsingh Chauhan (1655–1724): poet in Hindi; author of *Rupa-vilas* and *Chhanda-shastra*; translated *Mahabharata* and *Ritusamhara* into Hindi.

Sabayya (Hindi): generic name for a number of metres like 'hansi', 'mandarmala', 'madira', 'surendra-vajra', 'vagiswari', etc.

Sabhasadi bakhar (1697; Marathi) of Krishnaji Anant Sabhasad: prose chronicle about Shivaji, written at the behest of Rajaram. Because it was written within 12–14 years after the death of Shivaji, its information is generally authentic, particularly so about persons and places. It does not however give a complete account of Shivaji's life but of about 70 events.

Sabit Ali Shah (1740–1810): poet in Sindhi from Multan. He settled later in Sevhan town of Sindh. He knew Farsi, Arabi, Urdu and composed verses in these languages as well; more notably, he composed in Sindhi 'marsiya' and 'qasida' poems on Farsi models. He was the first Sindhi poet to do so, and he is best known in Sindhi for these poems.

Sabras (1635; Urdu) of Mulla Wajahi: a narrative prose-work, also known as "Qissa Husn-o-Dil", which presents allegorical treatment of the concept of love, human as well as divine. Its characters are either symbolic of the human attributes (viz., 'Dil', 'Husn', etc) or of moral concepts (viz., 'Sabr', 'Tauba', etc). In extent and significance, this is one of the greatest works in Dakhni; according to some scholars, it is not original but based on the Farsi 'nazm' *Dastur-e-usshak* (1448) of 'Fattahi' Nishapuri. The story deals with Dil (=heart), son of king Aql (=intellect) of Sistan. Impressed by his son's abilities, the father grants him the kingdom of Tan (=body). Dil now hears of the life-giving properties of Ab-e-Hayat (=elixir of life) and develops a craving for immortality; sends his spy Nazar (=sight) to locate its source. In his search Nazar lands up in the kingdom of Ishq (=love). Princess Husn (=beauty) of this kingdom knows where Ab-e-Hayat is to be found. After many obstacles are overcome, Dil is married to Husn.

Sachal Sarmast [Abdul Wahab (1739–1829)]: poet in Sindhi; adopted the poetic name 'Sachal' or 'Sachu' (=man of truth); was called 'Sarmast' because he was always in a trance. He is also known as 'Shair-e-haft Zaban' (=poet of seven languages) because he could compose in Sindhi, Hindi, Urdu, Panjabi, Farsi, Arabi and Saraiki; composed mainly in the form of dohas, kafis, ghazals and masnavis. None of his verses were written down in his own lifetime; they have been collected from various sources afterwards. A definitive edition of his poems in Sindhi, *Sachal-jo kalamu*, has been published by the Sindhi Adabi Board of Hyderabad (Sindh).

Sachchidananda Bada (early 14th): poet in Marathi. A contemporary of Jnaneswar, he wrote the first biography of the great sant-poet of Maharashtra.

Sadal Mishra (1764–1849): prose-writer in Hindi from Dhruvdiha village in Shahabad district of Bihar; later came to Calcutta and taught Hindustani at Fort William College. His two major works are *Nasiketopakhyan* or "Chandravati" and *Ramacharit*. His language bears the impact of Brajbhasa, Purabi and Bangla; there are many grammatical lapses in it. But he made a great contribution to the development of Khariboli prose.

Sadasukh Lal (1746–1824): early prose-writer in Hindi. Though he had mastered Farsi and Urdu well enough to compose 'sheir' in both, he chose to write prose in Hindi and developed it as a medium distinct from Urdu. His famous work *Sukhsagar* discusses some moral issues derived from *Vishnu-purana*; two other works are *Mantakhbuttavarikh* and *Hindibhasha-sar*. Unlike Lalluji Lal and Sadal Mishra who were employed by East India Company and wrote on commission, Sadasukh Lal, like Insha Allah Khan, wrote to please himself. He preferred that form of Khariboli which was the language of the educated middle class in the eastern Hindi region; known as Bhakha, it favoured Sanskrit words, as opposed to the Farsi-dominated Urdu patronised by East India Company.

Sadbhasa-chandrika (?C; Prakrit) of Lakshmidhara: a grammatical work.

Sadbhasha-nirmita Parsva'jina-stava (13th) of Dharmavardhana: a hymn which uses six languages—Sanskrit, Maharastri, Shauraseni, Paisachi, Apabhramsha.

Sad-bhashavibhushita Shantinatha-stava (*c*1340) of Jinapadma: a hymn which uses six languages (same as above).

Saddattha-bheda chinta (?C; Pali) of Thera Saddhammasiri: a grammatical work of the Kachhayana school.

Saddhamma-samgaha (late 14th; Prakrit) of Dhammakitti: work in prose and verse. It gives a historical account from the holding of the Buddhist councils in India down to 14th century.

Saddukada boli (Hindi): literally, speech of the sants. The utterances of Kabir would be good examples of this.

Sadukti-karnamrita (1206; Sanskrit) of Shridhara-dasa: anthology of 2380 devotional verses representing about 500 poets. The work is divided into five sections called 'pravaha', each of which is divided into several sub-sections called 'vichi'. The poet names his father as Vatu-dasa; they probably belonged to Bengal, because king Lakshmansena appears to have been the patron of both.

'Safir' Bilgrami [Saiyad Ahmad (1833–90)]: poet in Urdu; born in Merehra (Uttar Pradesh), moved later to Bilgram before making his home in Ara (Bihar). He composed in all genres of Urdu poetry; also wrote prose and produced a two-volume history of Urdu poetry, *Jalwa-e-khizr*.

Sagaranandin (11th): scholar of Sanskrit dramaturgy; author of *Natakalakshana-ratnakosha*, a treatise on the principles of drama. Nothing is known about his life; his date has been inferred from texts he cites in his work.

Sahaja-giti (?C; Bangla) of Santi, one of the *Charya* poets; a collection of verses.

Sahajananda-dohakosha-gitika (?C; Bangla) of Bhade, one of the *Charya* poets; a collection of verses.

Sahasa Bhima vijay (*c*980; Kannada) of Ranna: kavya work telling of the duel between Bhima and Duryodhan as given in 'Gada-purva' and 'Sauptik-parva' of *Mahabharata*. More than the original work by Vyas, *Pampa-Bharata* appears to have inspired Ranna. Though ostensibly based on only two parvan of *Mahabharata*, the work has in view the entire poem. It is also known as *Gada-yuddha*.

Sahasra'nama-vrittanta (16th; Asamiya) of Ananta Kandali: included in the *Kirtana* of Shankaradeva.

Saheb Namdas (mid-18th): sant-poet of Mithila, whose rasa compositions are very popular.

Sahib Kaul (17th): poet in Kashmiri; lived during the reign of Jahangir; author of *Krishnavatara* and *Janam-charita*.

Sahir (Marathi): name for persons who composed and sang 'powada' songs. They sang to the accompaniment of a simple one-wire instrument played by them.

Sahityadarpan (early 14th; Sanskrit) of Vishwanatha: work on poetics in ten chapters. There is little original thought contained in it, but it deals with important topics comprehensively and has served as a popular text book.
Tr. J.R. Ballantyne & P.D. Mitra, *Bib. Ind.* 1875.

Sahityalahari (?C; Hindi): popularly assigned to Surdas as a work based on his own *Sursagar*. However, its authenticity has not been established nor has its date of composition been determined. Dating has ranged between 1550 and 1750. It is a work of poetics which has not been granted much importance by scholars.

Sahridaya (Sanskrit): term for the ideal listener or reader or member of an audience; one who has the capacity for appreciating a dramatic performance or poetical composition.

Sahyadri-varnan (1330; Marathi): like *Riddhipurvarnan*, a long descriptive poem by a Mahanubhava author about the homeland and sacred places of the sect.

Saiful-mulk Badiuj-jamal (late 17th; Bangla) of Alaol: adaptation of a Farsi romance. The work was begun at the request of Magan Thakur and interrupted by his death, but resumed and completed at the request of Saiyad Muhammad Musah.

Saifulmuluk-wa-Badiujjamal (1624; Urdu): of Gavvasi, a poet of the Qutbshahi age of Golkonda (now Haidarabad, Andhra Pradesh). This is a masnavi poem featuring the romance between Egyptian prince Saiful Muluk and Chinese princess Badiya Chayal; it is modelled on the Alif-Laila story.

Saiyad Ahmad Khan, **Sir** (1817–1898): prose writer in Urdu; pioneered revitalisation of the Muslim community especially in North India; founder of Aligarh Muslim University. Born in Delhi and educated here; appointed 'seristadar' in 1838, subsequently 'sadr-e-amin' of Delhi 1846–54. Among his works are *Asarul sanavid, Jala-ul-kalub, Tuhfa-e-husn, Favayedul-afkar, Koule-matin, Kalmatul haq, Rahe sunnat*, etc. In a work entitled *Silsila-e-maluke-Hind* he gave an account of all the rulers of Delhi from Yudhisthir onwards.

Saiyad Ghulam Nabi Raslin (late 18th): poet of the riti convention in Hindi; author of *Angadarpan* (1737) and *Rasa-prabodh* (1741). He belonged to Bilgram village, near Hardoi (Uttar Pradesh).

Saiyad Hamza (late 18th): poet in Bangla. He completed the jangnama begun by Garibullah. He also wrote *Madhu-malati*, based on a popular folk-tale; *Jaiguner-punthi* (1797), the jangnama of Hanifa ; *Hatem-Tai'r kechha* (1804), stories about Hatim Tai.

Saiyad Sultan (*c*1600–66): poet in Bangla who was popularly known on account of the songs he composed celebrating the Radha-Krishna theme; also wrote *Jnan-pradip* or *Jnan-chautisa* which discusses tantric subjects. His major work is *Nabi-vamsa*, a translation of Muhammad Khan's work in Arabi *Mumtal Husain* which described the Karbala battle. As in Muslim shastras, here the story of creation and the advent of prophets have been described. Under the influence of Hindu shastras, the poet has also presented Brahma, Vishnu, Shiva and Krishna as prophets.

Sakal-katha samgrahamu (16th; Telugu) of Ayyalraju Rambhadradu: collection of stories featuring puranic kings and drawn from Sanskrit sources. The work was commissioned by Vijayanagar ruler Krishnadev Raya and references have been found to a work in Sanskrit with the same title attributed to him.

Sakal'vidhi-vidhan kavya (*c*1040; Apabhramsha) of Nayanandi, a Jain scholar of Avanti: kavya work containing 58 sandhis. Despite its stress on prayer and religious practices, its literary merit is to be found in the illustrations drawn by the author from ancient 'katha' and 'upakhyan' sources, including *Ramayana* and *Mahabharata*.

Sakalya (?C): Vedic scholar and grammarian; believed to have revised the Vedic texts and written their 'padapatha'. He is cited in *Ashtadhyayi*.

Sakhi (Panjabi): a form of prose.

Sakhi (Rajasthani): kind of poem composed by sants to express the truth experienced by them.

Salabega or **Salbeg** (16th/17th): poet in Oriya of Pathan origin; a devotee of Shri Jagannath. His father Jahangir Kuli Khan or Lalbeg was a Mughal subedar of Orissa; his mother was a Hindu widow; lost his father quite early and was brought up by his mother. According to legend, when Salabega fell very ill once, his mother prayed to Jagannath; after his recovery, he became a Vaishnav. For some years he travelled to many places before settling down in Puri.

Salva (mid-16th): poet in Kannada: among the more scholarly poets of his time. His works are *Bharata*, a Jain version of *Mahabharata* in shatpadi metre; *Rasa-ratnakar*, a discussion of rasa which ends by claiming the highest place for 'shringar'; *Sharada-vilas*, of which only a fragment has been recovered but enough to show that the poet was demonstrating the importance of 'dhvani' in poetry.

Samadauni (Maithili): class of songs representing the farewell songs sung to the daughter when she goes to her husband for the first time. Vidyapati composed many such songs and it is mostly his compositions that are sung on such occasions.

Samanta-pasadika (?5th; Pali) of Buddhaghosa: a commentary on *Vinaya-pitaka*. The work contains valuable historical, biographical and geographical information.

Samara rasu (*c*1316; Gujarati) of Ambadeva Suri: long poem which gives an account of the Jain merchant Samarasimha who renovated a number of Jain temples.

Samarataranga (*c*1760; Oriya) of Brajanath Badajena: unique work in Oriya, perhaps in all of older Indian literature, because it deals with a contemporary happening. The work narrates the victory of the raja of Dhenkanal over Maratha raiders led by Chimanji Bapu, son of Madhoji Bhonsla. The poet belonged to Dhenkanal state and may have participated in the action; he took up this contemporary theme to write a spirited war poem. The various sections are written in different heroic metres suited to situations; where Oriya does not suit the poet's purpose he has freely used Hindustani and Marathi. The work was obviously commissioned by his current patron, Trilochana Mohindra Bahadur, ruler of Dhenkanal, who is made out to be the hero of the action. There is very little historical truth in the account as given here of Dhenkanal's truimph.

Samaraditya-samkshepa (1214; Prakrit) of Pradyumna: a condensation of Haribhadra's *Samaraichchakaha*.

Samaraichhhakaha or **Samaraditya'katha** (8th; Prakrit) of Haribhadra Suri: a work of religious fiction ('mahadharmakatha') in champu style, perhaps the earliest extant champu work in any language. The main narrative depicts the fate of two characters, a hero and a villain, as they undergo many adventures through nine births. There are many subsidiary stories which, like the main narrative, illustrate and justify Jain ideas and beliefs. Interwoven with the stories are descriptions of customs, festivals, towns, jungles, lakes, etc., making the work a valuable source for the study of social life in North India in 8th.

Samartha Ramdas: see Ramdas.

Samashloki-Gita (mid-17th; Marathi) of Vaman Pandit: a simplified verse translation of *Bhagavat Gita*.

Samavakara (Sanskrit): one of the ten varieties of drama described in *Natya-shastra*.

Samayamatrika (11th; Sanskrit) of Kshemendra: verse work in eight sections. It tells of a young courtesan who, tutored by an old bawd, traps a rich young man and fleeces his parents. The work also depicts contemporary social conditions in Kashmir.

Samaya-parikshe (*c*1150; Kannada) of Brahmashiva: a philosphical kavya work, which seeks to establish the superiority of Jainism by pointing out the flaws and errors in all other forms of belief known to Karnataka of the time. At places its partisan fervour becomes quite harsh; at other places, touches of humour enliven the work. Incidentally, it presents a picture of contemporary life as lived by common people in Karnataka.

Samaya'sundara (*c*1560–1645): poet in Gujarati/Rajasthani. He also wrote scholarly commentaries as well as religious expositions in Sanskrit. Among 30 rasa works attributed by him are *Samba-Pradyumna rasa, Mrigavati charitra chaupai, Punyasara rasa, Valkalchiri rasa*, and so on. He also wrote many hymns and other religious poems.

Sambandha-chinta (?C; Sanskrit) of Samgharakkhita: a grammatical work dealing with Pali syntax.

Sambandhar (6th/7th): Shaiva sant-poet in Tamil and one of the four great Nayanmars; died very young (probably at 16) and is said to have performed several miracles during this short life. His hymns describe the natural beauty of the land where various shrines to Shiva were situated; mention puranic and other episodes associated with the shrines; expound Shaiva Siddanta philosophy in its devotional aspect; call upon the pious to chant the hymns. These Sambandhar set to music and sang them himself. Though popularly known as Sambandhar, his full name was Jnana-sambandhar and is some times referred to as Tiru jnana-sambandar; has also been called Aludaiya Pillaiyar. His 384 compositions have been collected in *Tevaram*.

Samchari-bhava (Sanskrit): see Vyabhichari-bhava.

Samhita (Sanskrit): term meaning 'collection' and traditionally used for the collection of mantras known as the Vedas. According to some orthodox belief, these mantras are of divine origin and were put together in four texts by the legendary Vyas (hence the name Vedavyas). The texts are *Rigved-samhita*, consisting mainly of eulogies; *Yajurved-samhita*, dealing mainly with yajna rituals; *Samaved-samhita*, about music; *Atharvaved-samhita*, with magic and related matters.

Sami [Bhai Chainrai Bachomal Utarani (*c*1743–1850)]: sant-poet in Sindhi from Sikarpur in North Sindh. He composed about 3500 'sloka' verses that were later collected in *Samiaw-ja salok*; originally written in Gurmukhi script, these were transcribed in Adabi-Sindhi by Kaudimal Chandanmal Khilnani and published in four volumes during 1885–90. In some slokas written to honour his guru, Swami Meghraj, the poet called himself Sami.

Samirkumar-vijayamu (18th; Telugu) of Pushpagiri Timmana: kavya work in seven 'aswas' glorifying the devotion and prowess of Hanuman. The poet claimed that Shri Ram had appeared to him in a dream and directed him to write this poem.

Samkhachura-vadh (17th; Asamiya) of Kaviraj Chakrabarti: kavya work. The original manuscript contains illustrations in three colours—red, yellow, ochre, blue.

Samkhitta Taramgavai kaha (Prakrit) or *Samkshipta Tarangavai Katha* (Sanskrit): pre-10th anonymous abridgements of the Prakrit 'katha' in verse, *Taramgavikava*, written by the Jain monk Padalipta in 1st or 2nd century A.D. This abridgement has 1641 verses in gatha metre.

Samkshepa vedartham (1772; Malayalam) of Clement Peanices (1714–82): the first printed book in Malayalam. It is a condensed scripture recast as a dialogue between a teacher and his disciple. It was printed in Rome.

Samkshiptasara (?12th; Sanskrit) of Kramadishwara: grammatical work in eight chapters, of which the eighth deals with Prakrit grammar. It appears to have been modelled on Bhartrihari's *Mahabhashya-dipika* and takes most of its illustrations from *Bhatti-kavya*. The work was particularly popular in western Bengal and the author came to be called 'Vadindra-chakra-chudamani'.

Sammara (Maithili): a term, derived from Sanskrit 'swayamvara', used for long poems in Maithili narrating episodes in which heroines choose their own bridegrooms or are willingly abducted by them. Well-known examples are *Usha-harana* of Chakrapani; the anonymous *Rukmini-swayamvara; Parijata-sammara*, extant in an incomplete manuscript; *Sita-Ram viraha* of Shivadatta.

Samraj (1613–1700): poet in Marathi; obtained the patronage of Shivaji as well as Rajaram. He wrote *Rukmini-haran* and *Mudgalakhyan*, both in Sanskrit kavya style.

Samudrabandh (13th/14th): a scholar of Sanskrit from Kerala who wrote a commentary on Ruyyaka's *Alamkar-sarvaswa*. He was probably a contemporary of Kerala ruler Ravivarma.

Samudra-manthan (13th; Sanskrit) of Vatsaraj: a 'samavakar' play in three acts dealing with the myth of 'samudra-manthan' (=churning of the ocean). Recommended by Bharata in *Natyashastra* as the ideal 'samavakar', it is the only known play of its kind in Sanskrit.

Samukham Venkata Krishnappa (early 18th): prose writer in Telugu; author of works like *Jaimini Bharatamu* and *Sarangadhara-charitramu*, written under the patronage of Vijayaranga Chokkanatha (r. 1706–32); also composed 'santvanam' works like *Radhika-santvanamu* and *Ahilya-santvanamu* which indulge in elaborate descriptions of love.

Samyaktva Kaumudi (*c*1510; Kannada) of Mangaraj: kavya work in shatpadi metre extolling the values of Jainism. This is done by retelling relevant stories drawn from Sanskrit sources.

Samyam-manjari (?C; Apabhramsha) of Maheshwar Suri: a short poetical work consisting of 35 doha verses. As the title suggests, the poem exhorts the virtues of 'samyam' (=self-control) and recommends 17 ways of practising it.

Sanamahi laikan (early 18th; Manipuri) of unknown authorship: prose work which tells the legend of the birth of Sanamahi, household deity of the Meitei poeple. He is born as the son of king Khagemba (1597–1652); when his divine origin becomes known, an idol is cast and worshipped. But when the Vaishnav influence is revived during the reign of king Pamheiba (1709–48), the idol is thrown away. As a result, civic disturbance breaks out; the king orders re-installation of the idol in 1733. Thereafter all forms of community worship is amalgamated and a Hindu form of worship emerges. From this develops a new stream of Manipuri life and culture. The text remained in manuscript form till 20th century.

Sanatkumar-charit (*c*1160; Apabhramsha) of Haribhadra: occupies verse 443 to 785 of this author's *Neminath-charit*. Though part of a larger work, it achieves independent existence as a typical 'charit' work. As in other such 'charit' work in Apabhramsha, Sanatkumar's appearance and brave deeds attract many young women; he indulges in earthly pleasures and also conquers the whole world; eventually, grows tired of achievements and retreats in to a life of eternal tapasya. The whole work is in 'radda' metre. The language contains elements of Old Gujarati which feature GurjarApabhramsha (Paschimi Shauraseni).

Sandesha kavya (Sanskrit): a literary form established by the celebrated *Meghadutam* of Kalidasa. In it, a lover separated from his beloved woman finds some way of sending a message of love to her.

Sandesha rasaka (12th; Apabhramsha) of Abdalla Rahman, an Arabic weaver who lived somewhere on the west coast. The work is a sandesha kavya of 223 verses in 'matra' metre; the language shows the early stage of Gujarati/Rajasthani. Hemchandra has cited this poem in *Siddha Hemavyakarana* as an example of language development: Apabhramsha developing into regional languages.

In the story, the heroine who lives in Vikrampur (in Jaisalmer division of Rajasthan) is separated from her husband who has been away for long to Khambat (on Gujarat coast). She conveys her sorrow through a messenger who is travelling from Multan (in undivided Panjab) to Khambat. The poet was probably born in Multan. The work is also known as *Saneha rasaka*.

Sandham (Tamil): verses composed to achieve the desired effect of sounds.

Sandhi (Sanskrit): term in grammar (for vowel combinations, as in 'vak' + 'artha' = 'vagartha'), also in dramaturgy; in latter, used for a juncture in the action of a drama. Corresponding to five 'avastha' and five 'artha-prakriti', there are five junctures—'mukha' (opening) 'pratimukha' (progression), 'garbha' (development), 'vimarsha' (pause), and 'upasamhara' (conclusion).

Sandhibandha (Apabhramsha): term for narrative poetry in Apabhramsha; corresponds to 'mahakavya' in Sanskrit. More specifically, the major units of a long narrative were called 'sandhi'; each sandhi was made up, in turn, of a number of shorter units called 'kadavaka'.

Sandhu Malo (16th): bardic poet in Rajasthani; obtained the patronage of Raja Rai Singh of Bikaner; wrote 'jhulna' poems and Dingal gits in praise of Rai Singh, Maharana Pratap and Emperor Akbar. His description of the famous battle of Haldighati was rousing but not authentic in many parts.

Sandhu Padma (16th): woman poet in Rajasthani. Betrothed to one Barath Shankar, a ward of Raja Rai Singh of Bikaner, she was abandoned by Shankar after he got a large money grant from the raja. However, the raja's brother Amar Singh gave her shelter and she wrote many gits in Dingal praising his generosity and courage.

Sandhyakar Nandi (1084–1130): poet in Sanskrit from Pundravardhan in northern Bengal. Two works of his have been recovered, *Rampal-charit* and *Ram-charit*, both dealing with Pala king Rampal. In the absence of historical evidence about this period, it is difficult to judge the authenticity of events narrated in these works.

Sangam literature (Tamil): The term 'sangam' (or 'cankam') refers, in relation to ancient literature in Tamil, to literary academies (or assemblies) in Tamilnadu which flourished from fairly remote antiquity. These sangams encouraged poets and apprised their compositions; were supported by Pandyan kings. The earliest mention of these was by Appar in his *Tevaram* but the first detailed (and rather fabulous) account is in Iraiyanar's *Kalaviyal urai*. There were at least three Sangams, the First (attended by 549 poets) at Ten Madurai, the second (59 poets) at Kapatapuram on the east coast, the Third (49 poets) at the present Madurai on the bank of the Vaigai river. The earliest extant Tamil works go back traditionally to the close of the Third Sangam period, about 500 B.C. and later. These works may be that old in their original form; but the language in which they have been preserved cannot be older than A.D. 300. Generally speaking, all Tamil literary composition before 3rd century A.D. is called Sangam literature.

Sangatya (Kannada): name of a popular metre which came into vogue in Kannada in 15th/16th.

Sangharakshit (12th): scholar of poetics in Pali. He lived in Sri Lanka during the reigns of Parakramvahu I and Vijayavahu III; was a disciple of Sariputta and later became head of the Undubargire vihara. Among his works are *Subodhalankar, Vrittodaya, Sambandhachinta*, etc.

Samgit-damodara (15th; Sanskrit) of Subhamkara: treatise dealing with a variety of topics in dance, drama and music. It seeks to attribute the origin of music and drama to Krishna (Damodara) and was very popular among the Vaishnavs of Bengal. The author belonged to this region.

Sangit-darpana (1625; Sanskrit) of Damodara: treatise on North Indian music. It appears to have borrowed freely from the first chapter of *Sangita-ratnakara*, while pictorial descriptions of ragas are based mostly on *Raga-vibodha*. The work was composed during the reign of Jehangir.

Sangit-makaranda (?11th; Sanskrit) of unknown authorship: treatise on music. It is in two parts, 'Sangita' and 'Nritya', of four chapters each. Ragas are divided into two kinds; musical sounds into five kinds according to the source of percussion. According to tradition the work is attributed to Narada, but has been assigned to 11th.

Sangit-parijata (17th; Sanskrit) of Ahobala: treatise on North Indian music. It recognises 29 srutis and gives 122 ragas; for the first time describes the 12 swaras in terms of the length of the string of the veena. It was translated into Farsi around 1724.

Sangit-raja (c1440; Sanskrit) of Kumbha: treatise on music. The work is divided into five chapters named 'Pathya', 'Gita', 'Vadya', 'Nritya' and 'Rasa'; each chapter divided into sections called 'ullasa'; each section divided into sub-sections called 'parikshana'. Altogether there are 16,000 shlokas, each shloka comprising 32 letters.

Sangit-ratnakara (*c*1240; Sanskrit) of Sharangadeva: voluminous treatise on music. Consisting of seven chapters ('adhyaya'), it deals with dance and music, vocal as well as instrumental, and is regarded as the most authoritative work on the subject. The chapters are named 'Swaragatadhyaya', 'Raga-', 'Prakirnaka-', 'Prabandha-', 'Tala-', 'Vadya-' and 'Nartanadhyaya'.

Sangita Madhava-nataka (early 16th; Sanskrit) of Govinda-das: short play on the Radha-Krishna story. This lost work is known only from a few references.

Sanjama-manjari (early 14th; Apabhramsha of Mahesara Suri: didaetic poem, in 35 doha verses, about self-control as the means to salvation. The work is particularly valuable because its exposition quotes profusely from Sanskrit, Prakrit and other Apabhramsha works.

Sanjibchandra Chattopadhyay or **Chatterjee** (1834–89): prose-writer in Bangla and elder brother of Bankimchandra. He wrote novels like *Rameshwarer adrista* (1877), *Kanthamala* (1877), *Jalpratapchand* (1883), *Madhabilata* (1884); but his best-known work is *Palamau* (1880–81), a travel-account.

Sankalpasuryodaya (*c*1300; Sanskrit) of Vedantadeshik: a symbolic drama, the subject of which is the defeat of 'moha' and the rise of 'vivek'. The author was a preponent of Vishista-advaita principles.

Sankardan Samaur (1824–78): charan poet in Rajasthani from Bobasar village in Sujangarh district. Apart from conventional verses in praise of Shakti or Bhairava, he composed many poems on contemporary events and persons, famine caused by locusts, British policy in social matters, etc. These are particularly notable because they reflect the prevailing chaos in the political and economic situation of the time.

Sanketa (Sanskrit): term in poetics

for conventional signification in the use of words. Opinions differ on whether the convention lies in 'jati' (genus) or 'guna' (quality) or 'kriya' (action) or in 'samjna' (name).

Sankusala Nrisimha Kavi (16th): poet in Telugu; said to have been ignored on account of the jealousy of Allasani Peddana; author of *Kavikarna-rasayana*.

Sanskrit: the most important and best-known (since its analysis by western scholars in 19th century) Indo-European language, widely spoken on the Indian subcontinent from about 1500 to 500 B.C. An older of form of the language, later called Vedic, was used composing the vedas, upanishads, brahmanas and aranyakas. The later form, more generally known as Sanskrit, is to be found in *Ramayana* and *Mahabharata*; it was the language used by poets such as Kalidasa, Asvaghosh, Magh, Sriharsha, Bhasa, Shudrak, Bhavabhuti and others. The word 'sanskrit' itself means that which has been refined. The definite form of Sanskrit was described and analysed by Panini in *Ashtadhyayi*, a grammatical work produced probably in 6th century B.C.

Sant-kavi or **Sant-poet** a 'sant', generally, is a pious person; more specifically, a pious person with a certain following, perhaps a sect. Much of the preaching of sants contains illustrative verses composed by them; hence the term 'sant-poet'. The sant believed in one god and gave the greatest importance to his guru; he opposed idolatry, caste systems and communal differences. He addressed the common man in the local speech of the time; hence the contribution of sant-poets to the literary development of a vernacular. In Hindi and related languages, Kabir is the typical sant.

Santalinga Swamikal (18th): sant-poet in Tamil. He probably belonged to Tirtturayur; spent the rest of his life in a hermitage in Tirupporur. Among his poetical works are *Kolai maruttal*, in 22 stanzas; *Vairekkiya dhipam*, in two sections of 50 verses each; *Avirota untiyar*, consisting of 100 three-line stanzas.

Santana Gopala (late 18th; Malayalam) of Mandavapalli Ittiraricha Menon: Kathakali play in eight scenes. The story involves Arjun who, on a visit to Dwaraka, met a brahman all of whose children had died at birth; Arjun promised that the brahman's next child would survive. When it does not, Arjun has to call upon Krishna to save his honour.

Santokh Singh, Bhai (1787–1849): poet in Panjabi and historian. Born in Nur-di-saran village of Amritsar district in undivided Panjab, he studied under Gyani Sant Singh, a well-known Sikh scholar of Amritsar; then spent five years in Kashi studying Sanskrit and Hinduism. He was honoured by Bhagwan Singh, chief of Buria, a Sikh principality near Jagadri (now in Haryana); later moved to Kaithal at the invitation of its chief and settled here. Among his works are *Nama kosh* (1821), a translation of *Amar kosh; Shri Guru Nanak prakash*, a long poem on the life and teachings of the guru; *Garab ganjani* (1829), a commentary on *Japji*; his greatest work, *Gurpratap suraj* (1843), which took eight years to complete. He also translated the Valmiki *Ramayana* into Panjabi. The medium of his literary composition was Braji written in Gurumukhi characters, and he is now acclaimed as the greatest poet in Braji ever produced by Panjab.

Sarab Loh Granth (?C; Panjabi) of disputed authorship: used to be attributed to Guru Govind Singh (d. 1706) but scholars have now inferred from internal evidence that it was composed after the tenth guru's death. Also known as *Mangla-charan puran* and *Sarab Loh*, this is a poetical work in five chapters, each of which describes a battle between a god or goddess or hero and demons. The fifth and longest chapter has Sarab Loh, an incarnation of Mahakal, coming to the rescue of the gods. The language is mainly Braji but other languages have also been used, making it difficult for the common reader.

Saradatilaka (11th; Sanskrit) of Lakshmana Desika: work on tantra, which begins with a theory of creation and the origin of human speech.

Saraha: see Sarhapa. He has also been referred to as Saroruhavajra, Sarojavajra, Padmavajra and Rahulabhadra.

Sarala Dasa (14th): the first great poet in Oriya. A 'chasa' (peasant) by caste, he had no knowledge of Sanskrit. According to legend one day while ploughing he felt inspired to write poetry and attempted not a song or a ballad but a version of *Mahabharata* in Oriya. Since he had no access to the original, he must have had to depend on what he had heard at recitals. When he wrote he believed he was being directed by the goddess Sarala, a local deity. He called himself Sarala Dasa (=servant of Sarala) rather than by his ancestral name, Siddheswar Parida. He composed two other works, *Vilanka Ramayan* and *Chandi-purana*. These three works provided the foundation for the use of Oriya as a literary language as opposed to Sanskrit. Sarala Dasa lived during the reign of Suryavamsi king Kapilendra Deva (1435–66).

Sarala Mahabharat (14th; Oriya): the adaptation of *Mahabharata* by Sarla Dasa. It is neither a translation nor an imitation but an adaptation which turns *Mahabharata* into a rural text, unfamilar with Sanskrit literature, whose characters are ordinary people living in the Orissa country side. Shri Krishna has a small role in the narrative; Bhim is the most heroic figure; the parvan are not named the same as in the Sanskrit text. Altogether, it is an original work, indicative of the awakening of regional culture consciousness in this part of India. No other Indian language had produced an 18-book *Mahabharata* prior to this.

Sarangadhar Charitramu (17th; Telugu) of Chemkur Venkat-kavi: kavya-work in three 'aswas' portraying the illicit love Chitrangi bore towards Sarangadharudu although she was married to Rajarajendrudu. With some revisions, the story has been performed very often as a play.

Sarangadhar-paddhati (14th; Hindi) of Sarangadhar: anthology of verse. In his own verses Sarangadhar often introduced 'desi' speech along with Sanskrit.

Sarangu Tammayya (early 17th): poet in Telugu; friend of Quli Qutb Shah, ruler at Golkonda; composed the celebrated love poem *Vaijayanti-vilasam.*

Saras Gita (end-18th; Gujarati) of Pritamdas: a 'bhramar-kavya' work which draws upon an episode from *Bhagavathapuranam.*

Saraswati-kantthavaran (early 11th; Sanskrit) of Bhojraj: work on poetics. It contains 643 'karika' divided into five 'parichhed'; the opinions of older scholars about poetic elements have been discussed and new principles proposed.

Sarhapa (?7th/8th): poet in Apabhramsha; foremost among the 84 siddhas who belonged to the Vajrayan sect of Bouddhas. Originally named Rehulbhadra (then Sarojvajra, when he became a monk), he retired to the forest near Nalanda (in Bihar) and lived with the daughter of an arrow-maker. Because he too began making arrows (=sara) he came to be known as Saraha, later Sarahapa ('pa' being the honourable suffix of siddhas). He is said to be the author of about 32 works; among these are: *Kaya-kos, Chitra-kos, Dakini-guhya vajra-giti, Doha-kos upades-giti, Charya-giti doha-kos*, etc. His *Charya-giti* poems are in eastern Apabhramsha while the *Doha-kos* poems are in western Apabhramsha. He is sometimes regarded as the first writer of Hindi.

Sariputra-prakaran (early 1st; Sanskrit): comic play ascribed to Ashvaghosh. From an incomplete text copied on a palmleaf MS found in Central Asia, it has been inferred that the play was in nine acts. Middle-class life portrayed here includes burglars, drunkards, gamblers, prostitutes, etc. Buddha's accepting Modgalayan and Sariputra as disciples is mentioned at one place. The Prakrit used in the play has been regarded as somewhat older than the literary Prakrit used in better-known texts.

Sarmaye-e-zuban-e-Urdu (18th; Urdu) of Hakim Saiyad Zamin Ali 'Jalal': dictionary which includes exemplary sentences, popular sayings and terminology. In explaining the meanings of words that have gone out of use, the lexicographer has indicated different pronunciations of such words. Famous ancient poets and writers have been quoted. Special attention has been paid to words used only by women.

Sarphoji Bhosale (1777–1832): also known as Sarabhendra Bhupale, was a poet in Marathi and ruler of Thanjavur from 1798 to 1832. Educated by a German missionary, he spoke English fluently; apart from Sanskrit and Marathi, he knew Telugu and Tamil. He collected many valuable MSS which are now preserved in the Saraswati Mahal Library at Thanjavur. He wrote narrative poetry, Yakshagana plays, dance-verses, a travelogue, a book on medicine. Among his works in Marathi are *Nilakanttha kulalvara charitra, Nilabhilla charitra, Kiratarjuniya, Panchakshari vibhuti Shivaratri katha, Uma Maheshwara varta.*

Sarphoji Maharaj (late 18th/early 19th): a prince of the Bhosla family, adopted (in 1781) by Maharaja Tulaji Rao of Thanjavur as his successor. After becoming ruler (in 1798), he devoted much time and money in establishing the famous library at Thanjavur. Also, he got English books translated into Marathi and printed.

Sarur: see Rajab Ali Baig 'Sarur'. This assumed name has also been used by Monshi Durge Sahay (1873–1910) of Jahanabad in Bihar and by Aley Ahmad (b. 1912) of Badaun in Uttar Pradesh.

Sarvajna (?14th): playwright in Sanskrit; may be the same as Simhabhupala, who is known by various other names. He wrote the play *Kuvalvali* or *Ratnapanchalika*; also *Sangit-sudhakara*, a commentary on Sarangadeva's *Sangit-ratnakara*.

Sarvajna (16th/17th): poet in Kannada who was popular enough at one time to be regarded as the national poet of Karnataka. Yet nothing is known about his life except that he was born in Ambalur village of Dharwar district; even his original name is not known, 'Sarvajna' being in all likelihood a title conferred upon him. His poems, mostly in 'tripadi' metre, have been collected in *Sarvajnan-vachanagalu*.

Sassi-Punnu: main characters of a folk-tale of Punjab, probably of Sindhi origin. In Sindh, they were known as Sasui and Punhu.

Satbara (Panjabi): a poetical form like the 'barah-masa'; here each day of the week is used to describe the woes of separation of lover from beloved. A version of this is the 'attbara' where a Sunday begins as well as ends the week, making eight days.

Sati Moyna: see Lor-Candrani.

Satravamshavali (Asamiya): verse as well as prose accounts of the heads of 'satra' (centres for religious propagation).

Sattaka (Prakrit): a form of drama, variant of the Sanskrit 'natika' as illustrated by *Karpura-manjari* of Rajashekhara. Bharata's *Natyashastra* does not mention this form.

Sattanar or **Sittalai Sattanar** (?C): poet in Tamil, author of *Manimikalai*. A grain-dealer by profession, Sattanar came to Madurai and was enrolled as a Sangam poet because of his proficiency in verse-composition; some stray verses of his are to be found in Sangam anthologies. It is said he was present in Madurai when the Kovalan story took place and he saw parts of the city in flames. Leaving Madurai he went to Vanchi, where he narrated the events to Chera king Senguttuvan and his brother IIango Adigal. In his own work Sattanar propounds Bouddha philosophy enthusiastically, hence it is assumed he was a Buddhist by faith.

Saturakarathi (1732; Tamil) of Father Beschi, also known as Veeramamunivar: a dictionary giving in four parts, 'Peyarakarathi' (word meanings), 'Porulakarathi' (synonyms and homonyms), 'Togaiakarathi' (compound words), and 'Todaikarathi' (rhyming words).

Though the work was completed in 1732, only the second part was published in 1819, then the whole in 1824.

Satvara: form of poetry in Panjabi.

Satyabhama-Santvanamu (*c*1660; Telugu) of Kameshwara Kavi: work which marks the beginning of the erotic 'santwanam' kavyas in Telugu literature. The story, derived from *Mahabharata*, tells of Satyabhama's woe in separation while Shri Krishna has gone away to slay Narakasur; after killing the asur, Krishna releases his 16,000 wives and marries them. This angers Satyabhama no end and Krishna has to exert a lot to mollify her.

Satyapirer panchali (Bangla): a form of religious poetry in West and North Bengal which developed in 18th, having to do with a new local deity called Satyanarain by Hindus and Satya Pir by Muslims. The writers of these poems were all Hindus. Among them were Ghanaram Kaviratna, Rameshwar Bhattacharya, Bharatchandra Raye.

Satyavati-ki katha (1489 or 1517; Hindi) of Ishwardas: perhaps the first kavya work in the language.

Sauda: see Mohammed Rafi Sauda.

Saundarananda (?1st; Sanskrit) of Aswaghosa: narrative poems in 18 sections. It deals with the conversion, by Buddha, of his half-brother Nanda, also called Sundara.
Tr. E.H. Johnston, London, 1928.

Saundarya-lahari (8th; Sanskrit) of Shankaracharya: a devotional poem of about 1000 verses in 'shikharini' metre. The first part, entitled Anandalahari, deals with tantric philosophy; the second part, carrying the main title, describes the beauty of Shakti (goddess). A favourite with scholars, there are more than 30 commentaries on it in Sanskrit.

Sayalavithi-vihana kavya (11th; Apabhramsha) of Muni Nayanandi: narrative poem in 58 'sandhi', which uses a large variety of metres. The author was from Dhar in the Malwa region and he also composed *Sudarshana-Chariu*.

Sayan (1315–87): scholar of Sanskrit, lived mostly in Vijayanagar kingdom. His main work is a commentary on the Vedas, sometimes referred to as "Sayan-bhashya". A feature of this work is that he has given all possible meanings of the more important words, thus allowing a reader of the Vedas to choose the meaning that he finds appropriate.

Sekasubhodaya (*c*1550; Bangla): earliest record of the tradition of Muslim pirs in Bengal. The work is written in a hybrid Sanskrit-Bangla language. Many of the stories relate to the spiritual powers of Sheikh Jalaluddin, who is said to have come to Bengal during the reign of Lakshmansena (late 12th).

Sekkilar (12th): Shaiva scholar and poet in Tamil; author of *Periya-puranam*. It is said that Sekkilar undertook this in order to wean away Chola king Kulottonga II's admiration for a 'heretical' work like *Jivaka chintamani*. Originally named Arulmoli Tevar, the poet was born into a Velala family of Kunrattur village; became a minister in the court of Kulottonga II; went to Chidambaram to write *Periya-puranam*: was later himself canonised and the work got included in the sacred canon.

Senpati (b. 1589): poet in Brajbhasa from Anupsahar in Panjab; author of *Kavi-ratnakar* and *Kavya-kalpadrum*; particularly admired because of his alamkar devices. He lived in Brindavan but was devoted to Shri Rama.

Senapati, **F.M.** see Fakirmohan Senapati.

Senavaraiyar (?13th): scholar of Sanskrit poetics; wrote a commentary on *Tolkappiyam*. Only a part of this (relating to the second book of *Tolkappiyam*) is available, but it was enough to establish his importance as a literary critic.

Setu mahatmya (18th; Malayalam) of Raghava Pisaroti: poem on the Rameshwaram temple.

Setubandha (5th/6th; Prakrit) of Pravarsen: kavya work in 15 'aswas' retelling the *Ramayana* story from Shri Ram's departure for Lanka to his return to Ayodhya and coronation. The language is Maharashtri Prakrit. The work, also known as *Ravana-vaha* or *Dahamuha-vaha*, was cited by Dandin in his *Kavyadarsha*.

Shabad (Panjabi): the term used for all the hymns in *Adi Granth*. Derived from the Sanskrit work *shabda* (=sound), 'shabad' pertains to the vibrations of the word uttered by the Guru.

Shabara Shankara-vilas (*c*1660; Kannada) of Shadakshardeva: a champu kavya in five 'aswas' based on a *Mahabharata* episode in which Arjun obtains the Pashupat-astra from Shiva. The poet was a Virshaiva, hence in this poem Shankara (Shiva) figures more prominently than Arjun.

Shabda-kalpadrum (7 vols, 1818–58; Sanskrit/Bangla) of Raja Radhakanta Deb, an orthodox Hindu socio-religious Sanskrit leader of Bengal. He organised this compilation work, which took 33 years to complete, in order to facilitate the study and teaching of Sanskrit in Bengal. In this lexicon of Sanskrit, words have been analysed into their base-forms; in some cases Bangla equivalents have been given.

Shabdamani-darpan (late 13th; Kannada) of Keshiraj: A grammar of Kannada which takes into account earlier grammars. It has eight 'adhyaya' (chapters); as in comparable works in Sanskrit, the 'sutra' portions are in verse while the 'vritti' portions are in prose.

Shabda-rasayan (late 17th/early 18th; Hindi) of Dev or Devadatta: work on poetics on the model of Sanskrit works like *Kavya-prakash, Sahitya-darpan*, etc. The author was a well-known poet in the riti tradition.

Shabdavritti (Sanskrit): the power or nature of a word by which the word indicates its meaning.

Shad Azimabadi (b. 1846): poet in Urdu from Patna (Azimabad) who studied not only Islam but also the faith of Hindus, Parsis and Christians. He excelled in marsiya and ghazal compositions. His collected poems *Nagm-e-ilham* do not convey his real worth as a poet because bad poems have been collected along with the good.

Shadakshari or **Shadakshar Dev** (mid-17th) Virshaiva poet in Kannada, known mainly for his champu-kavya works. These are *Rajshekhara-vilas, Sabara Shankara-vilas, Besavaraj-vijay* or *Vrishabhendra-vijay*, and *Virbhadra-dandak*. He is among the more learned poets of his time.

Shah Abdul Karim (1537–1626): poet in Sindhi from Tulari village; composed 'bait' poems of Sufi inspiration while remaining a householder and attending to his lands. Only 93 baits were recovered when, about six years after his death, his disciple Miyan Muhammad Raza included them in a book in Farsi entitled *Bayan-al-arifin va Tambih-al-Gafilin*. This book gives an account of his life.

Shah Abdul Latif (1689–1752): leading Sufi poet in Sindhi. Born in Hala Haveli village of Haidarabad (Sindh) district, he does not seem to have received any formal education; but he travelled a great deal in Sindh and nearby provinces with Sufi darveshes, other sanyasis and yogis. After his father's death, he made a home for himself, relations and disciples atop a 'bhit' (hillock); for this he came to be known as 'Shah Latif Bhitai'. His poetical works have been collected in the volume *Shah-jo risalo*.

Shah Ali Mohammad Jan Gamodhani (d.1575): poet in Dakhni from Gujarat; author of *Jawahirul-asar*.

Shah Husain (*c*1539–99): Sufi poet in Panjabi from Lahore; also known as Lal Husain because he always wore 'lal' (=red) clothes. He composed kafiya, shabad and doha poems, but was known mainly for his kafiya compositions.

Shah Inayat Allah Rizvi (1626–*c*1713): poet in Sindhi whose importance was realized only in mid-20th century when his verses were collected and it was demonstrated that his work had successfully blended Sufi elements with the 'charan' kavi tradition.

Shah-jo risalo (late 18th; Sindhi): collected works of Sindh's most famous poet, Shah Abdul Lalif. The poems are presented in various sections known as 'sur'. The work has run into many editions and is perhaps the most widely known work in the language.

Shah Muhammad (1782–1862): poet in Panjabi from Badala in Amritsar district. His father was a poet as was his son; many relations of his served in the court of Maharaja Ranjit Singh. His most substantial poetical work. *Jangnama sindha-te firangi-da* is popularly known as "Qissa Muhammad Shah"; it glorfies the bravery of Panjabis as displayed in Sikh-British battles of early 19th century.

Shah Saraf (*c*1724–94): poet in Panjabi from Batala in Gurudaspur district; composed poems in the Sufi tradition mostly in 'dohira' and 'kafi' forms.

Shahr-ashob (Urdu): a kind of poem describing the decay of a city, province or country. The poets Sauda and Mir excelled in such compositions.

Shair (Urdu): term for poet.

Shairkh Ganjulim (d. 1393): sometimes regarded as the earliest known writer of Dakhni. But his works, mainly religious tracts, have never been found.

Shakir Nazi [Saiyad Muhammad Shakir 'Nazi' (17th)]: poet in Urdu, also a warrior; served under an official of Mughal king Muhammad

Shah. When Nadir Shah invaded India, Nazi fought against him.

Shaktibhadra (?9th): playwright in Sanskrit; author of *Ascharya-chudamani*. Some scholars claim that two Bhasa plays, *Abhisheka* and *Pratima-nataka*, were written by Shaktibhadra; others believe that the play *Pratijna-yougandharayana*, attributed by some to Bhasa, was written by Shaktibhadra under the title of *Unmada-Vasavadatta*. He has referred to himself in the prologue to *Ascharya-chudamani* as a native of Dakshinpatha (South India).

Shakuntala (*c*1730; Asamiya) of Kaviraja Chakravarti: a kavya work composed at the behest of Ahom king Shivasimha (r. 1714–44) and his queen Phuleshwari. The narrative consists of two stories, one concerning Shakuntala, the other concerning Chandraketu and Kamakala. Chandraketu, king of Raktarati, saw Kamakala in a dream; similarly, princess Kamakala of Bhadravati saw Chandraketu in a dream; they long for each other and are united in the end. The tale shows indirect influence of Sufism.

Shakuntala-parinayamu (late 15th; Telugu) of Pinavirabhadrudu: an adaptation of *Abhijnan Shakuntalam*, with some changes, into kavya form.

Shalok (Panjabi):a popular metre of older Panjabi poetry, derived from the 'anushtup' metre of shlokas in Sanskrit. The section of *Guru Granth Sahib* entitled 'shalik' contains numerous verses in this metre.

Shalok-Farid: collective title of the 112 verses of Baba Farid included in *Granth Sahib*. These are the oldest samples of 'shalok' metre in Panjabi poetry.

Shamal (1636–1714): poet in Gujarati, esp. known for his 'varta' composition and recitation. Most of his poems relate to the contemporary social situation in Gujarat villages. Among his works are *Padmavati-ni varta, Simhasan battrisi, Nand battrisi, Vetal pachisi, Madan Mohna, Vinechar-ni varta, Rakhidas charitra, Shivapuran khanda, Angad vishti, Ravan'Mandodari samvad, Suda bahoteri.*

Shamsul-ushaq Shah Miranji (d. 1496): writer in Dakhni from Bijapur. Among his prose pamphlets are *Sharah marghoobul gulub* and *Gulbas*; among his poems, *Khush-nama* and *Khush-nagz*.

Shankara digvijay (1400; Sanskrit) of Madhavacharya: a verse-biography of Shankara in 16 'sarga'. It offers a convenient summary of

Shankara's religious and philosophic principles.

Shankara Panicker (late 14th): one of the Kannassan poets in Malayalam; composed *Bharatmala*, probably the first major work in the language based on *Mahabharata*.

Shankaradeva (*c*1449–1568): Vaishnav reformer and poet of Assam, who started a regional form of the pan-Indian bhakti movement. He composed 27 works in all, among which are translations into Asamiya of the last 'kanda' of *Ramayana* and portions of *Bhagavat-purana*; is said to have innovated the 'ankiya-nat' form in drama and the 'bar-git' form in poetry. His longer poetical works are *Rukmini-haran, Uddhav-samvad, Pashanda-mardan, Kurukshetra, Bali-chhalan, Ajamil-upakhyan, Bhakti-pradip, Anadipatan, Nimin-Vasishtha samvad, Gunamal*. Among his dramatic works are *Chinna-yatra, Patni-prasad, Kaliya-daman, Keli-Gopal, Rukmini-haran nat, Rama-vijay nat, Parijat-haran*. His most popular works are the kirtans composed by him; these were as widely known in Assam as *Ramcharitmanas* in Hindi-speaking areas.

Shankuka (early 9th): scholar and poet in Sanskrit; wrote an interpretation of Bharata's 'rasa-sutra', known as "Anumiti-vada". He may be the same Shankuka as the poet who is mentioned, along with his poem *Bhuvanabhyudaya*, by Kalhana in *Rajatarangini*. Shankuka lived at the time of king Ajitapida of Kashmir.

Shanti parva (18th; Asamiya) of Lakshminath Dvija: a verse rendering of this parvan of *Mahabharata*. It is notable partly because while all other parvan of *Mahabharata* had been rendered into Asamiya by 17th, the 'Shanti parva' was generally ignored by Vaishnav poets because it somehow did not agree with their world view. However, Lakshminath Dvija, although a Vaishnav himself, undertook to translate the sections dealing with 'Raj dharma', etc. Thus, it is a highly selective rendering.

Shanti-purana (10C: Kannada) of Ponna: champu work in 16 'aswas' dealing with Shantinath, the 16th tirthankar. The first nine 'aswas' describe Shantinath's 11 earlier births.

Shantishvar-purana (*c*1225; Kannada) of Kamalbhava: champu work in 18 'aswas' dealing with Shantinath. Some critics judge this to be better than Ponna's work on the same subject.

Sharadatanaya (12th): scholar of Sanskrit poetics; author of *Bhava-prakashana* which compiles the whole range of views on literature from Bharata (?2nd) to Kshemendra (11th). The author also incorporated views on music and dance, especially about the origin and development of these forms. It has not yet been possible to establish firmly his dates or the places where he was born and lived.

Sharngadeva (early 13th): authority on dance and music; wrote *Sangita-ratnakara*. Son of Sodhala and grandson of Bhaskara, his ancestors came from Kashmir, but he appears to have been a resident of Yajnapura village in northern Maharashtra. His patron was the Yadava king Singhana who ruled at Devagiri (1210–47); Sharngadeva was the king's chief accountant.

Shashanka-vijayamu (18th; Telugu) of Shesha Venkatapati: kavya work in five 'aswas' telling of the romance between the moon-god Chandra and a housewife named Tara. Erotic elements predominate in this work, sometimes in violation of propriety.

Shashisena (late 16th; Oriya) of Pratapa Raya: the only known work of this poet. It is an 'akhayika' in 14 sections, which tells of the princess Shashisena, her secret marriage with the Naga king's son Ahimanikya, and the adventures that follow thereafter. The work is unique inasmuch as it is a kavya based on a folk-tale of Orissa.

Shashisena (end-17th; Marathi) of Jagannath Kavi: long narrative in verse, which does not acknowledge any debt to Pratap Raya's kavya (see above) but uses the same hero and heroine. In the city state of Amaravati, the chief minister's son Ahimanikya and princess Shashisena are fellow-pupils of the same tutor. They fall in love and decide to marry but are opposed by their respective parents. They run away (with Shashisena in male dress) from Amaravati and undergo much hardship before they can settle down to peaceful married life.

Shashthi-mangal (1679; Bangla) of Krishnaramadas: narrative poem which seeks to establish the worship of goddess Shashthi deity of children's welfare.

Shastra (Sanskrit): a term denoting a genre as well as a species. It primarily meant scriptures or texts commanding religious authority; in its wider meaning the term is used for any department of knowledge or science. Thus, *Nyaya-shastra, Tarka-shastra*, etc.

Shata-prashnottari (*c*1570; Hindi) of Manohar: collection of doha verses. The poet was in the court of Akbar.

Shatikkachuppulvar (*c*1686–1723): poet in Tamil: associated with the court of Setupati kings of Ramnathpuram. He composed a sequence of 100 poems entitled *Tonttaimanhal shatakam* which provides much information about the society of the time in a part of northern Tamilnadu.

Shatrunjaya (18th; Asamiya) of Raghunath Mahanta: kavya work which discribes various explicits of the Vanara king Bali.

Shauq Tasadduq Husain Khan (1782–1871): poet in Urdu from Lakhnau. A practitioner of Yunani medicine, he was one of the court-physicians of Wajid Ali Shah and was popularly known as Hakim Nawab Mirza. He was a composer of masnavi works with erotic content, such as *Fareb-e-Ishq* (*c*1840), *Bahar-e-Ishq* (1849), *Zabar-e-Ishq* (1860).

Shauraseni: a dialect of Prakrit, spoken around Mathura in western modern Uttar Pradesh (area known in olden times as Madhyadesh). According to *Natyashastra*, the dialect used in a Sanskrit play should be Shauraseni and women characters should speak it. One of the earliest and best known works composed in this dialect is *Pavayanasara* of Kundakunda (1st).

Sheik Chilli: an imaginary person in many Hindi tales. He was a fool and there are many sayings about him.

Sheikh Khub Mohammad (early 16th): poet in Dakhni from Gujarat; author of *Khub-tarany*.

Sheir (Urdu): a poem or poetic statement in two lines; each line is called a 'misrah'.

Shibnath Shastri (1847–1919): writer in Bangla, educationist and social reformer. Born in Majilpur village of West Bengal into a Bhattacharya brahman family, he became a Brahmo in 1869 and also obtained the degree of 'shastri' on qualifying as a scholar of Sanskrit. Associated with many educational and religious institutions, he published *Mukul*, a highly successful pictorial magazine for children. He wrote poems, novels, essays, and a history of the Brahmo Samaj; but his best-known work is *Ramtanu Lahiri o tatkalin Banga samaj* (1897), a work of socio-religious history.

Shilanka (9th): poet in Prakrit. He wrote *Chauppana-mahapuri sachariya*, (868), the first work in Prakrit on the lives of illustrious persons aimed at setting models and thereby improving the moral life of people. The poet refers to himself also as Vimalamati and as Shilacharya. Perhaps he was originally called Vimalamati, was re-named Shilacharya when he became a monk, and gave himself the name Shilanka for his literary efforts.

Shilpa-ratna (16th; Sanskrit) of Shikumara: treatise in two parts on art and architecture. The first part is in 46 sections; deals with the construction of houses, villages, etc. The second part deals with iconography and allied topics. The author belonged to Kerala and was a protege of king Devanarayana.

Shilvati-ras (*c*1695; Gujarati) of Nemivijay, a Jain poet: prose kavya in which secular interest overrides the religious purpose.

Shirin-Farhad: main characters of a popular folk-story of Panjab, the subject of several qissa works.

Shirukkappiyam (Tamil): name of a literary form. These are poems that contain some elements of a mahakaya but never all.

Shishu-veda (?C; Oriya) of unknown authorship: ascribed by some scholars to Gorakhnath. An early work dealing with tantric themes, it has prose commentaries following each verse. This is the earliest extant literary prose in Oriya.

Shisupala-vadha (?7th/8th; Sanskrit) of Magha: mahakavya in 20 'sarga' based on a *Mahabharata* episode in which Shri Krishna kills the Chedi king shishupala.

Shishupala-vadha (14th; Marathi) of Bhaskaracharya or Bhaskar Bhatta: narrative poem on a *Mahabharata* episode. This is often regarded as the first truly literary work in Marathi.

Shishushankar Dasa (late 16th) poet in Oriya; author of *Ushabhilasha*. In this work he may be said to have innovated the ornate kavya style which became popular as courtly poetry in Oriya a century later.

Shitala-mangal (Bangla): a kind of mangal-kavya in honour of Shitala, the goddess of pox and other diseases.

Shitikantha Acharya (early 13th): poet in Kashmiri. According to some scholars he is the earliest known poet in the language and his *Mahanaya-prakasha* is the first literary text composed in Kashmiri. He was a Shaiva by faith and in this work he succeeded in using Kashmiri as a vehicle of philosophic expression.

Shiv Prasad, Raja (1823–95): writer in Hindi, but a scholar of many languages viz., Sanskrit, Farsi, Urdu, Bangla, English. Born at Banaras into a Parmar kshatriya family of Ranthambor (Rajasthan) which moved to Murshidabad (Bengal) before coming to Banaras, Shiv Prasad served the British in various capacities; earned from them the title of C.S.E. (Sitare-Hind) in 1870, later of Raja in 1874. He was editor of *Banaras akhbar* and *Shimla akhbar*; contributed poems in Urdu to *Awadh akhbar*; propagated the use of Hindi in administration; wrote a history of India in three parts, *Itihas timir-nashak*. Among his other works are *Bhugol hastamalak* (1855), *Vir Singh-ka vrittant* (1855), *Aaisiyon-ka koda* (1856), *Vama-manoranjan* (1856), *Man-bahalav* (1860), etc.

Shivalagan (*c*1850; Kashmiri) of Paramanand: poem in 380 stanzas telling the story of Shiva's wedding with Parvati. While retaining the puranic story and its basic details, the poet has interwoven elements of human concern to make it a philosophic poem as well.

Shivakalyana (17th): poet in Marathi: generally composed narrative poems. One of these, based on the 10th 'skandha' of *Bhagavat-purana*, dwells upon the amours of Shri Krishna in details bordering on the obscene.

Shivappirakasar (17th): poet in Tamil from Kanchipuram. Among his works are *Somasailamalai*, set in Tiruvannamalai; *Tiruvengai-kkovai* and *Tiruvengaikkalam-bakam*, both celebrating the deity of Tiruvengai; *Kuvattala-puranam*, a sthalapurana of Kuram; *Kalatti-puranam*, which celebrates Kalahasti (Andhra Pradesh). The last-named work was left incomplete by him.

Shivarajbhushan (*c*1670; Hindi) of Bhushan: work in poetics wherein all examples are verses in praise of Maratha king Shivaji who became the poet's patron. Through such examples, Bhushan manages to give an account of the 1713–30 period of Shivaji's reign, describing military as well as political events.

Shivaratri-mahatmyamu

(14th/15th; Telugu) of Shrinathudu: prabandha kavya, the story of which is drawn from the

'Ishansamhita' portion of *Skandhapurana*. The work is in five 'aswas'. In the first aswas, after the pre-eminence of Shiva over Brahma and Vishnu has been asserted, Shiva himself takes over the exposition and explains the importance of Shivaratri. The other four aswas tell the story of Sukumar, son of Yajnadatta, the chief minister of Ratnapuri.

Shiva'samkirtan (1710; Bengali) of Rameshwar Bhattacharya: narrative poem which deals with the Shiva-Parvati episode that generally prefaces a Chandi-mangal poem. The poet's keen observation reveals the low level of agrarian economy in South-west Bengal.

Shivasingh Sengar (1833–78): scholar in Hindi; author of *Shiva Saroj*, which is sometimes regarded as the first history of Hindi literature. About one thousand poets have been listed here, along with some information about their life and works. However, this information has not always proved reliable.

Shivatattva-saramu (12th; Telugu) of Mallikarjun Panditaradha: a sequence of 108 poems ('shatakamu') expounding a particular variety of Shaiva faith. Though the subject is religious, the literary importance of the work lies in its being the oldest known 'shatakamu' in the language.

Shivayana (1750: Bangla) of Rameswar Bhattacharya: the name of Ramaram Das is also associated with this work, which is a mangalkavya, one of the few Shaiva literary works in Bangla of this period. There is however no propagation of Shiva here: it describes the household of Shiva and Parvati and their social life. The divine pair is portrayed here as a peasant couple, and their life in a Bengal village reflects the realities of rural life in mid-17th century Bengal.

Shloka: the basic verse-line in Sanskrit.

Shodasha (Oriya): a poetical form.

Shraddharam Phullouri (1837–81): prose-writer in Panjabi and Hindi. He is important in the history of Panjabi literature because he sought to fashion modern Panjabi prose and wrote two books to demonstrate this, *Sikha-de raj-di vidhiya* and *Panjabi batchit*. He is also notable in the history of Hindi fiction because his work *Bhagyavati* is considered by some scholars as the first original novel in Hindi.

Shri Venkatesh Kalyan (?17th; Knk): one of the oldest poems in the language, which was first printed in Maḷayalam script. Because of Portuguese persecution in Goa, many Saraswat brahmans fled from there and took along their idols. Some settled in port-towns of Kerala, the largest number in Kochi. The Saraswat chief of Kumbhakonam mutth visited them in 1589 and presented them an idol of Shri Venkateshwara. This was installed in a temple and they became devotees of this god thereafter. The poem may have been composed originally about this time.

Shrichandra (*c*1100): poet in Apabhramsha author of *kathakasa*. He was probably the preceptor of Haribhadra.

Shricandra Bharati: another name assumed by Ananta Kandali.

Shridhar (1678–1728): poet in Marathi: author of *Pandava-pratap*, *Hari-vijay*, and *Rama-vijay*.

Shridhar (late 17th): also known as Muralidhar, he was a riti poet in Hindi from Prayag (Ilahabad). He wrote *Jangnama*, description of a battle between Farruksiyar and Jahandar; also composed *Nayika-bhed* and *Chitra-kavya*.

Shridhar Kandali (16th): poet in Asamiya who composed a metaphysical poem about Krishna using the folk-tale of the 'Kankhowa' (ear-eater). The poem became so popular that it came to be used as a lullaby.

Shridhar Vyas (14th/15th): poet in Rajasthani/Gujarati; author of *Ranmall chhand*, *Ishwar-chhanda* and *Saptashati*. A translation of the 10th skandha of *Bhagavat-purana* has also been attributed to him.

Shridhara Dasa (12th): scholar of Sanskrit, perhaps from Orissa. He compiled the earliest extant 'kosha kavya' (anthology), *Sadukti-karnamrita*, and initiated a new genre in Sanskrit literature. From his own account his father Vatudasa was a scribe and feudatory chief under Bengal ruler Lakshmansen. The poet himself was the administrative head of a district.

Shridhara swamin (*c*1300): Gujarati scholar of Sanskrit; author of *Bhavartha-dipika*, a commentary on *Bhagavat-purana*; also wrote commentaries on *Vishnu-purana* and *Bhagavat Gita*.

Shriharsha (early 7th): playwright in Sanskrit; author of *Ratnavali*, *Priyadarshika*, and *Nagananda*. He has been identified by many scholars with *Harshavardhana*, king of Thaneswhar, in the first half of 7th.

Shriharsha (late 12th): poet in Sanskrit; author of *Naishadha-charita*; also wrote the philosophical work *Khandanakhandakhadya*. He probably lived during the reigns of Vijayachandra and Jayachandra, rulers of Kanyakubja (Kanauj)

Shrikantha-charita (*c*1140; Sanskrit) of Mankha: mahakavya in 20 sections dealing with the puranic episode of the destruction of Tripura by Shiva. From the work we learn that the poet's brother, Alankara, was a minister of king Jayasimha of Kashmir (1127–50). The poet was a pupil of Ruyyaka.

Shrikara Nandi (16th): poet in Bangla at the court of Nasrat Khan, son of Pargal Khan. He was commissioned by the ruler to render a fuller version of *Mahabharata* into Bangla than the one done by Parameshwar Das.

Shrikrishna-charitam (early 18th; Malayalam) of Kunchun Nambiar: a re-telling of the Sanskrit work *Shrikrishna-vijaya* of Shankara Varier.

Shrikrishna gitavali (*c*1571; Hindi) of Tulsidas: collection of 61 unrelated poems in praise of Shri Krishna.

Shrikrishnakinkar (early 17th): poet in Bangla; elder brother Kashiram Das. He became a Vaishnav recluse and wrote a narrative poem following *Shrimad Bhagavat*.

Shrikrishnakirtan (16th; Bangla) of Badu Chandidas: extant only in a single and mutilated MS, the work is unique in many respects. Not a narrative poem, it is the nearest approach to dramatic poetry in Middle Bangla. The story is carried entirely through songs by the three characters (Krishna, Radha, Badai); the songs are generally connected by single or double verses in Sanskrit. The tone of the poem is human rather than devotional. The pair of lovers are common human beings, rather crude and unsophisticated. The available MS has been dated 16th but the original work may be older. The colophon mentions Badu Chandidas or Ananta Badu Chandidas as the poet.

Shrikrishna-mangal (16th; Bangla) of Madhav Acharya or Madhav Mishra: possibly a disciple of Shri Chaitanya. The work is an adaptation of the last three skandha of *Bhagavat-purana*, to which have been added stories from *Vishnu-purana*, *Harivamsha* and other sources. Popular semi-religious performances of Bengal such as 'dan-lila' and 'nauka-lila' have been described here.

Shrikrishna-vijay (1480; Bangla) of Maladhar Bosu: earliest narrative poem in Bangla, also the oldest Bangla poem on the Krishna legend. It is also known as "Gobinda-vijay" or "Gobinda-mangal" or 'Srikrishna-mangal'. The work, was undertaken under the patronage of a Muslim ruler of Bengal, Ruknuddin Barbak Shah. The poem is entirely narrative, written for the masses, and the tone is entirely devotional. It was so popular that Shri Chaitanya heard it frequently in his early years; by end-17th it was superseded by more popular poems on the same theme.

Shrikrishna-vilas (17th; Bangla) of Shrikrishnakinkara or Krishnakinkara: a long poem on Shri Krishna. The poet was a brother of Kashiram Das.

Shrikrishnavatar-lila (?17th: Asamiya) of unknown authorship: a poem in 'vatsan' form narrating the life of Shri Krishna based on the 10th skandha of *Bhagavat-purana*.

Shrinatha or Shrinathudu (*c*1365–1440): poet in Telugu, scholar of Sanskrit and Kannada. He occupied a position of honour in the court of the Reddy kings of Kondavidu; was awarded the title of 'Kavi-sarvabhauma'. He pioneered the 'prabandha kavya' form in Telugu. Many of his works are lost. Among those extant are *Shringara-naishadhamu*, a translation of the Sanskrit work of Shriharsha; *Harivilasamu*, based on Kalidasa and Bharavi; original works *Kashikhandamu, Bhimeshwar-purana*, *Shivaratri-mahatmyamu*. Among works not yet recovered are *Maruttaratth-charitramu, Shalivahan-saptashati, Palanativir-charitra, Kridabhiram-amamu, Panditaradhya-charitra*.

Shringara-manjari (?18th; Prakrit/Apabhramsha) of Vishweshwara: a 'sattaka' play which tells the love-story of king Rajasekhara and Shringaramanjari, the princess of Avanti. It is modelled on Karpura-manjari of Rajasekhara.

Shringara-prakasha (17th; Sanskrit) ascribed to Bhoja: the largest known work in Sanskrit on poetics, consisting of 36 sections; deals also with dramaturgy. Containing as it does ancient as well as more recent views of scholars, the work may be regarded as an encyclopaedia of poetics.

Shringara-shakuntalamu (15th/16th; Telugu) of Pillalmari Pinvir Bhadruda: kavya work based on the Shakuntala story. The poet has drawn from Vyasa and Kalidasa but added some matter of his own.

Shringara-shataka (?C; Sanskrit) of Bhartrihari: a sequence of 100 lyrics on the various stages of love.
Tr. C.H. Tawney, *Ind. Ant.*, 1876; B.H. Wortham, London, 1886; J.M. Kennedy, London, 1913; C.W. Gurner, Calcutta, 1927.

Shringara-tilaka (?C; Sanskrit): short poem on love in which the poet, while praising his beloved, also complains about her hard-hearted nature. The poem is ascribed to Kalidasa by some scholars.

Shringara-tilaka (?C; Sanskrit): work on poetics, ascribed to Rudra who is generally identified as Rudrata, author of Kavyalamkara.

Shringaramma (late 17th): woman poet in Kannada: author of *Padmini-kalyana*. She was among the poets associated with the court of Mysore ruler Chikkadevaraj (r. 1672–1704). She belonged to the Shrivaishnav community.

Shripadrayaru (16th): poet and song-writer in Kannada: also composed in Sanskrit. He was the head of a Madhva mutth in Mulagilu village of Kolar district. Though deeply read in Sanskrit, he was an ardent advocate of the mother-tongue. In the pseudonym of 'Rangavitthal', he composed many verses in Kannada to be sung by the assembly of preachers. His compositions in Kannada have been collected in *Bhramar-gite, Venu-gite, Gopi-gite* etc.

Shripati Mishra (early 18th): writer on poetics in Hindi, whose best-known work is *Kavya-saroj* (1720). Apart from this he wrote *Kavikul-kalpadrum, Rasa-sagar, Alamkar-ganga, Anupras-vinod, Vikram-vilas, Saroj-talika,* etc.

Shriramulu Dasu (1846–1908): poet and playwright in Telugu.

Shrirangapattanamu Krishnamacharya (b. 1800): scholar of Kannada. He was a lawyer in Madras and wrote several works on Kannada language and grammar. Among these are *Dhatumanjari, Shabdamanjari, Halamannad, Nudigannadi, Hosagannad.* His *Kannada vyakarana*, though more than a century old, is still respected as a scientific and authoritative grammar.

Shrivara (late 15th): poet and scholar in Sanskrit; compiled the anthology *Subhashitavali*; composed *Katha-kautuka*, a long poem; also *Jaina-rajatarangini*, a continuation of Kalhana's work. He claimed to have been a pupil of Jonaraja, hence probably belonged to Kashmir.

Shrutabodha (?C; Sanskrit): work on prosody in verse. It describes the features of different metres; the verses themselves illustrate the metres being described. The work has been ascribed to Kalidasa, also to Vararuchi, while some scholars ascribe it to Ajitasena who may or may not have been the Jain author of this name.

Shrukh (Kashmiri): didactic poems of Sheikh Nuruddin or Nund Rishi were known by this term.

Shukasaptati (?C; Sanskrit): folktale cycle, extant in three versions. One of these is by Devadatta; another, the Simplicior version, by a Jaina; another, the Ornatior version, by Chintamani Bhatta (?13th). The frame-story is of a man who goes abroad, leaving his young wife in charge of his pet parrot; some rogues seek to abduct her; they are asked by the parrot to wait until a story, told by it, is finished. One story follows another, each more interesting than the previous, until 70 stories are told; by this time the husband returns home and the crisis is averted. According to some scholars the work was originally composed in Prakrit verse and later rendered into Sanskrit prose, with occasional verse passages.

Shudraka (?C): playwright in Sanskrit; author of *Mrichhakatika*. He appears to have been a brahman king. According to some scholars the play was written by a court-poet but the king's name got associated with the work as the poet's token of gratitude. Other plays like *Padmaprabhritika* and *Vina-vasavadatta* have been attributed to Shudraka. Incidentally, Banabhatta's *Kadambari* has a prince called Shudraka; the pre-Kalidasa poets Parimal and Somil are believed to have jointly produced a text known as "Shudrak-katha".

Shunya-puran (Bangla): the first section of a Dharma-puran text, dealing with cosmogony. Also called 'shunya-shastra', it describes the creation of the universe from 'shunya'.

Shunya-puran (?C; Bangla) of Ramai Pandit: text of legendary origin; its author is the character of a Dharmapuran text. The main body of the work is in verse; its occasional prose-passages are regarded as the earliest known samples of Bangla prose, pre-dating the verse of the same work.

Shyamalik (800/900): poet and playwright in Sanskrit, probably from Kashmir. Kshemendra has quoted one of his poems in *Auchityta* *vichar charcha*. A lost play, *Padataditak*, has been attributed to Shyamalik.

Siddha: generally, one who has achieved 'siddhi' (=enlightenment or understanding). A siddha poet is one who belongs to the Vajrayan wing of Mahayana Buddhism. They lived mostly in Nalanda or Vikramshila (both in modern Bihar) from the late 8th to early 13th, and composed verses in an Apabhramsha close to local speech. This language is sometimes regarded as the first form of Hindi.

Siddha Hemachandra (*c*1150; Sanskrit) of Hemachandra: grammatical work, so named because it was written for Siddharaja Jayasimha, ruler of Patan. Popularly known as *Shabdanushasana*, its full title is *Siddha-Hemachandrabhidha-swopajna-shabdanushasana*. The work follows the arrangement and terminology of *Katantra*; omits Vedic grammar and accents; devotes eighth chapter to Prakrit grammar, using many Apabhramsha verses as illustration.

Siddhanta-kaumudi (early 17th; Sanskrit) of Bhattoji Dikshita: a commentary on *Ashtadhyayi*. It rearranges the sutras of Panini under appropriate heads and offers exposition that is orderly and easy to follow.

Tr. S. Vasu, Allahabad, 8 vols, 1891–98.

Siddhanta-saraswati (mid-17th): poet in Bangla; attached to the court of Govindamanikya, ruler of Tripura. He translated *Brihadnaradiya-purana* into Bangla verse around 1669.

Siddhantasutra-patha (13th: Marathi) of Chakradhara: his teachings collected by Mahindra Bhat. This and *Acharya-sutra* form the earliest works of the Mahanubhava sect.

Siddharam-purana or **Siddharam-charitrya** (late 12th; Kannada) of Raghavanka: kavya work dealing with Siddharam, a famous Shiva-devotee of Sonmalige or Sonnalapur.

Siddhar: class of mystic poets who arose in 14th century Tamilnadu. Their poems contained great philosophical ideas presented in simple language. Some of them were social reformers as well and they spoke out against the caste system and religious bigotry. Among them Sivakkiyar, Pattinattar and Bhadragiriyar adopted a direct and easy style of composition which would influence later Tamil poetry.

Siddhi Narasimha (mid-17th): poet-king of Lalitapura (or Patan) in Nepal. After ruling for forty years he renounced worldly affairs and went on a pilgrimage; became known as a sant-poet hence the prefix 'siddhi' to his name. He is believed to have started the song and drama festival at Patan known as 'Karttika Nacha'.

Sigrarya (early 18th): playwright in Kannada: wrote the earliest known play in the language, *Mitravinda Govinda*. It is modelled on the Sanskrit *Ratnavali* of Shriharsha.

Siharfi (Panjabi): a series of short poems forming an acrostic on the alphabet. This form, found only in Panjabi, is probably derived from Farsi or Arabi.

Silappadikaram (late 2nd: Tamil) of Ilango Adigal: a long poem with a tragic ending. It tells of the young merchant Kovalan of Puhar who marries Kannagi, but is distracted for some time by the favours of a beautiful dancing girl Matavi. Later he returns to his wife and they leave Puhar for Madurai. There Kannagi gives him one of her golden anklets to sell, so that they have some money for food and other purchases. Kovalan is arrested as a thief trying to sell stolen property and sentenced to death. When Kannagi hears of her husband's unjust end, she seeks an interview with the king and proves her dead husband's innocence. The king dies out of remorse and Kannagi curses the city of Madurai which catches fire and burns down. Later Kannagi is deified and a temple erected to honour the power of a chaste wife. The work, mainly in narrative form, has also been regarded as the earliest extant work in Tamil in the form of drama. Every excellence of ancient Tamil literature is to be found in this work.

Silovaesa-mala (?C; Prakrit) of Jayakirti: a series of 116 gatha verses. The work was composed earlier than 1337 because that year Somatilaka Suri wrote a commentary on it.

Simha Bhupala (early 14th): scholar and poet in Sanskrit; also called Singhadharanisa, Singaraja, Singamahipati or Singhabhupala. Some scholars believe he was king Singama Nayadu of Venkatagiri who ruled around 1330; his hereditary capital was at Rajachalam (Rachakonda). He is supposed to have written the work on alamkara, *Rasarnava-sudhakara*.

Simhagiri Narahari Vachanamalu (?13th; Telugu) of Krishnamacharya: a collection of devotional compositions in prose.

Simhasana-dvatrimsika (?C; Sanskrit) of unkonwn authorship: prose work consisting of 32 tales. Each is told by an image supporting the throne of Vikramaditya which has been dug out of the earth by king Bhoja; as Bhoja prepares to sit on it, each image narrates a tale in praise of Vikramaditya and implies that nobody should sit on this throne until he has acquired the merits of Vikramaditya. The original work is lost but two recensions are extant. The original is also known as *Vikrama-charit*.
Tr. F. Edgerton, *HOS*, 1926.

Sindhi: a language associated with the former province of Sindh in western British India (now in Pakistan). The same term is used for its speakers who number about 18 million in India and Pakistan and live in various parts of the country. The origins of Sindhi are a matter of controversy but it is generally accepted that the language, while being of Sanskrit-Prakrit origin, it absorbed many elements from neighbouring languages belonging to other language families. From Arab records it would appear Sindhi was spoken from 8th century and written in various scripts. In mid-19th century the British Govt. devised an Arabi-Sindhi (modified Perso-Arabic) script which continues to be used today.

Sinhal dvip: a story-line concerning the island (now called Sri Lanka; earlier Sinhala) has been used by many ancient Indian poets and playwrights. It consists of the hero's reaching Sinhal after overcoming many difficulties and facing much danger; on the way back the ship carrying the hero and heroine is damaged or destroyed and they get separated; some other accident or supernatural force brings them together again. Among works in Apabhramsha, this story-line has been used by Dhanapal in *Bhavisayat-katha*, Kanakumar in *Karakanda-chariu*, Lakhu in *Jinadatta-chariu*, Narasen in *Sripal-charit*. Sometimes the name of the island gets changed to Kanchan-dvip or Ratna-dvip or Hamsa-dvip.

Siraj-Aurangabadi [Shah Sirajuddin (1714–66)]: poet in Urdu from Aurangabad; came to Delhi and, like Wali, cultivated the local speech for literary purpose in the style of Dakhni. He took the place of Wali as the innovator of a new language and a new poetry. He left behind short poems adding upto about 10,000 lines; also a romance, *Bustan-i-khayal*.

Sirappuranam (18th; Tamil) of Umaruppulavar: kavya work dealing with the life of Nabi Muhammad. It is in three 'kanda'. The first,

'Viladat kanda', tells of his birth and childhood; the second 'Nubuvvat kanda' describes his being initiated into religious life by the angel Jibrail; the third, 'Hijrat kanda', narrates his departure from Makka and arrival in Madina. 'Sira' in the title of the work derives from sirat (=history) in Arabi.

Sirichimdhakavvam (13th; Prakrit) of Krishnalilasukha: poetical work in 12 sarga, dealing with the life of Shri Krishna. It is designed to illustrate the rules of Prakrit grammars written by Vararuchi and Trivikrama.

Siri Thulibhadra Phagu (*c*1330; Apabhramsha/Gujarati) of Jinapada Suri: the earliest work in this form, though it relates to the rainy season and not, as required by the convention of this form, to spring. It tells of the saga Sthulibhadra who lived in the company of the courtesan Koza during 'chaturmasa' as ordered by his guru but did not succumb to her charms, thus passing the test of his 'vairagya'.

Sirupanatruppadai (?C; Tamil) of Nattattanar of Nallur: the third idyll of *Pattuppattu*. The work is in the form of a well-rewarded poet addressing a fellow-poet. The patron celebrated here is Nalliyakkodan, a chieftain of Erumainadu.

Sishyalekha-dharmakavya (?7th; Sanskrit) of Chandragomin: an epistle in 114 verses instructing a pupil in the essential tenets of Buddhism. It is apparently aimed at prince Ratnakirti who was under delusion caused by wealth and power.

Sitaramcharyulu Bhujanapalli (1827–91): grammarian of Telugu, also famous teacher of the language whose whole working life was spent at the Pratikshan Patthshala of Madras. His major works are *Trilinga-lakshan seshamu*, which adds many explanations not to be found in Chinnaysuri's *Bal-vyakaranamu* and in a way completes that great work; *Shabdaratnakaramu*, which is the first complete lexicon of Telugu. He also wrote textbooks like *Bal-chandrodayamu* and *Aladhu-kaumudi*.

Sita-swayamvara (?C; Marathi) of Venabai: kavya work in ovi metre describing the marriage of Sita. This woman poet was a devotee of Shri Ram.

Sita-swayamvara (mid-17th; Marathi) of Vaman Pandit: narrative poem on the episode.

Sita-swayamvara (late 16th; Malayalam) of Kottarakkara Tampuran; Kathakali play in which only two scenes are generally performed. The first shows Rama winning Sita by bending the bow of Shiva; the second shows Rama withstanding Parasurama's challenge.

Sita-vijayam (16th; Malayalam): kavya work, at one time attributed to Ezuttachan.

Sitayan or **Sitaram-priya** (*c*1700; Hindi) of Rampriya Saran: long poem in eulogy of Sita.

Sitrilakkiyam (Tamil): a type of poem which describes a person, place or event.

Sivappirakasar (17th): belonged to the Virashaiva mutth at Turaimangalam; author of 23 works, some of which are literary, others religious. Among the former are *Nalvarnanmanimalai* and *Nanneri*.

Smritisthala (13th; Marathi) of Nagdeva: early prose work, a collection of reminiscences.

Sobagin sone (?C; Kannada) of Deparaj: a collection of seven 'katha' narratives, composed in 'sangatya' metre.

Sodhi Nathi (17th): woman poet in Rajasthani. From the MSS of her works it appears she was the daughter of Bhojraj of Umarkot and was married to Sundardas, son of the deposed Rawal of Jaisalmer. All her works are devotional in spirit, such as *Gudartha balacharita, Bhagat bhav-ra chandrayana, Hari-lila, Nam-lila*, etc. She generally composed in doha form.

Sohni-Mahiwal (1849; Panjabi) of Fazal Shah: qissa work, generally regarded as the best of some 70-odd such works based on his popular folk narrative.

Somadeva (10th): poet in Sanskrit; author of *Yashastilaka-champu*. A Digambara Jain, he was a protege of a son of Chalukya king Arikesarin II.

Somadeva (mid-11th): poet in Sanskrit; author of *Kathasaritsagara*. A brahman, he was attached to the court of king Ananta of Kashmir (1029–64).

Somadeva (early 12th): playwright in Sanskrit, author of *Lalita-vigraha-raja*. The play was written in honour of his patron, Vishaladeva Vigraharaja, Chahmana king of Sakhambari.

Somana Nachana (*c*1285/1355): poet in Telugu. who is ranked just after Tikkana and acknowledged his indebtedness to the earlier poet. Though at least four works are ascribed to him—*Uttara Harivamsha,*

Hari-vilasa, Adi-purana, Hara-vilasa—only the first has been recovered.

Someswar shataka (1299; Kannada): attributed to Palkuriki Somnath but this may not be correct. This sequence of 107 poems stresses the importance of morality.

Somnath [Somnath Mathur (mid-18th)]: poet in Hindi and scholar; his patron was Pratapsingh, youngest son of Bharatpur ruler Badansingh. Among his works are *Rasapiyushnidhi* and *Srinagar-vilas*, both on poetics; *Manav-vinod*, a verse play based on Bhavabhuti's *Malati-Madhav; Krishna-Lilavati, Panchadhyayi, Sujan-vilas*.

Somnath-charite (late 12th: Kannada) of Raghavanka: kavya work telling of a Shiva-devotee named Adayya who came from Saurashtra to Puligere, established the shrine of Saurashtra-Somnath here, and converted many Jains to Virshaiva faith. Written in 'vardhak shatpadi' metre, the poem is in five 'aswas' or 'sarga'.

Somprabhacharya (12th): scholar and poet in Apabhramsha, Prakrit and Sanskrit. Among his works *Sumatinath-charit* and *Kumarapala-pratibodha* are in Prakrit; parts of the latter are in Apabhramsha; *Suktimuktavali* and *Shatartha-kavya* are in Sanskrit.

Sori-charitta (15th or 17th; Prakrit) of Srikantha: a 'yamaka' kavya, with the eight matras in two metrical feet, having identical sound but different meaning.

Stephens, Thomas: see Thomas Stephens.

Sthala puranam (Tamil): also available in other languages of South India, this genre consists of stories about how temples came to be founded. More generally, it can be the account of a particular place ('sthala'). Among the more famous such collections are *Chidambar puranam, Setu-puranam, Tirukkalukunar puranam, Arunachal-puranam.*

Sthan-pothi (*c*1353; Marathi) of Muni Vyas: description of the 200 odd villages of Maharashtra visited by Mahanubhav sect founder Chakradhar in order to propagate his beliefs.

Sthayi-bhava (Sanskrit): term in poetics for the permanent or dominant human feelings. There are eight in number—'rati', 'hasa', 'krodha', 'utsaha', 'bhaya', 'jugupsa', 'vismaya' and 'soka'—corresponding to the eight rasas. For those who recognise 'santa' as the ninth rasa, the corresponding Sthayi-bhava is 'sama' or 'nirveda'.

Subandhu (6th/7th): early prose-writer in Sanskrit, whose only known work is the romantic narrative *Vasavadatta*. Very little is known about his time or place. In the introduction of his work he mentions one Vikramaditya whose career is over; this Vikramaditya has not yet been identified.

Subhadra-dhananjay (10th; Sanskrit) of Kulashekhar Varma: play in five acts dealing with the winning of Subhadra by Arjun.

Subhadra-haran (?C; Marathi) of Raghunandan-das: kavya work on Sanskrit model.

Subhadra-kalyanamu (late 15th; Telugu) of Timmamba; a work in dvipadi metre on the Subhadra story.

Subhashita-ratnakosha (early 12th; Sanskrit): of Vidyakara: anthology of verses of different poets, arranged under sections called 'vrajya'. It includes the work of poets (viz., Vallana, Buddhakara-gupta) who are not known from any other source. When first edited from an incomplete MS, it was given the title Kavindra-vachana-samucchaya. The compiler was probably a Bouddha monk of Bengal.

Subhashitavali (?C; Sanskrit) of Vallabhadeva: anthology containing 3527 verses by about 360 poets, arranged in 109 sections (paddhati). The verses, on a wide variety of topics, include the work of many poets of Kashmir who are otherwise unknown. The compiler himself was from Kashmir; has been dated anywhere from 12th to 16th century.

Subodhalamkara (?C; Prakrit): of Sangharakkhita; a work on rhetoric.

Sudama-charitra (*c*1545; Hindi) of Narottamdas: long poem in Brajbhasa about the reunion of Krishna and Sudama.

Sudamsana-chariu (?C; Apabhramsha): of Nayanandi Muni: a kavya style poem which glorifies the 'pancha-namaskara' ritual.

Sudan (18th): poet in Hindi. attached to the court of Bharatpur ruler and Jat chief, Sujansingh Surajmal. The poet composéd *Sujan-charit* or *Sujan-vilas* in praise of his patron.

Sufi: a sect among the Muslims who believe that love is the best form of worship and god should be regarded as one's beloved. Many romance writers in Old Hindi and Urdu were Sufis; they used the human story as an allegory of the spiritual meaning. The Sufis also influenced many non-Muslim thinkers.

Sugriva-vijayamu (*c*1568; Telugu): of Kandukuri Rudra Kavi: a Yakshagana work, the first in Telugu.

Suhini-Mehar: main characters of a folk tale of Sindh; they reappear with some changes as Sohni-Mahiwal in Panjab.

Sujan-charit (*c*1750; Hindi) of Sudan: a kavya work in praise of Sujansingh Surajmal, ruler of Bharatpur. The events described cover the period 1745–53, and feature all seven battles fought by Surajmal. The poet has demonstrated his skill by employing 103 different metres; his language, basically Brajbhasha, has many words from Purbi, Narwari, Panjabi and Farsi.

Sujan-hit (early 18th; Hindi) of Ghanananda: a collection of about 500 poems about the poet's beloved Sujan, a courtesan associated with the court of Mughal king Muhammad Shah Rangila.

Sukhadukha-charitam (?C; Kashmiri) of Ganaka Prasasta: didactic poem on the art of happy living.

Sukhamani (early 17th; Panjabi) of Guru Arjan Dev: a series of epistles in verse.

Sukhdev Mishra (1633–1703): scholar of poetics and poet in Hindi; author of *Vritta-vichar, Chhanda-vichar, Fajil Ali prakash*, *Shringarlata*, etc.

Sukta (Sanskrit): term for Vedic hymns. Its literal meaning is 'well-spoken utterance' (=su + ukta). Each sukta consists of some verses known as 'rik'. Thus, *Rigveda* contains about 10,552 riks making up 1028 suktas.

Sukti (Hindi): a statement offering advice in some striking manner.

Sukti-muktavali (?C; Sanskrit) also known as *Subhashita-muktavali*; attributed to Jalhana, but may have been compiled by one Bhanu. It is a collection of 2790 verses arranged in 133 sections; about 240 works and authors are represented.

Sukti-sudharnav (*c*1245; Kannada) of Mallikarjun: also known as *Kavysar*, this is an anthology of about 2500 verses prepared by

Mallikarjun at the behest of Hoysala king Vir-someshwar. The material is a testimony to the wealth of existing Kannada literature. Only half of the work, however, has been recovered in a reliable text.

Suleiman-Bilkis: a popular romance of Panjab.

Suman (late 18th/early 19th): Rambhakti poet in Hindi author of *Amar-prakash, Ashtayam, Lachhman-shatak, Hanuman-rakhsikh*, etc.

Sumangala-vilasini (?5th, Pali) of Buddhaghosa: a commentary on *Dighaniyaka*. The work is full of information on social, political, philosophical and religious history of Buddha's times.

Sumatinatha-charita (*c*1150; Prakrit/Sanskrit) of Somaprabha: a biography of the fifth tirthankar, Sumatinatha. More Prakrit is used in the work than Sanskrit.

Sumati-shataka (Telugu): a series of 100 poems on morals and wisdom; first series composed by Palakuriki Somnatha in *c*1180, second by Peddanna in *c*1260.

Sundardas (1596–1689): sant-poet for Hindi and scholar, from Dhausa near Jaipur; disciple of Dadu Dayal. He lived 30 years in Kashi studying shastras and puranas; also became proficient in Sanskrit, Farsi, Hindi, Panjabi, Gujarati and Marwari; was well-versed in poetics. *Sundar-vilas* is his major work, among others are *Daso dishaon-ki sabayya, Jnana-samudra*, and the collection *Sundardas-ki pada*. He composed mainly in sabayya and kavitta forms.

Sundarar (early 9th): sant-poet in Tamil, one of the four great Nayanmars. He composed 1000 hymns which constitute the seventh *Tirumurai*; also compiled *Tiruttondattogai*, which lists all the Nayanmars and explains their importance. Born into a brahman family of Tirunavalur village in South Arcot district, he regarded Shiva as his friend and confidant (as contrasted with Sambandar who regarded Shiva as father and Appar who regarded himself as the servant of Shiva). His full name is Sundaramurti Nayanar. A close associate of Chera ruler Cheraman Perumal, he died at an early age (probably 18).

Sundasan-chariu (*c*1040; Apabhramsha) of Nayanandi: kavya work which describes how Setth Sudarsan achieves 'moksha', A merchant's son being the hero of a kavya is a notable departure from convention.

Supasanaha-chariya (*c*1140; Prakrit) of Lakshmana Gani: a charitakavya dealing with the life of seven tirthankar, Suprashwanatha. The work consists of eight gathas and is divided into three 'prastava'. The language is strongly influenced by Apabhramsha.

Suppav (?13th): poet in Apabhramsha; author of *Vairagya-sar*. Nothing is known about his time or place. Though he was a Digambar Jain, his discussion of religious principles show that his was an open mind.

Suppirdip Kavirayar (18th): poet in Tamil. Born into a Vaishnav family of goldsmiths, he came under the influence of Christian priest and Tamil poet Beschi and converted to christianilty. His two works are *Virali-vittutu* which tells of the love-affairs of a prostitute; and *Kalappanayakkan katal*, which describes the indulgences of a feudal chieftain.

Surdas (1483–1563 or 1540–1620): foremost poet-singer of Krishna-bhakti in Hindi. Blind (perhaps not from birth), he belonged to Siri village in Ballabhgarh district near Delhi; lived mainly in Goughat, a village between Agra and Mathura. Vallabhacharya once heard him sing in Goughat and was so impressed that he took Surdas to the Shrinath temple on Govardhan hill and appointed him chief singer of the temple. The languages Surdas composed in was a Sanskritized form of literary Brajbhasha. Among 16 collections made of his verses, the more important are *Sur-sagar, Sahitya-lahari* and *Suri saravali.*

Sursagar (*c*1550; Hindi): a collection of all the lyrics sung by Surdas at the Shrinath temple. Many variants are available in different editions, but the two-volume text published by the Kashi Nagari Pracharini Sabha is regarded as the most authentic. This contains 12 'skandha' (sections), of which the 1st includes songs of humility, 2nd to 8th songs about the various avatars of various gods, 9th about Shri Rama, 10th about Shri Krishna from birth to his reaching Kurukshetra, 11th and 12th again about gods and goddesses.

Sursaravali (*c*1550: Hindi): index of the contents of *Sursagar*. The compilation is usually attributed to Surdas but may have been done by somebody else.

Suraj Prakash (1730; Rajasthani) of Kaviya Karanidan: long poem in eulogy of the ruling family of Jodhpur, the Rathods. Commissioned by the current ruler, Abhaya Singh, the poem centres on the battle between him and Sarbuland Khan, the then Mughal subedar of Gujarat, which ended in a victory for the Jodhpur king. Apart from a graphic description of the battle, the poem also describes Rajput life in great detail. The work contains 7500 stanzas in various metres.

Surajanji Puniya (1582–1691): poet in Rajasthani, also a religious leader. Among his works, *Katha Gajmokh, Katha Ushapuran, Ram rasau*, are narrative poems; *Katha prasiddha and Katha autar-ki* deal with the life of Jambhoji; *Katha chetan, Katha chitawani, Dharamchari*, are didactic poems; *Bhogolpuran* presents an account of the universe.

Surakavi [Adidamu Surakavi (1720–85)]: poet in Telugu. Author of *Kavijan-ranjanamu, Kavisamasya-vichhedamu, Chandralokamu, Ramalingeshwar-shatakamu.* The last-named is a critique of misdeeds committed by rulers of the time.

Surana Pingali (early 16th): poet in Telugu; one of the 'Ashta-diggaja' group. His works are *Kalapurnodayamu, Prabhavati-pradyumnayamu, Raghava-pandaviyamu.*

Suranga Kavi (early 16th): poet in Kannada; author of the champu work *Trishashti puratan charitre.* He was a Virshaiva by faith.

Surasundari-chariam (*c*1038; Prakrit) of Dhaneshwara; long poem in 16 'sarga', narrating the love-story of a Vidyadhara chief.

Surati Misra (early 18th): poet in Hindi and scholar from Agra; author of *Alamkar-mala.* He wrote detailed commentaries in Brajbhasha on *Bihari-satsai, Kavipriya* and *Rasikapriya.* He also translated *Vetal panchavimshati* into Brajbhasha prose. Among his other works are *Rasaratna-mala, Saras-rasa, Rasagrahak-chandrika, Kavya-siddhanta.*

Surendranath Majumdar (1838–78): writer in Bangla from Jasor (now in Bangladesh); educated in Calcutta where he learnt Sanskrit, Farsi and English. Among his works are the verse collections *Shadaritu-barnan* (1856) and *Barsha-barnan* (1872); a translation of Tod's book as *Rajasthaner itibritta* in five volumes (1872–73); a popular science book *Vishwa-rahasya* (1877); a historical play *Hammir* (1881); and the incomplete *Mahila* which is in praise of women.

Surpanakhangam (?C; Malayalam): early prose work in attaprakara form.

Surya Malla [Suryamal Mishran (1815–63)]: poet in Hindi from Bundi (Rajasthan); knew six languages; was also a scholar of grammar, logic, history, politics, etc. Among his works are *Mamsha-bhaskar, Vir-satsai, Balwant-vilas, Chhandomayush.* He wrote in both Dingal and Pingal styles; his glorification of local heroes helped to develop the spirit of nationalism in Rajasthan.

Surya-shataka (?7th; Sanskrit) of Mayura: a series of 100 verses. The work has been quoted by Abhinavagupta, Mammata and others. According to legend, Mayura was cured of leprosy after composing these verses.

Suthara (1615–*c*1700): humorous poet in Panjabi who generally made fun of things in order to draw some moral lesson. He belonged to Adiala village of Patiala district; abandoned by his parents as a child, he came into the care of sixth Sikh guru Hargovind.

Sutra (Sanskrit): a short statement which condenses an important or substantial idea into a few words.

Sutradhar (Sanskrit): the director of every aspect of a play, also its narrator. His functions are clearly set down in *Natyashastra*.

Sutta-nipata (?C; Pali): fifth book of *Khuddaniyaka*; contains narratives and dialogues, and is divided into five 'vagga' sections. There are 54 lyrics in the first four vaggas; the last one is a long metrical composition in 16 sections.

Sutta-pitaka (?C; Pali): a part of the *Tipitaka*. It is concerned with discourses; consists of five 'nikayas'; contains the essence of Buddhism. There have been many additions and alterations to this work through the ages.

Suvritta-tilaka (11th; Sanskrit) of Kshemendra: work on prosody; particularly valuable for literary history because it quotes abundantly from various existing works and gives names of their authors.

Swachha-telugu or Achha-Telugu: a form of literary Telugu from which all Sanskrit and Prakrit 'tadbhava' words have been eliminated. Ponnekanti Teleganna demonstrated in his *Yayati-charitramu* that it was possible to compose literature in this form of Telugu. Though his example was followed by Timmakavi and others, the innovation did not get established.

Swapna-vasavadatta (?3rd; Sanskrit) of Bhasa: perhaps his best known play; deals with the story of king Udayana in six acts. Although Udayana is happily married to Vasavadatta, his clever minister Yaugandharayana plans a second marriage for political advantage with Padmavati, daughter of the king of Magadh. He spreads the rumour of the queen's death, but arranges for Padmavati to look after the disguised Vasavadatta; the king believes in the rumour and agrees to marry Padmavati; afterwards he is reunited with Vasavadatta.

Tr. A. Baston, Paris, 1914; A.G. Shirreff & Panna Lal, Allahabad, 1918; C.R. Devadhar, Pune, 1926.

Swaramela-kalanidhi (1550; Sanskrit) of Rama Amatya: treastise which gives, for the first time, a detailed exposition of Carnatic music.

Swarochisa Manu-charitra (early 16th; Telugu) of Allaseni Peddana: work based on the romantic history of Swarochisa Manu derived from *Markandeya-purana*.

Swarupa Das (1801–63): poet in Rajasthani. A 'charana' by birth, his family belonged to Umarkot in Sindh (new Pakistan) but moved to Badali village near Ajmer. He was educated here, then initiated into the sect of Dadu Dayal. His most outstanding work was *Pandava yashendu chandrika* (1835), also known as *Ukti-chandrika*. Among his other works, *Rasa-ratnakar* (1826), *Varnartha-manjari* (1838), *Hrinayananjan* (1839), *Pakhanda-khanjan* (1833) are in verse; *Vritti-bodh* (1841), *Tarka-prabandha* (1842), *Aviveka-paddhati* (1851), *Sadharanopadesha* (1846), *Sukshimopadesha* (1848), combine poetry and prose. He was much esteemed by the rulers of Ratlam, Sitamau, Sailana, etc.

Swati Tirunal, Maharaja (1813–?): poet in Malayalam and patron of literature; belonged to the ruling family of Travancore. Among his works are *Raghav-charitam karyam, Kumarasambhavan-champu, Mudrarakohas-chhayel.*

Swayambhudeva (8th/9th): poet in Apabhramsha from Koshala; author of *Pauma-chariu* and *Ritthi Nemi chariu* (or "Arishtanemi charitra"), a version of *HvP*, both of which were completed by his son Tribhuvana. At one time he was considered the first poet in Hindi because he composed in an Apabhramsha which reflects an early form of Hindi.

Swayambhu-chhandas (8th/9th; Prakrit) of Sawayambhu: work in poetics, which discuss various metres and also gives many quotations mentioning the names of their authors.

T

Tabai (17th): poet in Urdu; regarded among the best poets of Haidarabad of his time. Though he was close to Tanashah Abul Hasan, he kept himself at a distance from the royal court. In 1670 he composed the masnavi work *Qissa-e-Bahram-o-Gul Andam*, which is considered one of the finest compositions in Dakhni.

Tadbhava (Sanskrit): name of one of the four classes of words in Indian languages (the other classes being 'tatsama', 'videshi', 'deshaj'). Tadbhava means 'arising from Sanskrit'. Thus, *ghar* in Hindi is from *griha* in Sanskrit.

Tagadur yattirai (?C; Tamil): co-authored by several poets among whom were Arisil Kilar and Ponmudiyar. The work describes the victorious march of the Chera army under Perunjeral Irumporai to Tagadur, capital of Adihaiman Neduman Anji. Mainly in prose, with some verse portions; the work is not extant; about 48 verses are known from commentaries and from *Purattirattu*.

Tahsin [Mir Muhammad Husain Ata Khan (late 18th/early 19th)]: prose writer in Urdu from Itawah in Uttar Pradesh. Not many details of his life are known, but his *Nau tarz-e-murassa* is famous as probably the first book of Urdu prose of North India. This work contains a version of 'The Chahar Darvesh qissa'. His several works in Farsi. (*Tarikh-e-kasimi, Zavabit-e-angrezi, Angsha-e-tahsin*) are no longer available.

Taj (mid-14th): a Muslim woman of Karouli in Uttar Pradesh who became a devotee of Krishna and composed songs and verses in an early form of Hindi. Only fragments of her work have been found.

Takkayagapparani (12th; Tamil) of Ottakkutar: a 'parani' work in prose of the battlefield triumphs of Chola kings. It also contains verifiable historical details about their regimes, especially their charitable deeds. According to legend, the poet wrote this work during the course of a night and in a Kali temple.

Talapaka Himmakka (mid/15th): an early woman poet in Telugu; composed a poem on a *Mahabharata* story, *Subhadra-kalyanamu.*

Tamasa (Marathi): a form of dance-drama, accompanied by song and music, which became popular in Maharashtra in 18th. Until the advent of women performers, boys dressed up as women sang vulgar lavani songs. This explains why the form is generally associated with low taste.

Tamil (also transcribed as Tamizh): main language of the modern state of Tamil Nadu (which formed part of Madras Presidency in British India) in South-east India. Spoken by about 71 million people in India as well as Shri Lanka, it is one of the oldest languages of the world today and has been in continuous use for over 2000 years. No evidence is available of its origins; reconstruction by modern linguists indicate that there was a source-language, Proto-Dravidian' which split up into three families—South Dravidian, Central Dravidian, North Dravidian Tamil belongs to the South Dravidian family and emerged as an independent language by about 5th century B.C. Its script is predominantly Brahmi, with additional scriptal symbols that denote peculiarly Tamil phonetic values.

Tanjaivanan kovai (13th/14th; Tamil) of Ponniamoshippulavar: poetical work in honour of Chantirvanan, a fendatory of the Pandyan king Kulasekhara (r. 1268–1311).

Tantrakhayayika (?C; Sanskrit) of unknown authorship: version of *Panchatantra* produced in Kashmir; regarded as the oldest, hence perhaps the nearest to the original. According to Winternitz, it was not composed before 3rd century B.C.; shows many features of ornate literary composition in Sanskrit.

Tapasa-vatsa-raja (?8th; Sanskrit) of Ananga Harsha Amatraraja: play in six acts which presents a variation of *Swapnavasavadatta*.

Tapati-samvaranam (late 16th; Telugu) of Addanki Gangadhara: a prabandha work sponsored by Sultan Ibrahim Qutb Shah of Golkonda.

Tappa (Bangla): a style of singing in which a more elaborate form (viz. dhrupad or khayal) has been condensed. The Bengali singer Ramnidhi Gupta (better known as Nidhi Babu) is said to have innovated this in early 19th.

Tappa (Panjabi): a form of folk-poetry in which a pair of lovers tease one another.

Tarah misra (Urdu): term for a line of verse from some famous poet assumed by an apprentice poet as his ideal.

Taraknath Gangopadhyay or **Ganguli** (1843–91): novelist in Bangla. He studied medicine and surgery and obtained an LMS; worked in various government hospitals all his life. His first and best-known work, *Swarnalata* (1874) is regarded as the first social novel in the language. Of his other works, *Lalit Saudamini* (1882) is a long story; *Harisha bishad* (1887), a novel; *Tinti galpa* (1889), three stories; *Adrishta* (1892), a novel; *Bidhilipi* an unfinished novel.

Tarangalata (?C; Prakrit) of unknown author: probably a much later re-telling of *Tarangavati* of Padalipta.

Tarangalola (13th/14th; Prakrit) of unknown author: a work of 1643 verses. It narrates the story of a female Jain ascetic and is probably based on the lost work *Tarangavati*.

Tarangavati (?5th; Prakrit) of Padalipta Suri: a prose romance, now lost. The work told a love story, concluding with a religious sermon; also known as *Tarangavai*.

Tarangavati Katha (Sanskrit) of Padalipta: one of the examples of a katha work, it was composed in the 1st or 2nd Century A.D. The story is narrated by a nun, Tarangavati, as her autobiography. She is the daughter of a rich merchant family of Kaushambi. The sight of some chakravaka birds recalls her previous life as a female chakravaka whose happy existence was cut short cruelly by a hunter who killed her male companions. She prepares and exhibits a picture panel depicting the main events of her previous life. The son of a leading merchant recognises himself in those pictures as the male bird. The human lovers establish contact secretly, plan to marry and have to elope when their families do not consent. They fall into the hands of some robbers and would have been sacrificed to these robbers' goddess if a prison-guard had not helped them to escape. They return home and are married. Later, they happen to meet a monk who tells them his life-story. He was the prison-guard who had helped them to escape; in his previous life he was the hunter who had killed the male bird. After hearing all this, the young couple decide to renounce worldly life and become monk/nun.

Tarangini (Malayalam): a metre of Malayalam verse used by the Niranam poets.

Taskin [Mir Husain 'Taskin' (1788–1849)]: poet in Urdu; born in Delhi but moved to Lakhnau and Meerut in search of a living before settling in Rampur where he won the patronage of Nawab Yusuf Ali. Initially a disciple of Shah Nasir, on his death sought the tutelage of Momin and remained Momin's disciple for the rest of his life.

Taslim [Munshi Amirulla (1820–1911)]: poet in Urdu from Mangalsi village in Faizabad district of Uttar Pradesh. Though he lived much of his life in Lakhnau, he accepted Nasim Dehlavi as his preceptor and composed in the Dilli style of Urdu poetry. His earliest collection of poems were lost during the disorders of 1857; later he became famous for his ghazal and masnavi compositions. *Nazme-arjumand, Nazme-dil afroz* and *Daftare-khayal* are his ghazal collections. His masnavi works are *Nala-e-Taslim, Sham-e-ghariba, Dil-o-jan, Nagma-e-bulbul, Shaukat-e-Shahjahani, Gohre-intikhab* and *Tarikh-e-Rampur*.

Tatsama (Sanskrit): name of one of the four classes of words in Indian languages (see 'tadbhava' above). 'Tatsama' means words 'like Sanskrit' or 'equal to Sanskrit'. These words have been absorbed without change of form or sound into another language.

Taylor [Joseph van Someran Taylor (1820–81): Scottish missionary who wrote a grammar of Gujarati entitled *Gujarati bhashanum vyakarana* (1867). Though this was not one among the early grammars of the language written by Westerners, it was meant for local use and was more comprehensive than any earlier grammar. Among his other publications are *Dhatusamgraha* (1870), an etymological dictionary compiled in collaboration with Kalidas Shastri; *Dharmagita* (1851) and *Kavyarpana* (1863), collections of hymns composed by him; translations into Gujarati of Barth's *Church History* (1862) and of *Westminster Shorter Catechism* (1878).

Tazkira (Urdu): biographical dictionary, or compilation of biographical notes on poets, based mainly on what is known to the compiler. Quite often, therefore, the information provided in one 'tazkira' may be at variance with what is provided in another. The earlier compilations listed poets in alphabetical order of names; later, they were grouped by eras. Generally, each entry provides information about the poet's life, seeks to describe his personality, and names his works. No critical evaluation is attempted.

Tazkira nikatusshoara (1752; Urdu) of Mir Taqi Mir: biographical dictionary listing about 100 Urdu poets, giving short biographics of each, quoting samples, and evaluating their literary merit. According to the compiler, this was the first such work dealing with Urdu poets.

Tazkiratusshoara (*c*1790; Farsi) of Mir Hasan: biographical dictionary listing about 300 poets, giving short biographies of each and quoting compilations in three time divisions: poets before Farrukshiyar, poets of the period between Farrukshiyar and Muhammad Shah, poets from then to the compiler's own time.

Tazmin (Urdu): word literally means 'to take responsibility of' or 'to make a promise'. As a literary term it refers to using well-known verses of another poet in one's own poem.

Tekchand Thakur: see Pyarichand Mitra.

Telakataha-gatha (?C; Prakrit) of unknown author: a poetical work of 98 verses, probably modelled on Sanskrit 'shataka' composition. The work is presented as the thoughts of and instructions given by a Mahathera. He had an illicit liaison with the queen of Kalanitissa, ruler of Kalaniya, and was thrown into a 'kataha' (large pan) of hot oil as punishment; hence the title.

Telugu: main language of the modern state of Andhra Pradesh (a large part of which includes the former princely state of Haidarabad) in South Central India. Also known as 'Andhra-bhasha', its speakers number about 74 million, ranking second only to Hindi as the mothertongue of the largest number of people in the country. Like Tamil, but at a much later date, it emerged from the South Dravidian branch of Proto-Dravidian and has been an independent language from about 6th century A.D.

Tempavani (1724; Tamil) of Constantius Beschi: a poetical work telling of the life of Jeses Christ. It contains 3615 verses divided into 36 'sarga'. The poet has used 90 different kinds of Tamil metre in this poem.

Tenali Ramakrishna (1485–1575): poet in Telugu whose literary achievement is generally overshadowed by his reputation as a prankster and fun-loving man, particularly quick at witty repartee. The latter gifts engendered stories that have turned him into a folk raman. His surname 'Garlapati' got changed by popular use to 'Tenali' which was his place of origin. He signed himself as 'Tenali Ramalinga Kavi' in his first poem, thus declaring that he was a Shaiva; later he appears to have become a Vaishnav, as indicated by another poem which honours a place of Vaishnav pilgrimage. His extant works are *Udabhataradhya-charitamu, Panduranga-mahatmyamu and Ghatikachala-mahatmyamu.*

Tevaram (Tamil): collective title of the first seven *Tirumurai* works, composed by the Shaiva sant-poets—Sambandhar, Appar and Sundarar.

Thakkayagapparani (?C; Tamil) of Ottakkuttar: a pioneer work in 'paranai' literature.

Thanjavanankovai (?C; Tamil) of Poyyamalippulavar: work illsutrating Narakaviraja Nambi's grammar on love.

Thayumanavar (17th/18th): philosopher-poet in Tamil, whose songs reveal devotional fervour without stressing sectarian zeal.

Thera-gatha (?C; Pali): eighth book of *Khudda'niyaka*, presenting 1273 gathas in 107 separate poems. The gathas express inner experiences of Bouddha monks and also offer beautiful samples of nature-description. The title means 'Songs of the Elders'.
Tr. Mrs. Rhys Davids, *PTS*, 1907.

Theri-gatha (?C; Pali): ninth book of *Khudda'niyaka*, presenting 522 gathas in 73 separate poems. The poems express the joys and sorrows of Bouddha nuns and describe the intimations of eternal life.
Ed. Oldenberg & Pischel, *PTS*, 1883, Tran. Mrs. Rhys Davis, *PTS*, 1909.

Thomas Stephens (1549–1619): foreigner who made a major contribution to Marathi literature by composing *Khrista-purana*. Born in Wiltshire, he was ordained as a Jesuit priest in Rome in 1575. He sailed for India from Lisbon in 1579 and was the first Englishman to come here round the Cape of Good Hope. His early letters home to his father (a leading merchant in London) were partly responsible for inducing mercantile interest in India, which led to the formation of the East India Company. Father Stephens did missionary work on the Malabar coast for 40 years. He learnt Marathi well enough not only to be able to preach but also to compose his great work in this language.

Thondaradipodi Alvar (?7th): sant-poet in Tamil; one of the 12

Alvars. His 55 hymns are included in *Nalayira divya-prabandham*. He was born into a brahman family of Mandangundi village in Thanjavur district and named Vipranarayana. On growing up he came to Shrirangam and made garlands for Shri Ranganatha, presiding deity of the temple there. It is said that he fell in love with a devadasi but was recalled to a devotee's life by Ranganatha himself.

Thulibhadda kaha (late 12th; Apabhramsha) of Somprabhacharya: a verse-tale contained within the larger work *Kumarapal-pratibodh*. The story is about Sthulibhadra, elder son of Shakatar, a minister of the ninth Nanda king who ruled at Pataliputra. On a spring day, the young and exceedingly handsome Sthulibhadra visited the palace of leading courtesan Kosha; charmed by her, he spent 12 years in her company. Meanwhile Shakatar died and the king decided to appoint Sthulibhadra's younger brother, Shripaka, as his minister. Shripaka would not accept this honour without the elder brother's consent. The king sent word to Sthulibhadra, who begged for some time to make a decision. On an impulse he came out of Kosha's residence and found he could no longer continue a life of self-indulgence. He took initiation into Jain faith from Acharya Samkhuti-vijay and applied himself thereafter to meditation.

Thupa-vamsa (early 13th; Pali) of Vachissara: prose work in three parts. The first part deals with the previous lives of Buddha. The second gives an account of events from the birth of Buddha to his death, the distribution of the relics of his body by Dona, and the construction of stupas at Rajagaha (by king Ajatsatru, at the instance of Thera Mahakssapa) over the relics brought from places like Vesali, Kapilavatthu, Pava, and Kusinara. The third part deals with the later history of the relics, also gives historical accounts of the theras sent by Thera Moggaliputta Tissa to different parts of India for propagating Buddhism. The latter offers valuable geographical information about important places of contemporary India like Tamralipta, Gandhara, Kasmira, Suvannabhumi, etc.

Tih-ahiya (Sindhi): the term literally means 'poem of thirty letters'. It is a kind of descriptive poem based on 30 letters of the Arabi alphabhet. (Actually, Arabi has only 28 letters but two are generally added to facilitate teaching.)

Tikkanna Somayyaji (*c*1220–1300): poet in Telugu and statesman; minister to a feudal chief of

Nellore, Manuma Siddhi (1200–58), who was a tributary to the Kakatiya king in Guntur. In his administrative capacity, he worked for the political unity of Andhra-desha as defence against Muslim invasion of the South; also worked for religious unity among Hindus by bringing together Shaiva and non-Shaiva poets, and promoted the cult of Hari-Hara. He undertook the task of rendering into Telugu the remaining books of *Mahabharata*, a work left unfinished by Nannaya. Other works attributed to him are *Niravachanottara Ramayanamu*, a kavya work; *Kavivag bandhana*, a treatise on prosody; *Vijaya-sena*, a poem.

Tilakamanjari (*c*970; Sanskrit) of Dhanapala: prose kavya work, perhaps in imitation of *Kadambari*. A continuous narrative, without any chapter divisions, it tells of the romance between princess Tilakamanjari and prince Samaraketu. The work offers some information about the Paramara king of Dhara; it is quite unique in style among Jain literary works. Another Jain poet named Dhanapal in 13th century wrote a summary of this work in Old Hindi and called it *Tilaksundari-kathasar*.

Tilism-e-hoshruba (?18th/19th; Urdu): a vast prose narrative, developed from the fifth part of the Farsi *Dastan-e-Amir Hamza* which appears in a single volume in the original. Elaborated in eight parts in Urdu, each containing more than 1000 pages, it has transcended the original work. There are several versions in Urdu. The one generally accepted is one published by Nawal Kishore Press of Lakhnau. The first four volumes, written by Munshi Mohammed Husain Jah, were published during 1881–90; the remaining volumes, written by Munshi Ahmad Husain Qamar, were published during 1891–93. The story depicts a struggle between the protagonists of Islam and the heathens. Amir Hamza is the Prophet's uncle while Laqa the magician is his chief adversary. Supernatural beings and events fill the narrative, in which goodness triumphs at the end. Apart from the supernatural, readers get an excellent view of the contemporary culture of Lakhnau.

Timmakka or **Tallapak Timmakka** (15th): regarded as the first woman poet in Telugu on the basis of her *Subhadra-kalyanamu*. This kavya work was composed in dvipadi metre and has 1163 verses. It is a special favourite of women and they sing its verses even today during marriages. Timmakka was the wife of Annamacharya, a famous poet and samkirtan leader.

Tipitaka: general term (meaning 'three baskets'; in Sanskrit, 'Tripitaka') for the three works *Vinaya-pitaka, Sutta-pitaka*, and *Abhidhamma-pitaka* in Pali. These constitute the religious philosophy and prescriptions of Theravada Buddhism. They appear to have been compiled through ages and may also reflect the deliberations of the Buddhist councils. The principal portions were completed at the Third Council (between 264 and 227 B.C.) held during the reign of Ashoka. From Tibetan and Chinese translations of the Pali work it has been inferred that a Sanskrit *Tripitaka* also existed. Only parts of this have been recovered, but enough to suggest that the Sanskrit work was not a translation of the Pali *Tipitaka* but an independent work.

Tirahuti, also Tirahuta (Maithili): the most popular kind of indigenous lyrics of the Tirhut area. The richest class of songs in Maithili, it comprises mainly love-songs abounding in descriptions of the nayika, her dalliance, her union with the nayak, her separation from him, etc.

Tirthakalpa (*c*1330; Sanskrit/Prakrit) of Jinaprabha Suri: a semi-historical work. It describes places of Jain pilgrimage; gives names of their founders; also of kings who repaired and restored them, along with dates and years.

Tirtha-mangal (1770; Bangla) of Bijoyram Sen Visarad: an account of a pilgrimage to Kashi by boat in 1768–69, undertaken by the poet when he accompanied his zamindar patron, Krishnachandra Ghoshal of Khidirpur.

Tiruchhendur Pillaitamil (15th; Tamil) of Pakalikkuttar: poetical work in the praise of the god Muruga (Kartikeya) of the temple in Tiruchhendur. As required by the 'pillai-tamil' form, ten stages of evolution of the infant Muruga are presented here.

Tirukkaruvappati truppattantati (16th; Tamil) of Ativir Ram Pandian: poetical work in praise of Shiva generally. More particularly, it expresses devotion to the idol in a temple in Karuvai village of Tirunelveli district.

Tirukkovaiyar (9th; Tamil) of Manikkavachakar: collection of verses, apparently of erotic sentiment, but dealing with sublime matters. In 'kovai' style, the work seems to deal with a loving hero and his beloved heroine; but the hero is Shiva himself and the poet is his beloved.

Tirukkural (?1st B.C.; Tamil) of

Tiruvalluvar: the major work in a group of 18 collections of didactic poems. Also called *Kural*, it is in the form of couplets and deals with three aims of life—'aram' (righteousness), 'porul' (wealth) and 'inbam' or 'kamam' (pleasure). It consists of 133 sections each containing ten couplets composed in 'kural-venba' metre. The first part gives the essentials of Yoga philosophy; deals with the happy household life as well as the path of renunciation. The second part deals with polity and administration, including citizenship and social relations. The third part deals with the concept of love; this is in the form of a dramatic monologue. It is generally regarded as the greatest ethical work in Tamil.

Tirukkural bhasha (16th; Malayalam) of unknown authorship: a prose rendering of the entire *Tirukkural*. The language is close to the spoken Malayalam of the time.

Tirukkutrala kuravanchi (mid-18th; Tamil) of Tirukutarasappak Kaviriyar: the first and the finest example of the 'kuravanchi' form of verse narrative in Tamil. It tells of the beautiful young girl Vasantavalli who sees Shiva in a temple procession and falls in love with him. While she is pining away, Singi the kuratti (=fortune teller) visits the household, reads Vasantavalli's palm and assures her that Shiva will come to her when it is time. Meanwhile Singam the kuruva (=birdcatcher) comes looking for his wife, Singi, and they are reunited after a long time. The story and its treatment is full of folk flavour, hence has always been popular. The form itself gained much popularity and gave rise to the 'kuravanchi' play which featured dances. From Tamil, the form and its offspring passed to Telugu and Marathi.

Tirukoneri Dasyai (?13th): woman poet in Tamil; author of *Vivarana shatakam.* She was a commoner and her real name remains unknown. The pseudonym she used means 'slave woman of the deity of Tirukoneri'.

Tirumalamba (16th): woman-poet in Sanskrit, queen of Vijayanagar ruler Achyutaraya; author of *Varadambika-parinaya champu*, a work which blends history and fiction in order to emphasise human concerns, especially love.

Tirumandiram (?C; Tamil) of Tirumular: the 10th *Tirumurai* collection, consisting of 3000 songs. Apart from Shaiva mystical thoughts, the work tells of medicine, physical culture, astronomy, etc.

Tirumurai (11th; Tamil) of Nambi Andar Nambi: corpus of Shaiva hymns and other poems by sant-poets, prepared as a series of collections in 11 groups. The first seven collections contain the work of Sambandhar, Tirunavukkaranar and Sundarar; the eighth, of Manikkavachakar; the ninth, of other sants of a later period; the tenth, of Tirumular; the eleventh, of poems by different devotees, including the compiler Nambi Andar Nambi. A work of the following century but not of the same nature, *Periya-puranam* or *Tirullontar-puranam* is sometimes referred to as the 'twelfth' *Tirumarai*.

Tirumangai Alvar (?7th/8th): sant-poet in Tamil; one of the 12 Alvars. His poems (hymns), numbering about 1250, were collected in *Nalayira divya prabandham*. Originally named Kaliyan, Tirumangai was born into a family whose hereditary profession was robbery. His father was a feudatory chief; Kaliyan succeeded him and became an army commander of the Cholas. Under the good influence of his wife Kumadavalli, the daughter of a Bhagavat, Kaliyan became a Vaishnav.

Tirumoli or **Tiruvaymoli** (Tamil): collective title of select 1000 Vaishnav hymns within the *Divya prabandham* anthology.

Tirumular (?C): sant-poet in Tamil: one of the 18 Siddhas. His *Tirumandiram*, a collection of 3000 verses, constitutes a body of thought from which Shaiva Siddhanta as known in South India draws its authority. Tirumular was also the first to name 'Shaiva Siddhanta' as such, and his work is practically a philosophical treatise stated in everyday language.

Tirumurugurruppadai (?C; Tamil) of Nakkirar: the first idyll of *Pattuppattu*. It is a work in praise of the god Muruga and of the various shrines where he is worshipped; incidentally, it also depicts the life of ancient Tamils.

Tirunavuk karasar (*c*610–91): sant-poet in Tamil; first of the great Nayanmars also known as 'Appar' (=father). He visited 125 Shaiva shrines and is said to have composed 49,000 hymns, of which only 3064 survive. Born at Tiruvamur in South Arcot district, he was named Marulnikkiyar; lost his parents when he was very young and was brought up by an elder sister. On growing up he felt drawn towards Jainism, was initiated and became a religious leader named Dharmasenar. According to legend, he was converted to Shaiva faith by Shiva himself and re-named Tirunavukkarasar.

Tiruppavai (?C; Tamil) of Andal: collection of 30 verses inbued with Vaishnav spirit.

Tiruppuhal (early 15th; Tamil) of Arunagiri Nadar: poetical work in praise of the god Murugan. It is said that the poet had composed 16,000 verses to express his devotion to Murugan, but only 2000 verses are extant.

Tiruttakka Tevar (late 9th/early 10th): Jain ascetic and poet in Tamil, author of *Jivaka-chintamani*, also of a short work entitled *Nari-viruttam*. No details are known about his life. According to Jain sources, he was born into the Chola ruling family, but became an ascetic in early life. Yet his great work is about Jivakan, who was fond of women and married many times. When it was first presented in the Pandyan court, suspicion rose about the poet's own private life.

Tiru'ttondattogai (early 9th; Tamil) of Sundarar: a compilation which lists all the Nayanmars and explains the importance of each. It was the first such work; gave a definitive list of the Shaiva sants of Tamilnadu, on which other works are based.

Tiruvachakam (9th; Tamil) of Manikkavachakar: one of 63 Nayanmar sant-poets. The work is a collection of poems which describe various stages of the poet's spiritual experience. Expressive of Shaiva devotion, these poems are addressed particularly to the Shaiva idea of the temple in Tiruppennuturai. The pious believe that Shiva himself wrote these poems as dictated by the poet, his devotee. The work is as famous among bhakti texts in Tamil as *Bhagavat-purana* is in Sanskrit.

Tiruvalluvar (1st/2nd B.C.): name attributed to the author of the ancient Tamil classic, *Tirukkural*. 'Tiru' is a respectful prefix, 'Valluvar' is the name of a low caste; hence the poet must have belonged to that caste. He has also been called Nayanar, Devar, Devappulavar, Nanamugnar, etc. Though his name is attached to such an important text, nothing is known yet about his life.

Tiruvilaviyadal-puranam (?C; Tamil) of Paranjoti: work celebrating Shiva's great deeds of grace; adaptation of the Sanskrit work *Halasya-mahatmyam*.

Tiruvisaippa (?10th; Tamil): the ninth *Tirumurai* collection, consisting of the hymns of Senthanar and eight other Shaiva devotees. One of these eight, Kandaradittanar, was a prince, descended from the Chola king Paranttakan I.

Tisatthi-mahapurisagunalamkara Mahapurana (10th; Apabhramsha) of Pupphadanta: a purana type work, divided into two parts, 'Adipurana' of 37 sections and 'Upapurana' of 65. It gives an account of the 63 great Jinas, who are of five categories—Tirthankara; Chakravarti; Vasudeva; Baladeva; Pratibaladeva. There is mention also of the Rama and the Krishna stories, both modified to propagate Jainism.

Tobhya-caritra (*c*1602; Telugu) of Ellana Rayudu: work based on the legend of St. Thomas, it is also known as 'Sarveswara-mahatmyamu'.

Tola (?C): poet in Sanskrit from Kerala; composed the Sanskrit work *Mahodaya-charitam*.

Tolan (?9th): poet in Malayalam at the court of Kulasekhara Perumal. His comic compositions are said to have started the Manipravala style in Malayalam.

Tolkappiyam (*c*500 B.C.; Tamil) of Tolkappiyanar: the oldest extant Tamil work on grammar and poetics. The date of the work remains a matter of controversy; some scholars consider it later than the Third Sagam, hence of A.D. 4th or later; others consider it assignable to 2nd or 4th B.C. From Paramparanar's 'payiram' (introductory verses) to the work, it seems that the author preceded Panini (5th B.C.). The work lays down rules for different kinds of poetical compositions drawn from the examples furnished by the best works then available.

Tolkappiyanar or **Tolkappiyar** (*c*500; B.C.): author of *Tolkappiyam*. Nothing is known about his life.

Topnidhi (mid-18th): poet in Hindi and scholar, from Sringberpur near Ilahabad; author of *Sudha-nidhi, Vinaya-shatak, Nakhasikha*.

Torana yuddha (late 16th; Malayalam) of Kottarakara Tampuran: Kathakali play in five scenes which show Hanuman visiting Lanka the first time in search of Sita.

Torve Ramayana (15th; Kannada) of Narahari, also known as Kumar Valmiki after he wrote this work: a re-telling of the *Ramayana* story in Kannada. This was the first such work in Karnataka in the brahmanical tradition; earlier all the re-telling of *Ramayana* stories had been done in the Jaina tradition. The poet belonged to a village named Torve near Bijapur.

Trilinga-shabdanushasana (?13th; Telugu) of Atharvana: a work on grammar.

Trilochan (late 13th): sant-poet from Pandharpur (in Maharashtra), some of whose verses in Hindi are found in *Granth Sahib*.

Tripitaka: see Tipitaka.

Tripura-daha (13th; Sanskrit) a play which according to *Natayashastras* was composed by Brahma himself. Another play with the same title and in four acts, composed by one Vatsaraja, deals with the destruction by Shiva of the capital of Tripurasura.

Tripura-dahan sangatya (*c*1185; Kannada) of Sishumayan: poetical work.

Tripurantakudu [Ravipati Tripuranatakudu (early 14th)]: poet in Telugu; probably a contemporary of Kakatiya king Prataprudra-II (r. 1295–1326). Among his extant works are *Premabhiramamu, Ambika-shatakamu, Tripurant'kodaharanamu*.

Trishashti-lakshanamahapurana (*c*978; Kannada) of Chavundaraya: early prose work which elucidates the basic tenets of Jainism and describes the lives of 63 sants. It is also known as *Chavundaraya-purana*.

Trishashtipuratan charitra (early 16th; Kannada) of Surang: champu work in which the lives of 63 eminent Shaiva sant poets have been described.

Trishashti-salaka purusha-charita (1160/1172; Sanskrit) of Hemachandra: mahakavya in ten parvan. It deals with the lives of 63 best men of the Jain faith—24 Jinas, 12 Chakravartins, nine Vasudevas, nine Baladevas and nine Vishnudvisas. The final parvan deals with Mahavira and offers some definite information about him.

Trivikrama Bhatta (9th/10th): poet in Sanskrit: author of *Nalachampu* (also known as *Damayantikatha*) and *Madalasa-champu*. Son of one Nemaditya (or Devaditya), grandson of one Shridhara, he appears to have been a court-poet of Rashtrakuta king Indra-III (r. 914-16). He mentions Bana and is cited by Bhoja.

Troilokyanath Mukhopadhyay or **Mukherjee** (1847–1919): prose writer in Bangla, best known as a writer of fantasies. Among his works are *Kankabai, Sekaler katha, Bhut-o-manush, Phokla Digambar, Muktamala, Maina kothaye, Majar galpa, Paper parinam, Damaru-charitra*. While working as a sub-inspector of police at Katak (Orissa), he became editor of the monthly *Utkal shubhankari*; later he was appointed head clerk in the office of the *Bengal Gazetteer*.

Tuk (Hindi): rhymed ending relating two or more lines of verse.

Tukaram (1588–1619): the greatest sant-poet of Maharashtra; composed about 5000 abhang poems, which in their totality form a kind of Bible for Maharashtrians. Born at Dehu near Pune, of humble shudra origins, he inherited the family's money lending business. After the great famine of 1630, in which he lost his wife and son, he withdrew into a life of contemplation and eventually emerged as a poet. He become a devotee of the god Vitthal and began the practice of giving public sermons known as 'Kirtan'.

Tullal: a solo dance of Kerala, supposed to have been innovated by Kunchan Nambiar in 18th century. In this the performer himself recites the verse and enacts the same with hand gestures and body movements. The text for recital generalises foibles of the time under the guise of telling a puranic story.

Tulsi Saheb of Hathras (b.1788): sant poet in Hindi; author of *Ghata Ramayan, Shabdavali, Ratnasagar*.

Tulsidas (*c*1523–1623): the greatest poet of Hindi, also known as Goswami or 'Gusai' Tulsidas; author of *Ramcharitmanas*. He was born into a brahman family of Sukarkhet (or Soro) village near Chitrakut in Uttar Pradesh; brought up (but not by his parents, Atmaram and Hulasi) in Rajapur village of Banda district; taken charge of by one Baba Naraharidas who took him to Kashi, where he studied with a scholar named Sesha Sanatan. He returned to Rajapur at the age of 15; married Ratnavali, daughter of Dinabandhu Pathak; left home because of some difference with his wife and travelled for 19 years. He began *Ramcharitamanas* in Ayodhya in 1574 but wrote the major part in Kashi, where he spent the rest of his life. He composed in Avadhi as well as in Brajbhasha 11 other works: *Ramlala nahachhu, Vairagya sandipani, Barvay Ramayan, Parvati-mangal, Janaki-mangal, Ramajnya-prashanavali, Dohavali, Kavitavali, Gitavali, Vinaya-patrika*.

Turawai (Panjabi): equivalent of the 'rubai' of Farsi poetry; a verse-stanza of four lines in which the first, second and fourth lines end on the same rhyme.

Turunavukkarasar: see Appar.

Tutinama (1639; Urdu) of Ghawwasi: a masnavi, derived from the Sanskrit work *Suka-saptati*.

U

Ud-e-hindvi (1868; Urdu) of Mirza Ghalib: the first collection of his letters. There are altogether 137, written from time to time to disciples and well-wishers. In addition there are some brief critical pieces on literature and three prefaces he wrote for other books. He died four months after the publication of this volume in October 1868.

Udaharana vangmayamu (Telugu): a minor kavya-form which became popular for some time in Telugu, beginning with *Basabodaharan* composed by Palkuriki Somnath in late 13th. Vidyanath, a Sanskrit scholar of Andhra, has described 'udaharan' in his work of poetics written in Sanskrit, *Prataparudriyam*. Though obviously based on a Sanskrit model, there are very few examples of 'udaharan', to be found in Sanskrit.

Udayan-kathai: see Perun-kathai.

Udayanakumara kaviyam (13th/14th; Tamil): by unknown author; long poem which tells, with slight variations, the story of Udayana as narrated in *Perun-kathai*, which in turn derives from the Prakrit *Brihat-katha*. It is regarded as one of the five minor 'epics' of Tamil.

Udayanath, Kavindra (b. 1679): poet in Hindi, son of Kalidas Trivedi; author of *Rasa-chandrodaya, Vinod-chandrika, Joglila.*

Udayaratna (17th/18th): poet in Gujarati; belonged to the Tapa Gachha sect of Jains. He wrote *Jambuswami rasa* (1693), *Sthulibhadra rasa* (1703), *Navakara rasa* (1706), etc.

Udayasundari-katha (*c*1000; Sanskrit) of Soddhala: prose kavya modelled on *Kadambari*, liberally interspersed with verse, but not a champu work. In eight sections it tells of the romance between Udaysundari, daughter of Naga king Sikhandatilaka, and Malayavahana, king of Pratisthana. The author was a Vallabha kayastha of Lata, and enjoyed the patronage of king Mummuniraja of Konkan.

Udbhat or **Bhattodbhat** (*c*800): literary theorist and critic in Sanskrit from Kashmir; according to Kalhana, Udbhat was the chief scholar in the court of Kashmir ruler Jayapida (r. 779–813). He is the author of the work on poetics *Kavyalamkara-samgraha*; also wrote *Bhamaha-vivaran* a commentary on Bhamaha's *Karyalamkar*, but this is not extant.

Udbhat-kavya (*c*1225; Kannada) of Somaraj; champu kavya in 'kanda' metre divided into 12 'aswas'. Also known as *Shringarsara*, it is a love-story which is given a bhakti ending; the story is derived from *Udbhat-ragale* of Harihar.

Uddhav Gita (*c*1310; Marathi) of unknown authorship: a philosophical poem based on the Sanskrit *Murtiprakash* composed in 1298 by Keshav Vyas, who derived his material from the 11th 'skandha' of *Shrimad Bhagavat*. The poem consists of advice rendered to Uddhav by Shri Krishna, hence came to be known as *Uddhav Gita*. The poet belonged to the Mahanubhav sect.

Uktivyakti-prakarana (early 12th; Hindi): oldest known work in Avadhi.

Ullasikama Thaya: see *Ajita'-shanti laghu'stavana*.

Umade Bhatiani-ri bat (1790; Hindi): prose narrative in Dingal. It tells of how queen Bhatiani, wife of Rao Maldey of Jodhpur, kept her vow of never having spoken to her husband all her life.

Umapatidhara (late 12th/early 13th): poet in Sanskrit. No single work of his is known, but verses composed by him were included in *Sadukti-karnamrita, Sukti-muktavali* and *Padyavali*. He was a contemporary of Jayadeva, who mentions him in *Gita Govinda*. Merutunga refers to him as a minister of king Lakshmansena of Bengal.

Umar-Marui: a famous love story of Sindhi literature in which the beautiful shepherd girl Marui is abducted by Amarkot ruler Umer.

Umaruppulavar (17th): Muslim poet in Tamil; born in Kalekkare village near Ramnathpuram town. He wrote *Sivappuranam*, an account of the life of Nabi Muhammad in the puranic form.

Unmada Vasavadatta (9th; Sanskrit) of Shaktibhadra: lost play referred to by the author himself.

Unnayi Varier (late 17th/early 18th): poet in Malayalam; author of the famous attakatha *Nalacharitam*. Not many details of his life are known. He lived permanently or occasionally at Triuvananthapuram; enjoyed the patronage of king Kartika Tirunal alias Dharma Raja of Travancore; probably earned a livelihood by making garlands and preparing other offerings for temple rituals.

Unnichirutevi-charitam (mid-14th; Malayalam) of unknown authorship: an early work in Manipravalam, in a form resembling the champu, but is entirely in prose. Unlike the prose of Sanskrit champus, however, this is a metrical prose with all the rhythmic and melodic organisation of verse. The story tells of a beautiful courtesan and how Indra himself comes down to earth on hearing of her beauty.

Unniyachi-charitam (*c*1325; Malayalam) of Shrikumar: a champu work in Manipravalam, which can also be regarded as the first kavya work in Malayalam. The story is about a young gandharva who comes down to earth when he hears of the beautiful dancer Unniyachi. A brahman student meets him and tells him about her family; next day the gandharva visits her house and sees her. The rest of the poem is a detailed description of the girl. This story has been used in two later champu works.

Unniyati-charitam (end-14th; Malayalam) of Damodar Chakyar: champu work composed in honour of the daughter of Kerala Varma, ruler of Kayamkulam. The story tells of how the apsara Pravrit attracts the attention of the moon-god Chandra but is cursed by his wife Rohini to be reborn as a mortal. She is reborn as the daughter of Kerala Varma and grows up into a beautiful woman, highly proficient in music and dance. Chandra hears her singing and sends an attendant to find out about her. The rest of the poem comprises of attendant's report to the moon-god.

Unnunuli-charitam (*c*1330; Malayalam) of unknown authorship: a sandesha kavya of 240 stanzas in Manipravalam. The poet is himself the hero; the heroine Unnunil is a princess of the Vadakkumkur royal family in central Kerala. They marry and live happily in Kaduthuruthy; but a jealous yakshi, enamoured of the hero, causes some problems but the couple is ultimately united. The poem is particularly important for the descriptions of medieval Kerala. The MS was discovered only in 1893.

Unnunuli-sandesham: another title for Unnunuli-charitam.

Upadesharasayana-rasa (*c*1150; Apabhramsha) of Jinadatta Suri:

didactic poem in 80 verses which explains the importance of human birth and how the soul may be saved. It also stresses the need to have a 'guru' in order to lead a proper life. There are many other items of advice to the householder.

Upanishad: a class of Vedic literature designated as 'Vedanta' because these were the last literary products of the Vedic period and mark the culmination of Vedic speculation. The word 'upa-ni-shad' literally means 'sitting down near'; the works in question grew out of confidential sessions between a preceptor and his disciples. Each of the Vedic samhitas has its upanishads and there are over 100 of them. Among these, the 10 commented upon by Shankaracharya, are regarded as the most genuine and authoritative. These are *Isha, Kena, Kattha, Prasna, Mundaka, Mandukya, Taittiriya, Aitareya, Chhandogya* and *Brihadaranyaka*. Some of the texts contain ancedotes which illustrate a particular exposition.

Upanyas (Hindi): the novel or long prose fiction. The term is also used in Bangla and some other Modern Indian languages.

Upendra Bhanja (1670–1720): great exponent of the highly sophisticated but artificial style which dominated Oriya writing from early 18th to first half of 19th century. Excelling in pedantry, play on words and erotic description, Upendra composed about 42 works altogether in which all known literary forms are illustrated. Ten great romances are among the most esteemed of his works: *Vaidehisavilasa, Subhadraparinaya, Kalakautuka, Arani-rasa-taranga, Lavanyvati, Rasika-hara-vali, Premasudhanidhi*. Two other works, *Rasa-panchanka* and *Gitabhidana* are meant to instruct young authors in poetical and rhetorical devices. He was desecended from a princely family of Ghumesar in Ganjam district. His grandfather and father were both poets.

Urdu: a language spoken in many parts of undivided India, but now more prevalent in North India while it was adopted as the national language of Pakistan. From humble origins as the speech of military camps, it developed into a literary language during 16th/17th first in the Deccan (Dakhan) where it was known as Dakhni. Subsequently it moved north and became established in and around Delhi as the language of authority as well as of culture. Its vocabulary and literary forms are influenced by Farsi and Arabi, while it is written in a

Perso-Arabic script. Urdu speakers in India would number about 102 million (28 million in India).

Urdu-e-mualla (1869; Urdu) of Mirza Ghalib: the second collection of his letters, published in two volumes after his death. The first, within 19 days of his death on 4 February 1869, was reprinted in 1891; the second volume was published in 1899 under the supervision of Hali. The combined volume published by Sheikh Mubarik Ali from Lahore in 1929 carries an appendix containing 23 hitherto unpublished letters.

Urubhanga (?C; Sanskrit) of Bhasa: one-act play on the mace-duel between Bhima and Duryodhan. It is the earliest known 'ekanki' (=one-act) play in Sanskrit; its ending with the death of Duryodhan marks a departure from Sanskrit literary tradition which did not approve of tragic endings.

Usha-haran (?C; Maithili) of Ratnapani: a kirtaniya play on the Usha-Aniruddha story.

Usha-haran (?C; Maithili):of Chakrapani: a 'sammara' work of about 200 lines which tells the Usha-Aniruddha story as a simple narrative.

Ushanirudda (mid-18th; Prakrit) of Rama Panivada: long poem on the story of Usha and Aniruddha.

Usha-parinaya (15th; Asamiya) of Pitambar: a series of love songs about Usha and Aniruddha.

Usman (early 17th): a Sufi poet in Hindi from Ghaziabad; composed the verse romance *Chitravali*. He tried to imitate Jayasi in his verses.

Uttara Harivamshamu (mid-14th; Telugu) of Nachan Somanna: a kavya work which is loosely related to the earlier portion of the Sanskrit *Harivamsha*, but otherwise offers material of the poet's own creation. Of its six 'aswas', the first contains an account of the slaying of Narakasura; the second features the rescue of Viprakumar; the third tells of Paundak Vasudeva, the fourth of Hamsadimbak, the fifth of Usha and Aniruddha, the sixth of the duel between Shri Krishna and Banasur. This kavya appeared at that phase of the history of Telugu literature when works based on puranic sources were making way for 'prabandha' works.

Uttarajjhayana-sutta (?C; Prakrit) of unknown authorship: Jain religious work in mixed prose and verse. It comprises various texts of multiple authorship and was composed at different periods. The older portion in verse contains aphorisms, parables, dialogues, ballads, sermons, admonitions, etc.

Uttara Rama-charita (7th/8th; Sanskrit) of Bhavabhuti: play in seven acts. It deals with the latter part of the *Ramayana* story from Rama's return to Ayodhya and coronation to the end. Bhavabhuti has introduced certain scenes that are not in the original.
Tr. C.H. Tawney, Calcutta, 1871; S.K. Belvalkar, *HOS*, 1915.

Uttara Ramayana (16th; Malayalam): of unknown author: a prose rendering of *Ramayana*.

Uttara Ramayanamu (early 17th; Telugu) of Kankati Paparaju: a prabandhakavya in prose as well as verse re-telling the *Ramayana* story in eight 'aswas'.

Utthanka (Panjabi): a form of prose.

Utthasoma (15th): poet in Kashmiri; belonged to the court of Zainul Abidin. He wrote his patron's biography; composed a series of lyrics; also wrote a treatise on music, Manaka.

Uvaes mal kahanae chhappay (12th/13th; Apabhramsha) of Vinaychandra Suri: a sequence of 81 didactic poems which cite examples from the lives of tirthankars and other eminent persons in order to teach moral lessons. Also known as *Upades mal kathanak chhappay*, the work is in chhappay metre.

Uvanga or **Upanga**: a class of Jain texts.

Uvavaiya (?C; Prakrit): the first 'uvanga', in two parts. The first part descibes Mahavira's departure for the Punnabhadda shrine and the pilgrimage of king Kuniya Bhimabisaraputta to that place to listen to Mahavira's sermons. The second part is in the form of questions and answers, dealing from bad and good deeds.

V

Vachana (Kannada): a form of lyrical prose which expressed some deeply felt personal experience. It was used most effectively by Virshaiva sant-poets and is often associated with them.

Vachana sampradaya kadai (18th; Tamil) of Muthukutti Iyer: an allegorical narrative in verse, which has no precedence in Tamil literature. The story is set in Ramanathapuram district where the monsoon has failed one year and drought conditions have set in; villagers perform the usual rites and offer sacrifices; the gods are propitiated and it rains again. By allegorical device, the clouds, gods, planets, etc., are all made into human characters, each with a caste name and appropriate station in life; even the failure of the monsoon is turned into the failure of a farmer to pay his annual rental dues to the landlord.

Vachanika (Rajasthani): a narrative form in verse mingled with poetical prose. It may have originated as a prose form in Apabhramsha but in late 16th it began to use rhymes and alliteration. *Jina Samudra Suri ri vachanika* is a good example of this mixed form.

Vachha-haran (*c*1280; Marathi) of Ramodar Kavi: narrative poem on an episode in Shri Krishna's life when he intercedes and retrieves for fellow-cowherds the cattle abducted by Adhasur. This is the earliest known 'prabandha-kaviya' in Marathi, also perhaps the only extant kavya featuring this episode. The poet belonged to the Mahanubhava sect.

Vadakkan Pattu (Malayalam): collection of ballads of medieval origin. These present the saga of heroes like Aromal Chevakar, Thacholi Otenan, Thachola Chantu, Palattu Koman and heroines like Unniyarcha, Mattu, etc. The oldest compositions do not date earlier than 16th but their idiom and vocabulary seem older. The Malayalam used is devoid of Tamil or Sanskrit, thus is probably close to the spoken idiom.

Vadakku Thiruveedi Pillai (*c*1217–1312): scholar of Tamil, a Vaishnav acharya of Shrirangam. He wrote *Mupatharayirappadi*, an exhaustive commentary on the more than 1000 hymns of the Nammalvars.

Vaddhamana chariu (*c*1130; Apabhramsha) of Vibudha Shridhara: prose narrative of 2500 verses in ten 'sandhi' dealing with the last tirthankara, Vardhaman Mahavir, and his previous lives.

Vaddharadhane (*c*920: Kannada) of Shivakotyacharya: prose work consisting of 19 stories which illustrate certain tenets of Jainism. Apart from their religious purpose, the stories are narrated in a lively manner and use vivid details. This is the second available ancient text in Kannada, the other being *Kavirajamarg*. Scholars believe that *Vaddaradhane* as well as the Sanskrit *Kathakosha* of Harishen are both based on an older work in Prakrit.

Vadha-kavya (Asamiya): the form presenting episodes from *Mahabharata* in which the Pandav brothers, chiefly Bhim, fight and kill demons. Many Asamiya works in this form are attributed to Rama Saraswati.

Vagbhata (?C): the name of several authors in Sanskrit. Two earlier ones, in 7th and in 8th, wrote on Ayrurveda; two later ones on alamkara. Of the latter, one in 12th wrote *Vaghbhatalamkara*, probably also a kavya entitled *Nemi-nirvana*; one in 13th wrote *Kavyanushasana*.

Vaidehisa Vilasa (*c*1700; Oriya) of Upendra Bhanja: re-telling of *Ramayana* in chitra-kavya form. Each line of this work begins with the consonant 'ba'; the number of stanzas in each section are figures that have 'ba' as initial when pronounced (thus, 'baro' for 12, 'battis' 32, etc.); the poem is supposed to have been completed in 'barmasa' (12 months). The work, an imitation of *Raghunatha-vilasa* of Dhananjaya Bhanja, the poet's uncle, is an extreme example of ornate poetry.

Vaijayanti (mid-11th; Sanskrit) of Yadavaprakasha: a voluminous lexicon which arranges words by syllables, genders and initial letters. The author appears to have been a former guru of Ramanuja, lived in Kanchipuram and wrote an independent commentary on *Brahmasutra*.

Vaijayanti-vilasamu (16th; Telugu) of Sarangu Somayya: kavya work in five 'aswas' relating an episode about Vipranarayan, one of the 12 famous Vishnu-bhaktas of

Tamilnadu. It so happens he is seen by two courtesans, Devadevi and Madhuravani, who are sisters, while they are walking in a garden. Madhuravani tells Devadevi that Vipranarayan is a pious man and unlikely to be drawn into romantic dalliance. Devadevi lays a bet with her sister and charms Vipranarayan into surrendering to her. However, alarmed by the situation, Shri Vishnu intervenes and rescues his devotee. The poem thus contains elements of bhakti as well as shringar.

Vairagya'sar (12th/13th; Apabhramsha) of Supravacharya or Suprav: poetical work of 77 verses which depict the transience of earthly life and its woes. The poet was a Digambar Jain.

Vairagya-shataka (?C; Sanskrit) of Bhartrihari: sequence of 100 poems on the hollowness of love and earthly happiness. It also offers valuable advice about practical life.

Tr. C.H. Tawney, *IA*, 1876; J.M. Kennedy, London 1913; C.W. Gurner Calcutta, 1927.

Vaishika-tantram (?13th; Malayalam) of unknown authorship: earliest known example of a poetical work composed in Manipravalam. No complete text has yet been found. It is a manual of prostitution, told to the courtesan Anangasena (or Anangalata) by her mother who has retired from the profession.

Vajid (mid-16th): poet in Panjabi who comsposed numerous poems expressing devotion to a non-sectarian god.

Vajihuddin Vajdi (early 18th): poet in Urdu from South India; composed several masnavi works. His *Panchhibachha* (1718) is a translation of the Farsi *Mantikul tir* of Fariduddin Attar; *Makhjan-e-ishk* (1731) is an original work; *Tohfa-e-ashika* (1740) is another translation from Farsi.

Vajja'lagga (?C; Prakrit) of unknown compiler: an anthology of 1330 verses arranged under about 95 different sections. The work was obviously modelled on *Sattasai* of Hala Satavahana; nearly all the verses are in Maharashtri Prakrit. No date has yet been fixed. It has been known variously as *Vijjalagga, Bhajjalagga, Vaggalagga, Vajjavagga*. The Sanskrit form of the commonly accepted title would be 'Vrajyalagna'.

Vakh (Kashmiri): the poetic form used by Lal Ded.

Vakenavis bakhar (late 17th; Marathi): prose chronicle which gives an account of Shivaji's life.

Vakpatiraja (early 8th): poet in Prakrit; author of *Mahumahavia* and *Gaudavaha*. He was probably a pupil of Bhavabhut.

Vakrokti (Sanskrit): a critical term propagated by Kuntaka in his *Vakroktijivita*. It stands for 'striking expression' which, according to Kuntaka, is the real test of poetry. This concept was debated throughout the history of Sanskrit poetics.

Vakroktijivita (10th/11th; Sanskrit) of Kuntaka: work on poetics. It seeks to establish that 'vakrokti' (striking expression) is the 'jivita' (essential life) of poetry. Only the first two sections of the work and parts of the third and fourth have survived. It is not known how many sections comprised the original work.

Vakrokti-panchasika (*c*850; Sanskrit) of Ratnakara: poem of 50 verses composed as a conversation between Shiva and Parvati during their love-sport.

Vakyapadiya (early 7th; Sanskrit) of Bhartrihari: work on grammar, in verse, dealing mainly with questions of the philosophy of speech.

Valaiyapati (?C; Tamil) of unknown authorship: one of the five major kappiyam. It is available in fragments (mostly quoted in *Purattirattu*) and the full story of the romance has not yet been reconstructed. Its high standing is inferred from references to it in important commentaries, in one of which it is stated that Ottakkuttar followed the *Valaiyapati* style. In another it is suggested that the author was a Jain.

Vallabha Bhatt (1690–1751): poet in Gujarati; composer of garba songs. A brahman, his name is remembered along with that of his twin-brother Dhola, in older shrines dedicated to the mother-goddess in Gujarat. According to tradition, he composed the famous *Ananda-no garbo* in 1653 when he was only 13 years old; his other compositions have been dated between 1710 and 1736.

Vallalar (1823–84): sant-poet in Tamil from Marudur village, in Arcot district of Tamilnadu. Among his works are *Tiruarutpa, Shivanesh venba, Mahadevmalai ingidmalai*, etc. Because of his kindly behaviour he came to be called 'Vallalar' (the kind one); his real name was Ramalingaswami.

Valmiki (?C): legendary first poet in Sanskrit; according to tradition, author of *Ramayana*. The legend makes him a bandit by the name of

Ratnakar, who gave up his nefarious livelihood at the bidding of Narada and started a long penance. While he sat at the same spot for this, a valmik (ant-hill) grew there to cover him; hence his name, Valmiki. After completing his penance, one day he happened to see a pair of krauncha (curlew) birds, engaged in love-making, killed by the arrow of a nishada (fowler). Moved to pity, he uttered the verse *'mah nishada pratistham tvamagamah'* etc.; this is regarded as the first ever poetic creation by man.

Vaman Pandit (1615–78): poet in Marathi and scholar of Sanskrit; composed narrative poems on puranic stories, also translated Sanskrit works into Marathi. He generally enriched Marathi prosody by introducing new metres based on Sanskrit. Born in Bijapur, he went to Banaras for studying Sanskrit and became a proficient debater on learned subjects. He used to compose in Sanskrit until he met Samartha Ramdas, who exhorted him to compose in Marathi. Among his philosophical works are *Samshloki Gita, Nigamsara*. He translated into Marathi the *shatakas* of Bhartrihari and *Ganga-lahari* of Jagannath. Among his narrative poems are *Gajendra-moksha, Sita-swayamvara, Venusudha*.

Vamana (*c*800): literary theorist in Sanskrit, author of *Kavyalamkar-sutra-vritti*. He was a minister of Kashmir ruler Jayapida.

Vamana Bhatta Bana (15th): writer of several forms in Sanskrit; obtained patronage of Vimabhupala who ruled (1403–20) in some part of Andhra Pradesh. Among his works, *Shringara-bhushana bhana, Kanakalekha-kalyanam, Parvati parinayam*, are plays; *Nalabhyudaya, Raghunatha-charita, Hamsa sandesha*, are poetical works; *Brihatkatha-manjari* is a prose work; *Shabdachandrika* and *Shabdaratnakari* are lexicons. He knew at least six languages and was given the title 'Shada-bhasha-vallabha'.

Vamsha-bhaskar (1840; Rajasthani) of Suryamall Misan (1815–68): verse chronicle of the Chauhan rulers of Bundi state in Rajasthan. The work, which was commissioned by Maharaja Ramsingh, also serves as a source of information regarding contemporary history and culture of the region.

Vamshamani Jha (1618–89): playwright and poet in Maithili, also musicologist. He appears to have gone to Nepal at the invitation of the ruler, Jagajjyotirmalla of Bhatagon (r. 1618–33); wrote in collaboration with him or in his name works on music in Sanskrit such as *Sangitasara-samgraha, Swarodaya-dipika, Sangita-bhaskara*. His plays in Maithili are *Mudita-kuvalayashva* (1628), *Hara Gauri-vivaha* (1629), *Kunjavihari-nataka, Gitadigambara, Mudita-madalasa*. He also wrote a number of devotional poems in praise of Shiva.

Vanchippattu (Malayalam): literally means 'boat-song'. This is sung especially on occasions like Onnam while moving across a body of water. Many narratives such as "Kiratam", "Nala'charitam", "Vyasotpatti", etc. have been composed in this form.

Vannakkalanji Pulavar (?C): Muslim poet in Tamil; author of *Muhaidin-puranam*, a work on Islam. His other name was Muhammad Ibrahim.

Var (Panjabi): term used in two senses in Panjabi literature. (1) It refers to hagiological poems in which the subjects could be divine or human (viz., "Var Shri Bhagouti ki", "Var Nadir Shah ka"); from this, the term 'var-kavya' means poems in praise of divine or eminent human personages. (2) Poems composed in 'poudi' metre glorifying heroic persons and deeds (viz., "Asa-di-var" in *Guru Granth Saheb*).

Var Nadarshah (?C; Panjabi) of Najavat: narrative poem describing the battle fought at Karnal in 1739 between the invader Nadir Shah and the Mughal emperor Muhammad Shah 'Rangile'. The poet dwells neither on the causes nor on the consequences of the battle but on the battle itself.

Varadambika-parinaya champu (1540; Sanskrit) of Tirumalamba: a kavya work telling about the royal family of Vijayanagar. The poet was the queen of the then ruling king Achyutaraya, and the story ends with the investiture of prince Chinna Venkatadri as heir apparent. This is the only known champu kavya to have been composed by a woman.

Vararucha kavya (?C; Sanskrit): lost work mentioned by Patanjali in *Mahabhasya*.

Vararuchi (?C): name of several authors in Sanskrit. One must be the author of *Vararucha-kavya* mentioned by Patanjali (see above). One Vararucha Katyana is supposed to have written the vartika-sutras added to *Ashtadhyayi*. The same name Vararuchi is assigned as the author of a *Niti-ratna*, a *Patra-kaumudi*, a *Linganushasana*, a *Simhasana-dvatrimsika*, a *Raja-niti*, a *Ubhayabhisarika*, though these works belong to different periods. According to tradition, one of the 'nine jewels' (nava-ratna) in the court of Vikramaditya was named Vararuchi.

Vardhamana (*c*1100): Jain poet in Prakrit; author of *Manorama-charita* and *Adinatha-charita*.

Vardhamana-puran (*c*1200; Kannada) of Achanna: an account of life of the 24th tirthankar, Vardhaman or Mahavira. The work was begun by the poet's father, Keshavraj, and completed by the poet.

Varna-ratnakara (early 14th; Maithili) of Jyotishwar Thakur: long prose work divided into seven 'kallola' (wave) sections to match the title which means 'ocean of descriptions'. The work is a compendium of life and culture in medieval India, particularly of Mithila; contains an interesting account of the function of the 'bhat' (court poet).

Varnak (Kannada): term for informal and indigenous literary composition, as distinguished from 'vastuk' which obeys formal requirements.

Varnana (Maithili): form of prose work, consisting of a set description. The origin of this form has been traced back to Prakrit literature of the Jains.

Varta (Hindi): a prose form, especially in Brajbhasha from 15th century onwards, used for biographical sketches of leaders of the Vallabhacharya sect.

Vartamana pustakam (1787; Malayalam) of Paremakkal Thoma Kalhanar: a prose account of the journey to Rome undertaken by Malpan and Kalhanar in about 1778. Apart from a description of the voyage via the Cape of Good Hope, Brazil and Portugal, the work also offers a description of the western world as seen by eastern travellers. This is probably the earliest known travelogue in any Modern Indian language.

Vasanta-vilasa (?C; Gujarati) of unknown authorship: earliest extant manuscript is of 1422. It is a 'phagu' work but unusual because its protagonists are an ordinary man and woman, who have not been given names.

Vasavadatta (?C; Sanskrit) of Subandhu: prose kavya of the katha type. It deals with the romance between prince Kandarpaketu and princess Vasavadatta. There is much uncertainty about its date of composition; both Patanjali's *Mahabhashya* and Bana's *Harsha-charita* mention a prose kavya of this name.

Vastuk (Kannada): term for the more fornal, convention-abiding literary composition, different from 'varnak'.

Vasu-charitra (?C; Telugu) of Bhattumurti: work in which the prabandha form is regarded to have reached its peak of excellence.

Vasu-charitramu (16th; Telugu) of Ramarajbhusanudu: a prabandha-kavya, one of the five most successful prabandha works in the language. The story, drawn from *Mahabharata*, tells of Chedi ruler Vasu, who as reward for tapasya was gifted an aerial chariot by the god Indra. Because of this he also came to be called Uparichar-vasu.

Vasudeva (?C): a poet in Sanskrit from Kerala who composed two yamaka kavyas, *Yudhisthera-vijayam* and *Nalodayam*.

Vasudeva-charia (4th B.C.; Prakrit) of Bhadravahu: lost work, probably a prose romance about the wanderings of Vasudeva.

Vasudeva Hindi (5th/6th; Prakrit): voluminous prose tale in 100 'lambhak' divisions. The first part consists of an autobiographical account of his travels by Vasudeva; this was composed by Samghadasa. The second part consists of the adventures of Narabahandatta. The work may have derived from the lost *Vasudeva-chariu* of Bhadravahu, but it also corresponds in form to *Brihatkatha* of Gunadhya; appears to have been composed before A.D. 600.

Vatakkamkur Rajaraj Varma (1822–70): poet in Malayalam, scholar of Sanskrit; author of poetical works in Malayalam *Raghabhyudayam, Raghuvir-vijayam, Uttar Bharatam*; prose work in Sanskrit *Kanyakumari-stavam.*

Vatavahan kavya (Sanskrit): type of Sanskrit kavya peculiar to Mithila. It is supposed to induce the wind to blow at particularly hot periods of the day.

Vatsabhatti (5th): poet in Sanskrit known by the Mandasor stone-inscription composed by him in A.D. 472. This composition, consists of 44 verses in Vaidarbhi style and they reveal the influence of Kalidasa. Though no other work of his has been recovered, Vatsabhatti is invariably mentioned in any discussion of Kalidasa's dates.

Vatsaraj (late 12th/early 13th): playwright in Sanskrit; was probably a minister of Kalinjar ruler Paramardi Deva and continued in this post during the reign of his son Trailokyavarma Deva. His six 'rupak' plays are *Karpurar-charit, Hasya-chudamani, Tripur-dahe, Kiratarjuniya, Samudra-manthan, Rukmini-parinaya*. Each is different from the other in dramatic form and purpose.

Vatsun (Kashmiri): form of folk-poetry dating back to 14th. The term is derived from 'vachan' in Sanskrit.

Vatsyayana (?3rd) also called Mallanaga: scholar of Sanskrit: author of *Kamasutra*. He is supposed to have pre-dated Kalidasa and belonged to Pataliputra. Another scholar of the same name, also from Bihar, lived in 4th century.

Veda: term for the four Vedic samhitas—Rig-veda, Yajur-veda, Atharva-veda and *Sama-veda*.

Vedanayakam Pillai (1826–89): the first modern novelist of Tamil, author of *Piratap Mudaliar charittiram* (1876). His other novel, *Chukuna chunlari*, is less known; it deals with the life of contemporary women. He also wrote some poetry, to be found in *Nitinul, Penamtimalai*, and *Charab chamay chamarachakkirtan*. A third generation Christian, he served the East India Company as a munsif.

Vedanta-rasayana (*c*1750; Telugu) of Mangalagiri Ananda Kavi: a kavya in four sections on the life of Christ and doctrines of the Christian church. The author was a brahman.

Veera Naikerin suya charitai (1778–93; Tamil) of Veera Naiker: a part-autobiography of the period 1778–93 in the author's life, written in the form of a daily diary. The author worked in the police department of the French administration in Pondicherry. His diary is a rich source of information on major historical and political events of the time. The language used by him includes words from French, English, Farsi and Urdu.

Veerama Munivar: the popular name of Father Beschi, the Italian missionary who mastered Tamil. See 'Beschi'.

Veli Krisan Rukmini-ri (1580; Hindi) of Prithviraj Rathod: work in 'veliyo git' form and in Dingal language, describing the marriage of Shri Krishna and Rukmini.

Vemabhupala-charita (early 15th; Sanskrit) of Vamana Bhatta Bana: prose work celebrating the 15th century Reddi ruler, Vemabhupala or Viranarayana of Kondavidu (r. 1403–20).

Vemana (?16th): sant-poet in Telugu. Though he was widely known, there is some doubt about his dates. He composed hundreds of didactic verses in a desi metre known as 'atalavedi'. His poetry makes a complete departure from the artifical verse of his contemporaries.

Vemulavada Bhima Kavi: see Bhima Kavi.

Venbappattiyal (11th; Tamil) of Gunavira Pandital: a work on grammar.

Venisamhara (8th/9th; Sanskrit) of Bhattanarayana: play in six acts, dealing with the *Mahabharata* episode where Bhima ties the loose braid of Draupadi's hair with hands besmeared with the blood of Dushasana whom he has just killed. According to unauthenticated tradition, the author was one of the five brahmans of Kanyakubja (Kanauj) brought over by king Adisura of Bengal.

Tr. S.M. Tagore, Calcutta, 1880. S. Viswanathan, Madras, 1961.

Venkata Krishnappa Nayaka (18th): poet in Telugu; also a warrior, attached to the court of Vijayaranga Chokkanatha (r. 1706–33) of his four works, *Radhika-santwana* and *Ahalya Sankrandanamu* are in verse; *Jaimini Bharata* and *Sarangadhara-charita* are in prose.

Venkatachar [B. Venkatachar (1845–19144)]: writer in Kannada; best known for his translations of novels from Bengali—first Vidyasagar's *Bhranti-vilas*, then many works of Bankimchandra.

Venkatacharyulu [Madbhushi Venkataryulu (1835–95)]: poet in Telugu, scholar of Sanskrit. Though at least five works are attributed to him (*Bharatabhyudayamu, Vamannatakamu, Pushpaban-vilasamu, Ramavaghuti nakshatramala, Hamsa-sandesamu*), only the first has been recovered so far.

Venkatapati (early 18th): poet in Telugu from Madurai, where he was a friend of a local chief, Vijayranga Chokkanath. Of his several works, only one is extant, *Shashanka-vijayamu*.

Venkatratanamu Pantulu [Kokkod Venkatratnamu (1842–1915)]: writer in Telugu also social reformer. He wrote one of the earliest novels in the language, *Mahasweta*, on the model of Sanskrit *Kadambari*. He rendered the Sanskrit *Narakasur-vijay* into Telugu and dramatised it, thus opening up a new path for Telugu drama. He wrote several long 'mahatmya' poems on places of pilgrimage. In emulation of Jayadev's *GitaGovinda*, he composed *Gita-mahanatnamu* in Sanskrit.

Venmanimahan Nambutiripad (1844–93): poet in Malayalam; son of another renowned poet, Venmani Achhan Nambutiripad. Though named Kadamban, he is known to the literary world as 'Venmanimahan'. He is associated with the Venmani movement in Malayalam poetry which was aimed at reducing the influence of Sanskrit and simplifying Malayalam in order to make it accessible to the common man. Most of his works were left incomplete; among the complete ones are *Puraprabandham, Ambopadesham, Bhutikhusa-charitram, Kamatilakam-bhanam*.

Vetala-charitam (late 18th; Malayalam) of Raghava Pisaroti: collection of stories derived from the Sanskrit works of Kshemendra and Somadeva.

Vetala-panchavimshati (?C Sanskrit) of unknown authorship: prose work in which 25 stories are set within the frame of the main narrative featuring king Trivikramsena (or Vikramsena) who later became known as Vikramaditya. Of four extant versions, three are by Shivadasa, Jambhaladatta and Vallabhadasa, none of whose identity or date is known; the fourth version is anonymous.

Jambhaladatta version Tr. M.B. Emeneau, New Haven, 1934.

Vibhava (Sanskrit): term in poetics for excitant or stimulant as a factor of 'rasa'. This is of two kinds, 'alambana' and 'uddipana'.

Vidagdha-chintamani (late 18th; Oriya) of Abhimanyu Samanta Simhara: kavya work on the Radha-Krishna story. Three sections covering 148 stanzas are devoted to love in various forms found in the human as well as in the animal world.

Vidagdha Madhava (?1589; Sanskrit) of Rupa Goswamin: play in seven acts depicting the entire Brindavan-lila of Radha and Krishna.

Vidagdha-mukhamandana (late 13th; Sanskrit): of Dharmadasa Suri: work on poetics, which pays special attention to 'chitra-kavya' and also describes the feelings of separation from the loved one. The author was probably a Bouddha ascetic.

Viddha-salabhanjika (9th/10th; Sanskrit) of Rajshekhara: play of the 'natika' type, named after the statue-device ('salabhanjika') used

in it. It tells of Vidyadharmalla, king of Karpuravarsa, who, though already married, falls in love with the Lata princess Mrigankavali, daughter of kind Chadravarman; after many difficulties, they finally marry.
Tr. L.H. Gray, *JAOS*, 1906.

Vidhi-nataka (*c*1420, Telugu) of Shrinatha: professedly a treatise on drama, it gives a vivid account of life in a town like Rajamahendi in the poet's own time; includes sketches of women the poet meets on the streets.

Vidya Sundar (*c*1752; Bangla) of Bharatchandra Raye: the second part of *Annada-magal*. The work is an erotic romance about Vidya, the beautiful daughter of king Virasimha, and Sundar, the handsome and clever son of king Gunasindhu, who set out to win the princess. This was the most popular theme of amorous poetry of the time among upper-class people in the townships along the Hooghly. There were many previous poems on the theme and several imitations afterwards, but Bharatchandra's poem remained supreme. It dominated poetic literature in Bengal even upto mid-19th and he was considered the greatest poet of Bengal. Other poems on this theme were composed by Shah Birid Khan, 17th; Govindadas, early 18th; Shridhar, early 19th; Krishnaram, early 19th.

Vidyavilas pavado (*c*1428; Gujarati) of Hiranand: long poem about the princess Vidya who is married off to a commoner, Vinay Bhatta, instead of to a minister's son; but Vinay ultimately proves worthy of her love.

Vidya-charavarti (early 14th) scholar of Sanskrit, probably belonged to the court of Hoysala king Vir Vallal III. He wrote *Sampraday-prakashini*, a commentary on Mammata's *Kavyaprakash; Alamkarsanjivani*, a commentary on Ruyyaka's *Alamkarsarvaswa*. Two other works in poetics, *Rasa-mimansa* and *Bharat-samgraha*, have been attributed to him.

Vidyachandra Bhattacharya, Kavisekhar (mid-18th): poet in Asamiya. During the reign of Ahom king Rajeshwar Singha (r. 1751–69); rendered Vishnu parvan of Harivamsha into Asamiya. He introduced the presence of Radha as mistress of Krishna, though she is not mentioned in this section of the Sanskrit original.

Vidyakalpadruma (1846–51; Bangla/English) of Rev. K.M. Banerjea: a bilingual encyclopaedia in 13 volumes. This one-man effort was aimed at strengthening the spread of 'vernacular education' in the face of English being made the medium of instruction in 1835. The compiler, Krishnamohan Bandopadhyay (1813–85), born into a brahman family of Calcutta, converted to Christianity in 1832.

Vidyakara (10th/11th): anthologist in Sanskrit; compiled *Subhashita-ratnakosha*, containing 1739 subhashita verses. Very little is known about him; he was probably a Bouddha and lived in East India.

Vidyapati (1360–1448): the greatest poet of Mithila and among the major poets of medieval India. Born into a family that had served the Oinavara dynasty for several generations, Vidyapati was a playmate of king Kirttisimha and later a close associate of king Sivasimha; after the latter's overthrow, he accompanied queen Lakhima to exile in the Nepal village of Rajbanauli; when she died, he lived in spells at the courts of successive kings. He wrote a number of works in Sanskrit relating to religious performances and household duties; his narrative poems are generally in Maithili-Avahatta; but most of his lyrics are in Maithili. A play by him in Maithili entitled *Gorakshavijaya* has been discovered recently. Although he wrote some devotional verse, he is primarily a poet of love and the 'pada' form was raised to excellence by him.

Vijayamuktavali (*c*1700: Hindi) of Chhatrasingh Kayastha: a re-telling of *Mahabharata*. The poet was from Bateswar.

Vijayaraghava-kalyanamu (*c*1680; Telugu) of Koneti Dikshita Chandra: a Yakshagana text on the theme of the marriage of Nayaka king Vijayaraghava, who was himself a composer and patron of Yakshagana.

Vijayaraghava Nayaka (*c*1633–73): Nayaka ruler of Thanjavur; poet in Telugu. He composed over 20 Yakshagana works and generally popularised the form by having Yakshaganas staged in his presence.

Vijaya-vilasamu (early 17th; Telugu) of Chemakura Venkata Kavi: prabhandha work dealing with the travels of Vijaya (Arjun) during which he meets and marries Ulupi, Chitrangada and Subhadra.

Vijaypal raso (*c*1300; Apabhramsha) of Nallasingha Bhatt: kavya work which describes the battles of Vijaypal, Yaduvamsi ruler of Vijaygarh (Karouli). The entire work has not been recovered.

Vijja, Vijjaka or **Vijjika** (7th): woman poet in Sanskrit, whose compositions have been praised by Rajshekhara and Bhoja in their works. She was probably the queen of Chandraditya, son of Pulakesin II who ruled about A.D. 660; her name is the Prakrit form of the Sanskrit name Vijaya.

Vikatanitamba (9th): woman poet in Sanskrit with this strange name (meaning a woman with ugly buttocks); it was probably a nickname. Her date has not been established nor have any separate works been found. But her verses have been cited by scholars, starting with Anandavardhan in *Dhvanyaloka*, and she also appears in many anthologies.

Vikramanka'deva-charita (1085; Sanskrit) of Bilhana: historical poem in 18 sections. It gives an account of the Chalukya kings of Kalyana, particularly of the poets patron, Vikramaditya VI Tribhuvanamalla (1076–1127).

Tr. S.C. Banerji and A.K. Gupta, Calcutta, 1965.

Vikramarjun-vijaya: see *Pampa-Bharata*.

Vikramarka-charitramu (late 14th/early 15th; Telugu) of Jakkana: hagiographical work about king Vikramark, who is presented through stories that highlight his courage, generosity and other virtues.

Vikramorvashiya (?5th; Sanskrit) of Kalidasa: play in five acts. It tells of king Pururavas who falls in love with the celestial nymph Urvashi, and of how after many difficulties they are permitted to live together during Pururavas' lifetime. The source is difficult to determine because the story occurs in *Rigveda, Satapatha-brahmana, Vishnu-purana, Bhagavata-purana, Matsya-purana, Hari-vamsha* and *Kathas-arit-sagara*. The author has introduced marked changes in the story in order to heighten the dramatic effect.

Tr. E.B. Cowell, Hartford, 1851.

Vila [Mazhar Ali Vila'; real name Lutf Ali (late 18th/early 19th)]: prose writer in Urdu probably from Delhi where he may have been better known as a poet. He came to Fort William College in Calcutta and wrote several books that were published by the college. Of these the most famous is *Vetal pachisi*, which he translated probably from a version available in Braj. Other works are *Madhavanal aur Kamakandala* translated from Hindi, *Tarikhe-Shershai* from Farsi; he also made a poetical version of Sheikh Sadi's *Karima*.

Vilanka Ramayana (15th; Oriya) of Sarala Dasa: the first retelling of *Ramayana* in this language. But the poet has introduced alterations, the most drastic of which is that Ravana is killed by Sita when Rama, Lakshman and Hanuman have all failed.

Vilasvati katha (*c*1060; Apabhramsha) of Siddhasen Suri: narrative poem of no particular religious purpose, though the author was an orthodox Swetamvar Jain. It tells of the handsome Sanatkumar, son of king Yasovarma of Swetambi. Rebuked by his father for some reason, the prince left Swetambi and, accompanied by his friend Vasubhuti, went to Tamralipti which was then ruled by Ishanchandra. Here the princess Vilasvati and he fell in love with each other. The chief queen Anangavati was also charmed by Sanatkumar and made advances to him; when he declined, she brought false charges against him and he was sentenced to death by king Ishanchandra. But the 'kotwal' Vinayandhar helped Sanatkumar to escape by boat, along with Vasubhuti, and they went to Swaradvip. The story continues like this with Sanatkumar and Vilasvati being separated and reunited several times.

Villi-bharatam (14th; Tamil) of Villiputturar: a re-telling of the first ten parvas of *Mahabharata*.

Villiputturar (14th): poet in Tamil; author of *Villi-bharatam*. A pious Vaishnav, he was born in some village in a central region of Tamilnadu.

Vimalsuri (1st): author of *Paumachariu*.

Vina Vasavadatta (?C; Sanskrit) of unknown authorship: play which is extant only in an incomplete version. Some scholars have proposed that this is the last play of Shaktibhadra (?9th) referred to by him as *Unmada-Vasavadatta*; others ascribe it to Shudraka. From the story it appears to be a variation on the theme of Pratijna-Yaugandharayana of Bhasa; the play also reveals some of the characteristics that feature Bhasa's drama.

Vinayachandra Suri (13th): Jaina sadhu and poet in Apabhramsha from Gujarat; author of *Mallinath-mahakavya, Parswanath charit, Kalpa-nirukta, Neminath-chaupai*.

Vinayapatrika (1609; Hindi) of Tulsidas: a collection of 279 poems, not all inter-related, in which the poet presents a petition to Shri Rama. Since Ram is master of the universe, he cannot be approached directly; so the poet addresses prayers to a number of deities like Ganesh, Surya, Shiva, Ganga, Yamuna, etc in support of his petition. He also appeals to Hanuman, Lakshman, Bharat and Shatrughna while addressing a separate prayer to Sita. Finally Lakshman, after consulting Hanuman and Bharat, presents the petition to Rama. The language used is Brajbhasha, with noticeable influence of Avadhi, Bundelkhandi and Rajasthani at places.

Vinayashri (b. 1168?): a poet of Mithila who is said to have composed 15 poems dealing with esoteric matters as in the *Charya* poems. These are the earliest available specimens of Maithili-Avahatta composition. The poet was a resident of Vikramshila 'vihar' and is reported to have fled in 1203 to Tibet, where these poems were discovered in a palm-leaf manuscript by Rahul Samkrityayan.

Vinodrasa (1670; Hindi) of Sumati Hans: long poem which tells of the romance between Jayasen, son of Vikramaditya, and Lilavati, daughter of Seth Shridatta.

Vinukonda Vallabharayudu (late 14th/early 15th): poet in Telugu; author of *Kridabhiramamu*. The better-known Shrinathudu, a close friend of his, may have collaborated in the writing of this kavya work.

Vipradas Pipalai (late 15th): poet in Bangla: author of a Manasa-mangal poem called *Padma-puran* around 1492. The work is also known as *Manasa-vijay*. There has been much controversy regarding the authenticity of the work.

Vir (11th) poet in Apabhramsha: scholar of Sanskrit. He belonged to Gulkhed village in Malwa; his father Devdatta was an established poet of his time. Vir could have composed in Sanskrit or Prakrit but, at the instance of his father and of friends, composed *Jambusami-chariu* in Apabhramsha.

Virgatha kavya (Hindi): long poems in praise of royal patrons, description of their battles, account of their romantic affairs and marriages. They form the earliest phase of Hindi literature.

Vira Kerala Varma (d. 1695): warrior prince of Kottayam, who was also a poet in Malayalam; composed several didactic poems.

Viraraghavakkavi (16th) poet in

Tamil; author of *Arichhandira-puranam*, a translation of the Harischandra story.

Virachozhiyam (?11th; Tamil) of Puttamittiranar: a work on grammar.

Viramanayana (Rajasthani): a form of memorial verses, that tell the story of Virama, a chief of the Rathod clan. This clan had sought refuge with the Joiya, a community that had converted to Islam, but later fought with them. Dhadhi Bahadara, a Muslim bard, originally composed these verses, which are known as 'nisani'; hence the body of works was also called *Dhadhi Bahadara-ri nisaniyan.*

Viramayan (*c*1400; Hindi): kavya work in Dingal in praise of Rao Viramji Rathod. The poet belonged to the Dahri tribe.

Viresh-charite (early 12th; Kannada) of Raghavanka: a relatively short kavya work (in two 'sarga' containing 127 verses) in uddanda shatpadi metre telling the Dakshayajna story. Virbhadra, created by Shiva to devastate the yajna, is the chief character here; hence the work has been named after him.

Vireshalingam [Kandukuri Vireshalingam (1848–1919): writer in many forms in Telugu who pioneered an era. Among his many contributions are the monthly, *Viveka-vardhini*, which aimed at the improvement of the position of widows; translation of *The Vicar of Wakefield* as *Rajashekhara charitra*, and of *Gullivers' Travels* as *Satya Raja Purva desha yatra*; an autobiography; three volumes of biographical sketches of poets in Telugu from Nannaya to his own time; and so on.

Virshaivamrit-puran (?C; Kannada) of Gubbi Mallanarya: expository work dealing with Virshaiva principles. But it also includes gatha poems on many subjects, tells 25 'lila' episodes from Shiva's life, narrates the lives of old as well as new devotees—thus, is not a purely philosophical text. This may be the reason for its being called a 'puran'.

Virsinghdeva-charit (*c*1600; Hindi) of Kesavdas: kavya work about the life and deeds of Virsingh, interspersed with reflections on charity, greed, etc.

Virud chhihattari (*c*1600; Rajasthani) of Adho Duraso: collection of 76 verses in honour of Rana Pratap of Mewar.

Virupaksha (14th/15th): playwright in Sanskrit: wrote the five-act

Narayana vilasa and the one-act *Unmatta-Raghava*. He has been identified as Bukka II, son of Harihara II, of the Sangama dynasty of Vijayanagar. There are at least two other authors in Sanskrit bearing this name who lived within a hundred years of one another.

Viruttam (Tamil): name of a verse metre.

Virutti (Tamil): long commentary on an important text.

Visaldev rasu (*c*1200; Hindi) of Narapati Nalha: kavya work in Dingal. It narrates the adventures of Visaldev, ruler of Ajmer; his marriage with Rupamati, princess of Dhara; his separation from her and final reunion. Only an incomplete text of the work is extant; the romantic rather than any heroic element is prominent. The language represents a crucial transitional phase where the Apabhramsha influence is clear, yet an early Hindi is also emerging. From this work it would appear that literary Hindi as represented initially by Braj and Khari-boli came into use in Rajasthan before in any other region.

Vishakhadatta (?4th/5th): playwright in Sanskrit, author of *Mudrarakshasa*. Although he mentions a king named Avantivarman (one in 7th, another in 9th) in the concluding verse, in some MSS the name Chandragupta occurs instead. This is taken to be the Gupta emperor, Chandragupta II (4th/5th) and the playwright placed accordingly. In the work Vishakhadatta names his father as the king Bhaskaradatta, his grandfather as Vateswaradatta. He may be the same as Vishakhadeva, to whom the play *DeviChandragupta* is assigned.

Vishnubhat Godse (1827–1904): prose writer in Marathi, known mainly for his travelogue *Majha pravas* which includes an eye-witness account of some of the battles of 1857.

Vishnudas (early 17th): poet in Gujarati. He is said to have composed 39 works, mostly 'akhyana' poems, but only two or three are extant, like *Mameru* and *Hurdi*.

Vishnupuri Sanyasi (425–1500): a poet of Mithila; contemporary of Vidyapati; composed devotional poems in Maithili. He became a Vaishnav sanyasi but wrote padas on Shiva as well and is the author of a work in Sanskrit, *Bhaktiratnavali*.

Vishnusharman (?C): according to tradition, author of *Panchatrantra*.

The introduction indicates that the stories comprising the work were told to the sons of king Amarashakti of Mahilaropya (or Mihilampya), somewhere in Dakhan. The original work appears to have been written prior to A.D. 531.

Vishwanath (early 14th): scholar of Sanskrit from Orissa; author of *Sahitya-darpana*. In the work he claims he was the son of Mahakavi Chandrasekhara, who was probably a high court official under a king of Kalinga. There are several authors in Sanskrit of this name. This Vishwanath may also have written a commentry on Mammata's *Kavyaprakash*; this commentry is called *Darpan*.

Vishwanath Kaviraj (mid-17th): scholar in Sanskrit; author of *Sahitya-darpan* which became a popular textbook and has had much influence on Hindi literature.

Vishwanathsingh, Maharaj (1789–1856): ruler of Rewa, patron of poets, himself a poet in Hindi and scholar. Among 32 works ascribed to him are *Ramayana-tika, Gita-Raghunandan pramanik, Kabir Bijak-ki-tika, Param-tatva, Ananda Raghunandan*; last named is a play.

Vishweshwara (?18th): playwright in Prakrit; author of *Shringara-manjari*, a sattaka, and *Navamalika*, a natika. He belonged to Almora in Uttar Pradesh.

Viswanath Jani (1721–71): poet in Gujarati, probably from Patan. Not much is known about his life. His known works are *Sagal-charitra*, which tells of Sagalsha Sheth, who sacrified his son to keep a vow; *Mosala-charitra*, an account of the preparations for the marriage of Kunvarbai, daughter of Narsi Mehta; *Chatur-chalisi*, a poem of 40 padas describing how Shri Krishna won over a gopi he had earlier offended; *Prema-pachisi*, another poem on a Krishna episode.

Vithi-natak (Telugu): an old dramatic form of the Andhra region which owes nothing to any Sanskrit model (it is unrelated to the kind of play defined as 'vithi' in Sanskrit texts).

Vithu Meha (16th): poet in Rajasthani; author of *Jaitai ro chhanda, Chhand trotak Babu Jindrava Rao*, and *Gogajirao rasavada.*

Vitthal [Vitthal Anant Kshirsagar (1628–60)]: poet in Marathi, author of *Rukmini-vilas, Sita-swayamvar, Panchali-stavan, Draupadi-vastraharan, Bilhana-charitra*, etc. His *Saundrya-lahari* and *Rasa-manjari* are translations from Sanskrit.

Vitthalnath (b.1458): sant-poet in Hindi and leader of Ashtachhap group; author of *Shringar-rasa mandan, Yamuna-shatak, Navaratna-shatak.* Son and disciple of Vallabhacharya, he propagated the use of Brajbhasha and helped to develop Brajbhasha prose.

Vivarana shatakam (?13th; Tamil) of 'Tirukoneri Dasyai' the pseudonym of a woman poet. The work, also known as *Tiruvaimozhi vachaka malai,* is a commentary on 100 out of 1102 hymns of Nammalvar. Perhaps because the author was a commoner, also a woman, the work was forgotten for about six centuries, until it was re-established in mid-20th as an important text.

Viveksindhu (13th; Marathi) of Mukundaraj: expository work on the basic tenets of Hindu philosophy; consists of 1671 verses in ovi metre; was composed to introduce the poet's patron Jaitrapal to the subject. He wrote this at the age of 60, when he probably lived at a place now known as Ambhor (in M.P).

Vividha tirtha kalpa (1330; Prakrit/Sanskrit) of Jinaprabha Suri: a travel guide written in mixed prose and verse, based on the author's own travels in North and South India. Of its 60 sections, 42 deal with places of pilgrimage; 38 tirthas are described in some detail. The author began writing it around 1300.

Vopadeva (13th/14th): scholar of Sanskrit; author of two grammatical works, *Mugdhabodha* and *Kavikalpadruma.* On account of the popularity of these works in Bengal, it is believed Vopadev belonged to that region.

Vrajlal Shastri (1825–1903): a philology scholar of Gujarati: who worked mainly at the Gujarati Vidya Sabha and Dharma Sabha, both of Ahmadabad; edited the journals published by these institutions—*Buddhi prakash* and *Dharma prakash.* Apart from studying Sanskrit grammar and poetry, through the reading of Jain religious texts he made a thorough study of Pali, Prakrit, Apabhramsha and Ardha-Magadhi before writing books on the philogy of Gujarati. These are *Gujarati bhashano itihas* (1866), *Utsargamala* (1870), *Gurjar bhasha prakash* (1892), *Dhatu samgraha.*

Vrind (b.1643): sant-poet in Hindi from Marwar; guru of Rajsingh, ruler of Krishnagad; author of *Vrindsatsai, Shrinagar-siksha, Bhavapanchasika, Rupak-chayanika, Alamkar-satsai* and *Hitopadeshnahtak.* The first is a didactic work, composed in dohas which became very popular among common people.

Vrishabhendra-vijaya (*c*1665; Kannada) of Shadakshardeva: champu work in 42 'aswas' consisting of about 400 verses. It is an account of the life of Basaveshwar.

Vrishabheshwar-shatakamu (13th/14th; Telugu) of Palkuriki Somanatha: the first 'shataka' work in Telugu which fulfils formal requirements of a shataka. While expressing devotion for Basaveshwar, it also praises many other Virshaiva devotees. The poet knew eight languages and at places in the poem he has used words and metres of Tamil, Kannada and Marathi well.

Vritta-ratnakara (11th/12th; Sanskrit) of Kedara Bhatta: work on prosody. Divided into six sections, it describes 136 metres; has been extensively quoted by commentators like Mallinatha. Son of Pibveka (Pathavaka), he probably belonged to Kashmir and lived sometime before 15th.

Vritti (Sanskrit): as a grammatical term, it means literal explanation of each word of a text. As a term in dramaturgy, it refers to dramatic style.

Vyabhichari-bhava (Sanskrit): term in poetics for the transient mood or subordinate feeling; a factor of 'rasa'. For example, 'shanka' (apprehension). It is also known as 'samchari-bhava'.

Vyakarana (Sanskrit): grammar. The word means 'the process of analysing', and in the context of language-analysis its purpose is to determine what is correct and what is not. Traditionally, it has been a prescriptive process.

Vyakti-viveka (11th/12th; Sanskrit) of Mahimabhatta: work on poetics. In three sections ('vimarsha'), the author seeks to demolish the theory of Dhvani and establish that the function of 'vyanjana' (suggestive meaning) posited by Anandavardhana is no other than traditional 'anumana' (logical inference). The author has identified himself as the son of Shri Dhairya and disciple of Mahakavi Shyamala; probably belonged to Kashmir and lived no earlier than first quarter of 11th to not later than the same of 12th century.

Vyanjana (Sanskrit): term in poetics for that function by which a word suggests a sense which is other than its primary sense.

Vyasa: according to tradition, author of *Mahabharata*; often referred to as Vedavyasa, because he is believed to have compiled the vedas for the first time. Because he was born on an island, he is also called Dvaipayana; because he was dark called Krishna Dvaipayana.

W

Waai (Sindhi): form of poetry peculiar to this language; possibly the oldest known in Sindhi.

Waisalul asiqin (early 18th; Urdu) of Shah Husain Zawqi: a new version, in Dakhni, of Mulla Wajhi's *Sabrås*. The work is also known as *Husn-i-dil*.

Wajid Ali Shah 'Akhtar' (1827–88): poet in Urdu and patron of the arts, last ruler of Avadh. He composed in a variety of forms—qasida, masnavi, ghazal, marsiya, thumri, git and dadra—and was ranked among the leading poets of his time. It is believed he wrote about 28 books of verse and prose, but only a couple have survived. Of these, the well-known *Hizn-e-Akhtar* is an account of his journey from Lakhnau to Calcutta which he made when Avadh was annexed by the British and he was exiled to Calcutta.

Wali Aurangabadi (?1688–1741) or Shamsuddin Waliullah of Aurangabad: sometimes called 'Baba-e-Rekhta' (the father of Urdu poetry) because he successfully employed the speech of Delhi to compose verse. Nearly one-third of his available work is in pure Dakhni, some in a mixture of Dakhni and Urdu, the rest is pure North Indian Urdu. Already an established poet in Dakhni while he was in Aurangabad, when he came to Delhi around 1720, he is said to have been advised by Shah Sadullah Gulshan, Sufi poet in Persian, to replace Dakhni idiom with Urdu. This innovation won Wali a number of followers and he started a school for poets in Delhi.

Wali Vellori (early 18th) or Mohammed Fyaz Wali of Vellore: poet in Dakhni; wrote a new version of Jayasi's *Padumavat* and called it *Ratan-wa-Padam*.

Waris Shah (*c*1720–1800): poet in Panjabi; composed the finest of the Heer-Ranjha poems generally referred to as "Heer Waris". No definite details are known about his life. It has been inferred that he was born in Jandiwala Sherkhan village of Shekhupura district (now in Pakistan); after primary education he sought initiation at the dargah of Babu Farid Shakarganj in Pakpattan; later settled in Malkahas village of Montgomery district and lived here until his death.

Wasokht (Urdu): poetical form in which the disappointed lover complains about the beloved's cruelty towards him.

Whengba Madhabram (1700–70): writer in Manipuri, who also knew Bangla and Sanskrit. His works are *Langlon*, a book of moral teachings; *Mahabharat Birat parva*, which adapts a parva of *Mahabharata; Chinthangkhomba Maharaj Ganga chatpa*, a travelogue; *Sonamanik* and *Sonakashi*, two romantic tales.

Y

Yadava (or Jadava) dynasty: a Maratha kayastha family who established their rule towards end-12th at Sinnar in Nasik district of Maharashtra; later transferred their capital to Deogiri (near Aurangabad). They are important to Marathi literature because they adopted Marathi as the court language and encouraged its wider use. The Yadava rule (1189–1320) can thus be regarded as a distinguished period in the history of Marathi literature.

Yadumani Mohapatra (?18th): best known as a wit among rural people in Orissa, his jokes and other sayings have been collected in *Yadumani-rahasya*. But he was also a scholar in Sanskrit and Oriya; composed a kavya *Prabandha-purnachandra* as ornate as any kavya of Upendra Bhanja. Born into a low caste of carpenters in Itumati village of the former Nayagara state, he rose on account of his wit, scholarship and other social qualities to be a favourite courtier in many states of Orissa.

Yaduram Barua (1801–69): scholar of Asamiya; compiled the first dictionary of the language in 1839.

Yamuna-shatak (*c*1500; Sanskrit) of Vallabhacharya: poetical work which was translated into Brajbhasha prose by his own son Vitthalnath.

Yapparunkalakkarigai (11th; Tamil) of Amutasagarar: work on prosody. The author was a Jain ascetic.

Yashastilaka champu (959; Sanskrit) of Somadeva Suri: champu kavya in eight 'aswas'. It tells of the legendary Yashodhara, the lord of Avanti, his deaths and rebirths, and final conversion to Jainism. The work was composed during the reign of Rashtrakuta king Krishna, and under the patronage of his feudatory, a son of the Chalukya king Arikesharin III.

Yashodhar Navakavishekhara (1493–1531): a poet of Mithila who called himself 'Navakavishekhara' in order to be distinguished from Jyotishwar Thakur already called 'Kavishekhara'. Some of Yashodhar's poems are to be found in *Ragatarangini*.

Yashodhar-charite (*c*1200; Kannada) of Janna: kavya work re-telling a popular story in Jain tradition. When a king named Maridatta decides to sacrifice his son Abhayruchi and daughter Abhaypati to the goddess Chandamari (a form of Kali), they seek permission to narrate their previous lives, on hearing their story, Maridatta gives up 'himsa' and becomes a Jain.

Yashodhara-kappiyam (13th/14th; Tamil) of Vennaval Vel: long poem, included among the minor epics. It tells of king Yashodhara, whose wife Amritapati, enchanted by the music played by an elephant-keeper, falls in love and goes to live with him; as counselled by his mother, Yashodhara plans to kill Amritapati but himself dies poisoned by her; mother and son then pass through many low lives. Finally, Yashodhara's son, on learning of his previous births, decides to renounce worldly life. There is not much literary merit in this work which, like *Chulamani* and *Nilakesi*, was composed for sectarian purposes.

Yashovanta Dasa (16th): one of the Pancha-sakha poets in Oriya; remembered now mainly through his narrative of Govindachandra sung by Nath mendicants. He also wrote works of religious philosophy like *Swarodaya, Premabhakti Gita, Atmaparache Gita*, etc.

Yashka (?C): scholar of Vedic; wrote the first commentary of *Rigveda*. His date is uncertain; it has not even been possible to establish whether he lived before or after Panini.

Yatharthadipika (mid-17th; Marathi) of Vaman Pandit: prose commentary of *Bhagavat Gita*. According to its author, the work offers a more correct interpretation than Jnaneshwar had in *Bhavarthadipika*. The real difference lies in Jnaneshwar's having emphasised 'bhakti-marga' while Vaman Pandit emphasised 'jnana-marga'.

Yayati-charitramu (1575; Telugu) of Ponnekanti Teleganna: a prabandha kavya, it tells the story of Yayati as given in *Mahabharata*. The work has 737 verse as well as prose stanzas divided into five aswas. The poet has demonstrated here that an entire kavya work can be composed in 'Swachha Telugu'. This is the earliest known work in this kind of Telugu. It was dedicated to Amin Khan, an official of the Muslim ruler of Golkonda.

Yodha Bhatta (15th): poet in Kashmiri in the court of Zainul Abidin; author of *Jaina-charita* and *Jaina-prakasha*.

Yogavashishtha, also known as **Yogavashishtha Ramayana** (?C; Sanskrit): sometimes claimed as an appendix to *Ramayana*. It deals with various topics, including 'moksha', discussed by Vashishtha with Shri Ram as listener. Its six sections ('prakarana') are entitled 'Vairagya', 'Mumukshu-vyavahara', 'Utpatti', 'Sthiti', 'Upasama' and 'Nirvana', indicative of the topics discussed. No authorship has been ascribed but it is regarded as a fairly old work, composed before 9th. Mughal emperor Akbar got the work translated into Farsi by Naquib Khan, Abul Fazl and Mulla Shiri.

Yusuf-u-Zuleikha (1680; Urdu) of Hafiz Barkhurdar: a romance of Farsi origin. It tells of Yusuf, a young man who was so handsome that Zuleikha, princess of Egypt, fell in love with him; due to some misunderstanding, he was put into prison; later he was exonerated, made king of Egypt and married off to Zuleikha.

Z

Zaban-e-Urdu-e-Mualla: or 'the language of the exalted Camp or Court', i.e., of the Mughal emperor; a polite name for Hindustani or the speech of Delhi. Later the name was curtailed to 'Zaban-e-Urdu'; finally, to 'Urdu'.

Zafar [Serajuddin Muhammad Bahadur Shah 'Zafar' (1775–1863)]: poet in Urdu and last Mughal emperor; ascended the throne in 1837 and remained till 1857, though his 'empire' had shrunk considerably; after the Sipahi Rebellion had failed, he was exiled to Rangoon by the British; died there. A disciple of Zauq, he was a good poet and his works have been collected as *Kulliyat-e-Zafar*.

Zainul Abidin, Badshah (1420–70): Muslim ruler of Kashmir during whose reign there was considerable revival of literary activity. He knew Sanskrit and Farsi, and encouraged the growth of literature in these two languages; set up a translation bureau for rendering Farsi works into Sanskrit and Sanskrit works in to Farsi; got *Rajatarangini* translated into Farsi and employed two Sanskrit scholars to continue the account beyond 1150 (where Kalhana had stopped). Among his court poets who composed in Kashmiri were Utthasoma, Yodhabhatta, Bhatta Avatara; some of them collaborated in rendering *Shahnama* of Firdausi into Kashmiri verse.

Zakaullah (1832–1910): prose writer in Urdu and mathematics teacher. Of his 143 books, 81 are on mathematics; the rest are mainly Urdu translations and adaptations from English, also textbooks on various subjects. His most substantial work is *Tarikh-i- Hindustan*, a 14-volume history of India, the first such book in Urdu.

Zamir [Mir Zamir (later 18th/early 19th)]: poet in Urdu, especially well-known for modernising the marsiya form. He introduced the use of Urdu that was close to the spoken variety; also began the practice of reciting rather than singing the marsiya. He belonged to Lakhnau and was a contemporary of

Nasikh; like Nasikh, he was an advocate of refined diction.

Zahir [Saiyad Zahiruddin Zahir (19th)]: poet in Urdu from Delhi. He had to leave in 1857 and went to many places (viz. Sonepat, Najibabad, Bareli, Lakhnau) in search of a living; briefly edited *Jalwa-e-nur*, a magazine published from Bulandshahr; spent four years at the Alwar court, 19 in Jaipur and 15 in Tonk. For a few months he was in Haidarabad and died there. Three of his four collections of verse have been published; in prose he wrote *Dastan-e-ghadar*, an eye-witness account of the Revolt of 1857.

Zauq [Sheikh Ibrahim (1789–1854)]: poet in Urdu from Delhi, where his father was a common soldier. His primary education was conducted by Hafiz Ghulam Rasul, who was himself a poet and his house a meeting-place for other poets. Thus Zauq grew up in an atmosphere favourable to literary aspiration; gained access to the royal court; was nominated literary mentor of Bahadur Shah Zafar. Despite this high honour, Zauq lived a life of hardship. He wrote a large number of poems but these were all lost during the disturbances of 1857. Some had been copied out by his favourite disciple 'Azad'; some other poems had been memorised by the blind disciple Hafiz 'Viran'. Reconstructed from these two sources, a divan was prepared consisting of 167 ghazals, 24 qasida and some stray verses. Zauq's fame rests on his qasida compositions.